PRACTICAL
LAW OFFICE
MANAGEMENT

The West Paralegal Series

Your options keep growing with West Publishing.
Each year our list continues to offer you more options for every course, new or existing, and on-the-job reference materials. We now have over 140 titles from which to choose.

We are pleased to offer books in the following subject areas:

Administrative Law
Alternative Dispute Resolution
Bankruptcy
Business Organizations/Corporations
Civil Litigation and Procedure
CLA Exam Preparation
Client Accounting
Computer in the Law Office
Constitutional Law
Contract Law
Criminal Law and Procedure
Document Preparation
Environmental Law
Ethics

Family Law
Federal Taxation
Intellectual Property
Introduction to Law
Introduction to Paralegalism
Law Office Management
Law Office Procedures
Legal Research, Writing, and Analysis
Legal Terminology
Paralegal Employment
Real Estate Law
Reference Materials
Torts and Personal Injury Law
Will, Trusts, and Estate Administration

You will find unparalleled, practical teaching support.
Each text is enhanced by instructor and student supplements to ensure the best learning experience possible to prepare for this field. We also offer custom publishing and other benefits such as West's Student Achievement Award. In addition, our sales representatives are ready to provide you with needed and dependable service.

We want to hear from you.
The most important factor in improving the quality of our paralegal texts and teaching packages is active feedback from educators in the field. If you have a question, concern, or observation about any of our materials or you have written a proposal or manuscript, we want to hear from you. Please do not hesitate to contact your local representative or write us at the following address:

West Paralegal Series, 3 Columbia Circle, P.O. Box 15015, Albany, NY 12212-5015.

For additional information point your browser to
http://www.westpub.com/Educate and **http://www.delmar.com**

West Publishing — *Your Paralegal Publisher*
an imprint of Delmar Publishers

an International Thomson Publishing company

PRACTICAL LAW OFFICE MANAGEMENT

Brent D. Roper, J.D.

WEST PUBLISHING

an International Thomson Publishing company I(T)P®

Albany • Bonn • Boston • Cincinnati • Detroit • London • Madrid
Melbourne • Mexico City • Minneapolis/St. Paul • New York • Pacific Grove
Paris • San Francisco • Singapore • Tokyo • Toronto • Washington

NOTICE TO THE READER

...he products described herein or perform any independent analysis in con- ...ined herein. Publisher does not assume, and expressly disclaims, any obligation to obtain and include information other ...an that provided to it by the manufacturer.

The reader is notified that this text is an educational tool, not a practice book. Since the law is in constant change, no rule or statement of law in this book should be relied upon for any service to any client. The reader should always refer to standard legal sources for the current rule or law. If legal advice or other expert assistance is required, the services of the appropriate professional should be sought.

The publisher makes no representation or warranties of any kind, including but not limited to, the warranties of fitness for particular purpose or merchantability, nor any such representations implied with respect to the material set forth herein, and the publisher takes no responsibility with respect to such material. The publisher shall not be liable for any special, consequential, or exemplary damages resulting, in whole or part, from the readers' use of, or reliance upon, this material.

Production Credits

Interior design by John Edeen

Copyediting by Allen Gooch

Composition by Parkwood Composition Services, Inc.

Art by Alice Thiede and William Thiede

Cover design by John Edeen

British Library Cataloguing-in-Publication Data. A catalogue record for this book is available from the British Library.

COPYRIGHT © 1995

By West Publishing
an imprint of Delmar Publishers
a division of International Thomson Publishing

The ITP logo is a trademark under license.

Printed in the United States of America

For more information, contact:

Delmar Publishers
3 Columbia Circle, Box 15015
Albany, New York 12212-5015

International Thomson Publishing–Europe
Berkshire House
168–173 High Holborn
London, WC1V 7AA
England

Thomas Nelson Australia
103 Dodds Street
South Melbourne, 3205
Victoria, Australia

Nelson Canada
1120 Birchmount Road
Scarborough, Ontario
Canada M1K 5G4

International Thomson Editores
Campos Eliseos 385, Piso 7
Col Polanco
11560 Mexico D F Mexico

International Thomson Publishing GmbH
Königswinterer Strasse 418
53227 Bonn
Germany

International Thomson Publishing – Asia
60 Albert Street
#15-01 Albert Complex
Singapore 189969

International Thomson Publishing – Japan
Hirakawacho Kyowa Building, 3F
2-2-1 Hirakawacho
Chiyoda-ku, Tokyo 102 Japan

4   5   6   7   8   9   10   XXX   03   02   01   00   99   98

Library of Congress Cataloging-in-Publication Data

Roper, Brent D.
　Practical law office management/Brent D. Roper
　　p. cm.
　Includes index.
　ISBN 0-314-04305-5 (soft : acid-free paper)
　1. Law Offices—United States.　　I. Title.
KF318.R66　1995　　　　　　　　　94-19945
340'.068—dc20　　　　　　　　　　CIP

To my beloved wife, Shirley Phelps-Roper
and my mom and dad

BRIEF CONTENTS

Preface   xiii

1   INTRODUCTION TO LAW OFFICE MANAGEMENT   1
     Case History—Experienced Litigation Legal Assistant   35

2   ETHICS AND MALPRACTICE   43

3   STAFF MANUALS, TOTAL QUALITY MANAGEMENT,
        MARKETING, AND PLANNING   79
     Case History—Solo Practitioner's Office   113

4   CLIENTS AND COMMUNICATION SKILLS   119
     Case History—Corporate Law Department   139

5   TIMEKEEPING AND BILLING   145
     Verdict Timekeeping and Billing   194
     Timeslips Timekeeping & Billing   209

6   CLIENT FUNDS AND LAW OFFICE ACCOUNTING   229

7   DOCKET CONTROL SYSTEMS   257
     Docket Software Program   283

8   HUMAN RESOURCE MANAGEMENT   297
     Case History—Legal Clinic Paralegal   337

9   LAW OFFICE INFORMATION SYSTEMS   345

10   FILE AND LAW LIBRARY MANAGEMENT   381

11   LAW OFFICE EQUIPMENT, OFFICE LAYOUT, SPACE MANAGEMENT, SECURITY, AND LEASES   417

APPENDICES:

Appendix A   Successful Strategies for the New Legal Assistant   457
Appendix B   National Law Office Management, Legal Assistant and Related
                Associations   469
Appendix C   IBM-Compatible Software Programs   471
Appendix D   Macintosh Software Programs   475
Appendix E   A Manual Law Office System   477

Glossary   491
Index   499

CONTENTS

Preface   xiii

1 INTRODUCTION TO LAW OFFICE MANAGEMENT   1

Introduction to the Legal Field   2
The Legal Team   4
Types of Law Practices   18
Law Practice Organization Structures   26
Law Office Management Principles   29
Case History—Experienced Litigation Legal Assistant   35

2 ETHICS AND MALPRACTICE   43

Why Is Ethics and Malpractice Important?   44
Legal Ethics and Professional Responsibility   45
Malpractice and Malpractice Prevention   67

3 STAFF MANUALS, TOTAL QUALITY MANAGEMENT, MARKETING, AND PLANNING   79

Law Practice Policies and Procedures—The Staff Manual   81
Total Quality Management   89
Marketing   93
Planning   105
Case History—Solo Practitioner's Office   113

4 CLIENTS AND COMMUNICATION SKILLS   119

Client Relationships   121
Communication Skills   126
Case History—Corporate Law Department   139

5   TIMEKEEPING AND BILLING   145

Kinds of Fee Agreements   147
Value Billing   158
Ethics of Timekeeping and Billing   158
Legal Expenses   164
Timekeeping   166
Billing   174
- Successful Billing Practices—Pleasing the Client and Avoiding
   Accounts Receivable Problems   178
Billing From the Corporate and Government
   Perspective   186
Verdict Timekeeping & Billing   194
Timeslips Timekeeping & Billing   209

6   CLIENT FUNDS AND LAW OFFICE ACCOUNTING   229

Client Funds—Trust/Escrow Accounts   231
Introduction to Bookkeeping/Accounting   236
Budgeting   240
Cash Flow and Accounts Receivable   244
Compensation and Profit Distribution   247
Internal Controls   247
Financial Management and Ethics   252

7   DOCKET CONTROL SYSTEMS   257

Appointments   259
Deadlines and Reminders   259
Hearing and Court Dates   261
Receiving Documents, Following Court Rules, and
   Calculating Deadlines   261
Ethical and Malpractice Considerations   264
Manual Docket Control Systems   269
Computerized Docket Control Systems   269
Docket Software Program   283

8   HUMAN RESOURCE MANAGEMENT   297

The Hiring Process   299
Performance Evaluations   310
Termination   320
Personnel Policies   326
Current Personnel Law Issues   327
Case History—Legal Clinic Paralegal   337

9 LAW OFFICE INFORMATION SYSTEMS 345

Computer Hardware   347
Size Classifications of Computers   350
Peripheral Devices   354
Computer Software   359
▪ Microcomputer Hardware: Putting It All Together   360
▪ Microsoft Windows   370
Considerations for Purchasing Application Software   373
Software as an Integral Part of the Law Office Information
    System   375
"Bugs" and Computer Viruses   375

10 FILE AND LAW LIBRARY MANAGEMENT 381

Introduction to File Management   383
Filing Methods and Techniques   383
File Management Equipment   395
File Management and Ethics   398
Form Files   399
Introduction to Law Library Management   400

11 LAW OFFICE EQUIPMENT, OFFICE LAYOUT, SPACE MANAGEMENT, SECURITY, AND LEASES 417

Law Office Equipment and Technology   418
Purchasing Equipment and Supplies   425
Law Office Layout, Space Management, Security, and
    Leases   432

APPENDICES:
Appendix A   Successful Strategies for the New Legal Assistant   457
Appendix B   National Law Office Management, Legal Assistant and Related
        Associations   469
Appendix C   IBM-Compatible Software Programs   471
Appendix D   Macintosh Software Programs   475
Appendix E   A Manual Law Office Systems   477

Glossary   491
Index   499

PREFACE

Another class, another boring text book. Right? Wrong! Law office management is a dynamic subject, and a great class. It will make you a better legal assistant. You will learn about real life problems you will encounter on the job and how to deal with them successfully. You will understand how important performing quality work for clients is. We'll explain how to improve your communication skills and how to work with clients successfully. You will be shown how to track and bill your time correctly, and how to use your time effectively. Throughout the book there are explanations about how to avoid ethical problems that will come up. Law office management is anything but boring.

The goal of Practical Law Office Management is to educate legal assistant students regarding law office management procedures and systems. Law firms, as well as legal assistants themselves, must have good management skills to survive in today's competitive marketplace. This text is written for the student that wants to understand effective law practice management techniques and systems whether or not he or she will go on to become a law office manager.

This text is not intended to be an "armchair" style text on the theories and principles of management, nor is it a text on how to set up a law office. Rather, this text presents a practical discussion of law office management from a legal assistant's view.

The information presented is national in scope and assumes no prior knowledge of management or the legal field. Sociology, theories, and jargon are kept to an absolute minimum. To present a flavor of how a real law office operates, step-by-step explanations are given, "how to" tips, practical charts, recent trends in law office management, case studies, software, and many practical ideas on law office management from the legal assistant's perspective is provided. Information is presented in a manner to encourage students to think independently and to learn by participating.

This book, among other things, will explain what management generally expects of legal assistants and will present good law office systems and practical information about law office management.

Legal assistants must learn to manage themselves in addition to performing their normal duties. This book will help the student manage his or herself in addition to teaching basic law office systems, such as timekeeping and billing, docket control, financial management, file and library management, computer systems and more. If the student takes the time to learn the management systems in this book, he or she will do things more efficiently, with greater accuracy, and with less work. Sound too good to be true? That is what good management is all about.

A book on law office management has inherent limitations because there are many different management styles, techniques, and philosophies depending on the size and type of firm (i.e., small, medium, and large firms, corporate legal departments), location of the firm (urban, rural, east, west) and so forth. In addition, law office management is such a diverse topic that most people cannot agree on all the topics that should be covered. In light of these inherent problems, a vast and varied amount of information from many different angles is presented.

ETHICS

The importance of ethics is stressed throughout the text. Assuring a high ethical standard in the law office is a major function of law office management. It is very important to your career to be educated regarding ethical issues and to adopt a high ethical standard as a way of life. Every chapter in the text has an in-depth section on ethics as well as real-life ethics problems at the end of the chapter. In "Chapter 2—Ethics and Malpractice" the codes of ethics for both the National Association of Legal Assistants (NALA) and the National Federation of Paralegal Associations (NAFPA) are included.

ORGANIZATION OF THE TEXT

The text is organized into 11 chapters. Chapter One is an introduction to the legal environment and to law office management. It is suggested that all students who are new to the legal field read this chapter first. However, from Chapter 2 on, each chapter stands on its own and does not depend on the chapter(s) before it. Thus, instructors can assign the chapters in whatever order he or she feels is appropriate.

CASE STUDIES

In an effort to move from theory to practice, case studies are presented throughout the text. These are not "a day in the life of" stories. The case studies examine law office management from corporate law offices, legal aid law offices, solo practitioner offices and more. They describe a particular law office, the needs of the office, the specific systems the particular legal assistant interviewed uses to get his or her job done, ethical situations they have had to deal with, and specific management problems and solutions the legal assistant has struggled with. They are intended to show how law office management applies to legal assistants. The case studies are an excellent opportunity to see how legal assistants work in real life in many different environments.

SUPPLEMENTS

Several supplements are available for use with the text, including an instructor's manual, student study guide, video tapes, and software.

- The instructor's manual includes outlines, teaching suggestions, discussion ideas and test questions.
- The student study guide contains chapter outlines, fill-in-the-blank, multiple-choice, and definition questions for each chapter to help test the student's knowledge of the material.

WESTEST 3.0 computerized testing program offers the complete test bank on disk.

"I Never Said I Was a Lawyer" Videotape, created by the Colorado Bar Association, uses a variety of scenarios to inspire discussion and give students experience dealing with ethical dilemmas. Topics explored include the unauthorized practice of law, identification of paralegals as nonlawyers, waiver of clients' rights through breaches of confidentiality, and lack of attorney supervision.

Drama of the Law II: Paralegal Series videotape includes 5 separate dramatizations intended to stimulate classroom discussion about various paralegal issues. Titles include Human Error, Strategic Information, Client Confidentiality, Unauthorized Practice, and Intake Interview.

SOFTWARE TUTORIALS

The text accommodates legal assistant programs that have access to computers by including software tutorials at the end of some chapters. However, these are simply an added feature and computer use is completely optional. This text can be used fully by legal assistant programs that choose not to use computers.

The software tutorials included in the text are completely interactive and allow the student hands-on experience with the software programs. In addition, all of the tutorials are specifically related to law offices and legal applications so the student not only learns how to operate the software, but also learns how to use it in a law office. Educational versions of the software programs used for the tutorials are provided free of charge for schools adopting the text. The programs include:

- Verdict (a timekeeping and billing program)
- Timeslips (a timekeeping and billing program)
- Docket (a docket control program)

A tutorial for a manual law office system is also included in the text.

TO THE STUDENT

Law office management is exciting and ever changing. It is my hope that you will find this book useful as a reference tool in your professional career and that you will use some ideas in it to climb the ladder of success. From my own experience, please remember that just because you graduate from a paralegal program, you do not get to start at the top. Everyone has to start at the bottom and work their way up. I started as a secretary and worked up from there. Do not be surprised or disappointed if you start in an entry level job. The experience you'll gain is priceless and through hard work and determination you'll move up, quicker than you think and you will be better for it because you will have earned it. Also, remember and help your co-workers, you will not be able to succeed without their help. Treat them like you would like to be treated and put the interests of your law office ahead of your own and you will go far.

If you have an interesting idea or have solved some problem in law office management, or just have a story to tell and you would not mind me using it as an example in a subsequent edition of this book, please do not hesitate to give me a call, I'm in the phone book. I am always interested in learning from you. I wish you the best of luck in your endeavors. Brent Roper, 3640 Churchill Road, Topeka, KS, 66604.

ACKNOWLEDGMENTS

One of my favorite parts of writing a book is to thank the people that helped me put it together. So to all the people listed below, who have worked on this project: Thank you for all of your help.

REVIEWERS

I would like to thank the following individuals who reviewed the text. Their thoughts, ideas and assistance were invaluable to me. They spent countless hours of their time and I owe them all a debt of gratitude:

Anna Boling
Athens Area Technical College, GA

June Brooks
Wallace State College, AL

Janet Cox
Northeast Mississippi Community College, MS

Donna Donathan
Marshall University Community College, WV

Holly Enterline
State Technical Institute of Memphis, TN

Beth Friedman
formerly of Jones College, FL

John Kellar
The Paralegal Institute, PA

Dorothy B. Moore
Ft. Lauderdale College, FL

Jean Morton
College of the Legal Arts, OR

Kathryn L. Myers
St. Mary-of-the-Woods College, IN

Zoran Perovanovich
North Central College, IL

Charlotte W. Smith
University of Maryland, University College

Bernard Sternin
Queens College, NY

Julia O. Tryk, Esq.
Cuyahoga Community College, OH

CASE STUDIES

A special thank you goes to the legal assistants and their offices who allowed me to interview them for the case studies. It was a pleasure to write about their careers, real life experiences, and accomplishments in the legal field.

- Betsy Horn, CLA, Harris, Finley & Bogle, Fort Worth, Texas
- Suzanne Sheldon, Woodbury College, Montepelier, Vermont
- Robin Saunders-Davis, Farnam Law Firm, St. Louis, Missouri
- Sherry R. S. Wehrle, Long John Silver's Inc., Lexington, Kentucky

WEST PUBLISHING

- A special thanks goes to the wonderful people at West Publishing including Elizabeth Hannan, Editor, Patricia Bryant, Developmental Editor, and Peggy Brewington, Production Editor. Without their long hours and help this book would not have been possible.

OTHER

- Elizabeth Phelps who spent hours of her time proofreading and editing the text and Betty Phelps who proofread and edited the instructor's manual and student study guide.
- My son, Sam Phelps-Roper, who spent many hours helping with the development of this text in various capacities (and "No," you cannot have a new car just because you helped).
- Pat Buser who spent hours copying manuscript pages and otherwise helping.
- Leanne Cazares and everyone involved at James Publishing Inc., publishers of Legal Assistant Today, 3520 Cadillac Avenue, Suite E, Costa Mesa, CA 92626, (714) 755–5450. Legal Assistant Today graciously granted me

permission to reprint many quotations contained in this text as well as many charts and figures.

- A. Jean Lesher of the American Bar Association (ABA). The ABA, as always, was extremely helpful and provided superb information and source material.
- Constance J. Anderson, of Webster University provided practical insight, advice, and wonderful course materials that proved very useful to me.
- Bill Statsky, who has unselfishly helped me develop my ideas and thoughts as a writer. Bill also provided me with a library of source material.
- I would especially like to thank James Cotterman and Altman Weil Pensa management consultants post office box 625, Newtown Square, PA 19073, (215) 359–9900, who provided me with outstanding source material.
- Robert Michael Greene for his outstanding ideas and books he has published through the ABA Section of Law Practice Management.
- Brad Koehn, CPA of Berberich & Trahan, CPAs, Topeka, Kansas, for his editing of the chapter on financial management.
- Legal Assistant Management Association for the information they provided to me.
- D. W. Darby, Jr. of Cantor and Company, Inc., Consultants, 110 Hopewell Road Downington, PA 19335, (215) 269–5100 for his Economics Study of Corporate Law Staffs.
- Dr. John L. Espy of Washburn University, for his ideas on management techniques strategic planning.
- The National Federation of Paralegal Associations and the National Association of Legal Assistants for their help and cooperation in writing this book.
- Dennis Erickson and Deluxe Business Forms and Supplies, (800) 833–3820 for permission to use forms from their legal catalog.
- A special thanks goes to Kris Kitchen, Jefferson Forrest, Cheryl Failer, Jan Michaelis, Jennifer Penry, Lora Baugher, and Tiffany Seeley for their patience and help with this project.
- A special thanks goes to my wife, Shirley Phelps-Roper, and children, Samuel, Joshua, Megan, Rebekah, Isaiah, Zacharias and Grace Elizabeth who put up with my long hours, and hectic schedule, and who also desperately wanted to see their names in print again (here they are!). Finally, a special thanks goes to my mom Nanci Toews (and step-father Jim), my dad Ed Fundis (and step-mother Gloria), and my father-in-law and mother-in-law, Fred and Margie Phelps. Without the love and cooperation of my family I never could have seen this project through.

Brent D. Roper
3640 Churchill Road
Topeka, KS 66604

INTRODUCTION TO LAW OFFICE MANAGEMENT

CHAPTER OBJECTIVES

After you read this chapter, you will be able to:

- Discuss the titles and duties of each member of the legal team.
- Explain the trends in legal assistant salaries and fringe benefits.
- Identify alternative law office organization structures.
- Identify the functions of law office management.
- Explain the "systems view" of management.

The firm was more than twenty years old and was well established in the legal community. Recently, however, the firm had moved to a particularly high-rent area and seemed to have an overabundance of attorneys and staff. The firm grew dependent on two large clients for most of its business. Unexpectedly, one of the clients moved its business to a competing law firm. Word had it that the client was less than pleased with the work it had received. Management decided a bold move was necessary to save the firm. Clients were interviewed to see how the firm's services could be improved. Budgets were developed to help project income and expenses better, a long-term business plan for the firm was drafted, staff discussions were held to explore ways to cut costs and increase productivity, and consultants were hired to help the firm's management increase its effectiveness. The firm was on its way to recovery.

INTRODUCTION TO THE LEGAL FIELD

The practice of law is diverse. Some attorneys are general practitioners and practice in many areas of the law. Other attorneys specialize in particular areas, including corporate law, tax law, labor law, and personal injury law to name just a few. It is difficult to describe exactly what lawyers, office staff, and law firms do, since a great deal depends on what area or specialty a case involves. However, Figure 1-1 gives a broad outline of many activities performed for any given client.

An attorney is ultimately responsible for the activities and outcome of a case, but legal assistants are involved in many aspects of it. Legal assistants frequently

1. A client engages a lawyer.
   a. A file is opened.
   b. A fee contract is signed.
2. Client information is gathered.
3. The client's problem is analyzed.
   a. Research is conducted.
4. The client's problem is handled through the following:
   a. Document preparation
      Letters
      Opinion letters
      Memorandums of law
      Briefs
      Pleadings
      Agreements
      Complete printed forms
   b. Court appearances
      Pleadings
      Information management
      Discovery
      Research
      Exhibits
      Admissions
      Interrogatories

      Expert witnesses
      Docket control
      Pretrial hearing
      Trial
   c. Miscellaneous
      Problem analysis
      Research
      Advice
      Written confirmation of advice
      Mathematical calculations
      Projects and estimates
      Forms completion
      Tax return completion
      Representation of client at
      closings
      Agreements
5. The lawyer and staff keep track of time and effort on behalf of the client.
6. The lawyer and staff send bills.
7. The lawyer and staff keep the law practice under control through the following:
   Timekeeping and billing
   Accounts receivable
   Calendar control
   File management
   Bookkeeping

   Payroll
   Tax returns
   Supplies purchasing
   Telephone bill reconciliation
   Management of the practice
8. The lawyer concludes the matter either because the work is completed or the client's case is decided by a judicial body.
9. Client materials are returned to the client and the file is closed.

FIGURE 1-1
What Attorneys and Law Firm Staff Do
Source: Robert P. Wilkins, R.P.W. Publishing Corp. Adapted and reprinted by permission of the publisher.

gather information through interviewing clients and witnesses. They conduct legal research and analyze cases. Legal assistants draft documents, make calculations, develop forms and procedures, monitor legislation, maintain the law library, and supervise clerical staff. Although legal assistants cannot replace the attorney, they are an important part of the legal team. A litigation legal assistant may help organize cases for trial, write interrogatories, prepare deposition summaries, draft chronologies of events, and organize witnesses and exhibits in a case. Additionally, legal assistants may produce billings, track appointments and deadlines, and manage files. In Figure 1-1, note that items five through seven specifically relate to law office management.

THE LEGAL TEAM

legal team
A group made up of attorneys, administrators, law clerks, librarians, legal assistants, secretaries, clerks, and other third parties. Each provides a distinct range of services to clients and each has a place on the legal team.

In a law office, there are many people who make up the legal team. The legal team consists of attorneys, administrators, law clerks, librarians, legal assistants, secretaries, clerks, and other third parties. Each person provides a distinct range of services to clients, and each has his or her place on the legal team. The positions and job duties in any law office depend on the type and size of the office. A list of job titles and a general description of common duties and responsibilities are provided in this section. It should be noted that job titles are just that, they are "titles" only. Attorneys and law office administrators are far more impressed with a person's actual performance than with a person's job title.

ATTORNEY

attorneys
Professionals who counsel clients regarding their legal rights, represent clients in litigation, and negotiate agreements between clients and others.

Attorneys counsel clients regarding their legal rights, represent clients in litigation, and negotiate agreements between clients and others. Depending on the size of the law office, attorneys may also have administrative duties. There are several kinds of attorneys.

partner or shareholder
An owner in a private law practice who shares in its profits and losses.

PARTNER/SHAREHOLDER   A partner or shareholder is an owner in a private law practice and shares in its profits and losses. In the partnership form of business, an owner of the business is called a partner. In the corporate form of business, an owner is called a shareholder. Partners and shareholders serve primarily the same purpose; it is only the legal structure that is different. For simplicity, "partner" will be used to refer collectively to partners and shareholders, but "shareholder" could also have been used.

managing partner
An attorney in a law firm chosen by the partnership to run the firm, make administrative decisions, and set policies.

Partners attend partnership meetings and vote in the management decisions of the firm. Partners must also make monetary contributions to the firm if the need arises. Partners are sometimes called "equity partners," since they share in the profits or losses of the firm. To become a partner, an attorney must either be an attorney who founded the firm or be voted into the position by the existing partners. Typically, partners do not receive a "salary" but may receive a periodic draw, which is an advance against future profits.

In some firms, a managing partner is chosen by the partnership to run the firm and make administrative decisions and set policies. The managing partner reports to the partnership on the progress of the firm. Managing partners are typically elected to serve a set time such as one or two years.

associate attorney
Attorney who is a salaried employee of the law firm, does not have an ownership interest in the firm, does not share in the profits, and has no vote regarding management decisions.

ASSOCIATE ATTORNEYS   An associate attorney does not have an ownership interest in the law firm and does not share in the profits. The associate is only an employee of the firm who receives a salary and has no vote regarding management decisions. Associates can be hired directly out of law school or come from other firms. Associates who are hired from other firms are known as lateral hires or lateral hire associates. Associates who are candidates for a future partnership are said to be on a partnership track. An associate is usually with the firm between three and ten years before he or she is a candidate for a partnership position, depending on the size of the firm. In large metropolitan firms, the time may be longer. An associate passed over for partnership may or may not leave the firm to practice elsewhere. Sometimes, to keep good associate attorneys who have nevertheless been

lateral hire associates
Associate attorneys hired from other firms.

FIGURE 1-2
The Legal Team

I. Attorneys
    1. Partners/shareholders
       a. Managing partner
    2. Associates
       a. Associate
       b. Lateral hire
       c. Nonequity partner
       d. Staff attorney
       e. Contract attorney
    3. Of counsel
II. Administrators (larger firms)
    1. Legal administrator
    2. Chief financial officer
    3. Human resource manager
    4. Director of marketing
    5. Information systems manager
III. Legal assistants
    1. Legal assistant
    2. Managing legal assistant
    3. Freelance legal assistant
IV. Office manager (smaller firms)
V. Law clerk
VI. Law librarian
VII. Secretaries
    1. Legal secretary
    2. Receptionist
    3. Word processing secretary
VIII. Clerks
    1. File clerk
    2. Calendar clerk
    3. Copy clerk
    4. Mail clerk
    5. Billing clerk
IX. Other legal team members
    1. Expert witness
    2. Investigator
    3. Litigation support service bureau
    4. Consultants

passed over for partnership, the firm creates a position known as a nonequity partner. A nonequity partner does not share in the profits or losses of the business but may be included in some aspects of the management of the firm and may be entitled to other benefits not given to associates. A staff attorney is another type of associate. A staff attorney is an attorney hired by a firm with the knowledge and understanding that he or she will never be considered for partnership. Finally, a contract attorney is an associate attorney who is temporarily hired by the law office for a specific job or period. When the job or period is finished, the relationship with the firm is over.

nonequity partner
One who does not share in the profits or losses of the firm but may be included in some aspects of management and may be entitled to certain benefits.

staff attorney
An attorney hired by a firm with the knowledge and understanding that he or she will never be considered for partnership.

contract attorney
An attorney temporarily hired by the law office for a specific job or period. When the job or period is finished, the relationship with the firm is over.

of counsel
An attorney affiliated with the firm in some way such as a retired or semiretired partner.

administrator
Person responsible for some type of law office administrative system such as general management, finance and accounting, human resources, marketing, or computer systems.

legal assistants
A distinguishable group of persons who assist attorneys in the delivery of legal services. They have knowledge and expertise regarding the legal system and substantive and procedural law that qualifies them to do work of a legal nature under the supervision of an attorney.

OF COUNSEL The "of counsel" position is a flexible concept but generally means that the attorney is affiliated with the firm in some way, such as a retired or semiretired partner. "Of counsel" attorneys lend their names to a firm for goodwill and prestige purposes to attract additional clients and business to the firm. An "of counsel" attorney may be paid on a "per job" basis or may be an employee of the firm. He or she does not usually share in the profits of the firm. The "of counsel" arrangement is also used when an attorney is considering joining a firm as a partner and wants to work on a trial basis first.

ADMINISTRATORS

Administrators are usually found in medium and large firms, although they are beginning to be used in small firms as well. Law office administrators are responsible for some type of law office administrative system such as general management, finance and accounting, human resources, marketing, or computer systems. Administrators are typically nonattorneys who have degrees in business or related fields or who have been promoted through the ranks. Administrators have a broad range of power to make management decisions with the approval of the partnership. Most report directly to a committee or a partner.

Administrators draft annual budgets, prepare and interpret management reports, and supervise the fiscal operations of the business. Administrators also hire, fire, train, and evaluate nonprofessional support staff and are responsible for implementation of effective management systems.[1] In short, administrators, are managers hired to relieve management burdens from partners or managing committees. Experienced legal assistants are sometimes promoted to administrative positions. Administration can be a positive career move for legal assistants with good management skills. An excellent source of information regarding law office administration is available from the Association of Legal Administrators (ALA); see appendix E.

LEGAL ASSISTANTS

Legal assistants are a distinguishable group of persons who assist attorneys in the delivery of legal services. Through formal education, training, and experience, legal assistants have knowledge and expertise regarding the legal system and substantive and procedural law, which qualifies them to do work of a legal nature under the supervision of an attorney.[2]

In 1968, the House of Delegates of the American Bar Association created a Special Committee on Lay Assistants for Lawyers (now called the Standing Committee on Legal Assistants). The House of Delegates stated

> that the legal profession recognizes that there are many tasks in serving clients' needs which can be performed by a trained, nonlawyer assistant working under the direction and supervision of a lawyer; that the profession [should] encourage the training and employment of such assistants . . .

Although legal assistants may perform many tasks, they are strictly prohibited from giving legal advise to clients, from representing clients in court proceedings, from accepting a client case, and from setting a fee in a matter. This is covered in more detail in the next chapter.

Some larger firms have legal assistant managers. A legal assistant manager supervises, recruits, trains, distributes assignments, sets priorities, and directs the overall management of a group of legal assistants.

> I like the freedom of movement and being able to be my own boss and set my own hours [as a freelance legal assistant]. I'm not restricted to a set schedule, though of course I set appointments with the attorneys or their clients. I can come and go as I please. The client's [i.e. the law firm's] only concern is that I get the work done. I charge an hourly rate, which the law firms bill to their clients. It's a win/win situation. I've never advertised, all my clients are people I knew before I became independent, or who found me by word of mouth or referral.
>
> —A freelance legal assistant in Carol Milano, "1993 Salary Survey Results," Legal Assistant Today, May/June 1993, 68.

Another kind of legal assistant is a freelance legal assistant. Freelance legal assistants, sometimes called independent legal assistants, are self-employed and market and sell their services to law offices on a per job basis. They work under the supervision of an attorney, but instead of working for one law office as an employee, they work for several or many law offices. There have been several cases that have held that freelance legal assistants who work under the supervision of an attorney do not violate the prohibition against practicing law without a license (see In re Opinion No. 24 of the Committee on the Unauthorized Practice of Law, 128 N.J. 114, 607 A.2d 962 (N.J. Sup. Ct. 1992).

LEGAL ASSISTANT ROLES, RESPONSIBILITIES, AND EMPLOYMENT

People unfamiliar with the legal profession might assume that legal assistants spend a great deal of time in trials and in court. This tends to be a misconception. No matter what kind of law a law office practices, a considerable amount of a legal assistant's time is spent researching background information, plowing through reams of files, summarizing depositions, drafting pleadings and correspondence, and organizing information and files. It is not always exciting, but it is always essential work in every case. Cases are won or lost on the facts gathered, researched, and presented.[3] Many duties a legal assistant may perform will never involve a courtroom, such as preparation of wills, real estate closing transactions, drafting discovery, and preparation of business corporation papers.

Defining the work legal assistants do is not always an easy task given the wide variety and versatility of the profession. Figure 1-3 shows sample legal assistant job descriptions. Notice the diversity of the tasks among the job descriptions. A recent survey asked practicing legal assistants what skills were the most important to them (see Figure 1-4). The top three skills were using correct grammar and spelling, having good oral communication skills, and having good written communication skills to draft documents. When asked what legal assistant courses were the most helpful once the legal assistant was on the job, legal research and legal writing were at the top of the list. Although there is diversity among legal assistant job duties, nearly all legal assistants spend a considerable portion of their time communicating either orally or in writing.

Most legal assistants practice in a particular area of the law. Figure 1-5 shows the areas in which legal assistants most frequently practice. The areas of the law

legal assistant manager
One who supervises, recruits, trains, distributes assignments, sets priorities, and directs the overall management of a group of legal assistants.

freelance legal assistants,
Self-employed legal assistants; they market and sell their services to law offices on a per job basis.

FIGURE 1-3
Legal Assistant Job
Descriptions

Source: William Statsky,
Introduction to Paralegalism
(Saint Paul, Minnesota: West
Publishing Company, 1992).

Bankruptcy Legal Assistant
- Interviews client and completes an extensive questionnaire on the person's assets and liabilities.
- Helps client assemble a list of creditors, a financial statement, loan agreement, security agreements, etc.
- Contacts creditors and confirms amounts of debts, handles creditor inquiries, and coordinates meeting of creditors.
- Identifies exempt property.
- Checks UCC (Uniform Commercial Code) filing at the secretary of state's office and at county clerk's office.
- Drafts bankruptcy petitions, schedule of liabilities, and status reports.

Estates, Trusts, and Probate Legal Assistant
- Prepares preliminary draft of wills or trusts from office form files or sample forms.
- Assembles a list of assets, bank accounts, insurance proceeds, and social security death benefits and assists in the valuation of the assets in probate matters. Notifies beneficiaries and maintains wills and trusts, powers of attorney, and other documents.
- Prepares preliminary draft of federal and state death tax returns and prepares final accountings.
- Draws checks for signature of executors, prepares and files tax waivers, and applies for the transfer of securities in to the names of the people entitled.
- Performs legal research, prepares sample pleadings, and assists with litigation.

Family Law Legal Assistant
- Interviews clients and collects information.
- Prepares initial pleadings, including petition, summons, and motions for temporary orders or injunctions.
- Compiles financial information and analyzes income and expenses information provided by client.
- Prepares discovery requests and responses to discovery.
- Assists in settlement negotiations and prepares analysis of proposed settlements.
- Helps prepare for hearings, conducts legal research, arranges for expert witnesses, and assists in preparing witnesses and clients for trial.
- Prepares the divorce decree.

Real Estate Legal Assistant
- Researches zoning regulations.
- Prepares draft of the contract of sale.
- Examines title abstracts for completeness, helps construct a chain of title noting defects, encumbrances, liens, and easements, or makes arrangements for a title company to prepare the title report.
- Assists in obtaining financing, reviews mortgage application, and assists in recording mortgage.
- Arranges for a closing time with buyer and seller, brokers and lender.

- Collects data for closings, including obtaining fees of the lender, title company, taxes, etc.
- Prepares closing documents, including deeds, settlement statement, notes and deed of trust, performance bond, etc.
- In foreclosure, prepares notice of election and demand for sale, compiles a list of parties to be notified, and monitors publication of the notice.

Paralegal Manager
- Hires, fires, and completes performance evaluations for all paralegal staff.
- Prepares a management plan and policy description for the paralegal department.
- Supervises paralegal staff on a daily basis.
- Prepares an annual budget for the paralegal department.
- Develops salary schedule for paralegal staff.
- Prepares annual billing rate for the paralegal staff.

What Specific Skills Are Important for You to Have in Your Position?

Skill	Very Important	Important	Very Important	Skill Not Utilized
1. Use of correct grammar and spelling	96%	4%	0%	0%
2. Oral communications	88%	12%	0%	0%
3. Document preparation	73%	25%	2%	0%
4. Analysis of documents	72%	25%	0%	2%
5. Typing skills	63%	32%	2%	3%
6. WordPerfect	60%	30%	5%	5%
7. Legal research	20%	63%	12%	5%
8. Interviewing	27%	38%	17%	18%
9. Use of law-specific programs	23%	27%	27%	23%
10. Use of spreadsheets	17%	11%	26%	46%

FIGURE 1-4
Legal Assistant Skills Survey
Source: Reprinted with permission. Susan H. Brewer, J. Sargeant Reynolds Community College, 1992. Survey of Richmond Association of Legal Assistant Members.

Now That You Are a Legal Assistant, What Course(s) Was (Were) Most Helpful to You?
1. Legal research
2. Legal writing
3. Real estate
4. Litigation
5. Torts
6. Estate planning
7. Ethics
8. Court system
9. Business organization
10. Trial preparation
11. Bankruptcy

FIGURE 1-5
National Survey—
Legal Assistant
Specialties

Source: "Legal Assistant
Today Salary Survey
Results, 1993" Legal
Assistant Today, May/June
1993, 60. Copyright 1993.
James Publishing, Inc.,
Reprinted with permission
from Legal Assistant Today.
For subscription information,
call (714) 755-5450.

What Area of Law Do You Primarily Practice In?

1.	Litigation-defense	27.3%
2.	Litigation-plaintiff	16.7%
3.	Corporate law	10.5%
4.	Personal injury	8.9%
5.	Real estate	6.5%
6.	Family law	4.8%
7.	Other	4.8%
8.	Employment & labor	3.3%
9.	Bankruptcy	3.2%
10.	Estate & probate	3.0%
11.	Environmental	2.4%
12.	Intellectual property	2.2%
13.	Workers' comp.	2.2%
14.	Criminal	2.1%
15.	Administrative/legislative	1.6%
16.	Banking & finance	.5%
	TOTAL	100%

practiced are highly localized and vary from city to city and state to state. Notice in Figure 1-5 that 44 percent of the legal assistants surveyed indicated that they specialized in either defense or plaintiff litigation. Litigation provides many employment opportunities for legal assistants.

In addition to practicing in many different areas of the law, legal assistants are employed in different kinds of law offices (see Figure 1-6). About three-fourths of all legal assistants work in private law offices. Figure 1-6 also shows that about 63 percent of the legal assistants surveyed worked in relatively small firms with nineteen or fewer attorneys. The size of the law office has an effect on the job duties and salaries of legal assistants. In small law offices, legal assistants

FIGURE 1-6
Legal Assistant
Employment

Source: "Legal Assistant
Today Salary Survey
Results, 1993," Legal
Assistant Today, May/June
1993, 58. Copyright 1993.
James Publishing, Inc.
Reprinted with permission
from Legal Assistant Today.
For subscription information,
call (714) 755-5450.

Legal Assistant Employment by Type of Law Office

Type of Law Office		
Private law firm		75.1%
Corporation		16.2%
Public sector/government		5.4%
Other		3.3%
	TOTAL	100%

Number of Attorneys in Office

Number of Attorneys		
1–4		32.8%
5–9		14.4%
10–19		16.2%
20–29		7.6%
30–75		18.4%
Over 75		10.6%
	TOTAL	100%

	Large firms	Medium-size firms	Small firms	Corporate law departments	Government law offices	Legal aid	All offices
By a particular lawyer	45%	17%	21%	22%	32%	6%	26%
By any lawyer in need of help	17	40	52	34	14	23	28
By a nonlawyer paralegal	16	3	0	10	14	2	8
By automatic routing	3	13	6	12	19	36	14
By social worker	0	0	0	0	0	2	0
Multiple responses*	15	24	15	17	11	28	19
No response	3	3	6	5	11	2	5
	(N = 92)	(N = 115)	(N = 33)	(N = 41)	(N = 81)	(N = 47)	(N = 409)

*The question requested one choice but 76 respondents indicated two or three choices. The most frequent of these multiple responses was by any lawyer, 52; followed by automatic routing, 50; a particular lawyer, 46; and a nonlawyer paralegal, 24.

FIGURE 1-7   How Work Is Assigned to Legal Assistants

Source: Quintin John Stone and Martin Wenglinsky, Paralegals, Progress and a Satellite Occupation, 1985, 26. An imprint of Greenwood Publishing Group, Inc., Westport, Conn. Reprinted with permission.

usually compose and draft their own documents on a computer or typewriter and do their own secretarial tasks. In larger firms, legal assistants may supervise secretarial personnel who transcribe documents and perform secretarial duties for the legal assistants.

Figure 1-7 shows how work is assigned to legal assistants. Notice in Figure 1-7 that in small firms, more than half the assignments come from "any lawyer in need of help" as opposed to large firms where nearly half the assignments come from a particular lawyer. Larger firms are more structured, and a legal assistant works under the direction of a specific attorney. Smaller firms tend to be less structured, and a legal assistant "floats" between attorneys as needed.

Figure 1-8 gives some insight into how legal assistants found their jobs. Notice that 27 percent of the legal assistants surveyed obtained their jobs by referral from a friend and approximately 80 percent found their jobs by means other than looking in the newspaper.

Where Was Your Present Legal Assistant Position Acquired Through?	
Referral from friend	27%
Other	25%
Newspaper ad	20%
School referral	14%
Employment agency	8%
Legal assistant assoc. job bank	6%
Total	100%

FIGURE 1-8
Paralegal Employment Survey

Source: Reprinted with permission of the Saint Louis Association of Legal Assistants. Fourteenth Annual Salary Survey Results, Saint Louis, Missouri, Association of Legal Assistants, 1993 (statistics gathered June 1992).

LEGAL ASSISTANT SALARIES AND BENEFITS

Figure 1-9 contains a national survey of legal assistant salaries. This survey found that the average salary in 1993 for a legal assistant with two years' or less experience was $23,182. The survey found that the average salary for all legal assistants was $29,548. The survey confirms that legal assistants in corporate law departments receive higher compensation on average than do legal assistants in other areas of practice. Figure 1-9 shows that more than half of all legal assistants (58.8 percent) do not receive overtime pay for hours worked in excess of forty hours a

FIGURE 1-9
Legal Assistant
Salary Survey

Source: Legal Assistant
Today, May/June, 1993, 54.

LEGAL ASSISTANT TODAY 1993 and 1992 Salary Comparison

By Education	1992 Average	1993 Average	% Increase or Decrease
High School	$27,404	$31,723	15.8%
College Credits	$29,242	$29,838	2.0%
Associate	$26,661	$26,933	1.0%
Bachelor's	$29,212	$29,343	0.4%
By Years of Legal Experience:			
0–2	$22,953	$23,182	1.0%
3–5	$26,978	$26,079	–3.3%
6–10	$30,627	$31,058	1.4%
10–15	$34,741	$33,939	–2.3%
Over 15	$38,927	$36,264	–6.8%
By Employer:			
Private law firm	$28,302	$29,071	2.7%
Corporation	$31,689	$32,939	3.9%
Public sector-govt.	$25,333	$27,954	10.3%
By Number of Attorneys:			
1–5	$27,920	$28,921	3.6%
6–19	$30,183	$30,773	2.0%
20–50	$32,526	$35,012	7.6%
50+	$30,669	$42,500	38.6%
By Practice Area:			
Litigation-plaintiff	$28,064	$28,408	1.2%
Personal injury	$26,382	$26,295	–0.3%
Corporate law	$30,932	$33,799	9.3%
Real estate	$27,666	$30,156	9.0%
Litigation-defense	$29,315	$30,039	2.8%
Estate & probate	$26,849	$28,689	6.9%
Bankruptcy	$27,641	$28,721	3.9%
Workers' comp.	$26,196	$24,713	–5.7%
Family law	$22,871	$24,753	8.2%
Employment/labor	$30,078	$32,009	6.4%
Environmental	$31,378	$27,184	–13.4%
Average Salary	$28,429	$29,548	3.9%

Are you required to bill hours?		
Yes	397	63.0%
No	233	37.0%
	630	
Average hourly rate	$62.00	
Average billable hours expected per year:	1,519	
Average hours billed:	1,628	
Average hours worked per week:	42	
Wage status		
Salaried	537	85.2%
Hourly	93	14.8%
	630	
Average gross paid overtime:	$4,590	
Average gross bonus:	$1,359	
How is overtime compensated?		
Paid		14.7%
Compensatory time off		16.5%
Not paid		58.8%
Other		10.0%

Source: Copyright 1993. James Publishing, Inc. Reprinted with permission from Legal Assistant Today. For subscription information, call (714) 755-5450.

week. The issue of whether legal assistants should be paid hourly and compensated for overtime as opposed to being paid a flat salary is a current topic of interest to legal assistants. Also, regarding compensation, some law offices award bonuses to legal assistants based on law office earnings or individual accomplishments. Among survey participants, the average bonus awarded was $1,359.

Figure 1-10 shows a wide range of fringe benefits offered to legal assistants. Health insurance and retirement plans are the most common types of fringe benefits. Many offices also offer payment of professional dues, such as dues for legal assistant associations, payment of continuing legal education seminars, and travel allowance. Compare the national average for all firms with the benefits offered by smaller firms in Figure 1-10. Benefits in medium, large, and corporate practices tend to be better than benefits offered in smaller practices.

Other trends in legal assistant salaries include:[4]

- Higher pay for legal assistants who work in large law offices as opposed to small law offices;
- Higher pay for legal assistants in cities than in rural areas;
- Higher salaries for legal assistants employed by large private law offices as opposed to government civil service positions;
- Higher salaries for legal assistants who are career oriented and willing to make a long-term commitment to legal assistant work.

	Small Firm Benefits 1993			
	Firms with 0–4 attorneys		Firms with 5–9 attorneys	
# Resp.	135		65	
Work Location:				
Metropolitan	51	37.8%	32	49.2%
Urban	62	45.9%	27	41.5%
Rural	22	16.3%	6	9.2%
Sex:				
Male	4	3.0%	4	6.2%
Female	131	97.0%	61	93.8%
Office Space:				
Private	92	68.1%	47	72.3%
Shared	23	17.0%	7	10.8%
Partitioned	14	10.4%	9	13.8%
Other	6	4.4%	2	3.1%
Secretarial Assistance:				
Personal	8	5.9%	4	6.2%
Shared	47	34.8%	32	49.2%
Computer terminal	63	46.7%	23	35.4%
Other	17	12.6%	6	9.2%
Benefits:				
Retirement	86	63.7%	50	76.9%
Profit sharing	78	57.8%	49	75.4%
Employer contributions to retirement plan	100	74.1%	56	86.2%
Health insurance	95	70.4%	60	92.3%
Life insurance	55	40.7%	51	78.5%
Dental insurance	32	23.7%	19	29.2%
Disability insurance	42	31.1%	34	52.3%
Vision insurance	13	9.6%	11	16.9%
Maternity benefits	40	29.6%	34	52.3%
Free legal representation	99	73.3%	40	61.5%
Business cards	78	57.8%	49	75.4%
Expense account	20	14.8%	11	16.9%
Flex time	47	34.8%	19	29.2%
Mommy track	0	0.0%	0	0.0%
Parking allowance	49	36.3%	29	44.6%
Travel allowance	92	68.1%	50	76.9%
Child care	2	1.5%	1	1.5%
Firm credit card	18	13.3%	9	13.8%
Job sharing	3	2.2%	0	0.0%

FIGURE 1-10a   Legal Assistant Fringe Benefit Survey

Source: "Legal Assistant Today Benefits Survey Results, 1993" Legal Assistant Today, July/August 1993, 42. Copyright 1993. James Publishing, Inc. Reprinted with permission from Legal Assistant Today. For subscription information, call (714) 755-5450.

Meal allowance	10	7.4%	9	13.8%
Professional dues	63	46.7%	49	75.4%
CLE courses	83	61.5%	44	67.7%
Firm retreat	8	5.9%	8	12.3%
Parental leave	28	20.7%	20	30.8%
Paid personal days off	68	50.4%	34	52.3%
Avg. # of vacation days	11.2		12.18	
Avg. # of sick days	6.37		9.79	
% resp. w/unlimited # of sick days		31.9%		10.8%

	Fringe Benefits All Employers 1993	
	# Resp.	%
Total # of Respondents:	630	
Work Location:		
Metropolitan	358	56.8%
Rural	40	6.3%
Urban	232	36.8%
Sex:		
Female	595	94.4%
Male	35	5.6%
Type of Present Employer:		
Corporation	102	16.2%
Private law firm	473	75.1%
Public sector-govt.	34	5.4%
Other	21	3.3%
Office Space:		
Private office	433	68.7%
Partitioned space	114	18.1%
Shared office	68	10.8%
Other	15	2.4%
Secretarial Assistance:		
Personal computer	194	30.8%
Personal secretary	30	4.8%
Shared secretary	331	52.5%
Word processing pool	37	5.9%
Other	38	6.0%
Benefits:		
Retirement plan	540	85.7%
Profit sharing	461	73.2%
Employer contributions to retirement plan	562	89.2%
Health insurance	571	90.6%
	(continued)	

**FIGURE 1-10b
Legal Assistant
Fringe Benefit
Survey**

Source: "Legal Assistant Today Benefits Survey Results, 1993" *Legal Assistant Today,* July/August 1993, 42. Copyright 1993. James Publishing, Inc. Reprinted with permission from *Legal Assistant Today.* For subscription information, call (714) 755-5450.

Life insurance	494	78.4%
Dental insurance	306	48.6%
Disability insurance	419	66.5%
Vision insurance	144	22.9%
Maternity benefits	379	60.2%
Free legal representation	304	48.3%
Business cards	493	78.3%
Expense account	138	21.9%
Flex time	210	33.3%
Mommy track	0	0.0%
Parking allowance	222	35.2%
Travel allowance	499	79.2%
Child care	16	2.5%
Company credit card	107	17.0%
Job sharing	23	3.7%
Meal allowance	91	14.4%
Professional dues	435	69.0%
Continuing legal ed.	423	67.1%
Firm retreat	79	12.5%
Parental leave	269	42.7%
Paid personal days off	375	59.5%
Avg. # of vacation days	13	13
Avg. # of sick days	9	9
% of resp. w/unlimited # of sick days		26.0%

LEGAL ASSISTANT ASSOCIATIONS

An indicator of the degree of professionalism of legal assistants is the existence of more than two hundred local, regional, state, and national legal assistant professional associations in the United States. A list of some of these associations is contained in appendix E. The two major national associations, National Association of Legal Assistants and National Federation of Paralegal Associations, represent more than thirty-two thousand members[5] and are very active in the development, training, regulation, and direction of the legal assistant profession.

THE JUDICIAL SYSTEM'S RECOGNITION OF THE LEGAL ASSISTANT PROFESSION

The United States Supreme Court case of *Missouri v. Jenkins*, 491 U.S. 274, 109 S.Ct. 2463, 105 L.Ed. 2d 229 (1989), established that the legal assistant profession has come of age. In that case, the plaintiff was successful on several counts under a federal statute in a civil rights lawsuit and was attempting to recover attorney's fees from the defendant. The federal statutory language allowed the prevailing party to recover "reasonable attorney's fees" from the adverse party. The plaintiff argued for the right to recover the time that both attorneys and legal assistants had spent working on the case. The defendant argued that legal assistant time was not "attorney's fees." Alternatively, the defendant argued that if required to pay for legal assistant time, the amount should be about fifteen dollars an hour, a representation of the overhead costs to the firm of a legal assistant.

The Court found that legal assistants carry out many useful tasks and "reasonable attorney's fees" refers to a reasonable fee for work produced, whether it be by attorneys or by legal assistants and could be compensable as long as the work was not of a clerical nature. The Court also found that under the federal statute, legal assistant time should be compensable at the prevailing market rates in the area for legal assistant's services. The Court noted that the prevailing rate for legal assistants in that part of the United States at that time was about forty dollars an hour and held that the plaintiff was entitled to receive that amount for legal assistant hours expended on the case. This important case defines a legal assistant position not as a secretarial or clerical position but as a professional, fee-generating profession.

Former Chief Justice Warren Burger stated that

> The "expanded use of well-trained assistants, sometimes called 'paralegals,' has been an important development. The advent of the paralegal enables law offices to perform high quality legal services at a lower cost. Possibly we have only scratched the surface of this development."[6]

Although the *Missouri v. Jenkins* case was a landmark decision for legal assistants, the opinion involved a federal court interpreting a specific federal statute, the Civil Rights Act. Fee questions occur under many different situations and in another court under a different statute a different decision might occur. This issue is discussed in more detail later in the book, but the *Missouri v. Jenkins* case is important to the legal assistant profession.

LEGAL ASSISTANT PROFITABILITY FOR LAW OFFICES

The use of legal assistants is a financially profitable proposition. Law offices charge clients for legal assistant time; however, they pay legal assistants a salary and do not share the profits of the firm with them. Also, legal assistant salaries are not as high as associate attorney salaries, and law offices are able to "sell" the use of legal assistants because of the cost-saving benefits they represent to the client over attorneys.

OFFICE MANAGER

Office managers *are found in smaller firms and handle day-to-day operations of the law office, including such activities as accounting, supervision of the clerical support staff, assisting the managing partner in preparing an annual budget, and making recommendations with regard to changes in systems and purchases.*[7] Office managers typically do not have degrees in business. Office managers are usually not given as much decision-making power as administrators, and unlike administrators, usually assist a managing partner in managing the law office. Nonetheless, good office managers are important to the survival of smaller firms. Experienced legal assistants are sometimes promoted into office manager positions.

LAW CLERKS

A **law clerk** *is usually a student who works for a law firm on a part-time basis while he or she is finishing a law degree. Law clerk duties revolve around legal research and*

office manager
Manager who handles day-to-day operations of the law office, such as accounting, supervision of the clerical support staff, and assisting the managing partner.

law clerk
A law student working for a law firm on a part-time basis while he or she is finishing a law degree. Law clerk duties revolve almost exclusively around legal research and writing.

writing almost exclusively. Law clerks perform legal research, write legal briefs and motions, and prepare memorandums of law.

LAW LIBRARIAN

law librarian
A librarian responsible for maintaining a law library. Maintenance includes purchasing new books and periodicals, classifying, storing, indexing, and updating the holdings, and coordinating computer-assisted legal research (i.e. WESTLAW, LEXIS, and other services).

A **law librarian** *is responsible for maintaining a law library. Maintenance includes purchasing new books and periodicals, classifying, storing, and indexing books, updating the holdings, and coordinating computer-assisted legal research (i.e., WESTLAW, LEXIS, and other services).*

SECRETARIES

secretaries
Employees who provide assistance and support to other law office staff by taking dictation, performing typing and filing functions, and aiding in scheduling of appointments.

Secretaries *provide assistance and support to other law office staff by taking dictation, performing typing and filing functions, and aiding in scheduling of appointments.* Secretaries include legal secretaries, receptionists, and word processing secretaries. Competent legal secretaries have highly specialized skills and perform many services to law firms. Legal secretaries, like legal assistants, have their own local, regional, state, and national associations. It is not uncommon for a person to start employment with a law office as a legal secretary and work his or her way up to legal assistant, office manager, or other positions. Receptionists are common in all law offices. Receptionist duties include answering the phone, greeting clients, opening the mail, and making photocopies. Word processing secretaries are common in larger law offices. They type, format, and produce documents using word processing software.

CLERKS

clerks
Employees who provide support to other staff positions in a variety of miscellaneous functions.

Clerks *provide support to other staff positions in a variety of miscellaneous functions.* Law offices may have a wide variety of clerks, including mail clerks, copy clerks, file clerks, calendar clerks, and billing clerks. Much of their work involves data entry and physically handling files and documents.

OTHER LEGAL TEAM MEMBERS

expert witness
A person who has technical expertise in a specific field and agrees to give testimony for a client at trial.

A variety of other people and organizations make up the legal team. Other team members may include expert witnesses, investigators, litigation support bureaus, and consultants. An **expert witness** *is a person who has technical expertise in a specific field and agrees to give testimony for a client at trial.* Professional investigators are hired in cases to gather facts and evidence regarding a case. Litigation support service bureaus are sometimes used in cases that have hundreds or thousands of documents to organize and records to computerize for trial. Law offices use business consultants, marketing consultants, and other types of consultants to give them advice on how to run their business efficiently.

TYPES OF LAW PRACTICES

To a certain extent, how law office management operates depends on the type of law office (see Figure 1-11). Therefore, it is necessary to review the different types of law practices and their functional effect on management. Usually, people think

	Number of Attorneys	Percent
Private practice	519,941	76.2%
Corporate practice	66,627	9.8%
Government practice	57,742	8.5%
Legal aid practice	7,369	1.0%
Other	30,746	4.5%
Total	**682,425**	**100%**

FIGURE 1-11
Active Attorneys by Type of Practice

Source: 1988 Lawyer Statistical Report. Printed with permission of American Bar Foundation.

only of the private law firm as a type of law practice, but there are others as well, including corporate law practices, government practices, and legal aid practices.

CORPORATE LAW PRACTICE

Some businesses have their own in-house law department, including large corporations, banks, retailers, manufacturers, transportation companies, publishers, insurance companies, and hospitals. In a corporate legal department, attorneys have just one client, the business. However, some corporate legal departments see each division or department in the corporation as a "client" that they must provide quality legal services for.

Corporations that have their own legal department are generally large, with millions of dollars in assets. Unlike private law firms, a corporate legal department is not involved in many administrative functions, such as accounting, since the corporation itself provides these services. Corporate legal departments do not record billable hours, since all costs are covered by the corporation. However, corporate legal departments must still budget, track, and plan activities, and they are responsible for the overall efficiency of their department. Corporate law departments handle a variety of legal concerns in such areas as labor relations, federal tax law, environmental law issues, SEC (Security Exchange Commission) filings, general litigation, real estate law, and workers' compensation claims.

> *The benefits of working for a corporation are really great. There is a lot of responsibility. . . . There is more opportunity for upward mobility within the company, since you can contribute your legal skills in other areas, such as sales and marketing. . . . The stress level is lower—it is not as frantic as at a law firm.*
>
> —A corporate legal assistant in **Carol Milano,** "1992 Legal Assistant Today Salary Survey Results," *Legal Assistant Today,* May/June 1992, 71.

Most corporate legal departments are too small to handle all the legal needs of the corporation, so the law departments hire private law firms that specialize in the additional areas they need. This is sometimes referred to as having "outside counsel." *The chief attorney for a corporate legal department is called the* **general counsel.** The general counsel, in addition to legal duties, may also be the corporate secretary.

Staffing in corporate legal departments includes secretaries, legal assistants, law clerks, administrators, and attorneys. Most corporate legal departments

general counsel
The chief for a corporate legal department.

employ one or more legal assistants (see Figure 1-12). The job duties a legal assistant performs in a corporate legal department are similar to those performed in other types of practices. Job duties might include preparing deposition summaries, performing legal research, interviewing witnesses, and drafting documents. Like legal assistants in private law firms, legal assistants in corporate legal departments might also specialize in specific areas such as litigation, real estate, or business law.

GOVERNMENT PRACTICE

Government attorneys, like corporate attorneys, have just one client. In most local, state, and federal agencies, there is a legal department that represents the interests of each particular agency. Government attorneys representing agencies or governmental bodies may be involved in contract law, bankruptcy law, tax law, employment law, property law, and environmental law to name a few. Each state also has an attorney general's office. The attorney general operates as the state's chief law enforcement officer and chief attorney. In many instances, when a state or state agency is sued, the state's attorney general's office represents the state. There are many other types of government attorneys, including prosecutors such as local district and city attorneys, state attorneys general, and United States attorneys.

In many ways, practicing for the government is similar to practicing for a large corporation. Government attorneys, like corporate attorneys, do not record billable hours and are not responsible for as many management duties as are their counterparts in private law firms. Government practices are different from the corporate legal department in that politics plays a role in governmental practices. Attorneys and legal assistants are paid according to their civil service classification. The political aspect of pay and advancement in a government bureaucracy sometimes affects expectations and aspirations.[8] Staffing for government legal departments consists of secretaries, investigators, legal assistants, law clerks, and attorneys. The job duties of legal assistants in government practices vary depending on the area of practice, and these duties may be tested for in various civil service exams that are a prerequisite to hiring.

FIGURE 1-12
Paralegals Employed by Corporations in Their Law Departments

Source: Special Report on Law Department Functions and Expenditures, 1989, Altman, Weil, Pensa, 14. Reprinted with permission of Altman Weil Pensa Publications, Inc. Copyright 1993 by Altman Weil Pensa Publications, Inc.

Sales Volume of Corporation	Average Number of Paralegals
Under $.5 billion	1
$.5 billion to $1 billion	2
$1 billion to $2.5 billion	3
Over $2.5 billion	7

LEGAL AID OFFICES

A **legal aid office,** sometimes called a legal clinic or public law office, *is a not-for-profit law office that receives grants from the government and private donations to pay for representation of disadvantaged persons who otherwise could not afford legal services.* In some cases, legal aid offices or clinics are operated by law schools, bar associations, or other nonprofit entities as a public service to the community. Clients pay little or no fees for legal services. Legal aid offices typically represent the disadvantaged in areas relating to child support, child custody, disability claims, bankruptcies, landlord-tenant disputes, and mental health problems. Staffing for legal aid offices includes secretaries, legal assistants, law clerks, and attorneys. In legal aid practices, legal assistants may be used fairly extensively and are usually given a wide variety of tasks because their use is cost effective.

legal aid office
A not-for-profit law office that receives grants from the government and private donations to pay for representation of disadvantaged persons who otherwise could not afford legal services.

After ten years of work at the Vermont Legal Aid, I seem to have accumulated cases that never close, clients that never stop calling. . . . "Can I run this by you?" So why does this work still seem fresh and new to me? Perhaps because no day is like any other. . . .

(A recent case of) helping [a] client through her housing crisis was a team effort, and that is a real benefit of working in this office.

—Printed with permission of Vermont Bar Association. This article appeared in the *Vermont Bar Journal & Law Digest,* vol. 19, no. 2 (April 1993): 20, by Joan C. Bauer, Esquire. A Legal Aid attorney.

PRIVATE LAW PRACTICES

The most common way that attorneys practice law is in a private law firm (see Figure 1-11). A private law practice is a firm that generates its own income from representing clients. Private law firms, like any business, are operated to make a profit for their owners. Private law firms represent a variety of clients and come in all shapes and sizes, from the solo practitioner to large group practices. See Figure 1-13 for a list of the different types of private law practices.

Group practices are usually differentiated according to the number of attorneys in the group. The terminology is somewhat arbitrary, but a small firm usually refers to a law office that has fewer than twenty attorneys; a medium-size

---

I. Sole practitioner
II. Office sharing
III. Group practices
    1. Small law firm
        a. Boutique firm
    2. Medium-size firm
    3. Large firm

FIGURE 1-13
Types of Private Law Practices

firm usually has from twenty to seventy-five attorneys; and a large firm can be from seventy-five to hundreds of attorneys. There are a few "megafirms" that have between five hundred and one thousand attorneys or more. Private practices, no matter the size, have their own unique styles, methods, clients, cultures, and ways of doing things. Almost half of all attorneys are sole practitioners (see Figure 1-14).

> *For over two years, I have worked for a sole legal practitioner. I am the only paralegal in the office and am directly involved in almost everything that transpires in our office. . . . My input is not only heard, but utilized. I have no billing quotas. While we do keep close track of billable hours, I don't have to justify every minute of my workday. . . .*
>
> —A sole practitioner's legal assistant. "Am I the Only Small-Firm Paralegal?" *Legal Assistant Today,* March/April 1993, 15.

SOLE PRACTITIONER

A sole practitioner is an attorney who individually owns and manages the practice. Anyone who works for the attorney is considered an employee. Sole practitioners sometimes hire another attorney as an employee. The employee attorney would not be entitled to any share in the profits of the practice. Although the sole practitioner has the advantage of freedom and independence, he or she is also ultimately responsible for all or nearly all the legal work performed by the law office and is also responsible for all the management duties. For the sole practitioner to succeed, it is important that overhead costs be as small as possible. Overhead costs are expenses incurred month after month and include such things as rent (thus the term "overhead"), utilities, the lease of equipment such as copiers and computers, and support staff salaries. These are costs incurred whether the attorney is serving one client or one hundred clients. Sole practitioners typically have small offices with a very small law library.

Sole practitioners are typically generalists, meaning they handle a wide variety of cases such as probate, family law, criminal law, and personal injury. The sole practitioner typically refers a case outside of his or her area of expertise to another attorney who is skilled in that matter. Sole practitioners need good management skills for their practice to survive. This may pose a problem because management duties take the sole practitioner away from the actual practice of law, which is the activity that brings in the money.

FIGURE 1-14
Attorneys Practicing in Each Size of Law Office

Source: 1988 Lawyer Statistical Report. Printed with permission of American Bar Foundation.

	Number of Attorneys	Percent
Solo	240,141	46.2%
2–5 lawyer law office	89,854	17.3%
6–10 lawyer law office	40,612	7.8%
11–20 lawyer law office	36,859	7.1%
21–50 lawyer law office	36,563	7.0%
51–100 lawyer law office	26,273	5.1%
100 or more lawyer law office	49,639	9.5%
Total	**519,941**	**100%**

Staffing can include a secretary, legal assistant, law clerk, and possibly an associate attorney. These positions may even be part time. Legal assistants working in a sole practitioner's office enjoy a great deal of responsibility and diversity in their jobs. Duties include legal research, drafting pleadings and discovery materials, word processing, and interviewing witnesses. Because sole practitioners are generalists, their legal assistants work in many areas of law. In a solo practice, the legal assistant has the opportunity to learn firsthand about law office management and to perform management functions.

OFFICE SHARING

An **office sharing** *arrangement is one in which two or more sole practitioners share office space and sometimes share support staff but do not share profits.* Sharing office space and support staff allows the sole practitioner to share overhead costs. Each sole practitioner contributes to the cost of rent, utilities, and support staff. Office sharing usually occurs in a small building or house converted to a law office, allowing attorneys to share suites or rooms in the building. A problem that sometimes arises with the office sharing arrangement is that some clients may think the attorneys are a partnership. Confidentiality can also be a problem if support staff is shared between the attorneys.

office sharing
An arrangement in which two or more sole practitioners share office space and sometimes share support staff but do not share profits.

> *I really enjoy my job (working for three sole practitioners). My employers keep me busy, and I am given lots of responsibilities. As the one support person for three attorneys, my job includes—you name it. I order supplies, maintain equipment, update the statutes, maintain the library, etc.*
>
> —Office sharing legal assistant in **Carol Milano,** "1992 Legal Assistant Today Salary Survey Results," *Legal Assistant Today,* May/June 1992, 63.

LAW FIRMS

Law firms have two or more attorneys in practice together. While there is not as much freedom as in solo practice, law firms do not have as much risk as a solo practitioner has. If a sole practitioner becomes ill, loses a large client, or faces other such catastrophes, the sole practitioner's income may be endangered. In law firms, these problems may be alleviated because more than one attorney is available. Law firms are usually categorized as either small, medium, or large.

> *The (small) size of the law office contributes to the fact that we, as paralegals, are appreciated for more than just our clerical or organizational skills. At times we do research or writing that an associate might do at a larger law office.*
>
> —Small law firm legal assistant in **Peggy N. Kerley,** "High-Profile Criminal Defense Cases Attract Top Paralegals," *Legal Assistant Today,* July/August 1992, 33.

**FIGURE 1-15
Law Firms by Law
Office Size**

Source: 1988 Lawyer
Statistical Report. Printed
with permission of American
Bar Foundation.

2–5 lawyers	32,729 firms	76.7%
6–10 lawyers	5,497 firms	12.9%
11–20 lawyers	2,583 firms	6.1%
21–50 lawyers	1,201 firms	2.8%
51–100 lawyers	381 firms	0.9%
100 or more lawyers	258 firms	0.6%
Total number of firms	**42,649 firms**	**100%**

THE SMALL LAW FIRM   The small firm usually has fewer than twenty attorneys. As you can see from Figure 1-15, 95 percent of all law firms are in this category. Most small firms have a staff member such as an office manager who helps with the day-to-day operations of the business. However, a partner or managing partner is usually responsible for major management decisions such as hiring, firing, distributing profits, and setting salaries. Small firms usually concentrate in a few areas of the law but may also have attorneys who are general practitioners.

A small law office that specializes in only one or two areas of the law is sometimes called a **boutique firm.** The boutique firm normally has several attorneys who practice in the same specialty. Legal assistants who work for boutique firms also usually become specialists in that particular area of law.

boutique firm
A small law office that
specializes in only one
or two areas of the law.

Disadvantages that hinder small firms include cash-flow problems, the lack of time to recruit, hire, and train new staff, little time for management, and long hours. Staffing positions include clerks, secretaries, legal assistants, office managers, law clerks, and attorneys. Small firms offer legal assistants a relatively large variety of tasks to perform.

THE MEDIUM-SIZE FIRM   The medium-size firm usually has from twenty to seventy-five attorneys. Typically, medium-size firms are organized into subject-area departments. Medium-size firms differ from small firms in that most medium-size firms have professional administrators who manage many aspects of the business. Administrators usually report to a managing partner or a committee that has overall management responsibilities. Medium-size firms typically have multiple offices, and it is not uncommon for them to have sophisticated computer systems. Staffing often consists of administrators, law librarians, receptionists, secretaries, legal assistants, law clerks, and attorneys. Legal assistants in medium-size firms have a more structured existence than in smaller firms. The diversity of duties and areas of practice are not as broad as in smaller firms. However, the legal assistant may learn a particular area of law in-depth. In addition, the internal structure and lines of communication are more intense and more important than in small firms where colleagues tend to be more familiar with one another.

THE LARGE FIRM   The large firm has from seventy-five to several hundred attorneys. A few large firms, sometimes called "megafirms" have five hundred to one thousand or more attorneys. Most large firms have practice groups or departments. The internal structure of these firms is more similar to the structure of business corporations than to other types of law firms. Staffing in large firms typically includes various classes of legal assistants, law clerks, and attorneys in addition to the positions shown in Figure 1-16. Large firms often have as clients large corporations. Many have offices throughout the United States, and some

Accounts payable clerk	Legal assistant supervisor
Accounts receivable clerk	Library aides
Analysts	Mail clerks
Bookkeepers	Messengers/pages
Chief financial officer/comptroller	Payroll specialists
Computer specialists	Proofreaders
Copy room clerks	Purchasing clerks
Credit/collections manager	Receptionists
Data processing operators	Records/file manager
Director of marketing	Recruiter
Docket clerks	Reservation clerks
Employee benefits manager	Risk manager
Equipment manager	Secretaries
Facilities manager	Telephone operators
File room clerks	Time and billing assistants
Human resource manager	Word processors
Legal administrator	Word processing supervisor

FIGURE 1-16
Large Law Firm Administrative Staff Positions

have international offices. Large firms also have resources such as large law libraries, a word processing department, and extensive technologically advanced computer systems connecting all their offices for information exchange.

Disadvantages encountered by large firms include recruiting and retaining good employees in the vital areas of the practice, getting departments to communicate and work together, and controlling the bureaucracy itself. Large law firms usually employ a large number of legal assistants and treat them formally and professionally, requiring them to attend department meetings, assist attorneys in depositions, and travel as needed. Computers are used extensively by legal assistants. The physical space occupied by a large firm is more lavish than in small and medium firms, usually including occupying several floors in a large office building.

PLAINTIFF/DEFENSE FIRMS

Private law practices may categorize themselves as either plaintiff or defense oriented no matter what the size of the law office. Plaintiff-oriented firms, as the name implies, represent clients who bring claims against others. Plaintiff-oriented firms tend to be smaller than defense-oriented firms, are generally not as well funded as defense-oriented firms, and have fewer employees. Cash flow in plaintiff firms may not be as stable as in defense-oriented firms because in many cases they take clients on a contingency fee basis. That is, the law office recovers fees for the case only if it wins.

Defense-oriented firms, on the other hand, have the luxury of billing defendants, who are typically businesses, according to the time spent on the case. This gives defense-oriented firms a more stable cash flow, enabling them to hire more personnel, purchase advanced equipment, and spend more on litigation services such as hiring expert witnesses and taking as many depositions as needed. Nonetheless, effective management is needed in both plaintiff- and defense-oriented firms.

Good management, including budgeting, fiscal planning, cost-efficient hiring and training of personnel, efficient use of people and equipment, and leadership, is important to all types of law practices.[9]

LAW PRACTICE ORGANIZATION STRUCTURES

Law practices have different organization or management structures. Private law practices are managed by a powerful managing partner, by all partners, or by committees. Corporate and government law practices have either a centralized or decentralized management structure.

LEGAL FORMS OF PRIVATE LAW FIRMS

Management structures of law firms are affected by the firm's legal status. A law firm can be formed as a sole proprietorship, partnership, corporation, or, in some states, a limited liability company. Before the management structure of law offices can be considered, the legal status of law offices must be explained.

SOLE PROPRIETORSHIP   In a sole proprietorship, the proprietor, in this case an attorney, runs the business and personally receives all profits and is personally responsible for all losses and liabilities of the law office. However, keep in mind that a sole proprietorship is a distinct type of legal structure. A sole practitioner does not have to use the sole proprietorship form of legal structure. Many sole practitioners are incorporated.

PARTNERSHIP   The partnership's legal structure allows two or more attorneys to associate themselves together and to share in the profits or losses of the business. Many group practices use this structure. When a law office is established as a partnership, the founding attorneys are usually named as partners. As growth takes place, the partnership may hire additional associate attorneys.

All the partners are jointly and severally liable for the actions of the firm. This means if one partner commits malpractice and injures a client, each partner may be held individually or jointly responsible. Partners are also personally liable for the debts of the partnership. Partnerships typically use committees to make policy decisions, and partners meet regularly to discuss partnership business.

PROFESSIONAL CORPORATION   The professional corporation allows a single shareholder or a group of shareholders from the same profession such as attorneys to join to share in the outcomes of a business. When a law office is established as a professional corporation, the founding attorney or attorneys receive shares in the business. As in a partnership, associates are not owners and are only paid a salary. Shareholders can vote to offer additional shares of the business to associates and expand the ownership of the law firm. All attorneys are employees of the corporation and are paid a salary. Besides a salary, shareholders are paid a dividend. The amount of the dividend depends on the profitability of the corporation and on the number of shares owned. Shareholders are not personally responsible for the debts of the professional corporation. The corporate form requires the election of officers and a board of directors.

LIMITED LIABILITY COMPANY   The limited liability company (LLC) is a hybrid form of legal structure. It is a combination of the corporate and partnership form. The LLC form of structure is valid in more than thirty states. The main advantage of an LLC is that it allows for limited personal liability of company debts for its owners (like a corporation) but is treated like a partnership for income tax purposes.

PRIVATE LAW FIRM MANAGEMENT STRUCTURES

The type of management or governing structure used to manage the business aspect of the firm is the choice of the firm, but the legal structure of the business may dictate some of that management structure. For example, a corporation by law must have a board of directors. Many law practices struggle with the problem of who runs the firm and who has the final say on firm decisions. Possible management structures include the powerful managing partner, rule by all partners/shareholders, and rule by management committee or board[10] (see Figure 1-17).

THE POWERFUL MANAGING PARTNER[11]   The **powerful managing partner** *management structure is one in which a single partner is responsible for managing the firm.* The managing partner is responsible for day-to-day operations of the partnership while partners vote on major firm decisions. The managing partner may have a specific term of office. In some firms, the position is rotated among the practicing partners. In many firms, the managing partner spends anywhere from 60 percent to 100 percent of his or her time on management responsibilities. This form allows other partners to spend more time practicing law but places the managerial duties on one partner and reduces the managing partner's time to practice law. The powerful managing partner structure is autocratic, meaning that power rests with one person. In some cases, the other partners may feel they are without a voice in the management of the firm.

powerful managing partner
A management structure in which a single partner is responsible for managing the firm.

RULE BY ALL PARTNERS/SHAREHOLDERS[12]   **Rule by all partners/shareholders** *is a management structure in which all partners/shareholders are included in decisions that affect the firm.* All the partners or shareholders meet whenever management policies or decisions need to be made. This is a democratic structure, since all the partners have a say in firm decisions and policies. Although this structure allows partners/shareholders involvement in all the decisions of the firm, as the number of partners/shareholders increases, the effectiveness of the group may decrease with more people added to the body. This may foster indecision and a lack of direction.

rule by all partners/ shareholders
A management structure in which all partners/shareholders are included in decisions that affect the firm.

RULE BY MANAGEMENT COMMITTEE/BOARD[13]   The **rule by management committee/board** *management structure uses a committee structure to make management decisions for the firm.* Committees are made up of five to ten members depending on the size of the firm. Committees are typically made up of partners or shareholders but may include administrators, associates, and legal assistants. Common committees include the library committee, automation committee, finance committee, and personnel committee. These committees usually report to a management or executive committee. If the committee gets too large, the actions of the committee slow down greatly and can hamper the effectiveness of the firm.

a rule by management committee/board
Management structure that uses a committee structure to make management decisions for the firm.

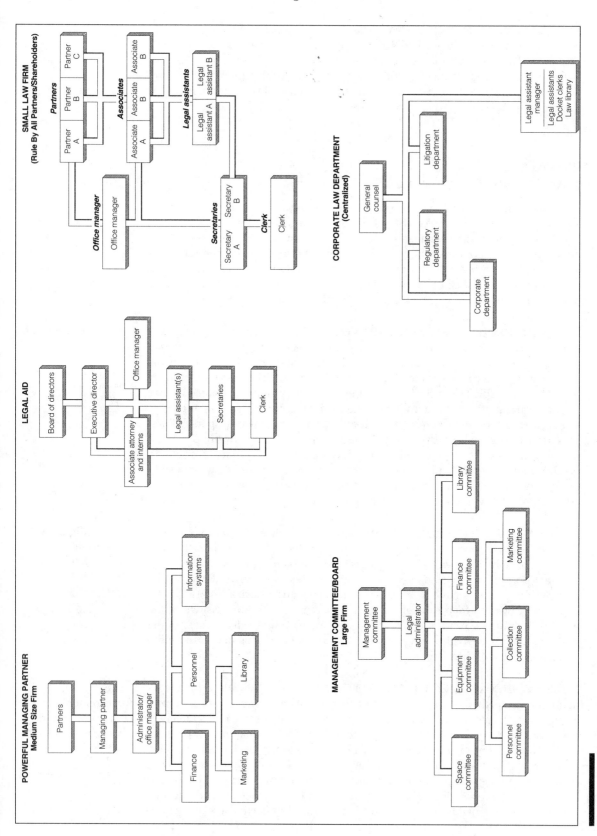

FIGURE 1-17　Organizational Charts

Source: *The Manager's Manual*, Legal Asst. Mgmt. Assoc., 1991. Printed with the permission of the Legal Assistant Management Association (LAMA).

CORPORATE, GOVERNMENT, AND LEGAL AID ORGANIZATION STRUCTURES

Corporate and government law practices have different organizational and management structures than do private law firms. Corporate law departments can be centralized or decentralized. In the past, many, but not all, were centralized, meaning they were usually located in the firm's corporate headquarters but provided legal services for the whole company. Many government practices take a decentralized approach. Most state and federal agencies have their own legal departments that provide legal services only to that particular agency. Like most private law firms, corporate and government practices can have different divisions within the practice such as litigation or labor law. Although many corporate departments are centralized and many government practices decentralized, the choice depends on the type, size, and dynamics of the organization.

The management structure of corporate and government practices is dependent upon the corporation's or agency's own organizational structure as well. Many corporate and government departments have a general counsel responsible for the overall management of the department. The power of the general counsel is similar to that of the powerful managing partner in private law firms. However, the power is diluted, since the general counsel must still act under the auspices of the overall corporate structure or of the legislative or other public body in the government practice.

Legal aid practices, because they are usually nonprofit corporations, are overseen by a board of directors. The board of directors might be made up of law professors, attorneys in private practice, judges, and other interested persons. The board usually hires an executive director who is responsible for the day-to-day operations of the practice. The executive director has attorneys, legal assistants, clerical staff, and administrators who report to him or her.

LAW OFFICE MANAGEMENT PRINCIPLES

There was a time when law office management was viewed as unimportant. Attorneys viewed management responsibilities as something that got in the way of providing legal services to their clients. In truth, some of this view still prevails. This is why a competent legal assistant, able to take over many responsibilities in office management, is a valuable member of the legal team. Today, the highly competitive nature of the legal field and the need to control costs make law office management an important topic. While you might think that management is more important in very large firms than in small law firms or corporate law departments, the opposite is true. Good management skills are equally important in every type of legal practice if the practice is going to be successful in serving clients, providing quality jobs for its employees, and producing profits for its partners or shareholders.

During the past ten years, there has been an automation revolution that has changed law office management. Until recently, law offices were generally unconcerned with computers, word processing, computerized accounting and billing, state-of-the-art telephone systems, copiers, and facsimile machines. However, during the past decade, law offices have spent millions of dollars purchasing this type of equipment. Law offices, like most other businesses, have discovered that purchasing state-of-the-art equipment gives them an edge over their competition, greatly increases staff productivity, and improves the quality of the services they can provide.

DISPELLING A MYTH

A myth about attorneys needs to be dispelled. Many people assume that attorneys automatically make good managers. In truth it is generally agreed that many lawyers are not very good managers.[14] Although lawyers have gone to school to learn about practicing law, most have no management skills or training. Practicing law and practicing management take very different skills. In fact, there is an adage that says: "The best system for law office management is the system that involves the lawyers least."[15] Although attorneys may realize that management is important, that does not necessarily mean they are proficient at it. As you read this chapter, keep in mind that many attorneys practicing today have never taken a course like this one. Although national and local bar associations are beginning to put emphasis on training attorneys in management skills, they still have a long way to go. Because of the general lack of management training for attorneys, legal assistants with good management skills can be very useful to law firms.

In today's medium- and larger-size firms, the situation is alleviated somewhat with the use of professional administrators. Unfortunately, most smaller firms do not have the resources to hire administrators and must rely on attorneys, legal assistants, and other staff members to deal with problems as well as their other duties. Given the increasing competitiveness of the legal market, effective law office management will be a prime concern for law firms for years to come.

WHY LEGAL ASSISTANTS NEED TO KNOW LAW OFFICE MANAGEMENT

If you think that good law office management does not affect legal assistants, reread the example at the beginning of the chapter about the law office. It is not an uncommon event to have a law practice close or merge. The cost of operating a law office is extremely high, and legal assistants depend on the viability of the law office for their economic survival. Management affects everyone in the practice. Other reasons why good management is important to legal assistants are that well-managed practices run with fewer problems and crises, work flows smoothly, billings and client payments are received in a timely manner, appointments and deadlines are met, staff members are adequately compensated, and there is less stress.

Practicing good management is hard; it takes time and teamwork but is well worth the effort. Some signs of poor management include frustrated and unhappy staff members and clients, daily "crisis," reduced attorney effectiveness, higher costs, low employee job satisfaction, high employee turnover, increased use of employee sick leave, and low staff morale. From the legal secretary to the law clerk to the legal assistant to the attorney, everyone has a stake in the action. In short, effective management is good for all and should be practiced by all.

practice management
Management decisions about how a law office will practice law and handle its cases.

PRACTICE MANAGEMENT V. ADMINISTRATIVE MANAGEMENT

There are two major aspects of managing a law office: practice management and administrative management. **Practice management (i.e. substantive or case man-**

FIGURE 1-18
Practice
Management v.
Administrative
Management

Practice, Case, or Substantive Management:
- What type of <u>cases</u> should we specialize in?
- Which <u>cases</u> should we accept?
- How will <u>case</u> files be organized?
- How will documents for each <u>case</u> be indexed for retrieval later?
- What form files will need to be created for each type of <u>case</u>?

Administrative, Office, or "Plant" Management:
- Purchasing equipment and supplies for the <u>law</u> <u>office</u>.
- Hiring and evaluating law <u>office</u> <u>staff</u>.
- Sending out invoices for the <u>law</u> <u>office</u>.
- Managing the finances and profitability of the <u>law</u> <u>office</u>.
- What administrative structure is the most efficient for the <u>law</u> <u>office</u>?

agement) *refers to management decisions about how a law office will practice law and handle its cases* (see Figure 1-18). Practice management decisions include determining the general types of cases the law office will specialize in, how many cases the law office should accept in a given area, and which clients should be accepted or rejected. Practice management is sometimes called "case management" or "file management" because this type of management centers on managing and controlling client files and client cases.

The cases and clients a law office takes on directly affect the profitability of the firm. If a law office undertakes to represent a number of client cases that do not generate any profits because the client did not pay, or the contingency case is lost, or the fees received are unexpectedly low, the economic effects on the law office are quite harmful. Also, if law office staff does not manage and organize cases effectively, then there may be poor quality legal services, reduced profitability, unhappy clients, and ethical complaints.

Administrative management (i.e. office management or "plant" management) *refers to management decisions relating to operating or managing a law office, including financial and personnel matters.* Administrative management is the focus of this text.

FUNCTIONS OF LAW OFFICE MANAGEMENT

Management *is the use of people and other resources to accomplish objectives.*[16] In private law practices (i.e. private businesses that provide legal services for a fee), the primary objective of management is to provide efficient, high-quality, affordable legal services to clients while earning a reasonable profit for the firm. In a corporate or government legal department, where generating a profit is not applicable, the objective of management is to provide efficient, high-quality legal services to its client at a reasonable cost. Law office management functions include providing financial management, practice management, and human resource (personnel) management, planning for the future, providing organization, setting policies, creating effective systems, providing marketing management, controlling the law office, and providing the law office with leadership. Figure 1-19 contains a detailed list of the duties of each function of management.

1. **Financial management** *is the oversight of a firm's financial assets and profitability to ensure overall financial health.* Financial management is important in any

administrative management
Management decisions relating to operating or managing a law office, including financial and personnel matters.

management
The use of people and other resources to accomplish objectives.

financial management
The oversight of a firm's financial assets and profitability to ensure overall financial health.

Financial Management
- Budgeting
- Forecasting
- Profitability analysis
- Financial reporting
- Cash disbursements
- Cash flow analysis
- General ledger accounting
- Billing rate analysis
- Accounts receivable control
- Banking relationships
- Investments
- Tax planning and reporting
- Trust accounting
- Payroll and employee benefit plans
- Lease negotiations
- Purchasing and inventory control
- Insurance

Practice Management
- Legal practice systems
- Legal practice quality control
- Planning client development
- Case management systems
- Practice management planning
- Case development

Human Resource Management
- Personnel recruitment, selection, and placement
- Personnel orientation, training, and development
- Performance evaluation
- Salary and benefit administration
- Employee relations
- Counseling
- Discipline
- Termination
- Workers' compensation
- Organization analysis
- Job design and development of job descriptions

Planning
- Short-term planning
- Long-term strategic and tactical planning
- Budgeting
- Forecasting
- Planning client development

Organizing, Making Policies, and Creating Effective Systems
- Policy making
- Operations analysis
- Systems analysis
- Procedures manual
- Computer systems
- Records and library management
- Office automation
- Document construction systems
- Information storage and retrieval
- Telecommunications
- Litigation support
- Conflict of interest docket systems
- Risk management

Marketing Management
- Business development
- Management of client-profitability analysis
- Forecasting of business opportunities
- Marketing legal services: Enhancement of the firm's visibility and image in the desired markets

Controlling and Determining the Effectiveness of the Firm
- Analysis regarding effectiveness of long- and short-range plans
- Operational audits
- Financial audits
- Analysis of financial reports

Leadership
- Firm leadership and direction
- Organizational development
- Motivation
- Development of firm identity and culture

FIGURE 1-19 Law Firm Management Duties

business. A business that does not earn a profit soon goes out of existence. Financial management includes preparing budgets for expected income and expenses, managing cash flow so there is money in the bank to cover payrolls and other expenses *when* the expenses come due, issuing invoices, purchasing goods and services necessary to provide legal services, keeping proper accounting and tax records, paying bills, setting proper fee schedules, and preparing financial status reports.

2. **Practice management**—Management must ensure that the firm's clients receive prompt, quality legal services at a fair cost. Law firms are service providers, and if clients do not receive quality legal services, they *will* go somewhere else to get the service they expect. A firm's lifeblood is dependent upon the ability of management to prudently choose the type of clients it serves, to keep existing clients, and to gain new clients.

A conviction that the client's needs must be placed above anything else is apparent in successful firms.

—A law firm consultant in **Thomas S. Clay,** "Profile of a Successful Law Firm," *The Law Firm Management Guide,* 1988, A-15.

---

3. **Human resource management** *refers to recruiting, hiring, training, evaluating, maintaining, and directing the personnel who will provide quality legal services to clients.* A law office cannot provide quality legal services without a well-trained staff.

4. **Planning** *is the process of setting objectives, assessing future needs, and developing a course of action to achieve the objectives.*[17] Planning is the road map for meeting the firm's goals. Law firms should have short-range and long-range plans or goals. A short-term plan might include raising staff salaries or increasing profitability by 10 percent. A long-term plan for a law office might include opening additional offices in other cities or expanding the practice into new legal areas. Without a plan, the law office goes about its business with no real direction. Successful law practices only happen by careful planning and the execution of good management decisions.

5. **Organization, determining policies, and creating effective systems**— **Organizing** *is the process of arranging people and physical resources to carry out plans and accomplish objectives.*[18] Management must make effective policy decisions to achieve its goals and carry out its plan. Part of this function is the process of creating systems that will bring this about. A **system** *is a consistent or organized way of doing something.* Establishing good systems is very important to effective law office management. Effective systems save time and money and ensure that all clients receive quality services. Systems are discussed in more depth later in this chapter.

6. **Marketing management**—**Marketing** *is the process of educating consumers about the legal services the law office provides.* It is not enough to simply service existing clients. Law firms, like other businesses in a competitive environment, must continue to bring in new business to grow and survive.

7. **Controlling** *is the process of determining whether the law practice is achieving its objectives.* Management must determine whether the law office is achieving its short- and long-range objectives so adjustments can be made to ensure that the office meets its goals.

8. **Leadership** *is the act of motivating or causing others to perform and achieve objectives.* Good, effective leadership inspires others, gives the law office vision and

human resource management
Recruiting, hiring, training, evaluating, maintaining, and directing the personnel that will provide quality legal services to the clients.

planning
The process of setting objectives, assessing the future, and developing courses of action to achieve these objectives.

organizing
The process of arranging people and physical resources to carry out plans and accomplish objectives.

system
A consistent or organized way of doing something.

marketing
The process of educating consumers on the quality legal services that a law office can provide.

controlling
The process of determining whether the law practice is achieving its objectives.

leadership
The act of motivating or causing others to perform and achieve objectives.

direction, and gives the law office an overriding purpose. Successful businesses have good leadership.

Notice that certain aspects of all these responsibilities (except marketing management) apply to corporate, legal aid, and government practices as well. All practices must provide financial management and quality legal services, must plan for the future, and must be adaptable as new problems arise. No law practice can ignore management problems and escape unharmed. If the practice is going to be successful, good management is necessary.

These management areas or responsibilities are interrelated. Performing only some is not enough. No matter how well a law office manages its human resources and ensures quality legal services to its clients, if financial management is lacking, the success of the law office is at risk. Likewise, good financial management is not enough to save a law office if the other management skills are lacking. Each of these management areas is developed more fully in this text.

THE SYSTEMS VIEW OF MANAGEMENT

A system is a consistent or organized way of doing something. A system allows you to create a set procedure for doing something as opposed to dealing with activities or problems in an ad hoc manner.

substantive task
A task that relates to the process of actually performing legal work for clients.

administrative task
A task relating to the internal practices and duties involved with operating or managing a law office.

Without a system, each time a legal service or an administrative function is performed, the person performing the task would rely solely on his or her memory to complete the task. Accuracy suffers and time is wasted while staff recreates the system each time a task is done.[19] By developing a system, staff members can take advantage of the experience and expertise of others in the law office. In essence, a system collects experience and expertise and passes it on to others. Systems preserve the procedures that have worked successfully in the past, but they also allow for future evolution.[20] Systems guarantee quality because the same mistakes are not made twice. Many law offices have a "systems" manual called a law office staff manual, which reduces the systems to writing. This way, the law office's systems are clearly established for all employees and can be passed down to new employees with less effort.

Systems can be used for both substantive tasks and administrative tasks. A **substantive task** *is one task that relates to the process of actually performing legal work for clients.* An **administrative task** *(or a business-related task) is one relating to the internal practices and duties involved with operating or managing a law office.*

Substantive systems include using form files, checklists, and detailed instructions to standardize many types of legal tasks. Certain areas of the law are particularly suitable for systems because of their routine nature, including: bankruptcy, divorces, adoptions, probate, estate planning, and workers' compensation.

Administrative tasks such as docket control, timekeeping and billing, purchasing, and human resource management can also be set up using an established system of procedures. A systems manual or staff manual establishes administrative procedures and documents how things will be accomplished administratively. Systems and staff manuals are covered in more detail in a subsequent chapter. However, it is important that you realize from the beginning how important good systems are to effective law office management.

From a financial point of view, proper use of "systems" allows attorneys to delegate more complicated work to legal assistants and in turn allows legal assistants to delegate clerical work to clerical employees. This is a financial benefit to the law office on the substantive side because it allows the firm to do the same amount of work with reduced cost to the firm and the clients. On the administrative side, a legal assistant can perform administrative tasks and relieve the attorney to do substantive legal work for clients. Efficient firms delegate work to the lowest competent level. For example, if an attorney, law clerk, legal assistant, and secretary all have the ability to perform a certain task competently, efficiency says that the work should be performed by the secretary, since the secretary's cost to the law office is the least. Although there is a "cost" to setting up a system, including the time and expertise to develop it, once it is in place the savings are substantial over time.

The legal assistant is in a perfect position to be an innovator of both administrative and substantive systems. Much of what a legal assistant does is amendable to systemization. Any member of a law office who creates or innovates usable and timesaving systems will gain a reputation for his or her ability to solve problems and will be a valued member of the law office team.

SUMMARY

Law offices depend on a legal team of effective players that includes attorneys, administrators, legal assistants, secretaries, clerks, and others to be successful. There are several types of law practices, including corporate, government, legal aid, and private, and each has its own management structures. Good management is necessary for the effective practice of law in all types of firms and for the overall survival of any type of law practice. Management is the use of people and other resources to accomplish objectives. Specific law office management functions include providing financial, marketing, and human resource management; providing leadership; controlling; organizing; ensuring quality legal services; creating effective systems; making policies; and planning for the future. Good systems are important to law practices since they save time, allow more work to be delegated, increase the quality of the legal services provided, and reduce costs.

EXPERIENCED LITIGATION LEGAL ASSISTANT

Betsy Horn, CLA

of Harris, Finley & Bogle, P.C.

Fort Worth, Texas

INTRODUCTION

Betsy Horn, CLA (certified legal assistant) has ten years' experience as a legal assistant, and currently works at Harris, Finley & Bogle, P.C., Fort Worth, Texas, as a litigation legal assistant. Betsy had six weeks of typing when she began her legal career as a receptionist. "I loved it, I kept asking for more work, and I was promoted to a legal secretary position," Betsy said. "When I took the legal secretary position, I told the firm up front that I wanted to move up and be a legal assistant when a position came available. Three years later I was promoted. It is a mistake not to tell people what you expect and where you want to go."

HARRIS, FINLEY & BOGLE— THE STRUCTURE OF THE FIRM

Harris, Finley & Bogle is a fifteen-attorney firm in Fort Worth, Texas. The firm began in 1977 when two attorneys left a larger firm to start their own practice. The firm has four legal assistants and two administrative staff members and employs thirty people. The firm has five practice sections separated rather casually as follows:

- Bankruptcy
- Trial/Litigation
- Oil and Gas
- Banking and Real Estate
- Probate and Estates

"We describe ourselves as a general practice," Betsy said. "We represent banks, oil and gas producers, individuals, investors, a seminary, and debtors and creditors, to name a few." The firm is set up as a professional corporation and a managing shareholder manages the firm on a day-to-day basis. However, Betsy says that "major firm decisions are made by the entire group of shareholders—each shareholder has one vote. This structure works well for our firm, it provides for diversity of opinion, and it allows the younger shareholders to have as much vote as more senior shareholders. It also allows the younger shareholders to learn from the more senior shareholders who have more experience, have been through economic crises, and have more temperance than younger members of the firm." The overriding philosophy of the firm is "to bring quality legal work to clients promptly and efficiently."

WHO BETSY WORKS FOR AND HOW SHE MANAGES ASSIGNMENTS

"I have two attorneys who are technically my supervising attorneys, but I work for all of the attorneys in the firm. While I can receive assignments from any attorney in the firm, there are six attorneys who work in the litigation, probate, and corporate sections for whom I particularly do a lot of work," Betsy said. It can be very difficult to manage assignments when a legal assistant has more than one attorney she is working for, let alone six.

"When you work for more than a couple of attorneys it can get really difficult. In our firm attorneys do not have priority—work has priority." That is, if a younger attorney has work that has a deadline or an immediate need, that work is done before a more senior attorney's work is completed that does not have an immediate need.

"I have an assignment log that I keep and when work comes in, the assignment is given a pri-

ority by the attorney when it is needed. I do not set priorities, I ask for them. 'When do you need this and what priority level is this, low, medium, or high.'" Since Betsy tracks all assignments including due dates and priorities, she can usually tell when she receives an assignment if there is a conflict. "If there is a conflict, the attorneys work it out. As a legal assistant, the way we are relieved of responsibility if we have a conflict is to immediately ask the attorney who just brought something in and say 'I have this work scheduled by so-and-so. Will you please go check with that attorney and see if that work can be set aside until later? Nine times out of ten the attorney who just brought the work in will say 'forget it.' This takes us out of the middle."

"Sometimes my caseload gets too big, and I have to go to my attorneys and say 'I am getting behind, I cannot get this done within the time frame you gave me, can I have more time or can you give it to someone else.' As soon as I see that I am not getting to it, I immediately go in and let the attorney know right then and say 'help'. That is the hardest thing for people to learn to do, to say 'help' or 'I made a mistake'. But you have to learn to do this and to be up front. Alternatively, you can say to the attorney 'I cannot accept this assignment right now given your deadline, please look at my work log and let's talk about it.' I have my assignment log in front of me at all times, and I always check things off as they are completed so I know where I stand."

HOW BETSY PRACTICES AS A LITIGATION LEGAL ASSISTANT

Betsy's time as a litigation legal assistant is spent drafting pleadings, drafting discovery, preparing deposition summaries, drafting correspondence, and using Summation Blaze, a computerized litigation-support program.

INITIAL PLEADINGS AND DISCOVERY ASPECT OF A CASE

"Our firm routinely represents both plaintiffs and defendants. Typically, an attorney will bring me a case that has recently been filed." Betsy is usually given the case after the "Petition" has been filed when the firm is representing the plaintiff. If her client is the defendant, she is usually given the file after the "Answer" has been prepared.

"The attorney will bring me the file and say 'I want you to draft interrogatories, requests for production, and requests for admissions,'" Betsy said. "The attorney will tell me what the case is about, will ask me to find out who the witnesses and experts are, and will tell me what documents our clients gave us. The attorney will also tell me what particular problems he or she sees with the case and what areas I should concentrate on.

"I will then read the petition carefully and read any documents our client may have given us. I will then begin preparing interrogatories to the opposite side. We have some standard questions we always ask regarding witnesses, documents, etc. I will ask them about any and all facts that support their allegations or claims. If we are representing the defendant, I will go through the petition and pick out the separate allegations that have been made and ask questions about each allegation and what facts or documents they have that support their allegation. If we represent the plaintiff, I will ask the defendant what specific defenses they have to our claim and facts or documents that support their defenses. I will then prepare a request for production of documents to get the documents identified and any other documents that might be relevant to the case.

"I will also ask interrogatory questions about damages, what damages they are asking for, and how they were calculated. Finally, I will prepare requests for admissions, when appropriate, depending on the case.

"I will send the draft interrogatories, requests for production of documents, and requests for admissions to my attorney. The attorney will review them, revise them, and often we will send them to the client to make sure we have covered everything; this is especially true if it is a complicated case." After all changes have been made, they are then sent out. "I will then calendar the response dates on my calendar and also send them to our firm docket clerk. I then give the file back to the attorney."

DEPOSITION STAGE OF CASE

"The attorneys handle the depositions, but I will get the file back to send out deposition notices. Occasionally, I will attend a deposition to keep track of documents," Betsy said. "When depositions have been taken, I do deposition summaries and also, if necessary, will prepare motions to compel discovery. Sometimes the firm will order the deposition transcripts on floppy disk. The disks are then loaded into the firm's litigation-support program, Summation Blaze. Summation Blaze has full-

text retrieval, so that I can search the deposition transcripts for specific things, and also a data base.

"I like to prepare deposition summaries myself. I either type them in WordPerfect or dictate them and give them to the word processing department."

TRIAL STAGE

"We very rarely go to trial. In the ten years I have worked as a legal assistant, I have gone to trial only twice. We try to settle when reasonable to do so, no matter if we are representing the plaintiff or the defendant. Trials are too expensive, too grueling and too risky unless it is absolutely necessary. We are a conservative law firm and this goes along with our conservative views. You can lose at trial even if your client is right."

"One time I did go to trial was in a federal court case that took three weeks to try. I went to court every day. The attorney asked permission of the judge to allow me to sit at the table, and the judge allowed me to do so. I managed the exhibits; it was a huge document case. There were 23 boxes of exhibits. I indexed the exhibits before we went, I had all of the depositions summarized, I prepared the witness lists, the exhibit list, and the actual exhibits themselves. I sat next to the lead attorney, and the attorney would ask me for documents that he needed. He listed the documents he would need for each witness, and I would have them ready for each person. I kept a log every day of what was offered, admitted, and objected to. Every day before I left, I would go over the exhibits accumulated at the court reporter's desk and sort them out and put them in the correct order.

"It is imperative to keep track of the exhibits. We would come back in the evenings and meet and decide what we were going to do the next day, and what exhibits we had to have. We also did this through lunch—I did not get to eat very much during that trial. We had our depositions in our litigation-support program, and we used the searching features of it quite a lot.

"Day-to-day organization and control was very important to the case," Betsy said. Our philosophy is to overprepare for trial. If we are representing the plaintiff, we want to know every possible defense, and we want to be prepared for it. And vice versa, if we are representing the defendant, we want to know everything that the plaintiff might bring up and be prepared for it. Quality is so important to winning. Cases are won as a team; it is important to have a well-prepared legal assistant and an innovative, intuitive attorney who can grasp the issues. You need both to expect to win.

"Having been a legal secretary for several years, I had no visions of grandeur regarding being a legal assistant because I knew what it was like. However, I think a lot of students think being a legal assistant is much more glamorous than it really is, and that is unfortunate. When I talk to legal assistants, I tell them straight out, for 95 percent of you, you will not spend much time in the courtroom."

PERSONAL PHILOSOPHIES TOWARD WORK

Betsy describes her personal philosophies toward work as follows: My attitude is that I only have one gear and it is wide open all of the time. I am not a maniac about work. I do not like to work overtime and I do have a family life, but when I am here, I give 100 percent to my firm. I care about my work, and I do not like sloppy work leaving my desk, and I am embarrassed when it happens. I enjoy the diversity of work, to get a new case, to figure out what is going on with it. I like to do new things and to do the investigation."

ETHICAL PERSPECTIVE

IMPERSONATING OTHERS

"I never use a fake name to obtain information. I use phone books, directories, directory assistance, Information America (which is a computerized on-line information service that has a people finder that uses information from phone directories, driver's license bureaus, and other information across the country), and other resources I have available to me and usually these will work.

"I have friends at the constable's office (police), friends at the courthouse who help me locate people. I work with the post office. I call the court clerk's office to see if there have been other lawsuits, where the person I am looking for may have been served."

KNOW YOUR ETHICAL BOUNDARIES

"You need to know the ethical boundaries you are working within, or you can get into a lot of trouble. I work for a very ethical firm, so this is not a prob-

lem, but this may not always be the case for all legal assistants."

THE UNAUTHORIZED PRACTICE OF LAW

The unauthorized practice of law also is a tough ethical problem for many legal assistants. "I make an extra effort to not give legal advice to clients. I stop myself and say 'I am sorry I cannot tell you, but I will check with the attorney and call you right back.'"

CONFIDENTIALITY

Betsy's firm is very protective of client confidences. "People are curious and they may ask you about cases your firm is handling," Betsy said. Legal assistants have to learn to keep client confidences. You should not even ask about other peoples files in your own office. It is none of your business. "We do not talk generally about cases in the firm or outside the firm. I was reading something recently that said that you should be careful about what you say in elevators. I thought it was the wrong advice. Do not say anything in elevators. You just do not talk about client cases there."

EQUIPMENT, OFFICE SPACE, AND SUPPORT STAFF

"I have a computer at my desk. I use WordPerfect, and I particularly like the tables features it has. I also use the Summation Blaze litigation-support program. I do not have my own secretary, but I do have access to our word processing department. However, I use it only for long documents. I have a private office and keep many of the active litigation files on which I am working. It saves time."

CLIENTS AND COMMUNICATION

Betsy's firm puts a high priority on client relationships. "We always treat our clients with respect, whether it is in person or on the phone. We treat them like royalty, we keep them advised of everything we do; they are copied on everything. We return phone calls promptly and our billings are also detailed. We try to keep our clients intimately involved with their case."

Communication is an important part of being a successful legal assistant. "I need to know myself and my limitations and then be able to communicate those to others. If I receive an assignment, and I do not understand it, I immediately ask questions. I say 'I don't understand this aspect of it' or 'I have never done this before. This may take longer than usual.' My philosophy is to ask questions all the time. Asking questions is how you learn."

CONCLUSION

Betsy enjoys her position as a legal assistant. Although it may not be as "glamorous" as sometimes portrayed, being a legal assistant has allowed her to earn an honest living, and gain the respect of people in her profession and has given her a job that she greatly enjoys.

QUESTIONS

1. What type of management structure does the Harris, Finley & Bogle firm have? The firm allows younger shareholders to have as much vote on issues as more senior shareholders. Given the weakness of this type of management structure, do you think this helps or hurts the firm?
2. What are the overriding philosophies of the firm?
3. What are the advantages of writing down all assignments and having attorneys prioritize work as opposed to legal assistants prioritizing the work? Can you think of any disadvantages?
4. What skills seem to contribute to Betsy Horn's success at drafting documents and taking on assignments she may not understand? What skills are important to legal assistants who help take a case to trial according to Betsy?

KEY TERMS

Legal team
Attorneys
Partner or shareholder
Managing partner
Associate attorney
Lateral hire associates
Nonequity partner
Staff attorney
Contract attorney
"Of counsel"
Law office administrators
Legal assistants
Legal assistant manager
Freelance legal assistants
Office managers
Law clerk
Law librarian
Secretaries

Clerks
Expert witness
General counsel
Legal aid office
Office sharing
Boutique firm
Powerful managing partner
Rule by all partners/shareholders
Rule by management committee/board
Practice management (i.e. substantive or case management)
Administrative management (i.e. office management or "plant" management)
Management
Financial management
Human resource management
Planning
Organizing

System   Leadership
Marketing   Substantive task
Controlling   Administrative task

PROBLEM SOLVING QUESTIONS

1. As a legal assistant/office manager in a small firm, you have recently become quite frustrated. The managing partner who has the final say on major management decisions is seldom in the office. You are having an increasingly difficult time making management decisions, since you cannot get her input. In addition, you do not know if you have the responsibility to make major management decisions or not. Work is beginning to back up. Discuss recommendations you might make for changing the structure of the law office.

2. For each of the following examples, state whether the situation involves a practice management or administrative management problem.

a) You go to the shelf to get a legal pad and the shelf is empty; none have been ordered.

b) You need a computer to computerize your discovery responses in a particularly large case.

c) You are looking for a particular kind of expert witness for a medical malpractice case you are working on and have not found one yet.

d) You think the firm is concentrating too much in bankruptcy cases. You are concerned that they will not produce enough revenue for the firm.

e) You are preparing for trial with your supervising attorney and you notice that the file is not organized well.

f) A client calls and says that his account was not credited for a payment he made last month.

3. As a legal assistant in a solo practitioner's office, you know that the attorney you work for works very hard. Unfortunately, although the attorney has a lot of clients, they do not seem to generate much money. Bill collectors often call the office and the practice has a hard time paying its bills. The attorney rents a house that he uses as his offices. The offices are plain but professional. The attorney has three rooms that are not being used except for storage. In talking with the attorney one day, he asks for your suggestions about what can be done to improve the firm's situation. What kinds of problems are these and what do you suggest?

EXERCISES

1. You are in your last semester of school about to graduate with a legal assistant degree, and you plan to begin looking for a job. Government practice would give you job security, a corporate law department would be interesting and provide opportunities for advancement, a legal aid office would give you the feeling that you were helping others, and a private law office would be exciting and fast paced. What type of law office would be your first pick and why?

2. Discuss the relative merits of being a legal assistant v. a freelance legal assistant. Compare the advantages and disadvantages of each.

NOTES

1. *Law Office Economics and Management Manual,* vol. 1, 1985, sec. 12:07, 1.

2. *NALA Manual for Legal Assistants,* West Publishing Co., 1992, 2.

3. Hal Cornelius, *Career Guide for Paralegals,* Monarch Press, 1983, 2.

4. Ibid., 34.

5. William Statsky, *Introduction to Paralegalism,* West Publishing Co., 1992, 765.

6. Ibid., xvi.

7. Ibid.

8. Deborah Heller and James M. Hunt, *Practicing Law and Managing People: How to Be Successful,* Butterworth, 1988, 20.

9. Richard C. Reed, *Managing a Law Practice: The Human Side,* American Bar Association, 1988, 16.

10. Joan Wagner Zinober, "Selecting a Firm Governance Structure," *Law Practice Management,* September 1991, 23.

11. Ibid.

12. Ibid., 26.

13. Ibid., 25.

14. Richard C. Reed, *Managing a Law Practice: The Human Side,* American Bar Association, 1988, 3. Citing *Law Office Economics & Management* (Summer 1977).

15. Ibid.

16. Louis E. Boone and David L. Kurtz, *Management,* Random House Business Division, New York, 1987, 3.

17. Thomas S. Clay, "Profile of a Successful Law Firm," *The Law Firm Management Guide,* 1988, 4.

18. Ibid., 7.

19. Charles R. Coulter, *Practical Systems—Tips for Organizing Your Law Office,* American Bar Association, 1991, 1.

20. Ibid.

2

ETHICS AND MALPRACTICE

CHAPTER OBJECTIVES

After you read this chapter, you will be able to:

- Define what the unauthorized practice of law is and list factors that are used to determine whether a legal assistant is "practicing law."

- Discuss the voluntary ethical codes established by national legal assistant associations.

- Explain the attorney-client privilege and to whom it applies.

- List guidelines that will prevent legal assistants from accidentally revealing confidential client information.

- Explain what a conflict of interest is and what a law office can do to limit conflict of interest problems.

- Discuss what the "Chinese Wall" is and when it applies.

- List the most common types of ethical complaints filed against law firms or attorneys.

Every day, paralegals run into minor or major roadblocks and are faced with situations requiring professional or ethical judgment. The consequences of ignoring or walking away from the sometimes subtle, fine, gray line can have serious ramifications and aftermath.[1]

WHY ARE ETHICS AND MALPRACTICE IMPORTANT?

The importance of high ethical standards and of following your state's ethical rules cannot be overemphasized. Clients and attorneys must have total confidence that a legal assistant understands the many ethical problems that might arise in the practice of law and that the legal assistant's ethical judgment is clear. Ethical problems routinely encountered by legal assistants include unauthorized practice of law questions, conflict of interest problems, and confidentiality problems. Unethical behavior of a legal assistant can cause an attorney to lose a case, destroy client confidence in the entire law office, or lead a client to dismiss the attorney. Unethical behavior on the part of a legal assistant could lead to sanctions, fines, and disciplinary action against the attorney and can cost a legal assistant his job. It also could result in damaging publicity for the law office and could even result in criminal charges being filed against him. Consequently, legal assistants must know how to work through and solve tough ethical problems.

A legal assistant must perform careful, high-quality work in everything he does. An error can be very costly and can subject an attorney or law office to a malpractice claim. Malpractice occurs when an attorney's or law office's conduct does not meet the professional standard for the area and injures a client. Malpractice claims can result in a law office being liable for thousands of dollars of damages to injured clients. It is important that legal assistants understand how malpractice occurs and how it can be prevented.

LEGAL ETHICS AND PROFESSIONAL RESPONSIBILITY

Legal ethics is an increasingly important and difficult topic for legal assistants in every type of law practice. There are many treatises that cover this topic in depth. This section will cover ethics only from a legal assistant's perspective and will give insight on common ethical problems likely to arise.

Ethics is an important topic not only because a law office or attorney can be disciplined for violating ethical rules but also because legal ethics bears on whether quality legal services are being provided to clients. If a law office or its employee engages in unethical conduct, the reputation of the office will be affected and clients will lose confidence in it. The unethical behavior does not necessarily have to be directly detrimental to the client or the client's case. If a client senses that the attorney or legal assistant is acting unethically toward an adversary, the client may suspect that the attorney or legal assistant could be guilty of the same type of practice toward her. The issues of trust and ethics are closely related and bear directly upon the attorney and client relationship.

When clients lose confidence, they may move their business to another law office, cease referring new clients to the law office, or even sue. Nearly 70 percent of all the new business a law office receives comes from referrals. When a client takes business elsewhere, it has an immediate as well as a long-term effect on the firm, since that source of revenue is also gone for future years. In short, legal ethics has a direct bearing on the "law office's bottom line" and on the long-term success of the firm. Thus, legal assistants and attorneys have both an incentive and a duty to act ethically and to develop systems that stress the importance of legal ethics on a daily basis.

ETHICAL STANDARDS FOR ATTORNEYS

An **ethical rule** is *a minimal standard of conduct. An attorney may not fall below the standard without losing his or her good standing with the state bar.* Attorneys who violate ethical rules may be disciplined. Such discipline for unethical conduct may include a permanent disbarment from practicing law, a temporary suspension from practicing, a public censure, a private censure, or an informal reprimand. Figure 2-1 shows a procedural example of ethical rules at work.

Ethics has had a long-standing place in the American legal system. In 1908, the American Bar Association (ABA), a voluntary association of attorneys, adopted the Canons of Professional Ethics. In 1969, the ABA updated and expanded the canons into the *Model Code of Professional Responsibility.* The *Model Code* was updated in 1983 and is now called *Model Rules of Professional Conduct.* Today, more than two-thirds of all states base their ethical rules on the ABA *Model Rules.* Attorneys in each state are regulated by their individual state bar association and state court system. Although state courts are free to create their own rules of conduct for attorneys, most simply modify either the ABA *Model Code* or ABA *Model Rules* to reflect the specific ethical conditions in their own states. For this text, the more recent ABA *Model Rules* are most often cited, even though some states still model their ethical/disciplinary rules on the older ABA *Model Code.* Although ethical rules are established by state bars or state courts, most states also have a disciplinary administrator who enforces the rules.

ethical rule
A minimal standard of conduct.

Model Code of Professional Responsibility Model Rules of Professional Conduct
Self-imposed ethical standards for ABA members, but they also serve as a prototype of legal ethic standards for state court systems.

The facts:	An attorney represented a client who was selling a piece of real estate. It was agreed that the attorney's fees would be $6,500. After completing the sale, the proceeds of the sale were placed into the attorney's trust account (i.e. a holding account for client funds). The attorney paid some proceeds to the client, withdrew $14,000 for himself, would not provide an accounting of the funds to the client, and would not respond to many messages left by the client.
The client:	The client, becoming increasingly frustrated with the attorney, calls the local courthouse and asks how to complain about the conduct of the attorney. The client is told to send a letter of complaint to the state's disciplinary administrator in the state's judicial branch. The client is told that the letter should clearly set out who the attorney was and exactly what happened. The client then sends the letter.
The disciplinary administrator:	The state's disciplinary administrator receives the client's letter. The administrator determines that if everything the client says is true, the attorney may have violated Supreme Court Rule 4-1.5 for his state that states "an attorney shall not charge an illegal or clearly excessive fee." The administrator sends a letter to the attorney asking for his side of the story but never receives a reply.
Investigation:	The disciplinary administrator then refers the matter to the State Bar's Investigation Committee, which investigates the matter including interviewing both the client and the attorney. The committee, after a full investigation, recommends that formal charges be filed before the state's bar court to discipline the attorney.
State bar court/ state supreme court:	The disciplinary administrator files formal charges and prosecutes the attorney for the ethical violations before the state's bar court, an arm of the state's supreme court. A hearing or trial is held where both sides present their evidence. The bar court determines that the attorney violated Rule 4-1.5 and disciplines the attorney by suspending him from the practice of law for two years and orders him to pay restitution to the client.

FIGURE 2-1   Example of Ethical Violation and Subsequent Ethical Proceedings Against an Attorney

ATTORNEY ETHICAL RULES NOT DIRECTLY APPLICABLE TO THE LEGAL ASSISTANT

State canons of ethics, the *Model Code of Professional Responsibility,* or the *Model Rules of Professional Conduct* do not apply directly to legal assistants, but to attorneys only. However, attorneys can be disciplined for the acts of their staff members including legal assistants because attorneys have the duty to adequately supervise their staffs. Rule 5.3 of the ABA *Model Rules of Professional Conduct* states:

Rule 5.3. Responsibilities Regarding Nonlawyer Assistants

With respect to a nonlawyer employed or retained by or associated with a lawyer:

(a) a partner in a law office shall make reasonable efforts to ensure that the firm has in effect measures giving reasonable assurance that the person's conduct is compatible with the professional obligations of the lawyer;

(b) *a lawyer having direct supervisory authority over the nonlawyer shall make reasonable efforts to ensure that the person's conduct is compatible with the professional obligations of the lawyer* (emphasis added); and

(c) a lawyer shall be responsible for conduct of such a person that would be a violation of the Rules of Professional Conduct if engaged in by a lawyer if:

    (1) the lawyer orders or, with the knowledge of the specific conduct, ratifies the conduct involved; or

    (2) the lawyer is a partner in the law office in which the person is employed, or has direct supervisory authority over the person, and knows of the conduct at a time when its consequences can be avoided or mitigated but fails to take reasonable remedial action.

This section of the *Model Rules* is important to legal assistants because it requires attorneys to ensure that their staff members operate within the bounds of these rules. See Figure 2-2 in which a law office was sued for malpractice and the attorney was suspended from practice because of the unethical acts of a paralegal. If a legal assistant is found to be acting unethically, especially when there is a pattern

---

In April 1984, Asphalt Engineers met with Robert Walston, a legal assistant with Lee and Peggy Galusha, doing business as Galusha Ltd., a private law firm. Asphalt Engineers advised Walston they wanted to file liens against real property involved in three construction jobs that they had not been paid on. They also requested that lawsuits foreclosing those liens be filed, if necessary. At trial, owners of Asphalt Engineers testified that they believed Walston was an attorney. Walston requested and received a retainer payment from Asphalt Engineers. A lien was filed on one of the projects, but not on the other two. The project where the lien was filed was settled.

In June 1984, Walston requested and received an additional retainer fee. Although Walston indicated that liens had been filed on the remaining two projects, no liens were in fact filed. The time for filing both liens expired. Before Asphalt Engineers discovered that the two liens had not been filed, they brought a fourth project to Walston to file a lien on. Again, no lien was filed on the project.

The court found that neither of the Galushas had ever met with Asphalt Engineers and that the Galushas allowed Walston, a nonlawyer, to provide legal advice to Asphalt Engineers, failed to file and foreclose liens, failed to adequately supervise Walston, and failed to prevent Walston from actually practicing law, among other things. Subsequently, a jury awarded Asphalt Engineers more than $75,000 in actual damages, attorneys fees, and punitive damages against the Galusha law firm. In addition, Lee Galusha faced ethical proceedings for failing to adequately supervise the legal assistant and for failing to adequately perform legal work for a client. Lee Galusha was subsequently suspended from the practice of law and eventually was disbarred.

FIGURE 2-2
***Asphalt Engineers, Inc. v. Galusha—*Attorneys Liable for Unethical Acts of Paralegal**

Source: See *Asphalt Engineers, Inc. v. Galusha,* 770 P.2d 1180 (160 Ariz. 134, 1989).

and practice of doing this, the attorney has an affirmative duty to remedy the situation, even if that means firing the legal assistant. Thus, there are many incentives for legal assistants to act ethically and to comply with the same rules as attorneys. In addition, this rule ensures that an attorney cannot avoid the ethical rules and accomplish an unethical act by delegating or allowing a staff member to do it.

So, although a legal assistant cannot be disciplined by state regulatory bodies for violating state ethical rules, he would be held accountable by the attorney who hired or supervised him. Legal assistants must understand and abide by any ethical rules governing the conduct of attorneys.

VOLUNTARY ETHICAL CODES ESTABLISHED BY LEGAL ASSISTANT ASSOCIATIONS

Legal assistants have self-imposed, voluntary ethical standards set out by national or local legal assistant associations. Both the National Association of Legal Assistants (NALA) and the National Federation of Paralegal Associations (NFPA) have adopted ethical canons for their members. Figures 2-3 and 2-4 show the codes of ethics for both associations. Legal assistants cannot be disciplined for not following such voluntary codes. However, following such a code will help the legal assistant avoid ethical problems.

CRIMINAL STATUTES REGARDING THE UNAUTHORIZED PRACTICE OF LAW

There are criminal statutes in nearly every state that provide sanctions for non-lawyers who engage in "practicing law." "Practicing law" usually includes providing legal advice to the public or representation of a client in a court of law. The topic of the unauthorized practice of law is covered in more detail later in this chapter.

So, there is no direct regulation of legal assistants, but they are indirectly regulated through state ethical standards for attorneys, nonbinding legal assistant association ethical standards, and criminal statutes barring nonattorneys from practicing law.

THE UNAUTHORIZED PRACTICE OF LAW

Most states have a criminal statute that prohibits a layperson from practicing law. The reason behind such a statute is to protect the general public from individuals who are not qualified to give legal advice because they do not have the proper educational training, have not passed the bar exam, or are not fit to practice law.

Besides criminal prohibitions, there are ethical prohibitions as well. Rule 5.5 of the ABA *Model Rules of Professional Conduct* prohibits attorneys from assisting nonlawyers in practicing law:

Rule 5.5. Unauthorized Practice of Law

A lawyer shall not:

(b) assist a person who is not a member of the bar in the performance of an activity that constitutes the unauthorized practice of law.

This rule draws a line that legal assistants cannot cross. Legal assistants are permitted to *assist* a licensed attorney in practicing law. The real question is at what

It is the responsibility of every legal assistant to adhere strictly to the accepted standards of legal ethics and to live by general principles of proper conduct. The performance of the duties of the legal assistant shall be governed by specific canons as defined herein in order that justice will be served and the goals of the profession attained. The canons of ethics set forth hereafter are adopted by the National Association of Legal Assistants, Inc., as a general guide and the enumeration of these rules does not mean there are not others of equal importance although not specifically mentioned.

Canon 1. A legal assistant shall not perform any of the duties that lawyers only may perform nor do things that lawyers themselves may not do.

Canon 2. A legal assistant may perform any task delegated and supervised by a lawyer so long as the lawyer is responsible to the client, maintains a direct relationship with the client, and assumes full professional responsibility for the work product.

Canon 3. A legal assistant shall not engage in the practice of law by accepting cases, setting fees, giving legal advice or appearing in court (unless otherwise authorized by court or agency rules).

Canon 4. A legal assistant shall not act in matters involving professional legal judgment as the services of a lawyer are essential in the public interest whenever the exercise of such judgment is required.

Canon 5. A legal assistant must act prudently in determining the extent to which a client may be assisted without the presence of a lawyer.

Canon 6. A legal assistant shall not engage in the unauthorized practice of law.

Canon 7. A legal assistant must protect the confidence of a client, and it shall be unethical for a legal assistant to violate any statute now in effect or hereafter to be enacted controlling privileged communications.

Canon 8. It is the obligation of the legal assistant to avoid conduct which would cause the lawyer to be unethical or even appear to be unethical and loyalty to the employer is incumbent upon the legal assistant.

Canon 9. A legal assistant shall work continually to maintain integrity and a high degree of competency throughout the legal profession.

Canon 10. A legal assistant shall strive for perfection through education in order to better assist the legal profession in fulfilling its duty of making legal services available to clients and the public.

Canon 11. A legal assistant shall do things incidental, necessary or expedient for the attainment of the ethics and responsibilities imposed by statute or rule of court.

Canon 12. A legal assistant is governed by the American Bar Association *Model Code of Professional Responsibility,* and the American Bar Association *Model Rules of Professional Conduct.*

**FIGURE 2-3
National Association of Legal Assistants, Inc. Code of Ethics and Professional Responsibility**

Source: *NALA Manual for Legal Assistants* (Saint Paul, Minnesota: West Publishing Co., 1992) 53.

point does one actually "practice law." The ABA, as well as most states, has been unwilling to give a specific definition of exactly what the "practice of law" is, preferring to consider the matter on a case-by-case basis. However, most courts look to the following items as determinants on the issue.

National Federation of Paralegal Associations Model Code of Ethics and Professional Responsibility

Preamble

The National Federation of Paralegal Associations, Inc. ("NFPA") is a professional organization comprised of paralegal associations and individual paralegals throughout the United States. Members of NFPA have varying backgrounds, experience, education, and job responsibilities which reflect the diversity of the paralegal profession. NFPA promotes the growth, development and recognition of the paralegal profession as an integral partner in the delivery of legal services.

NFPA recognizes that the creation of guidelines and standards for professional conduct are important for the development and expansion of the paralegal profession. In May, 1993, NFPA adopted this Model Code of Ethics and Professional Responsibility ("Model Code") to delineate the principles for ethics and conduct to which every paralegal should aspire. The Model Code expresses NFPA's commitment to increasing the quality and efficiency of legal services and recognizes the profession's responsibilities to the public, the legal community, and colleagues.

Paralegals perform many functions and these functions differ greatly among practice areas. In addition, each jurisdiction has its own unique legal authority and practices governing ethical conduct and professional responsibilities.

It is essential that each paralegal strive for personal and professional excellence and encourage the professional development of other paralegals as well as those entering the profession. Participation in professional associations intended to advance the quality and standards of the legal profession is of particular importance. Paralegals should possess integrity, professional skill and dedication to the improvement of the legal system and should strive to expand the paralegal role in the delivery of legal services.

CANON 1. A PARALEGAL SHALL ACHIEVE AND MAINTAIN A HIGH LEVEL OF COMPETENCE.

CANON 2. A PARALEGAL SHALL MAINTAIN A HIGH LEVEL OF PERSONAL AND PROFESSIONAL INTEGRITY.

CANON 3. A PARALEGAL SHALL MAINTAIN A HIGH STANDARD OF PROFESSIONAL CONDUCT.

CANON 4. A PARALEGAL SHALL SERVE THE PUBLIC INTEREST BY CONTRIBUTING TO THE DELIVERY OF QUALITY LEGAL SERVICES AND THE IMPROVEMENT OF THE LEGAL SYSTEM.

CANON 5. A PARALEGAL SHALL PRESERVE ALL CONFIDENTIAL INFORMATION PROVIDED BY THE CLIENT OR ACQUIRED FROM OTHER SOURCES BEFORE, DURING, AND AFTER THE COURSE OF THE PROFESSIONAL RELATIONSHIP.

CANON 6. A PARALEGAL'S TITLE SHALL BE FULLY DISCLOSED.

CANON 7. A PARALEGAL SHALL NOT ENGAGE IN THE UNAUTHORIZED PRACTICE OF LAW.

CANON 8. A PARALEGAL SHALL AVOID CONFLICTS OF INTEREST AND SHALL DISCLOSE ANY POSSIBLE CONFLICT TO THE EMPLOYER OR CLIENT, AS WELL AS TO THE PROSPECTIVE EMPLOYER OR CLIENTS.

- **Has the individual represented clients in court proceedings?** Legal assistants cannot appear in federal or state courts, or proceedings such as a deposition, on behalf of a client. Some administrative agencies allow a legal assistant to appear on behalf of a client, but this should not be done unless the rules of the agency specifically allow for such.
- **Has the individual prepared legal documents (without the direct supervision of a licensed attorney)?** Legal assistants cannot draft legal documents such as wills, briefs, motions, or contracts <u>without</u> the supervision of an attorney. Legal assistants routinely draft these types of documents; the distinction is that they do so properly under the direction and supervision of a member of the bar.
- **Has the individual given legal advice to a client?**[2] Legal assistants cannot advise clients as to their legal rights or advise clients on how they should handle a legal matter.
- **Did the individual accept a client case alone?** The function of agreeing to undertake the representation of a client may only be assumed by an attorney. The general rule is that the licensed attorney must maintain a direct relationship with the client so as to assume full professional responsibility for the case. The accepting of or rejecting of a client's case takes legal expertise that only an attorney has. It is the attorney's responsibility to determine whether in her opinion the client has a viable case.
- **Did the individual set the fee for handling the client's case?** Nonlawyers are generally prohibited from setting a legal fee. The matter of setting legal fees is sometimes complex and takes the experience and knowledge of a licensed attorney. An attorney is prohibited from accepting an unreasonable fee, so most states want the attorney to take responsibility for such an important aspect of the attorney-client relationship.

Canons 1 through 6 of the NALA Code of Ethics (see Figure 2-3) also reiterate these factors and prohibit legal assistants from performing these functions. Figure 2-5 contains a list of functions that legal assistants should not perform, since these acts could be construed as practicing law.

Additional factors and considerations that courts use to decide if there has been an authorized practice of law include:

- **Whether the activity is one "traditionally" performed by lawyers;**

Legal Assistants CANNOT:
1. Provide legal services directly to the public without the supervision of an attorney.
2. Give legal advice or counsel to a client. Legal advice is independent professional judgment based on knowledge of the law and given for the benefit of a particular client.
3. Represent a client in court or other tribunal or otherwise act as an advocate for a client.
4. Accept or reject cases for the firm.
5. Set any fee for representation of a client.
6. Split legal fees with an attorney.
7. Be a partner with an attorney.
8. Solicit cases for an attorney.

**FIGURE 2-5
Functions That a
Legal Assistant
Cannot Perform Re:
Unauthorized
Practice of Law**

Source: James W. H. McCord, *The Litigation Paralegal: A Systems Approach*, 2d ed. (Saint Paul, Minnesota: West Publishing Co.).

- **Whether the activity is one "commonly understood" to involve the practice of law;**
- **Whether the activity requires legal skill or knowledge beyond that of a layperson;**
- **Whether the activity is characterized by the personal relationship between attorney and client;**
- **Whether the activity is such that the public interest is served by limiting performance to only those who are attorneys.**[3]

A legal assistant ordinarily may interview witnesses or prospective clients, perform legal research, draft pleadings and briefs, and investigate the facts of cases without being accused of the unauthorized practice of law as long as a licensed attorney actively supervises him and the attorney maintains a direct relationship with the client.[4] The ABA also has been instrumental in setting guidelines for how attorneys can use legal assistants effectively as well as ethically. Figure 2–6 shows the *ABA Model Guidelines for the Utilization of Legal Assistant Services* adopted in 1991 (comments to the guidelines are not included). Like the *Model Rules,* these are simply model guidelines that states and other jurisdictions can use to model their own rules after.

Legal assistants who are employed by corporate law departments, private law offices, and the government will typically not encounter too many unauthorized practice of law problems as long as they work under the direct supervision of an attorney. Most unauthorized practice of law cases concern legal technicians or freelance legal assistants.

LEGAL TECHNICIANS, FREELANCE LEGAL ASSISTANTS, AND THE UNAUTHORIZED PRACTICE OF LAW

legal technicians
People who market their legal services directly to the public.

Recently, a new class of legal assistants, sometimes called "legal technicians," has emerged. What separates **"legal technicians"** *from legal assistants is that they market their services directly to the public and do not work under the supervision of an attorney.* Bar associations across the country have argued that since legal technicians do not work under the supervision of a licensed attorney but undertake to represent clients directly, they clearly violate criminal statutes regarding the unauthorized practice of law. Legal technicians argue that they simply provide forms that have been written by attorneys and help the clients fill in the forms. Cases are being decided on this issue on a case-by-case matter, but many courts have limited or greatly restricted what services legal technicians can provide.

Freelance legal assistants were defined in chapter 1 as self-employed legal assistants who market and sell their services to law offices on a per job basis. Freelance legal assistants are less likely to be accused of the unauthorized practice of law, since they are supposed to be acting under the supervision of an attorney. However, in instances where the freelance legal assistant is removed from the attorney, and where supervision is limited or nonexistent, unauthorized practice of law problems can occur.

Suggestions on how to avoid the unauthorized practice of law.

- **Always have your work approved by a supervising attorney**—No matter how routine the legal document is, always have an attorney review it. Remember, a legal assistant can do many types of activities as long as it is done under the supervision of an attorney, so take advantage of this and get everything

Guideline 1:   A lawyer is responsible for all of the professional actions of a legal assistant performing legal assistant services at the lawyer's direction and should take reasonable measures to ensure that the legal assistant's conduct is consistent with the lawyer's obligations under the ABA *Model Rules of Professional Conduct.*

Guideline 2:   Provided the lawyer maintains responsibility for the work product, a lawyer may delegate to a legal assistant any task normally performed by the lawyer except those tasks proscribed to one not licensed as a lawyer by statute, court rule, administrative rule or regulation, controlling authority, the ABA *Model Rules of Professional Conduct,* or these Guidelines.

Guideline 3:   A lawyer may not delegate to a legal assistant:
   (a)   Responsibility for establishing an attorney-client relationship;
   (b)   Responsibility for establishing the amount of a fee to be charged for a legal service;
   (c)   Responsibility for a legal opinion rendered to a client.

Guideline 4:   It is the lawyer's responsibility to take reasonable measures to ensure that clients, courts, and other lawyers are aware that a legal assistant, whose services are utilized by the lawyer in performing legal services, is not licensed to practice law.

Guideline 5:   A lawyer may identify legal assistants by name and title on the lawyer's letterhead and on business cards identifying the lawyer's firm.

Guideline 6:   It is the responsibility of a lawyer to take reasonable measures to ensure that all client confidences are preserved by a legal assistant.

Guideline 7:   A lawyer should take reasonable measures to prevent conflicts of interest resulting from a legal assistant's other employment or interests insofar as such other employment or interests would present a conflict of interest if it were that of the lawyer.

Guideline 8:   A lawyer may include a charge for the work performed by a legal assistant in setting a charge for legal services.

Guideline 9:   A lawyer may not split legal fees with a legal assistant nor pay a legal assistant for the referral of legal business. A lawyer may compensate a legal assistant based on the quantity and quality of the legal assistant's work and the value of that work to a law practice, but the legal assistant's compensation may not be contingent, by advance agreement, upon the profitability of the lawyer's practice.

Guideline 10: A lawyer who employs a legal assistant should facilitate the legal assistant's participation in appropriate continuing education and pro bono publico activities.

FIGURE 2-6
ABA Model Guidelines for the Utilization of Legal Assistant Services
Source: Reprinted by permission of the American Bar Association.

approved. Never let an attorney approve your work without reading it. If the attorney says, "I do not have time to review it, I'll sign it and you just send it out, I trust you," bring the document back at another time or find a tactful way to suggest to her that the document needs to be approved the right way.

- **Never let clients talk you into giving them legal advice**—Most legal assistants never intend to give a client legal advice. However, it is easy to give in when a client presses you. This is usually because the attorney is unavailable and the client "needs an answer now." Legal advice might be telling the client what he should or should not do, answering a legal or statutory question, or telling the client what defense or legal argument he should make. The way to handle this problem is to tell the client that you are a legal assistant and cannot give legal advice but that you will either have the attorney call him directly or you will talk to the attorney and call him with the attorney's advice. A frequent problem that can occur when a legal assistant does give legal advice is that if things go wrong, for any reason, many clients will not hesitate to turn on you and say that they relied on your advice. This is why this issue is such a critical one.

- **Do not start sentences with "You should" or "I think"**—When you hear yourself say "You should" or "I think," stop and realize that you probably are about to give legal advice. Again, it's not worth the risk.

> *They (clients) sometimes think they can call you and get the same advice they get from the attorney, and unless you have cleared things with your attorney, you are really getting yourself in hot water if you tell them, "Yeah, you don't have to do this, just do that . . . ." Well, that's legal advice . . . .*
>
> —**Cynthia Tokumitsu,** practicing legal assistant, in "How to Avoid the Top 10 Mistakes Paralegals Make on the Job," *Legal Assistant Today*, November/December 1991, 34.

- **Always clearly identify yourself as a legal assistant**—When you talk to clients or send letters out on a law office or company letterhead, <u>always</u> identify yourself as a legal assistant. It is very easy for a client to say "Well I thought he was an attorney" to a disciplinary administrator or in a malpractice case (see Figure 2-2).

Never represent to others either directly or indirectly that you are an attorney. In many states, legal assistants are allowed to have business cards and sign letters on the law practice letterhead as long as the title of "legal assistant" or "paralegal" is included. It would be unethical to represent to someone that you are an attorney.

- **Management should develop ethical guidelines and rules**—From a management perspective, law office managers should publish rules regarding the unauthorized practice of law, tell staff members what they can and cannot do, and provide a policy on the responsibilities of supervising attorneys.

- **Management should make periodic checks of ethical standards**—It is not enough to simply establish rules and then never monitor them to see if they are being followed. Occasionally, management must monitor its staff regarding compliance with law practice rules and state guidelines to ensure compliance. Management should keep staff members up-to-date on changes or clarifications in ethical standards by circulating recent state ethical opinions. Publications of legal assistant associations also report on recent ethical opinions. When appropriate, these should be called to the attention of management for general circulation. Another option is for law office management to hold workshops or seminars on ethics. Attorneys, legal assistants, and staff members should be constantly reminded about ethics.

CONFIDENTIALITY AND THE ATTORNEY-CLIENT PRIVILEGE

Another basic ethical concept is that of client confidentiality. **Client confidentiality** *refers to the need to keep information exchanged between a client and law office staff, including attorneys and legal assistants, confidential.* In addition to the ethical rules of maintaining client confidences, there is a rule of evidence, generally called the attorney-client privilege, that an attorney or legal assistant may invoke to avoid revealing the secrets of a client. The purpose of both the privilege and the ethical rules is to ensure that clients can consult with their attorneys without the fear that such statements would be passed to others or used against them later. If clients knew that what they told their attorney could be repeated to others, clients would be reluctant to tell their attorneys the truth. The attorney-client privilege and the ethical rules on confidentiality complement one another to achieve the same end.

client confidentiality
Keeping information exchanged between a client and law office staff confidential.

THE ATTORNEY-CLIENT PRIVILEGE RULE OF EVIDENCE

Generally, the **attorney-client privilege** *precludes the disclosure of confidential communications between a lawyer and a client by the lawyer.* Thus, if a criminal defendant confessed a crime to his attorney, the attorney-client privilege would prevent the prosecutor from calling the attorney to the stand to testify about the confession. In addition, courts have applied the attorney-client privilege to legal assistants.

attorney-client privilege
A standard that precludes the disclosure of confidential communications between a lawyer and a client by the lawyer.

> It has long been held that the [attorney-client] privilege applies . . . to members of the bar, of a court, or their subordinates . . . . Examples of such protected subordinates would include any law student, paralegal, investigator, or other person acting as the agent of a duly qualified attorney under circumstances that would otherwise be sufficient to invoke the privilege. 8 Wigmore, Evidence Section 2301 (McNaughton Rev. 1961).

> *Dabney v. Investment Corp. of America*, 82 F.R.D. 464, 465 (E.D. Pa. 1979).

For the privilege to be invoked, the communication must have been made in confidence between the client and the attorney for the purpose of obtaining legal advice.

ETHICAL PROHIBITIONS ON REVEALING CLIENT COMMUNICATIONS

There are several ethical rules regarding attorneys preserving client communications, including Rule 1.6 of the ABA *Model Rules of Professional Conduct*, which states:

1.6. Confidentiality of Information

(a) A lawyer <u>shall</u> not reveal information relating to representation of a client unless the client consents after consultation. . . . (emphasis added)

The older ABA *Model Code of Professional Responsibility* was more specific regarding law office staff members preserving client confidences:

DR 4–101(D)

A lawyer shall exercise reasonable care to prevent his employees, associates, and others whose services are utilized by him from disclosing or using confidences or secrets of a client. . . .

Canon 7 of the NALA Code of Ethics (see Figure 2-3) and section IV of NFPA's Affirmation of Professional Responsibility, although not enforceable, prohibit legal assistants from revealing client confidences.

Again, the purpose of these ethical rules is to encourage clients to be completely honest with their attorneys. You also should note that there are many nuances regarding the attorney-client privilege and the ethical rules, including some exceptions to the rules.

Legal assistants have an absolute duty to preserve the confidences and communications of clients. All information must be kept confidential and should not under any circumstances be revealed in casual conversations with anyone outside the workplace. In addition to the moral and ethical reasons for not disclosing client communications, there also is the issue of quality service to the client. If a client learns that her communications have been revealed to outside sources, by whatever means, even if it is by accident, she can lose confidence in the entire firm. If a client cannot trust her attorney, the client will quickly move on to another firm. Finally, remember that if confidential information gets out, it also could actually compromise your client's case; that the client is paying your fees and has hired your firm to represent her interests; and that the client could sue the law office for compromising the case.

Suggestions on how to avoid confidentiality problems:

▪ **Resist the temptation to talk about what goes on in the office whether or not it is client related**—There is always a temptation to talk about office politics and other office matters with people outside the firm. Resist this temptation. If you do this, it will only make it easier to talk about client-related matters. Consider that you are a professional and that both your firm and your clients demand anonymity.

▪ **Only talk about client matters to office personnel on a need-to-know basis**—Never go around your office talking about a client's case to employees who do not have a reason to know about it. You must get in the habit of keeping information to yourself. Why tell someone about client-related matters, even if it is a fellow employee, unless he needs to know for some legitimate reason? Also, even if you are talking to someone who has a need to know, avoid doing so in public places, such as waiting rooms, elevators, and restaurants, where your conversation can be overheard.

▪ **Never discuss the specific facts or circumstances of a client's case to anyone, not even friends or relatives**—There is a specific temptation to talk about interesting cases you have worked on with friends and relatives because you trust them. However, many client secrets have been unwittingly revealed by friends and relatives who have repeated information they never should have been told. The statement "I promise I won't tell anyone" does not work. People do tell. Former girlfriends or boyfriends may reveal knowledge you told them to spite you. Mother, fathers, brothers/sisters, or friends may inadvertently reveal a confidence you told them that gets back to the client, adverse party, or a member of your law office. When this happens, you will hear about it one way or another, and the repercussions can be severe. Do not take the chance: it is simply not worth losing a client or a job over. You should not even reveal the fact that an individual *is* or may be a client of your law office.

- **Always clear your desk of other case files when meeting with clients**—If case files are left in the open, other clients can read the files and access confidential information.

- **Do not take phone calls from other clients when meeting with a client**—Taking phone calls from other clients while a client is in your office also can expose confidential information. Be aware of who is in your office when talking about confidential information on the phone, and, when possible, keep your door closed when meeting or talking with clients.

- **Management must create policies and systems to ensure confidentiality**—Law office managers also have a duty to create systems that ensure confidentiality. Some of these systems may include locking file cabinets that contain client files, limiting access to client files on a need-to-know basis, requiring files to be checked out, having law office policies on client confidentiality, and developing procedures to ensure that the confidential information of clients is maintained (see Figure 2-7). Many law offices limit staff members even from revealing to persons outside the office that a particular individual is being represented. Even revealing the names of clients can give the appearance that the law office does not take confidentiality seriously. Although there is an affirmative ethical duty to maintain client confidentiality, there also is the potential for malpractice liability for firms that violate confidentiality. Under a legal malpractice theory, a law office through its employees reveals client confidences, accidentally or intentionally, it could be legally liable to the client for damages that result.

CONFLICT OF INTEREST

> *The exponential growth of law firms, particularly during the last decade, has spawned an increasing number of conflict of interest issues. As firms expand and their client rosters increase, so does the potential that new engagement will create conflicts with the interest of present or former clients.*
>
> **—Joseph H. Flom and Jonathan J. Lerner,** "Lawyers' Conflicts," *Law Practice Management,* March 1991, 28.

Conflict of interest problems also are an important ethical concept. A **conflict of interest** *occurs when an attorney or legal assistant has competing personal or professional interests with a client's case that would preclude him from acting impartially toward the client.*

Conflict of interest problems typically occur when:

- a) an attorney or legal assistant has a personal, financial, or other interest in a case;
- b) the attorney or legal assistant is a substantial witness in the case;

conflict of interest
A competing personal or professional interest that would preclude an attorney or legal assistant from acting impartially toward the client.

**FIGURE 2-7
Law Office
Confidentiality
Policy**

Source: Adapted from
*Complete Personnel
Administration Handbook for
Law Firms,* Altman Weil
Pensa, 1991. Reprinted with
permission of Altman Weil
Pensa Publications, Inc.
Copyright 1993 by Altman
Weil Pensa Publications,
Inc.

All employees must use extreme caution to ensure that client information in our possession does not become available to unauthorized third parties. The following rules should be followed to maintain client information in strict confidence:

- Do not discuss client affairs with a third party unless the client specifically authorizes such communication. Oral authorization should be noted in writing and placed in the client's file.
- Do not disclose confidential information to unauthorized personnel of the client.
- Do not discuss client affairs in public places.
- Do not talk about client affairs with spouses, relatives, or friends.
- Do not discuss client matters with law office personnel unless a legitimate need to discuss the matter exists.
- Client documents, files, notes, messages, and other information should not be put in places where persons not working on the matter may read them.
- Address all mail sent to a client to the attention of a specific individual and mark all envelopes "confidential" to ensure that the mail is opened by the specific individual instead of the mail department.
- Computer tapes or disks with confidential information should be passed through a bulk demagnetizer or burned instead of simply "erasing" the files from the disk (erasing only wipes out the directory listing—the file data is still left intact).
- Confidential documents such as client-related papers should be shredded.
- At no time should an attorney's or legal assistant's office be used by a client, vendor, or other unathorized person without the direct consent of that attorney, legal assistant, or, in his/her absence, his/her secretary.

    c) a law office, attorney, or legal assistant sometime in the past represented a client who is now an adverse party in a current case;

    d) an attorney and a client enter into business together.

If, for instance, an attorney represented a husband and wife in a legal action and then several years later the husband approaches the attorney to sue the wife for divorce, the attorney has a conflict of interest problem because he had at one time represented both parties. Not only would he have a question as to which client he should be loyal to, but the attorney may have during the first representation been privy to confidences and secrets of the wife that could be used in the divorce case against her.

Rule 1.7 of the ABA *Model Rules of Professional Conduct* speaks to the conflict of interest issue:

(a) A lawyer shall not represent a client if the representation of that client will be directly adverse to another client, unless:

(1) the lawyer reasonably believes the representation will not adversely affect the relationship with the other client; and

(2) each client consents after consultation . . .

Most case law in this area presumes that if a firm has represented both parties in the past, there is an actual conflict of interest. It is not necessary to prove that confidences and secrets were exchanged during the first representation. Usually when an actual conflict of interest occurs, the whole firm, not just the attorney involved, is prohibited from entering the case.

Rule 1.8 of the ABA *Model Rules of Professional Conduct* also speaks to the conflict of interest issue:

(a) A lawyer shall not enter into a business transaction with a client or knowingly acquire an ownership, possessor, security or other pecuniary interest adverse to a client unless . . .

(b) A lawyer shall not use information relating to representation of a client to the disadvantage of the client unless the client consents after consultation . . . .

It is important that attorneys and legal assistants are loyal to their clients and have no alternative motives that might influence their independent professional judgment to represent their clients. Figure 2-8 provides a few more examples of conflict of interest problems.

CONFLICT CHECKING

Since law offices and attorneys typically represent a large number of clients, it is often difficult for them to remember every client. As a result, it is possible for an attorney to have a conflict of interest but simply not remember the former client. Thus, it becomes the responsibility of management to ensure that before new cases are taken, a conflict check takes place. It is prudent to have a written policy regarding conflict checking (see Figure 2-9).

- Using Client Information to Harm the Client:
  An ambitious associate attorney regularly defends the X insurance company. Client comes into attorney's office and wants to sue X insurance company for a major personal injury claim, not knowing that the attorney has represented the company before. Attorney, in an effort to help X insurance company, intentionally allows the statute of limitations to take effect, then pays the client $2,500 from his own pocket and tells the client that the insurance company settled. Attorney had a clear duty to tell the client about his conflict of interest. Attorney was disbarred and the law firm was sued for malpractice.

- Financial Interest:
  Attorney is an employee of a county government water district. Attorney uses his position of authority to influence the water board's decision to purchase a piece of land that he owns through a partnership. Attorney also delays $300,000 of sewer connection fees to another of his pieces of land until after the sale of the land is completed to a third party. Attorney had a clear conflict of interest in both cases. Attorney was suspended for two years from the practice of law and pleaded guilty to using his official office to influence a governmental decision.

FIGURE 2-8
Conflict of Interest Examples

FIGURE 2-9
Sample Conflict of
Interest Policy

Source: *Law Office Staff Manual*, 2d ed.(American Bar Association, 1993). Reprinted by permission.

Before any new file can be opened, a conflicts check must be accomplished by checking the Alphabetic Client Index card files (current and closed) and the Adverse Party Index cards. Such conflicts check will be completed before requesting an internal file number from the Accounting Department.

No new file may be opened if such search discloses any potential conflict with any past or present client or adverse party. Any such conflict should be immediately reported to the responsible attorney. A log of each conflicts check will be maintained. Anyone opening a new file for a new client or new litigation matter without conducting the conflicts check will be subject to disciplinary action.

Many law offices maintain a list of all their former clients and adverse parties, so that when a new case is being considered as to whether it should be accepted, the firm will routinely check this list to ensure that there are no conflict of interest problems.

Manual conflict checking systems typically are compiled using index cards. An index card is prepared on each client and adverse party and filed alphabetically. Some firms have separate index card systems: one for current clients, one for past clients, and one for adverse parties.

Using a computerized data base program is an excellent way to set up a conflict checking system (see Figure 2-10). A data base program is application software that stores, searches, sorts, and organizes data. When using a data base program, it is advantageous to include the client's date of birth or social security number, otherwise a misspelled name may not be picked up by the program. Some accounting, billing, docket control, and case-management programs also can be used to perform conflict checking.

Some insurance companies that issue malpractice insurance to attorneys also require that before the policy is written, the firm have and consistently use a conflict checking device.

THE CHINESE WALL

Although it is the general rule that courts tend to disqualify a whole firm when a conflict of interest problem arises, some courts have carved out an alternative to

Last Name	First Name	Social Security	Adverse Party	Type of Case	Date
Allen	Alice	515722404	Hays, Jonathan	Personal injury	1/15/91
Allen	Mariam	093342872	Cox Construction	Contract	12/01/92
Barney	Larry	023234912	Barney, Cindy	Divorce	1/08/88
Johnson	Donald	505235682	Beckwith, Eric	Real estate	8/02/90
Kitchen	Jennifer	093239832	State	Admin.\ law	10/06/91
Hall	Electric	235648905	Den, Robert	Collection	3/16/92
Winslow	Harriet	452239423	—	Adoption	6/7/91

FIGURE 2-10   A Conflict of Interest Data Base

disqualification. The alternative is called the Chinese Wall theory. The **Chinese Wall** *alternative occurs when a firm effectively isolates the legal assistant or attorney with a conflict of interest from having anything whatsoever to do with the case, creating a "Chinese Wall" around her* (see excerpts of the *Rivera v. Chicago Pneumatic* opinion in Figure 2-11). This is typically done by instructing staff members not to talk to her about the case, and limiting any access she might have to the files of the case, such as locking file cabinets.

Chinese Wall

Term for a technique used to isolate the legal assistant or attorney with a conflict of interest from having anything to do with a case.

Rivera v. Chicago Pneumatic, 1991 WL 151892 (Conn. Super.).
The issue presented in this case is whether defendant's motion to disqualify plaintiffs' counsel should be granted where a paralegal formerly employed by defendant's attorneys, and who had been extensively involved in litigation concerning defendant, is now employed by plaintiffs' counsel, and where plaintiffs' counsel has set up screening procedures to ensure that confidences are not divulged.

Defendant Chicago Pneumatic Tool Company (hereafter Chicago Pneumatic) moves to disqualify plaintiffs' counsel, The Reardon Law Firm, on the grounds that plaintiffs' counsel has employed a paralegal formerly employed by defendant's attorneys, which employee had been involved extensively in the defense of similar product liability lawsuits brought against defendant. Chicago Pneumatic states that the employee, Patricia Lannon, "was privy to all stages of the development of (the prior) litigation" and that "(h)er duties included typing and/or filing of all correspondence, including materials which should be privileged as attorney-client communication; typing and/or filing of all internal office memoranda, including those which would be classified as attorney-work product, as they include discussions of strategy, tactics and the evaluation of legal theories and factual witnesses."

It also asserts that Ms. Lannon had access to documents of the client, and was exposed to interoffice conferences concerning the litigation. Ms. Lannon also was privy to discussions concerning trial strategy, the strengths and weaknesses of plaintiffs' case, and defenses to the action. Ms. Lannon in her affidavits annexed to Plaintiffs' Brief does not dispute that she acquired confidential information of the defendant while employed by defendant's attorneys. The matter at issue here is whether the "Chinese Wall" proposed by the plaintiffs is sufficient under the facts of this case to prevent disclosure of the confidential and privileged information . . .

To ensure that continued representation by plaintiffs' counsel does not threaten the integrity of the proceedings, plaintiffs' counsel has erected a Chinese Wall which incorporates the following:

(1)   Ms. Lannon will not be permitted to disclose or discuss any information she acquired while employed by defendant's counsel concerning the cases in question;

(2)   The files in question will be kept locked and will not be accessible to Ms. Lannon;

(continued)

**FIGURE 2-11
A Case Upholding the Chinese Wall Theory**

(3)   Ms. Lannon will not be permitted in the vicinity of the files when others are working on them;

(4)   Ms. Lannon's supervisors, Attorneys Horgan and Provatas, will not work on the cases in question, nor will they maintain any files involving defendant;

(5)   Ms. Lannon will sign an affidavit and agreement that she will have no contact with the files, nor will she discuss the files with anyone in plaintiffs' firm or disclose any information she acquired in her former position; and

(6)   The attorney who will be handling the files, Attorney Nazzaro, will have no direct contact with Ms. Lannon.

See Letter from Attorney Reardon to Attorney Boyce dated March 15, 1991, appended as Exhibit "B" to Defendant's Brief. See also affidavits signed by Ms. Lannon and affidavits of Attorneys Horgan and Nazzaro. Exhibits B and E; and C and D to Plaintiffs' Brief . . .

In this case, the defendant has not met its burden to show that Ms. Lannon has disclosed confidential information to her new employer. Nor has it sustained its burden of proving that the plaintiffs' law firm was tainted or "infected" by the hiring of Ms. Lannon, or that plaintiffs have obtained an unfair advantage over the defendant which can only be remedied by the removal of plaintiffs' attorneys. "The disqualification of a party's chosen counsel is a harsh sanction, and an extraordinary remedy which should be resorted to sparingly." The court in the state of this record is not persuaded to invoke such a remedy. Moreover, the "Chinese Wall" erected to ensure that confidences will not be revealed in the future appears sufficient and reasonable to accomplish that end. The court must presume that plaintiffs' counsel will scrupulously comply with the Rules of Professional Conduct. See, for example, the Preamble, sections 5.1, 5.2 and 5.3.

Accordingly, defendant Chicago Pneumatic Tool Company's motion to disqualify plaintiffs' counsel is denied, so long as the "Chinese Wall" set forth in Plaintiffs' Brief and affidavits remains in effect.

Not all courts accept the Chinese Wall theory. Again, it would be the duty of management to ensure that the office could lock up the files and to segregate the attorney or legal assistant with the conflict from the rest of the staff. Law offices must also effectively limit access to computers and client data files to build an effective Chinese Wall.

LEGAL ASSISTANT CONFLICT OF INTERESTS

Many courts have extended the conflict of interest issue to legal assistants as well as attorneys. Conflict of interest problems usually occur when a legal assistant changes employment. For instance in *In re Complex Asbestos Litigation*, a legal assistant worked for a law firm defending major asbestos litigation claims. He worked with discovery documents and was a part of the defense team from 1985 to 1988 and attended defense strategy meetings. Subsequently he was hired by a firm representing asbestos plaintiffs. The defendants moved to disqualify the plaintiff's attorney because of the legal assistant's conflict of interest, since he had knowledge of confidential information gained over several years. The motion was granted by the court.

Legal assistants should be ready to answer questions about their previous employers when interviewing for jobs to avoid conflict of interest problems. The ABA Committee on Ethics and Professional Responsibility recently issued an opinion regarding this matter:

> A law office that hires a nonlawyer employee, such as a paralegal, away from an opposing law office may save itself from disqualification by effectively screening the new employee from any participation in the case the two firms have in common.[5]

The legal assistant should be on guard for situations that might present a potential conflict of interest as a result of information gained in past employment and should disclose any questionable situation to the employer.[6]

I accepted a [legal assistant job] offer from another law firm, unaware that the attorneys on both sides knew about a potential conflict of interest. When I switched law firms, the former firm's client expressed major concern over the fact that I was now employed by the law firm representing his opponent. I was put behind an ethical wall and could hardly walk anywhere within the firm without having to shut my eyes and ears or look the other direction. Then one morning . . . a senior partner announced that I would be sent home for two weeks until the firm could get a conflict waiver from the other party. My new law firm would continue to pay my salary and benefits, but no one had any idea what was to follow. Finally, after sixteen weeks, the conflict waiver was granted. Do not take any chances with potential conflict of interest matters. Be sure to find out before you accept a job offer what the firm's policy is if a conflict of interest arises.

—**Susan L. Oder.** Reprinted in part from Los Angeles Paralegal Association Reporter, May 1992.

Ideas on how legal assistants can avoid conflict of interest problems include:

▪ **When changing jobs, bring up the issue of potential conflicts in the interview**—Tell the firm who you have worked for and what types of cases you have worked on. It is better to deal with potential conflict problems up front than for an employer to hire you and then find out there are problems.

▪ **Be absolutely honest about your past**—Do not hide or deceive employers about potential conflict of interest problems. Honesty is always the best policy.

▪ **If you later find out you may have a conflict, immediately inform your supervising attorney or legal assistant manager and do not have anything to do with the case**—If you later find out after you have been hired by a new firm that you may have a conflict problem, immediately raise the issue with your supervising attorney. Do not volunteer information to the new firm regarding the matter. If you can, approach your former employer and ask for an informed and express **written** waiver giving consent for you to work for the other firm. Verbal consents are hard to prove, so get it in writing.

- **Management must ensure that conflict of interest problems are checked**—It is also the duty of management to ensure that employees are not hired who have substantial conflict of interest problems, or if they do have such a problem, that the firm knows it up front. For instance, management might want to add a question to its employment form that asks potential employees to state any conflict problems in addition to establishing the conflict checking system mentioned earlier.

RESOLVING ETHICAL PROBLEMS

There is nothing easy about resolving an ethical problem. Typically, ethical issues are complex and messy; they are rarely "black and white." However, the following are several ideas that can help you deal with ethical problems.

> *I took a job in a ten-lawyer firm in a big city . . . . I soon sensed an undercurrent of shady activities by some of the lawyers. My way of dealing with it at the time was to terminate my employment. I got another job and left. I never discussed it with anyone. When you make your own decision in an ethical dilemma, you have to live with its aftermath. . . . At the time, I was not mature enough to handle such a sensitive situation. . . . I would [now] try to work through the problem with my employer because you don't leave problems behind. Your next employment situation will bring other problems. We need to learn how to deal with them to become better practitioners and better people.*
>
> —**Carol Milano,** legal assistant, in "Hard Choices: Dealing with Ethical Dilemmas on the Job," *Legal Assistant Today,* March/April 1992, 72, 78, 79.

- **Talk to your legal assistant manager or supervising attorney regarding ethical problems**—When you encounter an ethical problem, the first thing you should do is to talk to someone else about it to get a different perspective. Typically, this will be your legal assistant manager or supervising attorney. However, this is sometimes hard to do when the supervising attorney is the one asking you to do something you think is unethical or if the attorney is herself doing something unethical. One way to approach the issue is to discreetly ask the attorney if she thinks this might be a problem. It is important to not be accusatory but to simply inquire into the issue and to delicately try to prove your point. You always have the option, no matter how hard it is, to say "no" to the attorney if she asks you to do something that you know is unethical. Also, be sure to check your firm's personnel policy manual. Ethical problems and procedures for handling them are sometimes covered in this type of manual.

- **Talk to another attorney or legal assistant in the firm regarding ethical problems**—If you have a hard time talking to your supervising attorney about an ethical problem, talk to another attorney or legal assistant. It is important in dealing with ethical problems to take counsel with others, to bounce ideas off others, and to talk about it. It could be that the other people may have more experience than you and have had to deal with a similar situation. When talking to another attorney in the firm, use the same nonaccusatory approach. Also, be sure that you are talking to a person you can trust for sincere advice on how to handle the situation. You do not want to be perceived as spreading rumors or stirring up trouble. In larger firms you also have the option of asking to be transferred.

▪ **Join a professional legal assistant association**—Professional associations offer a good way to share information and experiences with others, including information about ethical problems. Most professional legal assistant organizations provide guidance on ethical concerns. Use these resources to help you solve your ethical problem.

FIGURE 2-12
Paralegal Ethics: The Ten Commandments of a Conservative

Source: William Statsky, *Introduction to Paralegalism* (Saint Paul, Minnesota: West Publishing Co., 1992), 264.

1. Know the ethical rules governing attorneys. If you understand when attorneys are vulnerable to charges of unprofessional conduct, you will be better able to help them avoid such charges.
2. Know the ethical rules governing paralegals. At the start of your paralegal career, promise yourself that you will adhere to rigorous standards of professional ethics, even if these standards are higher than those followed by people around you.
3. Never tell anyone who is not working on a case anything about that case. This includes your best friend, your spouse, and your relatives.
4. Assume that people outside your office do not have a clear understanding of what a paralegal or legal assistant is. Make sure that everyone with whom you come in contact (clients, attorneys, court officials, agency officials, the public) understands that you are not an attorney.
5. Know what legal advice is and refuse to be coaxed into giving it, no matter how innocent the question asked of you appears to be.
6. Never make contact with an opposing party in a legal dispute, or with anyone closely associated with that party, unless you have the permission of your supervising attorney and of the attorney for the opposing party, if the latter has one.
7. Don't sign your name to anything if you are not certain that what you are signing is 100% accurate and that the law allows a paralegal to sign it.
8. Never pad your time sheets. Insist that what you submit is 100% accurate.
9. Know the common rationalizations for misrepresentation and other unethical conduct:
   ▪ it's always done,
   ▪ the other side does it,
   ▪ the cause of our client is just,
   ▪ if I don't do it, I will jeopardize my job.
   Promise yourself that you will not allow any of these rationalizations to entice you to participate in misrepresentation or other unethical conduct.
10. If what you are asked to do doesn't feel right, don't proceed until it does.

- **Be familiar with the ethical rules of your state**—It is always a good idea to have a copy of the ethical rules used in your jurisdiction and to review them from time to time.

- **Subscribe to legal assistant periodicals that cover ethical issues**—Many national legal assistant publications routinely carry articles on ethical concerns. Some even have a regular column on the issues of ethics. This kind of timely information can be helpful when deciding ethical problems.

- **Report ethical violations to the state bar association as a last resort**—If you have tried to work out an ethical problem to no avail, you always have the option of reporting the violation to the state bar association. This is a very difficult decision to make, since there is a chance you will lose your job as a result. Ethical problems are not easy to deal with and you must be able to live with whatever decision you make.

- **When considering ethical questions, think conservatively**—When you are faced with a hard ethical question, be conservative and do that which you know is right, no matter how much it may hurt. Figure 2-12 contains a list of ethical "commandments" that may guide you in this direction.

- **Do not ignore the ethical problem**—A common way to handle ethical problems is to simply ignore them and hope they will go away. Unfortunately, this approach rarely works. In many instances, it simply makes the situation worse. For example, if you see a staff person charging time to a client's case when he is not working on it, it is better to bring the issue to a head then, rather than wait for him to do it to twenty clients. Ethical problems are better handled when they first occur as opposed to letting them fester and become far more complicated.

Suppose a paralegal, in the interest of job preservation, decides to engage in unethical or illegal activity that has been ordered by an attorney. At what point does that paralegal become liable criminally or civilly for such acts? . . .

Nothing at all would insulate the paralegal [from criminal prosecution if the acts are illegal]. Whether the individual is an attorney or a paralegal, the criminal liability is the same. We indict judges and we indict lawyers. There is no reason to believe we will not indict paralegals.—Robert P. Cummins, member of the ABA's Standing Committee on Lawyer's Professional Responsibility.

—Phillip M. Perry, "Should You Rat on Your Boss?" *Legal Assistant Today,* March/April 1993, 66.

ANSWERS TO COMMON LEGAL ASSISTANT ETHICAL QUESTIONS

The following are answers to some other common legal assistant ethical questions. The answers are based on general statements of law, but an answer may be different depending on your particular jurisdiction.

▪ **May legal assistants have business cards and may their names appear on law firm stationery?** In many states, the answer is yes. For business cards, care must be taken to ensure that the nonlawyer status of the cardholder is displayed prominently on the card. Regarding firm stationery, the name of the legal assistant(s) must be set apart from the lawyers' names, and the legal assistant's title must be shown clearly. Some firms print lawyers' names on one side of the stationery and print legal assistants' names on the other.

▪ **May a legal assistant sign letters prepared on firm stationery?** Yes, provided (1) the letter contains no direct legal advice or opinions, and (2) the legal assistant's status is shown clearly. The best practice is to include the title "Legal Assistant" or "Legal Assistant to X" directly below the typed name in the signature block of the letter.

▪ **May a legal assistant discuss fee ranges with a client on a preliminary basis, leaving the final discussion and decision to the supervising attorney?** All discussions related to fees must be deferred to the attorney. Even when a firm uses an internal fee schedule, it generally serves as a guideline only. It is solely the attorney's responsibility to measure the situation presented by each case and to set the fee.

▪ **How often and in what way must a legal assistant identify his or her nonlawyer status?** There is no single, correct way to identify the legal assistant's status. It seems prudent to do so at the beginning of all telephone conversations and at the beginning of every initial conference with a client or witness. For example, regarding a telephone call, one might say, "Hello. This is Jack Samson, Jane Mitchell's legal assistant." If it appears that the other party may think the legal assistant is a lawyer, that impression should be corrected right away. The issue is not how often identity must be clarified to comply with the rules, it is how often should identity be clarified to protect the legal assistant from charges related to the unauthorized practice of law.

▪ **May a legal assistant counsel a close friend or a relative about a legal matter when the friend or relative knows that the legal assistant is not a lawyer and when the legal assistant is not paid for the advice?** Other than suggesting that the friend or relative see a lawyer, the legal assistant cannot give advice or comment in any way that may be taken as a legal opinion. The problem arises most frequently at family dinners, parties, and other social events. Friends and relatives can create an extremely uncomfortable situation. Whether the legal assistant is paid or not is irrelevant; legal advice cannot be given by the legal assistant under any circumstances.

MALPRACTICE AND MALPRACTICE PREVENTION

legal malpractice
Possible consequence when an attorney's or law office's conduct falls below the standard skill, prudence, and diligence that an ordinary lawyer would possess or that is commonly available in the legal community.

Legal malpractice occurs when an attorney's or law office's conduct in representing a client falls below the standard skill, prudence, and diligence that an ordinary lawyer would possess or that is commonly available in the legal community. Figure 2-13 shows an example of legal malpractice. Legal assistants can play an active role in preventing legal malpractice. Figure 2-14 shows several examples in which legal assistants were directly responsible through mistakes or carelessness for large losses suffered by the law office's clients. Notice in Figure 2-14 that although the

FIGURE 2-13
Example of Ethical Misconduct Leading to Malpractice

An attorney was charged with disciplinary misconduct. In one case, the attorney was hired to file a bankruptcy action but failed to perform any legal services, file the bankruptcy petition, or communicate with his client after he was retained.

In another case, the attorney was paid $1,000 to file a case. The case was never filed. The attorney advised the clients that he had moved his office. The clients were unable to get their phone calls returned. When they attempted to visit the attorney's office, the address he gave turned out to be a coffee shop.

In another case, the attorney was paid advance attorney's fees to file a divorce case. Several months later the client received a purported petition for dissolution of marriage from the attorney with a court stamp on it. According to court records, no petition had been filed. The client sought information from the attorney, but the letter was not answered.

The attorney was disbarred and sued by his clients for legal malpractice.

mistakes were relatively minor in themselves, leaving off a couple of zeros on a lien, sending some stocks to the wrong person, and filing a document in the wrong county, the resulting losses to the clients were very large. It is for this reason that legal assistants must be very thorough in everything they do and have a high degree of professionalism.

Figure 2-15 shows areas of law that are more prone to malpractice than others. Plaintiff personal injury and real estate matters are among the highest. Practitioners in these areas should take particular precautions to prevent malpractice. Figure 2-16 shows the most common types of errors that resulted in a malpractice claim being filed. Notice in Figure 2-16 that 79 percent of malpractice claims are filed against small law firms with one to five attorneys.

The following is an examination of some of the more common causes of legal malpractice and some suggestions to prevent these types of malpractice claims.

▪ **Poor or no communication with client**—The attorney or law office failed to communicate with the client by returning phone calls, answering correspondence, sending out status reports or updates, and failing to keep the client informed of changes in the case.

Clients who feel isolated and uninformed sometimes start thinking malpractice.

—Barbara Rosen, "Lawyer Bashing," *The Docket,* September/October 1993, 9.

Clients should regularly be called and asked for their opinions on how to proceed with the case. Client phone calls and correspondence should be returned or answered the same day they are received. Status reports to clients should be routinely made at <u>least</u> once a month. In many instances, it may be the legal assis-

Understand that although paralegals are not sued for malpractice [yet], paralegals still can cause malpractice to occur. How do you avoid malpractice claims? Some things that have worked for me—keep paper trails, calendar and docket systems, and use them. Ask questions; I study the areas of law in which I work. I know the statutes and rules. I know the habits of the attorneys for whom I work. I know my own weaknesses. . . . I take extra measures to take those weaknesses into consideration. I take the time to do it right. But I remember I've made mistakes in the past. . . . I admit those mistakes, and I try to learn from them.

—**Betsy Horn,** CLA, "Legal Malpractice—A Paralegal's Perspective, *Fort Worth Paralegal Association Newsletter,* vol. 10, no. 2, March/April 1992, 8.

- A legal assistant at Prudential mistakenly left off the last three zeros on a mortgage used to secure a $92,885,000 loan made by Prudential to a company that took bankruptcy. Because of the mistake, Prudential had a lien for only $92,885. Attorneys working for Prudential are trying to convince the U.S. Bankruptcy Court in New York City to give them the lien for the additional $92,792,115.[1]
- To close a merger deal between Company A and Company B, the law firm representing Company A was to send several thousand shares of stock to a minority shareholder in Company B. The paralegal who was responsible for sending the stock certificates to the minority shareholder received a phone call from a women named "Janet" who told her to send 3,000 shares of the stock to a Florida address. The paralegal complied only to find out several weeks later that she'd been duped. The stock certificates were worth more than $40,000.[2]
- Attorneys represented a client in a real estate transaction in which the client was trying to clear the title of a piece of property so it could be sold. During the course of the transaction, a "lis pendens" was filed on the property (a lis pendens is a notice filed on public records for the purpose of warning all persons that the title to a piece of property is in litigation).

  The attorneys negotiated a settlement to clear the title and then prepared settlement papers together with a "Release of Lis Pendens" (the Release of Lis Pendens is necessary to clear the property's title so that it can be sold). Unfortunately, the attorneys' paralegal filed the "Release of Lis Pendens" in the wrong county.

(continued)

**FIGURE 2-14
"Malpractice" by
Legal Assistants**

Sources: 1. William Statsky, *Introduction to Paralegalism* (Saint Paul, Minnesota: West Publishing Co., 1992), 825, citing 17 *At Issue* (San Francisco Legal Assistants Ass'n, December 1990). 2. Mark Dowdy, "A Paralegal's Costly Mistake," *Legal Assistant Today,* November/December 1992, 27. 3. *Bonz v. Sudweeks,* 808 P.2d 876 (119 Idaho 539, 1991).

As a result, the original lis pendens was not released and continued to cloud the title to the client's property unbeknownst to the client. The cloud on the title to the client property was discovered by a third-party investor who had intended to invest $300,000 in the development of the property. As a result of the unreleased lis pendens remaining on the county records, the third-party investor refused to participate or have any further involvement in the development of the client's property. Further, the client was unable to obtain financing for the project and was unable to meet the financial obligation on the property. A foreclosure action was commenced on the property.

The client then filed a malpractice action against the attorneys for the misfiling of the Release of Lis Pendens in the wrong county because of the negligence of the paralegal.[3]

FIGURE 2-15
Malpractice Claim Data

Source: Reprinted with permission from *Characteristics of Legal Malpractice* by Gates and Swetin. Copyright 1989. American Bar Association.

MALPRACTICE CLAIMS BY AREA OF LAW:

	Number of Claims	Percent
Personal injury—plaintiff	7331	25.1%
Real estate	6808	23.3%
Collection and bankruptcy	3066	10.5%
Family law	2303	7.9%
Estate, trust and probate	2038	7.0%
Corporate/business organization	1554	5.3%
Criminal	976	3.3%
Personal injury—defense	942	3.2%
Business transaction commercial law	889	3.0%
Workers' compensation	624	2.1%
Securities (SEC)	582	2.0%
Taxation	458	1.6%
Civil rights discrimination	319	1.1%
Construction (building contracts)	228	0.8%
Labor law	193	0.7%
Consumer claims	192	0.7%
Local government	191	0.7%
Patent, trademark, copyright	167	0.6%
Government contracts/claims	101	0.3%
Admiralty	86	0.3%
Natural resources	62	0.2%
Antitrust	45	0.2%
Environmental law	31	0.1%
Immigration/naturalization	28	0.1%
International law	13	0
Total	**29,227**	**100.00%**

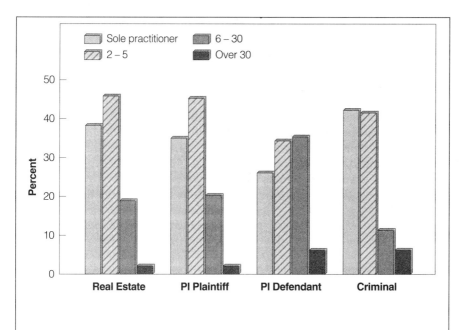

MALPRACTICE CLAIMS — by Firm Size

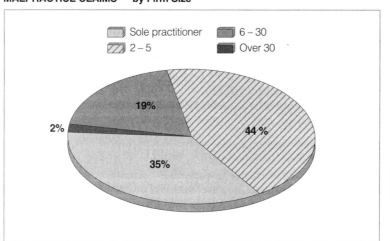

FIGURE 2-16A
Malpractice
Statistics

Source: Reprinted with
permission from *The
Lawyer's Desk Guide to
Legal Malpractice,* copyright
1992. American Bar
Association.

TYPE OF ALLEGED ERRORS

Administrative Errors	**25.76%**	**Intentional Wrongs**	**11.59%**
— Failure to calendar	11.14%	— Malicious prosecution	4.19%
— Procrastination	4.82%	— Fraud	4.16%
— Failure to file	4.21%	— Civil rights	1.73%
— Failure to react to		— Libel	1.51%
calendar	3.48%		
— Clerical error	1.45%	**Substantive Errors**	**43.59%**
— Lost file	.66%	— Failure to know law	9.47%
		— Inadequate investi-	
Client Relation Errors	**16.27%**	gation	8.96%
		— Planning error	7.66%
— Failure to obtain client		— Failure to know	
consent	9.19%	deadline	6.83%
— Failure to follow client		— Record search	4.73%
instructions	5.59%	— Conflict of interest	3.35%
— Improper withdrawal		— Tax consequence	1.84%
from representation	1.49%	— Math error	.76%

FIGURE 2-16B
Additional
Malpractice
Statistics

Source: Reprinted with
permission from *The
Lawyer's Desk Guide to
Legal Malpractice,* copyright
1992. American Bar
Association.

tant preparing the status reports. Constant communication with the client is an important aspect of malpractice prevention.

- **Neglected legal work**—The attorney or law office failed to perform the legal work required in a timely fashion. This can happen in many different ways. The law office personnel could forget to file a case before the statute of limitations ran out, an attorney could fail to attend a hearing, or a file could be lost.

Many would assume that instances of attorneys or law offices neglecting cases would be few. In reality, it is one of the top reasons that malpractice claims are filed. Law offices typically handle many cases at one time, so it is important that proper systems are set up to track each case. Any forgotten case can turn into a malpractice case. Automation, including computerized docket control programs that track deadlines, hearings, appointments, and things to be done can greatly help in this matter.

In some instances, neglect happens because law office staff duties and responsibilities are not clearly defined. Law office management must be sure that the staff knows who is responsible for each aspect of a case.

Neglect can be avoided by having good systems that track each client and each case in an organized manner and by having staff members who understand that each matter you work on must be regularly followed up on.

- **Fee disputes**—Arguments between the attorney and a client over how much the attorney should receive in fees is a common reason that clients sue attorneys for malpractice. If a client thinks the attorney collected an unfair fee, he is far more likely to file a malpractice claim. Fee disputes can be reduced by having written fee agreements, by sending monthly or biweekly accountings to the client of current fees so the client does not get "sticker shock" when you send a quarterly bill, and by being fair and honest. Many clients file malpractice claims because they are unhappy with how much the firm charged. Some malpractice claims possibly could be avoided if law firms tried more diligently to resolve fee disputes.

- **Incompetence**—Incompetence on the part of the attorney or a law office also leads to malpractice claims. Attorneys should not handle cases in areas in which they have no prior experience or expertise. A common way to handle this situation is to refer the case to an attorney who practices in a particular area or to secure cocounsel who has experience in handling that type of case.

Legal assistants can take an active role in avoiding incompetence problems. One way to avoid such problems is to have checklists and form files for every type of case or matter handled. Without checklists and form files, staff members may forget to do something, to file something, or to check something. Most state bar associations publish form files and checklists for all types of cases. In addition, legal assistants should be sure to use the law office's checklists/form files or create their own. Incompetence also can be avoided by education, going to seminars and workshops, reading law journals and legal periodicals, and belonging to professional associations. These things do not apply only to the attorney; they are just as important for the legal assistant.

Because the representation of clients is based on trust, it is critical that attorneys, legal assistants, and all law office staff be honest. This simply cannot be compromised on. When you see someone else being dishonest, it is your duty to inform others so that the conduct stops.

- **Conflicts of interest**—Attorneys sometimes ignore conflict of interest problems such as representing both parties in the sale of real estate or suing a former client. Either of these situations also can lead to a lawsuit for malpractice.

Figure 2-17 also provides some excellent suggestions for helping to avoid costly malpractice claims.

Accuracy is extremely important, but if you make a mistake . . . tell someone, don't just hide the problem. Remember, it's very hard for a human being to beat up on somebody who admitted they made a mistake. It's real easy to do it if they try to hide it.

—**Cynthia Tokumitsu,** legal assistant, in "How to Avoid the Top 10 Mistakes Paralegals Make on the Job," *Legal Assistant Today,* November/December 1991, 31.

▪ **Miscommunication regarding representation**—Clients sometimes think attorneys are representing them when in fact they are not. Law offices should always send an engagement letter or contract that clearly sets out when a case is taken, what the firm is going to do, and what the fees will be based on.

---

1. Gather factual information from the client to determine the basis of any legal claim and immediately determine and track when the statute of limitations takes effect.
2. Give the client a copy of the written fee agreement specifying the terms of employment and the basis of the attorney's fees in the case.
3. Conduct a thorough conflict of interest check before the client's case is accepted and immediately notify the client in writing if a conflict or a potential conflict is discovered.
4. Investigate the facts of the client's case and the law regarding the case diligently and promptly.
5. Keep the client informed regarding the status of his or her case by providing routine status reports and always inform the client of all developments that might affect the client's rights and ask for his or her participation throughout the case.
6. Charge a reasonable and fair fee for services performed and provide the client with a clear and detailed accounting of the basis for the fees charged.
7. Carefully and thoroughly proofread all documents before they go out for mistakes and whenever possible send a copy of the document to the client for his or her approval and review.
8. Immediately tell the client of problems or mistakes as they happen and offer solutions.
9. Do not overestimate the firm's capacity to take on cases outside its expertise and always determine whether there is sufficient time to handle the matter properly.
10. Provide the client with written notice upon the attorney's withdrawal from representation (obtain court approval in matters involving litigation) and promptly provide the client with his or her file and other property he or she is entitled to.

FIGURE 2-17
Ten Ways to Prevent
Legal Malpractice

Example 1: Disengagement Letter — New Client where Case Was Not Accepted

Subject: Potential Claim of *Client v. Johnson*

Dear Client:

Thank you for coming in to our office on Tuesday, November XX, 19XX, regarding your legal matter. We are interested in your concerns and appreciated the opportunity to meet with you. However, after further consideration we have decided to decline representation of your interests in the captioned matter.

We have not made a legal opinion as to the validity or merits of your case. You should be aware that any action in this matter must be filed within the applicable statute of limitations. We suggest that you consult with another attorney concerning your rights in this matter.

Again, we will not be representing you in the captioned matter and are closing our file.

Thank you again, and we wish you the best.

Kindest Regards,

Example 2: Disengagement Letter Following Representation

Subject: *Client v. Johnson*

Dear Client:

Thank you for allowing us the opportunity to serve you regarding the captioned matter. The case is now closed. We are closing our files and taking the case out of our active file drawers, in that our work in the matter is finished. We will be sending our file to storage shortly. If you would like evidence or other material that you have provided to us returned, please give me a call so I can get it to you.

We are interested in knowing how you feel about the quality of legal services you received from our firm. We would appreciate it if you would complete the enclosed client survey questionnaire. We are always interested in knowing how we can serve you better in the future.

Again, the captioned case is now closed, and we greatly enjoyed representing your interests.

If you have any questions, please feel free to give me a call.

Kindest Regards,

FIGURE 2-18
Disengagement
Letters

In addition, law offices should routinely send out disengagement letters for any type of case or legal matter even if the only thing the law office did was to meet with the client in an initial interview (see Figure 2-18). The purpose of the disengagement letter is to clearly set out in writing that the attorney-client relationship was not formed or has ended. A client may not understand that the firm is not pursuing the matter, then come back months or even years later claiming that the attorney committed malpractice against him by not following up on the case.

SUMMARY

Legal ethics is an increasingly important topic that comes up often for all types of legal assistants. Ethical problems routinely encountered by legal assistants include the unauthorized practice of law, conflict of interest problems, and client confidentiality problems. Although a legal assistant cannot be disciplined by state regulatory bodies for violating attorney ethical rules, she would be held accountable by the attorney who hired or supervised her. Voluntary ethical codes by national legal assistant associations can help resolve ethical problems.

Legal assistants must be careful to avoid unauthorized practice of law questions. They cannot give legal advise, represent a client in court, accept or reject cases, or set a fee in a matter. Legal assistants must maintain client confidentiality at all times and should not talk about client cases away from the office, since this can undermine client confidence and compromise the client's case. Legal assistants must avoid conflict of interest problems, especially when changing employment, and also should be careful to make sure that legal malpractice is avoided and that they act prudently and cautiously in handling all kinds of cases.

KEY TERMS

Ethical rule
ABA *Model Code of Professional Responsibility*
ABA *Model Rules of Professional Conduct*
"Legal technicians"
Client confidentiality

Attorney-client privilege
Conflict of interest
Chinese Wall
Legal malpractice

PROBLEM SOLVING QUESTIONS

1. You are a legal assistant in the real estate section of a corporate law department. Your company is a large retailer that owns thousands of small retail outlets across the country. You process the leases, review the contracts, and coordinate lease payments with the accounts payable to make sure the proper lease payments will be made. By the time the lease gets to you, the contract has been reviewed by the attorneys. Typically you assume that the description of the property is accurate even though you could pull the full file to confirm the description. This is the way that it has always been done. What are your thoughts regarding the adequacy of the description of the property? Is this

a good policy? What is the risk if the property description is not accurate? Does it change your answer if your supervising attorney thinks that you are in fact reviewing the contract for accuracy and completeness?

2.   You are a legal assistant at a law firm that is representing a company in the process of negotiating a deal to merge with a competitor. You inadvertently mention the possibility of the merger to your father. Without your knowledge, your father purchases a large sum of stock in the company you represent knowing that when the merger becomes public, the price of the stock will substantially rise. Several months after the transaction, your father gives you a check for five thousand dollars and explains how he made the money. He tells you that he only did it for your benefit. Forgetting the criminal statutes that have been violated, how would you handle the situation and how could the problem have been avoided?

3.   You work for a government agency and are responding to a plaintiff's request for production of documents. One of the requests specifically asks for any notes or memorandums arising out of the facts of the case. In one of the boxes of material the agency has collected on the matter, you find a particularly incriminating memorandum that will virtually win the case for the plaintiffs if it is produced. What do you do?

Assume you go to your supervising attorney about the matter. The attorney responds that she will take care of the matter and thanks you for your diligent work. Several months go by and you are now working on preparing the case for trial. You quickly realize that the document was never produced to the plaintiffs. Now how would you resolve this situation?

4.   You are working on a client's case when the client's accountant calls and asks you for information about the client. You have worked with this particular accountant before and know the accountant is trustworthy. Is there any problem with revealing the information to the accountant? How would you handle it?

5.   Your law office just signed an agreement to represent a famous athlete in contract negotiations with his team. A reporter from *Sports Illustrated* calls and asks if your firm is representing the athlete. You read *Sports Illustrated* all the time and are impressed that one of its reporters called

your firm. In fact, you are taken off guard by the question. Being typically honest and forthright, you begin to answer. What is your answer?

6.   You are a new legal assistant right out of school. You take the first job offered to you. It is at a small firm that is poorly run and not very well respected in the legal community. You work at the firm for only a month and quit. You apply for another position at a different firm and decide not to mention the employment at the small firm, since it was for only a month. You sign the Employment Application Form knowing that it says if you are found to have lied on the application form, you could be terminated. You are subsequently hired by the new firm. Later, you find out the two firms have a highly publicized case they are litigating against each other. What do you do?

7.   As a legal assistant in a medium-size law office, you have access to all the resources of the firm, including copy machines, telephones, and the postage meter. While the firm's staff manual states that the firm's equipment will only be used for firm business, you notice that the other legal assistants frequently use the copier, envelopes, and postage machine for personal use. When you asked one of the other legal assistants in the firm about it, the legal assistant said, "Don't worry about it, everyone does it." How would you handle the situation?

8.   Your law office represents a nonprofit corporation. The executive director of the nonprofit corporation calls you when your supervising attorney is out of the office. The executive director states that an employee is demanding overtime pay, since she worked more than forty hours last week, and saying that if she is not paid overtime, she will immediately file a wage-and-hour complaint with the appropriate state agency. The attorney will not be in the office the whole week but may call in. You recollect from previous experience that the Fair Labor Standards Act generally states that employees should receive overtime pay for hours worked in excess of forty hours a week, though you are not sure about exceptions to the rule. The executive director presses you and says that he absolutely has to have an answer immediately and that if your firm can't respond to emergencies, then maybe he will take his business elsewhere. How would you resolve the situation? Give options.

9. As a legal assistant for a legal aid office, one of your jobs is to screen clients. You routinely see new clients and report the facts of each client's case to one of the attorneys. The attorneys then decide which cases they have time to take on. On Monday, a client comes into your office. The client has no money but appears to need an attorney. The client advises you that she has been sued and needs legal counsel to represent her for a hearing in state district court on Friday at 10:00 A.M. before Judge Smith. From your experience, you are sure the attorneys do not have the time to accept this case. After listening to the client, you respectfully tell her that you do not think the office will be able to represent her. The client then leaves and you prepare a memo to the attorneys. The attorneys subsequently decide not to handle the matter and file is closed.

On Friday at 10:15 A.M., the office receives a phone call from Judge Smith. Judge Smith tells your receptionist that an attorney from your office has five minutes to get over to her courtroom to represent the client or she (Judge Smith) will hold the office/attorneys in contempt of court and levy a fine against the office. Apparently, the client told Judge Smith that she had met with a representative from the legal aid office and had told the representative about the hearing. It was the client's understanding that an attorney from the legal aid office would represent her. Please explain how this matter could have been avoided.

Practice Exercises

1. You notice one of your fellow legal assistants at the legal aid office where you work routinely using fake names and misrepresenting who she is when tracking down witnesses or when trying to serve subpoenas. Is this unethical or just uncouth? Analyze the situation using either the NALA or NFPA code of ethics.

2. You are a legal assistant for a sole practitioner. You have been working on a motion that has to be filed by 4:30 P.M. At 4:10 P.M., you hand the completed motion to the attorney. The attorney signs the motion and hands it back to you and asks you to copy it and file it. How would you handle this situation? List your options.

3. Analyze from an ethics perspective Figure 2-2, the case of *Asphalt Engineers, Inc. v. Galusha.* How many ethical problems do you see and what are they?

Notes

1. Nancy B. Heller, "Dealing with Ethical Dilemmas—Can You Sleep at Night?" October 1992, *On Point* (newsletter of the National Capital Area Paralegal Association) p. 1. Printed with the permission of Nancy B. Heller, paralegal.
2. Deborah K. Orlik, *Ethics for the Legal Assistant* (Scott, Foresman and Company, 1986), 26.
3. Ibid., 26.
4. Thomas W. Brunner, Julie P. Hamre, and Joan McCaffrey Wegrzyn, *The Legal Assistant's Handbook* (Washington, D.C.: Bureau of National Affairs), 171.
5. *NALA Manual for Legal Assistants* (West Publishing Co., 1992), 48, citing ABA Opinion No. 88–1526 (6/22/88).
6. Ibid., 49.

3

STAFF MANUALS, TOTAL QUALITY MANAGEMENT, MARKETING, AND PLANNING

CHAPTER OBJECTIVES

After you read this chapter, you will be able to:

- Discuss what a staff manual is and why it is important.

- Differentiate between a policy and a procedure.

- Discuss total quality management philosophies.

- Explain marketing and various marketing options that are available.

- Identify ethical problems that may arise in carrying out a marketing plan.

- Define "mission statement."

- Explain the planning process.

The law firm of Harris, Charlie & Baker was a ten-attorney firm that was experiencing growing pains. In response to the problems, the firm hired a consulting firm to offer solutions. The law firm suffered from the following problems.

Law firm staff members received changing and contradictory instructions from partners on policy matters and were frustrated with the lack of effective guidance on how legal services were to be provided. The consulting firm recommended the development of a staff manual to clearly set out what the policies of the firm were regarding a broad range of subjects. The manual would prevent partners from having to decide policy on a fragmented and daily basis and would be a resource for staff members to turn to when partners were unavailable.

There was a general lack of communication among the partners and among staff members. No one knew where the firm was headed. The consulting firm recommended that the firm draft a mission statement, a short-range plan, and a long-range strategic plan to help focus the firm on where it was headed and how it was going to get there. All partners and staff members were to help develop the plan to increase communication.

The firm was having a problem bringing in new clients. The consulting firm recommended developing an emphasis on total quality management. By making quality the number one priority, the firm could receive increased referrals from existing clients and have a product it could market better to the community. The consulting firm also recommended that the firm develop a detailed marketing plan that would help it cultivate new clients and expand into new areas. After implementing the strategies, the firm was back on track.

LAW PRACTICE POLICIES AND PROCEDURES—THE STAFF MANUAL

Read and digest any staff manual provided . . . . You should know what it says and keep it updated as new policies are published. Despite the comments you will hear describing the manual as out-of-date, it will give you a good overview of office policies. And if the firm bothered to publish the manual, it obviously was important to someone involved in the firm's future and yours. So until you are advised otherwise by someone in authority, presume that the manual states the rules.[1]

In Chapter 1, you were introduced to the "systems" view of management. A system was described as a consistent or organized way of doing something. A system allows managers to create procedures for doing something. By using a system, time is saved, efficiency is increased, and jobs are done uniformly.

One of the ultimate types of systems is a law office staff manual, also called a policy and procedures manual. The purpose of a staff manual is to set out in writing the standing policies and procedures of a law office. The types of policies covered by the staff manual depend on the office, but they can range from personnel policies and how files will be maintained to how letters and pleadings will be formatted (see Figure 3-1). Staff manuals establish and document an efficient and cost-effective way of handling the day-to-day operations of the firm. The manual allows everyone to operate under the same procedures and to quickly find consistent answers to common questions. Without a staff manual, each person develops her own particular method for accomplishing tasks. Law offices need uniformity so that elements are not missed or forgotten. Staff manuals can be used to guarantee each client the same high-quality legal services, every time.

One consulting firm reported that staff productivity increased by 30 percent in the first year after the firm adopted a staff manual.

—Robert G. Kurzman and Rita Gilbert, *Paralegals and Successful Law Practice* (Institute for Business Planning, 1984), 80.

Staff manuals are particularly helpful when training new employees. New employees can immediately get a feel for how the firm operates and what procedures are to be followed just by reading the manual. This makes the orientation process quicker and less difficult. It is a misconception that staff manuals are only needed in large firms. Small law offices, legal aid offices, and government and corporate law departments need written procedures as well.

FIGURE 3-1
Sample Law Office
Staff Manual Table
of Contents

Source: *Law Practice Staff Manual*, 2d ed. (American Bar Association, 1992). Reprinted by permission.

Chapter 1: Introduction
1.1 Purpose and Use of the Manual
1.2 Organization of the Manual
Chapter 2: Organization, Management and Administration
2.1 Firm Resume
2.2 Partners/Shareholders
2.3 Management Committee/Board of Directors
2.4 Officers
2.5 The Executive Committee
2.6 The Advisory Committees
2.7 Firm Offices
2.8 Administrative Management Organization
2.9 Administrative Personnel
2.10 Directory of Services
2.11 Office Facility Maps and Directory
2.12 The Firm's Legal Practice and Departments
2.13 Firm Meetings
2.14 Confidential Nature of Legal Work
2.15 Code of Personal and Professional Conduct
Chapter 3: Office Policies
3.1 Equal Opportunity Employer
3.2 Policy on Sexual Harassment
3.3 Policy on Disability
3.4 Office Hours
3.5 Overtime
3.6 Client Relations/Office Decorum
3.7 Weekly Time Report
3.8 Absence and Tardiness (Staff)
3.9 Attorney Absence
3.10 Lunch Hour
3.11 Rest Periods
3.12 Coffee and Lunch Rooms
3.13 Scheduling Vacations
3.14 Holidays
3.15 Personal Holiday
3.16 Alternative Work Schedule
3.17 Office Closing Due to Inclement Weather
3.18 Professional Attitude
3.19 Personal Appearance
3.20 Personal Use of Office Equipment and Supplies
3.21 Housekeeping
3.22 Adjustment of Workloads—Extra Help
3.23 Outside Employment
3.24 Employment of Relatives (Nepotism Policy)
3.25 Loans
3.26 Bulletin Boards

(continued)

3.27 Office Privacy
3.28 Charitable and Political Contributions
3.29 Attorney Publicity
3.30 Attorney Directory
Chapter 4: Personnel Policies and Benefits
4.1 Employee Classifications
4.2 Work Year Defined
4.3 Probation Period
4.4 Compensation
4.5 Leaves of Absence
4.6 AIDS/HIV and Other Life-Threatening Illnesses
4.7 Credit Union
4.9 Personnel Records
4.10 Payment of Relocation Expenses for New Attorneys
4.11 Bar Registration and Professional Memberships
4.12 Termination of Employment
4.13 Continuing Legal Education
4.14 Smoking
4.15 Substance Abuse
Chapter 5: Information Systems
5.1 In General
5.2 Removal of Files from the Record Room
5.3 The File Opening Form and Worksheet
5.4 Opening a New File
5.5 Returning Files to the Record Room
5.6 Closing Files
5.7 Retrieving or Reopening Closed (Inactive) Files
5.8 Long-term Follow-up System
5.9 Long-term Compressed Storage
5.10 Conflict of Interest Information System
5.11 Master Calendar and Early Warning System
5.12 Library
5.13 Form Files
5.14 The Firm's Records
Chapter 6: Word Processing Services
6.1 Purpose
6.2 Location
6.3 Equipment
6.4 Work Applicable for Word Processing
6.5 Work Not Prepared by the Word Processing Center
6.6 Submitting Work to the Word Processing Center
6.7 Revisions
6.8 Proofreading
6.9 Formats
6.10 Libraries of Word Processing Center Work
6.11 Finished Work

(continued)

Chapter 7: Duplicating Services
7.1 Types and Uses of Available Equipment
7.2 Location
7.3 Copying Procedures
7.4 Self-Service
7.5 Charges for and Recording of Copies Made
7.6 Equipment Maintenance and Repair
7.7 Out-of-office Document Reproduction Services
7.8 Paper Cutter
7.9 Binding
7.10 Hole Punching Equipment
Chapter 8: Office Security and Emergency Procedures
8.1 In General
8.2 Emergency Procedures
8.3 Medical Emergencies, Work Injuries or Accidents
8.4 Data Protection
8.5 Disaster Recovery
Chapter 9: Financial Management
9.1 In General
9.2 Timekeeping Records
9.3 Receipts
9.4 Disbursements
9.5 Petty Cash
9.6 Cash Advances and Reimbursement of Expenses
9.7 Billing Procedures
9.8 Trust Account
Chapter 10: Communication Systems
10.1 Telephones
10.2 Facsimile (Telecopier) Machines
10.3 Electronic Mail
10.4 Mail Services
10.5 Air Freight and Express Services
10.6 Messenger Services
10.7 Attorney Services
Chapter 11: Equipment, Maintenance and Supplies
11.1 Supplies
11.2 Furniture and Equipment
11.3 Requests for New Type of Supplies or New Products
11.4 Photographic Equipment
11.5 Computers
11.6 General Maintenance
Chapter 12: Support Personnel and Their Functions
12.1 Principal Switchboard Operator/Receptionist
12.2 Floor Receptionist
12.3 Librarian
12.4 Calendar Clerk

(continued)

12.5 Records Clerk
12.6 Mail Clerk
12.7 Office Attendant
12.8 Relief Personnel
12.9 Notaries Public
12.10 Litigation Service
Chapter 13: Travel
13.1 Automobiles
13.2 Travel Agency
13.3 Airlines
13.4 Hotel Accommodations
13.5 Overseas Business Trips
13.6 Reimbursement of Expenses
13.7 Taxicab Voucher
Chapter 14: Miscellaneous Guidelines
14.1 Solicitation of Funds
14.2 Office News Bulletin
14.3 Lost and Found
14.4 Dun & Bradstreet Reports
14.5 Index of Corresponding Attorneys
14.6 Publication of Law Review Articles
14.7 Charitable Services/Pro Bono Work
14.8 Community and Professional Activities
14.9 Memoranda
14.10 Kitchens
14.11 Parking

A small law office I know recently suffered a real crisis. The office had a law office manager that virtually ran all of the systems and procedures for the whole office. She handled all accounting and money transactions, staff payroll, billing, computer use and computer passwords, the firm's form files, everything. Unfortunately, she suffered an unexpected heart attack. She was the only one in the office that knew how all the systems worked. It took the rest of the staff months to piece everything together and the office itself really suffered.

—Kurzman and Gilbert

If a law office does not have a staff manual, consider developing one. Most employers appreciate employees who go beyond their normal job description and take on additional projects that benefit the office. Figure 3-2 shows the steps to put together a staff manual. These types of assignments can sometimes lead to career advancement.

FIGURE 3-2
How to Put Together
a Staff Manual

1. Approval Stage—Ask approval from your supervisor to begin to put together a list of office procedures. Tell her the benefits of having such policies in writing: to give new employees, to establish minimum acceptable standards in the law office, and to establish a consistent way to handle all client cases the same. You might want to tell your supervisor that you will work on this in your spare time and that it will not affect your regular work (if this is true—always be honest).

2. Information Gathering—Once you have approval to begin working on it, you must gather information. Below are ways to get information regarding your manual.

    a. Call Other Legal Assistants Outside Your Office—Begin by calling your legal assistant friends and acquaintances in other firms. Tell them that you are putting together a staff manual for your office and ask if you could copy or see their firm's staff manual. Many firms will be happy to do this. Some may not want to, but it never hurts to ask.

    b. Contact Any Associations You Belong To—Many legal assistant associations also have resources libraries that have this type of information or have had members that have had similar assignments, so contact them.

    c. Check out from a Law Library or Purchase the ABA *Law Practice Staff Manual* or *Cadence Policy and Procedure Manual*—The American Bar Association publishes the *Law Practice Staff Manual,* 2d ed., 1992. The manual comes on floppy disk and will work with all IBM-compatible word processors. The ABA's manual can be checked out from most law libraries or can be purchased from the ABA for less than one hundred dollars (American Bar Association, 750 North Lakeshore Drive, Chicago, IL 60611—(312) 988-5000. The *Cadence Policy and Procedure Manual* for law offices is compatible with Apple Macintosh computers and can be obtained from Greenlight Software, 79 West Monroe, Suite 1320, Chicago, IL 60603-4969—(312) 782-6496.

    d. Make Observations and Talk to Office Staff—Another way to gather information is to simply observe how the law office operates, how things are being done correctly, and how they could be improved. In addition, talk to all members of the staff (if possible) to get their ideas about how things are being done and how they could be done better. Good insight can be obtained from *all* staff members, including copy clerks, runners, etc.—no one is too low on the "totem pole" to talk to or to get ideas and input from.

3. Drafting Stage—After you have gathered information from many different sources, you are ready to begin drafting the staff manual. As you begin drafting, continue to get the input of other individuals and ask their advice.

4. Editing of the Rough Draft—Once you have a working rough draft completed, submit it initially to your supervisor or whoever is supervising the project. Once you have his changes, make the changes and

then submit the manual to all staff members for their comments and changes. Coordinate requested changes with your supervisor and make whatever changes are necessary. By including others in the idea and drafting stages, you will make implementing the manual much easier, since other staff members will have an ownership interest in the staff manual.

5. Final Approval by Partners/Executive Committee and Implementation— Before the manual can be finalized, it should be approved by the partners, shareholders or executive committee. Once this is accomplished, the manual should be copied, distributed to all staff, and implemented. During the implementation stage, you will typically find that many changes will need to be made. This is expected.

You will find that the actual writing of the [staff] manual will bring to light many of the current inefficiencies in your law practice. "It's the way we've always done it" philosophy will slowly give way to "We ought to do it this way, because it is obviously the most cost efficient in terms of time expended."

—Kurtzman and Gilbert

WHAT SYSTEMS OR SUBJECTS ARE INCLUDED IN THE STAFF MANUAL?

Figure 3-1 contains a list of systems that are often found in staff manuals. Staff manuals usually cover such items as how the office is organized, ethical and confidentiality policies, personnel-related policies, the use of office equipment, and office procedures for opening new files. Staff manuals can be adapted to the needs of the specific law practice. In general, if management has to reiterate a policy more than once or twice on a matter of importance, the policy should be put in writing.

DRAFTING POLICIES AND PROCEDURES

Staff manuals can contain both policies and procedures. Although the concepts are similar, they also are very different from each other. A **policy** *is a specific statement that sets out what is or is not acceptable.* A **procedure** *is a series of steps that must be followed to accomplish a task.* Some firms have separate manuals for policies and procedures. All policies and/or procedures should be detailed, accurate, and succinct (see Figure 3-3). Notice that the procedure in Figure 3-3 is clearly stated, is easy to read, and assigns specific responsibilities, stating *who* is responsible for the tasks. In addition, whenever possible, a due date also is included so that staff members know exactly *when* items are due. When writing policies and procedures, try to strike a balance between having too many details (i.e. overregulating) and having too few. The aim is not to make a bureaucratic detail-ridden manual but to have a usable, practical guide.

policy
A specific statement that sets out what is or is not acceptable.

procedure
A series of steps that must be followed to accomplish a task.

Docketing Forms

1. **Incoming pleadings.** All incoming pleadings, whether served personally or received in the mail, are entered by the firm's docket clerk in the permanent docket book or computerized record the same day they are received. It is the responsibility of the attorney to see that every incoming pleading reflects a docket date initialed by the docket clerk.

2. **Outgoing pleadings.** It is the responsibility of the secretary to see that a copy of every outgoing pleading is sent to the docket clerk for docketing. No office copy of a pleading is to be placed in the office file until the pleading has been docketed and reflects a docket date initialed by the docket clerk. The entry shall be no later than one day after the pleading is mailed out.

3. **Docket request slips.** All deposition dates, motion dates, hearing dates, etc. should be docketed as soon as they are scheduled. It is the responsibility of the secretary to complete a docket request slip and send it to the docket clerk. The slip will then be returned to the secretary with a docket date initialed by the docket clerk.

4. **Daily and Weekly Docket Reports.** It is the duty of the docket clerk to see that each attorney receives daily and weekly docket reports. Weekly docket reports will be generated and distributed by the docket clerk to attorneys on Fridays for the coming week.

ADDITIONAL IDEAS ON ASSEMBLING OR REVISING A STAFF MANUAL

Below are some ideas on putting together or revising a staff manual:

- **Loose-leaf or three-ring notebooks work well**—Staff manuals are typically put in loose-leaf form so that pages can be easily updated. Out-of-date staff manuals will not be of much use in a typical fast-moving law practice.

- **The manual should be accurate, complete, and clear**—The staff manual should be accurate and complete and should be a "how-to" document for the people using it. The manual must be readable and clear so that it can be used as a quick reference guide. Remember, everyone from a senior partner to a copy clerk will be using the manual; it must be able to be understood by all.

- **List steps to be followed and time frames**—Whenever possible, list a sequence of steps to be accomplished and time frames for each step. This organizes the task and lets the reader know exactly what the individual steps are and when they should be completed.

- **Prototype staff manual**—There are two prototype staff manuals currently available. The ABA publishes the *Law Practice Staff Manual*, 2d edition, which is available at most law libraries or from the ABA at (312) 988-5000. The manual is a good place to start if you are drafting one from scratch or redrafting an outdated one. It also comes on floppy disk (for IBM-compatibles) so that it can be edited quickly and easily. Likewise, Greenlight Software publishes the *Cadence Policy and Procedure Manual* for law offices. It comes on floppy disks, is available for both Apple Macintosh and IBM-compatibles computers, and is available by calling (312) 782-6496.

- **The manual should have a table of contents and an index**—The manual needs to be "user friendly." Also, use a simple numbering system so people can easily cite specific policies.

- **Clarify current questions of staff**—Try to address areas where current staff members have repeated questions.

- **Send it out for review**—Get everyone in the office involved in drafting or revising the manual. It never hurts to get the comments of others and to include them in the process. Consider their suggestions and be open about new ideas and new ways of doing things. The ultimate purpose of the manual is to make the firm as efficient as possible.

- **When writing policies, use titles**—When drafting the manual, never use a person's name to specify who is responsible for a duty; always use a job title.

- **Distribute the staff manual to all employees**—All employees should have a copy of the manual. Typically, staff manuals are handed out to new employees when they are hired.

- **The manual should be kept up-to-date**—One of the problems with written documents is that they are sometimes inflexible and hard to change. For the staff manual to be truly useful, it must be kept current. Encourage staff members to submit their ideas for new policies and for revisions in old policies. This is the only way they will truly use the document as it is intended. Law practices are constantly changing, and the staff manual must keep pace. This takes time, but it is time well spent.

STAFF MANUALS FROM AN ETHICS PERSPECTIVE

Staff manuals also are important from an ethical point of view. The manual allows management to draft policies that will deter ethical violations. For instance, a common ethical problem is neglect of client matters. A manual can address this by stating which person is responsible for keeping the calendar, how items will be put on the calendar, and what steps will be taken to avoid missing the deadline. In addition, the staff manual can be used to set out policies on ethical situations, such as the need for strict confidentiality of client information.

TOTAL QUALITY MANAGEMENT

We know exactly what we want in a product or a service, whether it is legal services, a car or a hamburger and fries: it's quality. Quality is not an accident of nature, nor a gift to the lucky; rather, it is the product of a well-managed organization. **We** *decide whether ourselves or our organization will have quality as its standard.*

—**Edward C. Manahan,** "Deciding to Train for Quality Service," *Cornerstone* (National Legal Aid and Defender Association), vol. 14, no. 2 (Fall 1992): 11.

WHAT IS TQM?

total quality management
Management philosophy of knowing the needs of each client and allowing those needs to drive the legal organization.

Total quality management *(TQM) is a management philosophy that is based upon knowing the needs of each client and allowing those needs to drive the legal organization at all levels of activity, from the receptionist to the senior partner.*[2] From the outset of this book, you have been introduced to the importance of meeting client needs and providing quality legal services to clients. TQM is just an expansion on this basic idea. The TQM philosophy of allowing clients' needs to drive an organization, instead of the other way around, was taught to major Japanese corporations in the 1950s by W. Edwards Deming. The emergence of TQM is what many think makes Japanese products more reliable than products made elsewhere.

The focus of the TQM philosophy is for businesses to compete on *quality*. That is, to compete against other firms on the basis of quality of the service that is provided, as opposed to price or other factors. A recent survey of more than one hundred of the Fortune 500 companies shows that more than 80 percent have adopted TQM programs. The survey also shows that of the law departments of these Fortune 500 companies, 80 percent are implementing TQM programs of their own and that when these companies hire outside legal counsel, 70 percent would be influenced by the fact that a law office had implemented a TQM program.[3] Figure 3-4 shows the difference between making management decisions based on client needs and based on what is easiest for the law practice to provide.

> *Many believe that quality management in the practice of law is a given. People always do their best—right? Unfortunately, doing your best doesn't necessarily constitute quality.*
>
> **—Cary Griffith,** "What TQM Means to Law Firms & Their Clients," *Law Office Management Administration Report,* issue 92–8, August 1992, 14.

FIGURE 3-4
Product-Centered v. Client-Centered Philosophies in a Law Office

Product-Centered Philosophy	Client-Centered Philosophy
1. Inner forces control the law office.	Client forces control law office decision making.
2. Emphasis is on short-run productivity.	Emphasis on long-range planning for quality and client satisfaction.
3. Law office decisions are forced upon clients.	Law office decisions are made based on client input and meeting clients' needs.
4. Law office provides services they have.	Law office develops new services and modifies existing services based on clients' needs.
5. Law office provides services but does not survey clients to discover whether clients were satisfied with the office's services.	Law office surveys clients before, during, and after services are rendered to ensure clients are satisfied with services and makes appropriate changes based on clients' needs.
6. Law office focuses on short-term profitability and financial success.	Law office focuses on long-range profitability by putting the priority on meeting client needs and providing quality legal services.

WHAT ARE THE SPECIFIC
TQM PHILOSOPHIES?

TQM has many nuances and subtleties, but there are several main points to the TQM philosophy.[4]

1. **Management has an overriding duty to ensure that the firm provides quality legal service.** Management must make decisions based on how the decision will affect the quality of the legal services being provided. The distribution of firm assets, including purchases, contracts, and staff employees, must be viewed from the client's perspective and be based on how these decisions will affect the *quality* of the services the firm provides.

2. **Quality service involves every person in the firm, and everyone must be involved and committed.** Providing quality services begins and ends with everyone. It is the idea of providing dedication and commitment in everything that is done. It is integrating quality methods into the daily working routine of every member of the staff. It begins with every person taking pride in her work.

3. **Quality service is based not on management's or our own perception of quality but on the perceptions of the client.** In the end, the only person who is going to bring business back to the firm, or refer your services to other businesses, is the client. Therefore, only the client's perception of quality is what counts. Because it is the client's opinion that counts, firms must regularly poll or survey their clients to find out what the firms are doing right, what they are doing wrong, and how they can provide better services to the client. This can be done by interviewing current clients and mailing out client surveys when matters have been resolved, but it is the client's opinions that motivate the firm to change. For a TQM policy to be effective, the firm must be willing to *listen* to the client and to institute *change* to meet the needs of the client. Keep in mind that client needs are constantly changing, so to keep up, the firm must also be willing to change.

4. **Quality service depends on individual, team, and ultimately the organization's performance.** In the end, the client will judge the quality of a firm's job based on the client's experience. Thus, everyone involved must be committed to the TQM idea and must be able to share in the financial or other types of benefits the firm receives. TQM eliminates the "we v. they" mentality and rewards all members of the team who contribute. TQM uses project teams to identify and solve problems and increase efficiency.

5. **Constantly improving systems.** Along with assuring absolutely high-quality services, TQM also seeks to increase performance and productivity by constantly improving the systems and the way in which services are provided. This may include purchasing technology, rethinking the ways in which work is performed or routed, deleting repetitive tasks, or doing other things that will increase productivity and efficiency. This is a vigorous process that never ends.

WHAT ARE THE BENEFITS OF THE
TQM PHILOSOPHY?

The benefits the TQM philosophy offers include:

- **Increased client satisfaction**—The ultimate benefit is that clients are completely satisfied beyond their expectations, and that based on this satisfaction, they will entrust all their legal services and will refer new clients to the firm.

- **Unity among the management, attorneys and staff**—TQM also seeks to break down the barriers among competing groups in a law practice by focusing everyone on the same goal (unity of purpose) and by allowing all involved to share in the profits and fruits of the business. This can be done by awarding bonuses, giving awards, or recognizing outstanding performance. The "we v. they" mentality should be a thing of the past. A recent survey found that more than 90 percent of all employees polled value recognition for a job well done, yet only half get any. Recognition and communication directly affect the level of quality.[5]

What is the legal assistant's role in delivering and assuring quality legal services? The legal assistant must accept responsibility for taking the initiative to do what needs to be done to resolve problems and extend first-rate service to the customer (the attorney and the . . . client).

—**Deborah C. Wahl,** "Managing for Quality," *The LAMA Manager,* Spring 1992, 21.

- **Continuously seeking to improve performance and productivity**—TQM seeks to improve the quality of legal services to clients by increasing staff efficiency and productivity, not just once or twice a year, but constantly to improve the system. This includes all members of the staff checking the quality of their own work, learning advanced technologies, and doing whatever is necessary to provide the client with the best service.

HOW IS TQM IMPLEMENTED?

TQM can be implemented by hiring professional consultants to develop systems for obtaining client feedback and for educating staff members on total quality management techniques. To a lesser degree, TQM also can be implemented by reading about the subject, by simply accepting the principles of TQM, by being responsive to client needs, and by recognizing the effect management decisions have on the quality of legal services being provided. In effect, never forget that quality services are what everything else in the firm depends on.

HOW TQM APPLIES TO LEGAL ASSISTANTS

Our organization's philosophy is that quality is not an option, but rather an expected and required performance criteria for all employees of the organization. As a legal assistant manager, satisfactory performance is dependent upon our ability to maximize lawyer and client satisfaction providing the highest level of service possible through the use of legal assistants and, through greater efficiency, to provide this level of quality to our clients at a reasonable and acceptable cost.

—**Deborah C. Wahl,** "Managing for Quality," *The LAMA Manager,* Spring 1992, 7.

Whether or not a legal assistant's firm has a formal TQM policy, TQM can still be an important concept. From a TQM standpoint, a legal assistant serves two clients: the attorney (i.e. the internal client) and the end client (i.e. the external client). For a legal assistant to succeed, it is necessary that she provide high-quality legal service that satisfies *both* of these clients. Quality should be a way of life whether or not it is officially endorsed by the law office. This philosophy of satisfying clients both internally and externally may lead to advanced career opportunities, increased pay, and better job evaluations. The TQM philosophy also leads to a better work environment, since all persons have a say in how things are done.

Marketing

In Chapter 1, **marketing** was defined as *the process of educating consumers on quality legal services that a law office can provide.* Twenty years ago, law office marketing was virtually nonexistent. Today however, it is a given. With more than one million attorneys projected to be practicing law by the year 2000, the "Why should we market our practice?" question has long since been forgotten. The increased competitiveness of the legal field has forced law practices to promote themselves or face the reality of getting left behind by losing business to more aggressive firms. In addition, law offices not only compete against other law offices, they also compete against accounting firms when it comes to handling some types of tax matters, real estate companies regarding real estate transactions, and other types of organizations as well. The only question truly left for a law office is *how* to market itself.

marketing
Educating consumers on quality legal services.

WHY IS MARKETING IMPORTANT TO LEGAL ASSISTANTS?

Marketing is the job of everyone in a private law office. Your job depends on the firm's ability to find and serve additional clients. Therefore, the legal assistant has a vested interest in the marketing function. Your friends, families, acquaintances, social groups, and your fellow legal assistants are worthy of your marketing effort. Make sure people know the name of the organization you work for, network with other professionals, and be prepared to talk to others about what your law office does. By marketing your firm, you will establish that you have an interest in and loyalty to the firm, and you also will be building in some degree of job security. Law offices cannot do business without new clientele.

MARKETING GOALS

There is a misconception that advertising and marketing are the same thing. They really are not. Advertising is simply getting your name out in the public eye. Marketing, on the other hand, includes advertising but is much more. Marketing encompasses providing quality services to clients, gaining insight and feedback into client needs, having a good reputation in the community, and having good public relations. Marketing also has focused objectives and goals. A law office may seek to:

- Educate clients and potential clients regarding the firm's array of services;
- Educate clients and potential clients as to the particular expertise of the firm in certain areas;

- Create goodwill and interest in the firm;
- Create positive name recognition for the firm;
- Create an image of honesty, ethics, and sincere interest in clients;
- Publicize the firm's accomplishments to the profession and community;
- Educate clients on changes in the law, thus creating client confidence in the firm;
- Improve the firm's competitive position in the marketplace;
- Obtain referrals from other attorneys;
- Maintain communication with existing clients;
- Increase client loyalty and client retention;
- Increase staff morale and reinforce your firm's self-image.

TYPICAL LAW PRACTICE MARKETING OPTIONS

Many larger firms have a marketing department or a marketing director who coordinates the firm's marketing efforts. The importance of having a well-prepared marketing plan is essential to effective marketing. However, you need to have an understanding of what kind of marketing is done in law practice before we get to the plan itself.

- **Quality legal services**—There's that word again: "quality." Before a firm can market its services, it is absolutely essential that it have something of quality to market! Keep in mind that it is always easier to sell a quality product that people want to buy than to sell a product you want to sell. Earlier in this book, it was explained how important existing clients are for bringing repeat business back to the firm and for making referrals to others. This is why quality is so important. Everything a firm does affects quality and therefore affects its marketing effort.

An employee who treats clients rudely, causing them to leave; a docket control system that does not work, causing deadlines to be missed and clients to leave; or billing practices that make clients upset, causing them to take their business elsewhere in the end are quality problems. It is this reason that law office management must ensure quality. Marketing and quality are parts of the same equation.

There is no substitute for the quality of the work of the lawyers [and paralegals]. No marketing ploy, no firm brochure, no slick public relations program will cover for the poor work of an attorney [or paralegal].

—**Deborah C. Wahl,** "Managing for Quality," *The LAMA Manager,* Spring 1992, 8.

So, assuming the firm has a commitment to quality, what marketing techniques can the firm employ to get the word out about its great services to clients (see Figure 3-5)?

- **Firm brochure/resume**—A firm brochure is typically a pamphlet that informs the general public about the nature of the firm (see Figure 3-6). In many ways, it is like a resume, and some even call it a firm resume. Firm brochures often contain the following types of information:

FIGURE 3-5
Marketing Options

Firm Brochures and Resumes
Firm Newsletter
Information Brochures
Public Relations:
  —Belonging to boards, associations, and community groups;
  —Speaking at public functions;
  —Issuing press releases;
  —Handling publicized pro bono cases;
  —Volunteering in "law day" activities;
  —Volunteering staff time to help with fund-raisers for community
    groups.
Promotional Materials (folders, pencils with law office logo)
Firm Open House
Business Cards/Letterhead/Announcement Cards
Public Advertising:
  —Yellow pages ads;
  —Newspaper ads;
  —Television ads;
  —Radio ads.
Client Seminars
Marketing to Existing Clients
Belonging to and Serving in Legal Associations
Direct Mail (not allowable in some states)

- History of the firm
- Ideology or philosophy of the firm
- Services offered by the firm (typically the types of law it practices or departments)
- The firm's fee or billing policies
- Description of the firm's attorneys (background, items of interest, awards, degrees, etc.)
- Description of the firm's support staff
- Address and phone number
- Whether the firm has a newsletter or other types of client services
- Notable firm accomplishments
- Important clients the firm has represented (must have client's permission)

Figure 3-6 is a firm brochure for a smaller law office. In some cases, this may be the only brochure the law office has. Larger firms typically take a different marketing approach. Instead of having one brochure that markets the whole firm, they may have separate brochures for each department or produce brochures that target specific industries. Figure 3-7 is an example of a large law firm's brochure that markets its legal health care department to the health care industry.

- **Firm newsletter**—Firm newsletters are a popular way of maintaining contact with clients and generating goodwill. Firm newsletters can be on a single topic, such as real estate, or on a potpourri of topics. Some firms focus on a different legal issue in each issue: family law, real estate, tax, and so on. It is important that

A Word About Our Firm

We are a general practice law firm, established in 1972 with four attorneys. We can handle almost every type of legal work that you, your family or your business may require. We take great pride in our team of lawyers, legal assistants, legal secretaries, and staff members. Each lawyer, legal assistant and legal secretary is an expert in one or more fields. This expertise allows us to provide superior legal services in a number of fields of law (See our "Legal Services" section). We hope you will meet our well-qualified team and allow them to work together for your benefit.

APPOINTMENTS: We prefer to work by appointment. Agreeing on the date and hour to get together allows both of us to make better use of our time. It is more efficient for us and more economical for you if we meet at our office. If due to illness or disability you are unable to come to our office, we can make arrangements to meet in the most convenient place for you. Our office is open from 8:30 to 5:00 Monday through Friday for appointments. If an unusual situation requires, an appointment can be arranged for other days and times. If you are confronted with a legal emergency, you won't need any appointment. Just give us a call!

S Selecting a Lawyer

We will help you select the right member of the firm to handle your work. Contact any of our lawyers that you know, or call the office number and speak to the receptionist. When you explain the type of legal matter that concerns you, you will be referred to someone in our firm who is well-qualified for that type of work. We will introduce you, at your convenience, to the lawyer we believe will be able to handle your legal need most effectively (See the bibliographical profiles in the "Our Lawyers" section). If you consider one of our lawyers to be your lawyer, continue to do so and feel free to consult with him at any time. We are here to serve you!

A ttorney-Client

between th...
however, ...
obligated t...
other.

Your w...
ever learn f...

We wil...
as we go a...
sometimes...
send out o...
heard or do...
important t...

O Our Work

When you retain our firm, there should be a clear understanding between us about the extent of the work we are authorized to do. We will discuss the types of legal remedies or legal work required by the situation and the estimated time and legal expense involved. It is a good time to be practical. If, as the work progresses, there are unexpected developments which result in a longer time period or greater expense than anticipated, we will tell you when we recognize this.

F

an hourly...
cases, such...
fee basis, ...
amount of...
arrangemen...
firm. In sc...
fee. In le...
matters, the...

DISBURSEMENTS: The work we do for you may require us to make disbursem... Sometimes the estimated disbursements are payable in advance. Sometimes they are...
RETAINERS: In many cases, our office policy requires an advance payment, kno... payments are deposited in our trust account and are paid to us periodically as your wor...

O ur Lawyers

Edward R. Parker (Ned), born Richmond, Virginia, June 19, 1929; admitted to bar, 1952, Virginia. Preparatory education, University of Virginia (B.A., 1951); legal education, University of Virginia (LL.B., 1952). Adjunct Assistant Professor, T.C. Williams School of Law, University of Richmond 1973-1979. Legal Specialities: Estate Planning, Administration of Decedent's Estate, Business Law and Taxation.

Henry R. Pollard, IV (Harry), born Richmond, Virginia, August 5, 1943; admitted to bar 1967, Virginia. Preparatory education, Hampden-Sydney College (B.S., 1964); legal education, University of Richmond (LL.B., 1967). Legal Specialities: Litigation, Business Law, Commercial Real Estate, Securities Law.

William N. Pollard, born Richmond Virginia, April 4, 1945; admitted to bar 1971, Virginia. Preparatory education, Hampden-Sydney College (B.S., 1967); legal education, University of Virginia (J.D., 1971). Legal Specialities: Real Estate, Business Planning and Corporate Law, Litigation, Estate Planning, Administration of Decedent's Estates, Family Law.

T. Lee...
1949; ...
educat...
legal ed...
1974). ...
Corpor...
istratio...
Comm...

Barry...
1955; ...
educat...
educat...
Legal S...
Planni...

Micha...
Decen...
ginia. ...
(B.A., ...
T.C.W...
(J.D., ...
ruptcy...

Park...

L egal Services

BUSINESS AND CORPORATE: Partnerships, incorporation of businesses, advising individuals, partnerships and corporations, business contracts.
PERSONAL INJURY CLAIMS: Investigation and evaluation of claims for injuries resulting from accidents, bringing lawsuits and conduct of trials to enforce claims.
GENERAL TRIAL WORK: Bringing or defending lawsuits in a variety of legal disputes, including bankruptcy.
WORKERS' COMPENSATION: The representation of persons injured on their jobs.
WILLS AND TRUSTS: The preparation of wills, and of revocable and irrevocable trusts.
ESTATE PLANNING: The preparation of a plan for the transfer of your assets prior to or upon your death to carry out your wishes in a cost efficient manner.

ESTATE ADMINISTRATION: Serving as executor or representing the executor or family of the deceased person in settling an estate.
TAX AND FINANCIAL PLANNING: Planning the shape of business and personal transactions for minimum tax impact, representation before Federal and State tax authorities, answering tax questions.
REAL ESTATE TRANSACTIONS: The sale or purchase of real estate, mortgage transactions, leases, contracts, title searches and title insurance.
INVESTMENT MANAGMENT: Offering investment counceling on your investment portfolio through your trust or directly.
FAMILY LAW: Adoptions; appointment of guardians, and conservators; separation agreements, divorces; annulments; and legal separations.

O ur Locations

We are easily accessible to you. Richmond: Take the Staples Mill Road West Exit off Interstate 64 and we are at 5511 Staples Mill Road between Southside and Northside Avenues. Tidewater: In Norfolk, travel east on Northampton Boulevard (Route 13) from its intersection with Interstate 64 to the northeast corner of Diamond Springs Road and Northampton Boulevard.

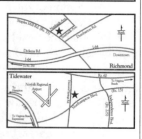

Parker, Pollard & Brown, P.C.
Attorneys at Law

5511 Staples Mill Road
Richmond, Virginia 23228
(804) 262-4042

1300 Diamond Springs Road
Northampton Executive Center
Virginia Beach, Virginia 23455
(804) 460-5050

Park...

Parker, Pollard & Brown, P.C.
Attorneys at Law

5511 Staples Mill Road
Richmond, Virginia 23228
(804) 262-4042

1300 Diamond Springs Road
Northampton Executive Center
Virginia Beach, Virginia 23455
(804) 460-5050

FIGURE 3-6

FIGURE 3-7

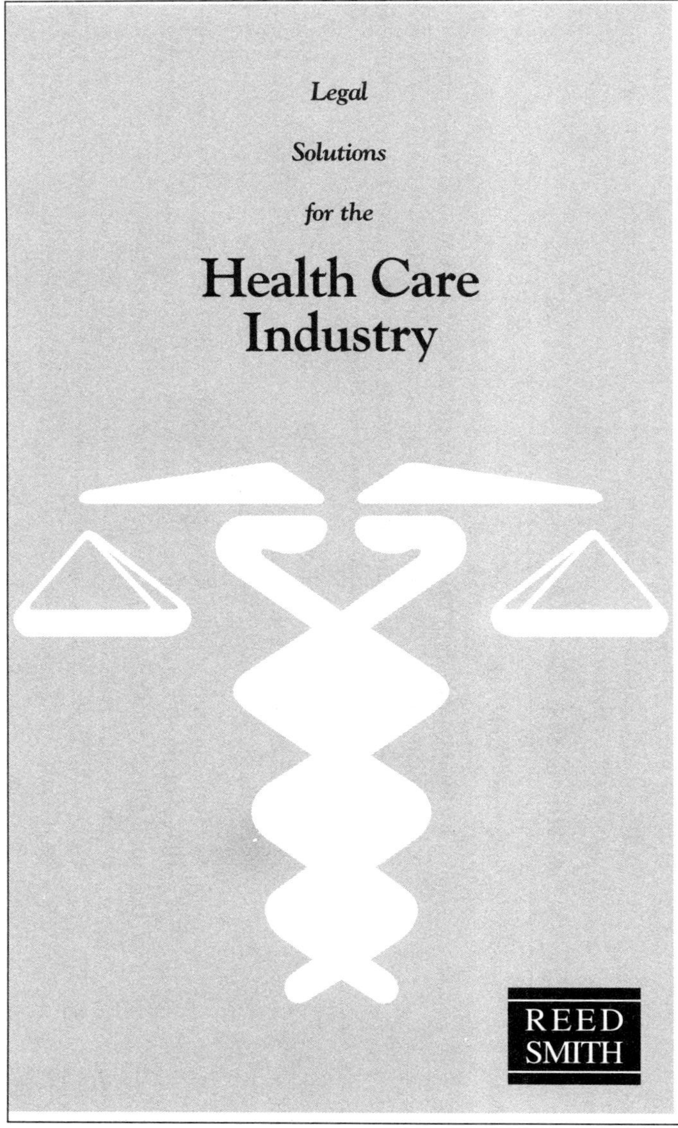

Legal
Solutions
for the
Health Care Industry

REED SMITH

Health Representation – Skills and Experience

Reed Smith's Health Care Group works to solve its clients' problems. Our representation begins by listening to you — the client. Systematically, our lawyers will analyze complex problems, advise you on various courses of action and, when necessary, advocate on your behalf to achieve a prompt and reasonable solution.

Legislative and Regulatory: Legislative representation for health care clients includes drafting and advocacy on proposed and enacted health care legislation. We have successfully challenged major regulatory actions through negotiations with federal agencies, including HCFA, OMB, the FTC, and others, and we regularly advise clients on a host of regulatory compliance issues. The firm assists clients throughout the legislative and regulatory process by drafting comments, testimony and legislative amendments, as well as presenting clients' positions directly to Members of Congress, Administration officials, and key regulatory personnel. A number of our attorneys previously served in high-level positions with both Republican and Democratic administrations, as well as in agency and various congressional positions.

Legal Fees

The particular backgrounds of our health attorneys make it possible for our clients to obtain comprehensive, targeted legal advice at competitive prices. Moreover, we believe that our wide range of specialties saves our clients money, if by using our services they have access to a coordinated team, and can thus avoid the need to consult specialists at a number of firms. Our health group is often retained by other law firms on specific projects requiring a high degree of technical advice, such as reimbursement, fraud and abuse, biotechnology, and the like. We are happy to provide more detailed information on our fee structure and billing procedures.

Future

Reed Smith attorneys welcome the opportunity to talk with you about your company, business, or organization. We would like to hear how the changing health care environment affects you, and discuss how Reed Smith can bring thoughtful, innovative, and responsive solutions to your health care problems. The lawyers in the Reed Smith Health Care Group are listed on the card at the end of this brochure. Please feel free to call any of them to discuss your particular needs.

Source: Reed Smith & McClay.
Printed with permission.

the firm know and understand who its clients are and what type of information would be beneficial to the clients. Another popular topic for newsletters is to inform clients of legislative changes, whether local, state, or national. Newsletters can be produced by using an in-house desktop publishing program, by hiring an advertising consulting firm to produce and help write the newsletter, or by purchasing ready-made legal newsletters. With a ready-made newsletter, all the law office has to do is add its logo and firm name and address. Newsletters can be purchased from several sources, including the ABA's Client Update, Section on General Practice, 750 N. Lakeshore Drive, Chicago, IL 60611 (312) 988-5000.

> *Newsletters are a good way of reminding clients that we are still here. I can't begin to describe the calls I get back. They come from both new clients and old . . . . We provide added value to our clients by educating them at our expense, through the newsletter . . . .*
>
> —**Anitra Rasmussen,** "Is a Newsletter for You?" *Oregon State Bar Bulletin,* December 1992, 15.

- **Informational brochures**—These are brochures that are aimed at informing clients about a specific topic such as "Why You Need a Will," "What to Do in Case of an Auto Accident," "How to Set Up Your Own Business," or "How to Protect Your Ideas through Copyrights, Trademarks, and Patents." They are informational pieces that are used to inform clients about legal problems.

- **Public relations**—Generating goodwill and a positive public image is a long-standing way that firms have marketed themselves. Being members of social groups, churches, committees, nonprofit boards, and associations is a way that legal assistants and attorneys can promote themselves and their firms.

  Speaking at public meetings and association meetings is also a way of attracting interest and goodwill. Handling pro bono cases and issuing press releases when a firm wins a case or achieves other accomplishments that the public would be interested in are other ways of generating and maintaining good public relations.

- **Firm open house**—Some firms hold annual open houses, where clients and visitors can come to the firm and socialize with attorneys and staff members outside the normal pressures of coming to the office with legal problems.

- **Business cards, letterhead, announcement cards**—Announcement cards are used quite frequently by law offices. An announcement card is usually a postcard that is sent to other firms when new attorneys have been added to the firm and it wants to publicize the change or when firms merge.

- **Public advertising**—yellow pages, newspaper, television, and radio ads—Public advertisements also are a popular form of marketing. They come in all sizes and shapes and in all price ranges.

- **Firm seminars**—Some firms put on seminars that are aimed at educating their clients or the general public (prospective clients) on legal issues. They can relate to any legal topic that is of interest. For example, businesses might be interested in the legal issues of hiring, firing, and evaluating employees and employee benefits. Individual clients might be interested in tax planning, trusts and estates, etc. Client seminars are usually put on to create client loyalty.

- **Direct mail pieces**—Some firms also send out direct mail pieces aimed at a specific audience. Usually, the pieces are unsolicited; that is, they are sent out to people without being requested. For example, if your firm primarily handles real estate matters, you might send out a letter to all real estate businesses. Note, however, that direct mail is very controversial, especially when the mailing is targeted to a specific group. Ethical rules in some states strictly prohibit targeted mailing under the theory that it is direct solicitation. Attorneys are specifically prohibited from directly soliciting clients.

- **Involvement in legal associations**—Attorneys and legal assistants also can market themselves by being active in local, state, and national bar and legal assistant associations. Many firms that involve themselves in these types of organizations gain the respect and goodwill of others and may gain referrals from another firm that may not have the expertise to handle a particular type of case.

- **Send information to clients that you know will be of interest to them**—Whenever you come across information that you think will interest clients, bring it to the attention of your supervising attorney and have the attorney send it to them. For example, if you come across a newspaper article that concerns their business or new laws that might affect them, clip it out and have the attorney send it to them. Or, if you come across a case that they might be interested in, get your attorney's approval and send it to them with a note (and do not bill them for it!). Clients appreciate when the law office takes a personal interest in them.

- **Marketing your services to existing clients**—A firm's current clients are among its biggest assets. Firms not only want to market to new clients but also need to keep the business of their current clients. Thus, firms will typically spend a great deal of time cultivating their existing clients using techniques described earlier such as newsletters and client seminars. Firms also have other techniques for marketing to existing clients:

  - **Cross-selling**—**Cross-selling** *refers to selling additional services to existing clients.* For instance, suppose a law office represented XYZ business in a tax matter. But XYZ used another firm to handle its personnel disputes. If possible, the law office would like to cross-sell XYZ to use its firm for both the tax matter and the personnel matters.

    cross-selling
    Selling additional services to existing clients.

  - **Client questionnaires**—Many firms send out client questionnaires at the end of a legal matter to see how the client felt about the services that were provided. In addition to this being a quality-control device, it also is a marketing technique, since it is aimed at correcting problems that the client might have had.

  - **Keep the firm's name in front of the client**—What happens if a client's case is completely finished and the client has no other business at the time? Should the firm forget about the client? No, most firms continue to try to keep in contact with the client with newsletters, seminars, letters, holiday cards, etc. Firms want clients to feel wanted and be reminded that the firm is there to serve them.

  - **Develop client relationships**—Who would you rather do business with, friends or strangers? Unquestionably friends, because you trust them and feel comfortable with them. It is this kind of relationship that firms want to promote.

  - **Thank clients for referring others to you**—Always send a thank you letter to clients (or other attorneys) for making referrals to the office.

THE ROLE OF THE RAINMAKER

rainmaking
Bringing in new clients
to a law office.

Rainmaking *refers to the ability to bring in new clients to a law office.* Some law offices bring attorneys into the firm for the sole purpose of being "rainmakers." Some rainmakers are well connected politically or have inroads into certain industries. Rainmakers use their influence and skills to bring new clients into the firm. However, a recent survey of successful "rainmakers" found without exception that helping their clients achieve their business goals and dreams was what made them a good "rainmaker." One rainmaker summed it up: "I like to think that I have a special relationship with my clients. My legal antennae are always sensitive to any issues which may affect them. . . . It gives them comfort to know we're here. They can sleep because the 'national guard' is awake." Many private law offices use rainmakers in their marketing scheme.

THE MARKETING PLAN

> *Sadly, although many [firms] would not admit it, they practice a haphazard approach to marketing. They proceed without direction, wasting valuable funds with an unfocused plan. These costly mistakes cause many . . . to question the value of marketing as a component in their firm's budget.*
>
> **—Leslee M. Stewart and Pamela J. Gonyea,** "Marketing for the Small Law Firm," *New Hampshire Bar Journal* (June 1992): 389.

marketing plan
The goals that a
marketing program is
to accomplish and a
detailed strategy of
how the goals will be
achieved.

Although there are many options a marketing program can take, it is important that a law practice develop a detailed marketing plan. A **marketing plan** *specifies the exact goals that the marketing program is to accomplish and establishes a detailed strategy of how the goals will be achieved.* The firm marketing plan should include:

- The overall goals of the marketing program;
- The strategies and activities that will be necessary to obtain the goals, including who, what, when, how, and in what order the activities will be implemented. To be successful, the marketing plan must be coordinated;
- The estimated cost of the marketing program;
- The estimated profit the successful marketing program would bring in.

The marketing plan and the strategic business plan are related documents. To develop an effective marketing plan, consider Figure 3-8. Additional information on law office marketing plans and law office marketing in general can be obtained from the National Association of Law Office Marketing Administrators (see Appendix E).

MARKETING—AN ETHICS PERSPECTIVE

Although ethical limitations on marketing have eased up during the past fifteen years, there are still many pitfalls that can occur from an ethical perspective, including making false or misleading statements in an advertisement, general requirements about any advertisement made, directly soliciting a client, or holding an attorney out as a specialist. Figure 3-9 contains a marketing ethics checklist.

FALSE OR MISLEADING STATEMENTS Attorneys are not allowed to make false or misleading statements in any kind of marketing or advertising piece. Rule 7.1 of the ABA *Model Rules of Professional Conduct* states:

1. **Develop a Strategic Business Plan for the Firm**—The firm needs to know who it is, what business it is in, who its competitors are, what areas are the most profitable, who its clients are, what the client's needs are, and in what direction the firm is headed. All of these things have a direct bearing on the marketing program.

2. **Determine Specifically What Target Market the Marketing Plan Will Be Aimed at and What the Goals of the Marketing Program Will Be**—The firm must decide exactly what the purpose of the marketing plan is. Is it to expand the firm's expertise into additional areas? Is it to expand into different types of clients? Is it into a new geographical area?

Types of Client Markets:
- Government—federal, state, local;
- Business Organizations—publicly owned, privately owned, non profit institutions, small businesses, large businesses;
- Labor organizations;
- Individuals—middle class, wealthy, disadvantaged.

Legal Specialty Markets
- Administrative law
- Admiralty law
- Antitrust law
- Banking law
- Bankruptcy law
- Civil rights law
- Collections law
- Contract law
- Corporate law
- Labor law
- Landlord and tenant law
- Litigation
- Military law
- Municipal finance law
- Oil and Gas law
- Real Estate law
- Criminal law
- Employee benefit law
- Entertainment law
- Environmental law
- Estates, trusts, and probate
- Family law
- Immigration law
- Insurance law
- International law
- Social Security law
- Tax law
- Tort law
- Water law
- Workers' compensation law

3. **Research the Market**—When you have determined what your goals are and what your target group is, you still need to find out about the target group. You need to know its wants and needs, who it is, where it is, and how you can serve it.

Researching the Market:
- Study your own marketing successes/failures;
- Study the marketing efforts of your competitors;
- Survey your target group members (talk to them, know their needs);
- Use in-house surveys to survey your own clients (what do they need/want);
- Talk to consultants;
- If it is a specific group, read its trade journals and find out what issues are important to it.

**FIGURE 3-8
Developing the
Marketing Plan**

Source: Austin G. Anderson, *Marketing Your Practice* (American Bar Association, 1986), 64. Reprinted by permission of the American Bar Association.

4. **Examine Problems**—Now that you know your goals and you have some market research, what problems will impede the firm from reaching those goals? Anticipate what the problems will be and devise solutions to them.

5. **Develop Specific Strategies and an Action Plan for Meeting the Goals**—In this stage you must set specific strategies for achieving the goal. How are you going to get there? What marketing techniques will convey your message and reach the target group the best? What pricing will you use? A plan or time line should be developed stating exactly when each step of each strategy or marketing technique is to be accomplished, and who is going to accomplish it. All the strategies should be coordinated and complement one another.

6. **Develop a Marketing Budget and Analyze Resources**—In this stage you must determine whether the firm's resources are large enough to carry out the specific marketing plan you laid out in the previous step. It is crucial that enough resources be available to carry out the plan. If the firm does not have the resources to carry out the plan, the plan may need to be scaled back.

A lawyer shall not make a false or misleading communication about the lawyer or the lawyer's services. A communication is false or misleading if it:

(a) contains a material misrepresentation of fact or law, or omits a fact necessary to make the statement considered as a whole not materially misleading;

FIGURE 3-9
Marketing the Law Office—Ethics Tips

1. **Do Not Use Examples of Past Performance**
   Do not use examples of past client successes. This may be interpreted as guaranteeing future results, even though every client's case is different and has a different set of factual and legal arguments.

2. **Keep Copies of All Marketing Pieces**
   Ethical rules in most states provide that a copy of the marketing piece or advertisement must be retained by the law office for a certain period of time (sometimes years) after the campaign is completed.

3. **No Direct Solicitation**
   Direct solicitation to unknown, prospective clients is not allowed.

4. **Language Should Be Carefully Drafted**
   The language of all marketing pieces should be carefully drafted to reflect only factual or quantitative information so that it is not subject to interpretation as being false or misleading. Words such as "specializing" and other such words cannot be used in advertisements in some states.

5. **When in Doubt, Have It Approved First**
   If you are uncertain if a marketing piece is ethical, most states will allow the firm to submit it to a disciplinary panel (before publication) where it can be reviewed to see if it complies with the state's ethics rules.

    (b) is likely to create an unjustified expectation about results the lawyer can achieve or states or implies that the lawyer can achieve results by means that violate the Rules of Professional Conduct or other law; or

    (c) compares the lawyer's services with other lawyers' services, unless the comparison can be factually substantiated.

This is a fairly straightforward ethical rule. Attorneys cannot promote themselves using advertisements that are less than truthful. Subpart (b) of the rule prohibits an attorney from running an advertisement about the results in a specific case, such as "I recently won a medical malpractice verdict of two million dollars." This type of information may create the unjustified expectation that similar results can be obtained for others without reference to the specific factual and legal circumstances.[6]

ADVERTISING IN GENERAL   Rule 7.2 of the *Model Rules* states some general guidelines that apply to all types of advertising.

Rule 7.2 Advertising

    (a) . . . [A] lawyer may advertise services through public media, such as telephone directory, legal directory, newspaper or other periodical, outdoor advertising, radio or television, or through written or recorded communication.

    (b) A copy or recording of an advertisement or communication shall be kept for two years after its last dissemination along with a record of when and where it was used.

    (c) A lawyer shall not give anything of value to a person for recommending the lawyer's services, except that a lawyer may (1) pay the reasonable costs of advertisements or communications by this rule . . . .

    (d) Any communication made pursuant to this rule shall include the name of at least one lawyer responsible for its content.

The reason for the two-year rule in subpart (b) is to ensure that if an ethical complaint is made against the law office, a copy of the ad will be available. In some instances, ethical complaints are made long after the initial advertisement has run. The rule also prohibits the lawyer from paying someone to refer cases to the attorney. Finally, the rule requires that at least one person's name be on the advertisement somewhere. This is so that if there is an ethical violation, the authorities will know who to hold responsible.

NO DIRECT SOLICITATION OR "AMBULANCE CHASING"   Rule 7.3 of the ABA *Model Rules* restricts attorneys from directly soliciting persons they do not know.

Rule 7.3 Direct Contact with Prospective Clients

    (a) A lawyer shall not by in-person or live telephone contact solicit professional employment from a prospective client with whom the lawyer has no family or prior professional relationship when a significant motive for the lawyer's doing so is the lawyer's pecuniary gain.

    (b) A lawyer shall not solicit professional employment from a prospective client by written or recorded communication or by in-person or telephone contact even when not otherwise prohibited by paragraph (a), if: (1) the prospective client has made known to the lawyer a desire not to be solicited by the lawyer; or (2) the solicitation involves coercion, duress, or harassment.

(c) Every written or recorded communication from a lawyer soliciting professional employment from a prospective client known to be in need of legal services in a particular matter, and with whom the lawyer has no family or prior professional relationship, shall include the words "Advertising Material" on the outside envelope and at the beginning and ending of any recorded communication.

Direct in-person telephone contact with individuals that the lawyer does not know is prohibited, since there may be the possibility of undue influence, intimidation, or overreaching when a skilled attorney contacts a layperson. However, prerecorded communications may be acceptable, since the attorney is not "live." This rule also squarely prohibits attorneys from making harassing communication or bothering persons that do not want to be solicited. Finally, the rule requires that advertisements soliciting business must be labeled as "Advertising Material" to inform persons up front that the communication is an advertisement.

A distinction is made in the rule between directly soliciting persons that are known by the attorney, such as family members or past clients, and soliciting unknown individuals. Attorneys and staff may solicit individuals they know. This is quite common, and there is nothing unethical about mentioning to friends and relatives that your law office handles certain types of cases and could help them if the need ever arose. What is prohibited is directly soliciting absolute strangers in person.

LAWYER CANNOT STATE HE IS A SPECIALIST   Rule 7.4 of the *Model Rules* prohibits attorneys from holding themselves out as specialists.

Rule 7.4 Communication of Fields of Practice

A lawyer may communicate the fact that the lawyer does or does not practice in particular fields of law. A lawyer shall not state or imply that the lawyer is a specialist . . . .

This rule allows attorneys to list what areas they practice in, but it prohibits them from holding themselves out as specialists or as attorneys who specialize in particular fields. The reason is that the word "specialist" has a secondary meaning, implying formal recognition (this rule would not apply in states that provide procedures for certification in particular areas).

Each state has specific ethical rules about lawyer advertising, so it is important that whoever performs the marketing be familiar with the rules of your state. One option to avoid ethical problems is to show the advertising to the disciplinary administrator for the state before it is run and ask her opinion on the matter.

PLANNING

The simple fact is that most law offices do not plan for the future. They wait for the future to come get them; then they get pulled into it kicking and screaming. These [firms] are the victims of change; they never truly succeed; they never quite get out of the rut.

—**Gary A. Munneke,** *Law Practice Management* (Saint Paul, Minnesota: West Publishing Co., 1991), 570.

When most people think of law practice management, planning is usually not at the top of the list of things management must do. However, planning is the difference between firms that stay in the past and firms that move ahead. In Chapter 1, **planning** was defined as *the process of setting objectives, assessing the future, and developing courses of action to achieve these objectives.* Planning is one of the most primary and important things that effective management must do to succeed. Unfortunately in the past, many law practices, including government, corporate, and private firms, have neglected this function. That may be why recently fifteen of the largest firms in the country have disappeared.[7] The reason that many firms neglect to plan is because it takes time and energy to do it right. It is easier to deal with the problems of today than to make strategies for the future.

planning
Setting objectives, assessing the future, and developing courses of action to achieve these objectives.

WHY LEGAL ASSISTANTS NEED TO LEARN TO DEVELOP PLANS

As a legal assistant's career expands, he will be given more complex assignments, job duties, and tasks. As the complexity of assignments increases, the ability to develop and execute plans is crucial. The following are some plans that legal assistants may prepare:

- **Budgets for a legal assistant department;**
- **Case budgets for a particular case (i.e. how much the law office will expend to bring a case to trial);**
- **Case plans (in conjunction with a supervising attorney), including what witnesses need to be deposed, what interrogatories, requests for production, and requests for admissions need to be issued and to whom, what experts need to be hired, what strategies the office should pursue, what further investigation needs to be conducted, etc.;**
- **Their own career plans**—where they want to be in two years or five years and how they are going to get there;
- **Large projects such as developing a litigation support data base in cases that have thousands of documents.** The legal assistants and others must plan how the documents will be entered into the computer, what program, service bureau, or technique will be the most successful, etc.;
- **Administrative projects that require planning, including computerizing a law office's time and billing system from a manual system, implementing a computerized docket control system, or setting up a new filing system or law library;**
- **In small law offices, the office's mission statement and some strategic plans.** These are important types of plans.

THE MISSION STATEMENT AND STRATEGIC PLANS

A mission statement is a particular type of plan. The **mission statement** *is a general, enduring statement of what the purpose or intent of the law practice is.*[8] The mission statement is a statement about the goals and objectives of the firm. It is a plan or vision stating what the firm is about. It sets out the fundamental and unique purpose that sets it apart from other firms, identifies the firm's scope, and sets out why it exists. For examples, see the mission statements in Figure 3-10.

All law practices need a vision, they need to know where they have been and where they are going. They need to have a few guiding principles and philosophies

mission statement
A general, enduring statement of what the purpose or intent of the law practice is.

FIGURE 3-11
Mission Statements

Law Office Mission Statements:

#1

The mission of the Davis, Saunders & Lavely law firm is to deliver high-quality legal services to business clients nationwide through personalized, value-added service and a strict adherence to the highest ethical standards.

#2

The KGLPE Law Department seeks to offer the Corporation the best legal services available while containing costs to a minimum. The law department will utilize four divisions—labor, environmental, litigation, and general business. The use of in-house staff will be maximized. Only matters of vital importance to the Corporation will be contracted out. The other departments of the Corporation will be defined as our "clients." Our clients will be given the same high-quality legal services as provided by outside counsel. Our clients will be surveyed on an annual basis, and we will obtain a 90 percent average approval rating.

#3

Woodsom and Stetson is a full-service, client-centered law firm. Our goal is to provide outstanding, responsive services to our clients at a reasonable cost. As a full-service law office, we offer many services for our clients. We represent clients as we ourselves would want to be represented. We use a team approach to provide legal services to our clients, including—lawyers, paralegals, and office associates—to ensure a professional level of response to our clients' needs.

that motivate and determine the direction of the firm. The mission statement represents the foundation for priorities and all other plans. If the firm you work for has a mission statement, memorize and use it. Every idea, new client, hiring of an employee, purchase of a piece of equipment, and everything you do should be judged as to whether it advances the mission of the firm. If it does not advance the mission, then it may not be right for the firm.

Successful firms typically have a few goals, which are understood by a broad majority of the firm . . . . Individual members . . . have a good understanding of what the organization is striving to accomplish and where it might be headed. This understanding allows individuals to orient their efforts to the benefit and acceptance of the organization.

—**Thomas S. Clay,** "Profile of a Successful Law Firm," *The Law Firm Management Guide* (Ardmore, Pennsylvania: Altman Weil Pensa, 1988), A–15.

Mission statements may include: when the firm began, who founded the firm, the philosophy of the founder(s), the nature of the practice (areas of experience and expertise), the geographic service area, the departments in the practice, the philosophies toward costs, income, growth, technology, client services, and personnel, and who specifically the firm's clients are. Mission statements do not have to be static; they can be changed and updated as long as everyone in the firm understands the change. A mission statement is a vision that keeps the firm headed in the right direction. Without one, a law practice may spend a considerable amount of time never knowing where it is headed.

Strategic planning has always been important, but the present circumstances make it imperative for law offices to consider strengths and weaknesses, evaluate the competition, and devise a game plan that will set the course to the future.

Strategic planning *is the process of determining the major goals of a firm and then adopting the courses of action and allocating resources necessary to achieve those goals.* In a strategic plan, a firm decides its long-range goals and prepares a plan of action of how to achieve those goals. For instance, a strategic plan may include expanding a firm's practice in additional areas of the law, such as adding a tax or labor law department. One thing to remember is that before you can sell a legal service to someone, you must have a buyer. That is, you should not focus on what you want to sell but rather on what the buyer or the client wants to buy. Strategic plans usually answer the questions contained in Figure 3-11.

strategic planning
Determining the major goals of a firm and then adopting the courses of action necessary to achieve those goals.

[In successful firms there is a] constant action or movement toward objectives . . . . Standing still is viewed as stagnating or losing ground to competitors. There exists a general perception that if the firm is not continually evaluating its position, problems, or opportunities, movement toward the goals might not exist. The old adage, "If it ain't broke, don't fix it," is ignored. [Successful] law offices realize that there are always better ways to accomplish goals more efficiently and effectively.

—**Thomas S. Clay,** "Profile of a Successful Law Firm," *The Law Firm Management Guide* (Ardmore, Pennsylvania: Altman Weil Pensa, 1988), A–15.

THE PLANNING PROCESS

Going through the planning process step by step is as important as the resulting plan itself (see Figure 3-12). The process of planning makes you wiser, and it forces you to think about and consider factors you might not otherwise.

The first step in the process is to gather as much relevant and timely information about the subject matter of the plan as possible. You can do this by researching the issue, hiring consultants, researching surveys of other similarly situated law practices, attending seminars, belonging to professional organizations, and reading periodicals. You should also talk to others in the firm about their ideas and opinions regarding the subject matter of the plan and get as many different angles and viewpoints as possible.

FIGURE 3-11
Strategic Planning

Source: Adapted from material supplied by John L. Espy, formerly professor of international business at the Chinese University of Hong Kong.

Key Questions a Strategic Plan Should Answer:

- What legal services will we provide? What services will we add or delete? How profitable are these areas?
- Who are our clients (individuals, businesses, government)? What market segments will we serve? What do our clients need? What do our clients want? What type of clients/cases do we want to pursue (type of clients—insurance companies, doctors, manufacturers; type of cases—personal injury, tax, family law).
- What are the long-term projections for these clients in these areas?
- How will we assure our clients receive quality services?
- How will we attract and hold customers (what will be our basis of competition)?
- Who will own the firm?
- Who will manage the firm? Is our governing structure adequate?
- What sources of finance will we use?
- Will we purchase or rent premises and equipment (new practices typically lease)?
- What kinds of technology and systems will we use to produce our services?
- What marketing channels will we use?
- How will we achieve continuing growth?
- What new area of the country/world will we enter?
- What kinds of insurance will we need to acquire (malpractice, disability, life, health)?
- How many employees will we require to accomplish our goals?
- How will we recruit, train, and retain the right people for our firm?
- Will the firm merge with another firm to obtain a competitive advantage?
- What type of additional staff will we need—attorneys, clerks, administrators?

Additional Factors a Strategic Plan Should Consider:

- Environmental Analysis—Consider demographic, political, and economic factors when considering your strategic plan. How will these things affect who we are going to serve and how we are going to serve them?
- Industry Analysis—Consider the legal environment as a whole, such as surveys of other law firms with average profit margins, growth rate, costs, etc., for your size of firm. How does your particular firm compare with industry averages?
- Competitive Analysis—Identify your major competitors; what are their strengths and weaknesses? What are your competitor's business strategies?
- Internal Analysis—Compre your own strategies with that of your major competitors and consider your strengths and weaknesses as compared with your competitors.
- Determine Threats and Opportunities—Consider what new markets are the most attractive for your firm and then analyze your firm's competitive position in the marketplace, identify any threats that competitors may have, and identify opportunities resulting from market conditions or a competitor's weakness.

1. Gather Facts and Opinions
2. Assess and Organize Information
3. Develop Goals
4. Assess Strengths and Weaknesses of Each Goal
5. Develop Objectives and Strategies for Obtaining the Goal
6. Consider the Resources Necessary to Achieve the Objectives
7. Develop an Action Plan
8. Monitor, Reevaluate, and Make Corrections in the Plan

FIGURE 3-12
The Planning Process

Source: Henry Ewalt, *Practical Planning* (American Bar Association, 1985), 23. Reprinted by permission of American Bar Association.

After you have gathered relevant information, the next step is to organize it and determine which pieces are the most persuasive.

Step three is to take the best information and opinions you have gathered and turn them into goals. These are typically statements of what the firm will accomplish. You should not be bothered with how the goals will be achieved at this stage, but only with what the specific goals of the plan will be (for example, to bring in a minimum of 15 percent more clients). At this stage you will begin to narrow down your ideas and determine exactly what you want to accomplish.

The fourth step is to assess each goal and determine its strengths and weaknesses. How will attaining these goals help or hurt the firm? Are there negatives? This is one more way to narrow the goals down to make sure you have completely thought through which goals will bring the firm the most benefit.

The next step is to develop specific objectives of how to accomplish each goal, including what will be achieved, when it will be achieved, how it will be achieved, who will be involved in achieving it, and where it will be achieved.

The sixth step is to look at each strategy or objective and determine whether the firm can allocate the resources (i.e. money, time, people, equipment, etc.) to accomplish each objective. Keep in mind that a plan will fail if it is too large and vast for the amount of resources the firm can devote to it.

Seventh, you must develop a specific action plan in writing as to how the firm will accomplish the goals. For each step, you should designate who is responsible for its achievement and when it will be achieved. You also may want to develop a time line so that you can track the progress of the plan. Last, you must monitor the plan, reevaluate the plan, and make needed changes as necessary. The planning process is a continuous process of refinement. Remember, for a plan to succeed, many people must be involved to increase support, enthusiasm, and ownership of the plan.

IDEAS ON HOW TO PLAN EFFECTIVELY

The following are some ideas on how to plan effectively:

- **Gather timely, relevant information**—It is axiomatic that without good information you cannot possibly make an effective plan. Too many times, people make plans based on faulty information. Gathering timely and relevant information is one of the most important things you can do to make sure your plan will succeed. You can gather information from public libraries, law libraries, the ABA, local, state, and national bar associations, law office surveys, consultants, other firms, and historical records from your own firm. Good information is a key to making good decisions.

▪ **All plans should be in writing**—Goals and plans should be in writing as constant reminders of where you are supposed to be headed.

▪ **Involve everyone in the planning process (ownership)**—Always ask for comments from anyone who would be affected by the plan. You want to build a consensus so that everyone will have input into the plan and will support it when it comes time to implement it. People promote plans that they perceive as being their own, either in part or as a whole. This is the "ownership" concept. Asking comments from others opens the lines of communication and allows everyone in the firm to feel that they have a stake in the action, that their thoughts are important, and that they are needed, from a copy clerk to the senior partner. When you are involving others in the process, do not judge their suggestions; listen to them and consider them. Your job is to facilitate communications and to provide a nonthreatening environment so everyone can participate.

▪ **Stick to the plan**—It takes an amazing amount of patience to stick to a plan and follow through with what you started. It does a firm little good to make a

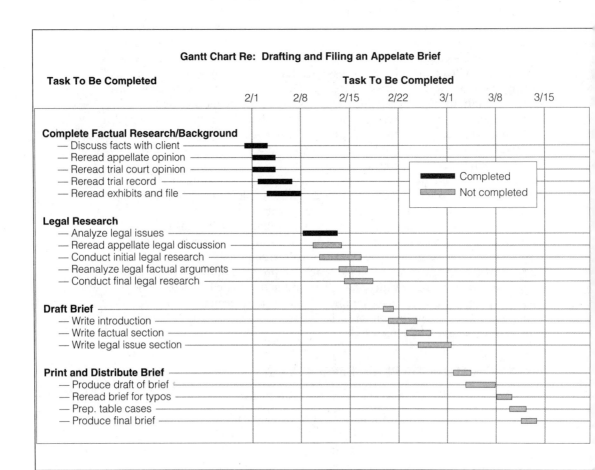

FIGURE 3-13

detailed and wonderful plan and then scrap it two months later. It takes commitment from everyone involved to give the plan a chance to succeed.

▪ **Planning is a continuous process**—Planning is a continuous process of making improvements; it is not a one-time thing in which you develop a plan and then never revisit it again. If all you do is make a plan and never follow it up or monitor it, all you have done is waste the firm's time.

▪ **Monitor the plan and communicate the results to others**—Always monitor the progress of the plan. One way to do this is to make a time line or Gantt chart to track the expected progress over time. A **Gantt chart** *is a plan or time line of projected begin dates and end dates of a project. A Gantt chart breaks a large project down into specific jobs or items that must be accomplished. As an item is finished, it can be marked completed* (see Figure 3-13). Gantt charts also are good at simplifying and communicating complicated projects. Most people find charts easier to read and more friendly than straight text.

Gantt chart
A plan or time line of projected begin dates and end dates of a project.

Periodically, you should check the progress of the project to determine whether the plan needs to be revised or completely overhauled to accomplish its objectives. One way to do this is to hold monthly planning meetings or to otherwise communicate the progress of the plan to others by keeping them informed of how the project is going. If possible, you want to build into the plan quantifiable means to show others that the plan is working as expected and that resources are not being wasted.

Summary

A law practice staff manual establishes written policies and procedures regarding the firm's personnel policies, filing procedures, billing procedures, general office procedures and more. The purpose of a staff manual is to ensure consistent treatment to all clients, to set out minimum standards that the law office expects, to help train new staff members, and to assign responsibility of certain tasks to specific persons.

Total quality management is a philosophy that is based on knowing the needs of the client and allowing those needs to drive the organization. It is the idea of providing quality legal services to clients, from the receptionist to the senior partner. Marketing is the process of educating consumers on the quality legal services that a law office provides. Marketing techniques include producing firm brochures, newsletters, and client seminars. Marketing works best when the firm establishes a written marketing plan and then sticks to the plan.

Planning is the process of setting objectives, assessing the future, and developing courses of action to achieve these objectives. There are many types of plans, including a mission statement and short- and long-range plans. Planning forces firms to anticipate change and to prepare for ways to handle the change.

SOLO PRACTITIONER'S OFFICE

Robin Saunders Davis

of the Farnam Law Firm

Saint Louis, Missouri

INTRODUCTION

Robin Saunders Davis is a paralegal at the Farnam Law Firm, an employee benefits firm in Saint Louis, Missouri. Robin's legal career started when she was in her late twenties. At the age of twenty-five, Robin decided to return to school as a full-time student to get a legal assistant's degree. She started at the junior college level and earned a bachelor of arts degree from a four-year university. After she received an associate's degree as a legal assistant, Robin began to look for work in the field.

"Law firms wanted paralegals with practical experience. Although I did not have any 'legal' experience, I did have good organizational and communication skills along with good clerical experience. Before returning to school, I worked as a talent coordinator for, at that time, one of the most successful advertising agencies in this area. There I gained the skills I did have. I highlighted those skills on my resume, talked about what I had been doing for the past year and was offered a part-time position. So there I was, my first job as a paralegal working part time earning four hundred dollars a month. The job market was tight, and I was willing to sacrifice to gain practical experience. I worked at that salary for a year. After a year I was offered a full-time position. It got a lot better as time passed. Those early years of experience helped me a lot. I learned to think and work independently. Those characteristics are most important in the industry."

THE FARNAM LAW FIRM

The Farnam Law Firm is a small firm that works exclusively with employee benefits matters. The firm is headed by Thomas C. Farnam, a Fellow of the American College of Tax Counsel who has been an attorney since 1970. The firm also has one associate attorney and a secretary, along with Robin as the firm's paralegal.

Being a very small firm, each of the four employees shares the firm's administrative duties. Each contributes and takes part in the firm's major decisions. "Here we discuss everything before the firm makes a move on any decision," Robin said. "Generally, we all think alike. Our firm operates like a family. We generally agree on what is best for the firm. Although Tom (Farnam) makes the final decision on most issues, he includes us in the decision-making process." For instance, when Robin began working for Tom three years ago, there was only the two of them. When the time came to add to the firm, Robin was included in the interviewing and selection process for both the associate attorney and the secretary.

The firm's organizational structure is relaxed but generally, Tom is at the top, then comes Robin, the associate and finally the secretary. "Administratively speaking, in Tom's absence, I wear his shoes." Hard work and loyalty is rewarded in this firm no matter what "level" the employee.

EMPLOYEE BENEFITS LAW

Employee benefits refers to retirement plans such as 401(K) plans, cafeteria plans including health insurance plans, profit sharing plans, etc., that organizations offer to their employees. Employee benefits is a highly regulated area. For example, the Internal Revenue Code and the Employee Retirement Income Security Act (ERISA) are the primary federal statutes that regulate employee benefits. There also are many Internal Revenue Service (IRS) and Department of Labor regulations that both employers and employees must be aware of.

The firm drafts retirement plans and other plans for businesses that typically have from fifty to a few hundred employees. The services that the firm provides depend greatly on the type of benefit plan the client has or wants. In some cases, the firm prepares a new plan, and, in other cases, the firm dissolves or amends an existing plan. Depending on its complexity, a new plan may take from two weeks to a year to bring into operation. This area of employee benefits law does not lend itself to litigation and court practice.

"We generally do not do plaintiffs work. We generally do not go to court. I have been with this firm for over three years, and we have only gone to court on one case."

ROBIN'S DUTIES AS A LEGAL ASSISTANT

PREPARATION OF PENSION PLAN DOCUMENT

Often clients come to the firm to get help with setting up a plan for their company. Plan documents generally are lengthy and very detailed. They describe specifically how the plan works in conjunction with applicable rules and regulations, who is eligible to participate, who contributes to it (the employer, employee, or both) and how much, when employees can take the money out and under what circumstances, and what benefits are available and when.

One of the first things the law firm does is to meet with the client to discuss the client's needs and desires and to advise the client regarding how the plan might work in his specific case. They also advise him regarding the complex regulations of the IRS and ERISA. One of the things that the firm strives to do is to break down complicated regulations so that clients can understand them.

To help in setting up and drafting plan documents, a detailed "checklist" has been developed that includes many different options that potentially can be included in any one plan. Once the checklist has been completed according to the needs of the client, the firm then generates the plan document. Robin works with Tom to complete the checklist. Once the plan has been developed, Robin helps to analyze the plan to make sure it has been drafted according to the needs and desires of the client and to ensure that each plan has the necessary components required by ERISA and IRS. Tom also meets with clients to explain in detail the draft of the plan.

IRS DETERMINATION LETTERS

Once a pension plan document has been prepared, adopted, and signed by the client, the next step is to request an IRS Determination Letter. One of the primary responsibilities Robin has is to organize, compile, and track the information necessary to complete an IRS Determination Letter Application for each plan that is to be filed on behalf of the client. Because plan sponsors and plan participants receive favorable tax advantages in that no federal taxes have to be paid on these funds until they are withdrawn from the plan or participant's account, it is advantageous for the plan sponsor (employer) to request a review by the IRS as to whether the pension plan is valid under the tax code (this is the basic purpose of a "determination letter"). However, a great deal of information has to be collected and analyzed for the IRS to rule on the validity of the plan, including the number of participants in the plan, when an employee becomes eligible to participate in the plan, how benefits are calculated, and the plan document itself. Receiving a favorable Determination Letter from the IRS is important to the law firm as well as the client, because if the IRS determines that the plan's terms are valid, the firm has done its job in helping client set up a proper plan.

ADMINISTRATIVE DUTIES

Because the firm is small, Robin also handles many administrative functions ranging from secretarial duties to reviewing documents before they go out.

Recently Robin coordinated the firm's move by working with the moving company and the vendors. "It was a lot of detailed work. I coached the staff to make sure that everything would go smoothly. It was really important to give them all the information they needed so that they could get packed and then unpacked quickly and efficiently. For all firms, no matter the size, downtime that is created by such things as relocating the office should be minimized. When you are moving, you cannot work; if you can't work, there are no billings and no income, so it is important that it goes fast and smooth." Robin planned the move for two or three months before it happened. The move went as planned, and the firm's downtime was minimal.

PERSONAL PHILOSOPHY TOWARD WORK

Robin describes her personal philosophies as follows: "One important thing to remember is to always consider what the client needs. I always keep in the back of my mind that I am here to serve each client to the best of my ability as efficiently as possible. It is important to keep my time minimal, which subsequently reduces the amount of money our client must spend for our services.

"At this firm or any firm, it is important that legal assistants have good organizational skills and good communication skills and be flexible and open to new ideas and new ways of doing things. Also, legal assistants have to be able to communicate with clients effectively, to be able to answer their questions, and to help them. I have found that a great deal of time is spent reading resources, researching, and keeping up with new developments and changes in the law. It is very important for us to keep abreast of new and changing laws because the rules and regulations we deal with are constantly changing. Many of those changes affect our clients in one way or another. If we see a change that may affect one of our clients, we immediately run and get the file to check it out and then contact them if necessary. We often use WordPerfect and our data base to notify each of our clients about the change and what they can expect as a result of that change.

HOW ROBIN WORKS

"I have my own office (with a nice view) and my own computer," Robin said. "I have secretarial support when I need it, but everyone in our office types his or her own work using WordPerfect 6.0 for DOS. Having our own computers allows us to be self-sufficient, including Tom." To track her schedule, she uses a simple weekly calendar and writes down all of her deadlines, appointments and things to be done. Generally speaking, Robin sets her own priorities, but the members of the firm are constantly talking with each other and discussing the work they are doing on a regular basis, so priorities are discussed with firm members on a daily basis.

WHY PEOPLE HAVE FAILED TO WORK OUT AT THE FARNAM LAW FIRM

"Because it is so small, it is crucial that all employees get along and that we 'click' with each other, and it is also important that you know what is expected of you in your particular role."

BILLING TIME

"In our firm, my time is up and down. A good month for me is to bill from eighty to one hundred hours (one thousand to twelve hundred billable hours a year). Sometimes I do not get there, but as long as my time is accounted for, I do not get into trouble. In our firm, I sometimes will not have enough billable work to keep me busy all of the time and Tom realizes that. However, whenever possible, I always ask for more work. I always try to find ways to relieve the attorney of work. If the attorney is doing all of the work, he will not see the advantage of having the paralegal around. So you must 'train' the attorneys to use a legal assistant.

"Sometimes, people think they should not charge a client for total hours spent completing a particular project," Robin said. "The legal assistant does not decide what is the appropriate amount of billing time. If I work on a project, I record the time no matter how much or how little time it takes to get the work done. I let the person responsible for the bills decide to reduce the time or to bill the client for the entire amount. Now, if for instance, Tom reduces my time and does not bill for the entire time spent, I get to hear it, but that is his decision."

ETHICAL CONSIDERATIONS AT THE FARNAM LAW FIRM

According to Robin, having a high ethical standard is very important to the success of any legal assistant. "We have a high ethics standard at this firm. If all you have is to sell your time and your services, then you need to walk on a straight and narrow. A person that deviates from that is not going to represent the client or the firm very well.

"One of the ways the Farnam Law Firm works out ethical problems is to encourage everyone in the firm to talk and discuss every problem. We are encouraged to discuss and ask questions about any problem in our minds. Not to ask or not to say something is a major mistake."

UNAUTHORIZED PRACTICE OF LAW

"I refrain from giving legal advice to clients. I know that I am a legal assistant and not an attorney. When I am in a situation where the client calls and asks what they should do, I merely tell them that I am the paralegal and that I can take down their concerns and questions and relay it to Tom, and then I make sure that Tom gets back with them."

Conclusion

Robin enjoys being a legal assistant at a small firm. It allows her to be involved with the management and direction of the firm in addition to practicing in substantive areas. However, she is considering going to law school.

Questions

1. Comment on Robin's decision to accept a part-time job to gain legal assistant experience. Was this a wise decision? Why or why not? If the job market was tight, would you be willing to make this type of sacrifice to work in this field?
2. According to the case study, Robin assumes a leadership role in the Farnam Law Firm. Her opinion is actively sought after and she participates in the administrative functions of the firm. How do you think this might differ if Robin worked in a larger firm and only performed strictly legal assistant functions? Would you rather work in a small firm where you might have more independence and do a variety of duties, or a larger firm where the duties tend to be more structured?
3. Discuss Robin's attitude toward clients and toward her work. Are her attitudes consistent with your own or are they different? Explain. Robin spends time just reading and keeping up on changes in the law. According to Robin, why is keeping up on changes in the law important?
4. Describe Robin's opinions on recording all of her time she actually works. Why is this process safer then trying to decide for herself to add or reduce time to her timesheet?

Key Terms

Policy
Procedure
Total quality management
Marketing
Cross-selling

Rainmaking Marketing plan
Planning
Mission statement
Strategic planning
Gantt chart

Problem Solving Questions

1. You are a legal assistant coordinator in a medium- to large-size law practice. You coordinate approximately fourteen legal assistants. Recently, attorneys in the firm have complained about the coordination of the legal assistants, including complaints of the attorneys needing assistance and no one being available to help them, too many legal assistants working on one particular case, a lack of effective priorities being set, and a lack of communication among the legal assistants. What general things could you do to help this situation?

2. As a legal assistant in a corporate law department, you are asked to begin working on a department staff manual and later to successfully implement it. You and your superiors are convinced that the department will benefit greatly from such a manual. However, your peers are disturbed that you were chosen to coordinate the effort instead of them. What is your next move and why? Be specific.

3. The attorney you work for asks if you have ever heard of something called "total quality management." The attorney would specifically like you to discuss what it is and what advantages it might have for the firm. The attorney also would like you to discuss what effect it might have on its marketing plans. Please discuss your understanding of the term and how it differs from the old philosophy the firm had about being well respected in the community and earning a good profit.

KNOW YOUR ETHICS

1. You and your supervising attorney have just spent three weeks in a complicated products liability trial regarding vaccine immunization shots for children. Your firm's client contracted the disease from the immunization shot. Your firm received the largest verdict in history for this type of case. Given the success of this case, the firm would like to handle more of these. When you get back to the office, you are shown a draft of an advertisement that is going to run in newspapers across the country that reads:

"MILLER AND HASTINGS Law Office SPECIALIZES IN PHARMACEUTICAL CASES!— Recently, our firm won a multi-million-dollar judgment against a drug company for producing an unsafe drug. Please call us if you would like us to represent your interests."

Your supervising attorney asks for your comment. How do you respond? Your client, who is absolutely ecstatic about the verdict, learns of your intentions and volunteers to appear in a television ad to do a testimonial about the verdict and the great services the firm provided.

2. Recently, a senior attorney was reading an article on legal malpractice that stated that every law office should have a person responsible for risk management. That is, someone in every law office should be responsible for thinking of ways to reduce the law office's exposure to legal malpractice. Because you are willing to take on additional responsibilities, you volunteer. Analyze briefly from an ethics and malpractice perspective why every law office should have a staff manual.

PRACTICE EXERCISES

1. As a legal assistant for a small-but-respected firm, you know that the firm wishes to expand and to move into more lucrative legal areas. You think that environmental issues such as toxic waste would be a very good area to expand into. However, before suggesting the idea, you know that you must present solid evidence of feasibility and present a plan for making this happen. Specifically, delineate what you would do to research this (be creative), then develop a draft plan of how you would sell the partners on it. How will you convince the partners that this can be accomplished?

2. As a legal assistant in a public legal aid clinic, you are asked to draft a policy/procedure regarding incoming and outgoing mail practices. The following should be addressed: who will stamp the incoming mail "received," how it will be stamped, how the mail will be routed, who will process the outgoing mail, when it should be delivered to the post office, and when overnight delivery will be used. Please draft the policy/procedure.

3. Your law office is considering placing a yellow pages ad. You are to research the issue by looking in the yellow pages under "attorneys." You are to pick out two ads that you think are outstanding. Consider what it is that you like about the ads and what the messages of the ads are. Do the same with television ads. What attorney ads are the best and why?

4. As you are considering Exercise 3-3, look for ads that you think are questionable from an ethics perspective or that are done in poor taste. Give explanations for your answer.

NOTES

1. Robert Michael Greene, *Making Partner* (American Bar Association, 1992), 3.
2. Adapted from *Total Quality Service* (Altman Weil Pensa, 1992), 6.
3. Ibid., 3.
4. Cary Griffith, "What TQM Means to Law Firms & Their Clients," *Law Office Management Administration Report*, issue 92–8, August 1992, 6.
5. Deborah C. Wahl, "Managing for Quality," *The LAMA Manager,* Spring 1992, 8.
6. *Model Rules of Professional Conduct* (American Bar Association, 1992), Rule 7.1, comment.
7. *Total Quality Service* (Altman Weil Pensa, 1992), 4.
8. Louis E. Boone and David L. Kurtz, *Management* 3d ed. New York: Random House Business Division, 1987), 119.

4

CLIENTS AND COMMUNICATION SKILLS

CHAPTER OBJECTIVES

After you read this chapter, you will be able to:

- Discuss factors that will promote effective client relationships.
- Discuss ways to communicate effectively.
- Identify communication barriers.
- Explain the importance of good listening skills.
- Identify the pros and cons of using groups to make decisions.
- Discuss the characteristics of a leader.

A sole practitioner lost a court case after months of preparation and weeks of trial. The attorney had been representing one of her best corporate clients, who had paid her faithfully each month during litigation.

The attorney did not relish the thought of visiting the owner of the company. But, when she did, she was stunned. The client offered his condolences and expressions of support. During the course of the litigation, the attorney and all the members of the attorney's staff had kept the client fully informed of everything that was transpiring in the case. The client knew that the attorney and her staff had worked hard on the case and how intent they had been on winning. He also knew that he had been treated fairly and that the attorney and the staff had acted honestly and ethically in representing his interests. While winning would have been better, the client felt well served.[1]

WHY DO LEGAL ASSISTANTS NEED TO FOSTER GOOD CLIENT RELATIONSHIPS AND COMMUNICATE EFFECTIVELY?

Fostering positive client relationships and communicating effectively with others are absolute necessities for legal assistants to be successful. Customer service and satisfaction are very important to the practice of law, especially considering the number of law offices and the fierce competition that exists. Legal assistants who mishandle client relationships, by not putting the client first, will cause clients to go elsewhere for legal services. Nearly every task a legal assistant performs requires communication skills such as writing correspondence, drafting briefs, interviewing clients and witnesses, and legal research. The ability to effectively exchange ideas and information with others is an essential part of being a legal assistant.

This section will present a basic but practical explanation of communication and will give you some ideas on how your communication skills can be improved. Also included in this section are related communication topics such as leadership qualities, the advantages and disadvantages of working with groups, and how to conduct client interviews.

CLIENT RELATIONSHIPS

A fundamental aspect of law office management is the commitment to provide quality legal service to clients. This is true whether you work in a private law firm or legal aid office with many clients or in a corporation or government practice where you have only one client: service is the key. Providing quality legal services begins with a good working relationship with each client, and this relationship is not just for attorneys. Everyone in the office, including legal assistants, should be committed to this. Remember, the client always comes first; she is the one paying your salary in the end. Clients may not have the legal background to know whether or not they are receiving good legal representation. However, clients do know whether their phone calls are being returned, whether documents in their case are poorly written and have typographical errors, whether deadlines are missed, or whether they are being treated respectfully. Merely providing good technical legal skills is not enough to please clients. Most clients are referred to attorneys and law offices by previous clients. If you provide poor service to existing clients, you will be depriving your firm of the best way to expand the practice.

Figure 4-1 shows a list of things that clients like and dislike about attorneys and law office staff. These likes and dislikes determine whether a client will come back for future business or refer others to the firm. Notice that the issue of winning or losing a case is not included in either list. This section will provide some ideas on how you can foster good client relations.

- **Treat each client as if he is your only client**—Every client should be treated individually. Behave as if that client's case is the only thing you are working on and as if the case is your most important one. People are usually more than a little apprehensive about coming to a law office and are potentially in some kind of trouble or in need of help. Everyone at the firm needs to put the client at ease. When you meet with a client, only have his file on your desk and give the client

Personality Traits and Work Habits Valued/Not Valued by Clients	
Likes	**Dislikes**
Friendliness	Acting Impersonal
Prompt and Businesslike Attitude	Bored or Indifferent Attitude
Courtesy	A Rude and Brusque Manner
Avoidance of a Condescending Attitude	A Superior Attitude
A Habit of Keeping the Client Informed	A Failure to Keep Client Informed

FIGURE 4-1
Work Habits Clients Like in Their Attorneys/Office Staff

Source: Reprinted with permission from *The Lawyer's Handbook*, copyright © 1983, American Bar Association.

your undivided attention. This is a good idea not only because it shows the client that you are interested in his case, but because the confidentiality of your other clients needs to be maintained.

Never tell the client how busy you are or how many other cases you are working on; the client's case is the only one he is concerned about and the only one you should be talking to him about. If a client calls and asks if you are busy, say something such as "I'm never too busy to take a call from a good client" (even if you are swamped). If a client comes in for an appointment, never make him wait in the waiting room. A good law practice makes prompt, *personal* service a high priority. Take a personal interest in the client's affairs and be empathetic. It is always best to be personable with clients because this fosters good working relationships that will continue for years to come.

One law firm's client reported that he was sending additional business—both his own business and referrals—to other law firms in town. When asked why he wasn't sending it to his primary firm, he replied. "Because they're too busy already. The lawyers [and legal assistants] are always telling me how busy they are, and are slow in responding to my requests."

—**Sally J. Schmidt,** *What Clients Say* (Burnsville, Minnesota: Sally Schmidt Consulting, Inc., 1989), 14.

■ **Send copies of all documents to clients**—As a matter of practice, it should be the policy of the law office to always send copies of all letters, memos, pleadings, and documents to the client. In nearly all cases, the client will appreciate this, and it will increase her confidence, satisfaction, and trust because although this might be just another case to you, this matter is of particular importance to the client. Although many people focus on the results of a case, the documents are a large piece of the product that the client is paying for. Even if the client does not understand everything sent, it still allows her to know what is happening in the case and how difficult the theories and complexities of the case are, and it lets the client know that you are actively working on the case. The cost of the copies can be charged to the client's account, so there is no real reason not to do it. Also, clients are usually more willing to pay their attorney's fees when they have seen the work done on the case. It can be frustrating when a client does not know what is happening and then receives a bill.

I like my lawyer and the law firm he works for. They send me copies of all memorandums of telephone calls and all correspondence in and out. They send me a letter once a week outlining what they have done during the preceding week. I am busy, and I am often out of town. I accumulate their letters to me, and I read them on a plane or whenever I have a few free moments. Their letters and memos allow me to keep abreast at my convenience of what is happening on my case. I do not always understand the specific details, but I get enough information. As a matter of fact, I don't even know whether they are doing a good job as lawyers, but I am happy.

—Adapted from **Jay G. Foonberg,** *How to Get and Keep Good Clients* (Washington, D.C.: Lawyers Alert Press, 1986), 308.

- **Do not use legalese**—Do not use legalese or legal jargon when talking with clients. Many clients do not understand legal jargon, and it is confusing and frustrating. Some clients may be too intimidated to ask what the terms mean. Try to explain legal concepts in words that a layperson will understand.

> *"They need to get explanations down to a level people can understand—I recently received an opinion letter from another law firm and was very impressed—it was succinct and easy to read."—A client*
>
> —**Sally J. Schmidt,** *What Clients Say* (Sally Schmidt Consulting, Inc., 1989), 19.

- **Return client phone calls immediately**—It is essential that you return client phone calls immediately. If that is not possible, at least return the calls on the same day that they are made. It is not uncommon for clients to call legal assistants. Usually, legal assistants are easier to reach than attorneys, and often legal assistants must work with clients quite closely depending on the type of case. Because legal assistants typically are very busy and may be working on many projects at once, you will be inclined to put client calls off, but do not do this. Always return a client's call first and then finish the job at hand. If you do not reach the client on the first try, continue to try to reach the client rather than letting the client call back for you.

> *Treat every call like a million-dollar fee; it could be, or it could generate that much over the years.*
>
> —**Jay W. Lewis,** "An Open Letter from a Frustrated Client," *Law Practice Management,* November/December 1990, 33.

> *Believe it or not, one of the key reasons clients feel rejected is the misuse of the telephone. Clients feel that calls are excessively screened. To them, the telephone represents accessibility. [One satisfied client said:]*
>
> *"He always calls me back the same day. I know I'm not his biggest client, but he makes me feel like my problems are important too."*
>
> —**Schmidt,** 19–20.

- **Be courteous, empathetic and professional at all times**—Some clients at times may be abusive. Do not take client comments personally. Never become impatient with a client, "snap" at a client, or act rudely. If you have a problem with a client treating you abusively, mention it to your supervising attorney or legal assistant manager and let him handle it. Act professionally in all situations.

Finally, never allow a secretary or receptionist to let a client stay on hold after calling for you. If you are on another call and cannot get to the client immediately, have the receptionist tell the client you will return the call as soon as you get off the phone, then follow it up and call the client.

- **Respond to client requests in a timely fashion and keep your promises**—It is not enough to simply return client phone calls. When clients request answers to questions, send letters, or need things from you, it is absolutely necessary that you respond as quickly as possible. If you tell the client that you will have something to her by a particular time or date, keep your promise. If an emergency comes up and you cannot make the deadline, always call the client and let her know and set a new deadline that you can meet.

▪ **Give clients periodic status reports**—Some cases can be sitting on appeal for months, waiting for a motion to be ruled on, or facing other things that make them lie in a dormant state. This will always frustrate clients, who would like quick remedies to their problems. So periodically, on a weekly or not less than a monthly basis, review your cases, and, with the approval or your attorney, write the clients letting them know what is happening in their cases. Word processors can be configured to make this a very quick process by having form letters on file for different situations or the ability to select prerecorded paragraphs. If the case is waiting for some kind of action, you should still write the client and let him know that you are still waiting and have not forgotten the case. If you do not review the case periodically, the case could very well sit for months with no contact with the client. Keeping in touch with the client never hurts, since it reiterates that his business is important to you.

▪ **Do not share personal or office problems with clients**—Always keep your personal problems to yourself and never make comments that are derogatory about your supervising attorney, firm, or other staff members. Clients need to know that their legal matters are in good hands and that everything is under control.

▪ **Preserve client confidences**—Preserving client confidences is very important and cannot be overemphasized. Apart from the ethics question, you should keep in mind that if a release of client information gets back to the client, the relationship is most likely finished.

▪ **The use of client surveys**—A client survey is a way to find out exactly what your clients think of your services (see Figure 4-2). Most client questionnaires are

**FIGURE 4-2
A Client
Questionnaire**

Source: Reprinted with permission from *The Lawyer's Handbook,* copyright © 1983, American Bar Association.

In order that we might provide efficient and skillful legal services to our clients at a cost which is not unreasonable, we are asking you to answer the questions listed below in the space provided. After doing so, would you please separate the top portion of this letter from the question section by tearing on the indicated line, and return the question section to us in the enclosed business reply envelope.

We are grateful for your time and effort involved in answering the questionnaire, and sincerely wish that your answers will help us obtain the results that we and our clients are striving for.

Sincerely,

1. Type of case: _____
2. Attorney: _____
3. Has any member of our firm represented you before? _____
   If so, how many months/years ago? _____
4. Why did you choose our firm to represent you? _____

5. Were your telephone calls to our office returned within a reasonable time? _____

6. Were you treated courteously by the members of our staff? _____
   If not, please explain: _____

7. Did you ever wait in the waiting room for an unreasonable period of time before seeing the attorney or legal assistant you had an appointment with? _____
   If yes, the number of times: _____

8. Were you informed, at the beginning of the case, as to the basis of our charges for legal services? _____

9. Were you sufficiently informed as to the progress of your case by the assigned attorney or legal assistant? _____

10. In your opinion, was the fee charged reasonable? _____
    If no, why not? _____

11. Were you satisfied with the results obtained in your case? _____
    If no, why not? _____

12. Would you recommend our law firm to another? _____
    If yes, why? _____
    If no, why not? _____

13. Please rate the general quality of the services performed by our law firm.
    (Excellent, Very Good, Good, Fair, Poor) _____

14. Comments: _____
    _____
    _____
    _____

given at the conclusion of a case. Anytime you get information directly from a client, you should take it to heart. Most firms allow the client to remain anonymous in completing the questionnaire to ensure truthfulness, and it is usually short, not more than a page long, to make completion as easy as possible.

▪ **Management must help promote good client relationships**—Management also has a duty to promote good client relationships. Figure 4-3 contains a list of possible firm policies regarding communication with clients.

**FIGURE 4-3
Policies for
Timeliness**

Source: Adapted from "The Power of Communication of the Billing Process," by Milton Zwicker, in *Law Practice Management*, copyright © 1992, American Bar Association.

- Clients should not be kept waiting in the reception area more than _____ minutes . . .
- Copies of documents should be mailed to clients within _____ days . . .
- A new case should be acknowledged in writing to a client within _____ days . . .
- Telephone calls should be answered within _____ rings . . .
- Clients should not be left on hold longer than _____ seconds . . .
- All telephone calls should be returned within _____ hours . . .
- A client should receive a status report every _____ days . . .
- When an existing client refers another person to the firm, the client should be thanked for the referral within _____ days . . .

▪ **Publish a client manual**—Some law offices publish a manual for their clients, which explains what to expect from the law office, such as how attorney fees are calculated, how the attorney-client relationship works, what discovery is, how to prepare for a deposition, and what to expect at trial. This type of manual is very beneficial and will save the attorney and legal assistant from answering the same questions over and over for different clients. For an example of an excellent client manual, see *The Compleat Lawyer,* vol. 10, no. 1, Winter 1993 (a magazine published by the ABA Section on General Practice).

COMMUNICATION SKILLS

> *Basically, the whole (legal assistant) profession is communication, and many of the problems that arise are going to be in that area.*
>
> —**Cynthia Tokumitsu,** quoting a legal assistant in "How to Avoid the Top 10 Mistakes Paralegals Make on the Job," *Legal Assistant Today,* November/December 1991, 27.

Possessing good communication skills is necessary in most professional jobs, but it is especially important in a law office. Legal assistants must communicate with clients, opposing counsel, supervising attorneys, office staff, court clerks, and witnesses on a daily basis regarding complex and important matters. Having good communication skills also bears directly on the effectiveness of law office management. Communication is the foundation of management,[2] because without it, management could not plan, organize, control, or direct the business. Thus, having good communication skills bears directly both on legal services to clients and on law office management.

COMMUNICATION GENERALLY

communication
The transfer of a message from a sender to a receiver.

Professionals, such as legal assistants and attorneys, typically spend about 79 percent of each day communicating (see Figure 4-4). **Communication** *is the transfer of a message from a sender to a receiver.* Although communication can be quickly defined, it is more difficult to explain why there is so much poor communication in the world.

communication barrier
Something that inhibits or prevents the receiver from obtaining the correct message.

Figure 4-5 is a flow chart that shows how information is communicated. The abundance of communication barriers shows why some messages are never properly received. *A* **communication barrier** *inhibits or prevents the receiver from obtaining the correct message from the sender.* These barriers include situations where the sender and receiver have different cultural backgrounds, different perceptions, different understandings, and different ages. Noise is also a communication barrier. **Noise** *refers to any situation that interferes with or distorts the message being communicated.*[3] An example of noise is when one person is trying to listen to several senders at one time. The messages are distorted, since the receiver cannot understand all the messages at the same time. There are many other communication barriers as well (see Figure 4-5). Effective communicators are able to overcome these communication barriers and make their point.

noise
Any situation that interferes with or distorts the message being communicated.

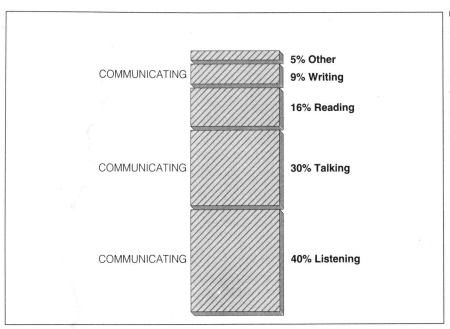

FIGURE 4-4
**How Professionals
Spend Their Time**

Source: Deborah Heller and
James M. Hunt, *Practicing
Law and Managing People*
(Butterworth, 1988), 210.
Courtesy of Heller, Hunt &
Cunningham.

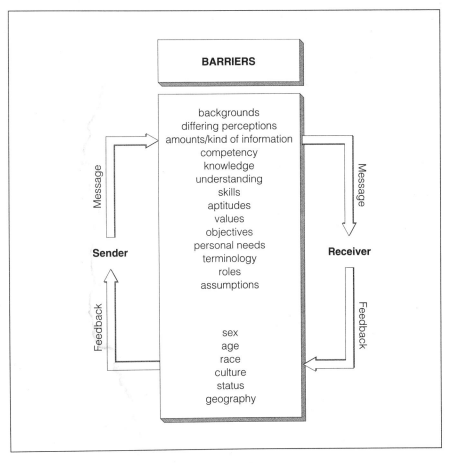

FIGURE 4-5
**Communication
Diagram**

Source: Deborah Heller and
James M. Hunt, *Practicing
Law and Managing People*
(Butterworth, 1988), 212.
Courtesy of Heller, Hunt &
Cunningham.

feedback
Information sent in
response to a message.

Feedback is an important part of effective communication. **Feedback** *is infor-mation sent in response to the sender's message.* There is no way for the sender to know whether his information has been properly received without feedback. Feedback allows the receiver to state his understanding of the message and also allows the sender to evaluate the effectiveness of the message and to clarify mis-understood points. Feedback does not have to be verbal; it can be as simple as a puzzled look on the receiver's face.

NONVERBAL COMMUNICATION

Communication is much more than just speech. There are many nonverbal com-municators, such as eye contact, facial expressions, posture, appearance, clothing, tone of voice, and gestures. All these nonverbal means of communication have a hand in determining whether or not a message is properly received.

IMPROVING YOUR COMMUNICATION SKILLS

> *Listening is the other half of talking, but in many cases it is not. For many people, listening is that agonizing time period they must survive before they themselves speak.*
>
> **—Louis E. Boone and David L. Kurtz,** *Management,* 3d ed. (New York: Random House Business Division, 1987), 464.

- **Listen**—Listening is one of the most important features of communicating effectively, and although it sounds easy to do, often it is not. The average person forgets 50 percent of what was said to her within just a few minutes. We have all caught ourselves in the middle of conversations thinking about something unre-lated to the conversation. We become "lazy listeners," only minimally listening. When this occurs, we are not communicating effectively.[4] Figure 4-6 contains some excellent rules on listening. A common problem that attorneys and legal assistants are guilty of is that instead of listening to what another person is say-ing, they formulate arguments and prepare for when they will speak. This effec-tively takes the listener out of good listening, and the listener may miss the total message.

- **Keep it simple and to the point**—Most people understand more of a message when the sender uses short, direct sentences rather than long, complex ones. You can explain complex issues to others, just use words and phrases they will under-stand. Avoid jargon and legalese when dealing with clients. In the same vein, research has shown that short letters are read sooner than are long ones, and the reader actually remembers the message of the short letter more accurately.

- **Consider your nonverbal signals**—Realize that when you are communicating with people, they look at you and your message as a total package. They are con-sidering how you are dressed, if you are nervous, if you are fidgeting, if you have your hands in your pockets, and if you have confidence in yourself.

- **Do not become emotional**—Try not to be emotional when communicating. Try to be objective and calm. The trick is to strike a balance between being non-emotional while not going as far as to be cold and distant.

1. **STOP TALKING!**
   You cannot listen if you are talking.
2. **PUT THE TALKER AT EASE.**
   Help the person feel that he or she is free to talk.
3. **SHOW THE INDIVIDUAL THAT YOU WANT TO LISTEN.**
   Look and act interested. Do not read your mail while the person talks.
   Listen to understand, rather than to oppose.
4. **REMOVE DISTRACTIONS.**
   Do not doodle, tap, or shuffle papers. Will it be quieter if you shut
   the door?
5. **EMPATHIZE WITH THE PERSON.**
   Try to see the other's point of view.
6. **BE PATIENT.**
   Alloy plenty of time. Do not interrupt. Don't start for the door or
   walk away.
7. **HOLD YOUR TEMPER.**
   An angry person gets the wrong meaning from words.
8. **GO EASY ON ARGUMENT AND CRITICISM.**
   This puts the person on the defensive. She may "clam up" or get
   angry. Do not argue: Even if you win, you lose.
9. **ASK QUESTIONS.**
   This encourages the speaker and shows you are listening. It helps to
   develop points further.
10. **STOP TALKING!**
    This is first and last, because all other commandments depend on it.
    You cannot do a good listening job while you are talking. Nature gave
    man two ears but only one tongue, which is a gentle hint that he
    should listen more than he talks.

FIGURE 4-6
The Ten Commandments of Good Listening

Source: Keith Davis, *Human Behavior at Work*, 4th ed., copyright © 1972, McGraw-Hill. Reprinted with permission of McGraw-Hill.

- **Make eye contact**—Make eye contact with everyone you are talking to, since it conveys honesty and interest. Juries, for instance, often cite the lack of eye contact as a reason that they did not believe a witness.

- **Body language**—Watch your body language. Crossed arms usually means you are feeling defensive, scared, or cold about something; poor posture is sometimes interpreted as lazy or slothful. One kind of body language that is more important than anything else is setting a positive tone is a simple smile. Smiling relaxes both your audience and you.

- **Be precise and clear**—Always try to be as precise as possible when communicating with others. How often have you heard someone say "Well, I thought you meant . . ." Speak clearly and do not leave anything to the imagination. For example, if you tell a delivery person you need something filed at the courthouse, be sure you are precise and tell him whether you need it filed at the federal courthouse, the local courthouse, or the state courthouse. These subtle differences can be very important in a law office, so be absolutely clear when you communicate. Look for feedback. If someone has a puzzled look on his face, explain your message again or ask him to repeat it to you.

- **Consider your audience**—Always tailor your communication to the specific audience with which you are communicating. You can have the best message in the world, but if you are delivering it to someone who does not care about it, you have wasted your effort. If possible, find out what is important to your audience, what concerns it has, and then tailor everything you say to address these concerns.

- **Consider the timing and context**—A good communicator must know when to communicate her message. Be patient and wait until the time is right. Time your message so that noise and barriers are kept to a minimum. You may want to wait until the receiver is in a good mood or has just received good news. Communication is an art; people will react to the same message in different ways depending on the timing. For your message to be effective, you must consider the context in which the communication is being made, such as:
    - Is the receiver "having a bad day?"
    - Where is the communication taking place, in a crowded hallway or in a private office?
    - What type of relationship have you had with the receiver? Do you respect each other, dislike each other, or distrust each other?

  Try to consider the other person's perception of your communication. Consider this: when you find yourself in a disagreement with someone, are you more likely to believe that *your behavior is motivated by context* (i.e. you had a bad day, you're tired, you're stressed out) while you believe that the *other person's behavior is motivated not by context, but by something personal* (such as spite, revenge, meanness, or unreasonableness)? Actually, this is a normal reaction. Consider the context in which the other person is viewing your communication; look at it from her point of view and be aware of your own biases. This will improve your ability to communicate with others.

- **Do not be judgmental/avoid negatives**—Do not start with negative or judgmental comments such as "That probably will not work." This will only make your audience defensive. Try to be positive and explore the conversation in a positive light. If you do not think an idea will work, ask a question about why you think it might not work, such as "Well, have you considered what would happen if this occurred . . .? Will your idea still be successful?" This allows the other person to consider your side but in a positive, constructive light.

- **Ask questions**—Never assume something based on unsupported evidence. It is very easy for people to misread or assume things about other people. Instead of assuming something incorrectly, ask questions and talk about it. This will allow you to verify whether or not your initial assumptions were accurate.

rephrasing
A technique used to improve communication by repeating back to a person what your understanding of the conversation was.

- **Rephrase things**—If you are not sure whether you truly understand what someone has told you, try rephrasing. **Rephrasing** *is the technique of telling the sender what your understanding of the conversation is. It allows the sender to clarify information that might not have been understood clearly.*

- **Importance of good communications with third parties**—A legal assistant deals with many types of people, including witnesses, court personnel, outside agencies, libraries, businesses, and other law offices. It is very important that you be professional at all times and have good relationships with these third parties, since they may provide information that will help you perform your job. When possible, cultivate these relationships.

- **Telephone techniques**

  Poor telephone techniques abound in many law offices. Here are some examples of what not to do:

- Office staff: "Law offices."
  Client: "May I speak to Mr. Smith?"
  Office staff: "Sure, just a sec."
- Office staff: "Law offices."
  Client: "May I speak to Mr. Smith?"
  Office staff: "He's yakking on the other line, you want to hold?"
- Office staff: "Law offices."
  Client: "May I speak to Mr. Smith?"
  Office staff: "He's not in, why don't you call back this afternoon."

Figure 4-7 contains a list of telephone technique suggestions. Keep in mind that these apply to receptionists, secretaries, attorneys, and legal assistants. Most law office staff members spend a great deal of time on the phone and need courteous telephone skills. In any conversation, try to portray a businesslike, courteous, professional attitude that puts the needs of the client first.

LEADERSHIP AND COMMUNICATION

Being a leader takes a special type of communication skill. In Chapter 1, leadership was described as the act of motivating or causing others to perform and

- Answer the phone pleasantly with *"Good morning/afternoon, (name of firm—if the firm name is long, say the first two names), may I help you?"* or when a call is transferred to you *"This is (your name), may I help you?"*
- When a person calls and asks to speak with someone, do not ask who is calling. First, tell the caller whether or not the person is available, then say *"Who may I say is calling?"*
- When the caller tells you his name, call him by name even if you have never met him before. It sets the caller at ease and is a personal touch. For example, *"Mr. Smith, I'll page her and she should get right on"* or *"Mr. Smith, I need to get your file, I'll get right back on."*
- Do not screen your calls. Either take all your calls, or, if you are busy, do not take any calls, but do not ask a secretary to screen your calls. It creates an almost unlimited potential for bad feelings on the part of your callers.
- If the person the caller is asking for is not available, give a short reason why she is not available: *"Mr. Smith, she's not in this morning, she's in court."* Avoid saying the person is "unavailable." This gives the caller the impression that the person is ducking his call.
- When taking a message, do not grill the caller about the subject matter of the call. Simply find out generally what the call is about. Many clients do not like to give out details about their problems.
- When taking a message, always get the area code and phone number of the caller, even if the caller says the person has her number. It's frustrating to hunt for a phone number when it could have been on the call slip.
- If the caller is referred to a legal assistant or other staff person, he should quickly identify himself as a nonlawyer.

FIGURE 4-7
Telephone Checklist for All Law Office Staff

Source: Adapted from Terri J. Olson, "Productive Use of the Phone Can Save Time," *The Florida Bar News,* May 1, 1993, 21. Reprinted by permission of Terri J. Olson.

achieve objectives. Leaders give us direction, vision, and motivation. Leadership is an important part of any organization or department. Legal assistants need to take leadership roles, and there are opportunities for legal assistants who have leadership skills. For instance, legal assistants can be legal assistant managers or law office administrators. Legal assistant "leaders" can take on projects and cases that need innovation and have never been done before. Legal assistants with leadership characteristics are sought after and are important to growing law offices.

> *Successful leaders . . . don't manipulate their people. They encourage small wins . . . striving to reduce the bureaucracy wherever possible. Their role is often coaching—unobtrusive leadership, stretching their players to their limits. As a result, their employees are inspired to perform far beyond ordinary capacity. [They] urge the importance of listening, teaching, facilitating, and providing more space in which subordinates can grow.*
>
> —**Gary A. Munneke,** *Law Practice Management* (Saint Paul, Minnesota: West Publishing Co., 1991), 112.

HOW DO I BECOME A LEADER?   Having identified that leadership qualities are essential for the legal assistant, the next question is "How does one become a leader?" This has been a hotly debated issue over the years. Early leadership theories said that only exceptional people were capable of assuming the leadership role (i.e. you either were or were not born with it). But current research overwhelmingly shows that leaders are not born, they are made. The following are some suggestions on how to be a leader.

1. **Be an expert**—Effective leaders are experts in what they do. They know precisely what they are talking about. People around them have confidence in their abilities and rely upon their knowledge and judgment. They are inventive and ingenious and are able to plan, organize, and manage resources to solve problems. Before they give opinions, they do research and master the subject they are talking about. Leaders must be competent, make good decisions, and be able to evaluate situations and act accordingly.
2. **Be honest**—Effective leaders have a reputation for being extremely honest and forthright and possessing a high degree of integrity. These are important qualities, since subordinates must respect them and must be motivated, inspired, and willing to follow their ideas.
3. **Stay calm**—Good leaders stay cool and collected even when they are "under fire." They have confidence in their own abilities and are not shaken by diversity but instead rise to the occasion.
4. **Trust and support those under you**—Good leaders choose effective and competent subordinates and then support them in their efforts. Subordinates know that they are trusted and their abilities and skills are appreciated and thus work even harder for the leader.
5. **Take risks and do not be afraid of failure**—Effective leaders take calculated risks. They focus on the positive and refuse to think about failure. Failures and mistakes are steps in the learning process and are to be expected. Leaders have the ability to make a bold decision and to stand by it when others are backpedaling.

6. **Encourage honest opinions from others**—Effective leaders encourage subordinates to be honest and to articulate their opinions even if those opinions are in disagreement with the leader's. Debate sharpens the decision-making process so that all alternatives are considered and evaluated based on their merits. This is the only way situations can be properly evaluated. Leaders encourage others around them to cooperate and communicate with each other by listening to everyone's ideas and opinions.

7. **Set goals and visions**—Effective leaders set goals and have specific visions of the future. The goals and visions inspire and empower others to accomplish the goals and to work toward the common dream.

8. **Be respectful**—Good leaders respect others and get along with and care for other people. They foster meaningful, personal, and professional relationships with the people around them.

"Communication is at the heart of leadership."[5] Leaders emerge when a new crisis arises or when a new challenge surfaces. Leaders are able to put together a solution, empower their subordinates to support it, reshape and retool their resources, and come up with a package that meets the new challenge and solves the problem. Figure 4-8 shows distinctions between bosses and leaders. These two functions, controlling and leading, are sometimes confused, but they are actually separate functions.

GROUP COMMUNICATION

Communicating in groups involves a whole different set of variables than when communicating one on one. Legal assistants must routinely work with groups, including working with groups of attorneys and legal assistants on trials and similar projects, working with clients and attorneys on cases, and serving on committees and associations. The following are some commonly known facts about working in groups.

Advantages of Groups:[6]

- Groups tend to make more accurate decisions than do individuals. As the adage says, "two heads are better than one." That is, there are more points of view to be heard and considered and a greater number of solutions offered and analyzed.

- Bosses drive their people.
  Leaders coach them.
- Bosses arouse fear.
  Leaders inspire enthusiasm.
- Bosses say, "Go."
  Leaders say, "Let's go."
- Bosses set up rules to follow.
  Leaders share values.
- Bosses set budgets.
  Leaders define a vision.

FIGURE 4-8
A Boss v. a Leader

Source: Reprinted with permission from "How to Be a Leader, Not a Boss," by Milton W. Zwicker, *Leadership & Management*, copyright © 1991, American Bar Association.

- Once a group has arrived at a decision, there is an increase in the acceptance of the final choice, since group members were involved in the process.
- Group members can communicate and explain the group's decision to others, since they were included.
- Once a decision has been made by a group, implementation is easier, since the group members were involved in the process and have a "stake in the action."

Disadvantages of Groups:[7]

- Decisions by groups take up to 50 percent longer to make than do decisions by individuals.
- Group decisions are often compromises between different points of view rather than the most appropriate alternative.
- Group decisions can sometimes result in groupthink. **Groupthink** *occurs when the desire for group cohesiveness and consensus becomes stronger than the desire for the best possible decision.*[8]
- Groups sometimes make more risky decisions than do individuals, especially when there is no one individual responsible for the consequences of the group decision.
- Groups are sometimes dominated by one or more individuals who rank higher in status in the organization.

groupthink
Term for when the desire for group cohesiveness and consensus becomes stronger than the desire for the best possible decision.

COMMUNICATION IN INTERVIEWING CLIENTS

Interviewing clients is a specialized communication skill that as a legal assistant you will need to know. In many firms, client interviews are conducted by experienced legal assistants or attorneys. However, new legal assistants sit in on interviews with an experienced legal assistant or attorney to learn good interviewing skills.

The initial client interview is very important, since it is usually the first real contact the client may have with the firm. The purpose of the interview is to relax the client, to convince the client that she has come to the right firm, and to gather enough information to decide whether your firm and responsible attorney are interested in representing the client or at least finding out more about the case. The following are some suggestions for handling each part of the interview and what to do should you encounter difficulties. Figure 4-9 is an evaluation sheet to evaluate your interviewing skills.

FIGURE 4-9
Self-Evaluation

Source: *A Practice Guide to Achieving Excellence in the Practice of Law*, ALI-ABA, 1990, 322, copyright © 1992 by the American Law Institute. Reprinted with the permission of the American Law Institute-American Bar Association Committee on Continuing Professional Education.

Client Interviewing
1. Planning for client interviews
    a. In planning for client interviews generally, do I consider
        (1) the length of the typical first interview?
        (2) the best seating arrangement?
        (3) how to minimize interruptions?
        (4) discouraging the presence of third persons unless absolutely necessary?
        (5) my personal appearance?

(continued)

(6) what information I will give to the client?
b. In planning for specific client interviews, do I
  (1) conduct an initial conflicts check?
  (2) conduct initial legal research or review?
  (3) note appropriate areas of factual inquiry?
  (4) consult checklists of general areas of inquiry?
  (5) identify which documents the client should bring to the interview?
  (6) consider giving the client a written questionnaire to complete and bring to the interview?
c. Do I have readily available sources to consult in preparation for client interviews, such as
  (1) treatises?
  (2) texts?
  (3) form books?
  (4) sample checklists?
  (5) sample questionnaires?

2. Interviewing skills
  a. Do I seek to develop rapport with a client by
    (1) putting the client at ease?
    (2) adopting an attitude of friendliness, courtesy, and patience?
    (3) demonstrating interest without becoming overly emotional or involved?
    (4) maintaining a receptive, nonjudgmental attitude toward the client as a person?
    (5) encouraging and allowing the client to talk openly?
    (6) listening attentively to the client?
    (7) interrupting the client only when necessary?
    (8) using language understandable to the client?
    (9) using active listening responses?
    (10) offering support to the client?
    (11) recognizing communication blocks?
    (12) showing respect for the client and avoiding condescension?
    (13) encouraging client questions?
  b. Do I seek to maximize information gathering by
    (1) encouraging a complete factual narrative?
    (2) avoiding premature diagnosis of the client's problem?
    (3) focusing on topics likely to elicit relevant information?
    (4) identifying additional topics as the interview progresses?
    (5) sequencing questions from general to specific or vice versa?
    (6) avoiding undue influence on client responses?
    (7) using open-ended questions, when appropriate?
    (8) using leading questions, when appropriate?
    (9) making sure that the client understands my questions?
    (10) making sure that I understand the client's answers?
  c. Do I periodically evaluate and attempt to improve my interviewing skills by
    (1) reading current literature on interviewing skills?

(continued)

---

        (2) transcribing an interview, with the client's permission?

        (3) reviewing the transcript?

        (4) with another lawyer, when permissible?

        (5) attending CLE programs designed to enhance interviewing skills?

3. Making a prompt, detailed, and accurate record

    a. Do I have a reliable system for preserving information gained in the interview by

        (1) taking notes during the interview?

        (2) without disrupting communication (e.g., by maintaining eye contact)?

        (3) making a detailed record immediately after the interview?

        (4) including follow-up plans in this record?

        (5) making this record sufficiently clear and detailed so that it could be reviewed or used by another lawyer?

- **Prepare for the interview**—One of the simplest things you can do to make sure an interview will go well is to prepare for it. Always try to get as much initial information as possible before the interview. Establish a checklist of questions you want to ask and specific information you want to gather. You must establish what the purpose or goal of the interview is, and then control the interview toward the direction of the goal. For example, if you routinely interview clients regarding workers' compensation claims, there is certain information that you must have. Establish exactly what information you need and then draft a checklist and an agenda to ensure that you obtain the information.

Many law offices also have an intake form on which the client generally describes why he has come to the firm. All this information will help you to prepare for the interview. Also, whoever is setting up the interview should always ask the client to bring in any documentation that may be relevant.

- **Breaking the ice**—The beginning of any interview brings apprehension both for the interviewer and interviewee. Ways to break the ice include: meeting the client in the waiting room and walking up to her; offering your hand for a handshake; accompanying the client back to your office; and talking to the client about the weather or other neutral topics such as whether she had difficulty finding the office. Always have a smile and be warm and friendly. Another interesting way to break the ice is to ask the client or witness about her family. This allows you to gain some background information. Some people may think this is nosy and/or may be suspicious. You may want to tell the person that the questions are not meant to embarrass her but to simply understand who she is and to get the "big picture." You also may want to explain about the confidentiality of everything that she tells you.

- **Always inform the person you are interviewing of your status as a legal assistant**—Once the client is relaxed and is ready to talk about why she is there, indicate your status as a legal assistant. Do not make a prolonged speech about it, which may demonstrate your lack of confidence; simply state "I am a legal assistant, and I work for Ms. Smith who is an attorney here." You should also tell the person what you will be doing and what the attorney is going to do, such as "I will be initially talking to you about your case. I will take down the facts of your case and then prepare a memo to the attorney about it. The attorney will then contact you to discuss it more in depth." Once you have done that, you are ready to begin the interview. Many people begin by asking an open-ended question such as "Why don't you tell me why you are here, start at the beginning."

- **Listen carefully**—Listening carefully to the client's story is sometimes hard to do, since the client may ramble, talk about events out of sequence, and talk about matters that may be irrelevant to the legal problem. However, refrain from leading the conversation at least during the first part of the interview. Be patient and let the client tell the whole story his own way. Then go back and fill in the details by asking questions. Do not take too many notes during the first part of the interview. You should give the client your undivided attention and try to make eye contact. Clients need to be reassured that you are interested in their case. As you listen, determine whether the client's story makes sense and think of what facts the client may be leaving out.

- **Communicate sincerity**—For any interview to be successful, you must communicate that you are sincerely interested in the client's problem. Characteristics such as dominance or defensiveness are counterproductive to establishing sincerity. One of the best ways you can communicate sincerity is to show you are really listening to what the person is saying by asking thoughtful questions. Avoid appearing as if you are "grilling" a client.

- **Be empathetic**—Be empathetic with the client, letting her know that you feel for her and for the situation she is in. This is distinguished from sympathy, which is feeling sorry for her. However, be sure to keep your objectivity. Sometimes the client may have to describe very personal, traumatic, or embarrassing information. In that case, you need to be extra sensitive and inform the client that everything said is confidential and is necessary so that you understand what happened.

- **Organizing the information**—Once you have listened to the client tell his story the first time through, you are ready to organize the information. A common way to organize the client's story is to build a chronology of events that starts at the beginning of the problem and works forward. This helps the client relive the facts in a particular order and may cause the client to remember more exact details. However, be aware that clients seldom remember things in exact order, so it usually takes several times through before your chronology is accurate.

- **Asking questions**—When you want to get detailed information about a particular event, remember to ask who, what, when, and where questions. However, do not ask leading questions that might suggest a particular answer, such as "You saw the traffic light as you were going through and it was green, right?" Ask your questions carefully. A better approach might be to say "Describe the intersection before the accident."

    Also, avoid compound questions that ask the client to answer two or more questions. For example, "How many cars were in the intersection and when was the first time you saw the blue car?" Ask your questions one at a time.

- **Do not be judgmental**—Never be judgmental to a client. Saying things like "You really need to get a grip on yourself,"—"You are acting like a child," or "You can't mean that," is the opposite of being empathetic, which is what you ideally want to be. Avoid questions that begin with "Why did you . . .". This type of question might be viewed as judgmental. These questions put the client on the defensive.

- **Never say "You have a great case"**—Be very careful about judging the client's case. Do not make any promises to the client and never tell the client what a great case she has, since this may be bordering on giving legal advice. At this stage you do not have enough information to make that determination. Lawsuits are usually too complex for this type of statement.

- **Fee discussions should be left to the attorney**—Discussions regarding whether the firm is going to take the case and discussions about the amount of the fee should be left to the attorney.

- **Closing the interview**—Do not close the interview too quickly. Before you close, be sure to:
    - Get copies of all the documentation that the client brought;
    - Instruct the client not to discuss the case with anyone else;
    - Reassure the client by telling him exactly what your office will be doing and when it will be done (For example: "I will draft a memo to the attorney, our office will do some preliminary legal research, and this will be completed by Friday. Our office will call you Friday to set up an appointment for early next week." Never tell the client that "the attorney will get with you as soon as he can." Clients want to know exactly what is going to happen and when it is going to happen.);
    - Review your checklist to make sure you have obtained all the information you need;
    - Have the client sign any release or authorization you would need to get information, such as a medical release for the client's files from a doctor or hospital, etc.;
    - List everything the client did NOT bring with her (Give a copy of the list to the client with a self-addressed return envelope.);
    - Thank the client for coming into the office, reassure the client that you will be in contact with her shortly, and instruct her that if she remembers anything else that she thinks is important to be sure to give you a call (Give her your business card).

SUMMARY

Legal assistants must be able to establish effective client relationships. Qualities that clients like most in attorneys and legal assistants include being friendly, being prompt and businesslike, being courteous, and keeping clients informed.

Effective communication is essential in law firms. Communication is the transfer of a message from a sender to a receiver. A communication barrier inhibits or prevents the receiver from obtaining the correct message from the sender. There are many different communication barriers, including the receiver and sender having different cultural backgrounds, using different terminology, and having different values. Interviewing clients is a communication skill that legal assistants use over and over.

CORPORATE LAW DEPARTMENT

Sherry R. S. Wehrle

of Long John Silver's Restaurants, Inc.

Corporate Headquarters—Lexington, Kentucky

INTRODUCTION

Sherry Wehrle is a legal assistant at Long John Silver's corporate headquarters in Lexington, Kentucky. During Sherry's legal career, she has worked for a very small law firm, a medium-sized law firm, a one-hundred-plus attorney firm, and a county prosecutor's office. Compared with working in other types of law offices, Sherry says that she likes her position in a corporate law department the best.

LONG JOHN SILVER'S RESTAURANTS, INC.

Long John Silver's Restaurants, Inc., is a private corporation (i.e., it is not openly traded on the stock market). It owns Long John Silver's, Inc., which in turns owns and operates Long John Silver's Seafood restaurants nationwide. The first Long John Silver's restaurant opened in 1969. The restaurants specialize in serving fish and chicken. Long John Silver's, Inc., has 1,461 restaurants in 35 states across the United States. It also franchises restaurants in Canada, Saudi Arabia, Singapore, and Mexico. It employees 26,000 "team members" worldwide and in fiscal year 1993 it had worldwide sales of $900 million.

Nine hundred ninety-five of the restaurants are company owned and 466 are franchise restaurants. A franchise restaurant means that the business is operated by a person or group of persons other than Long John Silver's, Inc., pursuant to a franchise agreement.

Besides Long John Silver's, Inc., parent company's corporate headquarters in Lexington, it has three regional offices in Atlanta, Georgia; Overland Park, Kansas; and Dallas, Texas. The regional offices handle operational questions and problems. However, all legal questions are referred to the law department at corporate headquarters. Long John Silver's, Inc., is run by its president and management committee that are responsible to the board of directors.

CORPORATE LAW DEPARTMENT AT LONG JOHN SILVER'S

Long John Silver's corporate law department is located at the company's corporate headquarters in Lexington, Kentucky. The law department serves the corporate offices and the divisional offices and answers questions from managers of the restaurants. Questions from restaurant managers range from contractors not performing work to asking whose responsibility it is in a lease to do maintenance on the restaurant.

The law department has fourteen staff members: the general counsel, associate general counsel, three corporate counsel, four paralegals, three administrative assistants, one word processor, and a file clerk.

The general counsel, along with the associate general counsel, handles much of the legal work related to the corporation itself, including working with and answering questions from other officers of the corporation including the president. The associate general counsel also is responsible for running the law department daily.

The law department has two internal sections: real estate and litigation. Two attorneys and two paralegals (including Sherry) handle real estate matters. Sherry reports directly to one of the two real estate attorneys, but she receives work from both of them.

OUTSIDE COUNSEL

Because the company has restaurants in thirty-five states, the law department must use local attorneys in other states to help with specific legal problems in that state or use attorneys and law firms that specialize in specific types of cases. The company typically has many types of cases where legal counsel is used, including labor law, regulatory disputes, workers' compensation claims, contract disputes, and many others.

REAL ESTATE LAW

The law department handles many real estate matters, including the purchase or lease of space for its restaurants. Each of its regional offices has a real estate director whose responsibility is to find property that is appropriate to either purchase or lease for one of its restaurants. The real estate directors also will initially be responsible for beginning negotiations on a deal for the property. The initial deal will be reviewed by the Real Estate Committee made up of the two attorneys who handle real estate matters, the general counsel, and some of the company's executive officers including the company president. They meet and discuss the relative merits of each potential real estate deal. Once a decision has been made to initially accept the deal, it becomes an active case and the real estate attorneys begin working on the contract/lease and on negotiation and getting a contract signed.

WHAT SHERRY DOES IN THE REAL ESTATE AREA

Once a contract is negotiated but not yet signed, the contract is turned over to Sherry (or to the other paralegal in the department). Her job initially is to read the contract and prepare a summary of the deal/contract for the company's chief financial officer (CFO), who will sign the contract for the corporation. Once it is signed by the CFO, Sherry sends the contract to the other party for signature. Sherry then orders a title search on the property and tracks important dates in the contract including, when construction is to begin (i.e. for undeveloped property), when earnest money must be deposited, when lease payments are to begin, when building construction permits are due, and when an environmental assessment must be prepared.

Because the company aims to open fifty new restaurants a year, Sherry will have anywhere from twelve to fourteen new contracts pending at a time. These new deals are a top priority, but, in addition to the new deals, work also must be done on the existing contracts and leases. Sherry gets calls from restaurant managers every day that require her to have a contract or lease file pulled

from storage to review the lease/contract and to either answer the question or refer the matter to one of the attorneys so that the manager gets a timely response to her question.

Sherry also has many other duties. One of the other things she does is to prepare contracts regarding "bridge loans" for high-level employees. From time to time, employees of the corporation must move from one area of the country to another. To help the employee move, typically before his house can be sold, the company will give the employee a "bridge loan" so that he can buy a new house in the new city. Sherry prepares the mortgage document and promissory note to make the loan.

SHERRY'S PERSONAL PHILOSOPHIES AND HOW SHE PERFORMS HER JOB

Sherry's personal philosophy is to always give 110 percent on whatever job she does and to take pride in her work. Sherry also believes that honesty is a very important part of how she works at performing her job.

To actually perform her jobs, Sherry uses a computer with WordPerfect for Windows. She uses WordPerfect to type memos, letters, and other documents. Sherry also has many "forms" in WordPerfect that she simply has to complete. She also is beginning to learn to use Lotus 1-2-3. Sherry has secretarial support to help her, and she has a cubicle/partition to work in. Sherry uses a weekly calendar and "to do list" to help her keep track of deadlines and commitments. Another way she manages her caseload is to keep a checklist in every file she is working on so that she knows exactly what has to be done and where she is with any given matter.

Some skills that Sherry thinks are important for real estate legal assistants wanting to work in a corporate law department include having a "thick skin" (i.e. not taking comments by others too personally), having a good work ethic, paying attention to details, and taking criticism professionally.

HOW SHERRY'S CAREER PROGRESSED

"I originally began my legal career working for a small law office as a secretary," Sherry said. "After several years, one of the attorneys in the firm asked me if I ever thought about going to paralegal school. This law firm, which I will be forever grateful to, paid my tuition and books to get my paralegal degree. After a couple of years, I moved to Lexington and began working in the same job I am now, except that then the corporation was called Jerrico, Inc., instead of Long John Silver's Restaurants, Inc.

"After several years I left and went to work for a twenty attorney firm in Lexington doing real estate work. I prepared title reports and other real estate work for commercial, residential, and farm real estate matters.

"After several years I moved to Louisville where I worked for one of the largest firms in Kentucky that had more than one hundred attorneys. I then moved back to Lexington where I worked for a county attorney's office collecting child support payments. After ten months there I came back to work for this company doing real estate work for Long John Silver's restaurants. I am very happy here."

CORPORATE LAW DEPARTMENTS V. PRIVATE LAW PRACTICE AND GOVERNMENT PRACTICE

"One of the pluses of working for a corporate law department is that you do not have to keep or track billable time. It is a real advantage for me. Another advantage to working for a law department is that we only have one client. It takes a lot of work to treat every client like he or she is your only client. In addition, a corporate office can be a lot more of a relaxed place to work in, since the work load tends to be more predictable. We can do many things at our own pace. In contrast, a private law office can be very hectic where every client must be pleased. I think the corporate law department setting is ideal for me at this point in my life where I have two small children."

ETHICS

"Ethics and honesty are very important in my opinion even when you make mistakes. In my experience, 99 percent of the mistakes made can be corrected, so admit the mistake and fix it. The attorneys that I work with are really good about ethics. . . . I can bring them problems or questions,

and they will always help me work through them. It is really nice to work in this environment."

CONFIDENTIALITY IMPORTANT

"At Long John Silver's, confidentiality is very important. Many of our attorney's offices are enclosed in glass, so you can see into the office. We are not even allowed to tell someone in another department whether a particular person was in our office or an attorney's office. We also have several written policies on confidentiality."

GIVING LEGAL ADVICE

"It is common for restaurant managers and others to try to get legal opinions from me. I bet I have said a thousand times 'I am not an attorney and I cannot advise you.' Instead, I tell them that I will check with an attorney and get back with them."

WORKING WITH PEOPLE AND COMMUNICATION SKILLS

"We always try to work with people and are pleasant with everyone around us," Sherry said. "Even if we are taking our fiftieth phone call of the day and have seven other things to do, we always try to be nice to the person on the other end of the phone and to not become frustrated with them.

"Every year our divisional offices and field personnel rate our corporate departments as to how fast their questions are responded to and what quality of service they get, and the law department always has a high rating, so this is really important to our department.

"Communication within our department is also good. If I do not understand an assignment, I will always ask questions so that I understand exactly what I need to do, and the attorneys are always very good about making themselves available."

CONCLUSION

"At this point in my life, the law department at Long John Silver's is a perfect place for me to be. It provides a relaxed environment, allows me to do things at my own pace, and gives me flexibility that I may not have at a private law office."

QUESTIONS

1. The case study states that Sherry receives phone calls from restaurant managers every day regarding questions that she needs to either answer or refer to an attorney. All questions must be responded to in a timely manner. Sherry has routine, normal duties such as contracts she also is responsible for. Comment on your own ability to work multiple tasks at the same time. Do you think the ability to be organized plays a greater or lesser role in jobs that require people to work multiple tasks at the same time?

2. According to the case study, describe how working at a corporate law department differs from working at a private law practice. Why does Sherry prefer working at a corporate law department?

3. From the case study, describe why communication skills are so important to a legal assistant working in a corporate environment similar to Sherry's. List the different "clients" that Sherry must work with. Take into account the office she works in, how work is assigned to her, and the fact that she must handle legal questions from people all over the country.

KEY TERMS

Communication
Communication barrier
Noise

Feedback
Rephrasing
Groupthink

PROBLEM SOLVING QUESTIONS

1. You are a legal assistant in a legal aid office. The executive director calls you in his office to let you know that he has received complaints from clients regarding legal assistants being less than courteous on the phone and in person. The executive director gives you one week to begin turning this situation around. He mentions on his way out the door that in addition to a short-term solution, he wants a long-term solution to the problem. How would you proceed?

2. Over the years you have become friends with one of your law office's best clients. The client likes you and believes in your ability as a competent legal assistant. Recently, you have spent many hours, including evenings and weekends, working on the client's case. The client comes in for an appointment to see you about his case. The client notices that you look very tired and ragged. You tell the client how many hours you have been working on the case to let him know about the hard work that the law office is doing. The client responds by saying that he is going into the lead attorney on the case and demand that you be given an increase for all the extra time you have spent on the case. You are flattered that a client would think of your interest and you could certainly use the money. How would you handle this situation?

3. You are a legal assistant manager at a medium-size law office. The Executive Committee thinks that the law office needs to put more emphasis on client services. You are a respected part of the firm and the committee thinks you interact with clients exceptionally well. The committee has approved the development of a client manual that will be given to all its clients. The committee has chosen you to be in charge of developing the manual at the initial stages. Your task is to prepare a client manual that will be presented to the Executive Committee within thirty days. In addition, once the committee approves the manual, you also will be in charge of implementing the manual's use. The committee is giving you control to research and develop the manual.

Assume you have never heard of or developed a client manual before. Assume you can choose to either accept the task or not accept it. Would you accept the assignment? Why or why not? How would you develop the client manual? Would you choose to use a work group or not? What sections or key points would you include in the manual? Give reasons for your answers.

KNOW YOUR ETHICS

1. From an ethical perspective, only analyze what the benefits are to a law office that routinely sends copies of all documents to its clients.

2. From an ethics perspective, differentiate between a law office that keeps a client informed and a law office that does not communicate with its clients. How do you think the client feels about the law office that does not communicate with her?

3. As a legal assistant in a busy office, you try your best to talk to clients when they call and to pass along information from the client to your supervising attorney, but sometimes you forget. On one such occasion a client called you because she was unable to talk to the attorney. The client called with vital information that the attorney needed regarding an important aspect of the case. Unfortunately, you failed to pass the information along. Discuss from an ethics and malpractice standpoint the importance of communication skills.

PRACTICE EXERCISES

1. Think of someone you know that you think is a good leader. Write down why you think this person is a good leader and what outstanding qualities she has. How do the qualities listed compare with the information in the chapter? What leadership qualities do you have?

2. Think about a group or committee that you have worked on. Write down the dynamics of how the group interacted. Who emerged as the leader and why? Looking back, do you see any evidence of groupthink? Did the group members communicate with each other effectively? Was the group successful at accomplishing its purpose? Why or why not? Did you feel like an active member of the group? Why or why not? If you could have changed one thing about the group, what would it have been?

NOTES

1. Adapted from Robert Michael Greene, *Making Partner* (Chicago: American Bar Association, copyright © 1992). Reprinted with permission.
2. Deborah Heller and James M. Hunt, *Practicing Law and Managing People* (Salem, N.H.: Butterworth, 1988), 209.
3. Louis E. Boone and David L. Kurtz, *Management,* 3d ed. (New York: Random House Business Division, 1987), 461.
4. Heller and Hunt, *Practicing Law and Managing People,* 210.
5. Milton W. Zwicker, "How to Be a Leader, Not a Boss," *Leadership & Management,* Newsletter of the Law Practice Management Section of the ABA, February 15, 1991.
6. Boone and Kurtz, *Management,* 180.
7. Ibid.
8. Ibid.

TIMEKEEPING AND BILLING

CHAPTER OBJECTIVES

After you read this chapter, you will be able to:

- Differentiate between timekeeping and billing.

- Recognize major types of legal fee agreements.

- Know the difference between billable and nonbillable time.

- Explain the concept of leveraging.

- Explain how to set an hourly billing rate using the Rule of Three.

- Discuss how the billing process works and what it entails.

- Differentiate between an earned and an unearned retainer.

When a Chicago-based law firm submitted its bill, the client company suspected something might have been wrong. Years later, an audit revealed that the invoice included nontechnical deposition summaries by paralegals at four to five pages per hour. The usual rate is twenty to twenty-five pages an hour. The paralegals were apparently working at 20 percent to 25 percent the normal rate, so the client company was being billed four times what it should have been for that service.[1]

A federal grand jury indicted two men allegedly conspiring to defraud an insurance company by having tens of thousands of dollars in checks issued for expenses and legal services that were never provided. The defendants are a former litigation supervisor for the insurance company and a former partner in the law firm representing the company. The grand jury indicted them on one felony count of conspiracy, three felony counts of mail fraud, and twenty felony counts of wire fraud as a result of checks written between May 1987 and July 1991.[2]

THE DIFFERENCE BETWEEN TIMEKEEPING AND BILLING

timekeeping
The process of tracking how attorneys and legal assistants use their time.

In the legal environment, **timekeeping** *is the process of tracking how attorneys and legal assistants use their time.* The obvious reason private attorneys and legal assistants keep track of their time is to bill clients. However, many corporate, government, and legal aid practices also keep time records for other reasons. Timekeeping can be used to manage and oversee what cases attorneys and legal assistants are working on and whether they are spending too much time or too little time on certain cases. Timekeeping can be used to evaluate the performance of attorneys and legal assistants and can be used in determining promotions and raises. Timekeeping also can be used to evaluate what types of cases are the most beneficial and profitable for the office.

Billing *is the process of issuing invoices for the purpose of collecting monies for legal services performed and being reimbursed for expenses.* The lifeblood of any organization depends on its ability to raise cash and be paid for the services it renders. In most cases, private law practices must be able to generate billings on at least a monthly basis to generate the cash they need to meet their expenses such as rent, utilities, and salaries. Attorneys and legal assistants in corporate and government practices also need to know about billing to ensure that when they hire outside counsel (private law firms), the corporation or government gets the most for its money.

billing
The process of issuing invoices for the purpose of collecting monies for legal services performed and being reimbursed for expenses.

WHY DO LEGAL ASSISTANTS NEED TO KNOW TIMEKEEPING AND BILLING?

There are several reasons why legal assistants need to know about timekeeping and billing. In most private law practices, legal assistants are required to track their time so it can be charged to the case(s) they are working on. Many law practices require legal assistants to bill a minimum number of hours a year. A 1991 survey of attorneys and legal assistants found that legal assistants were expected to bill about 1,410 hours annually. However, a 1993 survey of legal assistants found that legal assistants were expected to bill 1,519 hours.[3] Thus, it is necessary for legal assistants to understand how timekeeping and billing works. **Legal assistants are sometimes discharged from their jobs because they fail to charge the required number of hours**. The issue of tracking time and billing a minimum number of hours is very important in many offices.

In addition, legal assistants are sometimes put in charge of actually running the timekeeping and billing system, including managing the timekeeping process, and generating bills. This usually occurs in smaller law offices. In those cases, it is important for them not only to know the process but also to know how to actually run and operate the system. Timekeeping and billing are important issues, since the survival of law offices depends on their ability to track and bill time. However, before exploring the fundamentals of timekeeping and billing in depth, you first need a background in legal fee agreements, legal expenses, and trust accounts.

KINDS OF LEGAL FEE AGREEMENTS

Legal fees can be structured in many different ways. The kind of legal fee depends on the type of case or client matter, the specific circumstances of each particular client, and the law practice's preference toward certain types of fee agreements. Fee agreements can be hourly rate fees, contingency fees, flat fees, retainer fees, and others.

HOURLY RATE FEES

hourly rate fee
A fee for legal services that is billed to the client by the hour at an agreed-upon rate.

An **hourly rate fee** *is a fee for legal services that is billed to the client by the hour, at an agreed-upon rate.* For example, suppose a client hires an attorney to draft a business contract. The client agrees to pay $100 for every hour the attorney spends drafting the contract and advising the client. If the attorney spent four hours working on the contract, the client would owe the attorney $400 ($100 times 4 hours equals $400).

Hourly rate agreements can be complicated. Law offices have several specific types of hourly rate contracts, including:

- Attorney or legal assistant hourly rate;
- Client hourly rate;
- Blended hourly rate fee;
- Activity hourly rate.

Some law practices use a combination of these to bill clients.

attorney or legal assistant hourly rate
Fee based on the attorney's or legal assistant's level of expertise and experience in a particular area.

ATTORNEY OR LEGAL ASSISTANT HOURLY RATE *The* **attorney** *or* **legal assistant hourly rate** *is based on the attorney's or legal assistant's level of expertise and experience in a particular area.* Figure 5-1 is an example of this type of contract. If a partner or shareholder worked on a case, her hourly rate charge might be considerably more than that of an associate or legal assistant's hourly rate charge. Partners typically can earn from $150 to $400 an hour or more compared with associates who might work for $100 to $175 an hour. Legal assistants typically charge from $40 to $65 an hour. The difference in price is based on the expertise and experience of the individual working on the case and on locally acceptable rates. In this type of fee agreement, it is possible for a client to be billed at several different rates in a given period if several attorneys or legal assistants work on a matter, since they all may have different rates.

client hourly rate
Fee based on one hourly charge for the client, regardless of which attorney works on the case and what he does on the case.

CLIENT HOURLY RATE *The* **client hourly rate** *method is based on only hourly charge for the client, regardless of which attorney works on the case and what he does on the case.* For example, if an insurance company hired a law practice to represent it, the insurance company and the law practice might negotiate on a client hourly charge of $125 per hour for attorneys and $60 an hour for legal assistants. This means that no matter which attorney or legal assistant works on the case, whether the attorney or legal assistant has one year's or twenty years' experience, and regardless of what the attorney or legal assistant does (e.g., making routine phone calls or appearing in court), the insurance company would be charged $125 an hour for attorney time or $60 an hour for legal assistant time.

blended hourly rate fee
One hourly rate that is set taking into account the blend or mix of attorneys working on the matter.

BLENDED HOURLY RATE FEE *A* **blended hourly rate fee** *is one hourly rate that is set taking into account the blend or mix of law office staff working on the matter. The "mix" includes the mix among associates, partners, and sometimes legal assistants working on the matter.* Some states only allow the "blend" to include associates and partners, while other states allow legal assistants to be included. The advantage to this is that billing is simpler, since there is one rate for all legal assistant and attorney time spent on the case. The bill is easier for the law office to produce and easier for the client to read. Some states will allow legal assistants to have their own "blend" and have one rate for all legal assistants whether experienced or inexperienced.

HOURLY RATE CONTRACT FOR LEGAL SERVICES

This contract for legal services is entered into by and between H. Thomas Weber (hereinafter "Client") and Johnson, Beck & Taylor (hereinafter "Attorneys") on this _____ day of December, 199_. The following terms and conditions constitute the entirety of the agreement between Attorneys and Client and said agreement supersedes and is wholly separate and apart from any previous written or oral agreements.

1. Client hereby agrees to employ Attorneys and Attorneys hereby agree to represent Client in connection with a contract dispute in Jefferson County District Court of Client's claim against Westbridge Manufacturing.
2. Client agrees to pay a retainer fee of $2,000.00, which will be held in Attorney's trust account until earned.
3. Client agrees to pay associate attorneys at **$100.00** per hour, partners at **$150** per hour, legal assistants at **$50.00** per hour and senior legal assistants at **$65.00** per hour for legal services rendered regarding the matter in paragraph one. Attorneys are not hereby obligated to take an appeal from any judgment at the trial court level; if an occasion for an appeal arises, Attorneys and Client hereby expressly agree that employment for such an appeal must be arranged by a separate contract between Attorneys and Client.
4. Client agrees to reimburse Attorneys for all expenses incurred in connection with said matter; and, Client agrees to advance all expenses requested by Attorneys during the duration of this contract. Client understands that he is ultimately responsible for the payment of all expenses incurred in connection with this matter.
5. Client understands that Attorneys will bill Client periodically (usually on a monthly or quarterly basis, depending on how quickly the case moves through the system) for copying costs at the rate of $.25 cents per copy, postage and handling costs, long-distance telephone costs, travel costs, and other costs, and that Client is obligated to make payments upon said billing for said fees and expenses described at paragraphs (2), (3) and (4) above, or otherwise satisfy said fees and expenses. Attorneys will also bill Client for all deposition costs incurred and Client is solely responsible for said deposition costs and Client will be required to advance the sum of $1,500.00 (or more as necessary) for trial costs (including subpoenas, travel costs, and preparation costs) once the case is set for trial.
6. Client understands and agrees that this litigation may take two to five years or longer to complete and that he will make himself available for Attorneys to confer with and generally to assist Attorneys in said matter. Client agrees he will not discuss the matter of his litigation with any unauthorized person at any time or in any way. Client understands and agrees that Attorneys may withdraw from representation of Client upon proper notice. Client further understands that he can apply for judicial review and approval of this fee agreement if he so desires.
7. Client agrees that associate counsel may be employed at the discretion of Attorneys and that any attorney so employed may be designated to appear on Client's behalf and undertake Client's representation in this matter and such representation shall be upon the same terms as set out herein. **Client understands that Attorneys cannot and do not guarantee any particular or certain relief and expressly state that they cannot promise or guarantee Client will receive any money damages or money settlement.**

(continued)

FIGURE 5-1   Attorney/Legal Assistant Hourly Rate Contract

The undersigned hereby voluntarily executes this agreement with a full understanding of same and without coercion or duress. All agreements contained herein are severable and in the event any of them shall be deemed to be invalid by any competent court, this contract shall be interpreted as if such invalid agreements or covenants were not contained herein. Client acknowledges receiving a fully executed copy of this contract.

Date _____ _____

Date   Johnson, Beck & Taylor
NOTE: THIS IS ONLY AN EXAMPLE AND IS NOT INTENDED TO BE A FORM, CHECK WITH YOUR STATE BAR FOR A PROPER FORM.

---

activity hourly rate
Fee based on the different hourly rates depending on what type of service or activity is actually performed.

ACTIVITY HOURLY RATE *An* **activity hourly rate** *is based on the different hourly rates depending on what type of service or activity is actually performed.* For example, offices using this approach might bill attorney time to clients as follows:

Court appearances	$200 per hour
Legal research by attorneys	$150 per hour
Drafting by attorneys	$100 per hour
Telephone calls by attorneys	$75 per hour
Legal research by legal assistants	$60 per hour
Drafting by legal assistants	$50 per hour

This is sliding-scale hourly fee based on the difficulty of an activity. Hourly rate agreements, no matter what the type, are the most common kind of fee agreement.

CONTINGENCY FEES

contingency fee
Fee collected if the attorney successfully represents the client.

A **contingency fee** *is a fee that is collected if the attorney successfully represents the client. The attorney is entitled to a certain percentage of the total amount of money awarded to the client. If the client's case is not won, and no money is recovered, the attorney collects no legal fees but is still entitled to be reimbursed for all expenses incurred* (see Figure 5-2). Contingency fees are typically used in representing plaintiffs in personal injury cases, workers' compensation cases, civil rights cases, medical malpractice, and other types of cases in which monetary damages are generated. The individual who would like to bring the lawsuit usually has little or no money to pay legal fees up front. Contingency fees typically range from twenty percent to fifty percent.

For example, suppose a client hires an attorney to file a personal injury claim regarding an automobile accident the client was in. The client has no money but agrees to pay the attorney 20 percent of any money that is recovered (plus legal expenses) before the case is filed, 25 percent of any money recovered after the case is filed but before trial, and 33 percent of any money recovered during trial or after appeal. Suppose the claim is settled after the case is filed but before trial for $10,800. Suppose that the legal expenses the attorney incurred were $800. Under most state laws, legal expenses are paid first and then the contingency fee is calculated. The attorney would deduct the expenses off the top and the remaining $10,000 would be divided according to contingency fee agreement. Because the suit was settled after the case was filed but before the trial, the attorney would be

CONTINGENCY FEE CONTRACT FOR LEGAL SERVICES

Date:

Name: D.O.B.

Address: Phone:

1. I hereby employ **Johnson, Beck & Taylor** (hereinafter "attorneys") to perform legal services in connection with the following matter as described below:

    Personal injury claims arising out of an automobile accident which occurred January 12, 1993, on Interstate I-70.

2. I agree to pay a nonrefundable retainer fee of $1,000; plus,

3. I agree attorneys will receive ____ 20% of any recovery, if prior to filing suit;

    I agree attorneys will receive ____ 25% of any recovery, if prior to pretrial conference;

    I agree attorneys will receive ____ 33% of any recovery, if after first trial begins;

    I agree attorneys will receive ____ 33% of any recovery, if after appeal or second trial begins.

    Attorneys are not hereby obligated to take an appeal from any judgment at the trial court level; if an occasion for an appeal arises, attorneys and client hereby expressly agree that employment for such an appeal will be arranged by a separate contract between these parties. Further, I agree that attorneys will be entitled to the applicable above-mentioned percentage of recovery minus whatever a court may award, if I am a prevailing party and the court awards fees following my request therefor.

4. As to the expenses of litigation: I agree to reimburse attorneys for all expenses incurred in connection with said matter, and any expenses not fully paid as incurred may be deducted from my portion of any recovery. I agree to advance any and all expenses requested by attorneys during the duration of this contract. I agree to make an advance of expenses upon execution of this contract in the amount of $ 500.00. I understand that these litigation expenses do not pertain to the retainer fee or percentage of any recovery, and I am ultimately responsible for the payment of all litigation expenses.

5. I understand that attorneys will bill client periodically, and that client is obligated to make payments upon said billing for said fees and expenses described at paragraphs (2), and (4), or otherwise satisfy said fees and expenses.

6. I understand and agree that this litigation may take 2 to 5 years, or longer to complete, and that I will make myself available for attorneys to confer with, and generally to assist attorneys in said matter. I will not discuss the matter of my litigation with an unauthorized person at any time in any way. I understand and agree that attorneys may withdraw from representation of client at any time upon proper notice.

7. I agree that associate counsel may be employed at the discretion of Johnson, Beck & Taylor, and that any attorney so employed may be designated to appear on my behalf and undertake my representation in this matter and such representation shall be upon the same terms as set out herein. Attorneys have **not** guaranteed, nor can they guarantee, any particular or certain relief.

The undersigned herewith executes this agreement with a full understanding of same, without coercion or duress, and understands the same to be the only agreement between the parties with regard to the above matter, and that if any other terms are to be added to this contract, the same will not be binding, unless and until they are reduced to writing and signed by all parties to this contract. I acknowledge receiving a fully executed copy of this contract. Further, the undersigned Client under-

(continued)

FIGURE 5-2   Contingency Fee Contract

stands that said Client is entitled to apply for judicial review and approval of this fee agreement, if Client so desires.

Date _____   _____

Date _____   Johnson, Beck & Taylor _____
NOTE: THIS IS ONLY AN EXAMPLE AND IS NOT INTENDED TO BE A FORM, CHECK YOUR STATE BAR FOR A PROPER FORM.

entitled to receive 25 percent of any recovery. The attorney would be entitled to $2,500, and the client would be entitled to 75 percent, or $7,500 (see Figure 5-3).

Contingency fee agreements must be in writing. Figure 5-2 contains a sample contingency fee contract. Some states put a cap or a maximum percentage on what an attorney can collect in areas such as workers' compensation and medical malpractice claims. For example , some states prevent attorneys from receiving more than a 25 percent contingency in a workers' compensation case. Contingency fees by their nature are risky, because if no money is recovered, the attorney receives no fee. However, even if no money is recovered, the client must still pay legal expenses such as filing fees and photocopying. Contingency fees and hourly fees

FIGURE 5-3
Contingency Fee
Example

Written Contingency Fee Agreement Provisions
Attorney receives
- 20% of any money recovered (plus legal expenses) before case is filed;
- 25% of any money recovered (plus legal expenses) after case is filed but before trial;
- 33% of any money recovered (plus legal expenses) during trial or after appeal.

Settlement
Case is settled for $10,800 after case is filed but before trial.
Attorney has $800 worth of legal expenses.

Calculation of Contingency Fee
1. Legal expenses are paid first.

Settlement of	$10,800
Minus Legal Expenses	- 800
Balance	$10,000

2. Contingency fee is calculated as follows:

Total recovery minus legal expenses	$10,000
Attorney's 25% Contingency Fee ($10,000 x 25% = $2,500)	- 2,500
TOTAL TO CLIENT	$7,500

3. Total Fees and Expenses to Attorney.

Reimbursement of Legal Expense	$ 800
Contingency Fee	$ 2,500
TOTAL TO ATTORNEY	$ 3,300

also may be used together. Some offices reduce their hourly fee and charge a contingency fee.

FLAT FEE

A **flat fee** *is a fee for legal services that is billed as a flat or fixed amount.* Some offices have a set fee for handling certain types of matters, such as preparing a will, or handling an uncontested divorce, a name change, or a bankruptcy (see Figure 5-4). For example, suppose a client agreed to pay an attorney a flat fee of $200 to prepare a will. No matter how many hours the attorney spends preparing the will, the fee is still $200. Flat fee agreements are usually used when a legal matter is simple, straightforward, and involves few risks.

    Figure 5-5 shows a comparison of different methods of billing for drafting a routine or standard will. In routine matters, flat rates will typically be the least expensive for the client. In addition, flat rates and the blended methods are typically the easiest types of bills to both prepare and read.

flat fee
A fee for legal services that is billed as a flat or fixed amount.

RETAINER FEES

The word "retainer" has several meanings in the legal environment. Generally "retainer" fees are monies paid by the client at the beginning of a case or matter. However, there are many types of retainers. When an attorney or legal assistant uses the term "retainer," it could mean a retainer for general representation, a case retainer, a pure retainer, or a cash advance. In addition, all retainer fees are either "earned" or "unearned."

⌐ PRICE LIST ⌐

Initial Consultation with Branch Lawyer.......... $50.00

REAL ESTATE

Divorce - Uncontested...............................499.00
Domestic contracts and family litigation vary according to time involved.

REAL ESTATE

Purchase or Sale of House...........................499.00
Each Mortgage—Additional..........................199.00
Each Discharge of Mortgage—Additional........150.00
Refinancing...399.00

WILLS & ESTATES

Basic Will... 99.00
Estates, administrations, and estate litigation vary according to time involved

BUSINESS

Consultation...................................75.00—150.00
Incorporation...499.00
We provide many other business services, including:
- Commercial Leases
- Purchase and Sale of Businesses
- Trade Marks & Copyright

ADDITIONAL SERVICES

Collection—demand letter.............................150.00
Notarization (per signature)............................20.00
Power of Attorney / Promissory Note...............50.00

⌐ PAYMENT POLICY ⌐

We require a retainer before commencing work on your behalf, which amount is paid into trust. We then draw checks on the retainer to pay out-of-pocket expenses made on your behalf and our fees.

We will advise you of completion of our services to you and ask you to come in and pick up the documentation involved and pay any balance owing at the same time.

In real estate transactions the balance must be paid prior to closing. In litigation and criminal matters, any outstanding account and the estimated fee for the appearance must be paid prior to the court appearance.

FIGURE 5-4   Flat Fee Price List

Activities Provided:

1. Legal assistant interviews client (office conference) regarding the law office drafting a will for client. Legal assistant gets background information including financial holdings, heirs, family tree, etc . . . . .1.50 hours
2. Legal assistant drafts memo to Attorney itemizing the conference with client . . . . .0.25 hours
3. Attorney reads the legal assistant's memo and talk with client on the telephone . . .0.25 hours
4. Attorney conducts legal research, prepares a draft of the will that meets the expectations of the client . . . . .1.0 hours
5. Client reviews will and has office conference with attorney; attorney discusses client's changes to the will, makes client's changes to the will, and the will is executed, witnessed, and notarized . . . . .1.0 hours

                                   TOTAL HOURS . . . . .4.0 hours

- **CLIENT HOURLY RATE:**
Assume attorney agrees to charge the client to prepare the will for his time as follows:
- $80.00 an hour for the attorney's time;
- $40.00 an hour for the legal assistant's time.
TOTAL COST $250
(Legal Asst. 1.75 hours × $40 = $70; Atty 2.25 × $80 an hour = $180; $70 + $180 = $250)
- **ATTORNEY/LEGAL ASSISTANT HOURLY RATE:**
- Assume the attorney is an associate attorney and her normal hourly rate is $100.00.
- Assume the legal assistant assigned to the case has a normal hourly rate of $55.00.
TOTAL COST $321.25
(Legal Asst. 1.75 hours × $55 = $96.25; Atty 2.25 × $100 an hour = $225; $96.25 + $225 = $321.25)
- **BLENDED (Attorneys and Legal Assistant) HOURLY RATE:**
- Assume blended hourly rate for all attorney and legal assistant time is $70 an hour.
TOTAL COST $280 (4 hours x $70 = $280).
ACTIVITY HOURLY RATE
Assume:
- Legal Assistant Office Conference Rate is $40.00 an hour/Attorney's is $80.00;
- Legal Assistant Time for Drafting Memo is $30.00 and hour/Attorney's is $60.00;
- Attorney Time for Phone Conferences is $60 an hour;
- Attorney Time for Drafting Pleadings, Will, etc., is $100 an hour.
TOTAL COST $262.50
1.50 × $40 = $60.00; .25 × $30 = $7.50; .25 × $60 = $15; 1.0 × $100 = $100; 1.0 × $80 = $80; Total $262.50
FLAT FEE RATE:
Assume attorney and client agree on a flat rate of $200.00 to prepare the will.
TOTAL COST $200.00
CONTINGENCY RATE: $0.00 (No monetary recovery—not applicable)

FIGURE 5-5   Comparison of Legal Fees

EARNED V. UNEARNED RETAINERS   There is a <u>very</u> important difference between an earned retainer and an unearned retainer. *An **earned retainer** means that the law office or attorney has earned the money and is entitled to deposit the money in the office's or attorney's own bank account and can use it to pay the attorney's or law office's operating expenses such as salaries.*

An **unearned retainer** *is monies that are paid up front by the client as an advance against the attorney's future fees and expenses as a kind of down payment. Until the monies are actually earned by the attorney or law office, they belong to the client. According to ethical rules, unearned retainers may <u>not</u> be deposited in the attorney's or law office's normal operating checking account. Unearned retainers must be deposited into a <u>separate</u> trust account and can be transferred into the firm account as it is earned.*

A **trust** or **escrow account** *is a separate bank account, apart from a law office's or attorney's operating checking account, where unearned client funds are deposited.* As an attorney or law office begins to earn an unearned retainer by providing legal services to the client, the attorney can then bill the client and move the earned portion from the trust account to her own law office operating account.

The written contract should set out whether the retainer is "earned" or "unearned." However, in some instances the contract may be vague on this point. Typically, when a contract refers to a "nonrefundable retainer," this means an "earned retainer."

Additionally, in many contracts, "flat fee rates" as discussed earlier are said to be "nonrefundable" and thus have been treated as "earned." However, some state ethical rules regulate this area heavily, so it depends on the state. Some state ethical rules hold that all flat fees are a retainer, have been unearned, and must be placed in trust until they are earned. Whether a retainer is earned or unearned will depend on your state's ethical rules and on the written contract.

CASH ADVANCE RETAINER   One type of retainer is a cash advance. *A **cash advance** is unearned monies and is an advance against the attorney's future fees and expenses. Until the cash advance is earned by the attorney, it actually belongs to the client.* The cash advance is a typical type of unearned retainer.

For example, suppose a client wishes to hire an attorney to litigate a contract dispute. The attorney agrees to represent the client only if the client agrees to pay $150 an hour with a $2,500 cash advance against fees and expenses. The attorney must deposit the $2,500 in a trust account. If the attorney deposits the cash advance in his own account (whether it is the firm's account or the attorney's own personal account), the attorney has violated several ethical rules. As the attorney works on the case and bills the client for fees and expenses, the attorney will write himself a check out of the trust account for the amount of the billing. The attorney must tell the client that he is withdrawing the money and keep an accurate balance of how much the client has left in trust. So, if after a month the attorney billed the client for $500, the attorney would write himself a check for $500 from the trust account, deposit the $500 in the attorney's or the firm's own bank account, and inform the client that there was a remaining balance of $2,000 in trust. Look closely at the "payment policy" in Figure 5-4. The firm in Figure 5-4 requires a cash advance before it will take any case. Also, recognize that if the cases ended at this point, the client would be entitled to a refund of the remaining $2,000 in trust.

RETAINER FOR GENERAL REPRESENTATION   Another type of "retainer" is a **retainer for general representation**. *This type of retainer is typically used when*

earned retainer
Term for the money the law office or attorney has earned and is entitled to deposit in the office's or attorney's own bank account.

unearned retainer
Monies that are paid up front by the client as an advance against the attorney's future fees and expenses. Until the monies are actually earned by the attorney or law office, they actually belong to the client.

trust or **escrow account**
A separate bank account, apart from a law office's or attorney's operating checking account, where unearned client funds are deposited.

case advance
Unearned monies that are an advance against the attorney's future fees and expenses.

retainer for general representation
Retainer typically used when a client such as a corporation or school board requires continuing legal services throughout the year.

a client such as a corporation or entity requires continuing legal services throughout the year.[4] The client pays an amount, typically up front or on a prearranged schedule, to receive these ongoing services. For example, suppose a small school board would like to be able to contact an attorney at any time with general legal questions. The attorney and school board could enter into this type of agreement for a fee of $2,000 every six months, and the school board could contact the attorney at any time and ask general questions and the attorney would never receive more than the $2,000 for the six-month period. Retainers for general representation allow the client to negotiate and anticipate what her fee will be for the year. This type of agreement usually only covers general legal advice and would not include matters such as litigation (see Figure 5-6). Depending on the specific arrangements between the client and the attorney, and on the specific ethical rules in your state, many retainers for general representation are viewed as being earned, since the client can call at any time and get legal advice. Retainers for general representation resemble a flat fee agreement. The difference is that in a flat fee agreement, the attorney or law office is contracting to do a specific thing for a client such as prepare a will or file a bankruptcy. In the case of a retainer for general representation, the attorney is agreeing to make himself available to the client for all nonlitigation needs.

case retainer
A fee that is billed at the beginning of a matter, is not refundable to the client, and is usually paid at the beginning of the case as an incentive for the office to take the case.

CASE RETAINER Another type of retainer is a **case retainer**, *which is a fee that is billed at the beginning of a matter, is not refundable to the client, and is usually paid to the office at the beginning of the case as an incentive for the office to take the case.* For

**FIGURE 5-6
Retainer for General Representation Agreement**

Source: Adapted from Mary Ann Altman and Robert I. Weil, *How to Manage Your Law Office*, Matthew Bender, 1986, 4–6. Reprinted with the permission of Altman Weil Pensa Publications, Inc., copyright 1991 by Altman Weil Pensa Publications, Inc.

Ms. Gloria Smith, Chairperson
Unified School District
No. 453 School Board

   Subject: General Representation of the USD No. 453 School Board

Dear Ms. Smith:

Thank you for your letter informing us that the School Board would like to place our law firm on a general retainer of $_____ for the coming year. We will bill on a quarterly basis for the retainer plus any expenses incurred.

The retainer will include general advice concerning business operations, personnel questions, taxing questions, legislative initiative, and attendance at all Board meetings. It will not cover litigated matters requiring appearances at boards or commisions, court or state administrative agencies. Should any of the excluded services appear to be necessary, we shall be happy to discuss the cost of these services with you.

It is our hope that the knowledge that we are ready to serve you under the retainer will provide you with regular advice to avoid any serious problems or litigation. Please sign this letter and return it to us. If you have any questions, please feel free to give me a call.

Kindest Regards,

Sandra W. Johnson,
JOHNSON, BECK & TAYLOR

Accepted for Unified School District No. 453 School Board, by:

_____
Gloria Smith, Chairperson

example, a client comes to an attorney with a criminal matter. The attorney agrees to take on the case only if the client agrees to pay a case retainer of $500 up front plus $100 an hour for every hour worked on the case. The $500 is paid to the attorney as an incentive to take the case and thus is earned. The $100 an hour is a client hourly basis charge. Because the case retainer is earned, the attorney can immediately deposit it in the office's own bank account.

Another example of a case retainer is in a case involving a contingency fee. Suppose a client comes to an attorney to file a civil rights case. The attorney agrees to accept the case only if the client agrees to a 30 percent contingency fee and a nonrefundable or case retainer of $1,000. Again, the earned retainer is an incentive for the attorney to take the case and can be deposited in the attorney's or the office's own bank account.

PURE RETAINER   A rather rare type of retainer is a **pure retainer**. A pure retainer *obligates the law office to be available to represent the client throughout the time period agreed upon.* The part that distinguishes a pure retainer from a retainer for general representation is that the office typically must agree to not represent any of the client's competitors or to undertake any type of adverse representation to the client. Some clients, typically major corporations, think that listing the name of a prestigious law firm as counsel has a business value that they are willing to pay for.[5]

Retainers for general representation, case retainers, and pure retainers are usually earned retainers and a cash advance is an unearned retainer. However, the language of the contract will determine whether amounts paid to attorneys up front are earned or unearned. The earned/unearned distinction is extremely important and is one reason all fee agreements should be in writing.

pure retainer
A fee that obligates the office to be available to represent the client throughout the time period agreed upon.

COURT AWARDED FEES

Court awarded fees are another type of "fee agreement." *In certain federal and state statutes, the prevailing party (i.e., the party that wins the case) is given the right to recover from the opposing side reasonable attorney's fees. The amount of the attorney's fees are decided by the court.* This is called **court awarded fees**. Court awarded fees are provided for in civil rights law, antitrust, civil racketeering, and other statutes. The prevailing party must submit to the court detailed time records showing specifically how much time was spent on the case. If the prevailing law office did not keep such records, the court will not award fees. The purpose of court awarded fees is to encourage potential plaintiffs in public interest issues to pursue legitimate claims while discouraging frivolous claims. For example, if an employee brought a sexual harassment suit against an employer and subsequently won the suit, the employee's attorneys would be entitled to receive reasonable attorney's fees from the defendant.

court awarded fees
Fees given to the prevailing parties pursuant to certain federal and state statutes.

PREPAID LEGAL SERVICES

A prepaid legal service plan is another type of "fee agreement." **Prepaid legal service** *is a plan that a person can purchase that entitles the person to receive legal services (as enumerated in the plan) either free or at a greatly reduced rate.* In some cases, corporations or labor unions, for example, provide a prepaid legal service plan to its employees as a fringe benefit. For instance, if a person who is a member of a prepaid legal service plan needed a will drafted, that person would go to either an attorney employed by the prepaid plan or a private attorney that the prepaid plan contracted with and get the will drafted free of charge or at a greatly reduced rate.

prepaid legal service
A plan that a person can purchase that entitles the person to receive legal services either free or at a greatly reduced rate.

A Word About Value Billing

Recently, much has been written (in the legal press) about why private law practices should stop billing by the hour and use a different billing method. The reasons for the change from hourly billing include: a) the client never knows during any stage of the work how much the total legal fee will be; b) clients sometimes avoid calling legal assistants and attorneys because they know they will be charged for the time, even if it is a simple phone call; c) clients have trouble seeing the relationship between what is performed by the legal assistant or attorney and the enormous fees that can be generated; d) hourly billing encourages lawyers and legal assistants to be inefficient (i.e. the longer it takes to perform a job, the more revenue they earn); e) finally, many law offices force attorneys and legal assistants to bill a quota number of hours a year, which puts a tremendous amount of pressure on the individual legal assistant and attorney and may lead to burnout. A recent Louis Harris poll found that although 90 percent of legal services are compensated by billable hours, 68 percent of the lawyers surveyed want to be paid based on the value and quality of their work.[6]

value billing
A type of fee agreement that is based not just on the time required to perform the work but also on the complexity of the matter and the expertise of the attorneys required to perform it.

So what is value billing? *The* **value billing** *concept represents a type of fee agreement that is based not just on the time required to perform the work but also on the complexity of the matter and the expertise of the attorneys required to perform it. Value billing typically provides that the attorney and client reach a consensus on the amount of fees to be charged.* Because of the increased competition in the legal environment and because of the power of the client as a buyer, clients are demanding that they have a say in how much they are going to pay for legal services, what type of service will be provided, and what the quality of the legal services will be for the price.

The Ethics of Timekeeping and Billing

There are more timekeeping- and billing-related ethical complaints filed against attorneys and law offices than all other types of complaints. It is important that legal assistants completely understand the ethics of timekeeping and billing. In years past, timekeeping and billing complaints were viewed as simply "misunderstandings" between the client and the law office. In the early 1980s, state bars viewed timekeeping and billing disputes as having major ethical implications for attorneys. That is, such disputes were simply not misunderstandings, but law offices were sometimes flagrantly violating ethical rules regarding money issues.

Recently, as discussed further in this chapter, timekeeping and billing complaints by clients are leading not just to ethical complaints against attorneys but are also turning into criminal fraud charges filed against attorneys and legal assistants.

ETHICAL CONSIDERATIONS REGARDING LEGAL FEE AGREEMENTS

There are several important ethical considerations that need to be stressed about fee agreements. The first is that **all fee agreements should be in writing**, especially when a contingency fee is involved. Second, contingency fees should not be used in criminal or domestic-relation matters.

FEE AGREEMENTS SHOULD BE IN WRITING

It is highly recommended that as a matter of course all fee agreements be in writing. The days of a handshake between an attorney and the client are long over. There is no substitute for reducing all fee agreements to writing. If the firm and the client have a dispute over fees, there will be no document to clarify the understanding between the parties. The *Model Rules of Professional Conduct* state at 1.5 (b):

> (b) When the lawyer has not regularly represented the client [i.e. the lawyer has never represented the client before], the basis or rate of the fee shall be communicated to the client, preferably in writing, before or within a reasonable time after commencing the representation.

Although the *Model Rules* state that the agreement "preferably" be in writing, nearly every authority on this subject, as well as most attorneys who have been in business long, will tell you that the agreement absolutely should be in writing to protect both the attorney and the client. The reasons legal fee agreements should be in writing are that:

a) Clients file more ethical complaints against attorneys and law offices for fee disputes than for any other type of complaint;

b) The client and the attorney may (will) forget what the exact fee agreement was unless it is reduced to writing;

c) In a factual dispute regarding a fee between a client and an attorney, the evidence is typically construed in the light most favorable to the client.

CONTINGENCY FEE AGREEMENT MUST BE IN WRITING   When a contingency fee is involved, most jurisdictions state that the agreement <u>must</u> be in writing for the office to collect the fee. Rule 1.5 (c) of the *Model Rules* states:

> (c)… A contingent fee agreement shall be in writing and shall state the method by which the fee is to be determined, including the percentage or percentages that shall accrue to the lawyer in the event of settlement, trial or appeal. . . .

Even the *Model Rules* make a distinction between contingency agreements and other types of fee agreements and require that contingency agreements be in writing. The reason that a contingency fee agreement must be in writing is that in many cases, large sums of money are recovered and the difference between 20 percent and 30 percent may mean tens of thousands of dollars. Contingency agreements are risky for the attorney and they simply must be reduced to writing so that the client and the attorney know what the proper percentage of fees should be. It also is important that the contingency agreement state and the client understand that even if there is no recovery in the case, the client must still pay for expenses.

NO CONTINGENCY FEES IN CRIMINAL AND DOMESTIC-RELATION PROCEEDINGS IN SOME JURISDICTIONS   Many jurisdictions prohibit contingency fees in criminal and domestic-relation proceedings as a matter of public policy. Rule 1.5(d) of the *Model Rules* states:

> (d) A lawyer shall not enter into an arrangement for, charge, or collect:
>
> (1) any fee in a domestic relations matter, the payment or amount of which is contingent upon the securing of a divorce or upon the amount of alimony or support, or property settlement thereof; or
>
> (2) a contingent fee for representing a defendant in a criminal case.

For example, an attorney agrees to represent a client in a criminal matter. The client agrees to pay the attorney $10,000 if the client is found innocent, but the attorney will receive nothing if the client is found guilty. This is an unethical contingency fee agreement.[7] The thinking is that contingency fees in these types of cases are against the public policy and should be prohibited.

ONLY A "REASONABLE FEE" CAN BE COLLECTED

It is important to keep in mind that no matter what the contract or legal fee agreement is with a client, attorneys and legal assistants can only receive a "reasonable" fee. Unfortunately, there is no absolute standard for determining reasonableness, except that "reasonableness" will be determined on a case-by-case basis. However, Rule 1.5 of the *Model Rules of Professional Conduct* gives a number of factors to be considered in determining reasonableness:

(a) A lawyer's fee shall be reasonable. The factors to be considered in determining the reasonableness of a fee include the following:

(1) The time and labor required, the novelty and difficulty of the questions involved, and the skill requisite to perform the legal service properly;

(2) The likelihood, if apparent to the client, that the acceptance of the particular employment will preclude the other employment by the lawyer;

(3) The fee customarily charged in the locality for similar legal services;

(4) The amount involved and the results obtained;

(5) The time limitations imposed by the client or by the circumstances;

(6) The nature and length of the professional relationship with the client;

(7) The experience, reputation, and ability of the lawyer or lawyers performing the services;

(8) Whether the fee is fixed or contingent.

For example, in one case, a court found that a fee of $22,500 pursuant to a written agreement for a real estate matter that involved little time for the attorney and that was not unduly complex was unreasonable.[8] Figure 5-7 shows some additional examples of unreasonable fees.

FIGURE 5-7
Unethical/Highly Questionable Billing Practices

- **Firm Charges Client Twice the Going Rate for Legal Assistant Time**
  In Washington, D.C., a major law firm billed an insurance company client $3.5 million. Among the charges listed on the invoice was $125 per hour for each of 22 paralegals. The problem was, the usual rate in the nation's capital is $60–$65 an hour for the type of work the paralegals performed. Braxton Busch, "Questions Raised over Paralegal Billing," *Legal Assistant Today*, November/December 1992, 25.
- **Client Charged for Paralegals Doing Routine Filing and General Office Work**
  In Denver, a law firm charged a client the going hourly rate for research work carried out by staff paralegals. Only later did the client discover that

the "paralegal" tasks for which he was paying big bucks were routine filing and general office work. The firm charged the hourly rate to avoid the overhead of clerical work, a normal part of doing business. Braxton Busch, "Questions Raised over Paralegal Billing," *Legal Assistant Today,* November/December, 1992, 25.

- **Audit Questions Paralegal's 12-Hour Workdays**
An audit of a paralegal's time found that from September 1990 through July 1992 the paralegal worked (i.e. billed) an average of 12.45 hours each day, including Saturdays, Sundays, and holidays without details to support the hours. The paralegal only took one day off during this period (Christmas 1990). The audit estimated that the paralegal overbilled by 2,220 hours totaling $39,960. *Legal Assistant Today*, July/August 1993, 28–29.

- **Client Charged for Individual Attorneys Billing More Than the 24-hour Day**
A corporation recently received a monthly legal bill in excess of $300,000. The head of the corporate legal department was concerned. After hiring and outside audit firm to audit the billings, he discovered that:
  - Individual attorneys were billing in excess of the 24-hour day;
  - Attorneys were assigned to tasks that could have been provided by legal assistants at <u>greatly</u> reduced costs;
  - The client was billed by the firm for duplicate items;
  - Conferences were often attended by many attorneys who were not needed and time charged to the client;
  - The client was billed for the same expert witness fees multiple times;
  - The firm charged the client for the time the firm spent working with the auditor to show them their overcharges.

  ALA News, Association of Legal Administrators, vol. 12, issue 5, August/September 1993, 22.

- **Firm Bills Six Times the Actual Number of Hours Worked**
A real estate developer was sued six times arising out of the same development project. Although the cases where separately filed, the factual and legal allegations were identical. The client hired the same attorney to represent her in all six cases. The lawyer filed essentially identical answers in all six cases. Several weeks later, the developer-client received identical bills showing the same amount of time and hourly rate for each answer. The client was being asked to pay six times the actual number of hours worked. When she called the lawyer, he confirmed that she was billed six times the actual time spent. When she stated that she should only have to pay for actual hours worked, he replied that he should not be "penalized" for preparing similar answers. Peter R. Jarvis, "Overbilling Is a Losing Proposition," *The National Law Journal,* December 28, 1992–January 4, 1993, 13.

- **Firm Bills 348 Hours "Preparation" for a Deposition**
A firm billed a client a whopping 348 hours to prepare for a deposition. *Los Angeles Paralegal Assoc. Reporter,* vol. 22, issue 3, March 1993.

MANY STATE BARS' RULES PROVIDE FOR OVERSIGHT/ARBITRATION ON FEE ISSUES

One of the ways that state bar associations and courts have dealt with the abundance of fee disputes is to provide for immediate and informal review/arbitration of fee disputes without going through a long process. Many state ethical rules and court rules provide that clients have the right at any time to request that the judge in the case or an attorney representing the state bar review the reasonableness of the attorneys' fees. In many states, the attorney is required to inform the client of this right. In those states, the judge or attorney hearing the matter has the right to set the fee and determine what is "reasonable" under the particular facts and circumstances of the case.

FRAUD AND CRIMINAL CHARGES

> *If you bill someone for work you have not done, it is a fraud. That is a tort and a crime. You can be prosecuted by the government or by the client who was cheated.*
>
> **—Deborah K. Orlik,** *California Paralegal*, January–March, 1991.

criminal fraud
A false representation of a present or past fact made by a defendant.

Charging an "unreasonable fee" is no longer simply a matter of ethics. Recently, attorneys and legal assistants have been criminally charged for fraud for intentionally recording time and sending bills for legal services that were never provided. **Criminal fraud** *is a false representation of a present or past fact made by the defendant, upon which the victim relies, resulting in the victim suffering damages.*

Criminal charges for fraud are not filed against attorneys and legal assistants when there is simply a disagreement over what a "reasonable" fee is. Criminal charges are filed when an attorney or legal assistant acts intentionally to defraud clients. This usually happens when the attorney or legal assistant bills for time when she did not really work on the case or in instances in which the office intentionally billed a grossly overstated hourly rate far above the market rate.

> *One of the most common temptations that can corrupt a paralegal's ethics is to inflate billable hours, since there is often immense pressure in law offices to bill high hours for job security and upward mobility. Such "creative billing" [or "padding"] is not humorous; it's both morally wrong and illegal.*
>
> **—Smith,** AAfPE National Conference Highlights," 8 *Legal Assistant Today* January/February 1991, 103.

Interestingly, many of the criminal cases being brought are against well-respected large and small law offices specializing in insurance defense and corporate work. Some insurance companies and corporations, as a matter of course when a case has been concluded, hire an audit firm or independent attorney to go back and audit the firm's billing and files to be sure they were billed accurately. In some instances, these audits have concluded that intentional criminal fraud has occurred and have been referred to prosecutors where criminal charges have been filed. So, no matter what type of firm is involved, intentionally overstating bills can lead to very big problems.

> *Don't fall for the "everybody does it" theory. Not everybody does it. I don't . . . If your job is in jeopardy or you don't get the same bonus as the cheaters, this is definitely something that you must discuss with your supervising attorney.*
>
> —**Deborah K. Orlik,** *California Paralegal,* January–March, 1991.

ETHICAL PROBLEMS

There are several hard ethical problems with no definite solutions regarding time-keeping and billing that need to be explored. The rule in answering ethical questions such as these is to use your common sense and notions of fairness and honesty.

- Billing more than one client for the same time "double billing"—A situation happens from time to time in which a legal assistant or attorney has the opportunity to bill more than one client for the same time period. For instance, while you are monitoring the opposing side's inspection of your client's documents in case A, you are drafting discovery for case B. Another example: while traveling to attend an interview with a witness in case A, you work on case B.

 An argument (albeit not a strong one) can be made for billing the full time to each case. However, you or someone in your office may have to justify this in front of a judge who may say it is unreasonable. If you were the client, would you think it is fair for the attorney to charge full price for travel time related to your case while billing another case? More commonsense approaches are to bill only the case you are actively working on, to split the time between the cases, or bill the case you are actively working on at the regular hourly rate and bill the case you are inactively working on at a greatly reduced rate. Be fair and honest; your clients as well as judges and others looking at the time will respect you for it. If the law office has a policy to bill both clients full price, you may have no choice, but generally this practice should be discouraged.

- When billing by the hour, is there an ethical obligation to be efficient? Does the firm have to have a form file in lieu of researching each document each time? Must an office use a computer to save time?

 These types of ethical questions are decided on a case-by-case basis. The point is that billing by the hour rewards people to work slowly, since the more slowly they work, the more they are paid.

 Common sense tells you that if you were the client, you would want your legal staff to be efficient and to not "milk" you for money. The real issue is whether the attorney or legal assistant acted so inefficiently and charged so much, when compared with what a similar attorney or legal assistant with similar qualifications would charge in the same community, that the fee is clearly unreasonable. When a judge rules on the reasonableness of fees, there is no doubt that the judge will consider what a reasonably efficient attorney or legal assistant in the same circumstances would have charged. Use your common sense and be honest and efficient because someone in your office might have to justify your time and charges someday.

▪ Should you bill for clerical or secretarial duties?—Law offices cannot bill clients for clerical or secretarial tasks. The reason is that these tasks are viewed as overhead costs or are a normal part of doing business. An easy, but unethical way to bill more hours is for a legal assistant to bill time to clients for clerical functions such as copying documents or filing material. Legal assistants clearly should not bill for these types of clerical tasks. Legal assistants bill time for professional services, not for clerical functions.

▪ Should you bill for the mistakes of the law office?—This is another tough problem. People make mistakes all the time. Clients generally feel that they should not have to pay for mistakes, since the reason they went to an attorney was to get an expert to handle their situation. This is a decision that should be left for every law office to decide, but generally the practice of billing for mistakes should be discouraged.

▪ Must a task be assigned to less expensive support staff when possible? Common sense and efficiency will tell you that tasks should be delegated as low as possible. Clients should not have to pay for attorney time when the task could be completed by an experienced legal assistant. In addition, this practice is more profitable to the law office, since higher-paid persons are free to do tasks for which they can bill clients at their normal rates.

LEGAL EXPENSES

In addition to recovering for legal fees, law practices also are entitled to recover from the client reasonable expenses that are incurred by the office in representing the client. For example, in Figure 5-8 the office needed to make copies of a motion to compel and mail them to opposing counsels. The cost of making the copies of the motion and mailing them out is directly related to the case, so the office is entitled to be reimbursed from the client for this expense. In most offices, it is important that you fill out expense slips similar to the one in Figure 5-8 or fill out some type of log regarding expenses that the office can be reimbursed for. Such expenses typically include the costs of photocopying documents, postage, long-distance telephone calls, or travel expenses (see Figure 5-9).

The types of items to be charged back to clients are usually found in the law practice's staff manual. Most law offices charge what appears to be premium prices for legal expenses, such as copying costs of ten cents to twenty-five cents or more, especially when a client sees that print shops charge five cents for a photocopy. However, at five cents a page you (the customer) provide the labor; if you want the store to do the work it costs more. The same is true for a law office. One way to deal with this situation is to send jobs of fifty or more pages to a copy or printing service. This pleases the client, since he is not paying as much for copying costs; your copiers do not get as much wear and tear; and the invoice from the copy or printing service can be included on the client's bill for reimbursement.

In cases involving litigation, the expenses alone can run into the tens of thousands of dollars. Therefore, the careful tracking of expenses is no trivial matter. Consider the revenues that would be generated if you billed copies at twenty-five cents and the office made eighty thousand copies a year directly related to clients. This would be twenty thousand dollars. Consider also the additional overhead an office would have if it did not bill clients for the copies.

Johnson, Beck & Taylor
Expense Slip

Expense Type & Code:

1 Photocopies	4 Filing Fees	7 Facsimile	10 Travel
2 Postage	5 Witness Fees	8 Lodging	11 Overnight Delivery
3 Long Distance	6 WESTLAW/LEXIS	9 Meals	12 Other _____

Date _4-5-94_   Case Name: _Smith v. United_ _____   File No. _118294_ _____

Expense Code: ____1____   Quantity _20 pages_   Amount _File rate_   (Billable) Non-Billable

Expense Code: ____2____   Quantity _4 packages sent_   Amount _$4.66_   (Billable) Non-Billable

Expense Code: _____   Quantity _____   Amount _____   Billable Non-Billable

Name of Person Making Expense Slip: _____

Description of Expense(s) Incurred:
____Copies and postage re: Motion to compel   4/5/94_____

FIGURE 5-8   Expense Slip

As a legal assistant, you may be required to pay expenses for a case out of your own pocket from time to time. If this happens, be sure to ask for receipts. It also helps to know in advance what specific expenses the office will reimburse you for before they are incurred.

Court Reporter Fees (Deposition Transcripts)
Delivery Charges (Federal Express, etc.)
Expert Witness Fees
Facsimile Costs
Filing Fees
Long-Distance Phone Calls
Photocopying
Postage
Travel Expenses
WESTLAW/LEXIS
Witness Fees

FIGURE 5-9
Expenses Typically Billed to Clients

TIMEKEEPING

Timekeeping is the process of tracking what attorneys and legal assistants do with their time. Although this might seem like an incredibly easy task, it is not. Timekeeping is a necessary evil in most law practices. Keeping careful time records is important both for managerial reasons and for producing income.

From a managerial perspective, time records:

1. provide the office with a way to monitor the progress of a case, who is working on the case, and/or who is responsible for the matter;
2. allow the office to determine which cases are the most profitable;
3. allow office management to monitor the efficiencies of law practice staff.

From an income producing perspective, time records:

1. allow offices to bill their time to clients;
2. allow the office to document its fees in probate matters and in cases where legal fees will be decided by a court.

Notice that managerial reasons could apply to any type of law practice including corporate, government, or legal aid. And, it is not uncommon for corporate, government, and legal aid practices to be given court awarded attorneys fees from time to time.

timesheet or **timeslip**
A record of information about the legal services professionals provide to each client.

Figure 5-10 is an example of a typical timesheet. A **timesheet** or **timeslip** *is where legal professionals record information about the legal services they provide to each client.* Timekeeping entries must contain information such as the name of the case worked on, the date the service was provided, and a description of the service.

MANUAL TIMEKEEPING

There are many different types of manual timekeeping methods that can be purchased from most legal law office supply catalogs. Figure 5-10 is an example of a multiple-slip timesheet. The timeslips are recorded chronologically. Timeslips will be completed by different billing people within the office for a variety of different cases. At some point, typically once a week, the pages of timeslips will be turned in by everyone in the office to the billing department. Each individual slip can be separated and has adhesive on the back. Each slip is separated and is stuck to each client's timeslip page (see Figure 5-11). This provides a convenient way for tracking time for each client. All clients' timeslip pages can be stored in a three-ring notebook in alphabetical order by client name or stored in each individual client's accounting file.

It is important to point out that time records do not automatically get charged to clients. The supervising attorney in the case typically reviews the time records turned in and determines whether they will be charged as is or whether the time should be adjusted upward or downward. It should also be noted that it is common to have clients with more than one matter pending. Separate records need to be kept for each matter and typically separate invoices are generated.

COMPUTERIZED TIMEKEEPING

Some timekeeping and billing computer programs also can provide assistance in keeping track of time. In some programs, the user enters what case is being

PC - Phone Conference	R - Review
LR - Legal Research	OC - Office Conference
L - Letter	T - Travel
D - Dictation	CT - Court Hearing

Time Conversion

6 Minutes = .1 Hour	36 Minutes = .6 Hour
12 Minutes = .2 Hour	42 Minutes = .7 Hour
15 Minutes = .25 Hour	45 Minutes = .75 Hour
18 Minutes = .3 Hour	48 Minutes = .8 Hour
24 Minutes = .4 Hour	54 Minutes = .9 Hour
30 Minutes = .5 Hour	10 Minutes = 1.0 Hour

Date	Client/Case	File No.	Services Performed	Attorney	Time Hours & Tenths
5-7-94	Smith v. United Sales	118294	Summarized 6 depositions; Client; Δ (Defendant) Allen; Δ Barney, ΔRose; Witness Forrest & Johnson	BJP	6. 5
5-8-94	Marcel v. True Oil	118003	PC w/ Client Re: Settlement offer; Discussions w/ Attorney; Memo to file Re: offer	BJP	. 3
5-8-94	Johnson v. State	118118	PC w/ Client's Mother; PC w/ Client; L R Re: Bail; Memo to file; R correspondence	BJP	. 75
5-8-94	Potential claim of Watkins v. Leslie Grocery	Not Assigned Yet	OC w/Client; (New client); Reviewed facts; Reviewed medical records Re: accident; Conf. w/ atty	BJP	1. 50
5-8-94	Smith v. United Sales	118294	Computerized searches on depositions for attorney	BJP	. 75
5-8-94	Jay Tiller Bankrutpcy	118319	PC w/ Creditor, Bank One; Memo to file; Client; LT to Client	BJP	. 3
5-8-94	Potential Claim of Watkins v. Leslie Grocery	—	LR Slip & Fall cases generally; Standard of care	BJP	1. 00
5-8-94	Marcel v. True Oil	118003	Conf. w/atty. & Client Re: Settlement; Drafted & prepared LT to Δ's Re: Settlement offer	BJP	1. 10
5-8-94	Jay Tiller Bankruptcy	118319	Drafted Bankruptcy petition; OC w/Client; List of debts; Fin. Stmt; Conf w/ atty	BJP	1. 00
5-8-94	Smith v. United Sales	118294	Drafted and prepared depo notice to Witness Spring	BJP	.25
5-9-94	Seeley Real Estate Matter	118300	Ran amortization schedule to attach to 'Contract for Deed'	BJP	.25

FIGURE 5-10 Typical Timeslip/Time Record Form

Time Records for Case Name: _Smith v. United Sales_   Case No: ___118294___

5-1-94	Smith v. United Sales	118294	Prepared for & attended depo of Wilson	JJH	4.	0
5-7-94	Smith v. United Sales	118294	Summarized 6 depositions; Client; Δ (Defendant) Allen; Δ Barney, ΔRose; Witness Forest & Johnson	BJP	6.	5
5-8-94	Smith v. United Sales	118294	Computerized searches on depositions for attorney	BJP		75
5-8-94	Smith v. United Sales	118294	Drafted and prepared depo notice to Witness Spring	BJP		25
5-9-94	Smith v. United Sales	118294	PC w/ Client Re: Motion to compel Re: Several Ig's not answered	JJH		20

FIGURE 5-11   Timesheet Record for a Case

worked on and whether the time is billable or nonbillable and then turns the "meter" on. The computer keeps track of the time until the user is completed with the project for that client. The computerized timeslip is then stored in the program until a billing is generated. When a bill is generated, the computerized timeslip is automatically calculated and included in the client's bill. There are even some systems that use bar codes. The user simply scans in the client's bar code and the bar code for the type of activity he is delivering. When he is finished, the bar code for the activity is scanned back in to show that the work on the matter is completed.

billable time
Actual time that a legal assistant or attorney spends working on a case and that is directly billed to a client's account.

BILLABLE V. NONBILLABLE TIME

One of the basics of timekeeping is the difference between billable and nonbillable time. **Billable time** *is actual time that a legal assistant or attorney spends working on a case and that is directly billed to a client's account.* Any activity that you perform to further a client's case, other than clerical functions, is usually considered billable time, including: interviewing witnesses, investigating a case, serving subpoenas, performing legal research, drafting, and so forth. **Nonbillable time** *is time that cannot be directly billed to a paying client.* Nonetheless, it should still be tracked.

nonbillable time
Time that cannot be directly billed to a paying client.

There are typically three types of nonbillable time:

a) general firm activities;
b) personal time;
c) pro bono work.

General firm activities refer to time spent on personnel materials, planning, marketing, client development, staff/committee meetings, library maintenance, and professional development. Personal time refers to taking breaks, cleaning and organizing, and taking sick/vacation days. **Pro bono** *work is legal services that are provided free of charge to a client who is not able to pay for the services.* Typically, pro bono cases are taken to generate goodwill in the community for the office or to provide a community service. Although handling pro bono cases is a morally proper thing to do, nonetheless it is still counted as nonbillable time.

pro bono
Legal services that are provided free of charge to a client who is not able to pay for the services.

Figure 5-12 is an example of a chart comparing billable with unbillable hours for each of an office's timekeepers. Nonbillable time is sometimes referred to as overhead or office hours, since the cost of nonbillable time must be paid for by the office. **Overhead** *refers to general administrative costs of doing business. They are incidental costs regarding the management and supervision of the business. Overhead includes costs such as rent, utilities, phones, office supplies, equipment, and salary costs for administrators who manage the business and others. Overhead costs are sometimes defined as any cost not directly associated with the production of goods or services.*

overhead
General administrative costs of doing business, including costs such as rent, utilities, phone, and salary costs for administrators.

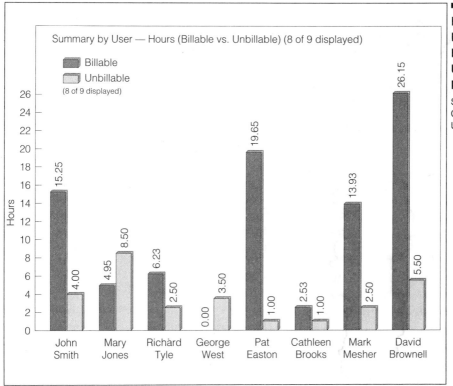

FIGURE 5-12
Bar Chart Showing Billable versus Unbillable Hours for Each Timekeeper

Source: Courtesy Timeslips Corporation, Essex, MA, USA, 508-768-6100.

*There are only approximately 1,300 fee-earning hours per year unless the lawyer works overtime. Many of the eight hours per day available for office work are consumed in personal, civic, bar, religious, and political activities, general office administration, and other . . . matters. Either five or six hours per day would be realistic, depending upon the habits of the individual lawyer. (Special Committee on Economics of Law Practice of the American Bar Association, **1959).***

The overwhelming majority of law firms today have a minimum billable hour or target that they like for their legal assistants to achieve. [It's] anywhere from 1,400 to 1,800 billable hours a year depending on the law firm. In the last couple of years, more and more firms have realized they have got to be more strict about billable minimums.

—**John P. Mello, Jr.,** "Paralegal Billing Trends," *Legal Assistant Today,* September/October 1993, 127.

MINIMUM BILLABLE HOURS

Many law offices have a preoccupation with the billable hour concept and set billable hour quotas that legal assistants must meet. Figure 5-13 (top) shows the average number of billable hours for legal assistants, associates, and partners/shareholders according to a 1991 survey. However, in some offices, legal assistant billable hours can be as high as 1,600 to 1,800 hours annually. Historically, this was not the case. In the early 1960s, 1,300 billable hours was thought to be realistic. The number of minimum billable hours depends greatly on location, the size of the law office, and the types of cases (see bottom of Figure 5-13 for the results of a 1993 legal assistant survey).

PARALEGAL TRAPPED

A paralegal, on his way to an assignment on another floor, became trapped in an elevator just after getting on. Fellow employees gathered around the elevator door. The time-conscious paralegal called out from inside the elevator, "Is this billable or nonbillable time?"

—**William Statsky,** *Introduction to Paralegalism,* 4th ed. (Saint Paul, Minnesota: West Publishing Co., 1992), 826, Citing *A Lighter Note,* NALA Advance 15, Summer 1989.

RECORDING TIME

There are several different ways to actually record and/or track your time. One method is to bill time in tenths of an hour with .5 being a half-hour and 1.0 being an hour. Every six minutes is a tenth of the hour, so you would be billing on six-minute intervals. Billing in tenths works out as follows:

Timekeeper	Average
Legal assistants	1,410 hours
Associates	1,807 hours
Partners/shareholders	1,711 hours

LEGAL ASSISTANT BILLABLE HOURS BY REGION—1993 *LEGAL ASSISTANT TODAY* SALARY SURVEY

		Minimum Expected Hours Billed	Average Actual Hours Billed
Region 1:	Connecticut, Delaware, Maine, Massachusetts, New Hampshire, New Jersey, New York, Pennsylvania, Rhode Island, Vermont	1,440	1,596
Region 2:	Maryland, North Carolina, Ohio, South Carolina, Virginia, Washington, D.C., West Virginia	1,384	1,525
Region 3:	Alabama, Florida, Georgia, Mississippi, Tennessee	1,538	1,656
Region 4:	Arkansas, Louisiana, Oklahoma, Texas	1,735	1,818
Region 5:	Illinois, Indiana, Kentucky, Michigan, Missouri, Wisconsin	1,565	1,687
Region 6:	Iowa, Kansas, Minnesota, Nebraska, North Dakota, South Dakota	1,592	1,691
Region 7:	Arizona, Colorado, New Mexico, Utah, Wyoming	1,546	1,583
Region 8:	Alaska, Idaho, Montana, Oregon, Washington	1,455	1,541
Region 9:	California, Hawaii, Nevada	1,516	1,572
National Average		**1,519**	**1,628**

FIGURE 5-13
Average Annual Billable Hours

Source: *The 1991 Survey of Law Firm Economics—A Management and Planning Tool,* Altman Weil Pensa. Reprinted with the permission of Altman Weil Pensa Publications, Inc., copyright 1991 by Altman Weil Pensa Publications, Inc.

Source: Carol Milano, "1993 Legal Assistant Today Salary Survey Results," *Legal Assistant Today,* May/June, 1993, 60. Copyright 1993, James Publishing, Inc. Reprinted with permission from *Legal Assistant Today.*

0–6 minutes	= .1 hour	31–36 minutes	= .6 hour
7–12 minutes	= .2 hour	37–42 minutes	= .7 hour
13–15 minutes	= .25 hour	43–45 minutes	= .75 hour
16–18 minutes	= .3 hour	46–48 minutes	= .8 hour
19–24 minutes	= .4 hour	49–54 minutes	= .9 hour
25–30 minutes	= .5 hour	55–60 minutes	= 1.0 hour

As an alternative, some offices will bill using a quarter of an hour as the basis, as follows:

0–15 minutes   = .25 hour

16–30 minutes   = .50 hour

31–45 minutes = .75 hour

46–60 minutes = 1.0 hour

Although the quarterly basis is easier to use, it is not as accurate as the tenth of an hour system. Suppose you took a five-minute phone call from a client and your average billing rate is $40 an hour. Using the tenth of an hour system, the fee for the phone call would be $4 (.1 hour times $40 equals $4). However, using the quarterly system, the fee for the phone call would be $10, since .25 is the smallest interval (.25 times $40 equals $10), or 60 percent more.

Figure 5-14 contains some stock billing phrases. It is important that you include as much detail as possible when completing your time records, that the language is clear and easily understood, and that the time record itself is legibly written. Clients are usually more willing to pay a bill when they know exactly what service was performed for them. For example, compare these general bill statements:

1. "Telephone conference—.50 hr. $20.00";
2. "Telephone conference with client on Plaintiff's Request for Production of Documents regarding whether or not client has copies of the draft contracts at issue—.50 hr. $20.00."

Which of these statements would you rather receive?

FIGURE 5-14
Billing Phrases

Telephone conference with _____, regarding _____.
Office conference with _____, regarding _____.
Interview of _____, regarding _____.
Review of file regarding _____.
Review of incoming correspondence from _____, regarding _____.
Review of incoming legal document entitled _____, from _____.
Review and approval of _____, prepared by _____.
Preparation of _____, regarding _____.
Appearance at _____, regarding _____.
Court appearance at _____, regarding _____.
Drafting of _____, regarding _____.
Revising of _____, regarding _____.
Preparation for _____, regarding _____.
Investigation of _____, regarding _____.
Legal research of _____ issue for the legal document entitled _____.
Travel to _____, regarding _____.
Negotiations with _____, regarding _____.
Status report to _____.
Advice and counsel to _____ concerning _____.
Handling miscellaneous details regarding _____.
Research and analysis of _____, regarding _____.

Many clients would prefer the latter, since they are able to see, and hopefully remember exactly what specific services they received. The problem with the longer format is that detailed timeslips take longer to complete.

TIMEKEEPING PRACTICES

If the average legal assistant is required to bill between 1,400 and 1,600 hours a year, it is very important that she take the timekeeping function extremely serious. The following are some suggestions to consider regarding keeping track of time.

- Find out how many hours you must bill annually, monthly, and weekly up front and track where you are in relationship to the quota—One of the first things you should do when you start a new legal assistant job is to find out how many billable hours you must have. If the office requires that you bill 1,400 hours a year, budget this on a monthly and weekly basis and keep track of where you are so that you will not have to try to "make it all up" at the end of the year.

- Find out when timesheets are due—Another thing you should do when starting a new position is to find out exactly what day timesheets are due so that you can submit them on time.

- Keep copies of your timesheets—Always keep a copy of your timesheet for your own file in case the original is either lost or misplaced. Having a copy also allows you to go back and calculate your number of billable hours.

- Record your time contemporaneously on a daily basis—One of the biggest mistakes you can make is to not record your time as you go along during the day. If you wait until the end of the day to try to remember all the things you did, there is absolutely no way you will be able to accurately reconstruct everything. In the end, you will be the one suffering, doing work you did not get credit for. So, be sure to keep a timesheet handy and fill it out as you go along.

- Record your actual time spent; do not discount your time—Do not discount your time because you think you should have been able to perform a job faster. If it took you four hours to finish an assignment and you worked the whole four hours, there is no reason to discount the time. **If the supervising attorneys think a discount is warranted, they can decide that, but it is not up to you to do that**. That is not your burden. However, if you made a mistake or had a problem that you do not think the client should be billed for, be up front and tell your supervising attorney and let him help you make the decision.

- Be aware if billable hours are related to bonuses or merit increases—Be aware as to how billable hours are used. In some law office, billable hours are used in distributing bonuses and merit increases and can be used in performance evaluations, so know up front how they will be used. Some offices discount or "cut" the time actually billed to the client. Always ask whether "billable hours" means the amount of time submitted or the amount of time actually billed to the client; there is a big difference.

- Be ethical—Always be honest and ethical in the way you fill out your timesheets. Padding your timesheet is unethical and simply wrong. Eventually wrongdoing regarding timekeeping, billing, or handling client funds will become apparent.

> *I worked closely with a paralegal who consistently had two or three more [billable] hours a day than I did, although we arrived around the same time and did similar work all day. We usually walked each other out at night (for safety reasons). I'd look at my time for a day: 10.5 hours; and she had 13. She didn't subtract for lunch or breaks. . . . An attorney called me in to ask about the discrepancy between her time and mine. . . . The lawyer talked to her. . . . Her timesheet was accurate after that.*
>
> —**Carol Milano,** "Hard Choices: Dealing with Ethical Dilemmas on the Job," *Legal Assistant Today*, March/April 1992, 79.

- Be aware of things that keep you from billing time—Be aware of things that keep you from having a productive day such as:

- People who lay their troubles at your feet or who are constantly taking your attention away from your work. An appropriate approach is to say "I would really like to hear about it at lunch, but right now I am really busy."

- Wasted time spent trying to track down other people or trying to find information you need.

- Constant interruptions, including phone calls. If you really need to get something done, go someplace where you can get the work done and tell others to hold your calls. However, check in every once in a while to return client phone calls. Clients should have their phone calls returned as soon as possible.

BILLING

To generate the necessary income to operate the firm, special attention must be paid to billing, the process of issuing bills for the purpose of collecting monies for legal services performed and for being reimbursed for expenses. This section shows how legal assistants are able to bill their time, how billing rates are determined, the difference between manual and computerized billing systems, the billing cycle, how management reports that are generated from many computerized billing systems can help the office make good administrative decisions, and what some successful billing practices are.

BILLING FOR LEGAL ASSISTANT TIME— LEGAL ASSISTANT PROFITABILITY

Many law offices bill for legal assistant time as well as for attorney time. A recent survey found that 77 percent of the 1,800 legal assistants responding to the survey stated that their law office billed clients separately for their work. Many clients prefer this, since the legal assistant hourly rates are much lower than attorney hourly rates. Figure 5-15 shows the average hourly rates for legal assistants, associates, and partners/shareholders throughout the country.

Region	Legal Assistants	Associates	Partners/Shareholders
California	$67	$140	$203
West	$56	$101	$149
South Central	$54	$107	$161
West Central	$54	$ 95	$135
East Central	$60	$101	$153
South	$53	$ 98	$147
Northeast	$62	$119	$175

FIGURE 5-15
**Average Hourly
Billing Rates**

Source: *The 1991 Survey of
Law Firm Economics—A
Management and Planning
Tool*, Altman Weil Pensa,
II–4. Reprinted with the
permission of Altman Weil
Pensa Publications, Inc.,
copyright 1991 by Altman
Weil Pensa Publications, Inc.

For example, assume an associate attorney and a legal assistant can both prepare discovery documents in a case and that the task will take seven hours.
Assuming the legal assistant bills at $55 an hour and the associate bills at $100 an
hour, the cost to the client if the legal assistant does the job is $385, and the cost if
the associate drafts the discovery is $700. Thus, the client will have saved $315 by
simply allowing the legal assistant to do the job. The client would still have to pay
for the attorney's time to review the legal assistant's discovery, but the cost would
be minimal. This represents substantial savings to clients.

The question of whether law offices can bill for legal assistant time was considered by the United States Court in *Missouri v. Jenkins*, 491 U.S. 274 (1989). In
that case, the plaintiff was successful on several counts in a civil rights lawsuit
and was attempting to recover attorney's fees from the defendant under a federal statute. The statutory language provided that the prevailing party could recover "reasonable attorney's fees" from the other party. The plaintiff argued for
recovery for the time that legal assistants spent working on the case as well as for
the time attorneys spent. The defendant argued that legal assistant time was not
"attorney's fees." Alternatively, the defendants argued that if they did have to
pay something for legal assistant time, they should only have to pay about $15 an
hour, which represents the overhead costs to the office for a legal assistant.

The Court found that legal assistants carry out many useful tasks under the
direction of attorneys and that "reasonable attorney's fees" referred to the reasonable fee for work produced whether it be by attorneys or legal assistants. The
Court also found that under the federal statute, legal assistant time should not be
compensated for at the overhead costs to the office but should be paid at the prevailing market rates in the area for legal assistant time. The Court noted that the
prevailing rate for legal assistants in that part of the country was about $40 an
hour and held that the office was entitled to receive that amount for legal assistant hours worked on the case. Thus, it is clear that offices can bill for legal assistant time if they choose to do so. The case also reminds us that purely clerical
tasks or secretarial tasks should not be billed at the legal assistant rate.

Although the *Missouri v. Jenkins* case was a landmark decision for legal assistants, the opinion involved the interpretation of a specific statute, the Civil Rights
Act. Fee questions occur in many different situations and if another court is deciding a fee question other than in the context of the Civil Rights Act, it may reach a
different decision. Figure 5-16 shows cases that have allowed for legal assistant
fee recovery and some that have not.

**FIGURE 5-16
Citations of Cases
Allowing and Not
Allowing Legal
Assistant Fee
Recovery**

Source: Adapted from
Susan French Koran,
"Recoverability of Legal
Assistant Time in Attorney
Fee Applications," *Journal of
Paralegal Education and
Practice,* American
Association for Paralegal
Education, vol. 9, no. 1, April
1993, 14–21. Printed with
permission of the American
Association for Paralegal
Education, P.O. Box 40244,
Overland Park, KS 66204.

CASES <u>ALLOWING</u> LEGAL ASSISTANT FEE RECOVERY:

Federal cases:

Missouri v. Jenkins, 491 U.S. 274, 285 (1989).

In re Meese, 907 F.2d 1192, 1202-03 (D.C. Cir. 1990).

Chambless v. Masters, 885 F.2d 1053, 1058 (2d Cir. 1989), *cert. denied,* 496 U.S. 905 (1990).

U.S. Football League v. National Football League, 887 F.2d 408, 415–16 (2d Cir. 1989), *cert. denied,* 493 U.S. 1071 (1990).

Blanchard v. Bergeron, 893 F.2d 87, 91 (5th Cir. 1990).

In re Olson, 884 F.2d 1415, 1426 (D.C. Cir. 1989).

Jacobs v. Mancuso, 825 F.2d 559, 563 (1st Cir. 1987).

Herold v. Hajoca Corp., 864 F.2d 317, 322 (4 Cir. 1988), *cert. denied,* 490 U.S. 1107 (1989).

Simmons v. Lockhart, 931 F.2d 1226, 1230 (8th Cir. 1991).

Kopunec v. Nelson, 801 F.2d 1226, 1229 (10th Cir. 1986).

Boyd Motors, Inc. v. Employees Ins. of Wausau, 766 F. Supp 998, 1000 (D. Kan. 1991).

Standard Oil Co. v. Osage Oil & Transp., Inc., 122 F.R.D. 267, 269–70 (N.D. Okl. 1988).

State cases

Genden v. Merrill Lunch, Pierce, Fenner & Smith, Inc., 741 F. Supp. 84, 86–87 (S.D. N.Y. 1990).

In re Telesphere Intern. Securities Litigation, 753 F. Supp. 716, 720 (N.D. Ill. 1990).

Continental Townhouses East Unit One Ass'n. v. Brockbank, 733 P.2d 1120, 1127–29 (Ariz. Ct. App. 1986).

Sundance v. Municipal Court, 237, Cal. Rptr. 269, 273 (Cal. Dist. Ct. App. 1987).

In re Marriage of Ahmad, 555 N.E.2d 439, 443–45 (Ill. App. Ct. 1990).

Merchandise Nat. Bank of Chicago v. Scanlon, 408 N.E.2d 248, 254–55 (Ill. App. Ct. 1980).

Landals v. George A. Rolfes Co., 454 N.W.2d 891, 898 (Iowa 1990).

Darmetko v. Boston Housing Authority, 383 N.E.2d 395, 400 (Mass. 1979).

Newport v. Newport, 759 S.W.2d 630, 636 (Mo. Ct. App. 1988).

Lea Co. v. North Carolina Bd. of Transportation, 374 S.E.2d 868, 871 (N.C. 1989).

Willamette Prod. Credit Ass'n v. BorgWarner Acceptance Corp., 706 P.2d 577, 580 (Or. Ct. App. 1985).

CASES <u>NOT ALLOWING</u> LEGAL ASSISTANT FEE RECOVERY:

Abrams v. Baylor College of Medicine, 805 F.2d 528, 535 (5th Cir. 1986).

Bill Rivers Trailers, Inc. v. Miller, 489 So.2d 1139, 1142–43 (Fla. Dist. Ct. App. 1986) [Now, superseded by statute as stated in *Lemoine v. Cooney,* 514 So.2d 391, 392 (Fla. Dist. Ct. App. 1987)].

Johnson v. Naugle, 557 N.E.2d 1339, 1344–45 (Ind. Ct. App. 1990).

LEVERAGING AND HOW HOURLY BILLING RATES ARE DETERMINED

Leveraging is an important concept in law office billing. **Leveraging** *is the process of earning a profit from legal services that are provided by law office personnel (usually partners, associates, and legal assistants).* Leveraging allows the office not only to recover the cost of an attorney or legal assistant's salary but also to pay overhead expenses and even make a profit on each such person.

One way to calculate attorney and legal assistant hourly rates using the leveraging concept is called the **Rule of Three**. *The* **Rule of Three** *billing formula says that for a fee earner to be profitable, she should bill at three times her pay.*[9] The formula multiplies the salary of the individual by three, and then divides it by the number of billable hours she will bill for, so that each timekeeper grosses three times her salary.[10] Why three times? One-third goes to the person's salary, one-third is allocated for the office's overhead (rent, utilities, equipment, etc.) and one-third is profit.

leveraging
The process of earning a profit from legal services that are provided by law office personnel (usually partners, associates, and legal assistants).

rule of three
Billing formula that says for a fee earner to be profitable, she should bill at three times her pay.

$$\frac{\text{Salary} \times \text{Three}}{\text{Annual Billable Hours}} \quad \frac{25{,}000 \times 3 = \$75{,}000}{1{,}400} \quad = \$53.57$$

Thus, if a legal assistant made $25,000 a year and wanted to bill 1,400 hours for the year, the hourly billing rate would be $53.57 per hour.

Another way to set billing rates is to use the salary plus overhead plus profit formula but to reach each figure independently of one another. For example, suppose your office determined that the person you are setting the fee for was paid $24,000 annually, that the overhead attributed to that person was $35,000, that the office wanted to make a profit of $20,000 from this position, and that the individual would bill 1,500 hours. The hourly rate would be:

$$\frac{\text{Salary} + \text{Overhead} + \text{Profit}}{\text{Divided by Billable Hours}} \frac{\$24{,}000 + \$35{,}000 + \$20{,}000}{1{,}500} = \$52.66 \text{ per hour}$$

There are many things that affect billing rates, including the size of the law office, whether the office is located in a large city, and other factors, but these are some simple and effective formulas for helping determine rates.

MANUAL BILLING SYSTEMS

Before legal billing software was widely available, billings were generated manually, using typewriters or word processors and timesheets. Law practices typically would store the timesheets in the accounting file of each case and then periodically send a statement. Although some offices may still produce billings manually, manual systems have certain inherent limitations. Manual billings typically are slow and cumbersome, are prone to mathematical errors, and can take a great deal of overhead time to generate the bill. Thus, manual billings are sent out less frequently than most offices would like, which can cause cash-flow problems. In addition, management reports on manual systems are burdensome to produce. Computerized billing systems automatically produce management reports that tell who is billing the most hours, which clients pay the best, and which types of cases generate the most money.

Successful Billing Practices— Pleasing the Client and Avoiding Accounts Receivable Problems

The following are some successful billing practices.

- Legal fees and expenses should be discussed early in the case

  Determining legal fees in a case must be performed by an attorney and should be done up front with a client. Clients know that legal matters are expensive, so many are nervous about the cost of the matter from the first time they walk into the office. The attorney involved should raise the issue first.

  Other matters that should be covered include:
  - What type of billing format the client would like to receive;
  - When billings should be sent: biweekly, monthly, bimonthly, annually, etc.;
  - Where the billings should be sent (Some clients do not want the billings going to their office or to their home, so the office needs to know where the billing should be sent.);
  - Introducing the clients to the people, including the legal assistant, assigned to their case;

- An estimate of the length of time it will take to complete the matter (days, months, years);
- Legal expenses, including exactly what costs they will be billed for, whether clients can pay for outside assistance, such as the costs of investigators and experts, and how much the total expenses might be.

- Clients should be asked point-blank whether they will be able to pay the costs as they go along

  When fee discussions are being held with clients, it is important that clients be directly asked whether they think they will be able to make payments on the case as the costs are incurred. If they do not think they can pay the balance as they go along, it is important that this is known up front to help decide what type of fee agreement is the most appropriate.

- Clients must be screened

  It is important to realize that some clients simply will not pay their bills. It is important for the law office to learn to screen out and minimize these types of clients. Attorneys and law offices cannot take every case presented to them. Attorneys and law offices must be able to pick out the cases that will be profitable.

- Get the fee agreement in writing

  There is no substitute for reducing everything related to the billing process to writing. All fee

COMPUTERIZED BILLING SYSTEMS

Computerized billing systems solve many of the problems associated with manual systems. Generally, timekeepers still must record what they do with their time on a timeslip or timesheet. The timeslips are then entered into the legal billing software on a daily or weekly basis. It is common for offices using computerized billing systems to produce monthly or even biweekly bills according to the wishes of the client. In addition to solving cash-flow problems, most legal billing software programs produce reports that can help the office make good management decisions (this is covered in more detail later in the chapter). Computerized timekeeping and billing also produces billings that are more accurate than manual methods, since all mathematical computations are performed automatically by the computer. The 1989 ABA *Office Automation in Smaller Law Offices* survey found that 54.6 percent of the small offices responding used legal timekeeping and billing software.[11] In the *1990 IIT Chicago-Kent Survey of Large Law Offices*, 100 percent of the offices responding to the survey used legal timekeeping and billing software.[12] Because legal timekeeping and billing software prices have plunged to below even one hundred dollars, nearly any office can afford these types of programs.

agreements, arrangements regarding when billing should be sent, and bill formats should be completed in writing and put into the client's file.

- Accurately track how much a client has paid the firm

A successful billing system must be able to accurately track how much clients have paid the firm. It is important that the firm take great care in what goes in and out of the billing system and that the information be accurate.

- The firm must send regular billings

Nearly all clients like to receive timely billings. Most clients like to receive billings at least monthly. Imagine the frustration of a client who receives a quarterly billing that is four or five times more expensive than what he planned on. Regular billings will alert the client as to how he is being billed and how much he needs to budget. In addition, if a client sees timely bills that are more expensive than he had planned, he can contact the firm to tell it how he wants to proceed to limit future bills before they are incurred. This at least gives the client the option of cutting back on legal services instead of getting angry at the firm for not informing him of the changes on a timely basis.

- Client billings must be fair and respectful

Billings that are fair and courteous are essential to a good billing system. If a client thinks that the firm is overcharging her for services or that the billings are curt and unprofessional, there is a good chance that she will not pay the bill or will hold payment. If you speak to a client regarding a bill, be courteous and respectful and try to understand the situation from her point of view. If there is a dispute, take down the client's side of the story, relay the information to the attorney in charge of the matter, and let the attorney resolve it. Also, it is usually not a good practice to bill time for the time spent discussing the bill with a client.

- Client billings must be clear

Billings should be clear and without legalese. The billings should be easy to read and provide the information that the client wants to see. Payments that are made based on billings that are complicated and hard to read are oftentimes help up while the client tries to decipher the bill.

- Build relationships with clients

Remember that everything you do to build relationships with your clients, including returning phone calls, listening and being responsive to client needs, keeping your promises, and providing quality services affects the client when he receives a billing. Clients are far less likely to complain or refuse to pay billings when they receive good service from someone they like and trust and who is sincerely interested in their best welfare.

THE TIMEKEEPING AND BILLING CYCLE

Although all law offices have their own timekeeping and billing practices, most computerized systems follow a cycle or process (see Figure 5-17):

a)   Client and attorney reach an agreement on legal fees—At the outset of most cases, the client and attorney reach an agreement regarding how much the attorney will charge for services.

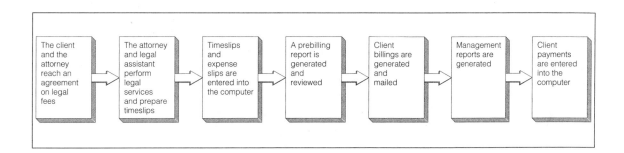

FIGURE 5-17   Computerized Timekeeping and Billing Cycle

b) Attorneys and legal assistants perform legal services and prepare manual timeslips—After the client and attorney reach an agreement on how legal fees will be figured, the attorneys and legal assistants begin work on the matter. When an attorney/legal assistant performs work, he fills out a timeslip to track the exact services performed for the client. As noted earlier, although some computer programs can keep track of time automatically and make computerized timeslips, many people still use the old manual method.

c) Timeslips and out-of-pocket expense slips are entered into the computer—Once the work has been performed on a case, and manual timeslips filled out, the timeslips must be entered into the computer. In addition, expense slips are entered into the computer to track the expenses an office incurs on behalf of a client.

d) Prebilling report is generated and reviewed by managing attorney (and discounted if necessary)—After legal services have been performed and recorded in the time and billing software, the next step is for a prebilling report to be generated. This is done before the final client bills are generated. A prebilling report is a rough draft of billings that eventually will be sent to clients (see Figure 5-18). The prebilling report is given to the attorney in charge of the case for review or to a billing committee to make sure the billing is accurate.

Attorneys may choose to discount bills for a variety of reasons, including thinking the task should have taken less time than it actually did. Discounts also are used for good customers, because of the client's hardship, for professional courtesy or for friends, or because the billing looks unreasonable. This can, however, be very frustrating to a legal assistant who has her time cut back. Typically, only the amount that is actually billed gets counted against her target or minimum billable set number of hours.

Changes can be made directly on the prebilling report and then entered into the computer.

e) Client billings are generated and mailed—Once the prebilling report has been reviewed and any changes made, formal client billings are generated by the computer (see Figure 5-19). There are many billing formats that most timekeeping and billing software can produce. The computer automatically prints the bills, and they are subsequently mailed to the clients.

f) Management reports are generated—Most computerized timekeeping and billing programs have a wide variety of management reports available. Management reports are not used for billing clients; they are used to evaluate the effectiveness of the office. For example, most programs generate a report that shows how much time is nonbillable. If an office has a great deal of nonbillable time, it might indicate the office is not productive and is losing valuable time from its timekeepers.

g) Client payments entered in computer—Finally, once the legal services have been performed and billings made to clients, payments made as a result of the billings must be recorded or entered into the computer, giving the client proper credit for the payment.

The timekeeping and billing process is a recurring cycle. Once billings are produced and payments made for a period, the process starts over if more work is performed on the case. The timeslips for the new period must be entered, billings generated, and so forth. Once a year or so, old timeslips should be purged or deleted from the computer. This allows the computer to operate faster.

```
                        JOHNSON, BECK & TAYLOR
                        Prebilling Report                    Page 1
  ----------------------------------------------------------------------

  Acme Refrigeration, Inc.                    Corporate Matters
  Miscellaneous Corporate Matters             Monthly
  Case Number:  ACME-002                      Trust Balance:  $2,825
  P.O. Box 10083                              Case Rate:  $125
  500 East Fifth Street                       Case Attorney:  MJB

  Los Angeles, CA  90014                      APR Interest:  18%
  Phone:  (213) 553-9342                      Discount:  10%


                              Previous Bill Owed $470.20




                          -- Legal Fees --

  7/6/91    MJB  Telephone conference with
                 Stevenson re:  June 1991 minutes     .50 hr    $ 62.50

  7/7/91    MJB  Preparation of June 1991 minutes;
                 prepared for review at next          1.00       $125.00 MJB
                 meeting of the board of directors    1.50 hr    $187.50

  7/9/91    MJB  Conference with Stevenson at home    .25 hr     none
                                                      1.75       $187.50 MJB
                 Total Legal Fees.....................2.25 hr    $250.00



                          -- Costs Advanced --

  7/7/91    MJB  Photocopy documents; June 1991
                 minutes (for board meeting)          $ .25 ea
                                                      100 items  $ 25.00

                 Total Costs Advanced.................           $ 25.00




                        Continued on Page Two
```

FIGURE 5-18 Prebilling Report—Corrections, if any, are made on the prebilling report by the supervising attorney or committee.

JOHNSON, BECK & TAYLOR
555 Flowers Street, Suite 200
Los Angeles, CA 90038
(212) 585-2342

Mary Smith
Acme Refrigeration, Inc.
P.O. Box 10083
500 East Fifth Street
Los Angeles, CA 90014

Billing Date: 08/15/91

Acct. Number: 4345AS3234
Previous Bal. in Trust $2,825.00

RE: Acme Refrigeration Miscellaneous Corporate Matters

DATE	PROFESSIONAL SERVICES	INDIV.	TIME	
7/6/91	Telephone conference with Stevenson re: clarifications to be made in June 1991 minutes regarding the purchases of additional refrig. units.	MJB	.50	$ 62.50
7/7/91	Preparation of June 1991 minutes; prepared for review at next meeting of the board of directors	MJB	1.00	$125.00
7/9/91	Conference with Stevenson regarding changes to the bylaws and voting rights	MJB	.25	$ -0-
TOTAL FOR THE ABOVE SERVICES			**1.75**	**$187.50**

DATE	PROFESSIONAL SERVICES			
7/7/91	Photocopy documents; June 1991 minutes (for board meeting)			$ 25.00
TOTAL FOR THE ABOVE SERVICES				**$ 25.00**
TOTAL BILLING				**$212.50**
CURRENT BALANCE IN TRUST				**$2,612.50**

FIGURE 5-19   Billing

BILL FORMATS

Generating bills is the most important aspect of any timekeeping and billing program. There is no uniform way that all law offices bill clients. The look and format of billings depend on the law office, its clients, the type of law it practices, etc. Thus, it is important that any timekeeping and billing system used, whether it is manual or computerized, be flexible in the number of client billing formats that are available. For example, some bill formats contain only general information about the services provided, while others show greater detail about what services were provided. In many computerized systems, the format of the bill is set up when the client's case is first entered into the system.

Historically, many offices did not itemize their billing, simply stating "For Services Rendered $XXX" on the bill. Although each client is different, most clients like to receive detailed billings of exactly what services are being provided. This allows the client to see what he is paying for. This also is beneficial to the office, since clients are more willing to pay the bill when they know what it is for. Producing detailed bills takes work. It requires timekeepers to make accurate, current timeslips of what work they have provided. Although this seems enough, it is not. It is very hard to persuade timekeepers to write down each service they perform (i.e. 12/22/91, Telephone call to Larry Jones, witness, regarding statement given 10/10/90.........15 minutes). Yet, the whole point of billing is to be paid. So, if an office produces a bill that is not itemized and therefore the client does not pay it, nothing has been gained. Although itemized billings are sometimes inconvenient for the timekeeper and take longer to produce, if the bill is paid in the end, the extra work has paid off.

MANAGEMENT REPORTS

Almost all timekeeping and billing software packages produce a wide variety of management reports. **Management reports** *are used to help management analyze whether the timekeeper is operating in an efficient and effective manner.* Management reports can be used to track problems an office may be experiencing and to help devise ways to correct the problems. The following are explanations of some common management reports and how they are used by offices.

management reports
Reports used to help management analyze whether the office is operating in an efficient and effective manner.

CASE/CLIENT LIST   Most billing packages allow the user to produce a case or client list. A list of all active cases an office has is very important in trying to effectively manage a large caseload. Most reports not only will list the client names but also will list the appropriate account number (also called "client identification number" by some programs). This is useful when trying to locate a client's identification number.

AGED ACCOUNTS RECEIVABLE REPORT   *The* **aged accounts receivable report** *shows all cases that have outstanding balances due to the office and how long these balances are past due* (see Figure 5-20). The report breaks down the current balances due and the balances thirty, sixty, and more than ninety days past due. Using this report, management can clearly see which clients are not paying and how old the balances are. This report also is helpful for following up on clients who are slow in paying their bills. Most programs allow the report to be run according to the type of case. Thus, management can see what types of cases (i.e. criminal, divorce, tax, etc.) have the most aged accounts. If one particular type of case has more than its share of aged accounts, it might be more profitable to stop taking that type. So,

aged accounts receivable report
Report showing all cases that have outstanding balances due and how long these balances are past due.

A. Aged Accounts Receivable Report

```
                    LAW OFFICES OF SMITH, SMITH AND JONES
 5/ 1/87                 Aged Accounts Receivable                    PAGE 1
------------------------------------------------------------------------------
 Entire Alphabet                                            All Bill Types
 All Attorneys                                              All Case Types
 Cycle:  All Cycles (All Months)                    Ignore Cycle Due Date
------------------------------------------------------------------------------
 Client/Matter                Balance   Current   30 Days   60 Days   Over 90
------------------------------------------------------------------------------
 All `Right Manufacturing C
   General Corporate Matt      127.50      None    127.50      None      None
   Hinge Division - Paten      975.00    975.00      None      None      None
                             ---------  --------  --------  --------  ---------
                             1,102.50    975.00    127.50      None      None

 Alta Loma Bookkeeping
   Purchase of Johnson Ch      800.00    175.00    175.00    450.00      None
 Burton, Sarah
   Divorce                     147.50      None    147.50      None      None
   Protective order            440.00      None      None    440.00      None
                             ---------  --------  --------  --------  ---------
                               587.50      None    147.50    440.00      None

 Carla's Hard to Fit
   Incorporation             1,500.00  1,500.00      None      None      None
 Chuck's Artist Supplies
   Liquidation                 607.50      None    505.00    102.50      None
 Drummond, Lester B.
   I.R.S. Matter               427.75    427.75      None      None      None
   Long Beach Property       1,775.00      None      None  1,775.00      None
   Possession                  500.00      None      None    500.00      None
                             ---------  --------  --------  --------  ---------
                             2,702.75    427.75      None  2,275.00      None
```

B. Timekeeper Productivity Report

```
                LAW OFFICES OF SMITH, SMITH AND JONES
 5/ 1/87          Attorney Time/Productivity Analysis       PAGE 1
------------------------------------------------------------------------
                                                    Fees      Hours
                                                    ----      -----
                        April 1987
                        ----------

 Arthur A. Alexander              Billed:        $8,852.50     77.75
                                  On Hold:          $100.00     1.00
   Payments Rec'd    $7,277.50    Non Chargeable:   $100.00      .75
   Standard Rate:    $  75.00     Written Off:      $125.00     2.00
   Realized Rate:    $112.00      Administrative:   $125.00     1.00

                         * * * *

 Byron B Brown                    Billed:        $9,527.75    101.50
                                  On Hold:            None      None
   Pyments Rec'd     $10,950.50   Non Chargeable:     None      None
   Standard Rate:    $  95.00     Written Off:        None      None
   Realized Rate:    $  93.00     Administrative:     None      None

                         * * * *

 Andrew B. Cabellero             Billed:        $12,750.00    101.00
                                 On Hold:         $1,250.00     10.00
   Payments Rec'd     $9,550.50   Non Chargeable:   $100.00     1.00
   Standard Rate:    $125.00      Written Off:      $250.00     2.20
   Realized Rate:    $125.00      Administrative:   $125.00     1.00

                         * * * *

 Monthly Summary - All Attorneys Listed
 ===========================================

                                 Billed:        $31,130.25    280.25
                                 On Hold:         $1,350.00     11.00
   Payments Rec'd                Non Chargeable:   $200.00      1.75
   This Month:       $27,778.00  Written Off:      $375.00      4.20
   Realized Rate:    $110.00     Administrative:   $250.00      2.00

                         * * * *
```

```
ng Servi
s                  175.00    175.00      None      None      None
Business
te                 725.00      None      None      None    725.00
                   112.50      None      None      None    112.50
                    75.00      None      None     75.00      None
                  --------  --------  --------  --------  ---------
                   912.50      None      None     75.00    837.50

 of Abe
te                 632.75      None    632.75      None      None
r chapt          7,500.00  7,500.00      None      None      None
s, Inc.
                 4,410.00      None  1,410.00  3,000.00      None
Agency
Fraud              475.00    475.00      None      None      None
Inc.
rative          12,550.00    550.00  9,405.00  2,425.00    170.00
ant
                   330.00    330.00      None      None      None

                   485.00      None      None    485.00      None
                  --------  --------  --------  --------  ---------
listed)         34,770.50 12,107.75 12,402.75  9,252.50  1,007.50
```

FIGURE 5-20   Aged Accounts Receivable Report and Timekeeper Productivity Report
Source: Courtesy CompuLaw, Ltd.

from a management perspective, this can be a very important report. It should be noted that aged account information should not appear on bills sent to clients. Bills that are more than thirty days old should simply say "past due."

```
  ┌─────────────────────────────────────────────────────────────────┐
  │                                                                   │
  │                  FENWICK, QUINT GERSON AND PECK                    │
  │    7/31/87            Case Type Productivity          PAGE 1      │
  │    ---------------------------------------------------------      │
  │                   Hours       Fees       Fees   %Total  %Total    │
  │    Case Type     Billable    Billed    Income  Fee Inc   Hours    │
  │    ---------------------------------------------------------      │
  │                                                                   │
  │                          July 1987                                │
  │                          ---------                                │
  │                                                                   │
  │    Bankruptcies        252.75  $26,450.00  $17,500.50  11.73  17.48 │
  │    Civil Matters        32.50   $4,142.75   $3,655.75   2.45   2.24 │
  │    Corporate Matters   125.75  $19,855.50  $12,500.25   8.38   8.70 │
  │    Criminal Matters     22.00   $1,875.00   $2,250.75   1.51   1.52 │
  │    Estate Planning      87.75   $9,475.00   $8,875.50   5.95   6.07 │
  │    Family Law           52.25   $6,175.75   $5,495.75   3.68   3.61 │
  │    General Business    108.70   $9,775.50   $8,975.50   5.95   7.52 │
  │    General Practice     61.00   $6,552.75   $7,275.50   4.88   4.22 │
  │    Litigation          225.00  $37,750.00  $44,550.75  29.87  15.56 │
  │    Personal Injury      35.00   $4,500.00   $4,125.25   2.76   2.42 │
  │    Probate Matters       0.00       $0.00       $0.00    .00    .00 │
  │    Real Estate Matter   18.00   $2,150.00   $2,100.00   1.40   1.24 │
  │    Taxation Matters     24.75   $2,650.00   $2,655.00   1.78   1.71 │
  │    --- Other ---         9.00   $1,253.00   $1,253.50    .84    .62 │
  │    Patents & Trademarks 36.50   $4,141.75   $4,155.50   2.78   2.52 │
  │    International Law    44.00   $8,645.25   $3,440.00   2.31   3.04 │
  │    Immigration Law      27.00   $3,150.00     $750.00    .50   1.86 │
  │    Insurance Defense   111.50  $10,950.75   $7,555.25   5.06   7.71 │
  │    Insurance Plaintiff  88.00   $8,125.00   $6,552.75   4.39   6.08 │
  │    Consumer Law          6.75     $595.00     $500.00    .33    .46 │
  │    Labor Unions         77.00   $5,845.00   $4,995.50   3.35   5.32 │
  │    ------------------------------------------------------------    │
  │    July Totals:      1,445.20 $174,058.00 $149,161.00             │
  │                                                                   │
  └─────────────────────────────────────────────────────────────────┘
```

FIGURE 5-21
Case Type
Productivity Report

Source: Courtesy
CompuLaw, Ltd.

TIMEKEEPER PRODUCTIVITY REPORT *The* **timekeeper productivity report** *shows how much billable and nonbillable time is being spent by each timekeeper* (see Figure 5-20). This report can be used to identify which timekeepers are the most diligent in their work. For example, notice in Figure 5-20 that "Arthur A. Alexander" billed a total of only 77.75 hours for the month, while the other attorneys billed more than 100 hours. Also, notice that "Byron B. Brown" produced the most billable hours and payments received by the office.

Finally, note the totals section, which shows that although the office billed 280.25 hours for a total of $31,130.25, the office received to date $27,778.00. Although the report in Figure 5-20 shows the results for only one month, most packages allow the productivity report to be run for a quarter or even for a year.

CASE TYPE PRODUCTIVITY REPORT *The* **case type productivity report** *shows which type of cases (i.e. criminal, personal injury, bankruptcy, etc.) are the most profitable* (see Figure 5-21). For example, in Figure 5-21 note that the bankruptcy and litigation areas of the law office brought in $17,500.50 and $44,550.75 respectively for the month of July, or 11.73 percent and 29.87 percent of the income earned. This report obviously shows which types of cases are the most profitable and which cases are the least profitable. Management will again use this type of report to decide which areas to concentrate more on to become more profitable.

TIMEKEEPING AND BILLING SERVICE BUREAUS

Some law offices use third-party timekeeping and billing service bureaus to generate their billings. *A* **timekeeping and billing service bureau** *is a company that for*

timekeeper productivity report
Report showing how much billable and nonbillable time is being spent by each timekeeper.

case type productivity report
Report showing which types of cases (i.e. criminal, personal injury, bankruptcy, etc.) are the most profitable.

timekeeping and billing service bureau
A company that for a fee processes attorney and legal assistant timesheets (usually on a monthly basis), generates billings, and records client payments for a law practice.

a fee processes attorney and legal assistant timesheets (usually on a monthly basis), generates billings, and records client payments for a law practice. Service bureaus are in the business of producing billings and tracking the financial management of other offices, including law offices. Whether it is cheaper to use a service bureau to produce billings or to do it in-house depends on the size of the office, type of clients, etc.

BILLING FROM THE CORPORATE AND GOVERNMENT PERSPECTIVE

outside counsel
Term referring to when corporate and government law practices contract with private law offices (i.e. outside of the corporation or government practice) to help them with legal matters, such as litigation, specialized contracts, stock/bond offerings, etc.

Corporate and government law practices sometimes hire outside counsel (i.e. private law offices). **Outside counsel** *refers to when corporate and government law practices contract with private law offices (i.e. outside of the corporation or government practice) to help them with legal matters, such as litigation, specialized contracts, stock/bond offerings, etc.* Thus, corporate and government law practices are purchasers of legal services and tend to look at billing from a different perspective. Figure 5-22 shows average expenditures for outside counsel for Fortune 500 companies by type of industry.

Corporate and government law practices are concerned with limiting the costs of legal fees. Many corporate clients will state that they will not pay more than a certain amount, perhaps $150 an hour, for any attorney regardless of experience. If the office wants to maintain the particular client, it will agree to the terms. Because corporations and governments have access to large sums of money and typically are good-paying clients, many offices will reduce the price to get and keep the business.

Corporate and government clients usually require very detailed bills to control what is being done on the case and to control costs. In some cases, corpora-

FIGURE 5-22
Average Expenditures for Outside Counsel/Legal Services for Large Corporations (Fortune 500)

Source: Altman & Weil, Inc. Management Consultants, *Special Report on Law Department Functions and Expenditures 1989.* Reprinted with the permission of Altman Weil Pensa Publications, Inc., copyright 1989 by Altman Weil Pensa Publications, Inc., Newtown Square, PA.

Industry	Average Expenditures
Petroleum	$ 5,941,812
Chemical/Pharmaceutical	8,494,339
Electrical/Computer	2,093,093
Machinery/Motors	7,368,842
Other Manufacturing	3,979,192
Retail/Wholesale	1,976,333
Finance/Stock Broker	1,608,830
Insurance	20,928,209
Banking	4,029,261
Telecommunications	2,246,213
Utilities	4,226,921
Transportation	5,600,263
Other Service Industries	3,147,144
Other Nonmanufacturing	3,984,814
Hospitals/Universities	954,912
All Industries	293,861

This list was developed by Sally Fiona King, the manager for legal administration of General Electric Co. in Fairfield, Conn., based on the author's experiences with the billing practices of a select group of law firms.

1. **Incomprehensible Format: Reams of Printout, No Clear Indication of What Was Accomplished**

This is everyone's worst nightmare, from the mailroom to the final recipient. Such an invoice takes months to read and will never be understood, and the in-house lawyer cannot hope to explain it to his or her business counterpart or internal auditor. This approach seems intended as justification for a big number on the bottom line. In fact, it merely enhances the negative beliefs about lawyers.

2. **Surprise Total!**

Sometimes an in-house lawyer is expecting an invoice for $10,000, and a $50,000 invoice arrives instead. Law firms should try to anticipate expectations, keep clients informed and avoid unpleasant surprises.

3. **Perceived Poor Work**

Some in-house lawyers are forced to spend considerable time rewriting and improving a brief, only to receive a bill for the full amount of time spent by outside counsel on an inadequate work product.

4. **Team Churning**

In some firms, the legal team, with the exception of the lead attorney, is constantly changing. This means additional time must be spent scaling the learning curve. It destroys any efficiency associated with the effects of experience.

5. **Too Much Conference Time**

Law firms need to look closely at the proportion of conference time to other activities reflected in the bill.

6. **Nickel-and-Dime Billing**

Some firms include line-item charges for postage, fax or the like, amounting to less than $10 in a bill for tens of thousands of dollars. A variation on this theme may be a bill for $50,000—which is readily acceptable—followed a few days later with a "supplemental invoice" for a de minimis amount.

7. **Errors in Arithmetic**

Such errors reveal that no real review has been conducted by the partner.

8. **Other Glaring Errors**

Some bills indicate time billed to the wrong client or matter. Others may show that an attorney has worked 26 hours in one day. As in Point 7, mistakes such as these raise questions about the entire bill.

9. **Bill Received Months after Work Completed**

When a bill is not timely, everyone who ever worked on or was involved in the matter has forgotten the complexity of the issues, as well as the results obtained.

10. **Bill Directed to the Wrong Person**

The in-house lawyer who works on a matter may not be responsible for getting bills paid. The bill should go to the person charged with this responsibility. That person, often the administrator, will obtain all appropriate reviews and approvals.

**FIGURE 5-23
Top 10 Reasons
Bills Are Unpaid**

Source: *The National Law Journal,* November 23, 1992, 55.

tions and governments use a competitive bidding process to select outside counsel. Thus, summary billings are usually not accepted. They also typically will limit the type and cost of expenses that are billed to them. For instance, some corporations require that computerized legal research (WESTLAW, LEXIS, etc.), postage, fax costs, and similar expenses be borne by the office.

It is not uncommon for a corporate law practice to publish policies and guidelines covering exactly what outside counsel will charge, when it will charge, how payments will be made, how much and what type of legal expenses will be reimbursed, and so on. Figure 5-23 shows the top ten reasons corporate law departments fail to pay private law offices.

SUMMARY

Although timekeeping, billing, and managing client funds are not glamorous tasks, they are essential to the survival of most law practices. Timekeeping is the process of tracking what attorneys and legal assistants do with their time. Billing is the process of issuing invoices for the purpose of collecting monies for legal service performed and being reimbursed for expenses. Typical kinds of legal fee agreements include hourly rate, contingency, flat, retainer, court awarded fees, and prepaid legal service plans.

A trust account is a separate bank account, apart from an office's general accounts, where unearned client funds are deposited. The use of trust accounts is mandated by ethical rules for all unearned monies that an office receives.

Leveraging is the process of earning a profit from legal services that are provided by the law office staff. The Rule of Three is a leveraging concept that states that fee earners should bill at three times their salaries.

Computerized billing programs allow offices to quickly and easily send out regular billings, produce management reports that administrators can use to help direct the office, and can typically produce many different types of bill formats.

KEY TERMS

Timekeeping
Billing
Hourly rate fee
Attorney or legal assistant hourly rate
Client hourly rate
Blended hourly rate fee
Activity hourly rate
Contingency fee
Flat fee
Earned retainer
Unearned retainer
Trust or escrow account
Cash advance
Retainer for general representation

Case retainer
Pure retainer
Court awarded fees
Prepaid legal service
Value billing
Criminal fraud
Timesheet or timeslip
Billable time
Nonbillable time
Pro Bono
Overhead
Leveraging
Rule of Three
Management reports

Aged accounts receivable report

Timekeeper productivity report

Case type productivity report

Timekeeping and billing service bureau

Outside counsel

PROBLEM SOLVING QUESTIONS

1. You are a new legal assistant and have worked for a medium-sized law office for three months. It has been a tremendous learning experience for you. It has taken time to learn how the office does business, its policies and procedures, what type of service you are expected to give to clients, where resources are and how to use them, such as the office's law library, copy machines, and form files. Although it has taken time for you to learn these things, you also have been productive and have received several compliments on the quality of your work.

One day, you read in the office's staff manual that all legal assistants are required to bill 1,500 hours annually or face possible discipline. You immediately contact your supervisor and ask whether as a new legal assistant you will be expected to bill this amount. Your supervisor responds "Of course, you were told that when you were hired." You immediately begin gathering copies of your timesheets to compile your total. You also request that the billing department send you the total numbers of hours you have billed to date. When you get the report from billing, you panic; you have billed only 300 hours. You are 75 hours behind where you should be (1,500 divided by four [i.e. one-fourth the way through the year] equals 375). What do you do now, and how could you have avoided this unfortunate situation?

2. On April 1, a billing goes out to John Myers, one of the clients whose cases you have been working on. Mr. Myers calls you a few days later and complains about the amount of time shown on the bill. He is extremely rude and discourteous. Mr. Myers flatly states that he thinks he is being over-billed. How do you handle the phone call?

3. Your office is on the same side of the city as a major manufacturing plant. You notice that many of the plant's employees come to your office for routine legal services, such as wills, adoptions, and name changes. Although the office has been charging these clients on an hourly basis, you think that there might be alternatives. You talk to one of the partners, and she suggests that you look into the alternatives. Prepare a memorandum to the partner discussing billing options for this situation.

4. You are interviewing a new client. The client wants to hire your office to help negotiate the purchase of a small business. The seller has offered $20,000. The new client would be willing to pay this amount, although she thinks it is a bit high, but does not feel comfortable negotiating with the seller and would rather have an attorney involved in the deal for her protection. The new client is suspicious of legal assistants and attorneys and is especially concerned about how much her case will cost. You inform the client that the attorney will be the one who actually talks to her about the fee issue, but that typically this type of case is taken on an hourly basis and that the attorney will only be able to give her a very broad estimate of what the total matter will cost. The client states that this would be unacceptable to her because she does not have a lot of money to pay overpriced attorneys. The client also states that she would like this matter settled as soon as possible. You must prepare a memorandum to the attorney outlining the facts of the case. What type of fee arrangement would you suggest to the attorney? Please keep in mind the client's anxieties and her particular needs.

KNOW YOUR ETHICS

1. Recently, your office has found a niche in representing spouses collecting on past-due child support. In most cases, your clients have little money to pay you with and are financially strapped, since they no longer have the income of their former spouses to support their children and do not have the child support. In some cases, large amounts of money are owed, but finding the former spouses has proved difficult. Your supervising attorney decides that the best way to handle these types of cases is on a one-third contingency basis. Your supervising attorney asks for your comments. How do you respond?

2.   You work for a firm with seventeen attorneys. The firm has always financially done well, but recently it is struggling. There is a great deal of pressure for you to meet your billing requirements of 1,550 hours, even if no one has work for you to do. The firm will not accept the answer "No one is giving me any work." You are being encouraged to go to each attorney's office and drum something up. Discuss the ethical situation you are being placed in and how you would handle it.

3.   Approximately three months ago you and another legal assistant, Jonathan, were hired in a medium-sized law office. You work very hard at your job, record your hours honestly, and always receive compliments on the quality of your work. However, your supervising attorney constantly compares you with Jonathan, who consistently bills more hours than you do. You suspect that Jonathan is padding his time. How would you handle the matter?

4.   A client contacts your law office for representation regarding the routine sale of a piece of property. The client appears to be fairly wealthy. Your supervising attorney charges the client what amounts to be about double what the firm regularly charges. You know this because the office uses an internal fee schedule to help the attorneys set a proper fee. Discuss the ethical considerations. How would you handle the situation?

5.   You work in a relatively small law office. The office is having a cash-flow problem and has requested that staff members bill as much as they can and really work on cases in which the firm may be able to solve some of its cash-flow problem. The office manager comes to you and tells you that a client whose case you are working on has several thousands of dollars in the trust account. Although not telling you directly, the office manager lets you know that she wants you to bill some hours to this client so the firm can get some of the money in the trust account. Discuss the ethical problems associated with this. Assume you bill the client when in fact no hours were worked on the case. What problems arise?

PRACTICE EXERCISES

1.   You just finished a hectic morning. Before you go to lunch, you fill out your timekeeping report for the day. Although you wanted to record your time earlier, you just could not get to it. Please record your time on a blank piece of paper; have columns set up for the date, client/case name, timekeeper, services rendered, billable or nonbillable, and the amount of time spent on the matter (see Figure 5-10). For each activity listed, decide whether it is billable or not billable. Record your time, first using tenths of hours. Also, you should fill out expense slips for items that should be charged back to clients. Record the expenses on a blank piece of paper and include date, client/case name, your name, type of expense, and cost. Please total the cost of each expense slip. The firm charges 25 cents each for copies and 50 cents per page to send a fax. Assume long-distance phone calls cost 25 cents a minute.

As best you can recall, this is how your day went:

8:00 A.M.—8:12 A.M.	Got a cup of coffee, talked to other law office staff members, and reviewed your schedule/things to do sheet for the day.
8:13 A.M.—8:25 A.M.	Talked to your supervising attorney (Jan Mitchell) about some research she needs done on the standards necessary to file a motion to dismiss in *Johnson v. Cuttingham Steel*. Ms. Mitchell also asks you

to find a bankruptcy statute she needs for *Halvert v. Shawnee Saving & Loan.*

8:26 A.M.—8:37 A.M.   A legal assistant from another office calls to remind you that the legal assistant association you belong to is having a meeting at noon and that you are running the meeting.

8:38 A.M.—8:40 A.M.   One of your least favorite clients, John Hamilton, calls to ask you when he is supposed to be at your office to prepare for his deposition tomorrow. You pick up the weekly schedule off your desk and read him the information he needs.

8:40 A.M.—8:50 A.M.   You find the information you need re: the motion to dismiss in *Johnson v. Cuttingham Steel* in a motion in another case you helped prepare last month. The research is still current so Ms. Mitchell will be pleased you found it so fast. You note that it took you two hours to research this issue when you did it the first time. You copy the material Ms. Mitchell needed (five pages) and put it in her box.

8:55 A.M.—9:30 A.M.   You get hold of a witness you have been trying to contact in *Menly v. Menly.* The call was long-distance. The call lasted fifteen minutes and the memo to the file documenting the call took twenty minutes.

9:30 A.M.—9:54 A.M.   Ms. Mitchell asks you to contact the attorney in *Glass v. Huron* regarding a discovery question. You spend ten minutes on hold. The call is long-distance but you get an answer to Ms. Mitchell's question.

10:00 A.M.—10:45 A.M.   One of the secretaries informs you that you must interview a new client, Richard Sherman. The person that was supposed to see Mr. Sherman got delayed. Mr. Sherman comes to your office regarding a simple adoption. However, in talking to Mr. Sherman you find out that he also needs someone to incorporate a small business that he is getting ready to open. You gladly note that your office has a department that handles this type of matter. You take the basic information down regarding both matters. You tell the client that you will prepare a memo regarding these matters to the appropriate attorney and one of the office's attorneys will contact him within two days to further discuss the matter. You also copy ten pages of information that Mr. Sherman brought.

10:45 A.M.—10:54 A.M.   One of the secretaries asks you to cover her phone for her while she takes a quick break. Because the secretary always helps you when you ask for it, you gladly cover the phone for a few minutes. Ms. Mitchell asks you to send a fax in *Stewart v. Layhorn Glass,* so you use this time to send the six-page fax.

10:55 A.M.—12:00 NOON   You were given the job of organizing some exhibits in *Ranking v. Siefkin* yesterday by Ms. Mitchell. You finally have some free time to organize the exhibits.

12:00 NOON—1:00 P.M.   You attend the legal assistant association lunch.

1:00 P.M.—2:00 P.M.   You work on a pro bono

2:00 P.M.—5:30 P.M.

criminal case that Ms. Mitchell is representing on appeal. In an effort to become familiar with the case, you read some of the transcripts from the trial. Ms. Mitchell hands you a new case. Ms. Mitchell says that we will be representing the defendant. She asks you to read the petition and our client file, analyze the case, and draft interrogatories to send the plaintiff. You spend the rest of the day working on this case.

2. You have just been hired by a private law practice. You begin to get a little worried because your employers say you should "hold on" to your paycheck for an extra day to make sure it will clear the bank. You notice that many times staff members "forget" to fill out slips for charging expenses back to the clients, that bills are usually done on a quarterly basis, and that many expenses (such as copying expense) are included in the overhead of the office and not billed to the clients at all. Please identify what the problems are with the office and give a detailed answer on how you would go about attacking the problems.

3. You work for an insurance company. The head of the legal department asks you to begin drafting some billing guidelines for private law practices that represent your interests. Currently the department reviews bills at varying hourly rates from firm to firm and law offices are passing on to your office all types of expenses that they should not be including. Please draft a set of guidelines as requested.

4. You are an office manager in a small law office. The office has two partners, four associates, two legal assistants, six secretaries, and several clerks. The offices does not use any billing formulas to set its rates; it charges approximately what the going rate is at other offices. You decide that this may not be a very good way of setting these rates, since the profitability of the office has decreased substantially every year. Below are the salaries for all the positions and the number of hours they will work. The salaries are largely determined by the experience and capability of the person involved. The partners set their own hourly rates, so do not bother with them.

Employee	Salary	Annual Billable Hours
Associate 1	$38,000	1,800
Associate 2	$40,000	1,750
Associate 3	$42,000	1,800
Associate 4	$60,000	2,000
Legal Assistant 1	$28,000	1,500
Legal Assistant 2	$24,000	1,600
Secretaries	$18,000	2,080 normal hours

a) Please set the billing rate for the above employees using the Rule of Three.

  Further, the office has never billed for overhead expenses, such as copying costs, long-distance costs, etc.; it has just absorbed these costs.

b) Should the office continue to do this? What are the alternatives?

  During your time there, you notice that once the office has taken on a case, the clients mysteriously quit making payments on their bills. This hurts the office's ability to pay staff and cover expenses. What do you suggest?

5. Using a national bar association magazine such as the *ABA Journal* or *Law Practice Management*, identify five timekeeping and billing packages and answer the following questions:

a) What are the major features of each package?

b) What features do the companies use to distinguish their products from one another?

c) Do the programs integrate with other software products from the same company, such as docket control and general ledger, or are they "stand-alone"?

d) For each package, identify whether it is aimed at small-, medium-, or large-sized practices.

e) Which packages look to be the most user-friendly (or easiest to use)?

f) Which product would you recommend purchasing if you worked for a:
- Large office (one hundred attorneys or more);
- Medium office (fifty attorneys);
- Small office (ten attorneys);
- Solo practitioner?

Give reasons for your answer and be sure and take into account the cost of the package.

6. Assume for this exercise that you can bill for all activities that relate to learning. Keep a detailed record for all your activities for one day, from when you wake up until you go to sleep. Record your time in tenths (i.e. on six-minute intervals). At the end of the day, calculate the amount due based on your timesheet.

NOTES

1. Braxton Busch, "Questions Raised over Paralegal Billing," *Legal Assistant Today*, November/December 1992, 25.
2. *Business Insurance,* October 18, 1993.
3. Carol Milano, "1993 Legal Assistant Today Salary Survey Results," *Legal Assistant Today,* May/June, 1993, 60.
4. Mary Ann Altman and Robert I. Weil, *How to Manage Your Law Office* (New York: Matthew Bender & Company, 1987), 4–44.
5. Altman and Weil, *An Introduction to Law Practice Management* (New York: Matthew Bender & Company, 1987), 71.
6. Jeff Schweers, "Lawyers Ready for an End to Billing by the Hour," *The Florida Bar News,* October 1, 1992, 17.
7. William Statsky, *Introduction to Paralegalism*, 4th ed. (Saint Paul, Minnesota: West Publishing Co., 1992), 271.
8. Statsky, *Introduction to Paralegalism,* 270.
9. John Tate, "Profitability Formulas and Paralegal/Associate Comparisons," *NFPA,* Spring 1991, 18.
10. Charlotte W. Smith, *Law Office Dynamics* (Dallas, TX, Pearson Publications Company, 1993), 96.
11. ABA Legal Technology Resource Center, *Office Automation in Smaller Law Offices: Survey Report* (Chicago: American Bar Association, 1989), 18, copyright 1989 by American Bar Association.
12. Ronald W. Staudt, *"1990 IIT Chicago-Kent Survey of Large Law Firms"* (Chicago: Illinois Institute of Technology, 1990), 3–8. 77 S. Wacker Drive, Chicago, IL 60606, (312) 567-6800.

WELCOME TO WALLACE AND SANDERS

TRAINING MANUAL OUTLINE

- Welcome to Wallace and Sanders
- Getting Started
- Lesson 1: Entering A New Client
- Lesson 2: Entering A Timeslip
- Lesson 3: Entering An Expense Slip
- Lesson 4: Entering Several Timeslips and Expense Slips
- Lesson 5: Printing A Pre-Billing Report and A Client Bill
- Lesson 6: Recording A Client Payment And Displaying An Account
- Lesson 7: Printing An Interim Time And Expense Summary Report

Welcome to Wallace and Sanders! We are an active and growing firm with four attorneys and two legal assistants. As you know, you have been hired as a legal assistant intern. We are very happy to have you on board, we can certainly use the help.

At Wallace and Sanders we put an emphasis on providing quality legal services to our clients. We bill our clients on a regular basis for these quality services, typically either on a bi-weekly or a monthly basis depending on the needs of the client. We strive to make sure our billings are timely and without errors. Because billings and fee disputes are some of the most common types of ethical complaints filed against lawyers we require that all staff members understand and fully appreciate the billing process. In addition, we want our staff members to have many job skills and to be flexible enough to enter timeslips into the computer should we be short-handed or need additional help. Thus, all staff members are required to have some minimal training on our billing system. We have developed this training manual to help you learn our system.

We currently use the Micro Craft VERDICT timekeeping and billing program. One of the reasons we chose VERDICT is because it is so easy to learn. Verdict is very easy to use and within a few minutes you will be entering information in it and generating client bills quickly and easily. Please note that during this training exercise you will be entering information for one attorney, RSS, to keep it simple.

We know you want to begin using VERDICT immediately, so there is only a short "Getting Started" section that you should read before you get on the computer. After the "Getting Started" section there are 7 short lessons, that only take between 5 and 15 minutes each to complete.

GETTING STARTED

OVERVIEW OF VERDICT

VERDICT is a timekeeping and billing system made specifically for law offices. It allows law offices to track attorney and legal assistant timeslips, to track expense slips, to issue client billings, to track client payments and to generally manage client accounts. VERDICT is menu driven. You see menus and can choose which option you want from the menu by typing a number or letter. Figure A-1 shows the main VERDICT menu. An explanation of the main VERDICT menu is described below:

A. **Create accounts -** This option is used to set up client accounts such as the client's name, address, type of case, billing format options and the like.

B. **Post to accounts -** This option is used to enter timeslips, expense slips, payments and to review client accounts. Much of your time is spent here entering information (see Figure A-2).

FIGURE A-1

```
                    V E R D I C T

            Legal Billing and Timekeeping System
            Copyright (c) 1991 by MICRO CRAFT, INC.
                Version 7.2 Serial No. 1699999

Master Menu

A - Create accounts                K - Back up hard disk
B - Post to accounts               L - Reload hard disk
C - Print bills and review statements  M - Print client summary statements
D - System maintenance             N - Batch transactions
E - Edit account information       O - Print a sorted client list
F - Delete or duplicate accounts   P - Print fee allocation reports
G - Print monthly and yearly summary  Q - Verify client data files
H - Print aged account report      R - Print audit reports
I - Print list of accounts         S - Print mailing and file labels
J - End of month clear

Select (backspace to exit):
```

FIGURE A-2

```
                    V E R D I C T
                      (LBSPOST)


Last Account No.: None yet

Transactions:

0 - Edit
1 - Review
2 - Service
3 - Expense
4 - Payment

Desired Transaction:
```

C. **Print bills and review statements** - This option is used to print pre-billing reports and to print final client bills (see Figure A-4).

G. **Print monthly and yearly summary** - This option is used to produce various management reports either for the current month or year-to-date.

Other Options - These items will not be used in this training manual.

Figure A-2 shows the "Post to accounts" submenu from the VERDICT main menu. The "Post to Accounts" menu is where timeslips (called "services" in VERDICT) is entered, expenses slips, payments and where a client's account can be viewed. Figure A-3 shows a complete "service" record (i.e., a timeslip) which has been entered into VERDICT. Figure 1-4 shows the "Print bills and review statements" submenu. This is where pre-billing reports, called "review statements" and final bills are generated and printed.

One of the things you will do in this training manual is to print the bill found in Figure A-5.

FIGURE A-3

```
                              SERVICE

   Account:  00010349 - Francis R. McDonald
                        McDonald's Red Mountain Hardware

   Min. Disk Space Remaining on DRIVE is 3054 Kbytes


                                                    Default Values

   Account No.              :00010349 (Type E to exit here)    :00010349
   Date                     :11-14-92                          :11-14-92
   Service Code (Part 1)    :Preparation of incorporation documents :Hand type
   Service Code (Part 2)    :First Meeting of Board of Directors.    :Hand type
   Timekeeper(FEE,RET,ADJ): SDM                                :SDM
   Time (decimal hrs.)   :3.5                                  :0.25

   All entries above correct? (Y/N)
```

FIGURE A-4

```
                        V E R D I C T
                           (LBSBILL)

   CHOICE OF STATEMENTS:

   0 - Change active attorney (all)
   1 - Billing statement only
   2 - Summary bill only
   3 - Billing statement and summary bill
   4 - Review statement
   5 - Billing statement only for To-Be-Billed accounts
   6 - Review statement for To-Be-Billed accounts
   7 - Review statement for Held accounts

   Select (press RETURN for menu):
```

GILBERT, SIMPSON & HOWELL
Attorneys at Law
232 Court Street
Huntsville, Alabama 35801
* * *
(123) 726-5000

Linda Smith   Billing Date: 12/31/94
P.O. Box 10083   Acct. No: RS000100
500 East Fifth Street
Cleveland, OH 90014

RE: Smith v. United Sales

PREVIOUS BALANCE $ 0.00

DATE	PROFESSIONAL SERVICES RENDERED	INDIV	TIME	
12-01-94	Phone Call and Letter to Expert Witness			
	re: Expert's Report on Causality	RSS	0.50	
12-06-94	Office Conf. with Client	RSS	0.50	
12-12-94	Investigation and location of Key Witnesses	RSS	4.00	
12-13-94	Preparation of Interrogatory Responses	RSS	5.00	
12-16-94	Deposition of Client	RSS	6.50	
12-19-94	Took Depostition of Defendant	RSS	3.50	
TOTAL FOR THE ABOVE SERVICES			20.00	$2,000.00

DATE	EXPENSES			
12-13-94	Copies of Interrogatories, 180 pages		$ 45.00	
12-13-94	Long Distance Phone Call Re: Expert		$ 5.00	
12-27-94	Copy of Deposition Transcripts		$450.00	
TOTAL FOR THE ABOVE EXPENSES				$ 500.00
			TOTAL	$2,500.00
	TOTAL PAYMENTS			$ 0.00
			AMOUNT DUE	$2,500.00

Please write the above account number on your check
and make your check payable to Gilbert, Simpson & Howell, P.A.
THANK YOU

FIGURE A-5

INTRODUCTION TO THIS TRAINING MANUAL

You are using a demonstration version of the program. This version is identical to the actual program except that you are limited to a maximum of 25 accounts or clients. For the training manual only you will be entering information for the imaginary law firm of Gilbert, Simpson & Howell. Some information has already been entered for you into the demonstration version of VERDICT. Throughout this training manual, information you need to type into the program will be designated in several different ways.

Keys to be pressed on the keyboard will be designated in brackets in all caps, bold and enlarged type (e.g. press the **[ENTER]** key).

Words or letters that should be typed will be designated in bold and enlarged (e.g. type: **Deposition of Client .25 hours**).

Information which is or should be displayed on your computer screen is shown in quotation marks and in *italic* type (e.g. *"press enter to continue"*).

You're now ready to get on the computer and use VERDICT!

LESSON 1: ENTERING A NEW CLIENT INTO VERDICT

You will begin to enter the information necessary to produce the bill in Figure A-5. In this short lesson you will load the VERDICT program and enter the client, Linda Smith into VERDICT.

LESSON 1:

1. Load the VERDICT program according to the instructions provided by your supervisor/instructor.

2. You will first see the VERDICT—Legal Timekeeping Logo which says to

   "press any key to continue."

3. Press the: **[ENTER]** key to go to the next step.

4. You are now asked to enter the current date (MMDDYY). For this training exercise, type: **123194** as the current date and press the **[ENTER]** key.

5. VERDICT responds with:

   "Note: Every user must enter a unique user number.
   Enter your user number:"

   Your supervisor/instructor will issue you a number. **Enter the number you have been given** and press the **[ENTER]** key.

6. You are now at the VERDICT main menu (similar to Figure A-1). The VERDICT main menu is displayed on the screen. The main menu allows you to access different options A through S of VERDICT by typing the letter to the left of the option.

   The first step in creating the billing shown in Figure A-5 is to enter the new client "Linda Smith" into VERDICT.

7. At the VERDICT main menu press: **A** (for "Create Accounts").

8. VERDICT responds with:

   "TOTAL NUMBER OF ACCOUNTS = 16
   Enter Account No. as XXXXXXX (press RETURN for menu):"

   VERDICT is telling you that there are currently 16 accounts already in VERDICT (these are accounts that have already been entered for you) and that it is ready to accept the account number of the new client you are about to enter.

Type the account number: **000100** and press the: **[ENTER]** key.

9. VERDICT responds with:

   "Enter responsible attorney:".

   You must tell VERDICT what attorney is primarily responsible for the case. Type: **RSS** and press the: **[ENTER]** key.

10. VERDICT responds with:

    "Enter income allocation percentage for RSS (press ENTER for 100%):"

    Income allocation is used when the firm wants attorneys to only receive the income they produced. Income allocation will not be used, simply press the **[ENTER]** key to go to the next step.

11. VERDICT responds with:

    "Enter working attorney (or type "COMPLETE" when done):

    VERDICT Is asking for the initials of another attorney who will work this case.

    Type: **COMPLETE** and press the **[ENTER]** key to skip this.

12. VERDICT responds with:

    "Client Name (40 char. max.)
    XXXXXXXXXXXXXXXXXXXXXXXXXXXXXXXXXXXXXXXXX

    VERDICT is asking you to enter the client's name exactly how you want it to appear on all bills and reports. Type: **Linda Smith** and press the: **[ENTER]** key.

13. VERDICT responds with:

    "Client's Address Line No. 1 (30 char. max.)
    XXXXXXXXXXXXXXXXXXXXXXXXXXXXXX

    Type: **P.O. Box 10083** and press the: **[ENTER]** key.

14. You are next asked to enter the client's address line no. 2. Type: **500 East Fifth Street** and press the: **[ENTER]** key.

15. VERDICT responds with:

    "Client's City, State Zip (30 char. max.)
    XXXXXXXXXXXXXXXXXXXXXXXXXXXXXX

    Type: **Cleveland, OH 90014** and press the **[ENTER]** key.

16. VERDICT then asks you to enter the: "RE Line 1." The program is asking you to enter what identifier should be put on all of the bills to identify this particular matter to the client. This will appear on the "subject" line of all bills.

    Type: **Smith v. United States** and press the **[ENTER]** key.

17. VERDICT then asks for a 2nd RE: line. Since one RE: line is enough press the: **[ENTER]** key to skip this. Press the: **[ENTER]** key again to skip the 3rd RE: line. Finally, press the: **[ENTER]** key one more time to skip the 4th RE: line.

18. VERDICT responds with:

    "Sort Name (15 Char. max., return for Client).
    XXXXXXXXXXXXXXX

    Because we want to sort this case using the client's name, just press the: **[ENTER]** key.

19. The next thing the program asks you for is the "Contact Name." This is typically only used if you are dealing with a company. To skip this, simply press the: **[ENTER]** key.

20. Next, enter the telephone number of the contact person. Type: **(913) 367-2344** and the press the **[ENTER]** key.

21. VERDICT responds with:

    Charge Codes:

    1-Standard Rate

    2-Discount Rate

    3-Flat Fee

    4-Retainer

    5-Contingent Fee

    6-No Charge

    7-Administrative Time

    VERDICT wants to know what type of fee arrangement this client has. In this case the client has agreed to pay the firm a standard hourly billing rate of $100.00 for all attorneys. Press: **1** (for "Standard Rate").

22. VERDICT responds with:

    "(1) hourly rate varies according to timekeeper.

    (2) Hourly rate fixed, regardless of timekeeper."

    Since the client agreed to pay a set rate for all attorneys on the case, Press: **2**

23. VERDICT now wants to know what the fixed hourly rate is. Type: **100** and press the **[ENTER]** key.

24. VERDICT responds with:

    "Rate to use for this account (A-J):

    In some types of cases such as flat fee or contingency fee cases, the attorney may want to know how much the services would have cost the client if he or she had billed at an hourly rate. This option helps to do that. To skip this, simply press: **A.**

25. VERDICT next asks if there is a previous balance on this account. Because this is a new client, press: **0** and press the: **[ENTER]** key.

26. VERDICT then asks what interest rate to charge clients for invoices that are not paid on time. Because we do not want to charge interest, press: **0** and press the: **[ENTER]** key.

27. Next, VERDICT asks whether to temporarily put this account on a "Hold" status. Since we do not want to put a "hold" on this account, press the: **N** key.

28. VERDICT then asks you to enter what type of default format the bills should be (this can later be changed when you go to print the bill also—but, this option sets the default or normal bill format for all bills sent to this client). Because we want to itemize the timekeeper and the time only, press: **2**

29. The program then asks you to enter what type of case this is. Press: **16** and press the: **[ENTER]** key since this is a product liability case. (Note: These are user defined and you can create what types of cases you usually handle).

30. VERDICT responds by displaying the account information with the prompt:

    "A-P to change. Any other key to post new account:"

    If you made a mistake entering any of the information you can now change it by typing the appropriate letter. If you did not make any errors, press the: **[ENTER]** key to post the client's account.

31. VERDICT then asks you to enter the account number of another new client. Press the: **[ENTER]** key and you will taken back to the VERDICT main menu.

This concludes Lesson 1.

TO EXIT VERDICT:

If you want to exit the program from the main menu simply press the **[BACKSPACE]** key.

TO GO TO LESSON 2:

To go to Lesson 2, stay at the VERDICT main menu.

LESSON 2: ENTERING A TIMESLIP

In this lesson you will enter the first timeslip shown in Fig. A-5 (e.g. "12/1/94 Phone Call and Letter to Expert Witness re: Expert's Report on Causality") into VERDICT.

If you exited from Lesson 1, follow steps 1-5 in Lesson 1 until you are at the VERDICT main menu.

LESSON 2

1. To enter a timeslip (VERDICT calls these a "service" slip) into the computer for work done on the case, press: **B** (for "Post to accounts") from the VERDICT main menu.

2. VERDICT responds with the "Post to account" submenu (i.e. "LBSPOST"), similar to Figure A-2. Because we want to enter and post a timeslip or service press: **2.**

3. VERDICT responds with:

   "Set Timekeeper Default Initials"

   Many times, a user will set down and post all of the time for a particular timekeeper at one time. This option allows the user to set a temporary default value to quicken the data entry process. Type: **RSS** and press the: **[ENTER]** key.

4 VERDICT responds with:

   "Set Time Increment Default"

   VERDICT allows you to set a default value for the amount of time timekeepers spend on a case. In some instances, this can speed up the data entry process. Type: **.50** and press the **[ENTER]** key.

5. VERDICT then presents you with a blank service or timeslip entry form (similar to Figure A-3, except the form is not completed). VERDICT responds with:

   Account No. ?

   VERDICT is asking you to enter the account number of the client you are entering a service entry form for. Type: **100** and press the: **[ENTER]** key.

6. VERDICT then asks you to enter the date that the service was performed. Type: **120194** and press the: **[ENTER]** key.

7. Next, VERDICT responds with:

   "Service Code (Part 1)?"

   VERDICT is asking you to identify what services were performed for the client. (VERDICT comes with default codes that you can enter here to speed up data entry—but to keep it simple we will enter our description of the service without using these codes). Press the: **[ENTER]** key.

   VERDICT responds by opening up a box called *"Powerpost."* This is simply a place to type the description of the services rendered. Type: **Phone Call and Letter to Expert Witness re: Expert's Report on Causality** and then press the: **[F7]** key. The computer responds by placing the text in the service slip.

8. VERDICT then responds with:

   "Timekeeper (FEE, RET or ADJ)."

   VERDICT is simply asking you for initials of the timekeeper that performed the services. Because we entered RSS as the default timekeeper earlier, just press the: **[ENTER]** key and RSS is automatically entered as the timekeeper.

9. You must now enter the amount of time the timekeeper spent on delivering the service. Because we entered the default time value of .50 earlier, just press the **[ENTER]** key.

10. VERDICT then asks whether the entry is correct. If your entries are correct press: **Y** and the service slip will be saved. If your entry is not correct type N and, the entry will be deleted and you can re-enter the entry.

11. You are now at another blank form which you can use to enter more service timeslips. At the: *"Account No.?"* prompt, press: **E** and press the **[ENTER]** key to go back to the "Post to accounts" submenu (i.e. "LBSPOST").

This concludes Lesson 2.

TO EXIT VERDICT:

If you want to exit the program press the **[ENTER]** key, which will take you to the main menu. To exit the program from the main menu simply press the **[BACKSPACE]** key.

TO GO TO LESSON 3:

To go to Lesson 3, stay at the "Post to accounts" submenu (i.e. "LBSPOST" similar to Figure A-2).

LESSON 3: ENTERING AN EXPENSE SLIP

In this lesson you will enter the first expenses shown in Figure A-5 (e.g. "12-13-94" Copies of Interrogatories Responses at .25") into VERDICT.

If you exited from Lesson 2, follow steps 1-5 in Lesson 1, and then press B to get to the "Post to accounts" submenu (i.e. "LBSPOST"—similar to Figure A-2).

LESSON 3:

1. In this lesson we will enter an expense slip into the computer. At the "Post to Accounts" submenu (i.e. "LBSPOST") press: **3** (for "Expense") to begin entering an expense slip.

2. The Expense form is very similar to the service entry form. You are first asked to enter the account number of the client you would like to bill the expense to. Type: **100** and press the **[ENTER]** key.

3. You are then prompted for a date. Enter: **121394** and press the: **[ENTER]** key.

4. You are then prompted with: *"Enter Expense Code (Part 1)."* Again, we will not use a code, but instead will type our own description of the expense. Press the: **[ENTER]** key.

5. VERDICT responds with:

   "What is the Expense Statement?
   XXXXXXXXXXXXXXXXXXXXXXXXXXXXXXXXX"

   You are being asked to enter what the expense slip is for. Enter: **Copies of Interrogatories, 180 pages** and press the **[ENTER]** key.

6. VERDICT then asks you for a check number. We will not enter check numbers in for any expense slips. However, if we had written a check to a copy

service for the copies we could have entered the check number here for reference purposes. To skip this, just press the: **[ENTER]** key.

7. You are then asked to enter the cost of the expense. Since the firm bills .25 a copy and 180 copies were made, type: **45.00** and press the: **[ENTER]** key.

8. You are now asked whether the slip was entered correctly. If the slip was entered correctly, press: **"Y"** to save the expense slip, if not press: N to re-enter the slip.

9. You are now at another blank expense form. At the: *"Account NO.?"* prompt, press: **E** and press the: **[ENTER]** key to go back to the "Post to accounts" submenu (i.e. "LBSPOST").

This concludes Lesson 3.

TO EXIT VERDICT:

To exit the program press the **[ENTER]** key to go back to the VERDICT main menu. From the main menu simply press the **[BACKSPACE]** key.

TO GO TO LESSON 4:

To go to Lesson 4, stay at the "Post to accounts" submenu (i.e. "LBSPOST").

Lesson 4: Entering Several Timeslips and Expense Slips

In this lesson you will enter on your own the remainder of the timeslips ("service" slips) and expenses slips in Figure A-5 following the instructions in Lessons 2 and 3.

When you have finished entering the timeslips and expense slips go back to the VERDICT main menu by pressing the: press the **[ENTER]** key at the "Post to accounts" submenu (i.e. "LBSPOST").

NOTE: If you made a mistake entering the service entries or wish to look at the entries you made and possibly edit them, go back to the Post to Accounts menu (i.e. "LBSPOST") and press: **0**.

VERDICT responds with *"Desired Account No.?"* Type: **"100"** and press: **[ENTER]**. A short menu of options that you can edit is listed. Press: 1 to delete or change a service entry or press 2 to delete or change an expense slip.

The current service slips or expense slips are displayed on the screen. Also, a menu of how to edit the timeslips is also listed. For instance, to change the date of the first timeslip you would type: **1DT**. You would then be allowed to change the date of the first timeslip listed. You can use this same menu to revise entries, delete entries and so on. To go back to the Post To Accounts menu, press the: **[ENTER]** key twice.

This concludes Lesson 4.

LESSON 5: PRINTING A PRE-BILLING REPORT AND FINAL BILL

(Note: this lesson requires a printer.)

In this lesson you will produce a pre-billing report (VERDICT refers to pre-billing reports as "Review Statements") and a final bill for the Smith v. United Sales case.

If you exited from Lesson 4, follow steps 1–5 in Lesson 1, to go to the VERDICT main menu.

Lesson 5:

1. In this lesson you will print a pre-billing report (referred to as a "Review Statement" in VERDICT) and, print the bill for services and expense items we entered in Lessons 2 to 4. This lesson begins at the VERDICT main menu. If you exited the program after Lesson 4, follow steps 1-5 in Lesson 1 to get to the VERDICT main menu.

2. At the VERDICT main menu type: **C** (for "Print bills and review statements").

3. You are then placed at the "Print bills and review statement" submenu (i.e. "LBSBILL"). The menu allows you to print several different types of bills and statements. For our purposes we will only print a review statement and a billing statement. To print a review statement, press: **4.**

4. VERDICT responds with:

   "Print timekeeper recap, (Y)es or (N)o."

   A timekeeper recap shows the total hours and the total charges by each timekeeper who worked on the account. Press: **N** since we do need a recap of the time spent by each timekeeper.

5. Next, VERDICT responds with:

   "Print by (C)harge code, (A)ccount number or (S)ort name:"

   VERDICT allows you to print review statements by charge codes, account numbers or by sort name. For our purposes, we only want to print the review statement for one client. Type: **A** (for account number).

6. You are then asked to choose either a range of account numbers or to select one account number. Press: **S** to select one account number.

7. Next, type: **100** and press the: **[ENTER]** key twice, to print the review statement for Smith v. United Sales.

8. You are then asked whether you want a blank line between each service listed. Type: **Y.** Allowing blanks between lines the review statements allows room to edit it later.

9. Finally, to printout the review statement (assuming you have a printer) press the: **[ENTER]** key.

10. Once the review statement is printed out, review the statement to make sure that the entries correspond to the bill shown in Figure A-5.

11. Once the review statement looks similar to Figure A-5 you will then be ready to print the bill shown in that Figure. To print the bill from the "Print Bills and Review Statements" submenu (i.e. "LBSBILL"), press **1** (i.e. "Billing statement only").

12. VERDICT responds with:

    "Print timekeeper recap, (Y)es or (N)o."

    Press: **N.**

13. VERDICT responds with:

    "Print by (C)harge code, (A)ccount number or (S)ort name:".

    Press: **A** (for (A)ccount number).

14. You are then asked to choose either a range of account numbers or to select one account number. Press: **S** to select one account number.

15. Next, type: **100** and press the: **[ENTER]** key twice.

16. You are then presented with a screen

    "Bill FORMATS FOR SERVICES RENDERED"

    The screen lists 0-9 billing format options. Notice that even though you listed a default billing format when you entered the client's account into VERDICT that you can now change that format and print any of the options listed. Press: **O** since we are satisfied with the default bill format we already entered (i.e. itemize timekeeper and time).

17. You are then asked whether you want to skip lines between each service listed. Press: **N.**

18. You are then asked:

    "Combine expense entries? (Y/N).

    VERDICT is asking you whether you want to combine all similar expenses (i.e. all entries for copying costs) into one entry. Press: **N.**

19. To printout the review statement (assuming you have a printer) press the: **[ENTER]** key. Your printout should look similar to Figure A-5 (depending on the type of printer you have). Go back to the VERDICT main menu by pressing the: **[ENTER]** key.

This concludes Lesson 5.

TO EXIT VERDICT:

To exit the program from the main menu press the **[BACKSPACE]** key.

TO GO TO LESSON 6:

To go to Lesson 6, stay at the VERDICT main menu.

LESSON 6: RECORDING A CLIENT PAYMENT AND DISPLAYING AN ACCOUNT

In this lesson we will record a client payment in the Smith v. United Sales case and then display the account to insure that the payment was saved to the account.

If you exited from Lesson 5, follow steps 1-5 in Lesson 1, to go to the VERDICT main menu.

LESSON 6:

1. In this lesson you will record a client payment and display the account to insure the payment was saved. This lesson begins at the VERDICT main menu. To enter a payment, type: "**B**" (i.e. Post to Accounts).

2. At the "Post to accounts" submenu (e.g. "LBSPOST"), press: **4** (for "Payment").

3. You are then asked to enter the account number of the client making the payment. Type: **100** and press the: **[ENTER]** key, to make a payment in the Smith v. United Sales case.

4. VERDICT responds by asking you for the date of the payment. Enter: **123194** and press the: **[ENTER]** key to enter the current date.

5. You are then asked to enter a description of the payment. Type: **Payment on Account** and press the: **[ENTER]** key.

6. You are then asked to enter the deposit number of the payment. Press: **[ENTER]** to skip this.

7. You are then prompted to enter the amount of the payment. Type: **500.00** and press the: **[ENTER]** key.

8. You are then asked whether the entry is correct or not, type: **Y** to save the payment entry or **N** to reenter the payment.

9. At the "Account No.?" prompt press: **E** and press the: **[ENTER]** key to go back to the Post to Accounts submenu (i.e. "LBSPOST").

10. To review the account on screen to insure that the payment was recorded press: **1** (for "Review").

11. Next, type the account number: **100** and press the: **[ENTER]** key. VERDICT will take you through several screens as you review the entire history of the case. Just press: **[ENTER]** to go to the next screen. When you have confirmed the $500 payment was made, go to the VERDICT main menu by pressing the: **[ENTER]** key.

This concludes Lesson 6.

TO EXIT VERDICT:

To exit the program from the main menu press the: **[BACKSPACE]** key.

TO GO TO LESSON 7:

To go to Lesson 7, stay at the VERDICT main menu.

Lesson 7: Printing an Interim Time and Expense Summary Report

In this lesson you will print an Interim Time and Expense Summary report for all accounts in VERDICT.

If you exited from Lesson 6, follow steps 1-5 in Lesson 1, to go to the VERDICT main menu.

LESSON 7:

1. In this lesson you will print an Interim Time and Expense Summary report for all timekeepers VERDICT. An Interim Time and Expense Summary report shows summary information containing the total amount of hours billed for each timekeeper. This report can be run in the middle of the month to get an idea of who is billing what and for how much. This is one of many management reports that VERDICT can run.

    This lesson begins at the VERDICT main menu. To begin, we must sort our records. Press: **O** (i.e. the letter O for "Print a sorted client list"). Then, press: **1** and press the: **[ENTER]** key to sort your records. Finally, press: **[ENTER]** to return to the VERDICT main menu.

2. At the VERDICT main menu, press: **G** (for "Print monthly and yearly summary").

3. At the "Print monthly and yearly summary" submenu (i.e. "LBSSUMM") press: **1** (for "Collect interim summary information"). VERDICT then runs through all of the accounts. Remember, some information was already entered before you started.

4. VERDICT then responds by letting you know that you have bills that need to be printed for some accounts. At the *"List these accounts? (Y/N):"*

    Press: **N.**

5. You are now taken back to the "Print monthly and yearly summary" submenu (i.e. "LBSSUMM") press: **2** (for "Print or Display summary information"). At the "LBSSUMM2" menu press: **1** (for "Interim Time and Expense Summary"). Press: **A** (for All categories). Press: **Y** to display the summary information on the screen. You can print a copy of the report if you wish.

6. Press the **[ENTER]** key two times to return to the VERDICT main menu. Press: **[BACKSPACE]** to exit VERDICT.

This concludes Lesson 7 and this training manual.

WELCOME TO WALLACE AND SANDERS

TRAINING MANUAL OUTLINE:

- Welcome to Wallace And Sanders
- Getting Started
- Lesson 1: Changing Settings to Legal Terminology
- Lesson 2: Entering a Timekeeper
- Lesson 3: Entering Activity Codes
- Lesson 4: Entering a New Client
- Lesson 5: Entering a Timeslip
- Lesson 6: Entering an Expense Slip
- Lesson 7: Entering Several Timeslips and Expense Slips
- Lesson 8: Printing A Pre-Billing Report and Final Bill
- Lesson 9: Recording a Client Payment

Welcome to Wallace and Sanders! We are an active and growing firm with four attorneys and two legal assistants. As you know, you have been hired as a legal assistant intern. We are very happy to have you on board, we can certainly use your help.

At Wallace and Sanders we put an emphasis on providing quality legal services to our clients. We bill our clients on a regular basis for these quality services, typically either on a bi-weekly or a monthly basis depending on the needs of the client. We strive to make sure our billings are timely and without errors. Because billings and fee disputes are some of the most common types of ethical complaints filed against lawyers we require that all staff members understand and fully appreciate the billing process. In addition, we want our staff members to have many job skills and to be flexible enough to enter timeslips into the computer should we be short handed or need additional help. All staff members are required to have some minimal training on our billing system. We have developed this training manual to help you learn our system.

We currently use the TIMESLIPS timekeeping and billing program. One of the reasons we chose TIMESLIPS is because it is so easy to learn. TIMESLIPS is very easy to use and within a few minutes you will be entering information in it and generating client bills quickly and easily. Please note that during this training exercise you will be entering information for one attorney, Rachel S. Simmons (RSS).

We know you want to begin using TIMESLIPS immediately, so there is only a short "Getting Started" section that you should read before you get on the computer. After the "Getting Started" section there are 9 short lessons, that only take between 5–15 minutes each to complete.

GETTING STARTED

OVERVIEW OF TIMESLIPS

TIMESLIPS allows law offices to track attorney and legal assistant timeslips, to track expense slips, to issue client billings, to trace client payments, and to generally manage client accounts. TIMESLIPS is menu driven. You see menus and can choose which option you want from the menu by typing the key letter of the menu item which is highlighted or by using the up or down arrow keys to highlight the item, and then pressing the: **[ENTER]** key. You can go back one level in the menus by pressing the: **[ESC]** key.

TIMESLIPS is made up of two separate but interconnected programs: *TSTimer* for recording times and expenses and *TSReport* for creating reports and bills. Although they can be run separately we will stay within *TSReport*, which provides instant access to *TSTimer* from its Main Menu. Figure 1 shows the TSREPORT Main Menu. An explanation of the TSREPORT Main Menu is described below:

> **Make Slips**—This option runs the *TSTimer* program, allowing you to enter, change, and search your time and expense slips.
>
> **Define Names**—This option allows you to enter, change, or delete new timekeepers. It also allows you set their default billing rates or enter default billing rates for clients. It also allows you to edit timekeepers history and to edit global references.
>
> **Enter Client Information**—This option allows you to set up client accounts and to describe the client's fee arrangements and billing options and is also where balances and payments are entered.

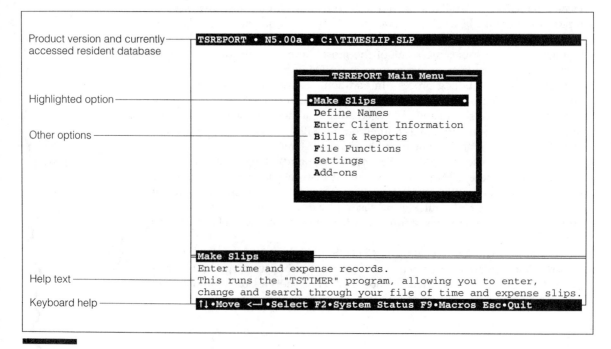

FIGURE 1 Timeslips/TS Report Main Menu

Bills & Reports—This is where bills and reports can be generated and printed.

File Function—This option is used to perform various functions on your files including accessing different data files, archiving and purging files, and to backup your data.

Settings—This option is used to customize the program including setting up security, preferences, printer settings, and performing other functions as well.

Add-ons—This allows you to access other programs which can be added on to TIMESLIPS.

INTRODUCTION TO THIS TRAINING MANUAL

You are using a demonstration version of TIMESLIPS. This version is identical to the actual program except you are limited to entering a maximum of 25 time or expense slips. You will be entering information into the company called "Your Company." We will assume this is the Wallace & Sanders law office. No information has been entered into the TIMESLIPS so you will be starting from scratch.

Throughout this training manual information you need to type into the program will be designated in several different ways.

- Keys to be pressed on the keyboard will be designated in brackets in all caps, bold and enlarged type (e.g., press the: **[ENTER]** key).
- Words or letters that should be typed will be designated in bold and enlarged (e.g., type: **Deposition of Client .25 hours**).
- Information which is or should be displayed on your computer screen is shown in either quotation marks (e.g., "press enter to continue") or in *italics* (e.g., *"press enter to continue"*).

TIMESLIPS sometimes refers to pressing the **ENTER** key on your keyboard with an arrow symbol with a vertical line at its tail. This is the universal symbol for pressing the **ENTER** key. When this tutorial is explaining what TIMESLIPS is displaying on your screen this arrow symbol will be represented by a left arrow symbol (i.e., <).

MOVING AROUND IN
TIMESLIPS ENTRY FIELDS:

When you are entering information in TIMESLIPS you can go between entry fields by pressing the **ENTER** key, by using the **ARROW KEYS,** or by using the **[TAB]** key to go forward or the **[SHIFT]-[TAB]** key to go backward.

OVERVIEW OF THE LESSONS
IN THIS TUTORIAL

TIMESLIPS is a timekeeping and billing program that can be used by any business needing to bill clients by the hour including accounting firms, consultants, and law offices. Because this program is generic and can be used by many types of businesses, in Lesson 1 we will customize the program for a law office so TIMESLIPS will use terminology utilized in a law office.

In Lesson 2 we will enter a timekeeper, an attorney, Rachel S. Simmons and set up her default hourly billing rate.

In Lesson 3 we will enter some timekeeper activity codes for work that will be completed such as "legal research", "phone calls," and "drafting." We will also enter some expense activity codes such as "copying," "postage," and, "long distance."

In Lesson 4 we will enter a new client into TIMESLIPS.

In Lesson 5 we will enter a timekeeping timeslip into the program and in Lesson 6 we will enter an expense slip into the program. In Lesson 7 you will enter several more timekeeping and expense slips.

In Lesson 8 you will print a pre-billing report and a final client bill and in Lesson 9 you will enter a client payment into TIMESLIPS.

When you have completed Lessons 1–8 you will printout a final bill similar to Figure 2.

You're now ready to get on the computer and use TIMESLIPS!

LESSON 1: CHANGING SETTINGS TO LEGAL TERMINOLOGY

In this lesson you will customize a part of TIMESLIPS to reflect terminology used in the legal environment. TIMESLIPS refers to people that are doing the work or incurring expenses for the law office as a "user." In the legal environment the people that are performing work for clients are usually called "timekeepers." TIMESLIPS also refers to "projects." A client may have multiple "projects" or matters. These "projects" are of course called cases in the legal environment. So, we will change timeslips so it calls a "user" a "timekeeper" and a "project" a "case" to reflect the terminology used in a law office.

LESSON 1:

1. Load the TIMESLIPS program according to the instructions provided by your supervisor/instructor (in most cases you will simply type: **cd\TIME-SLIP** and press the **[ENTER]** key and then type: **TSREPORT** and press the: **[ENTER]** key).

FIGURE 2
Blank Timekeeper/ User Form

Define User

Name   [   ]

Rate Information
     1 [   ]   3 [   ]   5 [   ]
     2 [   ]   4 [   ]   6 [   ]

Other
Initials   [   ]
Full name [   ]

2. You will first see the *TIMESLIPS 5—"It turns time into money"* Logo which says to *"Press Enter to continue or Esc to stop"*.

    Press the: **[ENTER]** key to go to the next step.

3. TIMESLIPS responds with a legal disclaimer that says:

    "IMPORTANT–PLEASE READ

    Timeslips Release 5 (TM) software is an outstanding tool to keep. . ."

    At the bottom of the screen it says:

    "Press < to continue. . ."

    Press the: **[ENTER]** key to go to the next step.

4. TIMESLIPS responds with:

    "TSREPORT DATE

    Please enter the date: [ ] press < if the date is correct. It is VERY IMPOR-TANT that the date is set correctly in order for aging and interest calculation to work. Is this date OK (Y/N)?"

    In this training exercise you will enter the date as 12/31/94 so type: **N.** TIMESLIPS will now allow you to enter the date you would like, type: **123194.** TIMESLIPS will respond with:

    "Is this date OK (Y/N)?

    Type: **Y**

5. TIMESLIPS responds with:

    "This is a DEMONSTRATION copy of Timeslips. It has all the features of the regular version with the following exceptions. . . ."

    Press the: **[ENTER]** key to go to the next step.

6. You are now at the TIMESLIPS/TSREPORT main menu (see Figure 1). The TSREPORT Main Menu allows you to access the different options of TIME-SLIPS by typing the first letter of the option or by using the arrow keys on your keyboard.

    The first step in changing the terminology in the program is to type: **S** (for "Settings").

7. TIMESLIPS responds by displaying the *"Settings"* menu. Type: **T** (for *"Terminology & Capacity."*).

8. TIMESLIPS responds by displaying the *"Terminology and Capacity"* settings screen. Your cursor should be under the "U" in "User". Type: **Timekeeper.** Then, press the: **[ENTER]** key **SEVEN TIMES** so the cursor is under *"Project."* Type: **Case** and then press the: **[F10]** key. TIMESLIPS responds with:

    "Is this OK (Y/N)?"

    Type: **Y**

    TIMESLIPS then responds with:

"The file:
C:/Timeslip/Timeslip.SLP was successfully updated. Press < to continue. . ."

Press the: **[ENTER]** key to go to the next step.

9. TIMESLIPS places you back at the *"Settings"* menu. Press the: **[ESC]** key to return to the TSREPORT Main Menu.

   TIMESLIPS will now refer to anyone doing work, recording time, or incurring expenses as a "timekeeper" and will refer to "projects" as cases.

This concludes Lesson 1.

   TO EXIT TIMESLIPS:

   If you want to exit the program from the main menu simply press the **[ESC]** key and type: **Y** at the *"Are you finished with TSREPORT (Y/N)?"* prompt.

   TO GO TO LESSON 2:

   To go to Lesson 2, stay at the TSREPORT Main Menu.

LESSON 2: ENTERING A TIMEKEEPER

In this lesson you will add a timekeeper, Rachel S. Simmons into TIMESLIPS. We will set up her default billing rate so TIMESLIPS will know how much to charge (assuming we are billing the particular client based on the timekeeper's default hourly rate).

   If you exited from Lesson 1, follow steps 1–5 in Lesson 1 until you are at the TSREPORT Main Menu.

LESSON 2:

1. The first step in entering a timekeeper into TIMESLIPS is to type: **D** (for *"Define Names"*) from the TSREPORT Main Menu.

2. TIMESLIPS responds by placing you at the *"Define Names Menu."* Because we want to enter a timekeeper type: **1** (for *"Timekeeper"*).

3. TIMESLIPS responds by placing you at a blank timekeeper entry form (see Figure 2). The top of your screen should say:

   "Define Timekeeper"

   Your cursor should be next to the *"Name"* entry field. In this field we will enter a name or nickname that we can identify the timekeeper by, such as the person's first name or a nick name they are called. Type: **Rachel** and press the: **[ENTER]** key.

4. TIMESLIPS responds by placing the cursor next to the *"1"* in *"Rate information."* TIMESLIPS is asking you to enter Rachel's default billing rate. Type: **100** (to make her default billing rate $100 an hour) and press the: **[ENTER]** key. TIMESLIPS responds by placing the cursor next to the *"2"* in *"Rate Information."* We could now enter several default billing rates, but for this exercise one rate is fine.

Press the: **[ENTER]** key **five times** so that your cursor is next to *"Initials"* under the *"Other"* category.

5. With your cursor next to *"Initials"* type: **RSS** and press the: **[ENTER]** key.

6. TIMESLIPS responds by placing the cursor next to *"Full name."* Enter Rachel's full name by typing: **Rachel S. Simmons** and press the: **[ENTER]** key. Press the: **[F10]** key to enter and save the timekeeper entry. Then, press the: **[ESC]** key.

7. TIMESLIPS responds by placing you back at the *"Define Names Menu."* Press the: **[ESC]** key to return to the TSREPORT Main Menu.

   Rachel Simmons has now been entered as a timekeeper into TIMESLIPS. This will allow us to begin making entries for her in the next lesson.

This concludes Lesson 2.

TO EXIT TIMESLIPS:

If you want to exit the program from the main menu simply press the **[ESC]** key and type: **Y** at the *"Are you finished with TSREPORT (Y/N)?"* prompt.

TO GO TO LESSON 3:

To go to Lesson 3, stay at the TSREPORT Main Menu.

LESSON 3: ENTERING ACTIVITY CODES

In this lesson you will enter some categories of activities for both timekeeping and for expenses. For example, you will enter some timekeeping activities such as drafting, phone call, office conference, investigation, deposition, court appearance, and legal research. Entering timekeeping activities is quite easy. You will also enter some expense activities such as copying, postage, long distance phone calls, filing fee, and court reporting fees. TIMESLIPS identifies an expense activity from a timekeeping activity by requiring that all expense activities start with a dollar sign. Thus, the expense activity for copying costs would be "$Copies."

The process for entering both timekeeping and expense activities is similar to entering timekeepers which we did in Lesson 2.

If you exited from Lesson 2, follow steps 1–5 in Lesson 1 until you are at the TSREPORT Main Menu.

1. The first step in entering an activity into TIMESLIPS is to type: **D** (for *"Define Names"*) from the TSREPORT Main Menu.

2. TIMESLIPS responds by placing you at the *"Define Names"* menu. Because we want to enter a timekeeper type: **3** (for *"Activity"*).

3. Your cursor should be located next to the *"Name"* field with *"Define Activity"* at the upper left of the screen. Type: **Drafting** and press the: **[ENTER]** key.

4. Your cursor should now be located next to the *"1"* field under *"Rate information."* TIMESLIPS is allowing you to enter default charges for this type of

activity. Because all of our clients will be billed according to whatever time-keeper is recording the time, we will leave these blank. In fact, all of the remaining information is fine so press: **[F10]** to enter the drafting activity.

5. TIMESLIPS responds by placing you back at the *"Define Activity"* screen. You can see that "Drafting" has now been added as an activity. Press: **[F3]** to create additional timekeeping activities.

   Follow the instructions in steps 3–5 of this lesson to enter the following additional timekeeping activities:

   - Phone Call
   - Office Conf.
   - Investigation
   - Deposition
   - Court Appear.
   - Legal Research

6. After you have entered the timekeeping activities you should be at the *"Define Activity"* screen with all of the activities listed on the screen that you just entered. You are now ready to enter some expense activities. At the *"Define Activity"* screen press: **[F3]** to enter a new activity.

7. Your cursor should be located next to the *"Name"* field with *"Define Activity"* at the upper left of the screen. Type: **$Copies** and press the: **[ENTER]** key.

8. Your cursor should now be located next to *"Price"* under *"Rate information."* Type: **.25** and press the: **[ENTER]** key. This will set a default rate of 25 cents per copy. All of the remaining information is fine so press: **[F10]** to enter the "$Copies" activity.

9. TIMESLIPS responds by placing you back at the *"Define Activity"* screen. You can see that "$Copies" has now been added as an activity. You are now ready to enter another expense activity.

10. Your cursor should be located next to the *"Name"* field with *"Define Activity"* at the upper left of the screen. Type: **$Postage** and press the: **[ENTER]** key. Since there are no default rates for postage, long distance, filing fees, or court reporter fees simply press the: **[F10]** key to enter the activity.

11. Follow the instructions in steps 10–11 of this lesson to enter the following additional expense activities:

    - $Long Dist.
    - $Filing Fee
    - $Ct. Rept. Fee

12. After you have entered the expense activities you should be at the *"Define Activity"* screen with all of the timekeeping and expense activities listed on the screen that you just entered. Press the: **[ESC]** key to return to the TSRE-PORT Main Menu.

This concludes Lesson 3.

TO EXIT TIMESLIPS

If you want to exit the program from the main menu simply press the **[ESC]** key and type: **Y** at the *"Are you finished with TSREPORT (Y/N)?"* prompt.

TO GO TO LESSON 4:
To go to Lesson 4, stay at the TSREPORT Main Menu.

LESSON 4: ENTERING A NEW CLIENT

You will now begin to enter the information necessary to produce the bill in Figure 3. In this lesson you will add a new client, Linda Smith, into TIMESLIPS.

```
Invoice submitted to:
Linda Smith
P.O. Box 10083
500 East Fifth Street
Cleveland, OH  90014


In reference to:  Smith v. United Sales
Invoice #10000

        Professional Services
                                            Hrs/Rate
                                            --------
12/01/94 RSS Phone Call to Expert Witness      0.50
                                            100.00/hr.
12/06/94 RSS Office Conf. with Client          0.50
                                            100.00/hr.
12/12/94 RSS Investigation and location of key witness   4.00
                                            100.00/hr.
12/13/94 RSS Drafting of Interrogatory Responses   5.00
                                            100.00/hr.
12/16/94 RSS Deposition of Client              6.50
                                            100.00/hr.
12/19/94 RSS Deposition of Defendant           3.50
                                            100.00/hr.
                                                        Amount
                                            ------      ------
        For professional services rendered    20.00    $2,000.00

        Additional charges:
                                                         45.00
12/13/94-Copies of Interrogatories                        5.00
        -Long Distance Phone Call re:  Expert           450.00
12/27/94-Copy of Deposition                          ----------
                                                        $500.00
        Total costs
                                                     --------------
        Total amount of this bill                       $2,500.00

                                                         Amount
                                                         ------
                                                     --------------
        Balance due                                     $2,500.00
                                                     ==============
```

FIGURE 3

You will enter her name, address, fee agreement information, and billing information.

If you exited from Lesson 3, follow steps 1–5 in Lesson 1 until you are at the TSREPORT Main Menu.

LESSON 4:

1. The first step in entering a new client is to type: **E** (for *"Enter Client Information"*) from the TSREPORT Main Menu. TIMESLIPS responds by placing you in the *"Enter Client Information"* screen. (See Figure 4.) This is where all new client accounts are set up. Notice that the only "client" listed on the left side of the screen is "Your Company." "Your Company" is not actually a client, this option allows the user to customize the new client information form and to set up default values which apply automatically to all new clients.

2. Press: **[F3]** to begin entering a new client.

3. TIMESLIPS responds by placing you at the *"Define Client"* screen. Notice that this screen looks nearly identical to the timekeeper entry form you completed in Lesson 2. At the *"Name"* prompt type: **Smith, Linda** and press the: **[ENTER]** key.

4. TIMESLIPS responds by placing you in the *"Rate information"* fields. Because the client will be billed according to who the timekeeper is press the: **[ENTER]** key **Six times.** You are now placed at the *"Default assignment"* field. Because the client will be billed according to who the timekeeper is press the: **[ENTER]** key **Two times.** Finally, press: **[F10]** to enter the information.

**FIGURE 4
"Enter Client
Information" Menu**

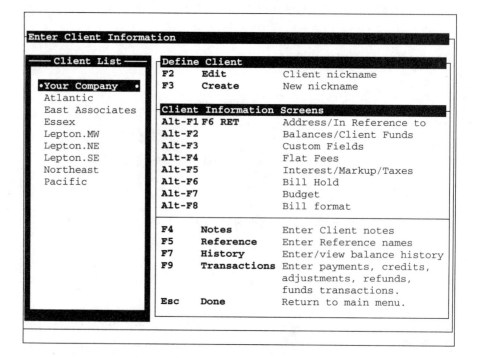

5. TIMESLIPS responds by taking you back to the *"Enter Client Information"* screen. Now you will complete the rest of the information TIMESLIPS needs to generate bills and reports for this client. You will enter the following information about the client including: name and address, balances and client funds information, flat fee arrangements, interest, mark up, tax information, bill formatting, client history, client transactions including payments and other information.

At the *"Enter Client Information"* screen "Smith, Linda" should already be highlighted under the *"Client"* field on the left side of the screen. If "Your Company" is highlighted simply use your arrow keys on your keyboard to highlight "Smith, Linda" and press the: **[ENTER]** key.

6. TIMESLIPS responds by placing you at the screen entitled *"Client Information for: Smith, Linda."* Notice in the far upper right of the screen it says "Screen 1 of 4." In all, we will enter four screens worth of client information. The actual entry of the screens is quite fast.

Your cursor should be next to *"Company name."* Type: **Linda Smith** and press the: **[ENTER]** key.

7. Your cursor should now be located next to the *"Address"* field. **P.O. Box 10083** and press the: **[ENTER]** key. Next, type: **500 East Fifth Street** and press the: **[ENTER]** key **Twice.**

8. Your cursor should now be located next to *"City."* Type: **Cleveland** and press the: **[ENTER]** key. Your cursor should now be located next to "State." Type: **OH.** Your cursor should now be located next to *"Zip."* Type: **90014** and press the: **[ENTER]** key **Twice.** Your cursor should now be located next to *"Phone 1"*. Type: **613/367–2344** and press the **[ENTER]** key **Twice.**

9. Your cursor should now be located next to *"In Reference to."* Enter the name of the case, type: **Smith v. United Sales** and press the: **[F10]** key.

10. TIMESLIPS responds by placing your cursor next to *"Last Bill"* under the *"Balances"* section. Because Linda Smith is a new client, she has no accumulated balance or past-due charges. Your screen should look like Figure 5. Press the: **[F6]** key to go to the second client information screen.

```
Client Information for:  Smith, Linda                Screen 1 of 4
Company Name    1[Linda Smith                    ]
Address         2[P.O. Box 10083                 ]
                3[500 East Fifth Street          ]
                4[                               ]
City            5[Cleveland      ]   State [OH]  Zip [90014]
                6[
Phone 1           [613/367-2344]     Phone 2   [            ]
In Reference to   [Smith v. United Sales    ]
 BALANCES                           CLIENT FUNDS
Last Bill [ / / ]  Use aging [N]o
120 days Overdue      [    0.00]   Automatic Payment [Nothing   ]
 90 days Overdue      [    0.00]   Funds Minimum     [    0.00]
 60 days Overdue      [    0.00]   Funds Balance     [    0.00]
 30 days Overdue      [    0.00]   Trans not Billed       0.00
Current Period        [    0.00]   Current Balance        0.00
Accum. Simple Interest [   0.00]
Trans not Billed           0.00
Current Balance            0.00
```

FIGURE 5
Completed "Client Information" Screen for Linda, Smith, Screen 1

11. TIMESLIPS responds by placing you at the screen entitled *"Client Information for: Smith, Linda."* Notice in the far upper right of the screen it says *"Screen 2 of 4."* Your cursor should be next to *"Controller: No Timekeeper Selected."* Press: **[F9]** to edit the field. A screen will pop-up entitled "Controller." Because "Rachel" will be responsible for this case, press: **DOWN-ARROW** key on your keyboard once to highlight "Rachel" and press the: **[ENTER]** key.

12. Your cursor should be next to *"Salutation"*. Type: **Dear Linda:** (your screen should now look like Figure 6) and press the: **[F6]** key to go to the third client information screen.

13. TIMESLIPS responds by placing you at the screen entitled *"Client Information for: Smith, Linda."* Notice in the far upper right of the screen it says *"Screen 3 of 4."* Your cursor should be next to *"Amount."* under the *"Flat Fee"* section of the screen. This screen can be used to indicate a flat fee arrangement, sales tax, whether your firm will charge interest, and other information as well. This screen shows the power of TIMESLIPS. Because Linda Smith's case has been taken on an hourly fee agreement and because the firm does not have to charge sales tax and will not charge interest (your screen should remain unchanged, see Figure 7) press: **[F6]** key to go to the fourth client information screen.

14. TIMESLIPS responds by placing you at the screen entitled *"Client Information for: Smith, Linda."* Notice in the far upper right of the screen it says *"Screen 4 of 4."* Your cursor should be next to *"Time style"* under the *"BILL FORMAT: TIME AND EXPENSE"* section of the screen. This screen describes the amount of detail your client wants printed on the bill. Generally, Ms. Smith would like to see what services are being performed, who performed them, the amount of time per entry, the expenses incurred including the amount of each expense, and a total. This section describes how to configure TIMESLIPS. There are several steps to do this. If you make a mistake it is okay, it will simply mean that the invoice you print out at the end of the lessons will not be formatted precisely like Figure 2.

   a. Your cursor should be next to: *"Time Style Itemize."* Because the options in the *"BILL FORMAT: TIME AND EXPENSE"* are all fine, press the: **PAGE DOWN** key to go to the next section.

FIGURE 6
Completed Screen for Linda Smith, Screen 2

```
Client Information for:  Smith, Linda              Screen 2 of 4

CUSTOM FIELDS
Controller                              [Rachel               ]
Salutation                              [Dear Linda:          ]
```

```
┌─Client Information for:   Smith, Linda              Screen 3 of 4─┐
│ ┌FLAT FEE─────────────────────────────────────────────────────┐  │
│ Amount     [    0.00]   Duration [None  ]    Override Hold [N]o   │
│ Type       [None    ]   Accum    [    0.00]  1st Bill sent [N]o   │
│ Covers     [Nothing ]   Message  [                           ]   │
│ ┌TAXES────────────────────┐ ┌PRECISION/MARKUPS────────────────┐  │
│ Sales Tax            [  0.0000]%  Round Timeslips to [M]inutes [ 0] │
│ Service Tax          [  0.0000]%  Full Precision       [N]o       │
│ Accum Service Charges [   0.00]                                   │
│ Service Tax Threshold [   0.00]   Markup slips         [ 0.000]%  │
│ ┌INTEREST─────────────────┐ ┌BUDGET INFORMATION───────────────┐  │
│ Annual Interest Rate  [ 0.00]%    Budgeted Hours       [   0.00]  │
│ Int. begins on period [1] 30d     Budgeted Fees        [   0.00]  │
│ Compound Interest     [Y]es        Budgeted Costs       [   0.00]  │
│ ┌BILL HOLD OPTIONS────────┐                                       │
│ Hold Full Bill        [N]o                                        │
│ Hold Time Charges     [N]o                                        │
│ Hold Expenses         [N]o                                        │
│                                                                   │
└───────────────────────────────────────────────────────────────────┘
```

FIGURE 7
Completed Screen for Linda Smith, Screen 4

b. Your cursor should be next to *"Description"* (under *"Time"*). Press: **1** to show only the first paragraph of times charges.

c. Your cursor should be next to *"Description"* (under *"Expense"*). Press: **1** to show only the first paragraph on expense charges.

d. Your cursor should now be on *"Dates"* (under *"Time"*). Press the: **[ENTER]** key **TWICE.**

e. Your cursor should now be on *"Initials"* (under *"Time"*). Type: **[Y]** and press the: **[ENTER]** key **NINE TIMES.**

f. Your cursor should now be on *"Charges"* (under *"Time"*). Type: **[N].**

g. Your cursor should now be on *"Charges"* (under *"Expense"*). Press the **[ENTER]** key.

h. Your cursor key should now be on *"Double space"* (under *"Time"*). Type: **[N].**

i. Your cursor should now be on *"Double space"* (under *"Expense"*). Type: **[N]** This completes the changes. No changes need to be made to the *"BILL FORMAT: OTHER SECTIONS"* so once you have the *"BILL FORMAT: TIME AND EXPENSE"* sections properly completed as above, press: **F10** to save your entry.

If you make a mistake you can use your arrow keys on your keyboard to go back and forth between the entries. When you are finished your screen should appear as follows (see also Figure 8).

	TIME	EXPENSE
Description	1	1
Dates	Yes	Yes
Initials	**Yes**	No
Activity	No	No
Hours/Qty	Yes	No
Rate/Price	Yes	No
Reference	No	No
Charges	**No**	Yes
Double Space	**No**	**No**
End Dates	No	No

FIGURE 8
Completed Screen
for Linda Smith,
Screen 4

```
┌Client Information for:   Smith, Linda              Screen 4 of 4─┐

 ┌BILL FORMAT : TIME AND EXPENSE┐ ┌BILL FORMAT : OTHER SECTIONS┐
                                    Payments and credits [Y]es
  Time style      [Itemize      ]  Balance               [Y]es
  Expense style   [Itemize      ]  Aging messages        [N]o
  Merge t & e     [N]o             Aging Table           [N]o

                   TIME    EXPENSE  Summary Table Rate    [N]o
  Description      [1]     [1]      Summary Table Hours   [N]o
  Dates           [Y]es   [Y]es    Summary Table Amount  [N]o
  Initials        [Y]es   [N]o
  Activity Name   [N]o    [N]o     Funds Style           [N]ot shown
  Hours/Qty       [Y]es   [N]o     Funds Replenish msg. [N]o
  Rate/Price      [Y]es   [N]o
  Reference       [N]o    [N]o     Msg1 [No message          ][Perp]
  Charges         [N]o    [Y]es    Msg2 [No message          ][Perp]
  Double Space    [N]o    [N]o     Override Invoice # [          ]
  End Dates       [N]o    [N]o     Separate Bill [N]o   New Page [N]o
```

15. TIMESLIPS responds by placing you back at the "Enter Client Information" screen. Press the: **[ESC]** key to return to the TSREPORT Main Menu.

This concludes Lesson 4.

TO EXIT TIMESLIPS:

If you want to exit the program from the main menu simply press the **[ESC]** key and type: **Y** at the *"Are you finished with TSREPORT (Y/N)?"* prompt.

TO GO TO LESSON 5:
To go to Lesson 5, stay at the TSREPORT Main Menu.

LESSON 5: ENTERING A TIMESLIP

In this lesson you will enter a timeslip into TIMESLIPS. You will enter the first timekeeping entry from the Figure 2 (e.g., "12/1/94, Phone Call to Expert Witness", RSS, .50).

If you exited from Lesson 4, follow steps 1–5 in Lesson 1 until you are at the TSREPORT Main Menu.

LESSON 5:

1. To enter a timeslip press: **M** (for *"Make Slips"*) from the TSREPORT Main Menu.

2. TIMESLIPS responds by placing you at a blank timeslip. Your cursor is at the bottom portion of the screen next to *"Go to slip [ ]"*. Press the: **[F3]** key (for *"Create a Slip"*).

3. TIMESLIPS responds placing the cursor next to *"Timekeeper."* Notice that since only one timekeeper has been entered in the system TIMESLIPS auto-

matically assumes "Rachel" will be the timekeeper. Because "Rachel" is the attorney recording the charges press the: **[ENTER]** key.

4. Your cursor is now next to *"Client."* TIMESLIPS is very adept at finding clients. You can enter part of the client's name, or press the F9 function key to see a list of all clients entered. Because the client, "Smith, Linda" is the first client entered type: **1** and press the: **[ENTER]** key.

5. TIMESLIPS responds by placing your cursor next to *"Activity."* In this example you will be entering an entry for a phone call. Press: **[F9]** to see a list of all available "activities." **Use your arrow keys to highlight the "Phone Call"** timekeeping activity and press the: **[ENTER]** key. (Note: be sure you do not select the "$Long Dist." category since this is an expense activity and you want to record time for the timekeeper).

6. TIMESLIPS responds by placing your cursor underneath the *"Activity"* category. This field allows you to type out a detailed description of the entry. Type: **Phone Call to Expert Witness** and press the: **[TAB]** key to go to the next field.

7. TIMESLIPS responds by placing your cursor next to *"Reference."* Press the: **[ENTER]** key to go to the "Date" field. Type: **120194.** Your cursor will automatically go to the "through": field. Type: **120194.**

8. TIMESLIPS puts your cursor next to *"Time estimated."* Press the: **[ENTER]** key to go to the *"Time spent"* field. Type: **.50** and press the: **[ENTER]** key.

9. TIMESLIPS responds by placing your cursor in the bottom portion of the screen next to the *"Billing Status–Billable"* field. This is where you tell TIMESLIPS whether the timeslip you are entering is billable or not. Because all of the fields in the lower portion of the screen are okay press the: **[F10]** key to enter and save the timeslip. Notice that the completed timeslip is now displayed on your screen.

10. Press the: **[ESC]** key **TWICE** to return to the TSREPORT Main Menu.

This concludes Lesson 5.

TO EXIT TIMESLIPS:

If you want to exit the program from the main menu simply press the **[ESC]** key and type: **Y** at the *"Are you finished with TSREPORT (Y/N)?"* prompt.

TO GO TO LESSON 6:

To go to Lesson 6, stay at the TSREPORT Main Menu.

LESSON 6: ENTERING AN EXPENSE SLIP

In this lesson you will enter an expense timeslip into TIMESLIPS. The process will be almost exactly like entering the timeslip you entered in Lesson 5. You will enter the first expense entry in Figure 2 (e.g., "12/13/94, Copies of Interrogatories", 180 copies).

If you exited from Lesson 5, follow steps 1–5 in Lesson 1 until you are at the TSREPORT Main Menu.

LESSON 6

1. To enter a timeslip press: **M** (for *"Make Slips"*) from the TSREPORT Main Menu.

2. TIMESLIPS responds by placing you at a blank timeslip. Your cursor is at the bottom of the screen next to *"Go to slip [ ]"*. Notice that TIMESLIPS has retrieved the last timesheet you entered. Press the: **F3** key (for *"Create a Slip"*).

3. TIMESLIPS responds by placing the cursor next to "Timekeeper." Notice that since only one timekeeper has been entered in the system TIMESLIPS automatically assumes "Rachel" will be the timekeeper. Because "Rachel" is the attorney recording the charges press the: **[ENTER]** key.

4. Your cursor is now next to *"Client."* Because the client, "Smith, Linda" is the first client we have entered type: **1** and press the: **[ENTER]** key.

5. TIMESLIPS responds by placing your cursor next to *"Activity."* In this example you will be entering an expense slip for copying charges. Press: **[F9]** to see a list of all available "activities." **Use your arrow keys to highlight the "$Copies"** timekeeping activity and press the: **[ENTER]** key.

6. TIMESLIPS responds by placing your cursor underneath the *"Activity"* category. This field allows you to type out a detailed description of the entry. Type: **Copies of Interrogatories, 180 pages** and press the: **[TAB]** key to go to the next field.

7. TIMESLIPS responds by placing your cursor next to *"Reference."* Press the: **[ENTER]** key to go to the *"Date"* field. Type: **121394.** Your cursor will automatically go to the *"through"* field. Type: **121394.**

8. TIMESLIPS puts your cursor next to *"Quantity"*. Type: **180** and press the: **[ENTER]** key. You are now at the *"Price"* field. We entered the default price of copies at 25 cents when we set up the $Copies activity so press the: **[ENTER]** key to accept this amount. (Note: if you made a mistake you can press [SHIFT]–[TAB] to go backward through the fields.).

9. TIMESLIPS responds by placing your cursor in the bottom portion of the screen next to the *"Billing Status–Billable"* field. Because all of the fields in the lower portion of the screen are okay and that this is a billable expense, press the: **[F10]** key to enter and save the timeslip. Notice that the completed timeslip is now displayed on your screen.

10. Notice that your completed expense slip is now on the screen. Press the: **UP ARROW** key on your keyboard to go back to the first timeslip you entered, the phone call to the expert witness. You can move between the timeslips you have entered by using the UP and DOWN arrow keys. You can also edit them by pressing the F2 key if you find that you made a mistake.

11. Press the: **[ESC]** key **TWICE** to return to the TSREPORT Main Menu.

This concludes Lesson 6.

TO EXIT TIMESLIPS:

If you want to exit the program from the main menu simply press the **[ESC]** key and type: **Y** at the *"Are you finished with TSREPORT (Y/N)?"* prompt.

TO GO TO LESSON 7:

To go to Lesson 7, stay at the TSREPORT Main Menu.

TO EXIT TIMESLIPS:

If you want to exit the program from the main menu simply press the **[ESC]** key and type: **Y** at the *"Are you finished with TSREPORT (Y/N)?"* prompt.

LESSON 7: ENTERING SEVERAL TIMESLIPS AND EXPENSE SLIPS

In this lesson you will enter on your own the remainder of the timeslips and expense slips in Figure 2 following the instructions in Lessons 5 and 6. All of the entries are for the "Smith, Linda" case and have been incurred by Rachel Simmons. Use whatever activity best describes the entry. On the long distance phone call expense, the quantity will be *"1"* and simply enter the $5.00 charge in the *"Price"* field.

The entries are as follows:

TIMEKEEPING TIMESLIPS FOR "Smith, Linda"

12/06/94	Office Conf. with Client	.50
12/12/94	Investigation and Location of Key Witness	4.00
12/13/94	Drafting of Interrogatory Responses	5.00
12/16/94	Deposition of Client	6.50
12/19/94	Deposition of Defendant	3.50

EXPENSE SLIPS FOR "Smith, Linda"

12/13/94	Long Distance Phone Call re: Expert	$5.00
12/27/94	Copy of Deposition	1,800 copies

When you have finished entering the timeslips and expense slips go back to the TSREPORT Main Menu by pressing the: **[ESC]** key **TWICE.**

This concludes Lesson 7.

TO GO TO LESSON 8:

To go to Lesson 8, stay at the TSREPORT Main Menu.

LESSON 8: PRINTING A PRE-BILLING REPORT AND FINAL BILL

In this lesson you will produce a pre-billing report (TIMESLIPS refers to this as a worksheet) and a final bill for the Smith v. United Sales case.

If you exited from Lesson 7, follow steps 1–5 in Lesson 1, to go to the TSREPORT Main Menu.

LESSON 8:

1. To print a worksheet press: **B** (for *"Bills & Reports"*) from the TSREPORT Main Menu.

2. TIMESLIPS responds by placing you at a *"Report Types"* screen. Press: **B** (for Bills and Worksheets).

3. TIMESLIPS responds by placing you at the *"Bills and Worksheets"* screen. Press: **F** (for *"Full Detail Worksheet"*). At this point you can tell TIMESLIPS which timeslips to include for which cases. For this example, we will print everything so, press: **P** (for *"Print"*).

4. TIMESLIPS responds by placing you at the *"Print Menu."* If you do not have a printer attached you can print it to the screen by pressing: **D** (for *"Display"*). If you have a printer press: **P** (for *"Primary printer"*—if you need to look at the print options screen before printing you can press F2). If you print to the screen you can use the ARROW KEYS and/or the PAGE UP and PAGE DOWN keys to view the full report. The report should look similar to the invoice in Figure 2. If you made a mistake on a timeslip you can go back and edit the timeslips as previously discussed in these lessons. If you printed the report to a printer "Demonstration Software" is printed at the top of the page—this is normal.

    Press: **ESC** so you are at the *"Bills and Worksheets"* screen.

5. You will now print the final client bill (assuming you had no errors). At the *"Bills and Worksheets"* screen press: **B** (for *"Bills"*). You are now at the *"Current Report: Default bill layout"* screen. Press: **P** (for *"Print"*). You are now placed at the *"Print Menu."* If you do not have a printer attached you can print to the screen by pressing: **D** (for *"Display"*). If you have a printer press: **P** (for *"Primary printer"*).

6. TIMESLIPS responds by printing the bill. It then asks you:

    "Do you want to finalize the billing (Y/N)?"

    Press: **Y.**

    TIMESLIPS then asks you if you want to backup, press: **N.**

    TIMESLIPS then asks you if you want to finalize anyway, press: **Y.**

You are now at the *"Current Report: Default bill layout."* Press: **[ESC]** **THREE TIMES** to return to the TSREPORT Main Menu.

This concludes Lesson 8.

TO EXIT TIMESLIPS:

If you want to exit the program from the main menu simply press the **[ESC]** key and type: **Y** at the *"Are you finished with TSREPORT (Y/N)?"* prompt.

TO GO TO LESSON 9:

To go to Lesson 9, stay at the TSREPORT Main Menu.

LESSON 9: RECORDING A CLIENT PAYMENT

In this lesson we will record a payment of $2,500 from Linda Smith.

If you exited from Lesson 8, follow steps 1–5 in Lesson 1, to go to the TSRE-PORT Main Menu.

LESSON 9:

1. This lesson begins at the TSREPORT Main Menu. To begin to enter a payment, type: **E** (i.e., *"Enter Client Information"*).

2. You are now at the *"Enter Client Information"* screen. **USE THE ARROW KEYS ON YOUR KEYBOARD TO HIGHLIGHT "SMITH, LINDA" ON THE LEFT SIDE OF THE SCREEN.**

3. Press: **[F9]** (for Transactions). You are now at the *"Enter transactions for: Smith, Linda"* screen. Your cursor should be under *"Date."* Press the: **[ENTER]** key to enter the current date.

4. A *"Transaction Menu"* screen will pop-up on the right part of the screen. Because Linda Smith has made a payment of $2,500 press: **1** (for Payment— thank you). *"Payment—thank you"* now appears under the *"Description"* field. Press the: **[ENTER]** to enter this description.

5. The cursor moves under the *"Amount"* field and enters $2,500 in the field as a default. TIMESLIPS defaults to the current balance due and owing. Because Ms. Smith is paying the balance in full press the: **[ENTER]** key. Notice that the screen now displays at the top of the screen that Ms. Smith's current balance (i.e., Cur Bal:) is now zero. Press the: **[F10]** key to enter the payment amount and save the payment.

6. Press: **[ESC]** to go back to the *"Enter Client Information Screen"*. Press: **[ESC]** again to go back to the TSREPORT Main Menu.

This concludes Lesson 9 and this training manual.

THANK YOU FOR COMPLETING THE TRAINING!

6

CLIENT FUNDS AND LAW OFFICE ACCOUNTING

CHAPTER OBJECTIVES

After you read this chapter, you will be able to:

- Understand the importance of trust/escrow accounts.
- Differentiate between gross income and net income.
- Discuss the importance of cash flow.
- Define income, gross income, and net income.
- Explain the budgeting process.
- Discuss what internal controls are.

As professionals, and as revenue producers within the law firm, it is very important that legal assistants have a basic understanding of the economics of the law practice. Recent recessions have caused attorneys to focus more attention on the financial aspects of practicing law and the need for sound financial planning and management. An understanding of law firm economics enables legal assistants to contribute more effectively to serving the clients as well as to the success of the law office.[1]

Hundreds of attorneys are disbarred and suspended from practicing law for failing to safeguard client funds. In one case an attorney was disciplined for grossly mishandling client funds. The court found that the attorney:

- Commingled client trust funds with his own personal funds;
- Used client trust funds to pay for personal expenses;
- Failed to maintain and keep appropriate records of client funds;
- Failed to return unearned attorney's fees back to the client;
- Failed to respond to reasonable status inquiries from the client.

The court found that the attorney's conduct in handling client funds amounted to gross negligence and significantly harmed the client. For this conduct, the attorney's license was suspended for two years.[2]

Why Legal Assistants Need a Basic Understanding of Law Office Accounting

Legal assistants need to have a basic understanding of law office accounting for several reasons. One reason is that legal assistants either directly or indirectly work with trust/escrow accounts on a regular basis and thus need to have an understanding of what they are and how they work. Another reason is that financial decisions drive the law office. It is important to understand how and why a law office operates and to know some basic accounting concepts. In smaller law offices, legal assistants may actually have some bookkeeping or accounting responsibilities. Finally, in some firms legal assistants will help prepare office or department budgets. Thus, it is important to have at least some knowledge of how to prepare a basic budget.

Client Funds—Trust/ Escrow Accounts

A trust account, sometimes called an "escrow account" or "client account", is an important part of how law practices manage money. *A trust* or *escrow account is a bank account, separate from a law office's or attorney's business or operating checking account, where unearned client funds are deposited.* Nearly all private law practices have at least two checking accounts, one checking account from which normal business deposits and expenses are paid and a <u>separate</u> trust account, which is typically a checking account as opposed to a savings account, where only client funds are kept (see Figure 6-1). Checks used with the trust/escrow account will carry the title of "Trust Account," "Client Trust Account" or "Escrow Account." Deposit slips also will have this designation. A separate bank statement also will be received for the trust account.

NO COMMINGLING OF CLIENT AND LAW OFFICE FUNDS

Ethical rules prohibit the commingling of client funds and law office funds in the same account. <u>This rule cannot be overemphasized</u>, and there is virtually no flexibility regarding this rule.

EXAMPLES OF HOW A TRUST ACCOUNT IS USED

There are times when clients will pay a cash advance or unearned retainer to an office to apply against future fees and expenses. Until the office has actually earned these monies, it must keep these funds in the trust account. The reason is simple: if client funds are commingled in the same bank account with general law practice funds, creditors could seize these funds to repay debts of the law practice.

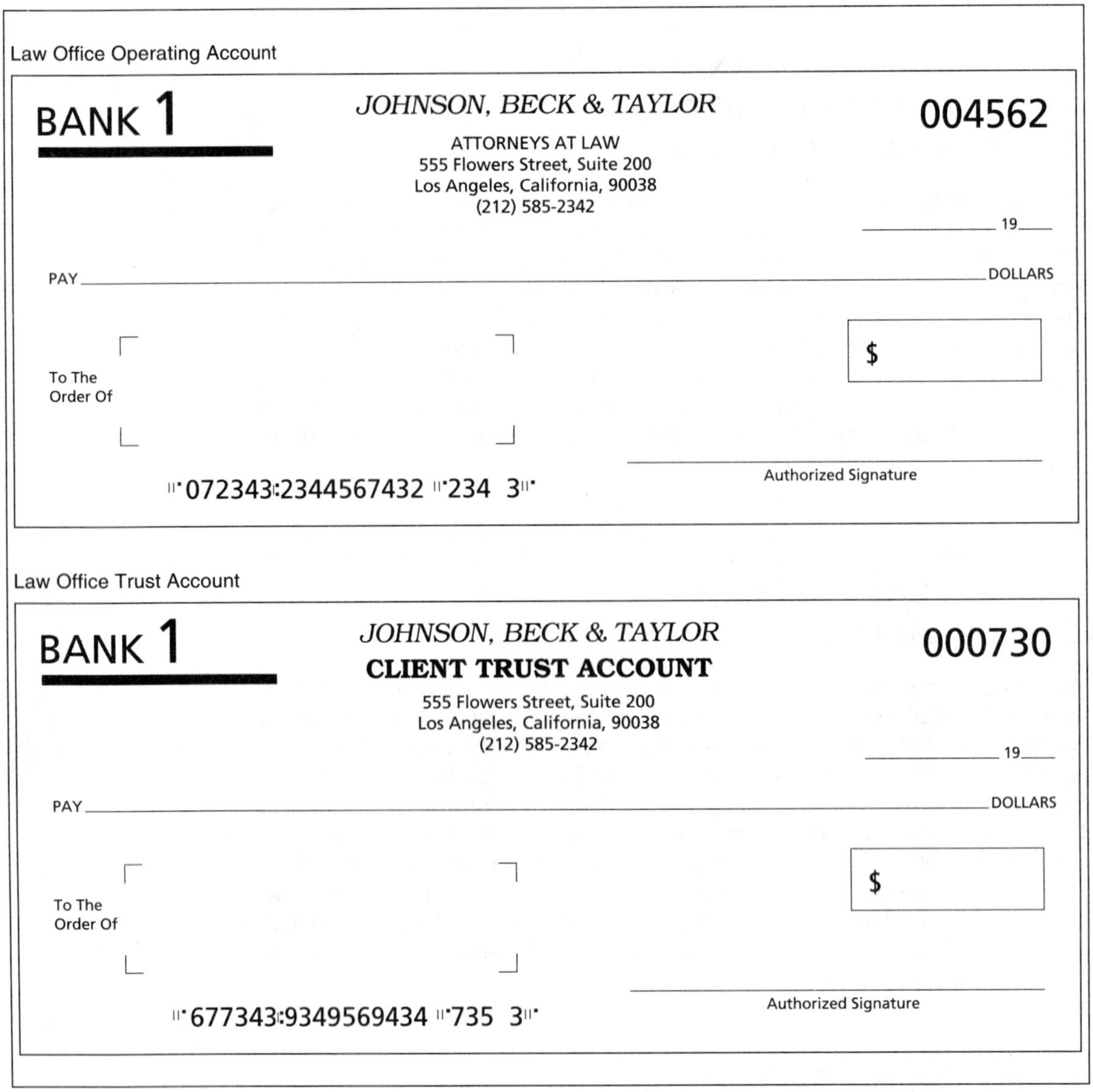

Law Office Operating Account

BANK 1 _____

JOHNSON, BECK & TAYLOR
ATTORNEYS AT LAW
555 Flowers Street, Suite 200
Los Angeles, California, 90038
(212) 585-2342

004562

_____ 19____

PAY _____ DOLLARS

To The
Order Of

$ _____

ıı·072343ı:2344567432 ıı·234 3ıı·

Authorized Signature

Law Office Trust Account

BANK 1 _____

JOHNSON, BECK & TAYLOR
CLIENT TRUST ACCOUNT
555 Flowers Street, Suite 200
Los Angeles, California, 90038
(212) 585-2342

000730

_____ 19____

PAY _____ DOLLARS

To The
Order Of

$ _____

ıı·677343ı:9349569434 ıı·735 3ıı·

Authorized Signature

FIGURE 6-1   Operating and Trust Checks

settlement
A mutual agreement to
resolve a dispute on
specified terms.

The cash advance is just one way that the trust account is used. Trust accounts also are used in other ways, such as for distributing settlement checks. *A **settlement** occurs when both parties in a dispute mutually agree to resolve the dispute on specified terms such as for one party to pay to the other party a certain sum of money.*

For example, suppose that an attorney represented a client in a personal injury case and the matter was settled out of court for $10,000. Suppose that the defendant issued a $10,000 check made payable to both the attorney and the client and that the attorney was entitled to $2,000 and the client to $8,000. The proper way to dispose of the monies would be for both the attorney and the client to endorse the settlement check. Then, the attorney would deposit the $10,000 settlement check in the trust account and subsequently write an $8,000 check from the trust account to the client and a $2,000 check from the trust account to the law office.

ETHICS AND TRUST ACCOUNTS

Every state bar's ethical rules prohibit the commingling of client and law office funds. Rule 1.15 of the *Model Rules of Professional Conduct* states:

(a) A lawyer shall hold property of client or third persons that is in a lawyer's possession in connection with a representation <u>separate from the lawyer's own property. Funds shall be kept in a separate account. . . . Complete records of such account funds and other property shall be kept by the lawyer and shall be preserved for a period of five years after termination of the representation</u> (emphasis added).

Notice in Rule 1.15 (a) that not only must the lawyer keep the client's and the lawyer's property separate from each other but that complete records regarding these accounts must be maintained for at least five years after termination of the representation. There is an affirmative duty not only to have the trust account but also to keep complete and proper records. It is permissible to use one trust account for all client funds as long as there is sufficient record keeping to know how much each client has in the trust account. Law practices do not have to have separate trust accounts for every client. In fact, many law offices have only one trust account for all client monies. Larger offices may choose to have several trust accounts to help organize and control the large numbers of cases they have.

For example, suppose "Attorney A" has twenty-five clients who have monies deposited in one trust account, and each client has differing amounts in the account. This is perfectly acceptable, as long as "Attorney A" knows and has records to prove exactly how much each client has in the trust account <u>and has a running ledger to show what money was taken out check by check and what amounts were deposited for each client (see Figure 6-2)</u>. This is why good record keeping regarding trust accounts is crucial. Law offices must know to the penny how much each client has in the trust account so that when it comes time to give the money back to the client, the money will be there. Most state bars require that the bank statement for the trust account be reconciled every month, showing exactly which clients have what amounts in the trust account. A failure of the law office to keep detailed records could result in a finding by the state bar that the attorney is subject to disciplinary action.

TRUST ACCOUNT CANNOT BE USED TO PAY LAW OFFICE OR PERSONAL EXPENSES   Ethical rules also prohibit attorneys from using trust funds to pay for general office expenses. For example, if an attorney had client money in the trust account but did not have enough money in the law office checking account to cover his rent, the attorney would be absolutely prohibited from writing the rent check on the trust account.

Sometimes attorneys will say that they are simply "borrowing" money from the trust fund and will pay it back. This, too, is a violation of the ethical rules, even if the money is in fact repaid to the trust account. Client funds simply cannot be used in any way for the personal use of the law office or attorney.

Rule 1.15(b) of the *Model Rules of Professional Conduct* states:

(b) . . . [A] lawyer shall promptly deliver to the client or third person any funds or other property the client or third person is entitled to receive . . . and, shall promptly render a full accounting regarding such property.

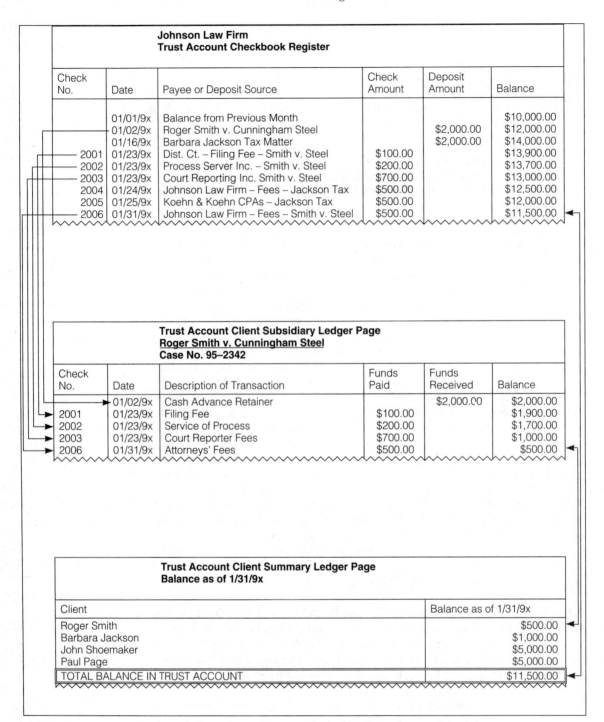

FIGURE 6-2 Trust Account Ledgers

Under Rule 1.15(b), once the client is entitled to receive monies held in trust, the attorney must deliver the monies promptly. For example, if a client's case is concluded and the client still has money left in trust from a cash advance, the attorney has a duty to promptly return the funds.

COMMINGLING OF CLIENT FUNDS A COMMON PROBLEM

The commingling of client funds with attorneys' or law office funds is not a trivial or uncommon matter (see Figure 6-3). Hundreds of attorneys are disbarred or suspended from practice every year for commingling client funds. In nearly every issue of every state's bar association journal you can read about an attorney being disciplined for commingling client monies. It is a common problem that nearly always results in harsh discipline being levied against the attorney.

BONDING FOR PEOPLE HANDLING FUNDS   Law offices should routinely buy a dishonesty bond from an insurance company to cover all employees handling client or law office funds. If an employee covered by an employee dishonesty

---

In the Matter of Long, 619 N.E.2d (919) (Ind. 1993) Attorney practiced law and owned two liquor stores . . . . Attorney wrote $21,000 worth of checks on the trust account payable to his liquor stores to purchase inventory . . . . Attorney was disbarred from practising law.

Committee on Professional Ethics and Conduct of the Iowa State Bar Association v. Minette, 499 N.W.2d 303 (Ia. 1993) Attorney was client's financial advisor, authorized to write checks on client's bank account . . . . When the complaint was received, Attorney had misappropriated about $88,000 in client funds. Attorney was disbarred.

In the Matter of Disciplinary Proceedings against Brown, 1993 WL 427056 (Wis.) The attorney repeatedly diverted client funds from his trust account to his own use and deposited his own funds into the trust account to pay over-

drafts . . . . Attorney was disbarred from practising law.

Non-Published California Case (California Lawyer, September 1993, p. 76) Attorney entered into an arrangement with a nonlawyer . . . . Both had signature authority on the office checking account; the office did not have a client trust account . . . . The non-lawyer embezzled $120,000 from clients' funds . . . . Attorney received a six-month suspension and was placed on three years' probation.

In re Petition for Disciplinary Action against Erickson, 1993 WL 408187 (Minn.) Attorney's trust account was overdrawn; trust account records were incomplete; on occasion the trust account contained both client and personal funds . . . . When there were no client funds in the account, only earned fees, attorney wrote checks on the account for filing fees, thus using the trust account

as a personal business account . . . . Attorney was suspended for 60 days.

In the Matter of Discipline of Tidball, 503 N.W. 2d 850 (SD 1993) Attorney practiced law for more than 20 years . . . . Attorney fell on hard times and to avoid garnishment attempts, he placed his personal funds in his trust account . . . . He failed to keep contemporaneous ledgers or other records regarding the account . . . . Attorney received a three year suspension.

Stegal v. Mississippi Bar, 618 So.2d 1291 (MS 1993) Attorney received a $2,500 payment from client . . . . Attorney did not perform the work or return the money; did not respond to letters and phone calls; had four prior complaint proceedings brought against him . . . . Attorney was disbarred.

FIGURE 6-3   Commingling and Misappropriation of Client Trust Funds

bond were to steal client or law office funds, the insurance company would cover the loss up to the amount of the bond. Bonding is a prudent way to protect funds.

INTRODUCTION TO BOOKKEEPING/ACCOUNTING

Accounting is needed in every type of business. Accounting and financial records must be maintained by law. The reasons accounting and financial records must be kept include:

- Reporting income and/or losses for federal, state, and local income tax purposes;
- Reporting payroll earnings and payroll taxes for employees;
- Securing bank loans;
- Managing cash flow;
- Making effective financial management decisions for the law office;
- Maintaining proper balances in checking and other types of accounts;
- Making deposits and paying expenses.

Proper accounting is required for every type of law practice: private, government, legal aid, and corporate. In large law firms, governments, and corporations, accounting may be provided by the firm's accounting department personnel who typically are CPAs (certified public accountants) or by administrators who either are CPAs or have a financial background. In smaller law offices and legal aid offices, accounting functions are typically handled by a bookkeeper. The bookkeeper usually performs most of the day-to-day accounting functions but works on a monthly or quarterly basis with a CPA to help prepare tax deposits, income tax returns, and other matters that the bookkeeper may need help with. Figure 6-4 shows a partial list of accounting/bookkeeping functions.

Some basic accounting principles are income, expenses, profit, and payroll. These functions can be handled with manual or computerized accounting systems.

income
Something of value that a law office receives from a client in exchange for the law office providing professional legal services.

gross income
Monies that are received before expenses are deducted.

net income
Monies that are left after expenses are deducted from gross income.

INCOME

Income is, of course, an important concept in law office financial management. **Income** (also called revenue or receipts) *refers to something of value that a law office receives from a client in exchange for the law office providing professional services.* In most cases, the "something of value" refers to cash, but it could mean a bartering of services with a client or other compensation such as realty, stocks, etc. **Gross income** (also known as gross receipts) *refers to monies that are received before expenses are deducted.* **Net income** (also known as net profit), *on the other hand, refers only to the monies that are left after expenses are deducted from gross income.*

Figure 6-5 shows average per lawyer gross income, expenses, and net income for various size firms. As detailed in Figure 6-5, it takes rather large amounts of income to operate an average-sized law office. Private law practices typically generate income by their professional staff, including partners, associates, and legal assistants producing billable hours, thereby earning and receiving fees.

Timekeeping and Billing Functions
- Prepares client billings
- Tracks client payments
- Tracks client disbursements

Law Office Expenses and Deposits
- Tracks and manages law office expenses
- Issues checks for law office expenses
- Makes deposits into the law office checking account
- Issues disbursements to partners/shareholders

Law Office Trust Account
- Maintains the law office's trust account
- Makes deposits into the trust account
- Issues proper trust account checks
- Tracks client funds

Payroll
- Issues payroll checks to law office staff
- Issues W2s to law office staff (once a year)
- Tracks law office salaries
- Tracks benefits for law office staff

Taxes
- Witholds proper taxes from law office staff payroll checks
- Pays in payroll taxes to federal, state, and local taxing agencies
- Completes payroll tax reports (typically quarterly)
- Completes income tax forms

Budgets
- Prepares annual budget
- Tracks and evaluates budget v. actual expenditures

General Management
- Produces fiscal reports
- Evaluates profitability of law office
- Communicates with vendors
- Communicates with partners/shareholders
- Establishes credit
- Secures loans

FIGURE 6-4
Law Office Accounting/Book-keeping Functions

EXPENSES

*An **expense** refers to a cost that the firm has incurred for the purpose of earning income.* There are generally two types of expenses, client expenses and overhead expenses. Client expenses directly benefit the client's case, such as filing fees, subpoena fees, copying costs, and long-distance phone calls. Most firms charge these directly back to the client.

Overhead expenses refer to general administrative costs of doing business. They are incidental costs regarding the management and supervision of the business. Overhead costs include salaries and benefits, rent, utilities, and equipment. Figure 6-5 shows that overhead expenses take up a large portion of gross income

expense
A cost that the firm has incurred for the purpose of earning income.

FIGURE 6-5

Average Per Lawyer Gross Income, Expenses, and Net Income

Source: Altman Weil Pensa, *1991 Survey of Law Firm Economics* and *1991 Small Law Firm Economic Survey*, 1991. Reprinted with the permission of Altman Weil Pensa Publications, Inc., Newtown Square, PA, copyright 1991 by Altman Weil Pensa Publications, Inc.

Size of Firm	Average Gross Income Per Lawyer	Average Expenses Per Lawyer	Average Net Income Per Lawyer
Sole Practitioner	$193,649	$104,889	$ 88,760
2–5 Lawyer	$175,843	$ 90,112	$ 85,731
9–20 Lawyers	$200,734	$ 90,756	$109,978
21–40 Lawyers	$216,831	$ 97,594	$119,237
75 or More	$249,481	$120,162	$129,319

from the sole practitioner to the large law firm. Expenses are quite large for corporate law practices as well (see Figure 6-6).

Figure 6-7 shows a rough average of where the majority of private law practices spend their money. Because of the increased competition among private law practices for clients and an increased emphasis on profitability, most law offices try to control and limit expenses. Note in Figure 6-7 that salaries for support staff and paralegals, together with lawyer income, add up to approximately 75 percent. Most businesses, not just law offices, spend approximately 75 percent to 80 percent of income on salary-related expenses.

> *Most firms are implementing policies and procedures to cut costs for the firm and for the client. Legal assistants are often in a good position to envision cost cutting measures that, if implemented, benefit the firm and the client. So speak up. Discuss your ideas with your firm administrator or other appropriate individuals.*
>
> —**Carol Milano,** "Hard Choices: Dealing with Ethical Dilemmas on the Job," *Legal Assistant Today*, March/April 1992, 17.

PROFIT

Private law practices are driven by profit. Profit (i.e. net profit or net income) refers to monies that remain after all expenses are deducted from gross income. It

FIGURE 6-6

Total Internal Costs for Corporate Legal Departments

Source: *1990 Economics Study of Corporate Law Staffs*, Cantor & Company, Inc., 236. Printed with permission of Cantor & Company, Inc., Downingtown, PA.

Size of Corporate Law Department	Average Expenses Per Lawyer*
10 Lawyers or Fewer	$199,439
11–25 Lawyers	$202,269
26–50 Lawyers	$197,398
51 Lawyers or More	$226,085

*Note that attorney compensation is counted in this amount.

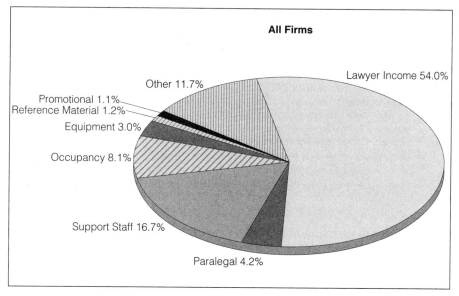

All Firms

Other 11.7%

Promotional 1.1%

Reference Material 1.2%

Equipment 3.0%

Occupancy 8.1%

Support Staff 16.7%

Paralegal 4.2%

Lawyer Income 54.0%

FIGURE 6-7
Average Expenses
as a Percent of
Receipts for Private
Law Practices

Source: Altman Weil Pensa, *1991 Survey of Law Firm Economics*. Reprinted with the permission of Altman Weil Pensa Publications, Inc., © 1991 by Altman Weil Pensa Publications, Inc.

is not uncommon for net profit to be referred to as the "bottom line." It cannot be stressed enough that private law practices are operated to make a profit.

PAYROLL

Producing staff payrolls has become an increasingly complicated task. Payrolls typically are produced either monthly or biweekly. In small to medium-sized law offices, payrolls typically are produced in-house, either manually or using a computerized payroll program. Large firms may produce their own payrolls but typically use an outside payroll service bureau. Payroll taxes are deducted using federal, state, and local withholding tax tables. Payroll taxes that are deducted from an employee's salary, together with employer taxes, must be paid according to federal, state, and local guidelines or stiff penalties may be incurred. Figure 6-8 shows an example of how much a typical employer pays in taxes, benefits, and salaries for a legal assistant. Some people are sometimes surprised at how much taxes and benefits add to the cost of an employee.

MANUAL V. COMPUTERIZED ACCOUNTING SYSTEMS

For many years, small law offices have used typical manual accounting systems, using checkbooks and ledger paper to track law office income, expenses, and profit. Unfortunately, accounting is a task-intensive process that takes a lot of time using manual systems. An alternative to the checkbook-and-ledger-paper manual system is a manual "one-write" system. A manual one-write system, using carbon forms, allows the user to write checks and record information in various accounts at the same time. One-write systems are available in nearly all law office supply catalogs.

Computerized accounting systems have been available for large law offices for many years. Recently, however, computerized systems have become extremely easy to use and can cost no more than two hundred dollars. Many of these systems automatically produce checks and fiscal reports, automatically calculate

**FIGURE 6-8
Payroll Example**

Assume a Legal Assistant's Gross Salary is $24,000 Annually	Annual Employer Cost
▪ Annual Salary	$24,000
▪ Employer's Share of FICA/MED FICA (i.e. Social Security Tax 7.65% of Salary)	$ 1,836
▪ Federal /State Unemployment Tax (Unemployment Insurance— Assume 3% experience rating & a cap at $7,000)	$ 210
▪ Workers' Comp. Insurance (assume premium is $100)	$ 100
▪ Single Health Insurance Policy (Assume $170 a month premium paid by employer)	$ 2,040
▪ Life Insurance (assume $20.00 a month premium paid by employer)	$ 240
▪ Retirement Plan (assume 3% paid by employer)	$ 720
▪ Vacation/Sick Leave (Assume 10 days a year for each— approx $11.53 an hr.—8 hrs a day=$92 a day at 20 days)	$ 1,840
TOTAL SALARY, BENEFITS & TAXES	**$30,986**

Summary:

	Amount	Percent
Salary	$24,000	$77.5%
Taxes (Social Security and Unemployment Ins.)	$ 2,046	06.5%
Benefits (Work. Comp., Health, Life, Retirement and Vacation/Sick leave)	$ 4,940	16.0%
TOTAL	$30,986	100%

These amounts will differ depending on your state, local laws, and individual situation.

payroll, and know the cash balance of checking accounts. In small law offices, a computerized system can be brought on-line with the help of a CPA and office staff members in only a matter of a few days or weeks.

BUDGETING

Budgeting in any kind of law office is a good tool to control expenses and make a profit. Although larger firms have routinely used budgets for years, smaller firms historically have failed to make detailed budgets. A survey conducted by the American Bar Foundation found that just 44 percent of all private practitioners surveyed said their organization prepared an annual budget of income and expenses. The survey also found that just 20 percent of solo practitioners and 29 percent of five-person firms used budgets. Interestingly, solo practitioners who did budget earned $5,500 more than ones who did not, and five-person firms earned $7,500 over their counterparts.[4] Firms that develop and use budgets recognize that the budgeting process allows them to project and manipulate the profitability they want.

budget
A projected plan of income and expenses for a set period of time, usually a year.

   A **budget** *is a projected plan of income and expenses for a set period of time, usually a year.* Budgets allow firms to plan for the future, to anticipate problems, needs, and goals for the firm, and to allocate and manage resources. A budget also is a management tool used to keep revenues and expenses moving toward the profit goal. Figure 6-9 shows an example of a typical law office budget. Notice that the budgeting process involves careful development of planned operating expenses, professional and administrative staff sizes, professional and administrative salaries, desired income, and planned capital expenditures for items such as computers, copiers, and furniture.

It is not uncommon for legal assistants to prepare budgets for their department, their office, or, in small firms, for the whole practice.

Step 1—Income Budget	Hours	Rate	Total
R. Johnson, Partner	1700	$175	$297,500
C. Beck, Partner	1700	$175	$297,500
J. Taylor, Partner	1700	$175	$297,500
J. B. Ring, Associate	1800	$125	$225,000
H. S. Hendershot, Associate	1800	$125	$225,000
B. D. Smith, Legal Assistant	1750	$50	$87,500
C. A. Sullivan, Legal Assistant	1750	$50	$87,500
Other Income			$35,000
SUBTOTAL (Total Billings)			1,552,500
Time to Billing Percentage			95%
TOTAL TO BE BILLED			$1,474,875
Realization Rate			90%
TOTAL GROSS INCOME			$1,327,388

FIGURE 6-9
Law Firm Budget
Master Budget

Johnson, Beck & Taylor
For Fiscal Year 1994.

Step 2—Staffing Plan	
EXPENSE BUDGET	
Salary Expenses:	
J. B. Ring, Associate	$52,000
H. S. Hendershot, Associate	$52,000
B. D. Smith, Legal Assistant	$27,500
C. A. Sullivan, Legal Assistant	$27,500
M. J. Johnson, Administrator	$32,000
J. T. Thomas, Secretary	$19,500
J. J. Statzman, Secretary	$21,000
H. V. Billingsley, Secretary	$20,250
B. J. Wickert, Librarian	$24,000
C. M. Hunt, Receptionist	$17,000

Step 3—Estimated Expenses	
All Other Expenses:	
Accounting/professional services	$3,500
Amortization of leasehold improvements	$1,000
Association/Membership Dues	$2,500
Client billings written off	$10,000
Continuing legal education	$13,000
Copying expenses (not billed to clients)	$18,000
Depreciation	$10,000
Employee benefits & taxes	$72,000
Entertainment	$2,500
Equipment purchase	$50,000
Equipment rental	$8,500
Forms & stationery	$6,000
General liability & property ins.	$3,000

(continued)

Housekeeping/cleaning services	$4,000
Malpractice/errors & omissions ins.	$70,000
Marketing	$10,000
Miscellaneous	$2,000
Office supplies	$12,500
Other taxes	$2,500
Postage	$10,000
Reference materials/subscriptions/library	$8,000
Rent expense	$94,000
Repairs and maintenance	$8,600
Telephone & fax exp. (not billed to clients)	$20,000
Travel (not billed to clients)	$3,000
Utilities	$34,000
TOTAL EXPENSES	$771,350

Step 4—Determine Acceptable Profit Goal

NET INCOME TO BE DISTRIBUTED	$556,038

BUDGETING AND PLANNING

Planning and budgeting go hand in hand. A budget is just a specific type of plan. For example, if a firm's long-term strategic plan and marketing plan call for $10,000 of marketing expenditures, the budget also needs to reflect the $10,000 planned marketing expenditure.

STEPS IN THE BUDGET PROCESS

income budget
Estimate of how many partners, associates, legal assistants, and others will bill for their time, what the appropriate rates of hourly charge should be, and the number of billable hours each timekeeper will be responsible for billing.

time to billing percentage
System of adjusting downward the actual amount that will be billed to clients during the budget process, taking into account the fact that timekeepers are not always able to bill at their optimum levels.

Income budget (step one)—One of the first steps in developing a firmwide budget is to draft an income budget (see Figure 6-9). *An **income budget** estimates how many partners, associates, legal assistants, and others will bill for their time, what the appropriate rates or hourly charge should be, and the number of billable hours each timekeeper will be responsible for billing.*

When preparing an income budget, it is recommended that you estimate as close to possible what the actual amount will be. However, if you are unsure of something, it is usually recommended that you be *conservative* in estimating the income budget. The reason for being conservative is that if you overestimate income and then rely on the overestimate in the expense budget and spend it, and income is actually lower than expected, you have a net loss. However, if you underestimate income and then the actual income is above the level (and expenses stay the same as budgeted), it simply means that the firm makes a larger profit than was estimated and there is no harm done. One way to minimize this problem is to use a "time to billing" percentage. *The **time to billing percentage** adjusts downward the actual amount that will be billed to clients, taking into account the fact that timekeepers are not always able to bill at their optimum levels due to vacations, sickness, and other unforeseeable events.* Notice in Figure 6-9 that the firm used a time to billing of 95 percent, thus reducing its billing estimate by 5 percent. The time to billing percentage for most firms ranges from 85 percent to 100 percent. The purpose of the time to billing percentage is to build into the budget the fact that the firm may not bill all the hours it would like to.

Reasons that timekeepers may not bill their required number of hours include:

- Extended medical leave of timekeepers;
- Too few clients;
- Procrastination or other bad work habits;
- Disorganization or inefficiencies in case management;
- Failure to consistently report all billable hours;
- Extensive use of the timekeeper on pro bono or other nonbillable tasks.

In some instances, legal assistants' and attorneys' actual hours end up being greater than the budgeted hours. When this happens, the firm makes an even larger profit than expected, as long as expenses remain as budgeted.

Realization also is an important concept in budgeting income. **Realization** *is what a firm actually receives in income as opposed to the amount it bills.* In Figure 6-9, the firm anticipates that it will actually receive or collect 90 percent of what it bills for. Some firms strive for a 95 percent rate, while others are comfortable with a rate as low as 80 percent.

realization
Amount a firm actually receives in income as opposed to the amount it bills.

Notice in Figure 6-9 that the firm usually sets the hourly rates for the year at this point. Setting rates in the income budget can be difficult. If a firm sets the rate too high, clients may take their business to a competing firm, but if rates are too low, it could mean a loss of revenue. It also is quite difficult to try to project income if the firm has many contingency fee arrangements. One way to do it is to look at gross income figures for contingency fees for the past several years to help in estimating future contingencies.

Staffing plan (step two)—A staffing plan also should be established early in the budgeting process. *A* **staffing plan** *estimates how many employees will be hired or funded by the firm, what positions or capacities they will serve, what positions will need to be added, what positions will be deleted, and how much compensation each employee will receive.* One of the largest expenses of any professional service business is salary costs, usually about 80 percent. Thus, it is important that the firm determine whether positions will be added or cut or whether existing staff members will receive cost-of-living adjustments or merit increases. A staffing plan also goes hand in hand with preparing the income budget.

staffing plan
Estimate of how many employees will be hired or funded by the firm, what positions or capacities they will serve in, what positions will need to be added, what old positions will be deleted, and how much compensation each employee will receive.

Estimating overhead expenses (step three)—Firms also must accurately estimate their general operating or overhead expenses. This can be fairly tricky, since in many cases the estimates are covering a period that ends at a minimum of a year in advance. For example, if a person is preparing a budget in November 1994, and the budget covers the period of January 1995 to December 1995, the person will not know until fourteen months later whether the estimates were accurate. The time problem makes budgeting difficult. For example, if insurance rates go up unexpectedly, if postage costs go up, or if large equipment breaks down unexpectedly, then your budget will be greatly affected. When discussing the income budget, it was noted that the preparer should be conservative in estimating income. However, when you get to the expense budget, the opposite is true. As always, you should try to be as accurate as possible in estimating expenses. However, if you question the validity of an item, you should be *liberal* in estimating the expense. This allows the firm to forecast unforeseeable events that might otherwise leave the budget short.

Profit margin (step four)—The last step is to calculate income and expenses so that the firm budgets the targeted profit margin it needs. That is, if after the draft budget the firm is not happy with the profit margin, the preparer can manipulate and make changes in the budget such as adding additional profit-making positions or cutting expenses further to reach the desired goal.

Here are some additional suggestions about budgets:

▪ **Budgets must be communicated to everyone involved**—For a budget to be effective, everyone in the firm should be aware of it, and there should be a consensus reached by the firm's management on major issues such as desired profits and equipment purchases. For instance, even if one timekeeper fails to charge the number of estimated hours, it could completely throw the budget off. Thus, it is very important that management stress the importance of the budget and communicate it effectively.

In a large firm, if each timekeeper is only two hours a week below budget, it could mean more than a million dollars of potential revenue lost.

—**M. J. Haught,** "Law Firm Economics,"
   San Francisco Association of Legal Assistants—At Issue, July 1991, 17.

▪ **Budgets must be tracked year-round and consulted regularly**—For budgets to be useful, they must be taken out of the desk drawer. That is, if a firm wants to purchase a piece of equipment, it is important that the budget be consulted to see if the purchase was planned or if there is "room" in the budget for it.

▪ **Track the progress of the budget on a monthly basis**—As suggested before, budgets are of little value if they are not updated and used throughout the year. One way to use the budget year-round is to compare "budget" v. "actual." This allows the firm to know whether it is staying in line with its budget and/or if it needs to make midyear adjustments.

▪ **Always document your budget**—Always document budgets well, making notes and narrative statements in the budget itself. It is common to make assumptions when formulating a budget, and unless the preparer notes why the assumption was made she may forget its purpose. It also helps in preparing the budget for next year.

▪ **Use zero-based budgets**—Although it is common for organizations to start the budgeting process of a new year by using the actual figures from the previous year and adding 4 percent or 5 percent, this is not an effective way of controlling costs and managing the firm. By using a **zero-based budgeting system,** *everyone in the organization must justify and explain his budget figures in depth without using last year's figures as justification. In short, each year's budget is taken on its own merit.*

zero-based budgeting system
Procedure that forces everyone in the organization to justify and explain his budget figures in depth without using prior year's figures as justification.

cash flow
The regular flow of revenue or monies into the law office and expenditures or disbursements flowing out of the office.

CASH FLOW AND ACCOUNTS RECEIVABLE

Cash flow *refers to the regular flow of revenue or monies into the law office and expenditures or disbursements flowing out of the office. When a law office has a cash-flow problem, it means that the firm does not have enough money on hand to pay all its current expenses that are due and owing.* As mentioned in Chapter 5, cash-flow problems are a common occurrence in law practices.

TYPICAL REASONS FOR CASH-FLOW PROBLEMS

Cash-flow problems can occur for several reasons, including:

1. **Failure to bill**—The law office is negligent in sending out regular monthly billings. The major source of cash in a law practice comes from client billings. Thus, if billings are not sent out regularly, payments will not be received when they are needed.
2. **Unhappy clients**—If the firm is performing low-quality legal services, clients will be unhappy with the service and will either delay or not pay the bills.
3. **Uneven flow of revenues**—In plaintiff-oriented firms, where contingency fees are involved, cash flow tends to be a problem because the firm receives one payment at the end of the matter (not regular payments throughout the case); in addition, the firm may be required to front client expenses such as filing fees, witness fees, expert witness fees, and/or depositions, also contributing to cash-flow problems.
4. **Unprofitable cases**—If the firm is generally accepting cases that are unprofitable, then there may be long-term accounts receivable problems. This also may lead to cash-flow problems. "Accounts receivable" refers to monies that have been billed to clients but that clients have not paid. This is particularly a problem when the firm has many accounts that are thirty, sixty, or ninety days or more past due. In some law practices, there literally can be tens of thousands of dollars tied up in clients who have not paid their bills (see Figure 6-10). Consider Figure 6-10 when looking at the accounts receivable problem for a ten-attorney practice. The practice would on average have $490,890 tied up in accounts receivable.

SOLUTIONS TO CASH-FLOW PROBLEMS

When a firm has a cash-flow problem, it typically looks for a quick fix. One thing it does is cut overhead costs. This is particularly hard to do in a law practice, since most expenses are tied up in fixed-costs items such as salaries, rent, utilities, etc. Fixed costs, like rent, are costs that are relatively constant and stay about the same

Size of Firm	Average Accounts Receivable
Sole Practitioner	$35,197
2–5 Lawyers	$36,850
6–8 Lawyers	$44,062
9–20 Lawyers	$49,089
21–40 Lawyers	$47,679
41–74 Lawyers	$48,721
75 or More	$53,664

FIGURE 6-10
Average Amount of Accounts Receivable Per Lawyer

Source: Altman Weil Pensa, *1991 Survey of Law Firm Economics* and *1991 Small Law Firm Economic Survey*, 1991. Reprinted with permission of Altman Weil Pensa Publications, Inc., copyright 1991 by Altman Weil Pensa Publications, Inc.

every month. No matter how much or how little work a law office is producing (i.e. whether it is producing five hundred billable hours a month or ten billable hours), the firm must pay the full rent. Most law practices cannot do away with these types of costs and still be able to stay in business. Firms also may try to limit supplies, copying expenses, etc., but this has an almost negligible effect. Firms also may try to produce more billable hours or even hire a new associate or partner to bring in additional clients. However, in the short run this immediately adds another large expense (i.e. salary, taxes, and benefits) to the firm's problem. Most of these are short-term solutions and are not effective.

There are several strategies to successfully solve a cash-flow crisis, but they are usually not one-time fixes. In many cases, the firm needs to change its philosophy or way of managing the firm in general to solve the problem.

practice management
Weeding out unprofitable cases, not accepting poor cases, and generally managing the case itself.

- **Practice management**—Effectively analyze what types of cases are the most profitable for the firm, and limit the cases that are not productive for the practice. *This idea of weeding out unprofitable cases, not accepting poor cases, and generally managing the case itself is sometimes referred to as* **practice management.** The firm must understand where and how it makes money. It helps to analyze the types of cases that are the most profitable for the firm and analyze which of the timekeepers are bringing in the most money as opposed to just issuing the most billings. Successful firms also have a mix of different types of cases. These firms accept cases that are both short in duration (real estate, criminal, or tax matters) and those that might last several years but may lead to large payoffs (personal injury or major litigation cases).

- **Regularly bill clients**—Ignoring cash-flow problems will not make them go away. Aggressively bill clients and track your accounts receivable at thirty, sixty, and ninety days and stay on top of the billing process. Although some firms may refer accounts receivable problems to collection agencies or even sue their clients for the money they are owed, be aware that many malpractice claims are filed by clients in retaliation for doing this. The whole point of regular billings is to minimize the time lag between performing work and collecting the fee.

- **Get nonrefundable retainers up front**—Consider requiring clients to pay a nonrefundable retainer so that they have an investment or "stake in the action." A client who has nothing invested in a case is usually the collection problem. In addition, it immediately increases your cash flow.

- **Get cash advances up front**—Get cash advances up front and place them in a trust account. Once a firm takes a case, it is sometimes very hard to get out of the case even if the client is not paying. So, before you get into a case, get cash advances on both fees and expenses. The money can remain in trust and then once it has been earned, it can be immediately disbursed to the firm. In most cases, the firm simply sends a billing to the client and informs the client that it is paying the bill from the trust account. Then, the firm writes itself a check payable from the trust account. The process is immediate.

- **Prepare a cash-flow budget or plan**—Budget your cash flow into the firm so that it matches the expenses or monies flowing out. Many firms produce a cash-flow budget. The whole idea is to match cash payments (i.e. expenses) with cash receipts so that they occur at the same time.

- **Bill one-fourth of your clients weekly**—An alternative to a true monthly billing cycle is a weekly billing cycle in which you bill one-fourth of the alphabet every week. This allows for a more constant stream of funds flowing into the firm.

- **Deposit checks immediately**—Always deposit all checks immediately into the bank account. Never accumulate checks for deposit until the end of the week. A check serves no purpose in a desk drawer, and, in the meantime, the client may be sued and have her account attached, or the check may bounce. By depositing the checks immediately, you immediately increase your cash flow.

- **Make payments as late as possible**—The magic rule of cash flow is to deposit monies at the earliest possible moment and forestall payments going out of the firm until the last minute. One way to forestall payments such as a large insurance payment is to pay them monthly or quarterly instead of paying them once a year in advance. Remember, "a dollar of expense deferred is a dollar earned."

COMPENSATION AND PROFIT DISTRIBUTION

The profit that a law practice earns is shared by the firm's partners, in a partnership structure, or shareholders, in a corporation. There are several ways that partners can share profits, and there usually is a committee that distributes or determines how this is done. One method is to use a **seniority system** (also known as a "lockstep" system), in which a partner's share in the profits of the practice is based on the partner's length of service. Another method is a merit system. In a **merit system,** profits are distributed to partners based on a determination of merit, such as who has produced the most paying clients, logged the most billable hours, etc. Many firms use the merit system because it tends to motivate partners to do more work, since they have a pecuniary interest in doing so. Other firms, especially professional corporations, distribute profits based on each partner's percent of ownership.

It also should be noted that some firms share the profits of the firm as a whole with all partners, while other firms share profits based on the amount of profit each office generated or each practice group earned, using the "eat what you kill" approach.[5] In any case, partners are entitled to receive a piece of the profit. However, in most cases, it is not known until the end of the fiscal year what any particular partner's share of the profit is. In most cases, it is simply not possible for partners to wait to receive income at the end of the year. Nearly all firms allow partners to draw monies throughout the year. *A **draw** refers to a partner receiving or drawing a certain monthly amount of his anticipated share of net income, which is then counted against his share of the profits at the end of the year.*

draw
A payment to a partner that represents a share of a partner's anticipated net income. The draw is counted against the share of the partner's profits at the end of the year.

INTERNAL CONTROLS

Law offices of every type—private, corporate, government, and legal aid—must establish good internal control procedures. **Internal control** *refers to procedures that an organization establishes to set up checks and balances so that no one individual in the organization has exclusive control over any part of the accounting system.* Internal controls discussions are usually saved for accounting professionals. However, embezzlement by law practice personnel has become a major issue (see Figure 6-11) and is quite prevalent. If embezzlement occurs in an organization, it signals that its internal controls were weak and ineffective.

internal control
Procedures that an organization establishes to set up checks and balances so that no individual in the organization has exclusive control over any part of the accounting system.

FORMER PARALEGAL SENTENCED IN EMBEZZLEMENT CASE

A former paralegal was sentenced to two months of home detention and one year of probation for having embezzled $8,000 in funds belonging to a bankruptcy debtor while employed as a paralegal at a East Coast law firm. The paralegal faced a maximum penalty of five years' imprisonment and a $250,000 fine. The paralegal was custodian of the bankruptcy debtor's account and was responsible for preparing checks for the bankruptcy trustee. The embezzlement was discovered a few months after the paralegal left the firm while he was working at another firm. "We discovered certain irregularities during a routine inventory of accounts and turned the information over to the proper authorities" said one of the firm's directors. The case was investigated by the FBI. At the time of sentencing the paralegal informed the U.S. attorney's office that he was no longer working at the new firm and that he voluntarily withdrew from law school entirely. *Legal Assistant Today,* July/August 1992, 27.

BOOKKEEPER ALLEGEDLY EMBEZZLES $2 MILLION OVER 15-YEAR PERIOD

A Boston personal injury attorney alleges that his bookkeeper of 15 years stole $2 million from him. The bookkeeper had complete authority over the office's finances. She was able to write and sign checks for unlimited amounts of money without the attorney's approval. The attorney felt confident about the bookkeeper. Then one day, he discovered that some checks were missing and that there were inaccuracies in the case settlement and disbursement records. One of the

bookkeeper's schemes was to write partial settlement checks between $3,000 and $6,000. She would then endorse these in clients' names, take them to the bank and cash them as a "favor" to the clients. But she kept the money. Among other things, the bookkeeper converted $30,000 which she used to make a down payment on a condominium in the Caribbean. "Stealing Your Practice Blind Embezzlement in the Law Office," *ABA Journal* 73, August 1987, 78.

BOOKKEEPER EMBEZZLES $84,000

$80,000 from office payroll accounts and $4,000 from trust accounts was embezzled from a North Carolina law firm. The embezzlement was discovered when the bank notified the attorney of an overdraft on the office account. An examination of the trust account revealed the checks had been taken out of sequence and written to the bookkeeper, and payroll checks were written for more than the bookkeeper was entitled to. To cover the embezzlements, false cash deposits were posted and copies of bank statements, canceled checks and check stubs were destroyed. **The bookkeeper had total responsibility for the maintenance of the accounts as well as signatory authority.** *North Carolina Newsletter,* vol. 18, no. 2, 1993, 5.

$400,000 EMBEZZLED FROM LEGAL AID ORGANIZATION

A neighborhood legal service's history of 25 years of service was overshadowed by the shocking revelation that the program executive director confessed that he was a compulsive gambler and had diverted nearly $400,000 in program funds to feed his addiction. Apparently the executive

director forged Board member signatures to documents that enabled him to open a false corporate account, giving a post office box as the program address. He was able to intercept and deposit program checks into the phony account and later withdraw such funds by using his own signature. The embezzlement took place during a two and a half year time span before the embezzlement was discovered. Lew Hollman, "Overcoming the Shock of Embezzlement," *Los Angeles Lawyer,* October 1992, 18.

EX-PARTNER EMBEZZLES $2 MILLION IN FIRM AND CLIENT FUNDS

An ex-partner with a prestigious law firm was recently charged by the U.S. attorney's office with embezzlement of more than $2 million in firm and client funds between 1986 and 1991. Some "irregularities" were turned up by the firm's accounting system. Once confronted, the ex-partner cooperated with the investigation. The ex-partner faces a maximum sentence of 11 years in prison and a $750,000 fine. Rex Bossert, "Ex-Partner Charged with Theft," *San Francisco Daily Journal,* October 19, 1992, 2.

LAW FIRM ADMINISTRATOR SUED

A law firm took bankruptcy due to a $56 million shortfall. The firm's ex-chief executive officer was sued by the bankruptcy trustee for deliberately misleading the firm's bankers for his personal gain. The trustee alleges the administrator used firm funds for his personal use including instructing the payroll department to pay him an unauthorized $650 per month without withholding taxes and renting an apartment with firm funds for his personal use. *National Law Journal,* vol.

FIGURE 6-11   Embezzlement Is Common in Law Practices

15, nos. 17 & 18, December 28, 1993.

ATTORNEY DEPOSITS $2,367 IN HIS OWN ACCOUNT
A new attorney in a large office had four clients make their checks to him instead of the firm. He then deposited the $2,367 in his own account. The attorney was convicted of grand theft and was disbarred. "Stealing Your Practice Blind Embezzlement in the Law Office," *ABA Journal* 73,

August 1987, 78.

BOOKKEEPER GOES FROM LAW OFFICE TO LAW OFFICE EMBEZZLING
A Miami bookkeeper went to one law firm, took a check for $650 made out to the firm, stamped it with a firm stamp, forged a partner's name, and deposited the check in her own account. At a Miami real estate law firm, she worked as a foreclosure secretary and stole $27,000 in two months.

If a client paid on a foreclosure to the firm, she would forge the name of someone at the firm and deposit the check in her account. To balance the books she would juggle firm accounts, diverting funds from one client and covering it up with money from another client. "Stealing Your Practice Blind Embezzlement in the Law Office," *ABA Journal* 73, August 1987, 78.

Internal controls must be established in both large and small firms. Interestingly enough, small law offices need internal controls more than large firms do. Why? Because fewer people handle the finances in a small office, and there are typically fewer written and strict procedures. Thus the opportunity to embezzle tends to be greater in a smaller office. Therefore, it is absolutely critical in a small law office to have exceptionally good internal controls. The downside of internal controls is that it takes time to do them right and they can slow down the financial process (i.e. such as requiring a partner to sign all checks instead of having a bookkeeper sign checks). This is particularly true in small firms. But, it is the <u>only</u> way to ensure that embezzlement and fraud do not start or take place.

So what type of internal control procedures could limit the possibility of embezzlement? There are several:

- **Never allow a bookkeeper or person preparing checks to sign checks or to sign on the account**

Never let the individual who writes the checks sign on the account. **A bookkeeper should never be allowed to sign on the account.** In addition, never let any one person record the check in the checkbook (or equivalent), prepare the check, obtain signature(s) on the check, and mail the check. Embezzlement is more likely to happen in that case. A partner or ranking member of the firm should sign all checks if possible. An alternative is to require two signatures on all checks.

- **Have careful, unannounced, routine examination of the books**

A partner or other ranking member of the law office with no direct accounting responsibilities should carefully look over the books on a weekly basis. A partner also should account for all monies on a regular basis (once a week or once every two weeks) by reviewing bank statements and canceled checks for the authenticity of the signatures, reviewing the reconciliation register, ensuring that check numbers out of sequence are not being cashed, and looking through cash disbursement records carefully. These procedures must be done for both the office business account and the trust account.

- **All documents must routinely be read and examined—no exceptions**

Never sign or let someone else sign checks, correspondence, or other important documents without carefully reading the material. It is <u>very</u> easy to hand documents to people and ask for their signature immediately. Don't do it and don't let someone else do it. It is very important that everyone involved always check all the supporting documentation of a check.

- **All checks should be stored in a locked cabinet**

All checks should be kept under lock and key at all times when not in use, and access for writing checks should be given to as few people as possible.

- **Never let the person signing the checks reconcile the account**

The person writing checks or the person signing the checks should not be allowed to reconcile the bank account. If the person who is preparing and signing the checks is allowed to reconcile the account, that person will be able to write herself a check, sign it, and destroy the check when it comes in the bank statement. This might even tempt a basically honest person. Oversight is the key. Never let anyone have the opportunity to embezzle; set up good procedures and follow them.

- **Use check request forms**

Check request forms also are used to bolster internal control procedures. If, for instance, an employee or attorney needed a check for a client expense or for an expense charged to the firm, the person would be required to complete a form similar to the one shown in Figure 6-12. Small law offices also should use check requests whenever possible.

- **Have guidelines for how the mail should be opened**

The mail should be opened by someone with no accounting duties such as a receptionist, secretary, or mailing clerk. When a check is received, the person opening the mail should be instructed to immediately endorse the check on the back "FOR DEPOSIT ONLY" in ink or with a stamp. If the bookkeeper or someone in accounting opens the mail, there is absolutely nothing to stop that person from taking the check and cashing it. This would be easy to do, since the firm would have no record of it.

- **Use nonaccounting personnel to help with internal controls**

An additional internal control would be for the receptionist, secretary, or another person to prepare the bank deposits, since he would be separated from the accounting department and would not have recorded the cash receipts in the accounts receivable system. In this way, all cash receipts and bank deposits are independently verified by someone completely outside the accounting department who has no access to accounting records.

A _very_ common way embezzlement occurs is on refund checks. For example, it is not uncommon for firms to receive large refund checks from insurance companies and other vendors. If a person in the accounting department opens the mail, he could endorse the check and deposit it in his own account with little possibility of someone finding out about it. Why? Because the original invoice would be shown as paid on the firm's books, and no one else would know that he had received the refund.

- **Require two signatures on checks over $5,000**

Checks over a certain dollar amount might also be required to be signed by a second individual (i.e. two signatures on the check). This is another example of an internal control. This would limit large checks from going out of the firm with the authority of only one individual.

- **Stamp invoices "Canceled"**

Once a check has been paid, the invoice should be stamped "CANCELED" so that no one could intentionally resubmit the same invoice for payment.

JOHNSON, BECK & TAYLOR
ATTORNEYS AT LAW
555 Flowers Street, Suite 200
Los Angeles, California, 90038
(212) 585-2342

CHECK REQUEST FORM

Client Name and File Number: _____

Date of Request: _____

Request Made By: _____

Bank Account: General Business Account   Trust Account   (Circle One)

Amount of Check: $ _____

Check Should Be Made Payable To: _____

Address of Payee: _____

Detailed Description: _____

_____

_____

_____

Accounting Use Only
Account No./Code: _____
Approved by: _____   Date: _____

FIGURE 6-12

- **Have an audit done once a year or hire a CPA to help you set up internal controls**

A yearly audit by an accounting firm can help find embezzlement and help strengthen and monitor internal control procedures. If your firm cannot justify the cost of an audit, hire a CPA to help you set up good internal controls and have her come in once a year to review them.

FINANCIAL MANAGEMENT AND ETHICS

Many of the ethics rules regarding financial management are related to safeguarding client funds, which was covered in the previous chapter. However, there are some other financial management issues that should be noted.

Attorneys are generally barred from directly sharing their legal fees with a nonlawyer such as a legal assistant. The ABA *Model Rules of Professional Conduct* state:

Rule 5.4 (a) A lawyer or law firm shall not share legal fees with a nonlawyer . . . .

(d) A lawyer shall not practice with or in the form of a professional corporate or association authorized to practice law for a profit, if:

(1) A nonlawyer owns any interest therein . . . .

In addition, all ethical rules for attorneys strictly prohibit them from committing fraud or misleading others, and attorneys should even avoid the appearance of impropriety. These general guidelines would, of course, also cover any type of financial management policies that were less than completely honest.

SPREADSHEETS

spreadsheet software
Computer software that calculates and manipulates numbers, using labels, values, and formulas.

In a modern law office, it is difficult to discuss financial management without covering the subject of computerized spreadsheets. **Spreadsheet software** *calculates and manipulates numbers, using labels, values, and formulas.* Law office managers and administrators use spreadsheets to prepare budgets, track inventory, produce financial related documents, project cash flow, and track payroll salaries and employee benefits. As word processors manipulate words, spreadsheets manipulate numbers. Figure 6-9 of this chapter was prepared using a spreadsheet program.

SUMMARY

Financial management is an important part of any successful law office, whether it be private, corporate, legal aid, or government.

Ethical rules require that client funds not be commingled with law office operating funds. This usually means that a law office must have a **trust** or **escrow account.** A trust account is a bank account, separate from a law office's or attorney's operating checking account, where unearned client funds are deposited.

Financial management consists of several key items, including income, expense, and profit. **Income** refers to something of value that a law office receives from a client in exchange for the law office providing professional legal services. An **expense** refers to a cost that the firm has incurred for the purpose of earning income. **Net profit** or **net income** refers to monies that remain after all expenses are deducted from gross income. Another key aspect of financial management relates to budgeting. A **budget** is a projected plan of income and expenses for a set period of time, usually a year. Most budgets consist of an income budget, staffing plan, general overhead expenses, and an estimated profit. Even with a budget, many law offices suffer from a cash-flow problem. A **cash-flow** problem occurs when a firm does not have enough cash on hand to pay all its current expenses. Finally, a firm must safeguard its assets by having **internal control** procedures that establish checks and balances so that no individual in the firm has exclusive control over any accounting system.

KEY TERMS

Settlement

Income

Gross income

Net income

Expense

Budget

Income budget

Time to billing percentage

Realization

Staffing plan

Zero-based budgeting system

Cash flow

Practice management

Draw

Internal control

Spreadsheet software

PROBLEM SOLVING QUESTIONS

1. You are a legal assistant in a five-attorney legal aid practice. The office manager who writes all the checks for the organization will not be back for several hours. Your supervising attorney asks you to get the checkbook out of the office manager's desk and issue a check that she needs right now. You fill in the manual check stub and type the check. Because the office manager is not there to sign the check, you hand the check to your supervising attorney to sign with several other papers. The attorney quickly signs her name while looking at the other documents. On your way to your office, the receptionist asks you to drop off the office manager's mail in his office. You notice that one of the envelopes appears to be a check from the local bar association that makes contributions to the practice as a community service. You also notice that another of the envelopes appears to be a bank statement and returned checks for the previous month. The office manager uses the returned checks and bank statement to reconcile the bank account. You place all the items on the office manager's desk as requested. Do you see any potential problems? Would it matter if the office manager had been there for twenty years, was extremely trustworthy, and refused to even take a vacation in that it might take him away from work? What recommendations would you make?

Know Your Ethics

1. Your office represented a business client in litigation. During the litigation, the client made several cash advances. The matter has been concluded for approximately two months and the client has a balance in the trust account of about $20,000. The client has requested that the money be returned but the supervising attorney has not gotten around to it yet. How do you analyze the situation and what would you do?

2. You have just been given the assignment to begin work on incorporating a new business. At the first meeting with the client, the client hands you a check for $1,000 and states that although no work has been performed on the case, this was the agreement that the client and your supervising attorney worked out last week on the telephone. Later, you hand the check to the supervising attorney. The attorney says to just deposit it in the office's account. What problems do you see, and what would you do and why?

3. As a legal assistant in a sole practitioner's office, you sometimes become "burned out" and tired. The attorney you work for is very appreciative of your hard work and would like to give you incentives when possible to keep you motivated. The attorney mentions that she will pay you a bonus equal to 10 percent of any new client retainers you are responsible for bringing in. How does this sound to you? Analyze this arrangement from an ethics perspective.

4. You are a legal assistant in a relatively small office. One day, one of the partners in the office instructs you to transfer $5,000 from the trust account into the office's general account. You ask him what case is involved. The partner says "There is no case name, but it doesn't concern you." What would you do? Explain your answer.

Practice Exercises

1. Using your state's bar association magazine, turn to the section that reports what disciplinary action has been taken against attorneys in your state and find one case wherein an attorney mishandled client funds (there is usually at least one in every issue). Answer the following questions:

a) Why was the attorney disciplined?
b) How were client funds mishandled?
c) What kind of discipline did the attorney receive?
d) Do you agree with the discipline? Why or why not?
e) How could the situation have been avoided?

2. At 8:00 on a Monday morning your supervising attorney rushes into your office. She states that at 10:00 A.M. she has a meeting with one of the firm's administrators to go over her draft version of the proposed budget for her satellite office. Although the office is relatively small, she must submit a budget that will produce a reasonable profit for the firm. Unfortunately, she has a meeting with a client and a court appearance to go to before the 10:00 A.M. meeting. She hands you a list of her notes and asks you to please come through for her on this one. You reluctantly agree, but then remember that your bonus at the end of the year will depend on how profitable your office is. Suddenly, you feel better about the assignment.

The attorney's notes:

- Rent is $3,000 a month, but halfway through the year the lease calls for a 5 percent increase.

- The legal assistants will bill at $58.00 an hour and must work a minimum of 1,750 hours. You think that they will do this, since they will not be eligible to receive a bonus unless they work this amount.

- Utilities are included in the lease agreement, so do not worry about these.

- Associates will bill at $115 an hour. You figure that they will bill no less than 1,900 hours, since if they do not, they will not look good for a partnership position.

- From past history, the firm has determined that its time to billing percentage is 98 percent and the realization rate is 92 percent.

- Telephone cost is expected to be $2,000 a month.

- Staffing is as follows:

  Two legal assistants
  Four secretaries
  Three associates

  Last year, legal assistants were paid on average $28,000, secretaries, $22,000 and associates, $50,000. Budget a 3.5 percent cost-of-living adjustment and a 2.5 percent merit increase.

- Fringe benefits and taxes are figured at 25 percent of the total of the salaries.

- Office supplies and stationery expenses will be about $20,000.

- The office must purchase four computers. Your best estimate is that they will cost about $3,000 each when all costs are included (installation, cabling, software, printers, training, maintenance contract, etc.).

- All other items such as malpractice and general liability insurance and professional services will be prorated to your office by the accounting office. You do not need to worry about this now.

What will the initial profit margin be before malpractice and other like items are added?

3. You are a legal assistant manager in a small-to-medium-sized firm. The firm administrator asks you to prepare a proposed income budget for your department of six legal assistants. You are not required to do an expense budget, since this is handled by the administrators and the accounting department. From years past, you know that you must sit down with each of the legal assistants and discuss billable hours, hourly rates, etc. You don't relish this much, since the firm has consistently pressed for more and more billable hours. Thus, this topic can be somewhat touchy for you as a manager. Below is the information you obtained to help you. Also, note that the time to billing percentage is figured at 95 percent and the realization rate also is 95 percent.

Legal assistant #1 typically works for one of the firm's general litigators. Because of her extensive background in this area, her hourly charge is about $60 an hour. However, during trial and trial preparation, her hourly charge is usually about $70 an hour. She figures that about 40 percent of her time will be either in trial or in preparing for trial. About 10 percent of her time is spent traveling to and from trials, finding witnesses, etc. Her travel time is billed at $35 an hour. She is a very hard worker, and although she billed 1,900 last year, she is requesting that her billable hours be lowered to 1,800. You tentatively agree.

Legal assistant #2 has recently been given a new assignment—to work almost exclusively on insurance defense cases. His typical hourly billing rate was $55 an hour. However, you know that the insurance company he will be primarily working for will only pay a maximum of $42 an hour for legal assistant time. In addition, the insurance company is extremely picky about its invoices and absolutely refuses to pay for anything even remotely close to secretarial functions. The legal assistant states he thinks that 1,750 is a reasonable number of billable hours when considering his present salary. You note that based on your experience, you figure the insurance company will either reasonably or unreasonably question about 40 hours that he bills. You reduce your estimate by this amount just to be safe.

Legal assistant #3 handles workers' compensation cases. Unfortunately, these cases are almost all taken on a contingency basis. The firm typically recovers 25 percent of these types of cases. You estimate that the firm will receive about $300,000 in revenues from this small part of its practice. You also note that about one-third of this is usually allocated to the work of the legal assistant.

Legal assistant #4 works mainly in the probate area. She typically receives about $50 per hour for her work. You note that although she billed more than 2,000 hours last year, she did not take any vacation and took very little time off. Your conversation reveals that she is going to take three weeks off for an extensive vacation and that she may need to take an additional week off for medical reasons.

Legal assistant #5 is new to the firm. From your past experience, you do not want to burn him out by putting too many billable hours on him at first. You also recognize that he will have many nonbillable hours during the first several months due to staff training and general unfamiliarity with the firm. You budget him for 1,600 hours. He will be a rover, working for many different people, and thus his hourly billing rate is hard to estimate, but you budget $40.00 an hour.

Finally legal assistant #6, yourself. You have many administrative responsibilities. You would like to set a good example, so you budget yourself at 1,400 hours. You are responsible for coordinating the efforts of the legal assistants under you, for handling personnel-related issues, and many other duties. You also remember that you are to take a greater role in marketing this year and that approximately 160 hours of your time will be non-billable handling this function.

Finally, you note that the economy may be turning down. So, you propose to lower your billable hour estimates by 10 percent. You will talk to the administrators about this.

4. Several years ago you were hired as a legal assistant in a small law office. Since that time you have been a good employee and have worked hard for the firm. Two weeks ago, the office manager "resigned." The firm's partners have offered you the position. However, the partners inform you that the office manager was actually fired for mismanaging the practice, and they want you to improve the financial performance of the practice.

The partners also tell you that the firm has a tremendous amount of aged accounts receivable. This has greatly affected cash flow and made it hard in recent months to pay expenses. The firm bills manually every six weeks.

After agreeing to take the position, you go into the office manager's office and notice that you cannot find any financial plans, budgets, or projections of any type. In addition, the firm's library has been ignored and is terribly outdated. You need a librarian but you are sure the firm cannot afford a full-time one. From your own experience you know that the firm seems to spend a great deal on postage costs—some of the staff members use the postage machine occasionally for personal use, but the office manager never enforced the rule about using equipment and supplies for personal use. One of the three attorneys seems to buy a lot of computer equipment and really enjoys tinkering with it. He always has to have the latest computer that comes on the market. The firms spends nothing on marketing costs to speak of.

The firm's partners are urging that you do something immediately. How would you go about saving the practice and keeping your new job? Please be specific, the firm's partners want to see a plan of how you will turn things around.

NOTES

1. M. J. Haught, quoting Nancy Siegel in "Law Firm Economics," *San Francisco Association of Legal Assistants–At Issue*, vol. 18, no. 7, July 1991, 1.
2. William Gilbert Burgess [#75969], (August 21, 1992), *California Lawyer*, November 1992, 77.
3. Ellan A. Panksy, "Client Trust Account Procedures," *Los Angeles Lawyer*, December 1992, 32, citing "Standard 2.2, Minimum Standards of Attorney Discipline."
4. Ezra Tom Clark, Jr., "Budgeting for the Small Law Firm," *Law Practice Management*, October 1991, 52.
5. M. J. Haught, "Law Firm Economics," *San Francisco Association of Legal Assistants–At Issue*, vol. 18, no. 7, 17.

DOCKET
CONTROL
SYSTEMS

CHAPTER OBJECTIVES

After you read this chapter, you will be able to:

- Explain how to make docketing entries.
- Discuss how to calculate court deadlines.
- Explain why a poor docket system is harmful to a law office.
- Differentiate between manual and computerized docket systems.
- Discuss how a computerized docketing cycle process works.
- Explain how a poor docket control system leads to ethical and malpractice claims.

A client sued his former attorney (and the attorney's partners) for legal malpractice for failing to timely file a medical malpractice claim. In October 1983 the client met with a Michigan attorney regarding a claim against a hospital for medical malpractice. After the initial meetings, the client made repeated telephone calls and sent letters to the attorney. However, the attorney never responded to the client's communications. In June 1985, the attorney finally responded. The client received a letter from the attorney.

> *My sincere apologies for the delay in responding to your earlier communications; however, we have been making a thorough inquiry into the facts of your alleged complaints. We have not been able to find an expert to make the appropriate causal relationship to support our theories of possible malpractice. Accordingly, we are not going to be proceeding on your claim and will close our file.*

Within two weeks, the client sought the advice of another attorney and filed a legal malpractice claim against the first attorney. A jury awarded the client $150,000 in damages against the attorney for allowing the statute of limitations on the medical malpractice claim to lapse.[1]

A Houston attorney accepted a reprimand when a grievance committee found that the attorney failed to adequately communicate with his client, failed to adequately prepare, willfully or intentionally neglected the legal matter entrusted to him, and failed to seek the lawful objectives of his client. The attorney was also ordered to pay restitution to his client.[2]

WHY LEGAL ASSISTANTS NEED TO UNDERSTAND DOCKET CONTROL

Have you ever awakened in the middle of the night wondering whatever happened to the "Smith" file that you haven't seen for six months? Are you wondering where it went and what deadlines you missed? This can be a nightmare waiting to happen if your office has an inadequate diary/tickler system.

—**Dee Crocker,** "Avoiding the Nightmare,"
Oregon State Bar Bulletin, August/September 1992, 31.

The practice of law is filled with appointments, deadlines, court dates, deposition dates, and other commitments. It is important to the survival of any law office and legal assistant to be able to track this information. Law offices control these events using a docket. *A* **docket** *is a calendaring or scheduling system that tracks and organizes appointments, deadlines, and commitments.* Law offices may refer to a docket or calendaring system as a "tickler" because it "tickles" the memory.

In many law offices, legal assistants operate the docket control system for the whole office, while in others, legal assistants only use the system to manage and track cases. Although the calendaring and docketing subject may seem trivial at first, the examples of dire consequences resulting from docketing system failures at the beginning of this chapter should indicate the grave nature and importance of this subject. Thus, it is critical for the legal assistant to know how to use docket control so that important deadlines are tracked and kept.

docket
A calendaring or scheduling system that tracks and organizes appointments, deadlines, and commitments.

APPOINTMENTS

During the course of a case or legal matter, a legal professional will have many appointments: meetings with clients and cocounsel, witness interviews, interoffice meetings, and so forth. Keeping appointments is very important. Law offices that must constantly reschedule appointments with clients may find their clients going to other attorneys who provide better service. *The concept of rescheduling appointments or legal deadlines is often called getting a* **continuance** *(e.g., "The deposition was continued because the witness was sick").*

continuance
Rescheduling an appointment or court date.

DEADLINES AND REMINDERS

The practice of law is filled with deadlines at practically every stage of a legal matter. One of the most important types of deadlines is a statute of limitations. *A* **statute of limitations** *is a statute or law that sets a limit on the length of time a party has to file a suit.* For instance, some states impose a five-year statute of limitations

statute of limitations
A statute or law that sets a limit on the length of time a party has to file a suit. If a case is filed after the statute of limitations, the claim is barred and is dismissed as a matter of law.

on lawsuits alleging a breach of a written contract. That is, if a lawsuit is brought or filed more than five years after a contract is breached or broken, the lawsuit is barred by the statute, and a court will dismiss the action. The purpose of a statute of limitations is to force parties to bring lawsuits in a timely fashion so that evidence is not destroyed, or before witnesses leave the area, and so forth. If an attorney allows a statute of limitations to run, or expire, without filing a case, she may be liable for legal malpractice.

There also are many deadlines that are set after a case has been filed. In some courts, the judge and the attorneys on both sides sit down and schedule a list of deadlines that the case must follow. The schedule may look something like the one shown in Figure 7-1. These deadlines must be tracked and adhered to. An attorney who does not adhere to the deadlines may cause the case to be dismissed or may be penalized. Some courts are very reluctant to continue deadlines once they have been set.

Because attorneys and legal assistants are busy, usually working on many cases, the law office must have a system of tracking upcoming deadlines. This is done not only by calendaring the deadline itself but also be creating reminder notices in the calendar so that a deadline does not catch a person by surprise. These reminders also are called warnings. For example, in Figure 7-1, regarding the January 30 motion to dismiss, the attorney or legal assistant may want to be reminded thirty, fifteen, and five days before the deadline. Therefore, reminder notices would be made on January 1, January 15, and January 25, in addition to the deadline itself being recorded on January 30. It is common for an attorney or legal assistant to request from one to four reminders for each deadline. If reminders are not entered in the docket system, it may make it hard to meet the deadline. Thus, logging reminder notices of upcoming events is crucial to the effective practice of law.

Some deadlines are automatically set by the rules of procedure that are in effect in any given court. Rules of procedure are court rules that govern and tell parties what procedures they must follow when bringing and litigating cases. For instance, in some courts, the rules of procedure hold that after a final decision in a case has been rendered, all parties have thirty days after that to file an appeal.

For a law office that practices in the tax area, April 15, the date that federal income tax returns are due, is an example of an automatic or procedural deadline that must be tracked. Thus, this automatic or procedural deadline must be

---

FIGURE 7-1
A Typical Case Schedule

Deadline Item	Deadline Date
All Motions to Dismiss must be filed by:	Jan. 30
Responses to Motions to Dismiss must be filed by:	Mar. 1
Discovery (depositions, interrogatories, request for production) to be completed by:	Dec. 20
Summary Judgment Motions to be filed by:	Feb. 1
Responses to Summary Judgment Motions to be filed by:	Mar. 1
Pretrial order to be filed by:	Jun. 1
Settlement Conferences to be completed by:	Jun. 30
Pretrial Motions to be completed & decided by:	July 15
Trial to start no later than:	Sept. 1

tracked by the office's docket system and appropriate reminders must be made so that returns are not filed late and penalties assessed.

HEARINGS AND COURT DATES

Hearings and court dates are formal proceedings before a court. It is extremely important that these dates be carefully tracked. Most courts have little tolerance for attorneys who fail to show up for court. In some instances, the attorney can be fined or disciplined for missing court dates.

In larger cases, especially when the case is being litigated in court, there may be hundreds of entries into the docket system. Figure 7-2 includes a list of common docket entries, including both substantive and law office management-related entries.

RECEIVING DOCUMENTS, FOLLOWING COURT RULES, AND CALCULATING DEADLINES

Receiving documents that need to be calendared, calculating deadlines, and following the local court rules are important aspects of docket control.

RECEIVING DOCUMENTS

It is important when documents come in the mail that response dates and other deadlines be immediately and systematically entered in the law office's docket system. For example, pleadings, motions, discovery documents, and other documents that need to be responded to within a certain time period should be immediately entered in the office's system.

Suppose your office received interrogatories (i.e. written questions that your client must complete and send back) for one of your clients in the mail. Also, suppose in the particular court where the suit is filed, interrogatory responses must be answered within thirty calendar days from the date they are received. It is important when the interrogatories are received by the mail department or whoever opens the mail that the documents with calendar entries be routed immediately to someone who has the responsibility to record the deadlines in the docket control system. If there is confusion as to whose responsibility it is to enter the calendar item or confusion as to when the documents should be calendared (i.e. no systematic system), there is an excellent chance the calendar dates will not be entered in the docket system. If that happens, it is virtually guaranteed that deadlines, response dates, etc., will be missed and ethical problems will follow.

KNOW THE LOCAL COURT RULES

It is imperative to know the local court rules for each court your office has cases in. Even courts in the same state can have vastly different rules depending on the internal operating procedure of each court.

**FIGURE 7-2
Common Docket
Control Entries**

Source: Kline Strong,
Docket Control Systems,
American Bar Association,
1981. Reprinted with
permission.

- Expiration dates for statutes of limitations
- Judgment renewal dates
- Charter renewal dates
- Renewal dates for copyrights, trademarks, and patents
- Renewal dates for leases and licenses
- Renewal dates for insurance coverage
- Trial court appearance dates
- Due dates for trial court briefs
- Due dates on various pleadings: answers; depositions; replies to inter-
  rogatories and requests for admissions; various motions and notices, etc.
- Due dates in probate proceedings such as inventory and appraisal dates
- Appearances in bankruptcy proceedings
- Action dates in commercial law matters
- Due dates in corporate or security matters
- Closing dates for real estate transactions
- Due dates for appellate briefs and arguments
- Tax return due dates
- Due dates in estate matters such as tax return dates, valuation dates,
  and hearing dates
- Dates of stockholder meetings
- Dates of board of directors meetings
- Review dates for wills
- Review dates for buy and sell valuations of business interests
- Review dates for trusts
- Renewal dates for lease on offices
- Renewal dates for attorney licenses
- Expiration dates on notary certificates
- Renewal dates for malpractice and other insurance
- Personal property tax return dates
- Dates for partners (and other recurring and nonrecurring) meetings
- Review dates for billings and accounts receivable
- Review dates for work-in-process
- Review dates for evaluation of associates and staff
- Review dates for raises and bonuses
- Quarterly payroll withholding reports due

CALCULATING DEADLINES

Calculating deadlines depends on the local rules. However, the following are
some of the different ways that deadlines can be calculated and some problems
that may arise in making calculations.

CALENDAR DAYS V. WORKDAYS   Some courts make a distinction between
calendar days and workdays. For example, if a court rule says that a party
responding to a motion has fifteen days from the file date to file a response, you
need to know if the fifteen days refers to all days (i.e. calendar days) or only to
workdays.

When calculating deadlines, **calendar days** *typically mean literal days, counting all days including weekends and holidays*. For example, if a motion is filed on the 1st and you have fifteen calendar days to respond, the response must be filed by Tuesday the 16th. When you count days, you count from one day to the next. For example, the 1st to the 2d is one day, the 2d to the 3d is two days, and so on. So, you actually start your count on the next day after you receive it. When using the calendar-day method, a deadline may fall on a Saturday or Sunday. In many courts, the due date would simply be the Monday after the Saturday or Sunday. If the deadline falls on a holiday, the deadline is typically the next day the court is open for business.

calendar days
System for calculating deadlines that counts all days including weekends and holidays.

When calculating deadlines, **workdays** *typically refer to only days when the court is open*. Since courts usually are not open on holidays and weekends, these days are omitted from the calculation. For example, if a motion is filed on the 1st and you have fifteen workdays to respond, and assuming the 1st is a Monday (with no holidays in between), the response would be due on Monday the 22d (see Figure 7-3).

workdays
System for calculating deadlines that refers to only days when the court is open.

Monday	Tuesday	Wednesday	Thursday	Friday	Saturday	Sunday
1 Motion filed	**2**	**3**	**4**	**5**	**6**	**7**
8	**9**	**10**	**11**	**12**	**13**	**14**
15	**16** Response Due if 15 Calendar Days	**17**	**18**	**19**	**20**	**21**
22 Response Due if 15 Work Days						

Sample Event:
Motion filed on 1st
Motion filed on 1st

Number of days:
15 Calendar Days
15 Work Days

Due Date:
Tuesday, 16th
Monday, 22nd

FIGURE 7-3 **Calendar for Calculating Calendar Days and Workdays Example**

As you can see, it is important that you know whether the court rules are figured on calendar days or workdays, since there is a big difference between the two.

FILE DATE V. DOCUMENT RECEIPT DATE

Typically court rules will state when deadlines are. Deadlines can be calculated either on the date the person actually receives the document or on the date when the document is actually stamped "FILED" at the clerk's office.

FILE DATE   A typical court rule may state for a civil action that a party has thirty days from when the judgment is "FILED" to file an appeal. Assume the court files a judgment on the 1st and that the party receives the judgment on the 3d. The deadline is calculated from the file date, and if there were thirty days in the month, the appeal would have to be filed by the 1st of the next month.

DOCUMENT RECEIPT DATE   Discovery document deadlines typically are calculated by receipt date. For example, a typical court rule may state that a party has thirty days to answer interrogatories. This is usually calculated when the document is actually received by the law office needing to respond to them. So, if the document was mailed on the 1st and actually received on the 3d, then the party has until the 4th of the next month to send his responses to the opposing side. Thus, it can be very important for the law office to establish when a document was received. All law offices should routinely stamp all documents that come into the office with a received stamp that shows the date the document was received (e.g., "RECEIVED 10/1/94").

DUE DATE—FILE DATE V. MAIL DATE

It is important when reading court rules to know whether documents can be mailed in or if they must be actually "FILED" within the specified deadline. For example, assume you receive a document on the 1st and the court rule says you have twenty days to respond. Thus, the response would be due on the 21st. In some courts it is acceptable to put the response in the mail on the 21st. That is, you do not actually have to get the document stamped "FILED" on the 21st. Some courts automatically give you three days' mail time before they say the document is late. Different courts have different rules; again, be sure you know if due dates are calculated on file dates or mail dates. This distinction becomes more important in rural areas.

ETHICAL AND MALPRACTICE CONSIDERATIONS

The ramifications of missing deadlines and otherwise failing to track the progress of cases can be severe. In fact, there are two types of negative outcomes that can result from case neglect: an ethical proceeding against the attorney and a legal malpractice claim filed against the attorney or firm. An attorney who neglects a case can be disciplined by a state ethics board. Such discipline in an ethics case may include reprimand, suspension, or even disbarment. In a legal malpractice case, the attorney involved is sued for damages for providing substandard legal work. These types of cases are not remote or obscure. There are thousands of legal ethics and malpractice proceedings filed throughout the country every year alleging case neglect.

ETHICAL CONSIDERATIONS

The Arkansas Supreme Court Committee on Professional Misconduct found that from 1981 to 1987, the number of complaints of attorney misconduct increased 40 percent. The committee also found that in 1981, only 19 percent of the complaints made resulted in some kind of disciplinary actions against attorneys for: 1) failure to perform work for clients; 2) total neglect of a client's case; and 3) failure of the attorney to communicate with clients.[3] In other words, attorneys and/or law offices represented to clients that they would take their case and help them, and then the attorneys either forgot the client's case or simply did not work on the cases as they should have. In many instances, an effective docket control system could have prevented such disciplinary action.

An Oklahoma study of complaints of misconduct against attorneys found that approximately 50 percent of all complaints were related to attorneys not taking timely action on cases.[4]

An attorney was found to have neglected a client in a probate case, where the attorney was specifically notified several times in 1983 to pay inheritance taxes on the case. The attorney failed to pay the taxes or to forward the matter to the client for payment. Between the time of 1983 and 1987, nearly $500 of interest and penalties accumulated on the unpaid inheritance taxes. The attorney received a reprimand from the grievance committee and was ordered to make restitution to the client.

—In the Matter of Respondent G., A Member of the State Bar,
  1992, WL 204655 (Cal. Bar. Ct. 1992).

The *ABA Model Rules of Professional Conduct* give direct guidance on these issues. The *Model Rules* state that attorneys should be competent in the area they are practicing in and that they be reasonably prepared to represent the client. The *Model Rules* state that the attorney must act with reasonable diligence and promptness when representing a client, and, finally, the *Model Rules* state that an attorney must keep the client reasonably informed with what is going on in the representation of the client. Each of these areas is explored in detail.

COMPETENCE AND ADEQUATE PREPARATION The *Model Rules* hold that an attorney must be competent to represent the client. That is, that she reasonably know the area of law that the client needs representation in and, assuming the attorney does know the area of law, that she take the preparation time to become familiar with the case to represent the client adequately. *Model Rule 1.1* states:

Rule 1.1 Competence
A lawyer shall provide competent representation to a client. Competent representation requires the legal knowledge, skill, thoroughness, and preparation reasonably necessary for the representation.

The purpose of this rule is to ensure that an attorney does not undertake a matter that he is not competent in and to ensure that the attorney has had adequate preparation. The amount of "adequate preparation" depends on what type of legal matter the client has. Major litigation, for example, will require far more preparation time that the amount of time it takes to prepare a will. The point is that attorneys should not undertake to represent a client if for some reason they cannot do it with the skill and preparation time necessary.

DILIGENCE   *Model Rule* 1.3 requires that an attorney act with a reasonable degree of diligence in pursuing the client's case:

> Rule 1.3 Diligence
> A lawyer shall act with reasonable diligence and promptness in representing a client.

Rule 1.3 specifically requires an attorney to act with commitment and dedication when representing a client and to avoid procrastination. Further insight into the rule is contained in the comment to the rule:

> A client's interests can be adversely affected by the passage of time or the change of conditions; in extreme instances, as when a lawyer overlooks a statute of limitations, the client's legal position may be destroyed. Even when the client's interests are not affected in substance, however, unreasonable delay can cause a client needless anxiety and undermine confidence in the lawyer's trustworthiness.

The comment to this rule also notes that the attorney should carry through to conclusion all legal matters undertaken for a client unless the relationship is properly and clearly terminated. If doubt exists about whether an attorney-client relationship exists, the attorney should clarify the situation "in writing so that the client will not mistakenly suppose the attorney is looking after the client's affairs when the lawyer has ceased to do so." The purpose of this rule is to ensure that attorneys put forth reasonable effort and diligence to represent a client. Attorneys cannot adequately represent the interests of clients if they ignore the case, if they are lazy and do not work the case, and so forth.

COMMUNICATION WITH CLIENTS   An attorney also must communicate regularly with a client. Rule 1.4 of the *Model Rules* states:

> Rule 1.4 Communication
> (a) A lawyer shall keep a client reasonably informed about the status of a matter and promptly comply with reasonable requests for information.
> (b) A lawyer shall explain a matter to the extent reasonably necessary to permit the client to make informed decisions regarding the representation.

This rule specifically requires the attorney to keep in reasonable contact with the client, to explain general strategy, and to keep the client reasonably informed regarding the status of the client's legal matter. The "reasonableness" of the situation will depend on the facts and circumstances of the particular case. The comment to the rule states:

> The guiding principle is that the lawyer should fulfill reasonable client expectations for information consistent with the duty to act in the client's best interests, and the client's overall requirements as to the character of representation.

Clients become extremely frustrated when they pay for legal services and then the attorney refuses to take their calls, answer their letters, or otherwise communicate with them in any way. The purpose of this rule is to ensure that attorneys talk to their clients, keep them informed about what is happening with their case, and keep them involved in their case. Often, legal assistants are more accessible to clients than attorneys are and can play an important role in communicating with clients. Figure 7-4 shows some examples of actual ethical and malpractice cases.

LAWSUIT NOT FILED TIMELY, STATUTE OF LIMITATIONS RUNS

▪ An attorney was hired to sue a business. By the time the attorney filed the suit, the applicable statute of limitations had run. The attorney was privately reprimanded. *Mississippi Lawyer*, April–May 1993, 32.

ATTORNEY FAILS TO FILE BANKRUPTCY PETITION TIMELY, CLIENT'S CAR REPOSSESSED

▪ Attorney failed to timely file a bankruptcy petition causing the client's vehicle to be repossessed. Attorney was privately reprimanded. *Texas Bar Journal*, July 1993, 756.

BRIEF NOT FILED, APPELLATE CASE DISMISSED

▪ In an action for emotional distress, Attorney did not file a timely opening brief on appeal. The appellate court dismissed the appeal. Attorney was put on 90 days' probation. *California Lawyer*, November 1992, 80.

LAWSUITS NOT FILED, ATTORNEY WITHDRAWS AFTER A YEAR

▪ Dallas attorney accepted a wrongful termination matter and advised the client that a lawsuit would be filed, but thereafter failed to file suit and withdrew from the case one year later. Attorney was given a private reprimand. *Texas Bar Journal*, July 1993, 756.

ATTORNEY FAILS TO TAKE DISCOVERY, FAILS TO TIMELY PRESENT DIVORCE DECREE TO COURT OR TO COMMUNICATE WITH CLIENT

▪ Regarding a client's divorce proceeding, attorney proceeded to trial and judgment without having first made proper discovery in order to protect his client's interest, waited an unreasonable length of time to prepare and present the divorce decree to the court, failed to inform the client of the debt figures he proposed to use even though he knew his client would dispute the figures, and failed to inform the court that he had been discharged by his client four months prior to the date the decree was filed. Attorney was ordered to pay the client $1,500 to compensate for fees and expenses in hiring another attorney. Attorney accepted a private reprimand. *Texas Bar Journal*, July 1993, 756.

ATTORNEY FAILED TO PERFORM LEGAL WORK, ACTS IN BAD FAITH, WILL NOT CONTACT CLIENT

▪ Attorney failed to perform legal services competently, to keep a client informed of significant developments regarding the client's case, and to respond to reasonable status inquiries from the client. Attorney withdrew from employment without taking reasonable steps to avoid foreseeable prejudice to client's rights. Attorney acted in bad faith and dishonesty and significantly harmed the client. Attorney displayed indifference to the client's interests and did not atone for the consequences of the misconduct. Attorney was suspended for 30 days, two years probation. *California Lawyer*, November 1992, 80.

FIGURE 7-4   Ethical Cases Regarding Lack of Diligence

LEGAL MALPRACTICE CONSIDERATIONS

> *[A] client sued his former attorney(s) alleging that they neglected his case by among other things: not taking the depositions of the defendants, not taking depositions of related witnesses, and failing to secure expert witness testimony which all led to the dismissal of the client's case. The client also testified that when he questioned the attorney about when the depositions would be taken, the attorney responded "all in due time." The client was awarded a judgment of $700,000.00 against his former attorneys.*
>
> *—Mayol v. Summers, 223 Ill. App. 3d 794, 585 N.E.2d 1176 (1992).*

legal malpractice
A claim that an attorney breached an ordinary standard of care that a reasonable attorney would have adhered to in that same circumstance.

In addition to the ethical considerations of neglecting a client's legal matter, the client may also have a legal malpractice claim against the attorney for negligence. The general theory in a **legal malpractice** *claim is that the attorney breached an ordinary standard of care applicable to a reasonable attorney under those circumstances.* In a legal malpractice case, both the plaintiff and defendant must rely on attorneys who are expert witnesses to testify that the defendant either did or did not act like a reasonable attorney would in the same situation.

Figure 7-5 shows some common deadlines that when missed may lead to malpractice claims. In fact, many malpractice insurers will refuse to write malpractice insurance for a law office that does not have an effective docket control system.

> *We [legal malpractice insurance carriers] believe that a majority of our claims come from poorly managed time and docket systems. . . . If we see evidence of a superior docket control system, we can reduce premiums up to five percent annually.*
>
> *—**Martin L. Dean,** "Software Guaranteed to Save Money," California Lawyer, November 1989, 77.*

**FIGURE 7-5
Common Reasons for Malpractice Claims**

Source: *The Lawyer's Handbook*, American Bar Association, copyright 1983. Reprinted with permission.

1. Expiration of the statute of limitations.
2. Failure to appear or plead resulting in a default judgment.
3. Dismissal of a lawsuit for lack of prosecution.
4. Failure to file tax returns or other documents within the time required.
5. Failure to file pleadings or to comply with an order within the time required.
6. Failure to answer interrogatories within the time required.
7. Failure to give timely notice when such notice is a precondition to a recovery of damages.
8. Failure to communicate with clients.
9. Not knowing what to do next (i.e. the attorney not being competent in an area).

In recent years, the number of legal malpractice claims that have been filed has gone up dramatically. In some cases, the amount of damages can be substantial. Some insurance companies that offer legal malpractice coverage actually meet with staff members who are in charge of docket control to ensure that a docket control system is being used. Thus, attorneys and law offices have two powerful reasons to maintain a quality docket system.

MANUAL DOCKET CONTROL SYSTEMS

There are many types of manual docketing systems, including a simple calendar, a card system, and others. Manual docketing systems work best for fairly small law offices. As a law office grows, manual systems become more difficult to manage.

CALENDAR   Small law offices regularly use a simple page-a-day calendaring system. Many calendars provide a section to record "things to do" or reminders, in addition to providing a place to schedule appointments.

As cases or legal matters are opened, deadlines and reminders (i.e. ticklers) are entered into the calendar. Notices from courts, attorneys, and so forth also are entered. In addition to the due dates or appointment date being entered, reminders also must be manually entered into the calendar. This process of manually entering due dates and reminders can be very time-consuming. For instance, if a deadline was entered that had two reminders, the whole entry would have to be manually entered a total of three times in three places.

In some offices, each attorney and legal assistant maintains his own separate calendar. The problem with this approach is that often the attorneys and legal assistants fail to coordinate their schedules and calendars. This can be a serious problem.

Finally, if attorneys wanted a short list of things to be done, appointments, or critical deadlines for a day, week, or month, it would have to be compiled and typed by a staff member.

CARD SYSTEM   A card system (sometimes called a "tickler card system") uses index cards or their equivalent to track deadlines and things to be done. A manual card or form, as shown in Figure 7-6, is used for each deadline or task to be completed and includes client name, action to be performed, client number, reminder date, and due date. In most cases, the card or slip of paper is kept in duplicate or triplicate. Copies are used as reminders and filed before the actual due date. An index card holder or expanding file folder with dividers for each month and for each day must be maintained to file each card under. When the date on which a card tickler is reached, the card is pulled and given to the appropriate person to perform the task or a list of the deadlines and things to do is made.

To work properly, the individual must check the system every day. However, if a slip is lost or is misfiled, the system breaks down. Although computerized systems also may occasionally break down, manual systems are far more likely to be error prone than their computerized counterparts. In addition, like the manual calendar, any daily, weekly, or monthly report must be typed by hand.

COMPUTERIZED DOCKET CONTROL SYSTEMS

Computerized docketing systems for law offices are available for many types of computer systems. The cost of docket control programs ranges from one hundred

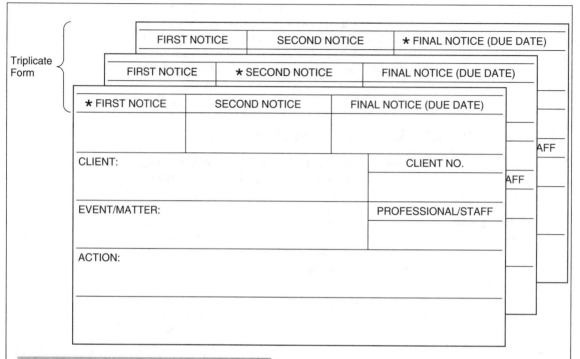

FIRST NOTICE	SECOND NOTICE	★ FINAL NOTICE (DUE DATE)
FIRST NOTICE	★ SECOND NOTICE	FINAL NOTICE (DUE DATE)
★ FIRST NOTICE	SECOND NOTICE	FINAL NOTICE (DUE DATE)

Triplicate Form

CLIENT:

CLIENT NO.

EVENT/MATTER:

PROFESSIONAL/STAFF

ACTION:

Complete a 3"×5" Reminder Slip with deadline information. Printed in blue ink on white paper, with room for dates, client data, and additional notes. Padded in 100's.

Make at least two carbonless copies with the folding Metal Clipboard. File one under the deadline, one under the date work preparation should begin.

File completed reminders in the Date Tracker File Box, organized by month and date. Check the file each day so no important date goes unnoticed!

FIGURE 7-6 Card Tickler System

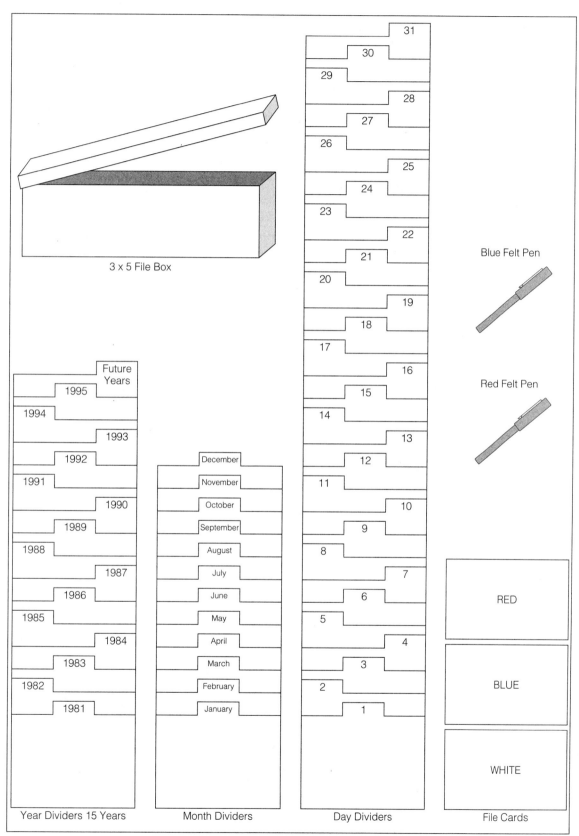

3 x 5 File Box

Blue Felt Pen

Red Felt Pen

Future Years

1995

1994

1993

1992

1991

1990

1989

1988

1987

1986

1985

1984

1983

1982

1981

December

November

October

September

August

July

June

May

April

March

February

January

31

30

29

28

27

26

25

24

23

22

21

20

19

18

17

16

15

14

13

12

11

10

9

8

7

6

5

4

3

2

1

RED

BLUE

WHITE

Year Dividers 15 Years   Month Dividers   Day Dividers   File Cards

Source: Printed with the permission of Deluxe Business Sytems, Saint Paul, Minnesota (800-336-4171)
and Kline Strong, *Docket Control Systems,* American Bar Association, 1981.

dollars to two thousand dollars or more for networked systems. Although each docketing software program is different, there are several popular features in these types of programs. The following is a discussion of some of the features.

DISPLAY SCREENS

Figure 7-7 shows a monthly display screen for a computerized docket system. Almost all docket control systems have some type of a monthly display screen or view. This allows the user to get an overview of his schedule. Notice in Figure 7-7 that this is the information for only one timekeeper, "RSS." Most programs also can display the same information for an entire office.

In Figure 7-7, small numbers appear below the date in each square of the top screen. October 5 shows "1" "1" "1." Using the legend at the bottom right of the screen, this means that on October 5 RSS had one appointment, one critical deadline (like a statute of limitations), and one self-imposed deadline (such as a reminder to do something). To see exactly what time the appointment is or what the critical deadline is, the user places the cursor on the appropriate date and presses the correct key to display all the entries for that day, which are shown in the bottom screen. The calendar display screen is quite useful in scheduling appointments and for getting an overview of an individual's or an office's schedule.

DATA ENTRY SCREEN   A typical data entry screen as shown in Figure 7-8 is where new docket entries are put into the computer. The data entry process usually is easy and straightforward. Most docket control programs are simple to operate.

PERPETUAL CALENDARS   Most computerized docketing systems have built-in perpetual calendars that allow a person to see and enter data that will be used many years into the future. Thus, contrary to some manual calendars, a computerized system does not have to be updated annually (although updated versions of the software may be desirable). The perpetual calendar is an important feature of a computerized system, since it allows the user to make entries concerning dates that are far in the future, such as a statute of limitations.

recurring entry
A calendar entry that simply recurs.

RECURRING ENTRIES   One advantage of using computerized docket systems is that the user can automatically make recurring entries. *A* **recurring entry** *is a calendar entry that typically recurs either daily, weekly, monthly, or annually.* For instance, if an office has a staff meeting every Monday morning, the entry could be entered once as a weekly appointment, since most computerized docket systems can make recurring docket entries daily, weekly, monthly, quarterly, and annually. Thus, an entry that would have had to be entered fifty-two times in a year could be reduced to one entry in a computerized system.

CONFLICT ALERT   Some docket systems automatically alert the user to possible conflicts. For instance, if a user mistakenly tried to schedule two appointments for the same date and time, nearly all computerized docket systems will automatically alert the user to the possible conflict. If the user knows of the conflict, most systems can be overridden and both appointments entered anyway. Some systems have a "lockout" feature that prevents users from scheduling more than one appointment for a given time period.

FIGURE 7-7
Typical Monthly
Calendar Display
Screen
Source: Courtesy
Micro Craft, Inc.

October   DOCKET for RSS

SUN	MON	TUE	WED	THU	FRI	SAT
						1 [1]
2	3 [4][1][1]	4 [1][1][2]	5 [1][1][1]	6 [4] [1]	7 [3][1][2]	8
9	10 [1]	11 [1]	12 [1]	13	14 [1]	15
16	17 [1][1]	18	19 [1]	20	21 [1]	22
23	24 [1]	25 [1]	26	27	28 [1]	29
30	31			**APPOINT-MENTS**	**CRITICAL DEADLINES**	**SELF-IMPSD DEADLINES**

Press the space bar to see a daily calendar for Wednesday, October 5...

Summary for RSS on Wednesday October 5

ITEM	TIME	ACCOUNT/CLIENT	SERVICE/INFO.
1	[A] 10:30 AM	00010000 JOSEPH TRIMBLE	DISCUSS TAX EVASION CHARGES
2	*[C] 02:00 PM	00011537 HILLTOP AUTO SALES	TRIAL - HILLTOP V. TRIPLE K JUDGE BERRY ROOM 306
3	[S]	00011024 AVERY INTERNATIONAL	AMEND COMPLAINT ADD DEFENDANTS

You can see there are three itmes scheduled for this day. To the far left of the screen, each entry is numbered. Then you see the letter A, C, or S. That tells you the item is an (A)ppointment, a (C)ritical deadline, or a (S)elf-imposed deadline. An asterik marks a critical deadline so you're aware of its significance. Next you see the time for the item. You can enter any time of day or night or no specific time at all. Then you see the account number. You don't have to use an account number if you don't know it yet. Finally, there is plenty of space for the name of the client or the style of the case, the description of the activity, and any extra information you desire.

Press the space bar to continue...

FIGURE 7-8
Docket Program
Data Entry Screen

Source: Courtesy
CompuLaw, Ltd.

```
┌─────────────────────────────────────────────────────────────────┐
│ ┌─────────────────────────────────────────────────────────────┐ │
│ │ Dec 24, 1990   9:02pm   Change or Delete Events   Audit trail is OFF │ │
│ └─────────────────────────────────────────────────────────────┘ │
│                                                                   │
│   Input Inits:   BDR                              Date: 12/24/1990│
│   Timekeeper :   Margie Jean Buck                                 │
│                                                                   │
│   Manager    :   ____                                             │
│   Category   :   Office Conference      Priority : 5              │
│   Location   :   OUR OFFICE             Extension: 1              │
│   Due Date   :   08/01/1991  (Thursday) Time    : 10:00am to 10:30am│
│   Reminders  :   07/30/1991  07/31/1991                           │
│                                                                   │
│  •Client Name:   Acme Refrigeration_____           │
│  •Matter/Case:   Miscellaneous Corporate Matters_____         │
│  •Docket ID #:   ACME-1_____                                 │
│   Other      :   _____                 │
│   Explanation:   This is a meeting with Stevenson to discuss the_____│
│                  upcoming board meeting and to go over the minutes_____│
│                  of the last board meeting._____│
│                  _____│
│                  _____│
│                  _____│
│                                                                   │
│ ════════════════════════════════════════════════════════════════ │
│                                                                   │
│   <Enter>:Change field    <F10>:Save changes    <Esc>:Cancel changes │
└─────────────────────────────────────────────────────────────────┘
```

Some systems even allow the user to enter such information as the individual's regular office hours and days of the week that are usually taken off. If, for instance, an individual's office hours were from 7:00 A.M. to 4:00 P.M. and an entry was made for 4:30 P.M., some systems will automatically recognize the conflict and alert the user.

SCHEDULING MULTIPLE PARTIES   Scheduling free time for an interoffice meeting can sometimes be difficult, since all parties must have an open block of time. Many docketing systems that operate on a local area network (i.e. where individual workstations are all linked together) can automatically bring up dates and times that a group of people have free, thus making scheduling meetings easy.

A computerized docketing system also allows other individuals working on a case to see what docketing entries have been made and to tell what is going on in the case. This eases the process of multiple people working on the same case.

CENTRALIZATION   Most docketing systems work well in a centralized system. That is, one person can make time entries for many individuals. A centralized system is beneficial because one individual is responsible for making the docketing entries and all the data are stored in one place and are accessible to the individuals in the office and to management. A decentralized system where the attorney or legal assistant enters her own deadlines also works well for some offices.

AUTOMATIC REMINDERS   Most computerized docketing systems allow the user to make one entry into the system that also contains the reminder dates. For instance, when an appointment or deadline is entered into the computer, the system automatically asks the user when he wants to be reminded of it. If a reminder date is entered, the computerized method automatically makes reminder entries.

REPORTING Most computerized systems allow the user to generate a variety of reports that manual systems cannot produce easily. Most systems allow the user to generate daily, weekly, or monthly schedules and things-to-do entries for one person or a group of people. Most systems also can search and sort the entries in a variety of different formats.

DAILY CALENDAR REPORT The daily calendar report is an in-depth listing of a timekeeper's or office's daily schedule. The daily report is sometimes called a "daysheet." Figure 7-9 is a daysheet for one timekeeper, RSS. Daysheets for an entire office also can be produced. Notice that at the bottom of the report, it says "ALL ITEMS"; this means that the daysheet contains all entries that were made. For instance, if the daysheet showed only critical deadlines or appointments, the report would note this. Many attorneys and legal assistants will use this report every day for an accurate listing of the day's events.

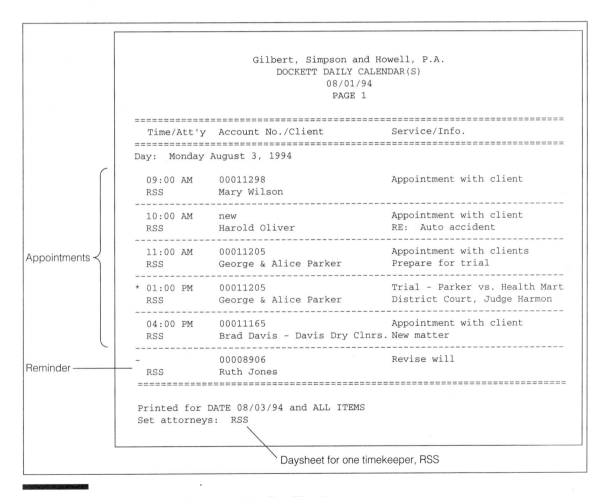

FIGURE 7-9   **Daily Calendar (Daysheet) for One Timekeeper**
Source: Courtesy Micro Craft, Inc.

DAILY CALENDAR REPORT FOR A WEEK   The daily calendar report for a week is similar to the daily calendar report except that the report shows docket entries for the entire week. Again, legal assistants and attorneys may want this report at the beginning of the week to get a "snapshot" of what their schedule looks like so they can plan accordingly.

PER CASE DOCKET REPORT   Most computerized docket systems allow the user to generate a docket report by case—that is, a report showing all the docketing dates for any one case (see Figure 7-10). This report can be very helpful in trying to determine how to proceed with certain cases. Figure 7-10 shows a listing of all entries for the client "Cooper International." This is particularly helpful when scheduling other events for the same case and also to give to clients. Keeping clients informed about their case is very important when it comes to client satisfaction and when it is time for the client to pay her legal bill. A client who is consulted often and kept aware of the progress of her case is more likely to pay her bill and generally will be more satisfied than a client who is not notified about a case's progress. Again, this report is very beneficial to clients who want to know what is going on in a case and to attorneys or legal assistants who have just been assigned to the case to see what has happened and where the case is headed.

PAST DUE REPORT   The past due report prints a listing of all docket entries that are past due (i.e. the deadline or due date has passed, and the entry has not been marked "completed"; see Figure 7-11). As mentioned earlier, the past due report is a safeguard against forgetting or not completing items. This report is used by legal assistants and attorneys to keep up on items that are past due.

FREE TIME REPORT   The free time report shows the times that one timekeeper or several timekeepers have unscheduled or open. This is useful when adding scheduling items or when setting up a conference of three or four individuals. Attorneys and legal assistants who have a lot of appointments and court dates also can use this report so they can see when free time is available for scheduling other matters.

SEARCHING   Most computerized docketing systems allow the user to search for entries. For instance, if a client called and wanted to know when his deposition is, the user could enter the client's name into the computer and the system would retrieve the entry showing the date of the deposition.

PRIORITIES   Most computerized systems also provide for prioritizing entries. An individual might want a list of all "priority 1" or critical deadlines, so that the priority items could be finished first. Prioritizing can be a critical task in busy law offices.

COMPUTERIZED DOCKETING CYCLE

A typical computerized docket cycle consists of completing manual docketing entry forms, entering the forms into the computer, generating reports that are used to operate and run the law office, and, finally, marking off items that have been completed so that they do not continue to show up on reports (see Figure 7-12).

   A docketing slip filled out (step one)—Although the docketing system is computerized, there still must be some way to get the docketing entries into the

```
                    Gilbert, Simpson and Howell, P.A.
                       DOCKETT ACCOUNT REPORT(S)
                             08/01/94
                             PAGE 1

==================================================================
   Date              Time              Service/Info.
==================================================================
Account:  00011254 - Cooper International          Att'y:  RSS

 * 08/05/94                            Cooper ats Sebco
                                       File answers to interrog.
------------------------------------------------------------------
 * 08/12/94          03:00 PM          Cooper ats Sebco
                                       Sebco production of documents
------------------------------------------------------------------
 * 08/12/94          04:00 PM          Deposition - David Morgan
                                       At law office
------------------------------------------------------------------
 * 08/12/94          05:00 PM          Deposition - Jim Smith
                                       At law office
------------------------------------------------------------------
   08/13/94          10:00 AM          Appointment with Jim Smith
                                       Witness list
------------------------------------------------------------------
   08/14/94                            Law research


------------------------------------------------------------------
 * 08/17/94                            Subpoena witnesses


------------------------------------------------------------------
 * 08/17/94          R                 REMINDER:  08/24/94
                                       Trial, Copper ats Sebco
------------------------------------------------------------------
   08/18/94          R                 REMINDER:  08/20/94
                                       Work on jury instructions
------------------------------------------------------------------
   08/20/94                            Work on jury instructions


------------------------------------------------------------------
   08/21/94          02:00 PM          Meet with clients
                                       at Cooper International
------------------------------------------------------------------
   08/21/94                            Prepare for trial


------------------------------------------------------------------
 * 08/24/94          09:00 AM          Trial, Cooper ats Sebco
                                       U.S. District Court
------------------------------------------------------------------
 * 08/25/94          09:00 AM          Trial, Cooper ats Sebco
                                       U.S. District Court
==================================================================

Printed for ACCOUNT 00011254 and ALL ITEMS
Set attorneys: RSS
```

FIGURE 7-10
Per Case Docket
Report
Source: Courtesy
Micro Craft, Inc.

computer. Timekeepers usually call information into a docket entry person or fill out a data entry form as shown in Figure 7-13. No matter how good a computerized docketing system is, if the attorneys and other professionals do not notify the data entry person of the information to be entered, the system will not work correctly.

FIGURE 7-11
Past Due Report

Source: Courtesy
Micro Craft, Inc.

```
                    Gilbert, Simpson and Howell, P.A.
                        DOCKETT PAST DUE REPORT
                              08/01/94
                              PAGE 1

==================================================================
   Time/Att'y   Account No./Client        Service/Info.
==================================================================
Day:  Monday July 27, 1994

                 00009080                Begin brief
      RSS        Karly Cooper
==================================================================
Day:  Wednesday July 29, 1994

                 00011210                Draft trust
      RSS        Gerald Patterson
------------------------------------------------------------------
                 00010023                Law Research - Custody dispute
      RSS        Susan Parker
==================================================================
Day:  Thursday July 10, 1994

                 00009969                Contract
      RSS        Jim Farrar
==================================================================
Day:  Friday July 31, 1994

                 00011318                Title work
      RSS        Brian Thomas
==================================================================
Day:  Saturday August 1, 1994

                 00009086                Review pension plan
      RSS        Third National Bank
==================================================================

Printed for DATES BEFORE 08/01/94 and ALL ITEMS
Set attorneys:  RSS
```

FIGURE 7-12
Computerized
Docket Cycle

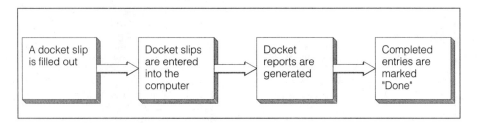

One way to keep an audit trail is to use triplicate forms. When a legal assistant or attorney completes a docket entry form, she keeps one copy and gives the original and one copy to the docket clerk. The docket clerk then makes the entry and returns one copy back to the individual for verification that the entry was in fact made.

Docketing slips entered into computer (step two)—Once the manual data entry forms have been filled out, the forms must be keyed or entered into the computer system. Some networked docket programs allow any user with a work-

---

JOHNSON, BECK & TAYLOR   DOCKET SLIP

Client/Case Matter: _____ *Smith v. United Sales* _____ File No.: *118294*

Event: _____ *Pre-Trial Hearing* _____

Date of Event: _____ *10/1/94* _____ Time of Event: _____ *10:00 AM – 11:00 PM* _____

Place of Event: _____ *U.S. Ct. House, Div. 2* _____

To Be Handled By: _____ *MJB* _____ Reminder Dates: _____ *9/1/94   9/15/94   9/29/94* _____

Priority: (1) 2 3 4 5 (Circle one, Top Priority is 1).

Slip Completed By: _____ *BRR* _____ Date Slip Completed: _*8/15/94*_

Notes: _____ *Meet client at 9:45 at Ct. House* _____

Docket Clerk Use Only
Date Entered in Docket: _*8/17/94*_
Entered By: _____ *JCC*

FIGURE 7-13   Sample Docket Slip

station or terminal to enter information into the docket system. In this type of system, the first step is completely removed.

Docketing reports generated (step three)—A hard copy of the timekeeper's docket must be generated. Some attorneys and legal assistants like to see a daily docket report of the things they need to do and the appointments they have, while others might prefer weekly or monthly reports.

Marking "completed" items that have been finished (step four)—Finally, the only thing left to do is to mark off those items that have been completed. This step allows the user to track items that are still outstanding. This can be done either by checking items as "completed" on the computer screen if a user has access to the docket control system or by sending a note or form to the docket clerk indicating that the item has been completed. The cycle is recurring, usually on a daily or weekly basis, since new entries are made regularly.

USING A WORD PROCESSOR FOR DOCKET CONTROL

Some law offices use a word processor to do docket control. That is, docketing entries are written down and given to the docketing clerk. The docketing clerk then records the docketing in a word processing document. This typically only works well for relatively small law offices. The docketing entries typically are arranged in the word processing document chronologically. Because the document can quickly become extremely long, reminder dates are sometimes not entered at all and only deadlines and appointments are entered. Word processors simply do not have the reporting capability or flexibility of a computerized docket system, but they typically are easier to use than a strictly manual system.

SUMMARY

The practice of law is filled with appointments, deadlines, hearings, and other commitments that must be carefully tracked. A docket is a calendaring or scheduling system that tracks and organizes these events.

Attorneys and law offices that fail to operate an accurate docket may be subject to ethical sanctions and malpractice lawsuits. In many offices, a legal assistant is responsible for maintaining a law office's docketing system.

Two types of manual docket control systems include calendaring and card systems. A card system uses duplicate or triplicate docket control slips that are filed according to the event's data. Manual docketing systems typically are only used for very small offices.

Computerized docketing systems have perpetual calendars that can make recurring entries with on entry, can alert the user to possible scheduling conflicts, and can generate past due reports, just to name a few of their features.

The computerized docket cycle consists of: 1) manually filling out entry forms; 2) entering the docket forms into a computer; 3) generating docket reports; and 4) marking "completed" items that have been finished.

KEY TERMS

docket
continuance
statute of limitations
calendar days

workdays
legal malpractice
recurring entry

PROBLEM SOLVING QUESTIONS

1. Your law office currently uses a manual docket system. It works fairly well, since the office is small. However, several clients have requested a detailed listing of what is going on in their case and what is coming up in the future. To do this, it takes a staff member quite a while to compile the information. Even though the office's manual system is working, should the office consider a change? What benefits would be realized? Please note that the office is driven by quality and productivity.

KNOW YOUR ETHICS

1. As a legal assistant in a legal aid practice, you notice that one of the attorneys in the office filed a case on behalf of an indigent client. The defendant's attorney has attempted on three separate occasions to take the client's deposition. However, the attorney asked for and received continuances on each occasion. The client's health is deteriorating and the client has anxiety over the deposition. The client's deposition is set for tomorrow and the attorney tells you that something has "come up" and to please call the defendant's counsel, the court reporter, and the client and get it continued. Although you have covered for the attorney on multiple occasions, you know that the client really wants to talk to the attorney and not to you and that the client would like to finish the deposition as soon as possible. Please respond to the attorney's request.

2. From time to time you see new clients that come into the office. On this one occasion, you interview a client who has a potential workers' compensation claim. After the client has left, you note that in a month the statute of limitations on the claim will expire. After discussing the case

with your supervising attorney, the attorney says that he does not believe that the client has a viable case. The attorney tells you to not waste anymore time on the matter and that you should simply call the client and tell her that the office will not be representing her. As you pick up the phone, you hesitate and then put the phone down. You go back into the attorney's office. What would you tell your supervising attorney?

3. You and your supervising attorney are overworked. You have two days to prepare for a trial that you really need eight to ten days to adequately prepare for. Your supervising attorney says "It's okay, we'll just do the best we can." Discuss this situation from an ethical perspective.

PRACTICE EXERCISES

1. One of the five attorneys you work for is taking on a new case. Unfortunately, the attorney has never handled a case like this before. This is particularly troubling to you, since you doubt if the attorney or you have the time or inclination to do the necessary research to handle the case properly. Please address any concerns you might have to the attorney and try to be diplomatic. Please give the attorney options that will address your concerns but will still allow the attorney to work on the case in some capacity.

2. Calculate the following due dates:

a) Motion for Summary Judgment filed 8/1/95; response due seventeen days from file date. Court rules in this case use calendar days.

b) Motion to Compel filed 3/5/95; response due ten days from file date. Court rules in this case use workdays only. Assume there is one weekend.

c) Request for Admissions is received 6/1/96; response is due twenty-five days

from receipt. Court rules in this case use calendar days. Response must be mailed by what date?

d) Request for Production of Documents is received 12/10/96; response is due within ten days. Court rules in this case use workdays only. Assume there is one weekend and two holidays.

3. Set up and maintain a docket of class assignments for a semester. Use index cards to represent each assignment and file them in chronological order. For quizzes and assignments give yourself one three-day reminder before the assignment or quiz is due in addition to recording the quiz or assignment itself. For exams or lengthy papers, give yourself three reminders—a ten-day reminder before it is due, a five-day reminder, and a three-day reminder in addition to docketing the deadline itself.

NOTES

1. *Gore v. Rains & Block,* 189 Mich. App. 729, 473 N.W.2d 813 (1991).
2. *Texas Bar Journal,* July 1993, 756.
3. Mary Ann Altman and Robert I. Weil, *How to Manage Your Law Office* (Matthew Bender & Company, 1990), 10–51, Newtown Square, PA.
4. *The Docket,* July/August 1992, 37.

WELCOME TO WALLACE AND SANDERS

TRAINING MANUAL OUTLINE:

- Welcome to Wallace And Sanders
- Getting Started
- Lesson 1: Entering Your First Docket Slip
- Lesson 2: Viewing the Docket Slip You Just Entered
- Lesson 3: Entering Many Docket Slips
- Lesson 4: Changing a Docket Slip Already Entered
- Lesson 5: Checking Off A Completed Item
- Lesson 6: Printing Reports

Welcome to Wallace and Sanders! We are an active and growing firm with four attorneys and two legal assistants. As you know, you have been hired as a legal assistant intern. We are happy to have you on board, we can certainly use the help.

At Wallace and Sanders we take our docketing system seriously. All appointments, deadlines, statutes of limitations, hearings, and other important matters, whether they are to be completed by an attorney or a legal assistant *must* be entered into our docketing system. Routinely using our docketing system enables us to track our clients' cases, keep our malpractice premiums down, make sure all deadlines are being met, insure quality services are being delivered to client cases since cases are not "forgotten", and helps us to avoid the ethical problems of missing client deadlines.

Since the use of the docketing system is mandatory, we have developed this training manual to help you learn it. We currently use the Micro Craft DOCKET 4.0 program. One of the reasons we choose DOCKET 4.0 is because it is so easy to learn. DOCKET 4.0 is very easy to use and within a few minutes you will be entering information in it and getting information out of it like a pro. Please note that during this training exercise you will be entering information for one attorney, RSS, to keep it simple. However, you will soon be required to enter your own deadlines into the program as well.

We know you want to get on and begin using the DOCKET immediately, so there is only a short "Getting Started" section that you should read before you get on the computer. After the "Getting Started" section there are 6 *very short* lessons, that only take between 5 and 15 minutes each to complete.

GETTING STARTED

OVERVIEW OF DOCKET

DOCKET is a calendar and reporting system made specifically for law offices. It allows law offices to track appointments, critical deadlines and self-imposed deadlines. DOCKET uses a menuing system to help you get around the program. Figure C-1 shows the main DOCKET menu. An explanation of the main DOCKET menu follows.

A.   **Enter, change, or display items**—You will use this option to enter docket slips into DOCKET, to change existing docketing slips and to display reports on the screen. Much of your time will be spent here. Figure C-2 shows what the "Enter, change, or display item" menu looks like.

B.   **Print calendars and account reports**—You will use this option to print reports.

C.   **Specify account number for new client**—This option allows you to enter account or file numbers for new cases.

D.   **Check off completed items**—You will use this option to "check off" items that have been completed so that they do not show up on "past due" reports.

E to H.   These items will not be used in this training manual.

Figure C-2 shows the "Enter, change, or display items" menu from the main DOCKET menu. This menu allows you to enter new docket slips into the computer, to change existing ones, and to display reports on your computer screen. Figure C-3 shows the "Enter new item" menu from Figure C-2. Figure C-3 is what you will complete to enter a new docket slip.

THREE TYPES OF ENTRIES

DOCKET categorizes your docket slips into three types, appointments, critical deadlines, and self-imposed deadlines as follows:

Appointments—Includes appointments, meetings, office conferences, etc.

Critical Deadlines—Includes statute of limitation deadlines, court dates, when an appeal must be filed, or anything that is a top priority.

Self-Imposed Deadlines—Includes "things to do" items, and other items that may not either be an appointment or a critical deadline but which still need to be tracked.

Figure C-4 shows a monthly calendar for the person "MM" which shows for each day how many appointments, critical deadlines and self-imposed deadlines the person has. Notice on March 19, that the person "MM" has 3 appointments, 1 critical deadline and 1 self-imposed deadline. Figure C-5 shows a daily calendar report for March 19, itemizing these entries.

INTRODUCTION TO THIS TRAINING MANUAL

You are using a demonstration version of the program. This version is identical to the actual program except that you are limited to a maximum of 100 entries. Throughout this training manual information you need to type into the program will be designated in several different ways.

Keys to be pressed on the keyboard will be designated in brackets in all caps, bold and enlarged type (e.g. press the: **[ENTER]** key).

Words or letters that should be typed will be designated in bold and enlarged (e.g. type: **Meeting With Client**).

You're now ready to get on the computer and use DOCKET!

LESSON 1: ENTERING YOUR FIRST DOCKET SLIP

In this short lesson you will load the DOCKET program and enter your first docket slip in the computer. You will enter the following docket slip for the attorney RSS:

Appointment on December 6, 1994, Account Number 100, Smith, Linda v. United Sales, the service is to discuss interrogatories with client, it will be held at our office in conference room 1, at 9:00 A.M.

LESSON 1:

1. Load the DOCKET program according to the instructions provided by your supervisor/instructor.

2. You will see a screen which states:

"At X hours, X minutes, X seconds, you are DOCKET user X.
There are X other DOCKET users.
If this is not correct, have all users exit, and run DKUSERM, Option 1.
PRESS RETURN TO PROCEED"

Press the **[ENTER]** key to go to the next step.

3. If you have a color monitor, you will see the Micro Craft Logo which says to *"press any key to continue"*.

Press the **[ENTER]** key to go to the next step.

4. Next, you will see the DOCKET logo. You are now asked to enter the current date (MMDDYY). For this training exercise, type: **120294** as the current date and press the **[ENTER]** key.

5. You are now ready to begin entering a docket slip. Press: **A** (for "A-enter, change, or display items").

6. You are prompted to *"enter attorney as XXXXX"*. The program is asking you to enter initials of a timekeeper you would like to make entries for. Type: **RSS** and press the **[ENTER]** key.

7. You are now taken to the DOCKET entry screen (i.e. DKTENTER) and given a list of options from 0 to 6. You will use option 1 to enter new items in to DOCKET. Press: **1** (for "Enter new item").

8. A blank entry form (similar to Figure C-3) is displayed. Notice it says *"Item for RSS:"* in the upper left hand corner of the screen. This means that you are currently entering items for the person whose initials are RSS.

The computer responds:

"Enter (A)ppointment, (C)ritical or (S)elf-imposed deadline, or 'E' to exit: DOCKET is asking you to enter the type of calendar item you want to enter.

Because you are entering an appointment, type: **A**

9. DOCKET responds with:

Enter date as MMDDYY

DOCKET is now asking you to enter the date of the docket entry you want to put in (i.e. when the service must be performed). Type: **120694** and press the: **[ENTER]** key.

10. DOCKET responds with:

Enter account (press 'N' for new client)

DOCKET now wants you to enter the client's account number (sometimes called a file number). Type: **100** and press the: **[ENTER]** key.

11. DOCKET responds with:

Enter client:
XXXXXXXXXXXXXXXXXXXXXXXXXXXXXX

Because this client is not in the system yet DOCKET is asking for a client name. Type: **Smith, Linda v. United Sales** and press the: **[ENTER]** key. From now on, any time you enter the account 100, DOCKET will automatically enter "Smith, Linda v. United Sales" into the client field for you.

12. DOCKET responds with:

Enter service:
XXXXXXXXXXXXXXXXXXXXXXXXXXXXXX

DOCKET is asking you to enter the kind of service to be provided. Type: **Discuss IGs With Client** and press the: **[ENTER]** key.

13. DOCKET responds with:

Enter info:
XXXXXXXXXXXXXXXXXXXXXXXXXXXXXX

DOCKET is asking you to enter any other kind of information about the entry. Type: **Our Office, Conf. Rm 1** and press the: **[ENTER]** key.

14. DOCKET responds with:

Enter time (XX is AM or PM)
HHMMXX

DOCKET is asking you to enter the time of the appointment. Type: **0900 am** and press the: **[ENTER]** key.

15. DOCKET responds with:

All entries correct (Y/N)?

If you entered all of the items correctly, press: **Y** and press the **[ENTER]** key. If you did not type the entries correct, press: **N** and press the **[ENTER]** key and you can start over.

16. After you press Y, DOCKET responds with:

Put on other attorney's calendar (Y/N)?

If multiple attorneys were going to handle this event you could automatically enter it on their calendar as well. However, because this appointment is only for one attorney, press: **N** and press the: **[ENTER]** key.

17. DOCKET responds with:

Enter reminder date as MMDDYY (press RETURN for Entry Screen)

DOCKET is asking you whether or not a reminder date should be automatically entered with this entry. In this instance, a reminder on December 5 would be nice to remind you of the meeting with the client the next day. To enter the reminder type: **120594** and press the: **[ENTER]** key.

18. DOCKET responds with the same message again. DOCKET wants to know if you want another reminder before that. Since one reminder is fine for this appointment, press the: **[ENTER]** key.

19. You are now taken back to step 8 above where you could either enter additional docket slips by typing a "A" for appointment, "C" for critical deadline, "S" for self-imposed deadline or you could enter an "E" to exit to go back to DOCKET entry screen. Press: **E** to go back to the DOCKET entry screen (i.e. "DKTENTER").

This concludes Lesson 1.

TO EXIT DOCKET:

To go back to the main menu from the DOCKET entry screen press the **[ENTER]** key. If you want to exit the program from the main menu simply press the **[ENTER]** key

TO GO TO LESSON 2:

To go to Lesson 2, stay at the DOCKET entry screen (i.e. "DKTENTER").

LESSON 2: VIEWING THE DOCKET SLIP YOU JUST ENTERED IN LESSON 1

In this short lesson you will make sure that the docket slip you entered in Lesson 1 has really been entered into the computer. You will do this by displaying a monthly calendar, similar to Figure C-4, then you will display the daily calendar similar to Figure C-5.

If you exited from Lesson 1, following steps 1–6 until you are at the DOCKET entry screen (i.e. "DKTENTER"), the screen should show options 0–6 (see similar to Figure C-2).

LESSON 2:

1. At the DOCKET entry screen (i.e. "DKTENTER", see Figure C-2), press: **6** to display the DOCKET monthly calendar.

(note: if you exited the program you will need to enter RSS as the attorney).

2. DOCKET responds with:

    Enter month and year MMYY (press ENTER for current month):

    DOCKET is asking you what month you want to display. Press: **1294** and press the: **[ENTER]** key.

3. DOCKET responds by displaying a calendar similar to Figure C-4. The screen should show one appointment for December 5, 1994, and one appointment for December 6, 1994. (This is a little confusing since there really is no appointment on December 5, but since the reminder on December 5 is connected to an appointment it shows it that way).

    DOCKET responds with:

    Enter Day to Display «for last month, » for next month:

    Docket is telling you that if you want to look at the specific events for one day, simply enter the day of the month (e.g. 6 for the 6th of the month), or to see the month before (e.g. November 1994, press the left arrow key), to see the next month (e.g. January, 1995, press the right arrow key).

    To make sure the appointment on the 6th is really entered, press: **6** and press the: **[ENTER]** key. DOCKET responds by showing you the docket slip you entered in Lesson 1 (similar to Figure C-5).

    To go back to the monthly calendar screen press the: **[ENTER]** key.

4. Now, let's insure that the reminder for December 5 is there. At the monthly calendar screen press: **5** and press the: **[ENTER]** key. Notice that an "R" is placed in the Time column. The "R" indicates that this is a reminder.

    Press the: **[ENTER]** key to go back to the monthly calendar screen.

5. Press the: **[ENTER]** key from the monthly calendar screen to go back to the DOCKET entry screen (i.e. "DKTENTER").

This concludes Lesson 2.

TO EXIT DOCKET:

To go back to the main menu from the DOCKET entry screen press the **[ENTER]** key. If you want to exit the program from the main menu simply press the **[ENTER]** key.

TO GO TO LESSON 3:

To go to Lesson 3, stay at the DOCKET entry screen (i.e. "DKTENTER").

Lesson 3: Entering Many Docket Slips

You now know the basics of entering docket slips and displaying information on the screen. In this lesson you will enter nine additional docket slips into the computer regarding three different cases for the timekeeper RSS.

Using the instructions in Lesson 1, please enter the following docket slips into the computer. Remember that once the client has been entered into the computer, the computer will automatically insert the client's name into the docket slip.

If you exited from Lesson 2, follow steps 1–6 in lesson 1 until you are at the DOCKET entry screen (i.e. "DKTENTER"), the screen should show options 0–6 (see similar to Figure C-2). Note: If you exited the program you will need to enter RSS as the attorney.

If you did not exit from Lesson 2, and you are currently at the DOCKET entry screen (i.e. "DKTENTER"), begin at Lesson 1, step 7 to begin entering new items.

Additional Docket Slips to Enter (read each docket slip entirely before beginning to enter it):

1. A—Type: Critical deadline

   B—Date: 121394

   C—Account: 100

   D—Client: (automatically entered by computer)

   E—Service: IGs of Client Due

   F—Info.: (nothing goes here press **[ENTER]** to skip)

   G—Time: (nothing goes here press **[ENTER]** to skip)

   This item as well as all other docket slips should not be placed on any other attorney's calendar.

   Reminder Date: 121294

2. A—Type: Critical deadline

   B—Date: 121694

   C—Account: 100

   D—Client: (automatically entered by computer)

   E—Service: Deposition of Client

   F—Info.: Our Office Depo. Rm. 2

   G—Time: 1000 am

   Reminder Date: 121594

3. A—Type: Critical deadline

   B—Date: 121994

   C—Account: 100

   D—Client: (automatically entered by computer)

   E—Service: Deposition of Defendant

   F—Info.: 100 Main St., Rm 4534

   G—Time: 0900 am

   Reminder Date: No reminder date needed.

4. Appointment on December 6, 1994, Account number 134, Johnson, Mary v. Elite Boating, meeting with new client, our office Conf. Rm. 1, 11:00 am, no reminder needed. Note: after talking to the client briefly, we have determined that the statute of limitations on this case will expire December 17, 1994. This should be entered as a critical deadline with a 5 day and 10 day reminder so we do not forget.

5. See "Note:" in number 4.

6. Self-imposed deadline, follow-up on finding witnesses in Smith v. United Sales, Account 100, 121394, no time, no reminder.

7. Appointment on December 8, 1994, Account Number 101, client's name is Wallis, Wendell. Preparation of will, 3:30 pm, our office, Conf. Rm. 1, no reminder.

8. Custody hearing (critical deadline), December 20, 1994, Account number 123, Taylor, Susan v. Taylor, John, Courthouse, Division 16, 10:30 am, no reminder.

9. Self-imposed deadline in Smith v. United Sales, Account 100, dated November 30, 1994, to Write Letter Expert Witness, no time, no reminder.

Lesson 3 is concluded.

To go back to the DOCKET entry screen (i.e. "DKTENTER"), press: **E**

TO EXIT DOCKET:

To go back to the main menu from the DOCKET entry screen press the **[ENTER]** key. If you want to exit the program from the main menu simply press the **[ENTER]** key.

TO GO TO LESSON 4:

To go to Lesson 4, stay at the DOCKET entry screen (i.e. "DKTENTER").

LESSON 4: CHANGING A DOCKET SLIP ALREADY ENTERED

In this lesson you will change the 7th docket slip you made in Lesson 3 (e.g. Preparation of a will for Wendell Wallis, Account number 101), from December 8, 1994 at 3:30 to December 9 at 11:30 A.M. The process is very simple and straightforward.

If you exited from Lesson 3, follow steps 1–6 in lesson 1 until you are at the DOCKET entry screen (i.e. "DKTENTER"), the screen should show options 0–6 (see Figure C-2). Note: if you exited the program you will need to enter RSS as the attorney.

LESSON 4:

1. At the DOCKET entry screen (i.e. "DKTENTER"), press: **3** ("change item by account").

2. DOCKET responds with:

Enter account as XXXXXXXX (press RETURN for menu)

DOCKET is asking you for the account of the client whose docket slip you would like to change. Enter: **101** and press the: **[ENTER]** key.

3. DOCKET responds by retrieving all of the docketing slips for that account. In this instance, we have only entered one docketing slip so the docketing slip for December 8, 1994, is displayed. DOCKET responds with:

Enter item no., Pg Dn for more items. . .

DOCKET is asking you to enter the number of the docketing slip you would like to change: Enter: **1** and press the: **[ENTER]** key.

4. DOCKET responds by retrieving the December 8, 1994, docketing slip to the screen with:

Select A-G to change, press space bar to save or RETURN for items:

To correct this entry with the change, press: **B** and then enter: **120994** and press the: **[ENTER]** key. DOCKET then enters the corrected date in the docketing slip. Note that you still have the "Select A-G to change, press space bar. . ." prompt on your screen. However, you also need to change the time.

5. To change the time of the appointment to 11:30, press: **G** and then enter: **1130 AM** and press the: **[ENTER]** key. The computer then responds with:

Select A-G to change, press space bar to save or RETURN for items:

To save your changes press the: **[SPACEBAR].** DOCKET responds by showing you your corrected docket slip. Press the: **[ENTER]** key to return other DOCKET entry screen (i.e. "DKTENTER"). Press the: **[ENTER]** key again go to the DOCKET main menu.

This concludes Lesson 4.

TO EXIT DOCKET:

If you want to exit the program from the main menu simply press the **[ENTER]** key.

TO GO TO LESSON 4:

To go to Lesson 4, stay at the DOCKET main menu screen.

LESSON 5: CHECKING OFF A COMPLETED ITEM

In this lesson you will check off (i.e. as completed) the docket slip for the self-imposed deadline, for December 13, in Smith v. United Sales, Account 100, to follow-up on finding witnesses. Checking off an item as completed prevents the entry from showing up on past due reports later.

If you exited from Lesson 4, follow steps 1–4 in lesson 1 until you are at the DOCKET main menu (see Figure C-1).

```
                    D O C K E T

           The Time Manager for Attorneys
          Copyright (c) 1993 by Micro Craft, Inc.
             Version 4.8  Serial No. 1599999

   Master Menu:

   A - Enter, change, or display items      [DKTENTER]
   B - Print calendars and account reports.  [DKTPRINT]
   C - Specify account number for new client. [DKTSPCFY]
   D - Check off completed items.            [DKTCHECK]
   E - Clear items from docket.              [DKTCLEAR]
   F - Search attorneys on a given day.      [DKTSERCH]
   G - Patch bad data files.                 [DKTPATCH]
   H - Enter event templates.                [DKTEVENT]

   Select (press RETURN to exit program):
```

```
                    D K T E N T E R

       Options:

       0 - Change active attorney (MM).
       1 - Enter new item.
       2 - Change item by day.
       3 - Change item by account.
       4 - Display daily calendar.
       5 - Display account report.
       6 - Display monthly calendar.

       Select:
```

```
          Item for MM:

          A - Type    : Appointment
          B - Date    : Friday March 19, 1993
          C - Account : 00000568
          D - Client  : John Abernathy
          E - Service : Appt. with client
          F - Info.   : His office - 300 Main St.
          G - Time    : 02:00 PM

          Select A - G to change, press space bar to save or RETURN
          for items:
```

FIGURE C-1
DOCKET Screens

LESSON 5:

1. At the DOCKET main menu press: **D** (for "Check off completed items").

   Note: if you exited the program you will need to enter RSS as the attorney.

2. DOCKET then places you at the "DKTCHECK" menu screen. You are allowed to either check off items by day (i.e. by the date of the docket slip) or by the client's account number. Press: **2** to check off the item by account number.

3. DOCKET responds by asking you to enter the account number of the client whose docket slip you want to check off. Enter: **100** and press the: **[ENTER]** key.

4. DOCKET responds by placing the current docket slips on the screen. You may need to press the [PgDn] key to see all of the entries. Read through the entries to find the December 13 deadline regarding following up on witnesses.

   Enter the docket slip number representing the self-imposed deadline on December 13, 1994, to follow-up on finding witnesses, and press: **[ENTER]**.

5. To go back to the "DKTCHECK" menu press the: **[ENTER]** key. To go back to the DOCKET main menu press the: **[ENTER]** key again.

This concludes Lesson 5.

TO EXIT DOCKET:

If you want to exit the program from the main menu simply press the **[ENTER]** key.

TO GO TO LESSON 6:

To go to Lesson 6, stay at the DOCKET main menu screen.

LESSON 6: PRINTING REPORTS

(Note: You must have a printer attached to your computer to run this lesson).

In this lesson you will print the following kinds of reports for the attorney RSS:

- **Past Due Report**—This report will show what items have not been checked off as completed. This is used to see what items you are behind on.
- **Future Due Report**—This report will show a list of items in all cases that are due in the future. This helps you plan and prepare for the future.
- **Daily Calendar Report**—This report will show all the activities for a single day. This report is used to tell you what items specifically are due for a specific day.
- **Account Report**—This report shows all of the activities for a single case. These are useful to give clients to let them know what is transpiring in the case and are useful in trying to strategize regarding a specific case.

   TO EXIT DOCKET:

If you exited from Lesson 5, follow steps 1–4 in lesson 1 until you are at the DOCKET main menu (see Figure C-1).

LESSON 6: PRINTING REPORTS

1. Printing reports is very simple. To start we will print a Past Due report. At the DOCKET main menu press: **B** (for "Print Calendars and account reports").

   Note: if you exited the program you will need to enter RSS as the attorney for whom you are printing reports.

2. DOCKET responds by taking you to the DOCKET print menu (i.e. "DKT-PRINT"). To print the past due report press: **1**

3. DOCKET responds with:

   Print (C)ritical deadlines only or RETURN for all:

   Docket is telling you that if you only want critical deadlines to show up on your past due report then press C. However, since we want all entries to show up on the past due report press the: **[ENTER]** key.

4. DOCKET responds with:

   Press spacebar for printout or RETURN for menu:

   To print out the past due report, press the: **[SPACEBAR]**. DOCKET asks you whether you want to allow space for Notes after items, press: **N** and then press the: **[ENTER]** key.

5. You are then taken back to the DOCKET print menu (i.e. "DKTPRINT"). Print the following reports using the same procedures. Remember to press the SPACEBAR to print the report.

   Future Due Report—Print the future due report by selecting **2** from the DOCKET print menu (i.e. "DKTPRINT"). Note that items with a dash mark have already been completed. Items that have an asterisk next to them are critical deadlines (or reminders for critical deadlines).

   Daily Calendar Report—Print the daily calendar report for December 6, 1994, by selecting **3** from the DOCKET print menu (i.e. "DKTPRINT"). Enter: **120694** as the date to be printed.

   Account Report—Print the account report for *Linda Smith v. United Sales,* Account Number 100.

   You can also print the monthly calendar report and sorted client list if you wish.

This concludes Lesson 6.

NOTES:

Tutorial assumes the attorney RSS is entered.

ADDITIONAL PRACTICE:

If you would like additional practice using DOCKET enter the following docket slips into DOCKET. Prepare reports and feel free to experiment with DOCKET features.

- 2/1/95; 9:00 AM; Appt. Client; Wilson, Mary; Acct #145

- 2/1/95; 10:00 AM; Hearing Motion to Suppress; Hall v. State; Acct #146, Div. 6

- 2/2/95; Prepare and File Bankruptcy Petition; Lauda, Frank; Acct #148.

- 2/7/95; 3:30 PM; Meet with Client re: Trial; Parker, Mary v. Health Foods, Acct #152.

- 2/8/95; Prepare Jury Instructions; Parker, Mary v. Health Foods, Acct #152.

- 2/9/95; 9:30 AM; Trial; Parker, Mary v. Health Foods; Acct #152; Div. 8 (5 day, 10 day, 20 day and 30 day reminder)

- 2/7/95; 10:00 AM; PreTrial Hearing; Hill, George v. Bell; Acct #136; US Dist. Ct., (5 day reminder)

- 2/8/95; Review pension plan; Bank Three; Acct #174

- 2/27/95; Statute of Limitations Runs; Wilson, Mary, Acct #145 (3 day and 5 day reminder)

- 2/22/95; Status Report to Client; Smith v. United States, Acct #100.

- 2/13/95; Prepare Contract; Graverson, Pete (House), Acct #156.

- 2/14/95; 12:30 PM; Meet with Client; Graverson, Pete (House), Acct #156.

- 2/27/95; 10:30 PM; Closing; Graverson, Pete (House), Acct #156.

**FIGURE C-4
Monthly
Calendar At-A-
Glance**

```
                    March 1993 DOCKET for MM

    SUN     MON     TUE     WED     THU     FRI     SAT

            1       2       3       4       5       6
            1 1 5   3 1             1       2     2

    7       8       9       10      11      12      13
            6       1       3

    14      15      16      17      18      19      20
                            6   1           3 1 1

    21      22      23      24      25      26      27
            1 1             2     3   1           3

    28      29      30      31
            1               1

                                    APPOINT-  CRITICAL  SELF-IMPSD
                                    MENTS     DEADLINES DEADLINES

Enter day to display,  for last month, → for next month:
```

```
              Summary for MM on Friday March 19, 1993

   ITEM    TIME        ACCOUNT/CLIENT        SERVICE/INFO.

   1    A 09:00 AM    new                  Prepare will
                      Mary Jones           New client

   2    A 10:00 AM    00000289             Appt. with client
                      Sam Wilson           Incorp. of Hexil Hardware

   3    A 02:00 PM    00000568             Appt. with client
                      John Abernathy       His office - 300 Main St.

   4    S             00000032             Prepare corporate documents
                      John Abernathy       Assignment of lease

   5   *C             00000415             REMINDER:  04/01/93
                      Darryl Hanson        Trial - District Court

Press ← for yesterday, press → for tomorrow.

Enter ITEM no., PgDn for more items, Home to start over, or Ins to add:
```

Appointment 1
Appointment 2
Appointment 3
Self Imposed Deadline
Critical Deadline

**FIGURE C-5
Daily Calendar**

8

HUMAN RESOURCE MANAGEMENT

CHAPTER OBJECTIVES

After you read this chapter, you will be able to:

- Define and discuss the term employment-at-will.
- Discuss the Americans with Disabilities Act of 1990.
- Define what sexually harassing conduct is.
- List questions that cannot lawfully be asked in an employment interview.
- List questions that should be covered when performing reference checks.
- Explain the coaching technique.
- Discuss when terminating an employee is appropriate.
- Explain what positive discipline is.

The field of employment law has developed only during the past twenty years and is changing rapidly. Hiring, firing, reference checks, evaluations—everything has to be done just right or you can find yourself in trouble with low morale, high turnover rates, and even lawsuits. Then there are all the federal regulations, ADA (Americans with Disabilities Act), FMLA (Family and Medical Leave Act), FLSA (Fair Labor Standards Act), the Civil Rights Act, the Age Discrimination in Employment Act, and many more. Law offices have to be very careful to manage their human resources carefully and lawfully.

INTRODUCTION TO HUMAN RESOURCE MANAGEMENT

A law office has many types of resources, including computers, books, financial resources, and information, yet none is more important than its human resources—its people. Because law offices are in a service industry, they must rely on the expertise and performance of their employees to provide quality legal services to clients. Like any resource, a law office's human resources must be carefully managed. Human resource management is particularly important, since in nearly every type of business, including law offices, roughly 75 percent of all expenses are on salaries and personnel-related matters.

In Chapter 1, **human resource management** was defined *as the process of recruiting, hiring, training, evaluating, maintaining, and directing the human resources (i.e. the personnel) that will provide quality legal services to the clients.* Some firms may refer to these duties as personnel management or employee relations. In larger law firms and in corporate and many government practices, there is a human resources department. In smaller law offices and in many legal aid practices, an

human resource management
The process of recruiting, hiring, training, evaluating, maintaining, and directing the human resources (i.e. the personnel) that will provide quality legal services to the clients.

office manager or partner will handle these responsibilities. It is important to note that this chapter contains general information about human resource, personnel, and labor-related subjects. Since every state has its own statutes and rules that cover these areas, it is important to research the specific statutes in your state.

WHY HUMAN RESOURCE MANAGEMENT FOR LEGAL ASSISTANTS?

The whole issue of human resources is profoundly important to most legal assistants. The obvious reason is that they personally are affected by human resource decisions, including being hired, receiving performance evaluations, and avoiding discipline problems. It is in a legal assistant's best interest to have an understanding of these issues. In addition, many legal assistants participate in hiring secretaries, clerks, and other legal assistants. Some law offices also have managing legal assistants who administer and run a legal assistant department. They typically are responsible for writing job descriptions for their department, interviewing and hiring personnel, and evaluating and disciplining people.

THE HIRING PROCESS

At some point in your career, you may be required to hire someone, such as a legal secretary, another legal assistant, or a clerk. It is important that you hire the right individual for the job the first time. A poor hiring decision can cost a law office literally thousands of dollars in wasted salary, wasted training expenses, and time. In addition, if the right person is not hired the first time, the firm must hire another individual and incur the cost of readvertising and retraining.

The hiring process is fairly detailed. Typically, a detailed job description is drafted, ads are placed in newspapers (or recruitment is started), resumes and employment applications are analyzed, candidates are interviewed, references are checked, and a final selection is made.

WRITING JOB DESCRIPTIONS

The first step in the hiring process is to write a detailed job description that explains what the duties of the position will be. If an employer does not know what the new hire is going to do, there is no way the employer can recognize the best person for the position. A detailed job description lets the employer match the strengths of candidates to the particular position that is being filled. Job descriptions also help the employee to understand her role in the firm and what will be expected. Most job descriptions include a job title, a summary of the position, a list of duties, and minimum qualifications that the new employee must have (a salary range is optional; see Figure 8-1).

All organizations should have job titles, even if there are only a few people in the law office. This gives each position an identity and a way to refer to the position itself. The "position summary" provides a brief overview of the position and describes who supervises the position. The list of "duties and responsibilities" is a list of the essential job functions. The most important job duties are listed first. **Essential job functions** *are job duties or tasks that are necessary for the completion of the job and that will take up a significant part of the employee's time.* Care should be

essential job functions
Job duties or tasks that are necessary to the completion of the job and that will take up a significant part of the employee's time.

FIGURE 8-1
Sample Job
Description

Source: Altman Weil Pensa,
*Complete Personnel
Administration Handbook for
Law Firms,* 1991. Reprinted
with the permission of
Altman Weil Pensa
Publications, Inc., copyright
1991 by Altman Weil Pensa
Publications, Inc., Newtown
Square, PA.

Job Title: Word Processing Supervisor
Position Summary: The Word Processing Supervisor works under the
                 direction of the Administrator and ensures scheduled
                 work flow, assists word processing personnel in docu-
                 ment production and in establishing and maintaining
                 quality standards.

Duties and
Responsibilities:

1. Manages department task work flow, direction, priorities, and coordination.
2. Prepares and conducts timely performance appraisals for all subordinates on or before due date.
3. Designs and coordinates a forms manual based on standard documents, formats, and boiler plate samples from attorneys and legal assistants.
4. Coordinates and implements necessary computer procedures for the effective operation of the department.
5. Manages the department's quality control procedures to ensure that all materials are of sufficient quality.
6. Answers all questions from firm personnel relating to the operation of the word processing software.
7. Revises form letters, pleadings, and other documents as needed.
8. Coordinates maintenance and service of equipment.
9. Trains new operators on computers and oversees their work.
10. Designs improved procedures to enhance quality and department work flow.
11. Maintains statistical data of word processing performance, including volume of work and quality.
12. Performs other department or company-related projects as assigned.

Qualifications:
High school diploma or equivalent, plus satisfactory completion of courses
in secretarial skills, word processing skills, and microcomputer courses,
plus two years' experience as a word processing operator.

Salary Range:
Pay Range 14–20

taken in drafting these essential job functions, especially when considering the Americans with Disabilities (ADA), which bans discrimination against persons with disabilities. If a job duty is included in the job description that is not essential and that might screen out otherwise qualified applicants who are disabled, the employer might be inviting an ADA complaint.

Suppose in the job description it is said that the paralegal must be able to lift fifty-pound storage boxes, but in fact the paralegal may only have to do this once or twice a year. This probably would not be an "essential job function" or a "significant" task. If a qualified applicant could show that he could perform all the truly essential job functions, the employer might be subject to an ADA complaint if the person is not hired because he cannot lift fifty pounds due to a disability.

When writing job descriptions, use simple, clear, concise, and easy-to-read language. When possible, use action verbs such as: prepares, maintains, performs, conducts, oversees, assists, and manages. Refrain from using technical language, since new employees and others will not be able to easily understand the job description. Cover the essential job functions and do not worry about duties that might be added later. There is no way to anticipate every job duty. A technique for drafting good job descriptions is to talk to people who already are in the position being covered or who are in similar positions. They will have the most accurate information about the position. Avoid using words such as "occasionally," "may," or "could," since they are ambiguous and do not specifically tell the applicant what the job consists of.

Always include as a job duty a "catchall" phrase stating that the position will be required to perform other functions not specifically listed as assigned by the supervisor or words to the effect that the employee will act in the best interest of the firm, even if doing so requires actions or responsibilities not listed in the job description. This prevents individuals from saying "It's not in my job description."

It is a good idea to periodically review existing job descriptions to monitor work load. It is important to note that job descriptions for existing positions should be made based on the *position* itself, not based on the individual holding the position. "Think *positions*, not people." Do not draft or redraft job descriptions for specific individuals. At this stage, you cannot think about who will fill the position, only what duties and qualifications will best meet the needs of the organization.

ADVERTISING AND RECRUITING

After a detailed and accurate job description is drafted, organizations begin the actual hiring process. This includes either promoting from within the organization or recruiting candidates outside the organization. Recruiting candidates can include using newspaper advertisements, interviewing candidates at specific schools or institutions, using employment agencies, contacting professional associations, or receiving referrals from the company's own employees on possible candidates.

Placing a newspaper advertisement is a very common recruiting method. Although drafting the newspaper advertisement or "help-wanted" ad is fairly simple, there are some pitfalls. Keep the following in mind:

- Make it clear exactly what you are looking for and always include the minimum qualifications. If you do not define exactly what you are looking for, you may spend hours looking through resumes of people who are not what you had in mind.

- Sell your organization in the ad with phrases such as "growing law office needs . . ." or "highly professional law office needs . . ." or "state of the art law office needs . . . ." The whole intent of the advertisement is to get applicants' attention so they will apply. Market your office's strengths.

- Always include the phrase "Equal Opportunity Employer" in the ad to emphasize that you are looking for all qualified applicants.

- Consider placing the ad in local or state bar association publications or similar legal associations in your area. This can enhance the quality of the applications you receive.

- Another alternative is to place the position with public employment agencies such as Job Services Offices, with private employment agencies (some employment agencies even specialize in the legal area), or with universities and private schools that train legal assistants.

- Avoid using language in the ad such as "If you work for our organization, you will have long-term and dependable employment" or similar wording. As described later in this chapter, this type of language might be considered an implied contract.

- Avoid references to gender or age in the advertisement. This might be construed as discrimination. Avoid listing physical requirements that might limit persons with disabilities from applying unless the requirement is an essential job function.

- Some law offices choose to use "blind ads" in which the ads do not use company names. Typically they will have the resumes sent to a title of a position with a post office box address (e.g., Human Resource Manager, P.O. Box 23453).

Advertising in the Sunday issue of the newspaper gets more response than advertising on weekdays. A common question is whether employers must advertise positions in the newspaper and other places. In many cases, employers hire from within their organizations and it is not necessary to advertise positions to the public. In fact, there is no requirement that employers advertise at all, and they generally are free to hire individuals anyway they like. However, if a business wants to demonstrate that it is truly an equal opportunity employer, public advertisements provide an excellent way of doing this.

EMPLOYMENT APPLICATIONS AND RESUMES

Once an employer has drafted a detailed job description and advertised the position, the next step is to review the employment applications or resumes received.

In many cases, an organization will receive a resume first and then subsequently have the individual fill out a formal application for employment. An application for employment is a good idea, since resumes are inconsistent and may not provide all the information needed to make a good decision.

Employment applications must comply with legal requirements and not ask for information that the employer is not entitled to have, such as information regarding race, religion, or age. Most office supply stores sell employment application forms that meet fair-hiring rules and regulations. It is a good idea for the application to contain a statement that it will be retained for only ninety days. This may protect the employer from discrimination charges brought by applicants who applied for a position in years past but were not considered for current positions. If the application is no longer active when the current position is filled, candidates generally cannot claim discrimination.[1]

Reading resumes and applications is not as easy as it might seem. The employer must learn to read between the lines of resumes. The following are some things to consider when reading resumes:

- **Look at the job titles of the positions the person has held.** Has the person consistently progressed and been promoted upward? If not, it might show that the individual lacks desire, skills, or motivation to advance.

- **Watch out for phrases like "had exposure to" and "had knowledge of."** These phrases indicate that the candidate may not have had actual hands-on experience with the skill in question.

RESUME EVALUATION FORM

Date: _____   Scoring: 70 points possible

Position: _____

Name of Candidate: _____

- SATISFIES MINIMUM QUALIFICATIONS OF THE POSITION:

  YES   NO
  If the candidate does not meet the minimum qualifications, do not continue.

1.   RESUME (0–10 points)

   (Circle the description that best describes the category and award points accordingly; numbers in parentheses show the points available for that selection)

   _____   (5–10)   neat, current, good format, professional looking
   _____   (3–7)   typos, unclear, long, grammatical problems, not current
   _____   (0–5)   unreadable, sloppy, careless
   _____   (0)   resume not included
   _____   (0–10)   other_____

2.   EDUCATION (0–20 points)

   _____   (15–20)   applicant's education — highly appropriate for the position
   _____   (10–15)   applicant's education — average qualifications for the position
   _____   (10–15)   applicant's education — overqualified for the position
   _____   (0–10)   applicant's education — underqualified for the position
   _____   (0)   no related education

3.   WORK EXPERIENCE (0–20points)

   _____   (15–20)   applicant's experience shows he/she is highly qualified
   _____   (10–15)   applicant's experience shows he/she has average qualifications
   _____   (10–15)   applicant's work experience shows he/she is overqualified
   _____   (0–10)   applicant's experience shows he/she is underqualified
   _____   (0)   no related work experience

4.   OTHER QUALIFICATIONS OR EXPERIENCES (0–10)

   _____   (0–10)   active in community, serves on social boards, has contacts or experiences
                          valuable to our organization
   _____   (0–5)   other_____

5.   OVERALL IMPRESSION (10)

   _____   (0–10)   this score shows my overall impression of the candidate

TOTAL SCORE_____   Reviewer's Name: _____

NOTES:

This is only a sample and is not intended to be all-inclusive. Always consult your attorney before using any personnel-related form.

FIGURE 8-2   Resume Evaluation Form

- **Consider using a resume evaluation form (see Figure 8-2).** Resumes can be hard to compare. Using an evaluation form will help quantify the distinctions between the applicants. In addition, the process tends to look more equitable, since all resumes are judged on the same objective criteria.

- **Gaps in employment may indicate that the person was incarcerated or has had other problems.** Ask about any significant gaps in employment. There may be a good reason for a gap, but you will not know unless you ask.

- **If references are listed, find out whether they are close friends or relatives.** These types of references obviously will not be as dependable as work-related references.

- **Look for things in resumes that are missing or are weak.** For instance, if the applicant is weak on education, she will stress her experience or vice versa.

- **Do not read things into a resume.** If an applicant has not put something in the resume, it usually means he does not have the skill or experience.

- **Read resumes carefully.** There is a large distinction between "attended" a school and "graduated" from a school.

- **Beware of trivia such as hobbies, sports, and so forth that might indicate the candidate is weak in skills and experience.**

- **Do not rely on statements such as "Have WordPerfect experience."** Candidates may overstate their knowledge of computer experience. If computer experience is important, give an objective test, such as having the candidate prepare a letter.

INTERVIEWING

Once resumes and employment applications have been analyzed and the field narrowed, the next step is the interview process. The interview typically is the most dynamic part of the hiring process. This is the point where the interviewer decides which applicant is the most qualified and which one will "fit" with the organization. The following are some general insights on how to conduct interviews and how to make the interview process truly productive.

SCREENING APPLICANTS TO BE INTERVIEWED   A common problem that occurs in interviewing is finding out that although the applicant may look qualified on paper, it is clear once in the interview that your organization will not be interested in the applicant. In that case, the whole interview is a waste of both the employer's time and the applicant's time. A way to avoid this is to conduct a casual preinterview on the phone of applicants who look qualified but who you are unsure about. By asking a couple of important questions on the phone, you can determine whether it is appropriate to have the individual come in for a formal interview. One way to do this when you call is to say that you are just confirming that you received her resume and that you had a few quick questions.

ALL INTERVIEWS MUST BE CONSISTENT   It is extremely important that all the interviews conducted for a position be consistently done. The interviewer must make sure that all candidates are asked the same questions, are treated fairly, and are treated the same. It is easy during the interview process to think of additional questions and to ask candidates who are interviewed at the end of the process different questions from those asked of candidates who are interviewed at the beginning. If interviews are not performed consistently, you may be giving preference or special treatment to one candidate over another. One way to maintain consistency is to have a script or interview checklist. This will ensure that everything done in each interview is the same (see Figure 8-3). Another way to use the checklist is to simply put more spaces between the questions on the form and record each applicant's answer on the checklist itself. The bottom line is that to avoid any appearance of impropriety, do not stray from your prepared interview format.

TALK LESS, LISTEN MORE   One thing an interviewer should do is to talk as little as possible. Anytime the interviewer is talking, she is giving up the opportunity to hear from the candidate, which is the whole purpose of the interview. Interviewers should avoid filling in pauses or completing sentences for candidates. If you are quiet, you may allow them to tell you something revealing or insightful about themselves. Also, do not give occupational or career advice to candidates. Your purpose is not to counsel them, you want to get only the information you need. Anything else complicates the situation.

OPEN-ENDED QUESTIONS   To find out information about a candidate, pointed questions must be asked. Open-ended questions that ask for concrete

---

Date:

Position Inteviewed for:

Applicant:

- Give applicants a copy of the job description to read while they are waiting for the interview to begin.

QUESTIONS:

1. Now that you have read the job description, do you have any questions about the position?
2. Why are you interested in this position?
3. Review your employment history and educational background and state why you think you are qualified for this position.
4. What personal characteristics do you feel are necessary for success in your field?
5. Where do you see yourself five years from now?
6. How do you feel about overtime work?
7. What is your concept of professional ethics?
8. Describe your concept of teamwork.
9. What have you accomplished that shows your ability and willingness to work hard?
10. What is your greatest strength?
11. What is your greatest weakness?
12. What specific skills would you bring to this position?
13. What do you know about our organization?
14. Do you have any questions you would like to ask?

FIGURE 8-3
Interview Checklist

Note: This is only a sample and is not intended to be an all-inclusive list. Always consult your attorney before using any personnel-related form.

examples relating to the person's personality, job history, and education are good ways of getting usable information (see Figure 8-4). It is not uncommon for candidates to draw a complete blank when answering an open-ended question. Although an interviewer's first thought is to let them off the hook and move on, the interviewer misses a chance to see how they handle the situation. A better idea is to let them know that they can take their time to answer. Sit back and relax. Another idea is to pose a real-life problem or situation that has happened in your office and then ask the applicant how he would handle it. For example, a question could be posed regarding how an applicant would respond to a client who is asking for legal advice. This will give you insight on how he would act in a real-life situation.

INVOLVE OTHERS IN THE PROCESS   It is usually a good idea to involve others in the interviewing process, such as other staff members. It is not uncommon for there to be two or three people on an interview team. They may see or hear things one person will dismiss or not hear altogether. Involving other staff members also makes them a part of the process and allows the new employee to join the team more easily. To ensure that you are considering applicants from all segments of the population, it is a good idea to have people on the interview team with culturally diverse backgrounds.

**FIGURE 8-4
Common Open-
ended Questions**

1. If you were hiring someone for this position, what attributes would you look for?
2. What have you done that shows initiative and willingness to work?
3. What are the disadvantages of your chosen field?
4. Who is your hero?
5. Tell me a story.
6. What do you know about our company?
7. What did you do to prepare for this interview?
8. What are your career goals?
9. Where would you like to be in five years?
10. Why do you want to work for our company?
11. What are your greatest strengths and weaknesses?
12. What areas would you like to improve upon?
13. What courses did you like the most in school?
14. What jobs have you held, and how do they relate to this position?
15. Why did you choose this type of work?
16. What involvement with the community have you had?
17. What personal characteristics do you feel are required to succeed in your profession?
18. Do you prefer working by yourself or with others? Why?
19. What type of supervisor do you like?
20. Have you ever had difficulty getting along with others?
21. Do you prefer to work in a small company or a large company?
22. How do you feel about overtime?
23. Tell me a difficult problem you experienced at your last job and how you solved it?

QUESTIONS TO AVOID   Take particular caution when deciding what interview questions to ask. There are many questions that should be avoided, since they might be considered discriminatory (see Figure 8-5). Figure 8-5 is not an all-inclusive list, since many states and local governments have additional antidiscriminatory laws.

As a rule, if a question is not directly relevant to the position or to job performance, do not ask it. There is no reason to take unnecessary risks. You should avoid all types of personal or family-related questions. There are ways around some of the prohibitions. For instance, although an interviewer cannot ask whether the candidate has a car (this might discriminate against lower-income individuals), she can ask whether the candidate has access to reliable transportation so he can get to work on time. The problem with most personal questions is that they relate to a person's race, color, religion, sex, national origin, age, or disability.

OBJECTIVE TESTS   Another strategy that can be helpful is to give candidates an objective test regarding the position, such as a typing test or punctuation or spelling test. These types of tests must be job related and nondiscriminatory. These frequently are used in the legal profession. For example, a law office might require the candidate to type a short letter to a hypothetical client to see whether he can set up a correct business letter, use software such as WordPerfect, and draft his own correspondence.

FIGURE 8-5
Interview Questions
You Should Not Ask

Race/Color/Religion/Sex:
Any question that is related to a candidate's race, color, religion, sex, national origin, age, disability, or veteran status.

Name/Marital Status:
- What was your maiden name?
- Have you ever used another name?
- Are you married? (permissible after hiring)
- What is your spouse's occupation?

Ancestry:
- Where were you born?
- Where does your family come from?

Residence:
- How long have you lived at this address?
- Do you own your house?
- Do you live with your parents?

Family/Personal:
- How many children do you have?
- How will you provide child care?
- Are you pregnant?
- Do you have a car?

(continued)

Credit/Financial:
- Describe your credit rating.
- Have you ever taken bankruptcy?
- Have you been garnisheed?

Age:
- What is your date of birth? (permissible after hiring)
- How old are you?
- When did you graduate from elementary or high school?

Organizations:
- What organizations do you belong to? (You can ask this if you instruct them to delete organizations related to race, religion, color, disability, age, etc.).
- Questions regarding union activity.

Religion:
- What church do you belong to?
- What holidays do you celebrate?
- Does your religion prevent you from working weekends?

Medical:
- Are you disabled or taking medication regularly? (You can ask whether they have the ability to perform the job.)
- Have you had any recent illnesses?

Arrest Record:
- Have you ever been arrested? (You can ask about convictions.)

Military:
- What type of discharge did you receive from the military?

REFERENCE CHECKS

Once the employer has narrowed the list to two or three final candidates, the only thing left to do is to check references. Checking references is an important part of the hiring process and should never be left out (see Figure 8-6). Some researchers have found that nearly 30 percent of all resumes contain exaggerated statements or misstatements about education or employment history. In addition, employers have been held liable for negligent hiring. **Negligent hiring** *is when an employer hires an employee without sufficiently and reasonably checking the employee's background.* In one case, an apartment complex was found liable after a new manager used a pass key to enter an apartment and rape a tenant. The apartment complex failed to check the new manager's references and reasonably investigate the person's background for felony convictions, fighting, and other criminal activity. Thus, references should always be checked and gaps in employment and other indicators of such behavior should be investigated.

The following are some hints on how to get good information when performing reference checks.

negligent hiring
Hiring an employee without sufficiently and reasonably checking the employee's background.

Applicant Name: _____   Date: _____

Employer/reference name: _____

Organization: _____

Dates known: From _____   To _____

Duties: _____
_____

Quality/quantity of work: _____
_____

Communication skills: _____
_____

Team player/relationship with peers: _____
_____

Dependability: _____
_____

Outstanding skills or abilities: _____
_____

Any problems or shortcomings: _____
_____

Describe applicant's work style or potential: _____
_____

Supervisory/managerial skills or potential: _____
_____

Reason for leaving: _____
_____

Eligible for rehire: _____
Recommendation for this job: _____
_____

Comments: _____
_____

By: _____   Date: _____

FIGURE 8-6   Reference Check Questionnaire

CALL PAST EMPLOYERS/SUPERVISORS   Typically, the most relevant information an employer can gather is from the candidate's last employer or supervisor. Call these people first. Although some of these people will refuse to give out any information for fear of being sued for defamation if they say something negative, many will still answer your questions. A way around this problem is to ask potential candidates to sign a release or waiver that allows the past employer to talk to you openly and freely without fear of being sued for defamation.

BE PREPARED AND KNOW WHAT YOU WANT TO ASK   Before you call, have a list of questions you want to ask. Ask specific questions about the candidate's dates of employment, job duties and responsibilities, quality and quantity of work, disciplinary problems, work attitude, communication skills, dependability, ability to be a team player, and reason for leaving. Also ask whether the former employer would rehire the person. You also might want to confirm the information in the candidate's resume. Always avoid questions related to race, religion, national origin, age, etc.

CALL INSTITUTIONS/SCHOOLS   If a candidate lists graduation from a school or institution, call the school and confirm it. This usually does not take a great deal of time. This is seldom done and many candidates claim that they have finished degrees when in fact they have not. Also, if a candidate claims she was in the top 5 percent of the class or received an honor, check on it.

BE FRIENDLY   When calling references, always be friendly and tell them that you are calling because a candidate has applied for a job with your organization. It is not necessary that you give them any other information. Your goal is to encourage the reference to give you information about the candidate's previous work.

CALL CHARACTER REFERENCES LAST   Candidates only give potential employers character references who will give them a glowing recommendation. Expect this, but ask specific questions as well.

AFTER THE SELECTION

Once the employer has checked references and selected an individual, and the individual has agreed to work for the employer, it is a good idea on the employee's first day of work to give him a thorough orientation to your office. Figure 8-7 shows an example of a orientation checklist. Special attention should be made to the INS (Immigration and Naturalization Service) I-9 Form. This form establishes that the individual can legally work in this country. An I-9 Form *must* be completed according to federal law and must be retained by the employer. In addition, a W-4 Form showing withholding deductions *must* be completed and retained for the employee file.

PERFORMANCE EVALUATIONS

Timely performance evaluations are a strong human resource development technique. Employees need to know on a regular basis what they are doing right and where they need to improve. Performance evaluations allow employees to know where they stand and help them to grow and progress. It is important to see a performance evaluation not as a heavy object to beat or threaten employees with, but as a part of the communication process of working with employees toward a common goal.

If done correctly, evaluations can strengthen ties with employees by allowing them to participate in the evaluation process. In the end, a well-defined evaluation process can make the organization more efficient. Employee evaluations should be conducted privately, and, when possible, the evaluation itself should be given to the employee before the meeting so that she is prepared to talk about the evaluation and its findings. The evaluation should always be performed in writing and should be kept in the employee's personnel file.

Name: _____   Hire Date: _____

Title: _____   Phone Number: _____

Address: _____

Employee Number: _____

WELCOME
- Welcome the employee to the company
- Introduce the employee to fellow staff members
- Show the employee his or her work area
- Give employee key to office/building
- Explain how to request supplies

FORMS, BENEFITS, POLICIES
- Give the employee a copy of the personnel handbook
- Give the employee a copy of the staff manual
- Complete Form I–9
- Complete Application for Employment
- Complete W–4
- Explain Insurance Plans/Complete Forms
  - Group Life
  - Group Health
  - Group Disability
  - Retirement Plan
- Explain Pay Procedures

GENERAL INFORMATION
- Assign parking
- Explain timesheets
- Explain telephone procedures
- Explain office hours
- Explain vacation and sick-leave policy
- Explain overtime policy
- Explain ethics and confidentiality policy
- Show employee location of restrooms
- Show employee break rooms and explain break policy
- Explain lunch policy
- Explain smoking policy
- Explain dress policy
- Explain probationary period
- Explain evaluation procedures

EVALUATIONS SHOULD BE DONE REGULARLY   To be effective, evaluations should be done on a regular basis. Some offices evaluate employees quarterly, biannually, or annually. Quarterly or biannually is recommended, since criticism or praise usually has more effect soon after an incident has happened. Doing an evaluation once a year for a few minutes does little to change behavior over a long period of time.

EVALUATIONS SHOULD BE OBJECTIVE AND MATCH RATINGS WITH PERFORMANCE   Evaluations should be based on objective performance by an employee and not on any personal likes or dislikes the employer has for an employee. It is particularly important to match ratings with performance and to be fair about it. Do not set quotas such as mandating that 70 percent of employee evaluations be "average," 20 percent "above average," and 10 percent "outstanding." Employees often complain about evaluations being unfair in that although they might have worked particularly hard, they were still given an "average" rating. This is very discouraging for most employees. It is important that employers communicate with employees on a regular basis and take a "hands-on" approach to knowing whether or not employees really deserve a certain rating. Using objective criteria and actual examples of the employee's performance will help in this process. Examples of how the employee earned the "excellent" or "average" performance rating will help identify what he is doing right and wrong.

EVALUATION METHODS SHOULD BE CONSISTENT   It is a good idea to use the same evaluation method so that evaluations done at different time periods can be compared. This will allow you to track the process of an individual consistently.

ELICIT OPEN COMMUNICATION AND SET MUTUAL GOALS FOR IMPROVEMENT   Any evaluation method must allow the employee to participate in the process by communicating how she feels about the evaluation, including what she likes or dislikes and what both parties can do to help solve problems. There must be a give-and-take relationship in the evaluation process to make it work. One technique is to ask the employee how she feels the year went; what went right or wrong. Let her do the talking. This will put her at ease and will let the person feel that she has taken part in the process. Setting realistic goals to solve the problems also helps to communicate what is expected of the employee in the future. One way of doing this is for the employer to set certain goals and then have the employee set certain goals as well.

GENERAL COMMENTS ON HOW TO CONDUCT EVALUATIONS   Always allow the employee to respond to your comments and always give reasons for *why* evaluations were made. Give specific examples if possible. When you get to negative comments, keep them specific but short. You do need to hash out every specific part. Sometimes talking about it more and more just makes it worse. Do not worry about hurting a person's feelings. You need to be completely honest with the employee. If the employee's performance is poor, you need to tell him that and discuss how to correct it. On the other hand, if the employee's performance is very good, you must be willing to put that in writing, too. Honesty is the key.

COACHING TECHNIQUE— ONGOING EVALUATION

coaching technique Counseling that focuses on the positive aspects of the employee's performance and explores alternative ways to improve her performance.

One way to help an employee succeed in her job is to coach and counsel the employee on a daily ongoing basis. *The* **coaching technique** *focuses on the positive aspects of the employee's performance and explores alternative ways to improve her performance.* Most people are more willing to listen to advice from a "friend" who is interested in their well being than from a disinterested and heavy-handed "boss."

1. Event—Describe exactly what happened; do not be negative, just state the fact.
2. Effect—Describe the impact of the event, who or what was adversely affected and why; be specific. Let the employee know why the behavior should be changed.
3. Advice—Describe exactly how the employee can improve performance in the future.
4. Remind—Emphasize that you believe the employee is competent and that this was just a lapse.
5. Reinforce—Monitor the employee's performance. If the employee corrects the mistake, let him know that he is doing it right. Reinforce the positive change he made.

FIGURE 8-8
The Coaching Technique

Source: Adapted from *Complete Personnel Administration Handbook for Law Firms,* Altman Weil Pensa, 1991, 8.4.2. Reprinted with the permission of Altman Weil Pensa Publications, Inc., copyright 1991 by Altman Weil Pensa Publications, Inc., Newtown Square, Inc.

The coaching technique is borrowed from sports, where a coach works with an individual to overcome her deficiencies by counseling her and by explaining problems to her.

The coaching technique works best when the supervisor has had direct experience in the employee's position. This allows the supervisor to give good concrete tips, examples, information, and opinions that the employee can use. Employees typically are more willing to accept the advice if the supervisor has been in the same position. When discussing areas that need improvement, try not to be judgmental, but instead give advice on exactly how to correct a deficiency. This technique is especially useful when an employee lacks knowledge about a situation. One of the most positive aspects of the coaching technique is that it does not place blame on the employee so that the employee is able to retain her self-esteem, which can be lost when an employee is simply reprimanded. Figure 8-8 explains how the coaching technique works. The coaching technique is not substitute for a regular evaluation, but it is a technique for helping an employee be successful in her job.

EVALUATION FORMS AND TECHNIQUES

There are many techniques and forms that can be used when completing a formal evaluation, including general performance evaluations, job-based/job-description aprals, and goal setting methods such as management by objectives (MBO). The evaluation technique used depends on the needs of the employer.

GENERAL PERFORMANCE EVALUATION FORM   Figure 8-9 contains a general performance evaluation form that could be used for many law office support jobs. This type of evaluation is quick to prepare and is straightforward. However, this type of checklist is not job specific and does not allow a great deal of interaction on the part of the employee. If possible, it is beneficial to allow the employee to make comments and to be an active participant in the evaluation process.

JOB-SPECIFIC FORM BASED ON THE JOB DESCRIPTION   One technique of analyzing performance is to use the job description as a guide for evaluating performance. Since the job description sets out the essential functions of the

**LAW OFFICE SUPPORT STAFF
PERFORMANCE EVALUATION**

Name: _____ Title: _____

Evaluation Type: Probation   Six Month   Annual   Special: _____

Date: _____ Score: _____

Evaluate the staff member's performance using the following rating criteria and make comments as necessary.

Rating: Description:
  5 — **Outstanding**—Employee's performance is exceptional and far exceeds normal expectations.
  4 — **Above Average**—Employee's performance is very good and exceeds expectations.
  3 — **Average**—Employee performs to normal expectations of the position.
  2 — **Below Average**—Employee's performance falls below acceptable levels from time to time.
  1 — **Unacceptable**—Employee's performance is completely unacceptable.

1. Competence in the Law Office

  _____   a. Is technically competent in all areas of work.
  _____   b. Other staff members have confidence in and trust the employee's work.
  _____   c. Continuously strives to learn and expand his/her competence level.
  Comments: _____
  _____
  _____

2. Quality of Work

  _____   a. Is accurate in all work.
  _____   b. Is thorough and complete in all work.
  _____   c. Takes pride in work.
  _____   d. Work is consistently of high quality.
  Comments: _____
  _____
  _____

3. Dependability

  _____   a. Highly dependable.
  _____   b. Good attendance.
  _____   c. Work is always turned in timely.
  _____   d. Can be counted on in a crisis.
  _____   e. Works independently without need of supervision.
  Comments: _____
  _____
  _____

(continued)

FIGURE 8-9   Evaluation Form

4. Work Habits/Attitude

_____ a. Has excellent work habits.
_____ b. Is neat in appearance and in work habits.
_____ c. Works hard and efficiently.
_____ d. Is conscientious and contributes new ideas.
_____ e. Accepts criticism professionally.
_____ f. Has a positive and enthusiastic attitude.
_____ g. Acts as a team player.
_____ h. Gets along with other staff members and supervisors.

Comments: _____

_____

_____

5. Communication/Relationships

_____ a. Treats clients professionally.
_____ b. Treats other staff members professionally.
_____ c. Can write effectively.
_____ d. Has good grammar skills.
_____ e. Listens effectively.
_____ f. Can make self understood orally.
_____ g. Develops and maintains efficient relationships.

Comments: _____

_____

_____

6. Judgment

_____ a. Makes sound judgment calls.
_____ b. Exercises appropriate discretion.
_____ c. Intelligently arrives at decisions.
_____ d. Thinks through decisions.

Comments: _____

_____

_____

7. Initiative

_____ a. Accepts new assignments willingly.
_____ b. Takes on new responsibilities without being asked.

Comments: _____

_____

_____

OVERALL RATING: **Outstanding   Above Average   Average   Below Average   Unacceptable**

(continued)

General Comments: _____

_____

_____

_____

_____

Employee's Strengths: _____

_____

_____

_____

_____

_____

Areas Which Need Improving/Recommendations: _____

_____

_____

_____

_____

Supervisor Signature: _____   Employee Signature: _____

Date: _____   Date: _____

Employee signature only verifies that this evaluation has been discussed and does not indicate agreement with the evaluation.

EMPLOYEE SELF-APPRAISAL:

A. What were your achievements this year?

B. List any goals you would like to achieve next year.

C. What strengths do you have in performing this position?

D. What areas do you think you can improve upon?

E. What can your supervisor do to help you reach your goals?

F. Overall, how would you rate your own performance level?

position, an employer should be able to go down the list of duties and responsibilities and talk about the employee's performance regarding each duty. This allows the employer to accurately break down the employee's performance so that he knows exactly what areas need improvement.

GOAL SETTING AND MANAGEMENT BY OBJECTIVES (MBO)   Another type of performance system is based on goal setting, also commonly referred to as management by objectives (see Figure 8-10). *In a* **management by objectives** *performance program, the employee and employer agree at the beginning of the evaluation period what the goals for the employee will be. Also included will be target dates for reviewing the employee's progress toward the goals and a determination for how it will be decided whether the goal was achieved or not.* An accomplishment report is prepared detailing which goals were accomplished, and rewards or incentives are given for meeting the goals. For example, a goal might be to reduce nonbillable hours by 5 percent or increase billable hours by fifty hours during the fourth quarter. MBO programs generally require quite a bit of time, planning, and paperwork, but they can be very successful programs if managed correctly.

management by objectives
A performance program in which the individual employee and the employer agree on goals for the employee.

EMPLOYEE ATTITUDE SURVEYS

If an employer is willing to evaluate the performance of its staff, it also should be prepared to allow the staff to evaluate it. *An* **employee attitude survey** *is a survey that is given to the employees of an organization asking them to rate the effectiveness of the organization in many specific areas.* Management can gain a great deal of information from its employees on how the organization can be run more effectively. Figure 8-11 shows an example of an employee attitude survey. These surveys allow employees to be critical of management and to suggest ways that management can improve the way in which it meets the needs of the staff. They allow the staff members to suggest and share ideas that they otherwise might not. They also are a very good way to test employee morale and discover how morale might be increased. Employee attitude surveys are another means of increasing communication between employers and employees.

In addition, employee attitude surveys help law offices keep the staff turnover rate down. Staff turnover is very costly. Every time a law office hires an employee, the office must invest a large amount of resources, including the time

employee attitude survey
A survey that is given to an organization's employees and asks the employees to rate the effectiveness of the organization in many specific areas.

1. Employee and supervisor agree on the employee's major performance objectives for the coming period, including target dates for accomplishing each part of them.
2. Employee and supervisor agree on how the objectives will be measured and how it will be decided if the objectives have been met.
3. Employee and supervisor meet periodically to discuss the employee's progress toward meeting the goals.
4. At the end of the period, an accomplishment report is prepared stating which objectives were met or not met.
5. Awards or incentives are given depending on whether the objectives were met.

FIGURE 8-10
Management by Objectives Process

Employee Attitude Survey

Introduction

The purpose of this survey is to give you a chance to express your feelings about various aspects of your work. These aspects include such things as working conditions, pay, benefits, etc. The survey consists of two sections:

In Section I, we ask several questions to determine what you like and don't like about your present job, and how satisfied you are with different aspects of your present job.

In Section II, we ask for your written comments in areas of general interest.

Your answers to the survey questions will be <u>confidential</u>. We want to encourage you to be completely frank in telling us how you feel about the different aspects of your job. Only then will our survey have any real meaning.

Thank you for taking part in this survey.

Section I

Following you will find statements about certain aspects of your present job. Read each statement carefully and decide how satisfied you are with the aspect to which it refers.

Circle "1"   if you are <u>not satisfied</u> with that aspect of your job
Circle "2"   if you are <u>only slightly satisfied</u> with that aspect of your job
Circle "3"   if you are <u>satisfied</u> with that aspect of your job
Circle "4"   if you are <u>very satisfied</u> with that aspect of your job
Circle "5"   if you are <u>extremely satisfied</u> with that aspect of your job

ON MY PRESENT JOB, THIS IS HOW I FEEL ABOUT:

For Each Statement
Circle a Number

1.	My job in general, considering all things.	1	2	3	4	5
2.	The chance to do something that makes use of my abilities.	1	2	3	4	5
3.	My present salary or pay rate.	1	2	3	4	5
4.	My pay when compared to the amount of work I do.	1	2	3	4	5
5.	How well my pay compares with that of others outside the office.	1	2	3	4	5
6.	How substantial my pay raises are.	1	2	3	4	5
7.	My overall benefit program.	1	2	3	4	5
8.	The way my vacation, sick leave and holiday schedules compare with those of other offices.	1	2	3	4	5
9.	The way my medical, dental and life insurance plans compare with those of other offices.	1	2	3	4	5
10.	My working conditions (heating, lighting, office equipment/supplies, work space).	1	2	3	4	5
11.	The opportunities for promotion for me.	1	2	3	4	5
12.	The degree to which my performance appraisal is based on what I do.	1	2	3	4	5
13.	The way my supervisor(s) treats me.	1	2	3	4	5
14.	The way my attorney(s) treat me.	1	2	3	4	5
15.	How the office values my opinions and suggestions.	1	2	3	4	5
16.	The personnel policies and practices of the office.	1	2	3	4	5
17.	The recognition I get for the work I do.	1	2	3	4	5
18.	How clearly I understand everything I am required to do.	1	2	3	4	5
19.	How clearly the offices aims and plans are stated.	1	2	3	4	5
20.	The orientation and training I receive.	1	2	3	4	5
21.	The way the office hires qualified people.	1	2	3	4	5
22.	My knowledge of what my supervisor(s) expects from me.	1	2	3	4	5
23.	My knowledge of what my attorney(s) expects from me.	1	2	3	4	5
24.	My job security.	1	2	3	4	5
25.	The ease of approaching personnel and management with work-related problems.	1	2	3	4	5

(continued)

FIGURE 8-11   Attitude Survey

Section II

On this and the following pages, you will be asked to comment on several general topics. This section gives you opportunity to express your opinions regarding both satisfaction and dissatisfaction in your working environment.

Your frank and thoughtful comments will be appreciated.

1. The one suggestion I would make to improve the office's physical environment is: _____

_____

_____

_____

2. My thoughts regarding the pay and benefit package are: _____

_____

_____

_____

3. What I like most about the supervisor for whom I work is (answer if applicable): _____

_____

_____

_____

4 What I like most about the attorney(s) for whom I work is (answer if applicable): _____

_____

_____

_____

5. What bothers me most about the supervisor(s) for whom I work is (answer if applicable): _____

_____

_____

_____

6. What bothers me most about the attonrey(s) for whom I work is (answer if applicable): _____

_____

_____

_____

7. What I need to get my current job done that I don't already have is: _____

_____

_____

_____

(continued)

8. My thoughts about the overall office management are:_____

_____

_____

_____

9. This law office could do the following to make my job more satisfying: _____

_____

_____

_____

10. Any other comments and/or suggestions concerning your work relationship with this law office?_____

_____

_____

_____

11. Any comments and/or suggestions concerning this survey? _____

_____

_____

_____

and energy of existing staff, to train the employee. Other factors are the time and cost of the mistakes of new employees as they learn about the employer's business, Social Security tax that every employer must pay on the employee, and additional seminars or other training the employee may need. Also, when a well-trained employee leaves, she takes with her all the knowledge that she gained from the employer (this hurts the employer, since her expertise is now gone and that employee must be replaced), and, in some cases, the employee actually may leave to go to work for one of the office's competitors. Another way of trying to reduce staff turnover is to hold an exit conference with employees who choose to voluntarily leave the law office. This allows the law office to find out why the employee was unhappy so the employer can take positive steps to prevent others from leaving.

TERMINATION

In all organizations it is necessary to terminate employees at some time or another. For many people, terminating employees is hard to do. However, it can be the only reasonable recourse in circumstances in which an employee is not "carrying his load" or is acting in a counterproductive manner to the goals of the organization. It can be a positive experience for the remaining employees of the organization, in cases in which the employee's conduct has brought down employee morale or when others have had to work harder to make up for the employee's poor performance. There are many nuances to terminating people correctly so that costly lawsuits and other unpleasant situations are avoided.

WHEN CAN AN EMPLOYEE BE TERMINATED?

In many states an employer is allowed to terminate an employee for any reason as long as it is nondiscriminatory and does not violate a public policy. This is called employment-at-will. In these instances, an employee serves at the leisure of the employer. Some states do not recognize the employment-at-will doctrine, but instead require that an employer terminate employees only when "just cause" exists. Employment-at-will does not apply if an employment contract exists between the employer and employee or in a collective-bargaining agreement. Instead, the contract or bargaining agreement determines when termination is allowed.

However, even if you are an employment-at-will employer, you should always avoid terminating an employee for arbitrary reasons. Terminating an employee for unjustified or arbitrary reasons can be as harmful to employee morale as the failure to terminate a nonproductive worker. Whenever possible, terminate employees as a last resort and for "just cause." That is, have a good reason for taking the action, follow your own rules, and give the employee notice and opportunity to be heard regarding the charges.

There are three general and justifiable reasons for terminating an employee[2]:

1. Disciplinary causes—This includes violating company policies or known company rules, such as acting dishonestly or unethically, falsifying records, fighting, being intoxicated, or using illegal substances.
2. Poor job performance—This includes failure to perform work, poor attitude, uncooperative behavior, excessive absenteeism, insubordination, and others.
3. Economic conditions—This includes layoffs and cutbacks because of poor economic conditions for the organization.

It is important that you include a list of unacceptable behaviors in your employee handbook. Employees also can be terminated for serious misconduct off the job, but the employee handbook should define what type of misconduct would lead to dismissal.

WHAT NOT TO TERMINATE EMPLOYEES FOR

An employer cannot terminate employees based on any kind of discriminatory reason related to race, color, religion, sex, or disability. The company should always avoid even the appearance of this. An employer should never terminate employees for petty or personal reasons, since it may appear that the termination was done for an unlawful purpose such as discrimination.

ALWAYS FOLLOW YOUR OWN PROCEDURES

Always follow the disciplinary procedures in your personnel handbook step-by-step. Most organizations have a progressive discipline policy that should be followed very closely and carefully (see Figure 8-12). Progressive discipline policies typically state that on the first occurrence of unacceptable behavior, an employee will be verbally warned; on the second occasion, the employee will be counseled and a written warning put in the employee's file; and on the third occasion, an employee typically is disciplined by either suspension or termination. Again, offices that fail to follow their own policies may appear to be discriminating against an individual for an unlawful reason even if they actually are not.

FIGURE 8-12
Progressive
Discipline Policy

If an employee's job performance or conduct falls below a satisfactory level but not to the level of requiring immediate suspension or termination (as covered earlier in this manual), the following progressive discipline policy will be followed:

1. Oral Warning—An oral warning will be given to the employee. A record of this shall be kept in the employee's personnel file.
2. Formal, Written Warning—If an employee fails to correct deficiencies after an oral warning has been given, a formal, written warning will be given to the employee and will include the steps necessary to correct the deficiency and a deadline when such steps are to be completed and reevaluated.
3. Suspension—If the employee has failed to satisfactorily correct the deficiencies itemized in steps 1 and 2, the employee may be placed on suspension either with or without pay. A deadline will be set when the situation will be reevaluated. The employee shall be informed that continued failure to correct the deficiencies will result in termination.
4. Termination—If the employee has failed to satisfactorily correct the deficiencies after oral warning, formal, written warning, and suspension, the employee may be terminated.

ALWAYS DOCUMENT ALL PERSONNEL ACTIONS, INCLUDING TERMINATION

Every aspect of an employee's employment history with an organization should be maintained. This includes employment applications, resumes, INS I-9 Forms, W-4 Forms, employee benefit records such as insurance and retirement records, performance evaluations, and salary increases. Performance evaluations are particularly important if the organization terminates the employee for poor performance and the organization must defend against discrimination or other types of lawsuits an employee might file.

The termination itself and the reasons behind the termination should be particularly well documented. This includes verbal conversations, formal office conferences, and everything in between. The purpose of the documentation will be to show that the employee knew the behavior was against a policy, was warned of the offense, and failed to correct the problem. The importance of clear, fair documentation cannot be overemphasized. The point is not to document a situation so you can fire someone—it is to document a situation in case you have to terminate someone and then defend a lawsuit.

BE CONSISTENT

It is important in the discipline and termination process that your actions be consistent from one employee to the next. Try to handle the same types of situations consistently. You never want to treat one employee differently from another; this may leave the organization open to discrimination suits.

Before terminating an employee, carefully consider the questions in Figure 8-13 to make sure you have correctly analyzed the situation and thought of all possibilities. This will help you avoid a wrongful termination lawsuit down the line. *In a* **wrongful termination lawsuit,** *the former employee alleges that an employer unlawfully terminated the employee. Depending on the former employee's allegations, she can recover back pay and punitive damages and be reinstated.*

wrongful termination lawsuit
A lawsuit in which a former employee alleges that an employer unlawfully terminated the employee.

HOW TO TERMINATE AN EMPLOYEE

If you have tried to work with an employee unsuccessfully, have followed your own progressive discipline policy, and have documented the situation, and you decide to actually terminate the employee, here are some pointers.

DO IT IN THE EMPLOYEE'S OFFICE AND MAKE IT EFFECTIVE IMMEDIATELY

When you terminate an employee, go into the employee's office if possible. This allows you to leave whenever you think it is appropriate. Also, an employer should make the termination effective immediately. The employer does not want to fire an employee in the morning and have the employee stay on the job through the afternoon or for some longer period of time. This only invites trouble and allows the employee the opportunity to get even by destroying company files or computer records. It also makes an uncomfortable situation for the employer and the person.

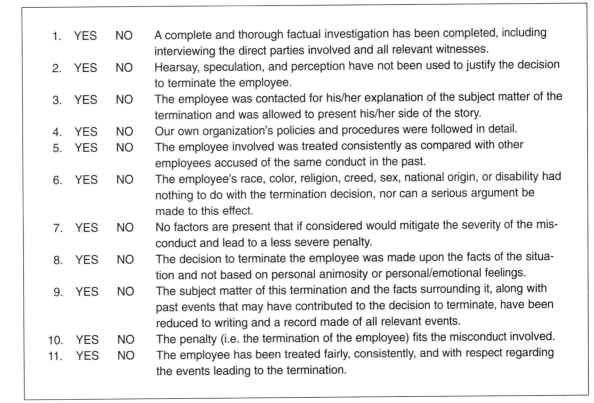

1. YES NO   A complete and thorough factual investigation has been completed, including interviewing the direct parties involved and all relevant witnesses.
2. YES NO   Hearsay, speculation, and perception have not been used to justify the decision to terminate the employee.
3. YES NO   The employee was contacted for his/her explanation of the subject matter of the termination and was allowed to present his/her side of the story.
4. YES NO   Our own organization's policies and procedures were followed in detail.
5. YES NO   The employee involved was treated consistently as compared with other employees accused of the same conduct in the past.
6. YES NO   The employee's race, color, religion, creed, sex, national origin, or disability had nothing to do with the termination decision, nor can a serious argument be made to this effect.
7. YES NO   No factors are present that if considered would mitigate the severity of the misconduct and lead to a less severe penalty.
8. YES NO   The decision to terminate the employee was made upon the facts of the situation and not based on personal animosity or personal/emotional feelings.
9. YES NO   The subject matter of this termination and the facts surrounding it, along with past events that may have contributed to the decision to terminate, have been reduced to writing and a record made of all relevant events.
10. YES NO   The penalty (i.e. the termination of the employee) fits the misconduct involved.
11. YES NO   The employee has been treated fairly, consistently, and with respect regarding the events leading to the termination.

FIGURE 8-13   Employee Termination Checklist

ALWAYS HAVE A WITNESS   Always have another staff member with you as a witness. You want to avoid situations in which it is your word against the employee's.

DO NOT DRAG IT OUT   Do not drag out the termination process or argue with the employee. Arguing will not help the situation, and you probably will not change the employee's mind anyway. Be brief and to the point, and do not get upset. Expect the employee's emotions to be high, so be under control.

GIVE OBJECTIVE REASONS FOR THE DISMISSAL AND BE RESPECTFUL
Give objective and clear-cut reasons for the dismissal when terminating an employee. Avoid name-calling or personal references. Avoid the "You're fired" approach or making accusations that can be used against you later. Terminations go best when the employee sees the termination coming because two or three meetings (progressive discipline) have been held, and you simply state why the termination is necessary. Do not try to soft-pedal the decision by suggesting that the employee can retire now, divert his attention to other topics, or use such conduct that might be viewed as discriminatory.

It is in your best interest to retain the employee's goodwill if possible. Do not become personal; you want the employee to preserve his self-esteem and self-respect, and you do not want to break the person down. If the employee wants to talk about it, and he feels better doing so, then listen but do not argue. When the employee is done, be respectful and thank him for the criticism and wish him good luck.

TAKE CARE OF ALL UNFINISHED BUSINESS THEN AND THERE   After you have announced the termination, collect office or building keys and so forth immediately. This point is to sever the relationship so that future contact is not necessary. The following is a checklist:

- Collect all keys such as those for the office, building, computer, or file cabinet;
- Give the employee her last paycheck or tell the employee when it will come;
- Take care of insurance forms or contact your group insurer to find out what to do (Under federal legislation called COBRA and state laws,

**FIGURE 8-14
Spotting the
Troubled Employee**

Source: Phillip M. Perry, "Dealing with Troubled Employees," *Legal Assistant Today,* May/June 1992, 82. Copyright 1992. James Publishing, Inc. Reprinted with permission from *Legal Assistant Today.*

- Sudden, extreme changes in behavior
- Wide mood swings from joviality to depression
- Absence from the workstation for many brief periods
- Easily frustrated
- Defensive posture in regard to criticism
- Inability to sit for long periods at a time
- Losing track of conversation
- Failure to control impulses
- Eyes glazed over
- Accident prone
- Drinks excessively at parties

employees and dependents may be entitled to continue coverage with your health insurance.);

- Collect any company property such as telephone credit cards;
- Change computer passwords, alarm codes, etc.;
- Have the employee clean out her belongings;
- Take care of any parking arrangements.

HOW TO HANDLE PROBLEM EMPLOYEES

> *Left unattended, the troubled employee can have a profound effect on a firm that is already struggling to remain profitable in a more competitive field. The employee's productivity can be cut in half. Inattention can lead to sloppy work and angry clients, accidents and workers' compensation claims . . . . All of this can be unsettling to a paralegal manager not accustomed to dealing with an employee's personal problems.*
>
> —**Phillip M. Perry,** "Dealing with Troubled Employees," *Legal Assistant Today,* May/June 1992, 80.

No matter how hard a supervisor or employee tries to get along with everyone in an organization, there are sure to be problem employees. A problem employee does not necessarily need to be terminated; it may be that the individual is going through a particularly hard time in his life. Reasons for employee problems can include family problems, stress, financial pressures, or alcohol and substance abuse problems. Figure 8-14 contains a list of signs that employees are troubled or are going through a crisis. This section provides insight on how to handle these situations.

DO NOT IGNORE PROBLEMS   Do not ignore an employee performance problem with the hope that it will go away. Problems should be dealt with as they occur. The problem only festers and gets worse if it is not addressed in a timely fashion, and client service will suffer in the meantime.

DOCUMENT THE PROBLEMS   As with any problem related to performance, the employer should document the job-related problems and then present the specific problems to the employee.

DISCUSS PROBLEMS WITH THE EMPLOYEE   After the employer has documented specific problems with the employee's performance, the next step is to talk to the employee about the problems. When talking to the employee, be specific as to exactly what problems are occurring. Give examples. Try to draw the employee into the conversation and get her to realize that there is a performance problem and that it needs to be corrected. Never talk about personality issues; always focus on the facts of the situation. Try to give a fair and actual account of the facts. Always discuss employee problems of any type privately with the employee. The fewer people who know about the matter the better. Allow the employee to defend herself and listen to her side of the story. It is possible that you are mistaken about the matter or that there is an acceptable explanation.

RECOMMEND COUNSELING OR USING AN EMPLOYEE ASSISTANCE PROGRAM   If employee problems are related to personal difficulties, recommend professional counseling to the employee. Some organizations have employee assistance programs. *An **employee assistance program** is a designated counseling service that an employer contracts with to provide counseling to its employees as a fringe benefit to employment.* Employers should avoid counseling the employee on personal problems. Leave that to a professional.

employee assistance program
A designated counseling service that an employer contracts with to provide counseling to its employees as a fringe benefit to employment.

> *Employee assistance programs are independent, outside organizations which shoulder the burden of counseling troubled employees and refer clients to longer term treatment programs when appropriate. Thanks to this structured way of dealing with troubled employees, law firms can concentrate exclusively on the job performance aspects of a troubled employee without feeling guilty about ignoring personal difficulties.*
>
> **—Phillip M. Perry,** "Dealing with Troubled Employees,"
> *Legal Assistant Today,* May/June 1992, 80.

PROGRESSIVE DISCIPLINE   The first time the performance problem comes to your attention, talk to the employee about the problem in a private setting or coach him. If the problem continues, meet with him on a more formal basis and prepare a written evaluation or a memo stating the problem in writing and outlining specific actions that will be taken to correct the matter. If the problem continues, discipline may be appropriate, such as suspension or termination. In all cases, always follow your own progressive discipline policies.

LEAVE WITH PAY (POSITIVE DISCIPLINE)   One option that some employers find beneficial is to give a one-day suspension *with* pay to an employee. This sometimes is referred to as positive discipline. The reasoning behind it is to let employees know that their actions are serious but that your intentions are positively motivated. Suspending them with pay avoids the animosity that an employee feels with a suspension so that she can focus on correcting the problem. Positive discipline also shows that you do not have an "ax to grind," that you have good intentions, and that you want to retain the individual. Punishing poor performance with a day off may seem to some to send the wrong signal. However, there are some advantages to it, including: 1) resentment and apathy problems are reduced; 2) adversarial relationships between management and staff are diminished; and 3) if termination occurs, fact finders typically will see that the individual was treated fairly.

PERSONNEL POLICIES

personnel handbook
A manual that lists the formal personnel policies of an organization.

One of the most useful things a law office of any type can do to effectively manage its human resources is to create a comprehensive and up-to-date personnel handbook. *A **personnel handbook** (sometimes called an employee handbook or it also can be a part of the law office staff manual) lists the formal personnel policies of an orga-*

nization. Personnel handbooks: 1) establish formal policies on personnel matters, so staff members will know what to expect of management and what management expects of them regarding personnel issues; 2) establish a standard so that all employees are treated fairly and uniformly; and 3) help to protect the law office if it is involved in litigation regarding personnel matters and to avoid government-compliance problems. In some law offices, the staff manual covers both substantive law office policies and personnel policies.

WRITING PERSONNEL POLICIES

Personnel policies are best when written in clear, specific language that is easy to read and understand. The drafter should explain personnel-related procedures leaving little for interpretation. Typical personnel handbooks cover the topics found in Figure 8-15. Figure 8-16 contains a sexual harassment policy. Notice in Figure 8-16 that the policy is quite specific in that it defines it, states how such complaints will be investigated, and gives the possible punishment for sexual harassment.

Generally, personnel policies should cover any matter that concerns the employee and employer relationship. This is particularly true of frequently asked questions regarding employee benefits (compensation and fringe benefits), vacation and sick-leave time, termination, and so on. It is axiomatic that if an employer develops and publishes a personnel handbook, the office must be willing to be bound by these policies and to follow its own rules and regulations.

Some courts have interpreted personnel handbooks as an enforceable contract between the employer and employee. Thus, careful thought must go into any personnel policy. It is imperative that personnel policies be kept up-to-date to reflect the rules and regulations of the company. It also is recommended that each personnel policy include the date it was put into effect. In this way, a reader can tell how old each policy is. This can be helpful when updating policies.

Personnel handbooks should be easy to use and include a table of contents and possibly an index as well to encourage employees to use it. Two excellent sources for drafting personnel policies are *Complete Personnel Administration Handbook for Law Firms,* 1991, Altman Weil Pensa, (215) 359-9900; and the *Law Office Staff Manual,* 2d. ed., American Bar Association, 1992, ABA, (312) 988-5555. In addition, several companies offer personnel manuals on computer disk; for a catalog of human resource products, contact G-Neil Companies (800) 999-9111.

CURRENT PERSONNEL LAW ISSUES

Personnel-related issues are highly regulated and often litigated. The following is a sampling of some of the more important areas related to federal personnel/labor law.

EMPLOYMENT-AT-WILL-DOCTRINE

The **employment-at-will-doctrine** *states that an employer and employee freely enter into an employment relationship and that either party has the right to sever the relationship anytime without reason.* If an employee is covered by a union collective-bargaining agreement, employment contract, or civil service regulations, the employment-at-will doctrine does not apply, and the employer must comply with

employment-at-will doctrine
Doctrine that states that an employer and employee freely enter into an employment relationship and that either party has the right to sever the relationship anytime without reason.

FIGURE 8-15
Typical Policies in a Personnel Handbook

Source: Altman Weil Pensa, *Complete Personnel Administration Handbook for Law Firms,* 1991, 4.1.7. Reprinted with the permission of Altman Weil Pensa Publications, Inc., copyright 1991 by Altman Weil Pensa Publications, Inc., Newtown Square, PA.

General Introduction
Welcome Statement
History of Firm
Mission Statement
Employment-At-Will
Equal Opportunity Employer

Role of Employee
Confidentiality
Conflict of Interest
Relationship with Clients

Rules, Polices, Procedures
Hours of Work
Attendance and Punctuality
Pay Period
Appearance and Attire
Sexual Harassment
AIDS Policy
Alcohol/Drug Policy
Computer Security
Smoking Policy
Fire Procedure
Accident and Injury Reports

Job Responsibilities
Outside Employment
Compensation
Overtime
Meal Allowance
Performance Appraisals

Promotions
Bonus Program

Benefits
Vacation
Holidays
Sick Leave
Leave of Absence

- Funeral, Jury Duty, Military Leave
- Child Care, Elder Care, Parental Leave

Insurance
- Health
- Life
- Disability

Expense Reimbursements
Membership and Dues
Education Assistance
Employee Assistance Program
Child Care Leave/Facilities

Termination
Notice Requirement
Exit Interview
Separation Pay

Administrative
INS Form I–9

the terms of the contract or regulations. Employment-at-will typically happens when an employee works for an employer without any type of written agreement or reference to how long the employee will work. For example, suppose a law office hired a legal secretary in an employment-at-will state. The legal secretary did good work, but the firm subsequently changed its mind and decided that it did not need the extra position and terminated the secretary. This would be perfectly acceptable, and the secretary would have no lawsuit against the law office. For another example, suppose that the legal secretary gets a better-paying job at another law office and quits without giving notice. This also would be acceptable under employment-at-will status.

Organizations should be careful when drafting their personnel handbook to state that the policies in the handbook are not a "contract" or that employees will be retained for a certain amount of time. For example, an employer should not include language such as "If you do your work satisfactorily, you will always have a job here." The reason is that if a court finds that the employer gave an expectation to an employee that he would have a job forever (as long as the work was satisfactory) or that the policies in the personnel handbook were a type of

This office prohibits sexual harassment of its employees in the workplace by any person in any form. Sexual harassment includes unwelcome sexual advances, requests for sexual favors, and other verbal or physical conduct of a sexual nature when:

1) Submission to or rejection of the conduct is made either explicitly or implicitly a term or condition of an individual's employment; or

2) Submission to or rejection of the conduct is used as the basis for employment decisions; or

3) The conduct has the purpose or effect of substantially interfering with the individual's work performance or creating an intimidating, hostile, or offensive working environment.

Employees should report any sexual harassment immediately to their supervisor or the Director of Human Resources, who will make every effort to resolve the complaint promptly and effectively. Any employee not satisfied with the action taken by the supervisor or Director of Human Resources should bring the complaint to the managing partner. The complaint will be investigated by the managing partner and the employee will be advised of the findings and conclusions. All actions taken to resolve complaints of sexual harassment will be confidential. Retaliatory action against an employee who charges sexual harassment will not be tolerated. Any employee found to have engaged in sexual harassment of another employee will be subject to appropriate sanctions which may include termination.

Effective Date 1/1/93

FIGURE 8-16
Sample Sexual Harassment Policy

Source: Altman Weil Pensa, *Complete Personnel Administration Handbook for Law Firms,* 1991, 4.1.7. Reprinted with the permission of Altman Weil Pensa Publications, Inc., copyright 1991 by Altman Weil Pensa Publications, Inc., Newtown Square, PA.

contract, this would upset the normal expectation of "employment-at-will." Personnel handbooks should contain a simple employment-at-will statement, typically near the front that states:

Employment-At-Will
It is understood that these personnel policies and any other firm document do not constitute a contract for employment, and that any individual who is hired may voluntarily leave employment upon proper notice, and may be terminated by the firm any time and for any reasons. I understand that any oral or written statements to the contrary are hereby expressly disavowed and should not be relied upon.[3]

In addition, some employers require employees to sign a statement such as the one above as of employment or place the statement on the employment application form.

The employment-at-will doctrine does, of course, have limitations. Courts have found that at-will employees may have legal rights against employers, even though the employer is supposed to be able to terminate the employee without any reason. Instances include when the employer violates public policies, such as firing an employee for filing a workers' compensation claim, firing an employee for refusing to commit perjury, or terminating an employee to avoid paying retirement benefits or sales commissions. Other instances include terminating an employee based on discrimination (see below) or terminating an employee when the employer promised to retain the employee as long as the employee did a good job. Thus, although employment-at-will is a strong doctrine that runs in favor of employers, it is by no means absolute. In addition, some states by statute limit the employment-at-will doctrine, so any organization should know its own state laws as well.

When employment-at-will is not in effect or if there is an employment contract in place, the typical standard is "just cause." An employment contract is a contract between the employer and an employee setting out the terms and conditions of the employment relationship. "Just cause" means that before an employer can terminate an employee, the employer must have "just cause" or reasonable cause to do so. "Just cause" can include many things such as violating the company's rules and regulations, insubordination, and dishonesty.

THE FAMILY AND MEDICAL LEAVE ACT OF 1993

Family and Medical Leave Act of 1993 (FMLA)
Legislation that allows employees in certain circumstances to have up to twelve workweeks of unpaid leave from their jobs for family or health-related reasons.

The **Family and Medical Leave Act of 1993 (FMLA)** *applies to employers with fifty or more employees (and any public agency and any private elementary or secondary school) and provides that eligible employees be allowed up to twelve workweeks of unpaid leave within any twelve month period for: a) the birth or adoption of a child or placement of a child for foster care; b) the care of a child, spouse, or parent with a serious health condition; and c) the employee's own serious health condition.* The FMLA requires that an employee granted leave under the act be returned to the same position held before the leave or be given one that is equivalent in pay, benefits, privileges, and other terms and conditions of employment. The employee also is entitled to health care benefits during the leave. The purpose of the FMLA is to assist workers to better balance the demands of the workplace with the needs of their families. Because the FMLA only applies to employers with fifty or more employees, many law offices will not be affected by the law.

FAIR LABOR STANDARDS ACT

The **Fair Labor Standards Act** sets minimum wage and maximum hours of work for employees. It also requires that overtime pay (one-and-one-half times their normal rate) be paid to employees who work in excess of forty hours a week. Employees do not need to be paid overtime if they fall into one of the four "white-collar" exemptions: executive, administrative, professional, or outside sales (see Figure 8-17).

If an employee is "exempt," it means that he or she is not required to be paid overtime wages. If an employee is "nonexempt," it means she is required to be paid overtime wages. Whether legal assistants are "exempt" or "nonexempt" is a hotly debated issue. One survey found that 59 percent of the legal assistants surveyed were not paid overtime, 15 percent were paid overtime, 16 percent received compensatory time (i.e. time off) for overtime hours, and 10 percent had some other type of arrangement.[4] Whether a legal assistant is or is not entitled to overtime pay depends on the particular job duties of the position.

equal employment opportunity
Concept that means that employers make employment-related decisions without arbitrarily discriminating against an individual.

EQUAL EMPLOYMENT OPPORTUNITY

Equal employment opportunity *means that employers make employment-related decisions without arbitrarily discriminating against an individual. This is a statement that is often seen in want ads, employment applications, and other employment-related*

There are four categories of employees who are exempt under the Fair Labor Standards Act of 1938: executive, administrative, professional and outside sales. The basic criteria for defining exempt employees are 1: Duties and responsibilities and 2: Amount of salary. A title or payment of salary does not determine exempt status. To be classified as exempt, an employee must meet **all** of the criteria in a category.

	Executive	Administrative	Professional	Outside Sales
Primary duties:	Management of the enterprise or recognized subdivision.	Nonmanual work directly related to general policies and operations or responsible work related to education or training.	Advanced knowledge requiring instruction; or original and creative work in a recognized artistic field; or certified teacher or recognized instructor.	Customarily and regularly work away from place of business selling or obtaining orders for goods or services.
Other duties:	Customarily and regularly direct two or more employees. Authority to hire and fire or to recommend either with particular weight, to avoid confusion and customarily and regularly exercise discretionary powers.	Customarily and regularly exercise discretion, independent judgment and authority for important decisions. Regularly assist a proprietor, executive or administrator, or perform under general supervision requiring special skills or perform special assignments under general supervision.	Customarily and regularly exercise discretion and judgment. Work is predominantly intellectual and varied rather than routine or mechanical.	
Time requirement:	20% of time can be spent on nonmanagerial duties, 40% for service or retail establishment.	20% of time can be spent on nonadministrative duties, 40% for service or retail establishments.	20% of time can be spent on nonprofessional duties.	20% of time can be spent on type of work done by nonexempt employees.
Salary requirement:	At least $155/week other than board, lodging or other facilities	At least $155/week other than board, lodging or other facilities.	At least $170/week other than board, lodging or other facilities.	None.
Short test for high salary (20% test does not apply if salary is greater than):	At $250/week, 20% rule above changes to majority of time must be spent on managerial duties.	At $250/week, 20% rule above changes to majority of time must be spent on managerial duties.	At $250/week, 20% rule above changes to majority of time must be spent on managerial duties.	

Figure 8-17 Who Are Exempt Employees?

Source: Altman Weil Pensa, *Complete Personnel Administration Handbook for Law Firms*, 1991, 7.3.5. Reprinted with the permission of Altman Weil Pensa Publications, Inc., copyright 1991 by Altman Weil Pensa Publications, Inc., Newtown Square, PA.

Family and Medical Leave Act of 1993	Provides that eligible employees be allowed up to twelve workweeks of unpaid leave within any twelve-month period for: a) the birth or adoption of a child or placement of a child for foster care; b) the care of a child, spouse, or parent with a serious health condition; and c) the employee's own serious health condition.
Civil Rights Act of 1964	Prohibits discrimination against employees on the basis of race, color, religion, sex, or national origin. The Equal Employment Opportunity Commission (EEOC) was established to enforce this law.
Equal Pay Act of 1963	Prohibits employers from basing arbitrary wage differences on gender.
Age Discrimination in Employment Act of 1967 (ADEA) (Amended 1978)	Prohibits employers form discriminating against persons age forty or more on the basis of their age unless age is a bona fide occupational qualification.
Pregnancy Discrimination Act of 1978	Prohibits discriminating against women because of pregnancy.
Americans with Disabilities Act of 1990 (ADA)	Prohibits employers from discriminating against persons with disabilities in several different areas.
Civil Rights Act of 1991	Relaxes the burden of proof in discrimination claims and allows for greater recovery of damages.
Fair Labor Standards Act	Sets minimum wage and maximum basic hours of work for employees, and requires overtime pay for nonexempt employees.

FIGURE 8-18   Partial List of Federal Employment Related Laws

Civil Rights Act of 1964
Legislation that prohibits employers from discriminating against employees or applicants on the basis of race, color, national origin, religion, or gender.

Americans with Disabilities Act of 1990 (ADA)
Legislation that prohibits employers from discriminating against employees or applicants with disabilities.

documents. Federal laws, including the **Civil Rights Act of 1964,** *prohibit employers from discriminating against employees or applicants on the basis of race, color, national origin, religion, or gender. The* **Americans with Disabilities Act of 1990 (ADA)** *prohibits employers from discriminating against employees or applicants with disabilities* (see the following section on the ADA). *The* **Age Discrimination in Employment Act of 1967** *prohibits employers from discriminating against employees and applicants on the basis of age where the individual is forty or older. The* **Equal Pay Act of 1963** *prohibits employers from paying workers of one sex less than the rate paid an employee of the opposite sex for work on jobs that require equal skill, effort, and responsibility and that are performed under the same working conditions* (see Figure 8-18). There are several other federal laws that legislate in this area. Most of the laws cited here make it unlawful for an employer to arbitrarily discriminate against employees or applicants.

Every personnel handbook should have a policy stating the law office's position on equal employment opportunity, such as:

Equal Employment Opportunity Statement
It is the policy of this organization to apply recruiting, hiring, promotion, compensation and professional development practices without regard to race, religion,

color, national origin, sex, age, creed, handicap, veteran status or any other characteristic protected by law.[5]

An exception equal employment opportunity is when age, sex, or religion is a **bona fide occupational qualification** (BFOQ).; *A BFOQ means that to perform a specific job adequately, an employee must be of a certain age or sex or a certain religion.* A BFOQ does not apply to race or color. An example of a BFOQ would be for a position as a Catholic priest. The employer could reasonably discriminate against non-Catholics, since the candidate must believe in and have knowledge of the Catholic religion to qualify. BFOQs generally have been narrowly construed by most courts, and there are few if any positions in a law office that would qualify.

AMERICANS WITH DISABILITIES ACT

The Americans with Disabilities Act of 1990 (ADA), among other things, makes it unlawful to discriminate in employment against qualified applicants and employees with disabilities. Under the ADA, a person has a "disability" if he has a physical or mental impairment that substantially limits a major life activity, such as seeing, hearing, breathing, speaking, walking, performing manual tasks, working, or learning. This does not include a minor impairment that is of short duration such as a broken limb, infection, or sprain. An individual with a disability also must be qualified to perform the essential functions of the job, with or without reasonable accommodation. That is, the applicant or employee must be able to satisfy the job requirements, including education, experience, skills and licenses, and be able to perform the job. The ADA does not interfere with an employer's right to hire the best-qualified applicant but simply prohibits employers from discriminating against a qualified applicant or employee because of his disability.

The ADA also requires that employers "reasonably accommodate" persons with disabilities. An employer must make **"reasonable accommodation"** *for a person with a disability, which may include existing facilities readily accessible, restructuring the job, or modifying work schedules.* The ADA provides that individuals with disabilities have the same rights and privileges in employment as employees without disabilities. For example, if an employee lounge is in a place inaccessible to a person using a wheelchair, the lounge might be modified or relocated, or comparable facilities might be provided in a location that would enable the individual to take a break with co-workers. This is an example of "reasonable accommodations."[6] The ADA went into effect July 26, 1992, for employers with twenty-five or more employees, and after July 26, 1994, the ADA will apply to employers with fifteen or more employees. Persons who have been discriminated against because of a disability can receive back-pay damages, reinstatement, punitive damages, and other remedies.

SEXUAL HARASSMENT

Sexual harassment *means unwelcome sexual advances, requests for sexual favors, and other verbal or physical conduct of a sexual nature that creates an intimidating, hostile, or offensive working environment.* Federal guidelines make it clear that an employer is responsible for the acts of its supervisory employees, regardless of whether the specific acts complained of were authorized or even forbidden by the employer and regardless if whether the employer knew or should have known of their occurrence. It is the responsibility of the employer to take immediate and

---

Age Discrimination in Employment Act of 1967
Legislation that prohibits employers from discriminating against employees and applicants on the basis of age when the individual is forty or older.

Equal Pay Act of 1963
Legislation that prohibits employers from paying workers of one sex less than the rate paid an employee of the opposite sex for work on jobs that require equal skill, effort, and responsibility and that are performed under the same working conditions.

bona fide occupational qualification
An allowable exception to equal employment opportunity. For example, for an employee to perform a specific job, the employee must be of a certain age or sex or of a certain religion.

"reasonable accommodation"
Accommodating a person with a disability, which may include making existing facilities readily accessible, restructuring the job, or modifying work schedules.

sexual harassment
Unwelcome sexual advances, requests for sexual favors, and other verbal or physical conduct of a sexual nature that create an intimidating, hostile, or offensive working environment.

FIGURE 8-19
What Firms Can Do
to Discourage
Sexual Harassment

Source: Phillip M. Perry,
"Sexual Harassment," *Legal
Assistant Today,* July/August
1992, 66. Copyright 1992.
James Publishing, Inc.
Reprinted with permission
from *Legal Assistant Today.*

1. **Detailed Sexual Harassment Policy**—Have a detailed sexual harassment policy that defines what sexual harassment is; that explains how complaints are to be reported and how they will be investigated; that ensures confidentiality; that details what the ramifications are if the charges are found to be true; and that ensures that complainants will not be retaliated against for making honest complaints.

2. **Train Employees**—The policy should be regularly reviewed with new hires and existing employees through memos, speeches, bulletin board notices, videotapes and other means. The organization must continually emphasize that this kind of conduct will not be tolerated and provide training to employees on it. Videotapes on sexual harassment are available from the American Bar Association, the American Law Institute-ABA and the NOW Legal Defense and Education Fund.

3. **Establish Alternate Reporting Routes**—Employees must be provided with a comfortable means for reporting incidents of sexual harassment to management. This can be a problem if the employee's supervisor is the one involved in the sexual harassment. Thus, it is appropriate for firms to set up alternate people that can be notified of the sexual harassment such as a supervisor, a particular partner, a department head, or others. If possible, the alternate people should be different sexes. Harassed individuals may shy away from reporting sexual harassment to a supervisor of another sex.

4. **Investigate Complaints Immediately**—Sexual harassment complaints should be investigated immediately and thoroughly without delay and with confidentiality.

5. **Take Action**—If a complaint is found to be true, the organization must take appropriate action. Simply having a policy against sexual harassment is not enough. The organization must discipline the party involved ranging from counseling to suspension to termination. In addition, consider transferring the individual involved in the harassment away from the other party. Finally, if the complaint is found to be utterly false, discipline against the accuser should also be taken.

appropriate corrective action.[7] Law offices should have a policy prohibiting sexual harassment (see Figure 8-19). Federal guidelines state that an employer can be liable if it did not have a written policy prohibiting sexual harassment at the time an employee filed charges of harassment. If the firm receives a complaint of sexual harassment, it has a legal duty to immediately investigate the situation, to initiate corrective action, and to reprimand or discharge the employee involved if warranted.

Many people typically think of sexual harassment as a male supervisor sexually coercing a female subordinate in order for her to keep her position or to be promoted. Sexual harassment is much broader than this, however. Sexual harassment can include unwelcome sexual jokes, inappropriate sexual remarks, innuendos, insults, leering and subtle forms of pressure for sexual activity, vulgar or indecent language, sexual propositions, displaying sexually oriented photographs, and unwelcome and inappropriate touching, patting, and pinching.

Sexual harassment does not have to involve a subordinate and a supervisor; it also can take place with persons at the same job level. In addition, sexual harassment can involve clients as well. It has been reported that clients sometimes sexually harass law office staff. The law office also has as a duty to investigate a client harassing a staff member. The law office may be liable if it does not take appropriate action to protect its employees. Finally, although the majority of sexual harassment cases involve male employees harassing female employees, women also have been accused of sexually harassing male subordinates. In any case, the employer is responsible for taking corrective action.

> *Paralegal managers play a key role in preventing harassment by communicating policies and by keeping the door open to complaints . . . [W]e need to convey to legal assistants that we are sensitive to the situation and to assure them that they do not need to tolerate harassment. . . . The way to preempt problems down the road is to develop policies which prohibit sexual harassment, then communicate the policies to employees. Firms with a policy in place are less likely to face litigation because people have a place to go and feel as though they will be treated fairly.*
>
> —**Phillip M. Perry**, "Sexual Harassment,"
>   *Legal Assistant Today*, July/August 1992, 66.

PREVENTING SEXUAL HARASSMENT

Figure 8-19 contains a list of things that law offices can do to discourage sexual harassment. Preventive training is one of the most important things an organization can do. Some employees may not be aware that behavior constitutes sexual harassment. With appropriate training on the subject, they can realize that their conduct makes others feel uncomfortable, and they may stop.

Video trainings on how sexual harassment in the workplace can be avoided include *Preventing Sexual Harassment in the Workplace,* published by the Society for Human Resource Management, (800) 444-5006; *Guidelines for Management: Eliminating Sexual Harassment from the Work Environment*, published by the National Organization for Women Legal Defense and Education Fund, 99 Hudson Street, New York, New York, 10013 (cost is $15); and *Law Firm Policies on Sexual Harassment,* published by the ALI-ABI, (800) 253-6397.

> *Harassment, like all abuse, is an invasion of your personal worth. By being direct, acknowledging that you do have power, setting limits, and being willing to take action, you can empower yourself to heal. The emotional damage from harassment is progressive. The longer you tolerate it without taking action, the worse you will feel. Ignoring the situation never works.*
>
> —**Anna Sobkowski,** "I've Been Sexually Harassed. How Do I Get Back on
>   Track? *Executive Female,* July/August 1993, 60.

Books on the topic of sexual harassment recovery include *The 9 to 5 Guide to Combating Sexual Harassment,* John Wiley & Sons, (800) 522-0925 (cost is $9.95); and *Sexual Harassment on the Job: What It Is and How to Stop It,* Nolo Press, (800) 992-6656 (cost is $15).

INVESTIGATING A SEXUAL HARASSMENT CLAIM

Legal assistant managers must sometimes investigate sexual harassment claims. Figure 8-20 shows some common steps involved in investigating a sexual harassment claim. The most important point during the investigation is to be completely neutral and objective and to interview both the parties and witnesses carefully, listening to all people and documenting the entire investigation. The American Bar Association also publishes a thorough video on how to investigate a sexual harassment claim (ABA, (312) 988-5555, cost is $175). If your investigation deter-

FIGURE 8-20
Step by Step: Dealing with a Sexual Harassment Complaint

Source: Ann Meyer, "Getting to the Heart of Sexual Harassment," *Human Resource Magazine,* July 1992, 83. Reprinted with the permission of *HRMagazine* (formerly *Personnel Administrator),* published by the Society for Human Resource Management, Alexandria, VA.

No training program, no matter how effective, will eliminate sexual harassment. But the action a company takes to handle a complaint can be more important than any written policy, experts say. Though you must take every complaint seriously, it's important not to overreact or make any promises until you've heard both sides of the story.

No matter how convincing the complainant is, keep in mind that there may be other reasons the victim came forward. The only thing worse than a sexual harassment suit just might be a defamation lawsuit by the alleged perpetrator.

Step 1: Listen to the complaint carefully without judging. Take notes. Do not make any promises. Tell the complainant what the process involves. Begin the process promptly.

Step 2: Use a third party to conduct an investigation. Many experts advise having at least one man and one woman on each case. Maintain your objectivity and take precautions to protect the privacy of the people involved.

Step 3: Interview the accused party and any people he or she believes would have information pertinent to the case. Again, listen carefully.

Step 4: Decide whether the employee's complaint is credible and what action to take, if any. If you can't determine who's being truthful, issue a warning and follow up.

If you agree that harassment occurred, consider appropriate disciplinary action (reprimand, suspension, termination) which will be based on the seriousness of the offense and whether or not it was a first offense. In addition to informing the accused, the complainant also should be notified of the outcome.

Step 5: Document the entire investigation. In addition, you'll want to keep track of the complainant and perpetrator to make sure no further offenses occur and the complainant is not penalized for coming forward.

mines that sexual harassment has occurred, immediately and decisively deal with the situation by disciplining the individual, including reprimand, suspension, or termination depending on the severity of the situation. You do not want to be accused of either ignoring the situation or issuing a "slap on the wrist."

SUMMARY

Because a poor decision can cost an organization literally thousands of dollars, it should take great care in hiring individuals, including writing detailed job descriptions, advertising positions, analyzing resumes, interviewing candidates correctly, and checking references to select the best candidate available.

Performance evaluations are an important human resource technique that is designed to communicate with employees what they are doing right and where they need to improve on a timely basis. In some situations, termination actually can be positive for an organization, getting rid of employees who are "deadwood" or who do not contribute. Termination is no light matter and should be done with careful thought and attention to the legal ramifications.

Human resources are regulated by many rules, regulations, and statutes. The **employment-at-will doctrine** states that an employer and employee freely enter into an employment relationship and that either party has the right to sever the relationship at any time without reason. However, there are many exceptions to employment-at-will, including laws aimed at equal employment opportunity. The **Americans with Disabilities Act of 1990** is one such law that makes it unlawful to discriminate in employment against a qualified individual with a disability. **Sexual harassment** is another type of conduct that is prohibited by law. This includes unwelcome sexual advances, requests for sexual favors, and other verbal or physical conduct of a sexual nature that creates an intimidating, hostile, or offensive working environment.

employment-at-will doctrine
Doctrine that states that an employer and employee freely enter into an employment relationship and that either party has the right to sever the relationship anytime without reason.

CASE HISTORY

LEGAL CLINIC PARALEGAL

Suzanne Sheldon

Woodbury College Legal Clinic

Montpelier, Vermont

INTRODUCTION

Suzanne Sheldon is the Weekday Paralegal Program director for Woodbury College, Montpelier, Vermont. For two and a half years she worked as the staff paralegal at the Woodbury College Legal Clinic. In addition to her legal assistant duties, Suzanne also was the clinic's administrator.

"Our philosophy at the clinic was to provide quality legal services to clients who otherwise might not have had access to legal assistance," Suzanne said. "We wanted to ensure that our client's impression of the legal system was a favorable one. We did not want our clients to think they had to have anything less than first-class legal services because they were coming to a clinical setting. We wanted them to feel good about their case; our documents, for instance, looked like they came from any other law firm in town."

Unfortunately, the clinic closed in early 1992 because of a funding cut, but Suzanne's story typifies how legal aid practices operate, the community service they provide, and the funding problems that many legal aid practices have.

Woodbury College Legal Clinic

The purpose of the Woodbury College Legal Clinic was to provide legal services to low-income residents in a three-county area in Vermont. The clinic handled family law, bankruptcy, landlord/tenant disputes, and minor administrative law matters. The clinic was funded by the Vermont Bar Foundation. The Vermont Bar Foundation approved the clinic's budget and awarded a grant to the clinic once a year. As a condition of the grant, the foundation directed the clinic as to what type of cases it had to handle and how many, as well as placing other requirements on the clinic.

The clinic operated as a component of the Woodbury College paralegal program, so the college also had an active role in the clinic. The clinic's staff consisted of one part-time attorney (Jan Sensenich), Suzanne, who was the staff paralegal, and one legal secretary, who also worked part time. In addition, typically one legal assistant student intern worked in the clinic. Suzanne's position as staff paralegal was a dual role of paralegal and administrator. The attorney also operated as the clinic's executive director.

The clinic served clients using a team approach. Suzanne was actively involved with clients from the time they came in the door. "Everyone at the clinic was directly involved in making decisions about cases. We routinely had staff meetings and case conferences together where we would discuss the progress of each case. This team-model approach to serving clients worked excellently. It was very supportive for staff members, but it was also supportive for clients. Clients got a greater depth of service, because whoever they encountered in the environment was knowledgeable about their specific case. The clients really appreciated that whoever picked up the phone knew about their case. We conducted client satisfaction surveys and found that 98 percent of the people receiving services rated our services as overly satisfied or excellent."

Legal Services to Clients

DIVORCE CASES

Suzanne developed a system in WordPerfect using macros that expedited divorce cases. A macro refers to computer abilities to recall a series of commands or steps at one time. She had programmed macros for different provisions of a divorce petition and other pleadings. When a client came into the office regarding a divorce, Suzanne and the attorney would check off which macros/provisions applied to the client's case, so she would know what the petition (sometimes called the complaint) or the "temporary stipulation" pleading should include. A "temporary stipulation" is the next pleading that must be filed after the petition (usually within thirty days in Vermont) to establish temporary child support, custody, and so forth. Suzanne would then assemble the petition using the appropriate macros. This made preparation of the documents fast and relatively easy.

"We gathered as much information as possible in the initial client interview for all of the successive pleadings. The clients liked this, as transportation was sometimes a problem for our clients. This was the only way that we were able to file forty new divorces a year. We had to be extremely organized and have a great system to get this many cases filed."

BANKRUPTCIES

"We used 7–11 Plus, a computerized bankruptcy program, to file and litigate bankruptcies. In a client's first intake interview, the client would meet with Jan (the attorney) and me. Jan would outline the bankruptcy law and the remedies. In the second half of the interview, I would take the client into my office and using 7–11 Plus would ask them the questions that the computer asked for. In about an hour the initial client interview was typically complete and when the client walked out the door, he or she knew they could file for bankruptcy and even had a draft version of the bankruptcy petition. Our clients really appreciated this promptness.

"It also helped us, since we knew exactly what information we needed from them to complete the petition. Typically, the client would be scheduled an appointment in a few days to allow them time to gather the other information we needed. When the client came back in with the information, it was entered into the computer, the bankruptcy petition was finalized and reviewed by the attorney, and the client signed the petition, and it was then ready to be filed.

"Our system was really efficient. As the paralegal, I was able to enter the information into the computer with the client present. This definitely saved the client time, but it also saved the attorney time."

SCREENING AND INTAKE

Both Suzanne and the legal secretary screened cases. The nature of a legal clinic is that there is no way to take all of the hundreds of cases that are referred. "We had to screen cases to make sure our clients were eligible for our services using income guidelines, such as poverty guidelines, what type of case it was (since we only handled family law, bankruptcy and landlord/tenant cases), and the contested nature of the case," Suzanne said. "If a divorce, for example, contained a lot of contested issues such as a long custody battle, we could not take the case. "Our grant required that we file forty divorce cases a year, so there was no way we could file this many cases and still have time to litigate a lot of lengthy legal issues."

The secretary did the first level of case screening and Suzanne did the next level of screening, which included a conflict check and getting specific information about the case. If clients made it through both levels of the screening process, they were typically scheduled for an appointment.

GOING TO COURT

"I went to court frequently with Jan. This was part of the team approach we used. It was Jan's philosophy that he needed me in court and this made sense because I was deeply involved in some cases. I organized the case, reinforced different theories and ideas he had and did many other things. I routinely went to contested family law hearings, probate guardianship hearings, and some bankruptcy hearings."

SUZANNE'S ADMINISTRATIVE RESPONSIBILITIES

Suzanne ran the clinic on a day-to-day basis as the clinic's administrator. In addition, she had responsibilities for setting systems up in the office such as the filing system and the time and billing system and purchasing substantive bankruptcy and other types of programs the office needed.

"I really enjoyed office administration. I had one day where all I did was office administration." Because Suzanne was able to do office administration and still participate in the practice area, she had many different tasks and jobs to do. The diversity in her position made the job interesting and enjoyable.

LEGAL CLINIC PART OF PARALEGAL PROGRAM

The legal clinic was a part of the paralegal program at Woodbury College. So, not only did low-income clients receive quality legal services that they may not have received, students in the paralegal program were able to participate as interns with the delivery of services to the clients. This aspect of the clinic made it a win-win situation for both the community and the paralegal program at the college.

EQUIPMENT, OFFICE SPACE, AND COMPUTERS

Everyone in the clinic office had a computer. WordPerfect was used for word processing. Suzanne also had her own office. Suzanne had secretarial support but would prepare her own letters and pleadings on the computer. "The one thing I did use secretarial support for was help with administrative duties, and I dictated narratives or conversations and meetings with clients."

WHAT LEGAL ASSISTANTS NEED TO HAVE TO BE SUCCESSFUL IN A LEGAL AID PRACTICE

"As a paralegal, you need to be flexible and to go with the flow. In a legal aid practice, there will be many different skills you will need and demands on your time. It is pretty important to be well organized to manage the diversified work flow. Working in a legal aid practice can be a demanding role, and you have to manage your time and develop a system that works for the practice.

"For instance, I discovered early on that I had to arrange my time so I could take a lot of calls on Monday mornings. I always received calls Monday morning on family law cases regarding visitation problems that happened over the weekend. I figured out if I returned those phone calls right away, I did not have to do it on Tuesday when we were trying to interview new clients. I would return the phone calls, pull the case files, and I had a form that I created called a 'Case Activity Sheet.' I would write up what my conversation was with the client and give it to Jan for his information. If there was a need for him to respond to a legal question, I would put the form on top of the file and put it on Jan's desk for him to respond to on Tuesday mornings when he came (because Jan was a part-time attorney, he only came in on certain days). So, Jan knew exactly what was going on and what he had to do. He said that this system worked really well for him because he knew that if there were legal questions that had to be answered, he was seeing them in a timely fashion and he was adequately supervising my work and complying with the ethical considerations."

ETHICS

CONFIDENTIALITY

"Confidentiality was very important to our firm given the environment we operated in. Vermont is an extremely small place. It was absolutely critical that we and our legal assistant interns never talk about a case, even if the person only talked about the facts of the case and did not reveal names. No one could talk about a case at all outside of the office, not to their family, not to anyone. In a small community if you go home and tell your partner about a great case where X happened, they may know instantly who you are talking about just because it is such a small town."

UNAUTHORIZED PRACTICE OF LAW

"Because I was involved with the delivery of services to clients, the 'Client Activity Sheet' was very important to keep the attorney informed of what I was doing. I felt it was critical to document my conversations with clients. If I had any conversation that there was a need for the attorney to respond, I had a section on the form that specifically provided for that, where I would check 'Action Needed.' So, he not only had to read that form but he had to respond to the matter I had marked.

"We also had general ethical guidelines that, for instance, stated that no pleadings or documents left the office without the attorney reading them."

CHINESE WALL

"One time a woman came into the clinic to file for divorce. I had been close personal friends with her husband's mother and the woman filing also had been my neighbor. So, I had intimate knowledge about the marriage, not so much from her viewpoint but from her husband's viewpoint, the adverse party. To be safe, I totally removed myself from the case. The clinic handled the case but I did not have anything to do with it at all. We put up the so called Chinese wall in that case. The day she came in for her client interview, I did not go into the clinic." In addition, Suzanne did not have access to the file. "We knew this case had serious ethical implications and had to be handled properly. In addition, I never talked to the attorney or

other staff about what I knew about my experience with any of the parties. Everything went fine once we took these precautions."

HELPING PEOPLE AND BEING INVOLVED

"I loved working in the legal clinic. We were very committed to the clients we served. It gave me a wholesome and rich experience because I was able to help people that really needed it and because I was able to participate in the practice end of cases. I got to be as involved with cases as I wanted to be. I could make a difference. If I thought I needed to go research at the law library for a half a day on a case because I felt there was a particular angle to the case that needed research, I could do that."

A CLIENT'S CASE AS AN EXAMPLE OF HOW A CLINIC OPERATES

"We had a client who we represented in a Chapter 7 bankruptcy. In my initial telephone call with her I established that it appeared she had enough debt to file for Chapter 7 bankruptcy and I took down as much basic information about her case that I could. I then gave the information to Jan. With his approval I scheduled the client for an initial client interview. I had her bring in all of her bills, which she did. In the initial client interview Jan outlined with her the remedies that were available to her which took about a half-hour. Then, I took her into my office and interviewed her putting the answers to my questions into the bankruptcy program which prepared the bankruptcy petition. So, when she left the office she not only knew she could file for bankruptcy, but she knew what it looked like and had it with her. This gave her peace of mind. She only had to get one or two more pieces of information before we could finalize the bankruptcy. She got the information back to me the next day and we filed the petition the next week.

What made this case interesting was that she had a very large bank as a creditor (they had loaned her money to buy a car). The bank happened to call the day she came in for her initial client interview and she advised the bank that she was going to see an attorney about filing bankruptcy. The bank documented the call into their computer log. A couple of days later they called her again. She told them she had signed her bankruptcy petition and that the petition was being filed. In addition, the attorney called the bank and informed them that the bankruptcy petition had been filed. These calls were also documented into their computer log by the bank.

About a week after the bankruptcy petition was filed the bank called the client's home early in the morning, impersonated a UPS driver to get her address, which she gave them. They came out, hooked a tow bar to her car, knocked on the door to let her know they were repossessing the car and even asked for the key. This was a clear and blatant violation of the bankruptcy code which puts an automatic stay on all creditors from levying the person's property when a bankruptcy petition is filed.

After they took her car away, the client called the clinic. The attorney called the bank, who acknowledged that they knew the client had filed bankruptcy, which was also put in the bank's computer log. The bank refused to give the woman her car back which she needed.

The clinic's attorney then filed an action asking for sanctions against the bank. Because all the action was documented in the bank's computer log, the facts of the case were not in dispute. The bankruptcy court. awarded the client $10,000 in punitive damages against the bank and the legal clinic was awarded attorneys fees. As a part of the attorneys fees the clinic was awarded fees for Suzanne's time. The part that was particularly satisfying about the case was the punitive damage award without an award of compensatory damage and that the client was awarded enough money to buy a new car!

CONCLUSION

Suzanne's experience shows why working in a legal clinic can be very rewarding and satisfying on a personal level. Being directly involved in a client's case and helping people can make this a satisfying job for some.

KEY TERMS

Human resource management
Personnel handbook
Employment-at-will doctrine
Equal employment opportunity
Family and Medical Leave Act of 1993 (FMLA)
Civil Rights Act of 1964
Americans with Disabilities Act of 1990 (ADA)
Age Discrimination in Employment Act of 1967
Equal Pay Act of 1963
Bona fide occupational qualification

"Reasonable accommodation"
Sexual harassment
Essential job functions
Negligent hiring
Coaching technique
Management by objectives
Employee attitude survey
Wrongful termination lawsuit
Employee assistance program

PROBLEM SOLVING QUESTIONS

1. As a legal assistant manager in a large law firm, you have the opportunity to see pay scales, budgets, and other financial data. During your long career with the firm, you have had many positions. From your experience, you know that the file clerks in the probate department perform substantially the same functions as the file clerks in the tax department. The only difference is that the file clerks in the probate department are nearly all female, while most of the file clerks in the tax department are male. In looking through the firm's budget for next year, you notice that the file clerks in the tax department are paid nearly $1.50 more an hour than are their counterparts in probate. You know that the firm is only motivated by good intentions. However, does this pose any potential problems for the firm? Is there any other information you would like to know?

2. You are a new legal assistant at a medium-sized law firm. You are currently making just enough for you, your spouse, and your children to get by but hope in a year or two that the firm will recognize your hard work and promote you. Your supervising attorney is well respected at the firm. Recently, you have had to work many long hours on a particular case with the attorney. One evening when you are alone, the attorney unexpectedly propositions you. You politely refuse. However, the propositions continue. They are quite annoying and unsettling and are affecting your performance. You worry about whether anyone will believe your story, since you are new and the matter concerns a well-liked and respected attorney in the firm. What are your options and what would you do?

3. You are a legal assistant manager, and one of your top assistants just quit to take another job at a competing firm. You must fill the position in at least three weeks with a qualified candidate. You would like the candidate to be "young and aggressive." You know of an acquaintance who is a legal assistant and who is looking for a job. Please state exactly how you would fill the position.

4. As a legal assistant, you need to hire a temporary document clerk to help you with a particularly large case. You expect the position to last about six months. After carefully drafting a detailed job description, advertising, and interviewing, the best candidate happens to be an individual who uses a wheelchair. This presents some problems, since your firm is somewhat wheelchair accessible but not entirely so. You figure that the improvements would cost about two thousand dollars. You doubt that your office will want to put in the necessary improvements. Briefly, what are your obligations?

5. You are a new legal assistant manager at a medium-sized law firm. The individual who managed the department before you did an incredibly poor job. Morale is low, and people under you are threatening to quit. The situation looks bleak. You must take quick action to ensure that people do not quit and that they understand you are here to make changes and to listen. Can you think of anything you can do relatively quickly that might help in this situation? Explain your answer.

6. Your office has put you in charge of hiring a clerk. You advertise for the position, conduct interviews, and make a selection. Because you have all your regular job duties to perform in addition to hiring the clerk, you only casually call his references and do not call his past employers at all. You do, however, feel very confident that you have hired the best individual for the position. After three weeks, one of the other staff members quits, stating that the new clerk has been harassing her and threatening her into going out with him. You feel particularly bad about the situation, since you were responsible for hiring him and she had always been a good employee. You feel even worse when the law office is served with a negligent hiring lawsuit. The lawsuit alleges that the clerk spent the last two years in prison for a sexual-related crime and before that had been fired from a job for sexual harassment. What could you have done to prevent this?

KNOW YOUR ETHICS

1. The law office you work for failed to perform routine evaluations on a certain legal assistant. The firm subsequently received a complaint from a client regarding the legal assistant's work. The office investigated the matter and found that the legal assistant had been performing work far below an acceptable level and in some cases had even compromised a client's case. Discuss the law office's ethical duties to adequately supervise a legal assistant.

2. Recently, your firm terminated an employee. Unfortunately, the employee's keys were not taken and the locks were not changed. Later, the employee returned and stole vital information from the office's files regarding a client. The information, if released, would be very detrimental to the client. Did the office act in a prudent way to safeguard client confidences?

PRACTICE EXERCISES

1. You are a legal assistant manager and a subordinate, legal assistant one, comes to you and reports that legal assistant two propositioned her. He became belligerent when she refused and threatened to get her fired if she told anyone. You have never had any trouble with either one of them. They currently are working on the same case together. It is your job to investigate the complaint. You initially call in legal assistant two and tell him about the complaint. Legal assistant two appears shocked and states that it is completely unfounded, that he would never do such a thing, and that he is completely innocent. He further states that legal assistant one has a vendetta against him and wants him fired and that no one else in the firm has ever complained about his conduct in any regard. Both individuals appear completely honest and their stories are believable. Please indicate what steps you would take to further investigate this matter; be specific. What steps would you take if there were no other credible evidence available and nothing else to corroborate either story? What steps would you take to keep this from happening in the future?

2. You work closely with a secretary in your office. During the past three weeks, the secretary's quality of work has gone substantially down. Three assignments you have given to her were late and not completed correctly. The secretary also has been moody, belligerent to other staff members and clients, and generally hard to get along with. You have avoided her on several occasions and have seen others doing so, too. You have been asked by the firm to handle the situation. You have looked for the right opportunity to talk to the secretary but have not done it yet. Today, a client complained about the secretary's poor quality of work. You know that the situation must be dealt with now. On your way to the secretary's office, you meet her in the hall. Please state step-by-step how you would handle the situation. Explain your answer.

3. You have worked for a law office for several years and your hard work finally has paid off. The office is going to create a legal assistant manager position to manage the firm's other legal assistants. The law office has selected you to fill that position. The office has asked that since you are the one filling the position and doing the job, you should have the first crack at writing the job description. Keep in mind that you must supervise other legal assistants, do performance evaluations, manage and coordinate their caseloads, prepare a budget for your department, and handle your own cases and many other duties. Please draft the job description.

4. You are a legal assistant manager and must prepare interview questions for a new legal assistant position you are filling. You want to find out the following information about the candidates but do not want to ask a question that is illegal. Please draft legal questions to find out the following information:

- You have had trouble with employee's cars breaking down, making them late for work; you want to make sure this is not a problem.
- You want to make sure the person is stable, committed, and will not leave town after you have trained him.
- You want to make sure that the person will not be continually receiving phone calls from children, relatives, and others, taking him away from his work.
- You want to hire persons that are interested in community projects and organizations, since it looks good for your firm to have employees who are involved in community affairs.
- You want to make sure that the person will be able to work on Saturdays, even if the person has religious observances on that day.
- You want to make sure that if you invest your time and train this individual, he will not have to take a medical leave of absence after you have trained him.
- You want to make sure that you hire a reputable person who does not pose a treat to co-workers.

5. After looking at your firm's performance evaluation procedures, you realize that they desperately need to be updated. Please draft an evaluation policy stating who will conduct performance evaluations, what the evaluations will involve, and when, where, and how they will be conducted. You want to make sure the employee not only knows how she is performing but also takes an active part in the process and knows exactly what she should be accomplishing or working on for her next evaluation.

6. It has recently come to your attention that your secretary has stolen money out of the petty cash fund that your office keeps. In addition, the secretary has recently on at least two occasions violated the firm's confidentiality policy by telling people outside the office about cases that your office handles. Your supervisor thinks the secretary should be fired but will defer to your judgment for now. After investigating the petty cash allegation, you find out that the secretary claims he borrowed the money to pay for an emergency and that he then put the money back. You do confirm, however, that the confidentiality policies were in fact violated and could have serious implications to your clients. Please state how you would handle the matter.

NOTES

1. *Build a Better Staff* (Los Angeles: Aspen Publishers, Inc., 1992), 27.
2. *Complete Personnel Administration Handbook for Law Firms,* (Newtown, PA: Altman Weil Pensa, 1991), 8.5.1.
3. Ibid., 4.4.3.
4. Carol Milano, "1993 Legal Assistant Today Salary Survey Results," *Legal Assistant Today,* May/June 1993, 60.
5. Altman Weil Pensa, *Complete Personnel Administration Handbook for Law Firms,* 4.3.3.
6. U.S. Equal Employment Opportunity Commission, *The Americans with Disabilities Act—Questions and Answers* (Washington: Government Printing Office, July 1991).
7. Altman Weil Pensa, *Complete Personnel Administration Handbook for Law Firms,* 4.3.4.

Law Office Information Systems

CHAPTER OBJECTIVES

After you read this chapter, you will be able to:

- Distinguish between RAM and ROM.

- Explain what LAN is.

- Define hard and floppy disk.

- Understand different types of printers.

- Discuss what a computer virus is and how it starts.

- Discuss application software used in a law office information system.

One of our top priorities was to have an information system that connected all of our office's computers and branch offices together, even if they were located in different cities halfway around the world.[1]

The smaller the office, the greater the need for software power because absent human resources must be replaced with technology.[2]

My general suggestion [to legal assistants] is to get as much experience on computers as possible. This is true for litigation . . . but all areas use computers now.[3]

WHY DOES THE LEGAL ASSISTANT NEED AN UNDERSTANDING OF MANAGEMENT INFORMATION SYSTEMS?

During the past ten years, computers have had a dramatic effect on law practices, both on the substantive practice of law and on law office management. Both of these topics are important, since some legal assistants will have administrative duties and may be required to use law office management software. Legal assistants who practice in substantive areas also are being required to use computers for word processing, litigation support, and other duties as well. Legal assistants who want to be competitive in the marketplace are finding that having an understanding of computers and having computer skills are necessities.

It is important to realize just how pervasive computers are in the practice of law. A 1987 study by the American Bar Association indicated that only 75 percent of the offices surveyed owned or leased a computer.[4] By 1989 that amount had risen to 91 percent. Much of this rise can be attributed to the increased power, decreased costs, and increased "user-friendliness" (i.e. ease of use) of computers. Notice in Figure 9-1 that law offices use computers for a wide variety of management functions.

As we begin, it is necessary to dispel a common myth about computers. This myth is that a person has to know about computer programming to operate a computer. This is not the case. Most people who use computers know nothing about programming. Instead, they learn how to use application programs that programmers have written.

COMPUTER HARDWARE

A **computer** *is an electronic device that accepts, processes, outputs, and stores information.* The goal of computers is to take disorganized raw information, process it, and output it in a method that is organized and relevant. A computer system is made up of hardware and software elements. **Hardware** *refers to the actual physical components of a computer system.* Most computer systems have a central processing unit (CPU), sometimes referred to as "the computer," a keyboard, a monitor, and a printer. These are all examples of hardware.

Computer programs (also referred to as **computer software** or just **software**) *are the step-by-step instructions that direct the computer to do certain tasks.* Two types of computer programs make the computer function: operating system software and application software. **Operating system software** *instructs the computer how to operate its circuitry and how to communicate with input, output, and storage devices.* In essence, operating system software performs housekeeping and internal functions to make the computer work properly. *An* **input device** *(e.g., a keyboard) enters information into a computer,* whereas *an* **output device** *(e.g., a printer) outputs information from a computer after it has been processed. A* **storage device** *stores data so that it can be retrieved later (e.g., a floppy disk).* **Application software,** *on the other hand, instructs the computer to perform a specific application or task, such as word processing.*

computer
An electronic device that accepts, processes, outputs, and stores information.

hardware
The actual physical components of a computer system.

computer programs
The step-by-step instructions that direct the computer to do certain tasks.

operating system software
Instructs the computer how to operate its circuitry and how to communicate with input, output, and storage devices.

input device
Enters information into a computer.

output device
A piece of equipment that outputs processed information from a computer.

storage device
Stores data that can be retrieved later.

application software
Instructs the computer to perform a specific application or task, such as word processing.

Type of Software	Percentage of Total Respondents
Word processing*	60.7
Timekeeping & billing*	46.5
Accounting—general ledger*	43.3
Spreadsheets*	25.1
Docket control*	24.6
Payroll*	19.5
Data-base management*	18.5
Litigation support software	14.4
Trust accounting software	9.1
Desktop publishing*	8.7
Law practice management*	6.2
Probate & estate planning	6.2
Tax software	5.3

FIGURE 9-1
Computer Software Owned by Law Firms

Source: "ABA Journal Primary Readersh Study," *ABA Journal* (March 1989): 14. Adapted and reprinted with permission from the *ABA Journal,* the Lawyer's Magazine, published by the American Bar Associated.

•Used in whole or in part for law office management tasks.

Hardware and software are interdependent and cannot function without each other (see Figure 9-2).

A computer by itself will not solve problems; instead, the user needs an information system to be effective. *A* **law office information system** *is a combination of human involvement, computer hardware and software, and raw information that work together to solve problems in a law office.* The key to an information system is that all the components must be present, but more important, they must work together to achieve a common objective. Computers by themselves are useless pieces of technology. Only when humans interact with them can they become productive.

Electronic computers are mathematically based. All data that are transmitted to a computer eventually must be converted into a numerical representation. Once the data are in a numerical format, the computer must process and organize them. The component of the computer that does this task is called the central processing unit, and it is part of the system unit (see Figure 9-2).

law office information system
A combination of human involvement, computer hardware and software, and raw information that work together to solve problems in a law office.

SYSTEM UNIT COMPONENTS

A computer or system unit works together with peripheral devices such as storage devices (e.g., floppy disks, hard disks, etc.) and input and output devices to receive, process, store, and output information. The system unit of a computer contains a central processing unit (CPU) and main memory. Each is covered in detail in this section.

central processing unit (CPU)
The "brains" of the computer. It organizes and processes information.

CENTRAL PROCESSING UNIT (CPU)   The **central processing unit (CPU)** *organizes and processes information. It is the "brains" of the computer. It performs logical operations—in accordance with the operating system software—and coordinates and*

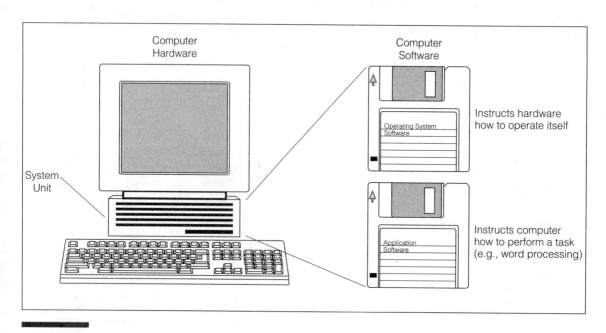

FIGURE 9-2   Interrelation of Hardware and Software

Source: William M. Fuori and Lawrence J. Aufiero, *Computers and Information Processing: Transparency Master* (Englewood Cliffs, N.J.: Prentice-Hall, 1989), transparency 7, Copyright 1989 by Prentice-Hall. Adapted and reprinted by permission of Prentice-Hall, Inc., Englewood Cliffs, N.J.

communicates with storage devices and input, output, and communication devices (see Figure 9-3).

At the heart of the CPU is the processor chip (see Figure 9-3). *The **processor chip** performs the actual arithmetic computations of the computer.* Some recognizable processor chips come from microcomputers, such as the Intel 80286, 80386, and 80486 (used in many IBM-compatible microcomputers) and the Motorola 68000 (used in the original Apple Macintosh microcomputer). *The processor chips used in microcomputers are called **microprocessors.*** Many other types of processor chips are available.

MAIN MEMORY *The function of the **main memory** is to hold or store information that the computer is processing.* This is accomplished through memory chips. **Memory chips,** *like processor chips, are made up of tiny electronic circuits, but instead of processing information, they store or hold information.* As information is entered into a computer, it is temporarily stored in memory locations, also called memory addresses, while the computer is processing it. Main memory is made up of two types of memory: "read only memory" (ROM) and "random access memory" (RAM).

Read only memory (ROM) *is permanent, unchanging memory that is used internally by the computer to operate itself.* It is permanently installed by the manufacturer and cannot be changed or altered, thus the name *read only.* A computer reads ROM, but you cannot enter information into it or change the data. The data contained in ROM are not lost when the computer is turned off. Practically speaking, the user never realizes ROM exists.

processor chip
Performs the actual arithmetic computations of the computer.

microprocessors
The processor chips used in microcomputers.

main memory
Holds or stores information that the computer is processing.

memory chips
Tiny electronic circuits that store or hold information.

read only memory (ROM)
Permanent, unchanging memory that is used internally by the computer to operate itself.

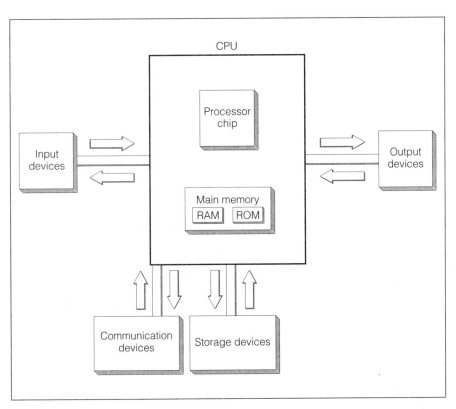

FIGURE 9-3
Central Processing Unit

**random access
memory (RAM)**
Temporary memory
that is used to store
application programs
and data that are
entered into a
computer.

Random access memory (RAM) *is temporary memory that is used to store application programs and data that are entered into a computer.* When a user loads a program, such as a word processing program, into the computer or enters information from the keyboard, RAM is where the information is temporarily stored. RAM refers to memory locations that are volatile in that they are erased every time the computer's power is turned off. This can be particularly frustrating when a user has information in RAM and power is interrupted, such as it is when the lights flicker. When power to the computer is interrupted, the computer turns off and any information in RAM is lost. Information in RAM that the user wants to save must be stored on a storage device (e.g., a hard disk or floppy disk).

SIZE CLASSIFICATIONS OF COMPUTERS

Computers are used for a variety of purposes, both large and small. Computers that support small applications require limited capabilities, whereas computers that support large applications require the ability to digest, store, and process tremendous quantities of information at a time.

Computers are classified based on speed, main memory capacity, and storage capacities. Storage capacity refers to the amount of information that can be permanently held by the storage device. Computers generally come in three sizes: mainframe computers, minicomputers and microcomputers (see Figure 9-4). Size classifications are important, since in almost every case the larger the law office, the larger its computing needs.

MAINFRAME COMPUTERS

mainframe computer
A large computer that
is more powerful than a
minicomputer and is
capable of processing
enormous volumes of
data.

A **mainframe computer** *is a large computer that is more powerful than a minicomputer and is capable of processing enormous volumes of data.* Mainframes require a full-time operator or staff to operate them. At one time, mainframes were the only kinds of computers available. Organizations that need the computing power of a mainframe are typically quite large and need to store and use enormous quantities of information. For example, mainframe computers are used by a few extremely large law offices, by the federal government for military purposes and by state governments for tax-return processing.

service bureau
An outside or third-
party office that sells
computer time—usually
mainframe computer
time—to others.

Although most law offices cannot afford to purchase their own mainframe computer, they nevertheless are able to use a mainframe through the use of a service bureau. *A* **service bureau** *is an outside or third-party office that sells computer time—usually mainframe computer time—to others.* West Publishing Company provides a computer-assisted legal research service through WESTLAW, which is the

	Mainframe Computer	Minicomputer	Microcomputer
Main memory	5–150 Mb or more	1–50 Mb or more	64K–16 Mb or more
Auxiliary storage capacity	100 Gb or more	10 Gb or more	500 Mb or more
Cost	$350,000–$15,000,000	$20,000–$350,000	$200–$20,000
Maintenance staff	Full time	Part time	None

FIGURE 9-4   Computer Size Classifications

equivalent of a computerized law library, and has the full text to millions of judicial opinions, statutes, and law-related works. WESTLAW sells computer time to attorneys and law offices. The computerized library resides on WESTLAW's mainframe computer system and law offices are billed according to the amount of time spent on the system.

Mainframe (and minicomputers) users use terminals to communicate with the computer. *A* **terminal** *has a keyboard and monitor but may or may not have computing capability of its own.* A mainframe computer, depending on the size, can serve more than one hundred terminals or users at a time (see Figure 9-5). Terminals are linked to the mainframe either by cabling or by phone lines.

terminal
A keyboard and monitor that are used to communicate with computers.

MINICOMPUTERS

A **minicomputer** *is a medium-sized computer that is not as powerful as a mainframe computer but can still process large volumes of data.* Minicomputers are smaller to house than mainframes are and generally do not require special environmental controls as mainframes do. Minicomputers typically have from one to fifty megabytes of main memory and up to ten Gb (gigabytes) of storage capacity. (A megabyte equals one million bytes of storage; a gigabyte equals one billion bytes of storage.) The cost of a minicomputer system ranges from $20,000 to $350,000 or more. Minicomputers usually require at least one part-time computer operator to perform maintenance on them. Minicomputers are used for medium-sized data-processing needs. For example, law offices with fifty or more attorneys would most likely use a minicomputer system.

minicomputer
A medium-sized computer that is not as powerful as a mainframe computer but can still process large volumes of data.

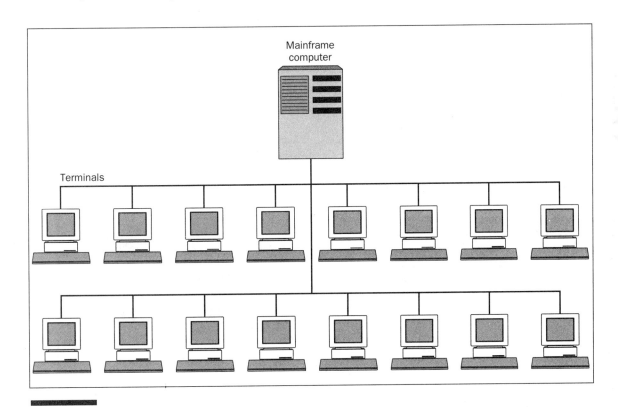

FIGURE 9-5   A Mainframe Computer Serving Multiple Terminals

MICROCOMPUTERS

microcomputer
A small computer that
is cheaper and less
powerful than a
minicomputer or a
mainframe computer
and is sometimes
referred to as a
personal computer or
"PC."

A **microcomputer** *is a small computer that is less expensive and less powerful than a minicomputer or a mainframe computer and is sometimes referred to as a personal computer or "PC"* (see Figure 9-6). Microcomputers typically have from sixty-four to sixteen Mb of main memory and have storage capacities from 360 K to 500 Mb or more. "K" refers to Kilobytes or *thousands* of bytes of storage, "Mb" refers to megabytes or millions of bytes of storage, and "Gb" refers to gigabytes or billions of bytes of storage. The price of microcomputers ranges from $200 to $20,000 depending on the size of the microprocessor, main memory, and storage devices. Unlike mainframes and minicomputers, microcomputers do not ordinarily need a professional computer operator to operate them (see Figure 9-4).

Microcomputers are very popular because they are inexpensive, relatively powerful, and able to perform numerous and varied tasks. As a result of the widespread use of microcomputers, many software programs have been written for microcomputers. In addition, many software programs currently are available for microcomputers that are specific to the legal field, such as timekeeping and billing packages and docket control.

Microcomputers are the overwhelming choice of small law offices. A 1989 study by the American Bar Association showed that 89.3 percent of the small law offices surveyed use microcomputers, compared with just 13 percent that use minicomputers. Some law offices may use both minicomputers and microcomputers—mainframe use in law offices is below 1 percent.[5] One of the main reasons for the popularity of microcomputers is that they are extremely flexible. Many microcomputers have access to literally hundreds of computer programs

FIGURE 9-6 Microcomputer System
Source: Courtesy IBM Corporation.

that can be used in a law office. Most microcomputers also can be upgraded to add a variety of devices to meet practically any need. Microcomputers also can be networked together so that users in the law office can exchange information.

Microcomputers started as single-user systems. *A* **single-user system** *is a computer that can accommodate only one person at a time and is not linked to other systems or computers.* Microcomputers can now be linked or networked together. *A* **local area network** *(LAN) is a multiuser system that links independent microcomputers together that are close in proximity for the purpose of sharing information, printers, and storage devices.* Primary reasons to install a LAN include: a) to share data and software among multiple microcomputers and b) to share peripheral devices such as expensive printers and hard disks among multiple computers. There are many kinds of LAN methods for connecting the computers. Some of the more popular network links include a star network, a ring network, and a bus network. Although the specifics of networking go beyond this introductory text, a diagram of a horizontal ring network is shown in Figure 9-7. Another advantage of a LAN is that different types of computers (IBM-compatible machines and Apple Macintosh computers, for example) can be linked together to share data in some LAN configurations. LANs are used by law offices of all sizes, even very small offices. Prices have dropped so significantly that even small offices can afford the benefits of a LAN.

There are other types of networks as well. *A* **wide area network** *(WAN) is a multiuser system that can link independent microcomputers together that can be located thousands of miles apart.* Wide area networks can be used by large law offices that

single-user system
A computer that can accommodate only one person at a time and is not linked to other systems or computers.

local area network
A multiuser system that links independent microcomputers together that are close in proximity for the purpose of sharing information, printers, and storage devices.

wide area network
A multiuser system that can link independent microcomputers together that are located thousands of miles apart.

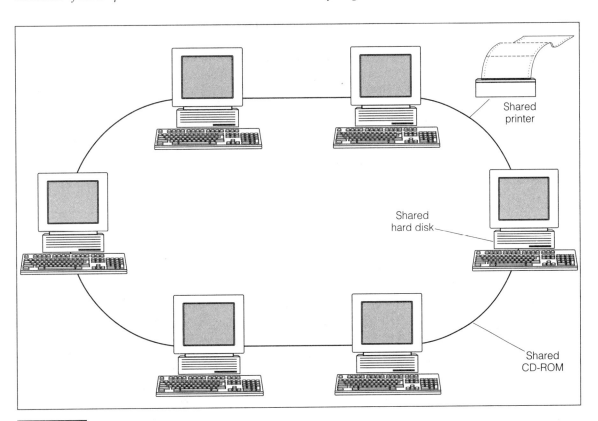

FIGURE 9-7   Horizontal Ring Network

have several offices across the country or across the world to connect and communicate with one another.

A network is a convenient way for microcomputers to share information, storage devices, printers, and other devices among machines automatically. A network enables otherwise independent single-user systems, such as a particular microcomputer, to store information in a single location so that other microcomputers on the network can access the information. LANs and WANs can connect branch offices across town or across the world with the main office to share billing information or files. Networks, whether they are local or wide area, usually have a "host" computer or a file server. The file server acts as a "traffic cop" in that it directs incoming and outgoing signals among the other computers. Some of the new networks, however, do not need a file server.

PERIPHERAL DEVICES

peripheral devices
Pieces of equipment that are connected to a computer to perform specific functions.

Peripheral devices *are pieces of equipment that are connected to a computer to perform specific functions.* They include storage devices, input devices, output devices, and communication devices.

STORAGE DEVICES

A storage device is used to permanently store information. Storage devices and RAM are sometimes confused with each other. RAM is where information is stored temporarily, and it is erased every time the computer is turned off; a storage device stores it permanently. The two are sometimes confused because they both use kilobytes or megabytes to refer to their respective storage capacities and they both store information although for different purposes. **Storage capacity** *refers to the maximum amount of data that can be stored on the device.* A microcomputer might have 640 K RAM, and a storage device such as a floppy disk might have 360 K space available. A floppy disk is a storage device that stores data on a plastic disk. Although RAM and storage devices serve very different purposes, they both use "K" to show the maximum amount storage. Also, RAM stores user information on a temporary basis, and a storage device saves that same information on a permanent basis.

storage capacity
The maximum amount of data that can be stored on a device.

There are many types of storage devices, including floppy disks, hard disks, and compact disk read-only medium (CD-ROMs) (see Figure 9-8), and more. Each type of storage device has a different storage capacity and a different access time. **Access time** *refers to the amount of time it takes to transfer data between a storage device and RAM.* Many computer systems will have several types of storage devices.

access time
The amount of time it takes to transfer data between storage device and RAM.

FLOPPY DISKS   A **floppy disk drive** *stores data on a plastic magnetic disk called a floppy disk or diskette.* Floppy disks are used in almost all microcomputers. They can read and write data. Writing data means saving information to the disk. Reading data means reading information previously stored on the disk back into the computer's main memory. Most microcomputers today use floppy disks that are 5¼ inch, 3½ inch, or smaller. Some 5¼-inch diskettes have a storage capacity of only 360 K, while some 3½-inch disks have a storage capacity of up to two megabytes. Floppy disks are often used in law offices even when other storage devices such as hard disks are available. For example, when you buy a new com-

floppy disk drive
Device that stores data on a plastic magnetic disk called a floppy disk or diskette.

puter program, such as a word processor, it is stored on floppy disks that come with the package. Floppy disks also are used to back up copies of your data so that you have an extra copy of your information. If a disaster happens, such as a fire or a theft, and you have made a backup copy, the data will still be intact. Many law offices back up their data on a daily basis.

HARD DISKS   *A* **hard disk** *stores data on a rigid magnetic material.* Hard disks are very reliable and have faster access times than floppy disks. They can read and write data. Hard disks usually are mounted inside the computer and can only be identified by a small light that turns on when information is to be either accessed or saved to the drive. Hard disks have storage capacities ranging from ten megabytes to well over 500 megabytes. Many microcomputers will have both a floppy disk drive and a hard disk.

> **hard disk**
> Device that stores data on a rigid magnetic material.

Hard disks usually are an absolute must for a law office of any size. This is because law offices usually work with such large quantities of information spanning many, many cases, and the vast number of forms they use requires the storage capacity hard disks can provide. In addition, law offices usually require hard disks because they give users quick access to information. Finally, many of the sophisticated computer programs law offices use, such as high-end word processors, cannot run on a computer without a hard disk. The prices of hard disks have fallen so dramatically during recent years that they are standard equipment on most computers sold now.

TAPE BACKUP   Tape backup systems store data on cartridges or reels. Tape cartridges look similar to cassettes used in a stereo. Tape backup systems primarily are used for making copies of information on other storage devices. For example, many law offices use the system to back up their hard disk so they have an extra copy of their data. Tape backup systems are faster than backing up with floppy disks.

CD-ROM   *A* **CD-ROM** *uses optical technology, or laser beams, to store large quantities of data on a small laser disk.* CD-ROMs have a storage capacity ranging from 100 Mb to one Gb, and each CD-ROM disk can hold approximately 100 to 125 average-sized books. A typical CD-ROM disk has a storage capacity of about 550 Mb. It would take well over 1,250 360 K floppy disks to equal the storage capacity of one CD-ROM disk. The potential of CD-ROM on the legal market is astounding. State reporters, bankruptcy reports, federal regulations, and many other law-related topics already are in CD-ROM format. Not only does CD-ROM allow users access to the information but also it allows users to access information the same way information is accessed on WESTLAW or LEXIS, using computerized search techniques. However, WESTLAW and LEXIS, which are on-line mainframe systems, are updated all the time; CD-ROM users must purchase updates separately.

> **CD-ROM**
> Peripheral device that uses optical technology, or laser beams, to stores large quantities of data on a small laser disk.

Storage Device	Capacity	Ability to Read & Write Data	Access Time
Floppy disk	360K–2 Mb	Read & write data	Medium
Hard disk	10–500 Mb	Read & write data	Fast
Tape backup	1–100 Mb	Read & write data	Slow
CD-ROM disk	200 Mb–1 Gb	Read data only	Medium

**FIGURE 9-8
Auxiliary Storage Devices**

INPUT DEVICES

input device
Enters information into a computer.

Input devices *are used to enter information into a computer.* Most people consider a keyboard the only means for entering information into a computer, but many ways have been developed, including optical character recognition scanners and mice.

COMPUTER KEYBOARD   At present, the keyboard is by far the most-used method for entering data into a computer. Most computer keyboards are similar to the keyboard of an ordinary typewriter with a few additions. A computer keyboard is basically made up of alphanumeric keys, function keys, cursor movement keys, and a numeric keypad (see Figure 9-9). Keyboards are inexpensive and come in a variety of types and styles. For instance, replacement keyboards for many microcomputers cost less than $100.

optical character recognition scanner (OCR scanner)
Device that scans or reads printed material into a computer's memory.

OPTICAL CHARACTER RECOGNITION SCANNER   *An* **optical character recognition scanner (OCR scanner)** *scans or reads printed material into a computer's memory.* Through the use of OCR technology, it is possible to scan printed information into a computer much faster than a keyboard operator could enter the information. Large OCR scanners can scan hundreds of pages of text into a computer in a day.

An OCR scanner reflects light onto the printed text, then compares the letters of the text with the letters in its memory and writes the information into the computer. If the printed text that is being scanned into the OCR system does not exactly match the letters in its memory, an error will occur and the right letter may not be entered into the computer.

Some OCR scanners can even scan human handwriting. OCR scanners are quite accurate at scanning in documents that have been produced on most type-

FIGURE 9-9   Keyboard
Source: Courtesy IBM Corporation.

writers and printers. Small low-volume OCR scanners cost about $1,500, while large high-volume OCR scanners can cost more than $50,000.

OCR scanners can be used very productively in a law office setting. For instance, suppose you need to enter a 1,000-page document into a computer so that you can use a litigation-support program during a trial to search for specific information in it. Although the document might take more than a week to enter into a computer using a keyboard, it could be entered using an OCR scanner in a relatively short amount of time, depending on the type of scanner. Some law offices use an OCR service so that they do not have to purchase a scanner. Unfortunately, the cost can be quite high in some cases.

MOUSE   *A* **mouse** *is used to move the cursor on a monitor and otherwise enter information into a computer.* A mouse is sometimes called a pointing device. A mouse is approximately the same size as the palm of your hand and contains a ball that rotates inside the mouse (see Figure 9-6). As the mouse is moved, it transmits a signal to the computer that correspondingly moves the cursor in the same direction. If the mouse is moved to the right, the cursor moves to the right, and so on. The mouse also has two or more buttons along the top. When a mouse button or buttons are pushed, the computer program acts accordingly. The type of action the buttons produce is determined by the software the computer is running. A mouse for a microcomputer is quite inexpensive, usually costing under $100.

OUTPUT DEVICES

Output devices *provide the user with the data that the computer has generated.* Like input devices, they come in many different types. The type you select depends on the application you are using it for. Popular types include video display screens, or monitors, and printers.

MONITOR   A monitor uses the same technology as a television. These monitors are either monochrome or color. *A* **monochrome monitor** *displays information in one color, usually green, amber, or white.* **Color monitors** *display information in a variety of different colors.* Which type of screen you use is a question of personal preference; color screens are more expensive, but they may make some programs much easier to use.

Monitors also have different resolutions or screen qualities. High-resolution monitors have more pixels, or dots, that make up the screen than do low-resolution monitors. For this reason, high-resolution monitors have a better quality of display than do low-resolution monitors. Most people find that monitors with a higher resolution are easier on their eyes.

PRINTERS   *A* **printer** *produces data onto paper (sometimes called "hard copy").* A tremendous number of printers are available. There is a vast number of methods, speeds, and print quality. Choosing a printer is again a personal decision based on the law office's specific needs. There generally are two categories of printers, impact printers and nonimpact printers (see Figure 9-10).

Impact printers—*An* **impact printer** *prints data onto paper by physically impacting or striking the paper, like a typewriter does.* Impact printers are specifically suited for instances when the user needs a carbon copy or multiple copies. There are two principal kinds of impact printers, dot-matrix printers and daisy wheel printers.

A **dot-matrix printer** *prints data by forming rows and columns of dots.* The dots are formed when the pins or wires in the printhead of the printer strike the paper

mouse
Device used to move the cursor on a monitor and otherwise enter information into a computer.

output device
A piece of equipment that outputs processed information from a computer.

monochrome monitor
Monitor that displays information in one color, usually green, amber, or white.

color monitors
Monitors that display information in a variety of colors.

printer
Peripheral that produces data onto paper (sometimes called "hard copy").

impact printer
Prints data onto paper by physically impacting or striking the paper, like a typewriter does.

dot-matrix printer
Prints data by forming rows and columns of dots.

FIGURE 9-10
Impact and
Nonimpact Printers

Printer	Type	Speed	Cost	Quality
Dot matrix	Impact	50–1,000 CPS	$100–$2,500	Average
Daisy wheel	Impact	10–200 CPS	$200–$2,000	Average—good
Ink jet	Nonimpact	100–300 CPS	$400–$2,000	Good
Laser	Nonimpact	4–20 PPM	$600–$15,000	Excellent

through the ribbon. The more pins in the printhead, the better the quality of the print. Therefore, a 24-pin dot-matrix printer has much better quality print than does a 9-pin printer (Figure 9-10). Dot-matrix printers are inexpensive, ranging between $100 and $2,500. They also are fairly fast (but not as fast as a laser printer). A medium-priced dot-matrix printer can print about 250 characters per second (CPS). Law offices typically use dot-matrix printers for billing purposes, producing mailing labels, and for printing rough drafts of documents. Dot-matrix printers do not print as high a quality of print as laser printers and ink-jet and daisy wheel printers do, but the quality has continued to get better. Another disadvantage of dot-matrix printers is that they are quite loud, which can pose a problem in an office.

daisy wheel printer
Printer that uses a daisy wheel or "print wheel."

A **daisy wheel printer** *uses a daisy wheel or "print wheel" to print data.* Daisy wheel printers are quite slow (10 to 200 CPS), but they produce letter-quality print. The cost ranges from $200 to $2,000. Daisy wheel printers probably will soon be obsolete because of the new high-quality dot-matrix printers and nonimpact printers. Daisy wheel printers, like dot-matrix printers, also are quite loud.

nonimpact printers
Print data onto paper without physically striking the paper.

Nonimpact printers—**Nonimpact printers** *print data onto paper without physically striking the paper.* Several methods are used for doing this, including ink-jet printing and laser printing.

ink-jet printer
Sprays ink onto a page to form letters.

An **ink-jet printer** *sprays ink onto a page to form letters.* The print quality of ink-jet printers is letter-quality and surpasses both dot-matrix and daisy wheel printers. The print speed is fairly good, at about 150 CPS for most ink-jet printers. Ink-jet printers cost between $500 and $2,000. Ink-jet printers are used in some law offices, since they produce a good print quality and are very quiet.

laser printer
Uses a laser beam to form characters on a page.

A **laser printer** *uses a laser beam to form characters on a page.* This process is very similar to that of a copy machine. The quality of laser printers is outstanding compared with all other methods. They produce text that is called near-typeset quality because it looks like it was prepared by a professional typesetter. Also, laser printers are much faster than other printers, printing from four to 20 pages per minute (PPM). The price of laser printers continues to spiral downward. The cost is between $750 and $15,000. Laser printers are quite often used in law offices because of their outstanding quality and fast speeds (see Figure 9-10).

Laser printers also can print in different fonts. A font is a complete set of characters that are all of the same typeface, or design. This means that instead of only being able to print documents in either Elite or Courier like a typewriter, a laser printer can print documents in literally hundreds of different typefaces like a print shop.

communication device
Device that allows computers to exchange information with one another. It is technically both an input and an output device.

COMMUNICATION DEVICES

A **communication device,** *such as a modem, allows computers to exchange information with one another. It is technically both an input and an output device, since it can receive data from other computers (input) and also send data to other computers (output).*

Modem—*A* **modem** *allows computers in different locations to communicate with one another using a telephone line.* Modems can transmit data at a variety of speeds. Many can transmit data at 9,600 BPS (bits per second); just a few years ago the standard was only 1,200 BPS. Modems can be either external units, which sit next to the computer, or internal units that are housed inside the computer itself. Modems use telecommunication software (e.g., Procomm and others) to transmit information between the computer and the modem.

COMPUTER SOFTWARE

As mentioned earlier, computer software (i.e. a computer program) amounts to step-by-step instructions that direct a computer to perform a task. There are two basic types of software: operating system software and application software. Computer hardware is useless without computer software to make it operate. Quality software is extremely important in determining how beneficial a computer will be to the user. *A* **programmer** *is a person who writes computer programs.* Most people who use computers are not programmers. Instead, they buy and use **"off the shelf"** (or preprogrammed) **software** *that someone else has developed and written.*

OPERATING SYSTEM SOFTWARE

Operating system programs, as defined previously, instruct the computer how to operate its circuitry and how to communicate with input, output, and storage devices.

When the computer is turned "on" (sometimes called being "booted-up"), the operating system is loaded into RAM. Operating systems are necessary to the operation of a computer, and computers cannot even turn themselves on properly without them. The manufacturer of the computer usually supplies the operating system, although this is not always the case. Recently, some microcomputers have a choice of what system can be used. Some operating systems are pleasant and easy to use, while others are frustrating, slow, and cumbersome. Users communicate with the operating system using a keyboard or mouse. When a user types in a command to load or run a program, she is communicating with the disk operating system. Thus, operating systems communicate with the hardware and with the end user.

Operating systems are usually unique to each type of computer. For example, an Apple Macintosh microcomputer uses a different operating system than do IBM-compatible microcomputers (see Figure 9-11).

DUTIES OF THE OPERATING SYSTEM   The operating system is a cross between a traffic cop, who directs traffic between the computer and different input, output, and auxiliary storage devices, and a housekeeper who organizes and maintains the system. Specifically, operating systems control main memory; input, output, and auxiliary storage devices; and management of the CPU.

TYPES OF OPERATING SYSTEMS   Operating systems can be classified many different ways. One way is to classify operating systems as to whether they provide for a single-task environment or a multitask environment (see Figure 9-11).

CLOSE-UP

Microcomputer Hardware: Putting It All Together

Microcomputers are used in law offices because they are inexpensive, readily available, and able to greatly increase productivity and efficiency. Legal assistants are frequently required to have microcomputer skills.

Many types of microcomputers are available, each having its own strengths and weaknesses. A typical microcomputer system used in a law office will have from twelve to sixty-six MHz (megahertz) or greater microprocessor speeds, one to sixteen Mb (megabytes) of RAM, at least one floppy disk drive (typically a 5¼ inch, 3½ inch, or smaller floppy disk), a forty to five hundred Mb hard disk, at least one serial port, one parallel port, a compatible monitor and a display adapter, an open architecture with system-expansion potential, a printer, and possibly a sound board, modem, CD-ROM, or tape backup unit.

Microprocessor

Microcomputers have different speeds and capabilities. The speed depends on how fast the microprocessor processes information. For example, a 486 IBM-compatible class machine uses a thirty-two bit microprocessor, compared with the original IBM-PC, introduced in 1982, which had only an eight-bit microprocessor.

The speed of the computer also is determined by the microprocessor's clock speed or how fast the microprocessor executes commands. Clock speed is measured in megahertz. Many of the first microcomputers such as the IBM-PC had a clock speed of about four MHz. Currently, microcomputers including IBM-compatible and Apple Macintosh computers have clock speeds of from thirty-three to sixty-six MHz or more.

The difference in the size of the microprocessor can make an enormous difference. For example, consider a user who needs to work with a data base that has two thousand records or a time and billing program that has to process thousands of

timeslips for hundreds of clients. It might take an original IBM-PC, which used a 8088 microprocessor, hours and hours to process this information, whereas a 486 IBM-compatible microprocessor or an Apple Macintosh 68040 microprocessor could process it in a quarter to a tenth of the time. Further, larger microprocessors are required for applications that use a great deal of RAM, such as powerful word processors and data bases, desktop publishing programs, and other graphic-based programs.

RAM

Most microcomputers come standard with from one to ten Mb of RAM. A minimum of one to eight Mb of RAM is necessary to run most software programs. As software programs continue to develop and become more complex, the amount of RAM required will continually be pushed higher. Nearly all microcomputers allow the user to install additional memory.

Floppy Disks and Hard Disks

Almost all microcomputers come with at least one floppy disk drive and one hard disk. A floppy disk is a plastic disk that stores information and that goes into a floppy disk drive. Floppy disk drives come in standard sizes of 5¼ inches and 3½ inches and some drives are being developed that are even smaller than this. Floppy disks also come with different storage capacities. For example, older 5¼-inch disk drives had a storage capacity of 360 K (K refers to thousands of bytes), whereas newer high-capacity 5¼-inch disk drives have a storage capacity of 1.2 Mb. Most new IBM-compatible computers come standard with a 3½-inch, 1.44 Mb floppy disk drive. Floppy disks can be easily destroyed by mishandling them.

Floppy disks are inexpensive and can be used in almost all kinds of microcomputers. For this reason, they must be formatted for the user's particular type of computer before they can be used to store data. When a disk is formatted, the

(continued)

computer simply prepares it to be used in the user's particular type of machine.

Hard disks also are common on nearly every type of microcomputer. Hard disks are much faster than floppy disks and are generally more reliable, since they are stationary and permanently reside in the computer. They come in many different sizes, ranging from forty Mb to five hundred Mb or more. The size of the hard disk a user may need depends on how the user intends to use the computer. An adequate amount of hard disk space is especially important because software programs continually take up larger and larger amounts of hard disk space. Users are sometimes surprised at how easy it is to fill up a hard drive.

Serial and Parallel Ports

Peripheral devices, such as printers and modems, must be connected to the computer to communicate with it. They are connected by either a serial or a parallel port at the rear of the microcomputer. Nearly all microcomputers come standard with at least one serial and one parallel port. Some peripheral devices, such as a modem and a mouse, are connected to the computer by a serial cable that attaches to the serial port at the rear of the computer. Some printers also use the serial method. Many printers are connected to microcomputers using a parallel cable that is attached to the rear of the computer at the parallel port.

Monitors and Display Adapters

Either monochrome or color monitors can be purchased for microcomputers. Many computers come standard with a color monitor, but monochrome monitors are cheaper. Most programs can take advantage of color monitors and some programs even require them. Many people think that color monitors are easier to look at than monochrome screens. A display adapter allows a computer and monitor to display detailed graphics on the screen. The display adapter and monitor must be compatible. Many computers use VGA or

SVGA color monitors and adapters for IBM-compatible computers. Monitors also come in a variety of sizes depending on your needs and your pocketbook, from fourteen-inch models to twenty-inch or greater models.

Open Architecture and System Expansion

Many microcomputers are built with an open architecture, which means that they can be easily expanded. Most of the components of a microcomputer are on boards that can be easily added to and removed from the computer. The mother board contains the essential elements of the computer, including the CPU, RAM chips, and more. The boards fit into electrical slots. Most microcomputers come standard with at least three open slots so that the user can add additional hard disks, additional RAM memory boards, or sound boards. In addition, many computers have the ability to upgrade the microprocessor in it as well. For instance, some 386 class IBM-compatible computers can be upgraded to 486 class machines.

Sound Board, Modem, and CD-ROM

A sound board is a computer board that fits into one of the open slots in the computer and gives the computer professional-quality sound. The speaker found in many computers is simply not adequate for complex sounds. A sound board allows the computer to produce high-quality music, synthesized speech, and other complex sounds.

A modem is a device that allows a computer to hook into phone lines and communicate with other computers across the country or across the world. For example, a modem is used to communicate with legal data bases such as WESTLAW and LEXIS. Most new modems come in different speeds, ranging from 2,400 to 14,400 baud rate or higher.

A CD-ROM drive allows a computer to access information on CD-ROM disks. Many CD-ROM

(continued)

(continued)

drives for computers can use data disks made for (computers, but they also can typically play CD-ROM music disks through the computer. Large amounts of data can be placed on CD-ROM data disks.

Sounds boards, modems, and CD-ROM drives typically are optional on most computers and depend on the needs of the user.

Compatibility

Compatibility is a key feature when considering microcomputers. Compatibility means that files and devices used on one kind of computer can be used by another computer without modifications. For instance, an Apple Macintosh and an IBM-compatible microcomputer are not compatible because a file saved on a Macintosh cannot be read by an IBM-compatible machine without modification. In addition, peripheral devices made for the Macintosh will not work with IBM-compatible machines.

For microcomputers to be compatible, they must be of the same type or use an agreed-upon standard. For instance, microcomputers that are IBM compatible, whether or not they actually are manufactured by IBM, are compatible and can exchange data and peripheral devices with one another. A file saved on one IBM-compatible machine could be read and used by a different IBM-compatible machine.

Recently, efforts have been made to improve compatibility among different kinds of computers. For example, some networks have the ability to link together different types of otherwise incompatible computers. In addition, some computer manufacturers are working together to solve their compatibility problems.

Printers

There are literally hundreds and hundreds of printers on the market. Laser printers, ink-jet printers, and dot-matrix printers are the most common. Dot-matrix printers are very inexpensive but typically do not have the quality of print that ink-jet or laser printers have. Laser printers are very common in law offices because of their high-quality output and their quietness. Printer speed also is a factor. For example, some laser printers print eight pages a minute, while others print four pages a minute. The prices of laser printers have dropped dramatically, so many users can afford them.

Tape Backup

A tape backup is used to back up or store an extra copy of the information on your hard disk onto tape cartridges. If your computer's hard disk fails or the computer is stolen, and if you have made a backup of your data, you at least have your data intact. A backup can be made using floppy disks, but this is very slow and requires large numbers of disks, say thirty or more to back up an eighty Mb hard disk.

---

single-task operating system environment
System that allows the execution of only one application program at a time.

multitask operating system
System that allows the execution of several application programs at the same time.

A **single-task operating system environment** *allows the execution of only one application program at a time.* If a user wants to load another program into memory, he must usually close the first program out of memory. For example, if a user wants to load a word processor program while a spreadsheet program is already running, he will have to exit the spreadsheet program before the word processor program can run. MS-DOS for IBM-compatible microcomputers is an example of this type of operating system.

A **multitask operating system** *allows the execution of several application programs at the same time.* This is useful to many users who like multiple applications running at a time and then switching in and out of each program at will. For example, in a multitasking environment, a user who wanted to refer to a word

Tape backups are quick and easy to use and ensure that your data are intact. Your data are only as safe as your last backup.

IBM Compatible and Apple Macintosh

Currently, the microcomputer market for law offices, as well as the market as a whole, is dominated by the IBM-compatible line of microcomputers (made by a variety of computer companies including IBM, Zenith, and Compaq) and the Apple Macintosh line. A recent survey showed that IBM-compatible machines have about 80 percent of the law office market.

However, there are many law offices, including some very large ones, that swear by the Apple Macintosh. Apple Macintosh machines have an easy-to-use, almost intuitive interface that makes learning and using them generally easier than IBM-compatible machines. Ease of use is the main selling point for the Macintosh over the IBM compatibles. Macintosh machines offer a wide variety of software, have good graphics, and have a wide variety of peripheral devices (including tape backup units, hard disk drives, sound boards, modems, CD-ROMS, etc.) available as well. There are many legal-specific programs available for the Macintosh, but not near the quantity and depth that are available for IBM-compatible machines.

IBM-compatible machines have a huge variety of software products, including a large market of law office-related software. The difference between software availability for the IBM and the Macintosh is that for every legal-specific type of program, there may be two or three products available for the Macintosh whereas in the IBM-compatible market there may be eight or ten. The breadth of the IBM-compatible software market is unparalleled. IBM-compatible machines also are cheaper than similarly equipped Macintosh machines. This is largely because many manufacturers produce IBM-compatible machines, which increases competition in the marketplace and forces prices down. On the other hand, Apple Computers is the sole manufacturer of Macintosh machines and has a virtual monopoly on them, so it has more flexibility in pricing. IBM-compatible machines, like the Macintosh, offer good graphics, a great deal of computing power, and many peripherals. Both IBM compatibles and Apple Macintosh are excellent lines of microcomputers. Either one will meet the needs of most users; the decision depends on the unique needs of each user.

Conclusion

Microcomputers increase the productivity and efficiency of the law office, no matter what kind of specific hardware is used. They are widely accepted and used in all sizes and types of law offices.

processing document while a spreadsheet was running could load both programs into the computer's memory and simply switch in and out of each program when needed. OS/2 for the IBM-compatible microcomputer is an example of this type of operating system.

APPLICATION SOFTWARE

Application programs make a computer useful. They can be custom-made, which means a programmer writes the application specifically for a particular user, or off-the-shelf, which is generic and will fill the needs of many users. Off-the-shelf software can be purchased from hundreds of software vendors, and prices are

FIGURE 9-11
Popular
Microcomputer
Operating Systems

Source: James F. Clark,
Warren W. Allen, and Dale
H. Klooster, *Computers and
Information Processing:
Concepts and Applications,*
2nd ed. (Cincinnati:
Southwestern Publishing
Co., 1990), 163. Adapted
and reprinted by permission
of the publisher.

*Limited multitasking
capabilities.

Operating System	Type of Computer	Multitasking
MS-DOS or PC-DOS	IBM compatible	No
MS-Windows	IBM compatible	Yes*
OS/2	IBM compatible (80286 & later microprocessors)	Yes
Multifinder	Apple Macintosh	Yes*
Finder	Apple Macintosh	No
Pro-Dos	Apple II	No
Unix	Workstations	Yes

more affordable than those for custom-made programs. Off-the-shelf legal software tends to be slightly higher priced than general business software, but there is still a wide selection of legal-specific software currently available for all types of law offices, including software that makes life administratively easier, software that makes practicing law easier, and software that connects the law office to the world. Some types of software, such as word processing, spreadsheets, and database program, can be used for administrative purposes and in the actual practice of law. Docket control software and timekeeping and billing software have already been covered in the text.

accounting software
Program that uses a
computer to track and
maintain the financial
data and records of a
business.

ACCOUNTING SOFTWARE   **Accounting software** *uses a computer to track and maintain the financial data and records of a business.* Accounting information is crucial to any type of law office. It is required for income tax purposes, to obtain loans, and to help in the operation and control of an organization. Computerized accounting programs are often less time-consuming to use than manual methods, are more error free, and usually produce better and faster final reports than do manual methods. Such accounting software can include a general ledger, accounts payable, accounts receivable, payroll, and trust accounting.

SPREADSHEET SOFTWARE   A spreadsheet is a computer program that calculates and manipulates numbers. Because a large part of law office management is related to financial management, spreadsheet software is used greatly by many law office managers. Figure 9-12 shows an example of a very simple law office budget. In addition to budgets, law office management uses spreadsheets for comparing financial alternatives (i.e. rent v. purchase decisions), tracking rents and other types of payments, managing cash flow, tracking profit distributions among partners, tracking payroll-related data, and many other uses. The power of spreadsheets is that they allow users to enter formulas that automatically add, subtract, multiply, divide, and perform other complex mathematical calculations on columns or rows of numbers quickly and easily. Once a formula is in place, individual numbers or values can be changed and the formula will automatically recalculate the new totals. Information in a spreadsheet also can be edited, copied, moved, graphed, saved, and much more. Spreadsheets also are used in the substantive practice of the law, such as calculating damages, calculating income taxes, and calculating loan payments and amortization schedules in a real estate transaction.

	B	C	D	E	F	G
3		BUDGET				
4	Item	Jan.	Jan.	Jan.	% Of	
5		Budget	Actual	Difference	Budget	
6	EXPENSES					
7	Utilities	$1,000	$400	$600	40%	
8	Equipment Rental	$500	$600	($100)	120%	
9	Insurance	$500	$450	$50	90%	
10	Rent	$1,500	$1,450	$50	97%	
11	Marketing	$200	$200	$0	100%	
12	Salaries	$15,000	$14,750	$250	98%	
13	Office Supplies	$750	$875	($125)	117%	
14	TOTAL EXPENSES	$19,450	$18,725	$725	96%	
15						
16	INCOME					
17	Fees	$22,000	$23,500	$1,500	107%	
18	Retailers	$5,000	$4,000	($1,000)	80%	
19	TOTAL INCOME	$27,000	$27,500	$500	100%	
20		=======	=======	=======	=======	
21	PROFIT/LOSS	$7,550	$8,775	$1,225	116%	
22		=======	=======	=======	=======	

FIGURE 9-12
Spreadsheet
Software

DESKTOP PUBLISHING   **Desktop Publishing** *is page layout and design using a* *computer.* Designing documents is sometimes referred to as page layout, since graphic art and text must be placed or "laid out" on each page of a document (see Figure 9-13). Desktop publishing allows the user to produce documents that look as if they came from a professional print shop and has the ability to produce a variety of typestyles or faces, graphics, and more.

Desktop publishing currently is being used in law offices to inexpensively produce professional-quality documents in-house without the expense of hiring outside offices. Desktop publishing is a relatively new application program that now has widespread acceptance. Desktop publishing also is being used in law offices to produce brochures, advertisements, newsletters, and briefs. For example, before desktop publishing, important briefs that needed to be filed with a court had to be sent out to be typeset by a professional printer. In addition to the office having to pay for the brief to be typeset, there also was a long turnaround time incurred, since once the brief was completed it had to be typeset by the printer, sent back to the office for corrections, sent back to the printer, and so on. With desktop publishing, a brief can be typeset in-house with virtually no turnaround time, with no fee, and without the security and confidentiality problems associated with using an outside service. All this is achieved with practically the same quality as with a professional printer.

DATA BASE MANAGEMENT SOFTWARE   *A* **data base** *is a computer program* *that organizes, searches, and sorts data.* A data base allows a user to enter information and then organize that data as she sees fit. For example, a law office might use a data base to track all its clients' names and addresses. Once the clients' names and addresses were entered into the data base, the names could be alphabetically sorted by the client's last name and printed (see Figure 9-14). A data base also can be used to search for specific information. Law office managers may use a data base for a variety of tracking purposes, including the number and types of cases they have, when certain office supplies will need to be reordered, tracking witnesses and exhibits (e.g., litigation support), creating a conflict-of-interest data

desktop publishing
Page layout and design using a computer.

data base
A computer program that organizes, searches, and sorts data.

FIGURE 9-13
Sample Firm
Brochure Produced
with Desktop
Publishing
Equipment

Johnson

Beck &

Taylor

Attorneys At Law

Dallas

New York

Los Angeles

JOHNSON, BECK & TAYLOR

Johnson, Beck & Taylor, with over a hundred and forty years of legal experience, is a cohesive team of attorneys in the business of practicing law with emphasis in commercial, contract, and legislative lobbying.

SERVICES

We provide a full range of legal service to you, our clients. Our services separate us from the rest. We take great pride in communicating with our clients at all stages of the proceedings, and by sending our clients copies of all documents filed. We strive to keep you informed.

- Dallas Office

  1700 First State Plaza
  Suite 1950
  Dallas TX 56424-2342
  (342) 942-5234

- New York Office

  1200 Prospect St. #242
  New York, NY 89323-2342
  (234) 543-5543

base for tracking past and current clients, creating a card catalog for a law library, or indexing past legal research topics.

Data bases can be used to organize virtually any type of information. Data bases can do this because they allow the user to tell the computer what kinds of information she will be working with (i.e. whether it is text, dates, money, etc.) and how the data are to be presented. Because the user actually sets up the system for each new type of information, the data-base program can be used over and over to track all types of data.

word processing program
Program used to edit, manipulate, and revise text to create documents.

WORD PROCESSING   A **word processing program** *is used to edit, manipulate, and revise text to create documents* (see Figure 9-15). Word processors allow the user to enter text and edit text without having to retype the entire document. Word processors are used heavily in law offices because nearly everything a lawyer or legal assistant does must be put in writing at one time or another. Word proces-

Last Name	First Name	Address	City	State	Zip	Work Phone	Home Phone	Case Number
Allen	Alice	P.O. Box 2342	San Diego	CA	95336	619-998-2589	619-465-4434	91-5234
	Mariam	2341 Huntoon	La Jolla	CA	92039	619-234-5345	619-764-3424	91-2342
Barney	Larry	23492 12th SE	Ocean Spray	CA	95334	619-293-2435	619-234-3332	90-2342
Davis	Karl	2941 Lane	La Jolla	CA	92039	619-443-9944	619-234-3455	90-3424
Johnson	Donald	32455 Coastal	Miami	FL	65773	673-256-2355	673-552-5489	91-2343
Kitchen	Jennifer	2342 45th St. NW	San Diego	CA	95334	619-887-4566	619-342-7521	91-2342
Robert	Den	23332 Westside Road	Marina Bay	CA	93442	615-933-5355	615-933-6500	90-3423
Winslow	Harriet	89404 Humbolt	Las Vegas	NV	78524	204-345-8624	204-346-9908	91-3424

FIGURE 9-14   A Data Base that Tracks a Law Office's Client List

sors allow attorneys and legal assistants the flexibility to change and edit documents whenever needed. A typewriter does not. In addition to being able to insert, delete, save, and retrieve information, there are many other features word processors have, such as automatic spell checking (i.e. checking a document for misspelled words), a built-in thesaurus, text copying, footnoting, line numbering, and tables of authorities.

In short, word processors are easy and convenient to use and let the user concentrate on the content of what he is writing. More word processors are used in law offices than any other type of computer software. In fact, many law offices require that legal assistants have some word processing skills as a minimum requirement for qualifying for the job. Common word processors include WordPerfect, Word, Display Write, and Ami Pro.

```
Word processors are easy to use and have many features such as:

                        Automatic Centering


Word processors have other features, such as automatic insertion
and deletion, and spell checking for misstakes.

Word processors can even copy whole blocks of text such as below
(notice that the text is double indented - another word processing
feature that is great for quotations):


          Word processors have other features, such as
          easy editing, automatic insertion and
          deletion, and spell checking for misstakes.

With a word processor you can change line spacing automatically,

such as this.  Finally, word processors have automatic page

numbering features, the ability to underline and embolden and more.
                              Doc 1 Pg 1 Ln 1" Pos 1"
```

**FIGURE 9-15
A Word Processing
Screen**

LITIGATION SUPPORT SOFTWARE   Litigation support systems assist attorneys in organizing, storing, retrieving, and summarizing information that is gathered in the litigation of a lawsuit. Because during the course of a lawsuit large quantities of documents and information are gathered, it is necessary that this information be organized to be used at the time of trial. For example, suppose you have a case with ten thousand documents in it, and you are requested to find all the documents that refer to a person named "John Doe." Using manual methods such as looking through all ten thousand documents could take weeks. Computerized litigation support software automates this process so that this search could be done in a matter of seconds. Computerized litigation support works much like a data-base management system. Once the data have been entered into the computer, the user simply tells the system what information she would like found or sorted and the system performs the request without affecting the data. Clerks, typists, or, in small offices, legal assistants may enter the information in the litigation support program. In addition, deposition transcripts on disk can be ordered from many court reporters so no data entry is required. The transcripts on disk are simply transferred to the computer with the litigation support system, and the system uses the transcripts to search for keywords.

CASE MANAGEMENT   Case management software organizes information to help the legal assistant and attorney manage or work the case. Notice in Figure 9-16 that case management software in that example helps the law office track client information, witness information, expert witness information, information about deposition and exhibits, and much more. Figure 9-16 refers to "modules." A module refers to a separate program that works in conjunction with another program.

DOCUMENT ASSEMBLY SOFTWARE   Document assembly refers to a computer program that merges information (such as a client's name and address) into

**FIGURE 9-16
Main Menu from a
Case Management
Program**

Source: Courtesy Micro
Craft, Inc.

```
Press the space bar to continue...

                    L I T I G A T O R


                    Master Menu:

A - Load Client module          J - Load Document module
B - Load Plaintiff module       K - Load Physical Exhibit module
C - Load Defendant module       L - Load Miscellaneous module
D - Load Attorney module        M - Load Issue module
E - Load Court module           N - Load Points & Authorities module
F - Load Court Filings module   O - Load Notes for Trial module
G - Load Witness module         P - Load Settlement Negotiations module
H - Load Expert Witness module  Q - Load Sort, Verify & Transfer module
I - Load Deposition module      R - Load Conflict and List module

Select (X to exit):  A
--------------------------------------------------------------------
The 18 options above make up the LITIGATOR Master Menu.  Options A
through P are used to enter, change, delete, and review data for any of
the sixteen categories listed above.  Option A is the Client module
which contains information about the client.  We have chosen Option A
for you.

Press the space bar to continue...
```

form documents or templates. Document assembly is similar to using the merge feature in many word processors, except that document assembly is more powerful and flexible. For instance, document assembly programs come with premade computer templates for workers' compensation cases, wills, trusts, deeds, corporate forms, leases, and other documents.

PRESENTATION GRAPHICS SOFTWARE   **Presentation graphics software** *allows a computer to produce professional quality charts and diagrams.* Presentation graphics programs take words and numbers and present them in a visual or graphic fashion. Most presentation graphics programs can produce pie charts, bar charts, line charts, area charts, or organization charts. In addition, once the information is entered into the program, it can be saved and edited if changes occur.

> **presentation graphics software**
> Software that allows a computer to produce professional-quality charts and diagrams.

Many law offices regularly use presentation graphics software because visual effects can be used to make complex or difficult information easier to understand. Further, visual effects, such as charts, help keep a jury's or an audience's attention and can be very persuasive. Presentation graphics can be used for both substantive and administrative purposes.

INTEGRATED SOFTWARE   **Integrated software** *combines several application functions into one.* For example, many integrated programs combine a word processor module, spreadsheet module, and data-base module into one program. There are several advantages to integrated software. One advantage is that the command structure in each module is the same. That is, the commands that are learned in one module of the program are the same or similar to the commands in the other modules. This is important, since the time it takes to learn the program would be less than when trying to learn the commands for three or four application programs that have completely different command structures. For example, the commands to move text in the word processor generally would be the same to move numbers in the spreadsheet.

> **integrated software**
> Software that combines several application functions into one.

Another advantage is that information can be exchanged between the modules very easily. If, for example, a legal assistant wanted to include a section of a spreadsheet in the word processing document, this task could be easily accomplished by simply copying the information from the spreadsheet into the word processor. Exchanging data between regular application programs is usually difficult. Another advantage is that integrated programs tend to cost less than individual programs that do the same applications.

The main disadvantage to integrated software is that the individual modules of the program are usually less powerful than the single application programs. This is an important consideration. The choice between using single application programs and an integrated program will depend on the needs of each particular user.

SUBSTANTIVE LEGAL-SPECIFIC PROGRAMS   Substantive legal-specific programs also are available. That is, these are programs that are designed for legal assistants and lawyers for a specific legal application. There are hundreds of types of programs, such as software designed for law offices that specialize in tax work, which calculates tax returns; bankruptcy software that automates the filing of bankruptcy petitions and other bankruptcy-specific documents and work; software for personal injury lawyers that automates personal injury litigation; or software that calculates different estate plans (see Figure 9-17). No matter what specialty a law office is in, there probably is a software program that will help automate it.

Microsoft Windows

What Is Windows?

Microsoft Windows is an IBM-compatible software application. Windows gives IBM-compatible computers a graphical interface much like an Apple Macintosh computer (see insert Figure 1). Without Windows, IBM-compatible computers use a text-based and sometimes hard-to-learn operating system called DOS. Windows acts as a manager for all the programs that you use. That is, when Windows is loaded, it runs in the background and allows other programs to operate "over the top" of it.

Graphical Interface

Many users prefer a graphical interface, since it is user-friendly, uses a mouse, and does not require users to memorize complicated DOS commands. Windows uses icons to depict programs. An icon is simply a picture that represents a particular computer program (see insert Figure 1). For example, ordinarily, to run a program in DOS, a user must know and enter the proper DOS commands to load the program. Using Windows, the user would simply use the mouse to point at the program's icon and press the mouse button twice.

In Windows, unlike many DOS programs, you see on the screen exactly what will print out. This is called WYSIWYG (What You See Is What You Get). That is, you will see information on the screen exactly as it will print, including seeing different font sizes (i.e. different styles and sizes of type), on-screen formatting such as centered text, page numbers, and so forth.

Windows Compatible Programs Offer Common Command Structure

There are many programs that are made to specifically run under Windows, such as WordPerfect for Windows and Lotus 1-2-3 for Windows. A wide variety of software companies currently produce versions of their programs specifically for Windows. Windows-compatible programs have similar menus, similar appearances, and similar command structures. This is a real benefit, since users do not have to learn totally new command structures for each new program. Many of the techniques and procedures learned in one Windows program will work in others as well. This standardization makes learning new programs easier and allows users to work among programs easily. In addition, many think that Windows versions of programs are easier to learn and use than their DOS counterparts.

Windows-Compatible Programs Can Share Information Between Each Other

Windows-compatible programs such as WordPerfect for Windows and Lotus for Windows can share information between each other. There is no such compatibility in most DOS applications.

Multiple Programs Running at the Same Time

DOS prohibits users from running more than one program at the same time. For example, if you were in your spreadsheet program and wanted to quickly type a letter on your word processor, you would have to quit the spreadsheet program, load the word processor, type your letter, quit the word processor and load the spreadsheet program again. However, Windows allows the user to run more than one program at a time. It is possible to have a word processor running in one "window" and a spreadsheet program running in another "window" at the same time.

A window is simply a place or box on the screen where a particular program is running. Users can control the size and shape of each window. They can make one window take up the entire screen and force the other open windows to the background where they cannot be seen, or they can make all the windows small so that more than one window can be displayed at the same time. Finally, an interesting feature of Windows is that it can run multiple DOS programs at the same time as well. So, even if users do not want to purchase the new Windows versions of programs, they can still take advantage of the Windows interface.

Windows Comes with Several Utility Programs

Windows comes with several utility programs that determine how Windows operates and even includes a Solitaire program, an easy-to-use but limited word processor, a drawing program, and a Rolodex-type card file.

Hardware Requirements

Windows is a complex program that requires large amounts of hard-disk space, large amounts of RAM, and quite a bit of computing power to run properly. 386 or higher microprocessors are recommended. Most new computers, even very inexpensive ones, come standard with a 486 or higher microprocessor, so most new computers can run Windows.

Conclusion

Windows is a powerful program that extends the capability of DOS. It provides users with a graphical interface, the ability to run multiple programs at the same time, many built-in programs, and a standardized command structure among Windows-compatible programs. Windows has become a useful and powerful force in the microcomputer market and offers users many advantages.

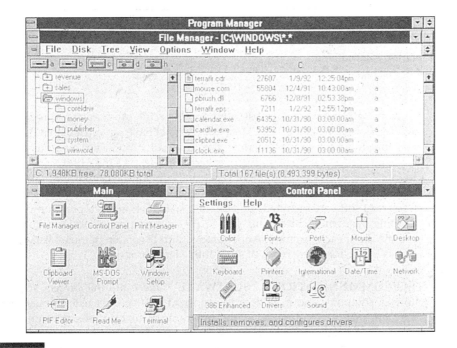

FIGURE 1   Windows 3.0 Application Programs

Source: Screen shot reprinted with permission from Microsoft Corporation.

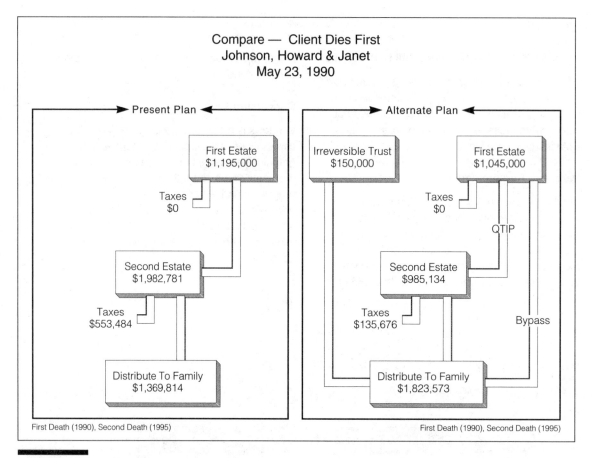

**Compare — Client Dies First
Johnson, Howard & Janet
May 23, 1990**

Present Plan

First Estate $1,195,000

Taxes $0

Second Estate $1,982,781

Taxes $553,484

Distribute To Family $1,369,814

First Death (1990), Second Death (1995)

Alternate Plan

Irreversible Trust $150,000

First Estate $1,045,000

Taxes $0

QTIP

Second Estate $985,134

Taxes $135,676

Bypass

Distribute To Family $1,823,573

First Death (1990), Second Death (1995)

FIGURE 9-17   Estate Planning Alternatives

Source: Courtesy Benefit Analysis, Inc., Wayne, PA.

Although finding such substantive legal-specific programs used to be difficult, that is no longer the case. Most bar journals have advertisements for these programs. In addition, the American Bar Association publishes an annual directory of law office computer software called *LOCATE. LOCATE* lists legal-specific programs for nearly every type of legal specialty and every kind of computer. Although a full review of each program would not be possible given the large numbers of software included, general information about each program is listed, including the manufacturer's name, address, and telephone and technical specifications about each program. Appendixes C and D contain itemized lists of software available for many types of substantive legal programs.

TELECOMMUNICATIONS SOFTWARE Telecommunications software allows a computer and a modem to send and receive data using phone lines. There are many telecommunications programs available. Telecommunications software, for instance, allows a user to access WESTLAW and LEXIS.

With a computer, modem, and telecommunication software, in addition to accessing WESTLAW and LEXIS (once you have properly subscribed), a user also can go "on-line" and have access to literally hundreds of different information services, including ABA/net, Compuserve, Dow-Jones, and DIALOG. An information service usually refers to a large host computer that stores large amounts of information and allows users access to that information for a fee. "On-line" means that a user is connected to a service and accessing information.

COMPUTER-ASSISTED LEGAL RESEARCH Legal research using manual methods is performed in a law library using books, periodicals, statutes, indexes, and digests. Manual legal research has many drawbacks, including having to go to a law library (during operating hours), trying to find appropriate key words and indexes that match your topic, finding the appropriate books (assuming they are not checked out), and then reading case by case until the information you are looking for is found.

Computer-assisted legal research searches the words of cases, statutes, and documents themselves. In addition, the research can be done at any time, day or night, and the user does not have to use indices. The user enters words that describe the issue and that would appear in the text itself, and the cases or statutes that use the words that were entered are retrieved. Although this may sound simple, it sometimes is not. For example, you may be searching for cases about "organ donation" and cases actually use the phrase "anatomical gift." Computer-assisted legal research does have some drawbacks, but it can be very beneficial.

ABA/NET ABA/net is an information system offered through the American Bar Association that is aimed exclusively at the legal market. Services on ABA/net include an electronic mail system (for sending electronic mail to other ABA/net users), a bulletin board system (this allows users to read and leave messages on "electronic bulletin boards"—useful for exchanging and reading interesting information and having ongoing discussions on topics that are available for all to read), and a gateway access to WESTLAW and LEXIS. A gateway access means an information service provides a "gateway" to another information service without requiring a separate password or subscription.

COMPUSERVE, DOW-JONES, DIALOG Compuserve is a large information service that offers hundreds of features to users, including on-line banking, weather reports, news, shopping, games, and bulletin boards. Dow Jones News/Retrieval is an on-line service designed to provide business and financial information such as up-to-the-minute stock quotes and financial news. For example, using this service, a user can get a corporate profile, an income statement, or a list of officers and directors for many publicly traded corporations. DIALOG is a large information service that provides access to thousands of different data bases. DIALOG provides articles and abstracts of articles on science, technology, engineering, chemistry, medicine, and hundreds of other areas.

Having access to these different information services means that users have instant access to millions of different services, resources information, other users, and products worldwide.

CONSIDERATIONS FOR PURCHASING APPLICATION SOFTWARE

Purchasing computer software can be difficult. Without taking proper precautions, it is easy to purchase a great-looking software package that does not meet your particular needs. You should do more than just rely on the word of a friend. Take the following considerations into account.

DETERMINE NEEDS

Many purchasers of computer software approach the buying process by reading advertisements and looking at what software products are on the market. Instead, the first step should be to determine exactly how you would like to use the software and identify what specific problems the software program will solve for you. Write down what features or capabilities the program you purchase should have. You also should consider future needs in addition to the capabilities you need currently. Once you have determined your needs and the capabilities the program should have, you are ready to begin looking for the right software product.

SURVEY THE MARKET AND OTHER FIRMS

The purchaser should begin the search for the right product by completely surveying the software market. This can be done by talking to software salespeople, reading computer magazines, and talking to users of the software programs you are considering. One of the most helpful sources is to find a review or an article on the product you are considering. Most computing magazines have reviews of software products in each issue. Also, some trade associations, such as the American Bar Association, have a committee that reviews software products. The reviews will offer insight into the product that you may not have considered yet. In addition, contact other law offices and professional associations in the area to see what programs are being used. This can be the best source of information, since a local law office may have recently implemented a program you are looking at. Computer users at other offices may be able to tell you what mistakes they made and how to avoid them.

LOOK FOR PRODUCTS WITH GOOD CUSTOMER SUPPORT

Good customer support is important. Too often, "customer support" means paying an extra fifty dollars to five hundred dollars a year on top of the purchase price of the software. The best kind of customer support is from companies that provide a toll-free (800) number with no extra charges. They also should have enough support staff to handle the number of calls they receive, otherwise a caller may be kept on hold for thirty minutes or longer. Try to buy software from manufacturers who really support their product.

CONSIDER TRAINING TIME

Before a product is purchased, the user should look at how long it will take to learn the program and what kind of learning aids the manufacturer has included. Good software will include a tutorial disk that teaches the user to use the product in an interactive environment. Other learning aids include a workbook, a separate quick reference card or template, a well-organized reference manual that is indexed, a well-documented installation guide, and a context-sensitive help key. Having a **context-sensitive help key** means that when the "help" key is pressed, the program displays messages that reflect the portion of the program you are in.

This is opposed to a help key that always displays the same message, no matter where the user is in the program. All these features will greatly reduce the amount of training time it takes to learn the program.

CONSIDER AVAILABILITY AND PRICE

Availability is another factor to consider when purchasing software. Do not buy a product based on features that may be in the next version of the program. Many times manufacturers will promise "revolutionary" products for a certain release date and then miss the release date by months or years. Generally, buy the product you see before you, not something a salesperson or an advertisement offers you in the future.

Finally, consider price and overall value of the program. If a program meets your needs, has been reviewed well, has good customer support, will be easy to learn, and is available now, it is worth a few extra dollars in the long run to buy the product over a product that is less expensive and questionable.

SOFTWARE AS AN INTEGRAL PART OF THE LAW OFFICE INFORMATION SYSTEM

A **law office information system** *is a combination of computer hardware, software, procedures, and human interaction that work together to solve problems in a law office.* The emphasis is on *system,* which means that all the separate components work together to achieve a common goal. Software is an integral part of a law office information system. It is important to note that no one piece of software can solve every problem. Instead, there must be a number of software products that go together to make up the law office's information system. The needs of each law office are separate and distinct, so there is no one information system that is best for all offices. The model system produces organized, relevant information that is available to all who need it, when they need, and in a useful form.

Figure 9–18 is an example of some of the main components of many law office information systems. This list is not meant to be exhaustive. Most law offices must be able to handle these types of problems and functions whether they use a computerized or a manual method.

law office information system
A combination of human involvement, computer hardware and software, and raw information that work together to solve problems in a law office.

"BUGS" AND COMPUTER VIRUSES

A **"bug"** *is computer slang for a programming error or glitch.* If a program is full of "bugs," it simply means that the program does not work correctly, "freezes up," or quits working for no apparent reason. Bugs are typically found in new programs or in new versions of existing programs.

A **computer virus** *is a computer program that is destructive in nature and can bury itself within other programs.* Computer viruses are intentionally programmed by people, usually as a joke or prank. Unfortunately, the damage they can do is tremendous.

bug
Computer slang for a programming error.

computer virus
A computer program that is destructive in nature and can bury itself within other programs.

FIGURE 9-18
The Main Components of a Law Firm Information System

Type of Software	Function
Word processing	Draft & edit documents, store documents, retrieve documents
Computerized legal research	Conduct legal research using a legal research data base (e.g., WESTLAW or LEXIS)
Timekeeping & billing	Track staff & attorney time records, produce client invoices
Litigation support	Tracking documents, testimony, & other information necessary for cases
Data base	Maintain a conflict of interest list, a client list, a case list, a legal research list, a library catalog, an expert witness list
Docket control	Track attorney schedules, appointments, deadlines, & commitments
Spreadsheet	Compile financial projections, prepare budgets, track financial information
Desktop publishing	Prepare brochures, advertisements, marketing pieces, briefs
Accounting	Track financial information necessary for the operation of a law firm

Computer viruses are small programs that bury themselves within other software, usually operating system software. The viruses can delete information, damage data on files, or harm hardware. Because the virus usually attaches itself to the operating system software, the program will execute each time the operating system loads (every time the computer is turned on). A computer virus can automatically spread itself when users exchange information or programs that contain the virus. A virus is usually spread by on-line bulletin boards or diskettes that have the virus on them. Some computer viruses can lay dormant for months until they are triggered by a certain date (like April Fools' Day).

There are several ways to protect your computer from computer viruses. Some of the ways are to carefully inspect the software programs you buy, use only programs by national manufacturers, and keep a regular backup copy of all your data. Another way is to buy an antivirus program, sometimes called a vaccine. A vaccine program notifies the user when a virus program is attempting to attach itself and blocks the virus from doing any damage. Some vaccine programs actually can delete or remove viruses if they do attach. Unfortunately, vaccine programs do not work 100 percent of the time.

Additional information on computer software is included throughout this text, including appendix G, which covers learning word processing, and appendix H, which covers data-base management.

SUMMARY

A computer or system unit works along with peripheral devices such as auxiliary storage and input, output, and communication devices to input, process, store, and output information. Every computer has a system unit, which contains the CPU and main memory. The CPU organizes and processes information in addition to coordinating storage, input, output, and communication devices. The main memory is made up of ROM and RAM, which hold information that is being processed.

Computers are available in three general size classifications: mainframe computers, minicomputers, and microcomputers. Storage devices store information so that it can be retrieved at a later time and include floppy disks, hard disks, and CD-ROMs.

Output devices provide the user with the data that the computer has generated. These include video display screens, printers, and modems. Printers are broken into two categories: impact and nonimpact.

Quality software is important for a computer system to function well. It is not necessary to understand how a software program works to use it. Operating system software manages the internal operations of the computer, whereas application programs accomplish a stated task. Some application programs used in law offices include word processing, spreadsheets, data bases, accounting software, timekeeping and billing software, and docket control.

A law office information system is a combination of computer hardware, software, procedures, and human interaction that work together to solve problems in a law office. The systems approach means that separate components work together to achieve a common goal.

KEY TERMS

Computer
Hardware
Computer programs
Operating system software
Input device
Output device
Storage device
Application software
Law office information system
Central processing unit (CPU)
Processor chip
Microprocessors
Main memory
Memory chips
Read only memory (ROM)
Random access memory (RAM)
Mainframe computer
Service bureau
Terminal
Keyboard
Monitor
Minicomputer
Microcomputer
Single-user system
Local area network
Wide area network
Peripheral devices
Storage capacity
Access time

Floppy disk drive
Hard disk
CD-ROM
Optical character recognition scanner (OCR scanner)
Mouse
Monochrome monitor
Color monitors
Printer
Impact printer
Dot-matrix printer
Daisy wheel printer
Nonimpact printers
Ink-jet printer
Laser printer
Communication device
Modem
Programmer
"Off-the-shelf" software
Single-task operating system environment
Multitask operating system
Data base
Word processing program
Presentation graphics software
Integrated software
Desktop publishing
Bug
Computer virus

PROBLEM SOLVING QUESTIONS

1. Three people in your office would like to economically share a large printer among them and to share information. The office is fairly small, but great productivity gains could be made by having access to one another's word processing and other types of documents. What do you recommend? If it was a large law office and you wanted to share information among branch offices in different cities, would your answer change?

2. You have been consulted by your law office to help choose a new computer system. You have not decided what size of computer you will need. What additional information would you like to have before you make a recommendation?

3. Your office needs to purchase at least three new printers that are at least letter quality or the same quality type that a typewriter would produce. Recently, office staff members have complained about the noise level being too high, so you should consider this fact. One of the printers needs to print quite fast and deliver outstanding quality documents. The office does not want to spend more than it has to. What do you recommend?

4. Having just graduated from a legal assistant program, you start work at a small law office. You notice that the office has a few computers. However, you notice that the only program that is used is a word processing program. The program is used to do word processing, but it also is used to do other things, such as limited data-base management. The office uses the sorting features of the word processor to make client lists and other data bases. The office also uses the word processor to prepare its billings and uses it to set up its budget. The office uses a manual accounting package and prepares financial statements (whenever they are needed) on the word processor also. The office uses its word processor as a total information system. After you have been with the office for several months, you speak to the partner of the office to make some gentle recommendations. What would they be?

5. As the manager of the legal assistant department in a large office, you are to plan and track the discovery process in a class action case that involves more than fifty parties. Your office is defending the action. Your job is to make sure that discovery documents, such as interrogatories, are sent out to each party; that each party responds in a timely fashion; and that any discovery documents any party sends to your client are answered in a timely fashion. You are overwhelmed by the task of trying to track all these deadlines and manage this job. What kind of software program(s) might help you with this project and how would it do so?

KNOW YOUR ETHICS

1. Your firm is considering purchasing a computer and software necessary to run a computerized docket control and conflict-checking system. The system will cost about four thousand dollars. One of the partners in the firm thinks that this is an unnecessary expense and that the simple calendar system the firm has used for years has always been sufficient. Using an ethics-related argument, "sell" the system to the partner.

PRACTICE EXERCISES

1. Contact a law office in your area and find out what types of computers, computer programs, and printers it uses. Be sure to ask which of these programs, printers, etc. it likes the best and why.

2. Using a state or national bar journal magazine, look for legal-specific reviews and advertisements regarding substantive legal programs. Journals such as *ABA Law Practice Management* and law office computing magazines such as *The Lawyer's PC* and *Law Office Computing* also are good sources.

3. Use a national computer magazine to compare and contrast three top word processing, data base or spreadsheet software programs for features, productivity, price, customer support, training, and other related topics. How do you think they would work in a law office? If you had to purchase one for an office, which one would you purchase and why?

NOTES

1. Brent D. Roper, *Computers in the Law* (Saint Paul, Minnesota: West Publishing Company, 1992), citing "Case History" by Andy Peterson of Paul, Hastings, Janofsky & Walker, 352.
2. Jack Baldwin-LeClaim, "Back to Basics: The Components of an Efficient Law Office," *Legal Assistant Today*, September/October 1992, 57.
3. Diane Patrick, "What's Hot and What's Not—Legal Assistant Hiring Trends," *Legal Assistant Today*, March/April 1992, 46.
4. David R. Hamourger, *Office Automation in Smaller Law Firms: A Survey Report*, 11. Prepared by the ABA Legal Technology Resource Center. Copyright 1989 by the American Bar Association, Chicago
5. Hamourger, *Office Automation in Smaller Law Firms: A Survey Report*.

FILE AND LAW LIBRARY MANAGEMENT

CHAPTER OBJECTIVES

After you read this chapter, you will be able to:

- Discuss alphabetic and numerical filing systems.

- Explain centralized and decentralized filing systems.

- Discuss the importance of closing and purging files.

- Explain why library ordering should be centralized.

- Give example of how law library costs can be reduced.

- For 2½ hours I searched for our file on tax issues in the State of Maine. I found it under "S."

- We finally located the agreement with Boeing under "N." It was labeled 1979 Aircraft Contracts by the lawyer and filed under "N" for "Nineteen" by the secretary.

- I waited two weeks for Alice to return to ask her about her previous work on a particular issue. She told me that Alan was the one who worked on it. He [Alan] said that his work would probably help me but that it wasn't the main issue in his case and he couldn't remember the file name.[1]

- The library is, without a doubt, the heart of the law office. Lawyers [and legal assistants] are in the business of doing legal research and reporting the results of that research to the courts, to their clients, and to each other.[2]

WHY LEGAL ASSISTANTS NEED AN UNDERSTANDING OF FILE AND LAW LIBRARY MANAGEMENT

Legal assistants work with files every single day. It is crucial that they know how to organize, track, and store client files. If a file or parts of a file are lost, misplaced, or misfiled, the effects can be devastating both to the office and to the client's case. Information must be stored so that it can be quickly found and retrieved. In many instances, legal assistants are responsible for organizing case files.

Like file management, legal assistants also must have a basic understanding of law library management. Legal assistants use the law library to conduct legal research, so it is important that they know how libraries work. In addition, many legal assistants, especially in smaller offices, actually may be in charge of maintaining the library.

INTRODUCTION TO FILE MANAGEMENT

Law offices of all types need a file system that allows them to store, track, and retrieve information about cases in a logical, efficient, and expeditious manner. The outcome of many legal matters depends on the case information gathered, including evidence, depositions, pleadings, discovery requests, and witness interviews. File information generally is worthless unless it is organized and available to the legal assistants and attorneys who will use it. File management is a large task no matter the size of the law practice.

Figure 10-1 contains characteristics that a good file system has. Each of these areas is vital to a law office, and none can be compromised. A poor file system has some or all of the following problems:

1. files are lost and cannot be found;
2. files are messy and disorganized;
3. office staff is unclear about how the filing system works;
4. attorneys and legal assistants do not trust the file system and keep their own files or keep the office's files in their possession;
5. staff is constantly aggravated and frustrated over the file system;
6. large amounts of time and money are wasted trying to find the file and information;
7. poor-quality legal services are given to clients because of the poor filing system.

> *Files are the nerve center of any law office. Therefore, the proper storage, safekeeping, and expeditious retrieval of information from the files is the key to the most efficient operation.*
>
> —**Paul Hoffman,** *Law Office Economics & Management Manual,* 1986, sec. 41:04, p. 4. Clark, Boardman and Callaghan, New York.

File management is an important topic, since law office management is responsible for providing an effective system that adequately supports its attorneys and legal assistants. Files and file systems represent a tool that the attorney and legal assistant use to provide their services.

FILING METHODS AND TECHNIQUES

There are different variations or filing methods that accomplish the objectives in Figure 10-1. Which filing method is used depends on the particular needs of each

FIGURE 10-1
An Effective File
Management System

Source: Adapted from
Deborah Heller and James
M. Hunt, *Practicing Law and
Managing People: How to
Be Successful* (Butterworth,
1988), 62. Courtesy of
Heller, Hunt & Cunningham,
Stoneham, MA.

1. **Completeness**—The files are complete and contain all of the information relevant to the case or matter.
2. **Retention**—Filing procedures ensure that all items are retained for the appropriate length of time.
3. **Integrity**—Files are maintained so that they are accurate, sound, and reliable.
4. **Ease of Use**—The file structure and file access provide for quick and easy location of files.
5. **Security**—Files are maintained in a safe environment which prevents unauthorized access to the system as a whole or to individual files.
6. **Ease of Learning**—The file system is candid, straightforward, and easy for others to learn.
7. **Adaptability**—The file system is flexible and easy to modify if structural or functional changes in the organization are necessary.

law office. These needs may include such factors as the number of attorneys in the firm, the number of cases that will be tracked and stored, the size and length of time typical cases are kept open or active, how much paper typical cases generate, the amount of space available for storage, whether the files will be kept in a central location, or whether departments or attorneys will keep their own files.

EACH LEGAL MATTER IS MAINTAINED SEPARATELY

No matter what filing method is used in a law office, it is essential that each case or legal matter be maintained separately. Even if one client has several legal matters pending, each case/legal matter should have its own separate file and should be given its own file number. Otherwise, there is the danger that documents will be misplaced or lost if all documents are commingled together.

When matters are commingled together, it affects other law office systems, such as conflict-of-interest checking (which determines whether the law office has a conflict of interest), docket control, and billing. Each case should be checked for conflict-of-interest problems, should have its own distinct and separate deadlines entered into the docket control system, and should be billed to the client separately.

ALPHABETIC SYSTEMS

alphabetic filing system
Filing method in which cases are stored based on the last name of the client or organization.

In an **alphabetic filing system** *cases are stored based on the last name of the client or name of the organization.* There is a natural tendency to alphabetize, since it is a system that most people understand. In addition, staff members do not need to memorize case numbers or use numerical lists, since a user knows exactly where the file should be in the drawer. Figure 10-2 contains some alphabetic filing rules.

The larger the number of cases the law office is handling, the more problems it will experience with an alphabetical system. This is because names are not all that unique; many clients may have the same last name. It is not efficient to look through four or five file drawers or cabinets of "Smith" files looking for the right

Rule 1. Alphabetize by arranging files in unit-by-unit (a word or individual letter) order and alphabetically within each unit.

For example, when filing a person's name, consider each word an individual unit:

Jackson	Wayne	T.
Unit 1	Unit 2	Unit 3

Company names are likewise filed in units:

Marilyn's	Doll	Shop
Unit 1	Unit 2	Unit 3

Rule 2. Each filing unit in a filing segment is to be considered. This includes prepositions, conjunctions and articles. The only exception is when the word "the" is the first filing unit in a segment. In this case, the "the" is the last filing unit.

	A	Moveable	Feast	Men's
Shop	The			
	Unit 1	Unit 2	Unit 3	Unit 1
Unit 2	Unit 3			

In the preceding examples, "A Moveable Feast" would be filed under "A." "The Men's Shop" would be filed under the "M" disregarding the "The."

Rule 3. File single unit segments before multiple-unit segments. In other words, a single name would be found in the file before an identical name with an initial. Initials go before names beginning with the same letter. if the last names (the first unit) are identical, the first name or middle initial (second unit) determines the order. If the last and first names are identical, the middle name or initial determines the sequence. For this rule to become more clear, review the following examples:

Thompson		
Thompson	M.	
Thompson	M.	S.
Thompson	Michael	
Thompson	Michael	B.
Thompson	Mitchell	B.
Thompson	R.	John
Thompson	Richard	F.
Thompson	Richard	Henry
Unit 1	Unit 2	Unit 3

If there are two identical names in the same file, file first by order of the town or city, then by the state, next by the street name and last by the numeric order of the house or building:

Indexing

By	Conley	Katherine	G.	Lexington	Kentucky

(continued)

FIGURE 10-2
International Alphabetic Filing Rules

Source: Copyright 1972, 1985, 1986. Extracted with permission from *Alphabetic Filing Rules*. For information on the complete publication contact: Association of Records Managers and Administrators, Inc., 4200 Sommerset Dr., Suite 215, Prairie Village, KS 66208 (913) 341-3808.

Town or City	Conley	Katherine	G.	Louisville	Kentucky	
Indexing By State	Kinney	Martha	T.	Decatur	Georgia	
	Kinney	Martha	T.	Decatur	Illinois	
Indexing By Street Name	Low	Glen	S.	Canton	Ohio	Oak St.
	Low	Glen	S.	Canton	Ohio	Wren Ln.
Indexing By House Or Building Number	Benson	Ted	R.	Houston	Texas	Rose St. 244
	Benson	Ted	R.	Houston	Texas	Rose St. 311

Rule 4. Ignore all punctuation hen alphabetizing. This includes periods, commas, dashes, hyphens, apostrophes, etc. Hyphenated words are considered one unit.

Below are some examples. Note that the left column is how the company names are commonly seen written and the right column is how they should appear in your files:

A.A.A. Printing	AAA	Printing	
A T & T Company	ATT	Company	
A-1 Tire Company	A1	Tire	Company
B & B Restaurant	BB	Restaurant	
Unit 1	Unit 1	Unit 2	Unit 3

Rule 5. Arabic and roman numerals are filed sequentially before alphabetic characters. All arabic numerals precede roman numerals. For example:

| 21 Club | III Estate | IV Brigade |

Rule 6. Acronyms and radio and television station call letters are filed as one unit, as follows:

| WGN | WTR |

Rule 7. File under the most commonly used name or title. Cross-reference under other names or titles that might be used in an information request. For example:

American Telephone & Telegraphy

File under: "ATT" and cross-reference in your files.

If an alphabetic entry is especially difficult, check the phone book. The phone book has strict guidelines and makes an excellent reference guide.

Source: Copyright 1972, 1985, 1986. Extracted with permission from *Alphabetic Filing Rules*. For information on the complete publication contact: Association of Records Managers and Administrators, Inc., 4200 Sommerset Dr., Suite 215, Prairie Village, KS 66208 (913) 341-3808.

case. It also is not uncommon for clients to have the same first and last names. Other systems, such as a numerical system, can track an infinite number of cases with a unique number and also can protect the confidentiality of the client better, since the client's name is not the identifier for the file and is not on all the files. In offices with a large number of cases, an alphabetic system may not be the best kind of filing system. Alphabetic systems also are difficult to expand and can mean constantly shifting files to make room for more.

NUMERICAL SYSTEMS

In a numerical filing system, each case or legal matter is given a separate file number. This is similar to when a case is filed with a court; a clerk assigns each action or lawsuit a separate case number. Case identifiers can be, but do not necessarily have to be, all numbers (i.e. 234552). Variations can be used such as alphanumeric in which letters and numbers are used. For instance, a letter might be used in the case number to reflect which branch office is handling the case and two of the numbers might reflect the year the case was filed, such as LA94–990004. The "LA" might stand for the office's Los Angeles office, and "94" stand for 1994, the year the case was initiated.

Letters also may stand for types of cases—"PB" for probate, "TX" for tax—for a particular attorney—"Patricia Burns"—and so forth. Even in a numerical system, however, legal matters for the same client can be kept together. For instance, in the example "LA94–990004," "99" could represent the client's personal number and "4" could mean that this is the fourth case that the office is handling for the client.

Some offices use a client number system followed by a matter number. For example, an office might use a case number such as 2343.001. The first set of numbers, "2343," represents the client number and the last three digits represent the legal matter number. Finally, another numerical filing method is to assign a range of numbers to a particular type of case, such as 000–999 for trusts; 1,000–1,999 for tax matters; and 2,000–2,999 for criminal matters.

A filing rule that sometimes bears out is that the longer the case number, the more misfiling and other types of errors occur. Also, shorter numbers can be remembered easier. Numerical filing also solves the shifting problems with alphabetical systems. When a new case is taken, the next sequential number is given to the file, and it is stored accordingly. This is opposed to an alphabetic system, where a new file is stored by the client's name. When the new file is added to the existing drawer, the drawer already may be filled an d then someone must shift or move files to make room for the new file.

Law offices also may have billing codes or numbering systems that reflect internal matters such as time spent on personnel-related issues, marketing, or whatever. These types of matters also may be given a file number. It is important to remember that there is no set way for designating files; it all depends on the needs of the office.

BAR CODING

Bar coding *is a file management technique in which each file is tracked according to the file's bar code.* Each time a user takes a file, the file's bar code and user's bar code are scanned into a computer. The computerized system then tracks which user checked out which file. When the file is returned, the file's bar code is scanned back into the computer. A report can be generated anytime listing what files are

bar coding
A file management technique in which each file is tracked according to the file's bar code.

checked out and by whom. Using this system, it is possible to find the location of files quite easily. Bar codes are used in many libraries to track the library's collection, and bar coding of law office files works much the same way.

CORPORATE, GOVERNMENT, AND LEGAL AID FILING METHODS

Corporate law departments and government departments may arrange their matters differently. They may file matters by subject, by department, or by other means that suit their particular industry or need. Legal aid offices typically file cases alphabetically or even geographically, by city or county.

CENTRALIZED V. DECENTRALIZED

centralized file system
Method in which a file department or file clerk stores and manages all active law office files in one or more file rooms.

decentralized file system
System in which files are kept in various locations throughout the law office.

A fundamental law office filing consideration is whether the filing system will be centralized or decentralized. *A **centralized file system** is where a file department or file clerk stores and manages all active law office files in one or more file rooms. In a **decentralized file system,** files are kept in various locations throughout the law office, such as each department storing its own files or each attorney keeping his own files.*

A centralized system is typically used when the law office has a high secretary turnover rate (in decentralized systems, secretaries do much of the filing); when the office has a complex filing procedure best handled by one department or file clerk staff; when the office wants a highly controlled system; or when several attorneys or legal assistants work on the same cases. Even though a law office may want a centralized system, the office must have the physical space to accommodate it. Law offices in which a single attorney or legal assistant works on each case, such as real estate matters, or needs the case files for long periods of time may use a decentralized file system where the files are located in an individual's office or in a secretarial area. Some offices use a "pod," or team filing system, where several people, perhaps two or three attorneys, a secretary, and a legal assistant or two, have offices located close to one another and have their files stored next to them. Some offices may use a combination. Whether an office uses a centralized or decentralized system depends on the size of the office, type of cases handled, and the needs of the personnel involved. Closed files are almost always kept in a centralized location.

OPENING FILES

When a new or existing client comes into the office with a new legal matter, a new file should be immediately opened. The opening of a file should be standardized and should require certain information about the legal matter. A file opening form (sometimes called a new client/matter form or casesheet) is customarily completed when opening a new file (see Figures 10-3 and 10-4).

file opening form
A standardized form that is filled out when a new case is started. The form contains important information about the client and the case.

*The **file opening form** is used for a variety of purposes, including to check potential conflicts of interest, to assign a new case number and attorney to the matter, to track the area or specialty of the case, to set forth the type of fee agreement and billing frequency in the case, to enter the case in the timekeeping and billing system, to make docketing entries such as when the statute of limitations in the matter might run, and to find out how the client was referred to the law office.* Although file opening forms are commercially available, most law offices choose to customize the form to reflect their own needs.

Billing No. _____
Date_____Opened _____Closed

New File

New File (Check one)
___ INDIVIDUAL
_____
    Last   First   Middle Initial

___ ENTITY
_____
    (Use complete name & common abbreviations; place articles [e.g., The] at end.)

___ CLASS ACTION
_____
    (File Name, ex.: Popcorn Antitrust Litigation)

Matter (Check one)
___ NON-LITIGATION _____
___ LITIGATION _____
_____ Approved for litigation by—MUST BE INITIALED by submitting attorney!!

Nature of the Case

Area of law code _____   Summary of work or dispute: _____

_____

Client Contact (N/A for Class Actions)
Name: _____
Company: _____
Street: _____
City, State, Zip: _____
Telephone: _____

Billing Address (N/A for Class Actions)
Name: _____
Company: _____
Street: _____
City, State, Zip: _____
Telephone: _____

Team Information (Use initials)
___ ___ ___   Managing Attorney(s) (for non-litigation cases only)
___ ___ ___   B II Review Attorney(s)
___ ___ ___   Originating Attorney(s)
___ Calendar Attorney (for litigation cases only)
___ Legal Assistant (for litigation cases only)
___ Secretary to Calendar Attorney (for litigation cases only)

Referral Source (Check one)
___ Existing Client _____
                    Name
___ Non-Firm Attorney _____
                    Name
___ Firm Attorney or Employee _____
___ Martindale-Hubbell
___ Other _____

FIGURE 10-3   File Opening Form

Fee Agreement (Check those that apply)

___ Hourly

___ Contingent _____ %

___ Fee Petition

___ Fixed Fee $ _____ or Fixed Range from $ _____ to $ _____

___ Retainer $ _____

___ Letter of Retainer sent by _____ on _____

___ ___   (Initials)   (Date)

Statement Format (Check those that apply)

Do you want identical disbursements grouped?   _____ Yes _____ No

Do you want attorney hours relflected on *each* time entry?   _____ Yes _____ No

Do you want fees extended on *each* time entry?   _____ Yes _____ No

---

Conflict check	Docket Entries

Conflict Check Completed By: _____   **Date:** _____

        (Initials)

Conflict Check Not Needed: _____

    (Initials of Submitting Person)

Statute of Limitations

_____

Other deadline:

_____

Check One:

___ No conflicts

___ Potential conflict with the following existing parties (from computer system):

_____

_____

    (Or attach computer printout from Conflict Check System.)

*New Adverse Parties

_____

_____

_____

*New Related Parties (for Class Actions, Named Plaintiffs Only):

_____

_____

_____

*Will be entered into computer system by Bus. Dept. *AFTER* approval by Managing Partner.

Closed File

Retain File For: 3, 5, 7, 10 yrs.

Date Closed: _____   Atty. or Sec. Initials: _____

_____ Attach Pleadings and/or File Indexes. If indexes are not available, attach brief description of what is contained in the file(s). SEND FILES, THIS FORM, AND INDEX TO FILE ROOM.

FIGURE 10-3   File Opening Form *(Continued)*

Source: Intro. to Paralegalism, Statsky, West Pub., 1992.

CASE NO. ASSIGNED _____

CLIENT MASTER INFORMATION

CLIENT NAME _____

ADDRESS _____   DATE OPENED _____   RESPONSIBLE ATTORNEY _____

_____   REVIEWING PARTNER _____

ATTENTION _____   BILLING PARTNER _____

PRESENT CLIENT

TELEPHONE NO. _____   ☐ NEW CLIENT   ☐ NO _____

CASE MASTER INFORMATION

RESPONSIBLE ATTORNEY NO. _____   BILLING PARTNER NO. _____

DESCRIPTION OF MATTER _____

ADVERSE PARTY OR OTHER CROSS-REFERENCE _____

FIELD OF SPECIALTY (2) CIRCLE AS APPROPRIATE)

01 ADMIN. AGENCIES	11 LABOR	19 REAL ESTATE
02 ANTITRUST	12 MUNICIPAL	20 SECURITIES
03 BANKS AND S. & L.	13 PATENT & TRADEMARK	21 TAX
04 BANKRUPTCY	14 PERSONAL INJURY — DEFENSE	22 WORKMEN'S COMP.
05 COLLECTIONS	15 PERSONAL INJURY — PLAINTIFF	23 I.C.C.
06 CORP., PART., PROP.	16 MINOR SUBROGATION	24 OTHERS (SPECIFY)
07 CRIMINAL	(UNDER 10,000.00)	
08 DOMESTIC RELATIONS	17 MAJOR SUBROGATION	
09 INVESTMENT	I(OVER 10,000.00)	
10 WILLS & ESTATES	18 INSURANCE LAW	

TYPE OF FEE

☐ 1 PER DIEM
☐ 2 PER DIEM WITH RETAINER
☐ 3 FIXED BILL
☐ 4 FIXED PERIODIC BILL
☐ 5 CONTINGENT
☐ 6 NONBILLABLE

TO BE COMPLETED BY ATTORNEY OPENING FILE

BILLING FREQUENCY — SERVICES   BILLING FREQUENCY — DISBURSEMENTS

☐ 1 MONTHLY   ☐ 1 MONTHLY
☐ 2 QUARTERLY   ☐ 2 QUARTERLY
☐ 3 SEMIANNUALLY   ☐ 3 SEMIANNUALLY
☐ 4 ANNUALLY   ☐ 4 ANNUALLY
☐ 5 ON DEMAND   ☐ 5 ON DEMAND

UNBILLED SERVICES CONTROL AMOUNT $ ____   DISBURSEMENT CONTROL AMOUNT $ ____

TYPE OF FILE: ☐ CONTINUING TYPE ☐ WILL BE CLOSED UPON COMPLETION OF A SPECIFIC ITEM

ESTIMATED FEE POTENTIAL $ ____   SOURCE OF CASE ____

TYPE OF FILE HOLDER TO BE USED: ☐ EXPANSION ☐ MANILLA ☐ ORANGE

ENTERED INTO MASTER INDEX BY ____   DATE ____

ENTERED INTO DATA PROCESSING BY ____   DATE ____

MASTER INDEX CHECKED FOR CONFLICT BY ____   DATE ____

REMARKS

ALL COPIES TO ACCOUNTING OFFICE — White copy retained in Accounting Office; Canary Copy to reviewing partner; Pink Copy to client's file.

FIGURE 10-4   Another File Opening Form

Source: *The Lawyer's Handbook*, 2d ed. (American Bar Association, copyright 1963). Reprinted with permission.

Copies of the file opening form may be sent to the managing partner, other attorneys, accounting department, docket-control department, and the responsible attorney.

FILE FORMAT/INTERNAL FILE RULES

The format or how case files are set up and organized depends on the needs of the office and how the office thinks the organization will best be served. The type of file format will depend on the filing system that is used. As an example, vertical file drawers require the tab at a different place than does an open-shelf filing system that requires tabs on the side.

Many offices use separate manila files as subdivisions in the same case to differentiate information in the same file, such as having files for "Accounting," "Discovery," "Pleadings," "Client Correspondence," and others (see Figure 10-5). The individual manila files are stored in one or more expanding files, so that all the files for one case are kept together. Also, many offices use metal fasteners in the manila files to hold the papers securely in place. The exception to this is that original documents should not be punched. Instead, they should be maintained separately and a copy put in the regular file. Finally, information typically is placed in each manila file in chronological order with the oldest on the bottom and newest on top of the file. This gives the user a systematic way of finding information. It is routine to find duplicate and draft copies of documents in a file. However, duplicates and drafts only make the organization process harder. If duplicates must be kept, they should be in a separate file folder called "duplicates."

COLOR CODING

Color coding files is a simple but effective way to reduce the number of misfiled documents. Files can be color coded in a variety of ways, such as determining that red-labeled files are probate or green files are criminal matters. Color coding also can be done according to the year the case was opened or according to the attorney handling the matter.

**FIGURE 10-5
Typical
Subcategories of
Files**

Accounting
Correspondence with Client
Correspondence with Attorneys
Deposition Summaries
Discovery
Evidence
General Correspondence
Investigation
Legal Research
Memorandums
Notes & Miscellaneous
Witnesses

The High Cost of Misfiling

A recent survey found in the average office that:

- *19 paper copies are made of each original;*
- *7.5 percent of paper documents are lost completely;*
- *3 percent of paper documents are misfiled;*
- *$20 in labor in spent filing or retrieving a document;*
- *$120 in labor is spent finding a misfiled document;*
- *$250 in labor is spent recreating a lost document.*

—*Via Fedex*, Summer 1993, 2.

Color coding also can be used for cases that are especially sensitive or that need to be especially secure. For example, if the law office is trying to create a "Chinese wall" to keep a staff member from participating in a case, it can alert others to the need for security by assigning a certain color of file label to the case. Finally, color coding can be used in an alphabetic filing system. For example, A to E equals blue; F to J equals green, and so forth. Many law office supply catalogs carry all types of color-coded files for the law office.

CHECKING FILES OUT

In some law offices where many people have access to files, users are required to complete checkout cards similar to library cards, which state the file number checked out, who is checking the file out, how long the file is expected to be needed, and other information. This is similar to most court systems, where the original documents are filed with the court clerk, but the file can be checked out by anyone. It can be quite frustrating to search and search for a client file and discover that someone else took the file home to work on it.

CLOSING, STORING, AND PURGING FILES

After a legal matter has come to a conclusion, and after the final bill has been paid, the file is closed and taken out of the storage area of active files. It is boxed up and kept in the office's basement or an off-site storage facility (for a certain number of years until it is destroyed) or put on microfilm or microfiche.

A closed file is sometimes called a "dead file" or a "retired file." When a case is closed, some offices give the case a new number to differentiate it from active cases. The closing of cases represents a problem for many law offices. Attorneys like to have access to closed files in case they need the information in them someday. Storage space can be quite expensive. Most law offices are continually opening and closing cases, which means that the flow of files never stops and that the required storage area gets larger and larger. To reduce file storage requirements, duplicate copies of documents should be removed.

> *Most attorneys cannot rest comfortably knowing that closed client files have been destroyed, yet the actual frequency of need for a file which has been closed for more than one year is very low. Because of unwillingness to authorize file destruction, most law offices build up huge quantities of old paper which often end up in lofts, basements, barns, abandoned buildings, or worst of all, on the office's premises in increasingly expensive space.*
>
> —*via Fedex,* Summer 1993, 2.

One solution is to purge or destroy files after a certain period of time (see Figure 10-6). One researcher estimates that every file cabinet that is emptied will save the organization six hundred dollars a year in storage-related costs.[3] Some law offices purge all files after a certain number of years, such as seven or eight, while others purge only selected files. Destroying files usually means shredding, burning, or recycling them. Simply throwing them away does not protect the client's confidentiality and should not be done. Another alternative is to microfilm closed files. Drawbacks are that the cost of microfilming can be fairly expensive and that the information is not as usable as the original document. However,

FIGURE 10-6 Sample Record Retention Periods

Source: Adapted from Association of Legal Adminsitrators. Reprinted with permission.

Source: Adapted from Association of Legal Administrators. Reprinted with permission.

Law Office Administration	Retention Period
Accounts Payable and Receivable Ledgers	7 yrs.
Audit Reports	Permanently
Bank Statement and Reconciliations	3 yrs.
Cash Receipt Books	Permanently
Canceled Checks (except for payments of taxes, real estate, and other important payments—permanently)	7 yrs.
Contracts, mortgages, notes, and leases (still in effect)	Permanently
Contracts, mortgages, notes, and leases (expired)	7 yrs.
Correspondence, general (except important matters—permanently)	7 yrs.
Deeds, Mortgages, etc.	Permanently
Employment Applications	3 yrs.
Financial Statements (Year End)	Permanently
Insurance policies (expired)	3 yrs.
Invoices	7 yrs.
Minutes of directors and stockholders meetings	Permanently
Payroll records	7 yrs.
Retirement and Pension Records	Permanently
Tax Returns	Permanently
Timecards	7 yrs.

Client Files and Documents

- Retention of client files and client-related documents depends on the ethical rules in your state.
- Before destroying a client file, contact the client to make sure she does not want the file or want something out of the file.
- When destroying client files, burn, shred, or recycle them to ensure client confidentiality.

when considering the cost of long-term storage, microfilming actually may be less expensive in the long run.

ORGANIZATION OF FILES— A MAJOR LEGAL ASSISTANT DUTY

File organization is a large part of what many legal assistants do. They must use files on a daily basis. Therefore, for most legal assistants to become efficient at what they do, they must be able to organize and in some cases index case files in a logical and systematic fashion so they can quickly find information. Case material also must be organized in such a way that others, such as attorneys, can find the information quickly. A file that is an unorganized mess is useless in a law office. For instance, if the legal assistant is assisting an attorney at a deposition and the attorney asks her to find a specific answer in the discovery request, she must be able to quickly locate it. If the legal assistant is not familiar with the case, does not have the file organized, or misfiled the document, she will not have the ability to find the information quickly, and the client's case may suffer.

FILE MANAGEMENT EQUIPMENT

There are several types of equipment used to manage and store files, including file drawers, shelf files, automated filing equipment, micrographics, imaging, and bar coding.

> *The combined costs of filing equipment, supplies, floor space taken up by the equipment, and clerical help necessary to maintain the files form a considerable portion of overhead expenses. It is mandatory to give careful consideration to filing equipment in order to have the most efficient system for the least possible overall cost.*
>
> **—Paul Hoffman,** *Law Office Economics and Management Manual,*
> 1992, sec. 41:04, p. 1. Clark, Boardman and Callaghan, New York

FILE CABINETS

Many law offices still use standard file cabinets for storage of active files. File cabinets come in varying sizes from two to five drawers in either legal or letter size. File cabinets have an advantage over some other kinds of storage equipment in that they can be fire retardant (although they are more expensive than regular models) and lockable. File cabinets can be either vertical or lateral style.

Vertical file cabinets can be from two to five drawers high. Drawer depths range from eighteen to twenty-eight inches. Vertical file cabinets are relatively inexpensive, offer a neat appearance, an can be locked for security purposes. Unfortunately, they waste the most amount of space, require large aisles (so the drawers can pull out), and have several other disadvantages as well.

Lateral file cabinets are wider than they are deep, and folders are placed across the length of the drawer. They take less floor space and contain more internal file space than vertical file cabinets. They also can lock and have a neat appearance. They typically are the most expensive type of filing system, sometimes twice as much as vertical file cabinets.

shelf filing
Method in which files are stored on a shelf, much like books in a library would be stored.

Shelf filing *is where files are stored on a shelf, much like books in a library, rather than in closed drawers that are pulled out.* The file tab projects out on the side instead of from the top like in file drawer files. Larger offices use shelf filing because shelf files take up 50 percent less floor space than drawer files with the same maximum capacity. The space savings is because shelves will rise above five feet, since the tabs are read from the side and not the top, and because only thirty inches is needed between the rows of shelves, whereas file cabinets need fifty-four to sixty inches to allow for the drawers to open comfortably.[4] In addition, the shelves can be stacked higher than drawers and still be reachable, since there are no drawer fronts to hinder access to high shelves. Shelf files come in models with and without fronts or doors on them. Figure 10-7 shows a filing space comparison chart of a vertical filing cabinet, a lateral filing cabinet, and shelf filing.

MOBILE STORAGE SYSTEMS

Mobile storage systems are movable shelving that use wheels and that roll on tracks in the floor. This allows shelves to be moved as needed and allows adjustments in aisle width; they are generally more flexible than normal shelving or file drawers.

AUTOMATED FILING EQUIPMENT

automated filing equipment
File shelving that automatically moves the files to the individual using the equipment.

Various **automated filing equipment** *is available where the file shelving automatically moves the files to the individual using the equipment.* Although the equipment is very expensive compared with other more conventional methods, time and energy are saved and a large number of files can be maintained by one person. Automated systems are used in courthouses and in law offices that have a large volume of cases. In addition to the equipment being expensive, the floor-load capacity must be from four hundred to five hundred pounds per square inch. The average floor-load capacity in many buildings is about one hundred pounds per square inch.

MICROGRAPHICS

micrographics
Means of storing files photographically using microfilm or microfiche on small pieces of film or plastic.

Micrographics *is a means of storing files photographically using microfilm or microfiche on small pieces of film or plastic.* Micrographic storage requires about 3 percent of the space required for hard copy documents. Offices can buy their own photography equipment and use their personnel to shoot the documents or they can hire a service bureau to perform the microfilming. A typical initial investment for a law office is twenty thousand dollars. A service bureau will charge approximately three to five cents per page.

Both of these methods are fairly expensive, but if documents must be kept for long periods of time, the initial investment may be cheaper than paying very high storage costs for years to come. It is estimated that the cost of producing microfilm is prohibitively expensive in law offices with fewer than forty attorneys.[5] In addition to the photography equipment needed, a reader also must be purchased to read the microfilm or microfiche. If hard copies of the documents are needed, a reader with a copy-machine-like device attached is needed.

FILING SPACE EFFICIENCY

FILE SYSTEM TYPE	Vertical - 4 Drawer	Lateral - 4 Drawer	4 Shelf - Open
Size (Height, Width, Depth)	52" x 15" x 26"	54" x 36" x 19"	50" x 36" x 13"
Internal Filing Space	100 Inches	144 Inches	180 Inches
Floor Space	5.50 Sq. Ft.	9.00 Sq. Ft.	3.25 Sq. Ft.

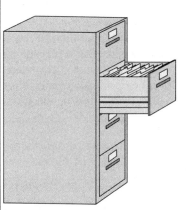

Vertical File

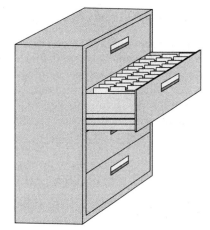

Lateral File

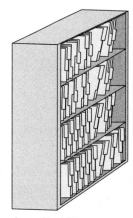

Open-Shelf File

FILE SYSTEM TYPE	ADVANTAGES	DISADVANTAGES
Vertical File Cabinet	• Inexpensive • Neat appearance • Can be locked	• Requires the most amount of room • They "stick out" and can take up as much as 44 inches of aisle space • Filing time is slow due to opening and closing drawer • Only one person is allowed to access documents at a time • Waste a lot of space if space is important • Contain far less internal file space than other methods
Lateral File Cabinet	• Saves floor space • Contains more internal file space than vertical file cabinets • Can be locked • Neat appearance	• More expensive than either vertical or open shelf • Filing time is slow due to opening and closing drawer • Only one person can access documents at a time
Open Shelf	• Takes up less floor space than either vertical or lateral cabinets • Contains more internal space than vertical or lateral cabinets • More than one person has access to documents at a time • Are relatively inexpensive	• Open shelves without doors may pose a security risk • Must use side tabbed folders instead of top tabbed folders • If you need to remove a document you must remove the whole folder

FIGURE 10-7   Filing Systems

IMAGING

imaging
The capture, retrieval, and storage of document images.

Imaging *refers to the capture, retrieval, and storage of document images.* Images are captured and stored on optical disks (CD-ROM), which greatly reduces storage needs. Document and images retrieval time is greatly improved and almost no misfiling of information is possible. Once the images are captured and stored, they can be viewed using a computer. Imaging is a quickly emerging technology.

FILE MANAGEMENT AND ETHICS

There are several ethical questions that should be addressed when considering filing and filing systems. These issues include performing conflict-of-interest checks before a new case is taken, maintaining client-related property that is turned over to the law office during representation, maintaining trust and client-related accounting records, returning a client's file to him if he decides to change attorneys, and ensuring that the office's filing system and/or file destruction procedures maintain client confidentiality.

CONFLICT-OF-INTEREST CHECKS

It is important when a new case is being considered that a conflict-of-interest check be made immediately to ensure that the law office has not represented an adverse party or would not have another type of conflict such as an attorney having a financial interest in the case. This was covered in detail in Chapter 2.

Small offices may check an index card system that contains the names and addresses of all clients the office has ever represented, as well as adverse parties. The index system also may contain other information regarding potential conflicts such as stocks or other ownership interests that office attorneys have an interest in.

Data-base software also can be used to perform this function. A data-base program is software that stores, searches, sorts, and organizes data. A typical conflict-of-interest data base might track all the office's past clients, first name and last, a client's Social Security number or birthday, the name of the case or matter that the office handled, the date the case was closed, and the adverse party in the case. Periodically, the data base is sorted and printed according to the client's last name. Thus, when a file is opened, the list can be checked to make sure the office has no conflict.

Finally, some software companies that produce software for attorneys put out conflict-of-interest programs that manage this information for the office without having to use a data base program.

CLIENT PROPERTY

Offices should be careful when closing files and especially in destroying files where documents or other information were given to the attorney by a client. Rule 1.15 of the *Model Rules of Professional Conduct* states:

Rule 1.15 Safekeeping Property
(a) A lawyer shall hold property of clients or third persons that is in a lawyer's possession in connection with a representation separate from the lawyer's own

property. . . . Other property shall be identified as such and appropriately safe-guarded. . . .

A law office has a duty at the end of a case to give the client the option to pick up information that was delivered to the attorney for representation in the matter. Generally, unless the client consents, a lawyer should not destroy or discard items that clearly or probably belong to the client. In addition, an attorney should be especially careful not to destroy client information where the applicable statutory limitations period has not expired.

DUTY TO TURN OVER FILE WHEN CLIENT FIRES ATTORNEY

An attorney also has a duty to turn over to a client her file when the client decides to fire an attorney and hire another one. What must be turned over to the client depends on the ethical rules and case law in each state. For example, Rule 3-700(D) of the *California Revised Rules of Professional Conduct* states:

> (a) [An attorney] whose employment has terminated shall . . . promptly release to the client, all the client papers and property. Client papers and property include correspondence, pleadings, deposition transcripts, exhibits, physical evidence, expert's reports, and other items reasonably necessary to the client's representation, whether the client has paid for them or not.

In most states, the attorney must turn over the documents the new counsel will need to reasonably handle the matter. In some states, such as California, a law office cannot refuse to release a client's file just because the client still owes fees and expenses.

DESTRUCTION OF RECORDS OF ACCOUNT

Rule 1.15(a) of the *Model Rules of Professional Conduct* states the minimum rules for how long attorneys should keep client account/fund information:

> . . . Complete records of . . . account funds and other property shall be kept by the lawyer and shall be preserved for a period of [five years] after termination of the representation.

Law offices should carefully maintain accurate and complete records of the lawyer's receipt and disbursement of trust funds in every case.

CONFIDENTIALITY

An attorney's duty to maintain the confidentiality of client-related matters should be a factor when considering a law office file management system. Files must be maintained so that sensitive information about a case or client is maintained. Also, the confidentiality rule does not stop once the case is closed. Law offices should be careful to destroy or dispose of files in a manner consistent with the confidentiality requirements.

FORM FILES

A **form file** *contains examples of documents that are commonly used in the law office, including pleadings, contracts, letters, discovery documents, wills, and incorporation*

form file
A file that contains examples of documents used in a law office, including pleadings, contracts, wills, and discovery documents.

papers. As a practical matter, anytime a new type of document is prepared, a copy of the document should be placed in the form file. Depending on the size of the law office, the office itself may keep a form file, or attorneys, legal assistants, and legal secretaries may keep their own form files. Form files are critical to practicing law efficiently, since if a firm does not keep a form file, staff members are forced to recreate documents over and over. Sometimes hours of research go into producing a new document. Thus, the law office does not want to duplicate this research time over and over.

Form files are kept in three-ring notebooks, expanding file folders, or manila files. Form files can be arranged alphabetically or can be grouped according to type, such as bankruptcy. Any form file should have some type of alphabetical index so that users can quickly find the document they are looking for. In addition to keeping hard copies of documents, many offices also keep copies of the documents on a word processor so that they can be quickly pulled up and edited as needed. This, too, can save hours of time. Although form files are great time-savers, users must be sure to update the forms and/or research on a regular basis to keep forms current.

Finally, in addition to each office keeping a form file, many state bar associations or legal secretary associations publish forms for their particular state. The cost of such forms is usually several hundred dollars, although in many states the set contains literally hundreds and hundreds of different forms and checklists for many areas of law. This type of form file can pay for itself in legal research savings very quickly. Most law libraries have form books, but in many cases the books are not specifically made for a particular state.

INTRODUCTION TO LAW LIBRARY MANAGEMENT

> *Even though the library remains the single most valuable tangible asset of a law office or corporate legal department, it must justify the continuing investment that it requires.*
>
> **—Richard Sloane,** "The Law Office Library," *The Lawyer's Handbook* (American Bar Association, 1983), B3-1. Chicago

Nearly every law office has some type of law library. From an administrative standpoint, the library must be managed correctly to ensure that the law office gets its money's worth from it, especially when considering the high cost of maintaining a law library. In medium-sized to large law offices, professional librarians may coordinate and manage the law library. In smaller law offices, legal assistants or associate attorneys may perform these duties. Figure 10-8 contains a list of librarian-related duties.

Depending on the structure of the law office, the library may be supervised by a library committee, a managing partner, or an office administrator, or all functions may be controlled by the librarian.

Law libraries generally are thought of as an overhead expense and, regardless of size, are costly to maintain. Proper library management can, however,

- Trains and supervises staff.
- Explains research techniques to lawyers and legal assistants, answers questions, and performs some research for them.
- Compiles legislative histories and bibliographies.
- Selects and orders books.
- Reviews and approves bills for payment.
- Plans library growth.
- Catalogs books.
- Routes library-related materials to appropriate staff.
- Files loose-leaf services and other library-related documents.
- Manages check out of books and reshelves material.

FIGURE 10-8
Librarian-Related
Duties

Source: *The Lawyer's Handbook*, 2d ed. (American Bar Association, copyright 1983). Reprinted with permission.

reduce overhead expenses and increase the quality of services to clients at the same time. Proper library management includes having proper policies and procedures so that the library is maintained in a productive and efficient manner. Figure 10-9 contains a sample list of policies for a law library. All library policies must be developed for the specific needs of the particular law office.

Some legal assistants may be put in charge of the law library. Managing a law library may not seem at first like a difficult job but in many instances it is. Material must be ordered on a regular basis to ensure the library is kept current, supplements to books (sometimes called pocket parts) must be ordered and replaced regularly, the collection must be tracked using some type of computer or card catalog system (this requires quite a bit of time), books must be shelved and maintained, a library budget must be kept and tracked, and, from time to time, books must be tracked down and found. Proper law library management can be a time-consuming task.

DEVELOPING A LIBRARY COLLECTION

What distinguishes an excellent library from a mediocre one . . . is not its size but its usefulness to the practitioners who rely on it. Its worth depends not merely on the amount of information they can find there but on the quality of that information and the ease of gathering it.

—**Richard Sloane,** "The Law Office Library," *The Lawyer's Handbook* (American Bar Association, 1983), B3-2.

There are many different types of materials that can be found in a law office library. The office's collection should mirror the type of practice and specialties it practices in. As a law office's practice changes, the library also will need to change to keep information that is current with the needs of the law office. Figure 10-10 shows typical types of publications that are found in many law office library collections.

The extent of an office's collection will depend on many factors. Larger offices that have been in existence for many years will have much larger collections than will newer or smaller law offices. Some offices think that most, if not

Circulation

Any publication or series of publications may be removed from the library and taken to one's office. There are no "library use only" materials in the library, although high frequency use items such as court rules and legal newspapers should be returned to the library promptly. No publication may be taken to your home or loaned to a "friend." However, with the authorization of a partner, it is permitted to loan a publication as a matter of "professional courtesy" to a colleague at another firm.

Check-out System

Books removed from the library must be "checked out." This procedure is absolutely mandatory. Knowing the whereabouts of library books, at all times, is tremendously important and needlessly complicated by the failure to properly check out borrowed books.

Routing System

After journals, loose-leaf services, summary sheets, and advance sheets have been entered into the library catalog system, they are circulated to those staff members who have asked or need to receive them. The entire contents of a "case summary reporter" are copied for each person who has requested to be on the routing list for this type of publication.

Acquisitions

If you become aware of a publication or know of one that you think the library should contain, please inform the librarian. By centralizing all orders for publications, we are able to monitor expenditures, avoid duplication, and control purchases.

Data Bases

The library has access to various "on-line" data bases including WESTLAW and LEXIS. It is highly recommended that if you anticipate using these systems, you attend the training programs available. At all times the librarian can assist you in structuring and performing searches on these systems by framing queries.

In-house Data Bases

The library also has several in-house data bases. The Legal Research File contains hundreds of memorandums of law and opinion letters. If you prepare a document that you would like to contribute to this system, request the Word Processing Department to provide the librarian with a copy of it. The librarian will assign index terms to the document, summarize it, and enter the full text of the document into the data base. The index to the documents in this system is available in the library.

Reference and Research

The reference and research assistance that the librarian can provide for you includes: a) conducting computerized data-base searches; b) finding cases, statutes, and regulations; c) cite-checking and shepardizing briefs; d) locating obscure facts or statistics; e) searching jury verdict reports for decisions involving a particular attorney, party, expert, or type of injury; and f) providing sample jury instructions, sample pleadings, and sample interrogatories.

Penalty Clause

You are strongly encouraged to abide by the policies and procedures. Failure to follow them may result in the library staff being unwilling and reluctant to provide you with the services you need.

FIGURE 10-9 Sample Law Library Policies

- Case Law
- Citators
- Digests
- Encyclopedias
- Index to Periodicals
- Periodicals
- Reference Works
- Statutes
- Treatises

FIGURE 10-10
Possible Holdings in
a Law Library

all, research should be performed in their own library, while other law offices that have large collections nearby, such as a law school or state or county law library, may want to keep their costs low and use these resources to the fullest extent possible.

One option to keep overhead costs low in the library, especially for new offices, is to purchase only current reporters, buy used, older reporters as money allows, or purchase reporters on CD-ROM and use WESTLAW and LEXIS to make up the difference.

ACQUISITIONS   Library acquisitions may be made by a library committee, a managing partner, a librarian, or by administrators. However, no matter what kind of structure is used, careful acquisition of materials is needed for cost-effective library management. In many cases, attorneys and others in the office will make recommendations about what purchases should be made. However, any such recommendation should be carefully considered. Figure 10-11 contains a list of sample questions and considerations that should be made when purchasing new materials.

ORDERING   As indicated previously, all purchasing decisions should be well thought out and justified. Although a committee may decide on what materials

- Does the author have proper experience and authority to write the material?
- What is the reputation of the publisher?
- Does the material appear to be logically organized?
- How important is the material to the law office's practice?
- Is the expense comparable to the benefit that will be received?
- Does the library already have something similar that can be used instead of purchasing new material?
- Does the law office have access to the material through another library such as a state, county, law school, or bar association library?
- Will the material be used for one case (and when the case is finished be useless) or will the material have continual use?
- Does the firm have physical room for the material?

FIGURE 10-11
Checklist for
Purchasing Library
Materials

are purchased, all library orders should be centralized and handled by one individual to ensure that duplicate orders are not made. An important part of the ordering process is to ensure that once the office has ordered and paid for the material, the office actually receives it and is not charged for any additional costs. One way to do this is to keep order forms of purchase information, such as the one shown in Figure 10-12. Library supply houses also sell preprinted order forms. In addition, some law offices use data-base management or law library management programs to track this information.

ROUTING MATERIAL TO INTERESTED PERSONS A typical law office may subscribe to a costly newsletter to keep up on current changes in the law. However, if the information is never passed on to the appropriate individual or only passed on to one person instead of everyone in the department, then the office is really not getting what it is paying for. Thus, it is a good idea to make sure that information is routed to interested and appropriate attorneys and legal assistants.

Depending on the law office, complete publications may be routed or just summaries or their tables of contents. Both have advantages and disadvantages. When a table of contents is routed, the user does not get to read the full publication but is put on notice of the publication if he is interested in it. In law offices where the complete publication is routed, the system may break down if the material is not passed along quickly, since it may become out-of-date or get lost or misplaced. This is particularly true if the material is routed through many individuals. In larger offices, library staff members may publish a library newsletter or abstracts that contain recent purchases.

DEVELOPING AN INTERNAL LEGAL RESEARCH DATA BASE OR BRIEF BANK Some of a law office's best information consists of research and materials that it has prepared. This can be a tremendous resource of information. It is quite common for attorneys and legal assistants to encounter the same legal issues in other cases. Unfortunately, it also is common for practitioners to forget

Author	Title	Vendor	Date Ordered	Date Received	Cost	Check # or Payment Method
						January, 1994
Black, Henry C..	Black's Law Dictionary	West Local Rep.	10 Jan 94		$19.95	Credit

FIGURE 10-12 Order Form—Notebook Format

Source: Adapted from Mickie Voges, *Building Your Law Library* (Amerian Bar Association, copyright 1988).

LEGAL RESEARCH DATABASE

RESEARCH TOPIC	SUB- TOPIC	CASE NAME	DOC NAME	DOC DATE	FILE NUMBER
ANTI-TRUST	Generally	Smith v. Jones	Mot. Sum. Judg	4/3/93	93-2341
ANTI-TRUST	St. Act. Doct.	Dunn v. Jones	Mot. Sum. Judg	6/1/92	92-7853
APPEALS	Standard of Review	Bud v. John	Brief. Appell.	1/23/93	93-5032
APPEALS	Jurisdiction	King v. Head	Brief. Appell.	6/30/94	94-0089
DAMAGES	Present Vlaue	Copp v. USD 201	Mot. New Trial	3/2/93	93-0838

FIGURE 10-13   Internal Legal Research Index

which prior case the research might be in. Thus, it is highly desirable to keep and track research that has been prepared in the past. This is sometimes called a brief bank or an in-house data base. There are many ways to do this. Some offices keep word processing files that contain the brief or research and then use the word processor to search for information; this technique is similar to using WESTLAW or LEXIS, and many full-featured word processors can perform this.

Another way is for an office to simply keep an index of what research was performed in each case. Figure 10-13 shows an example of a simple index that is sorted by research topic and allows the practitioner to pull the document that contains the research.

CD-ROM   CD-ROM is a technology that is having a major impact on law office libraries. Currently state statutes, federal statutes, state reporters, bankruptcy reporters, tax reporters, federal reporters, and many other legal publications are available on CD-ROM. A single CD-ROM is able to hold about three hundred thousand typed pages. It takes up almost no space on the bookshelf and can be searched using keywords just like WESTLAW or LEXIS. CD-ROMs also are typically less expensive to purchase and easier to update than a set of reporters or statutes. CD-ROMs offer many advantages to the law office over traditional books. The disadvantages include that CD-ROMs require the equipment to access them and that this equipment can be costly.

CATALOGING AND CLASSIFYING THE COLLECTION

Proper classification and organization of a collection are imperative for the office to know what material it has and where it is. If information is not arranged or organized in such a manner so that attorneys and legal assistants can easily find it without wasting time, the whole purpose of an in-house library is thwarted.

Cataloging is the process of listing and organizing the inventory of a library. This usually includes giving each book a separate call number and listing the book's author, title, publisher, subject, publication date, and so forth. Some offices classify and catalog their collections according to the Library of Congress classification system or the Dewey decimal system. The Library of Congress system uses the alphabet as its general divisions. For instance, "K" is the letter that represents American Law. Figure 10-14 contains a list of selected Library of Congress legal classifications. Other offices may simply group materials together, such as having a tax section, labor section, or real property section. This is sometimes called a "neighborhood" classification system.

The cataloging process can be either manual or computerized. One of the most popular types of catalog systems is the card catalog system. However, typing title, author, and subject cards for each book or piece of material can be quite time-consuming. One alternative to making cards (if you use the Library of Congress classification and catalog method) is to purchase from the Library of Congress each book's accompanying index cards. Although it appears to cost more, this saves time, since the cards are prepared by experts in their field and law library staff members do not have to prepare them.

A card catalog is just one way a law library can be cataloged. Some smaller law offices use a notebook-style catalog system. For instance, the notebook has a

Administrative Law	KF2120
KF5401	Estate Planning
Agency	KF746
KF1341	Evidence
Appellate Advocacy	KF8931
KF9050	Federal Courts
Civil Procedure	KF8700
KF8810	Future Interests
Commercial Transactions	KF604
KF871	Income Tax
Conflict of laws	KF6200
KF8810	Indian Land Titles
Conservation of Natural Resources	KF5660
KF5505	Labor Law
Constitutional Law	KF3301
KF4501	Local Government Law
Consumer Law	KF5300
KF1601	Partnership
Contracts	KF1371
KF801	Professional Responsibility
Corporations	KF305
KF1384	Property
Criminal Law	KF560–720
KF9201	Soil Conservation
Criminal Procedure	KF1686
KF9601	Torts
Decedents' Estates & Trusts	KF1246
KF746	Water Resources/Conservation
Energy & Natural Resources	KF5551

FIGURE 10-14 Modified Library of Congress Classification Numbers

Source: Mickie Voges, *Building Your Law Library* (American Bar Association, coyright 1988).

title section, an author section, and a subject section. Each book would be entered into each section separately (see Figure 10-15). Although the system is easy to use, it is usually only used for collections that are quite small.

Notebook Catalog by Title

TITLE _____A-C_____   Holdings as of _____March 1985_____

Title	Author	Location
BLACK'S LAW DICTIONARY	BLACK, H.C.	c.1-Libn
		c.2-Indexes
		c.3-Smith
COLLIER'S ON BANKRUPTCY	COLLIER	
[SHEPARD'S] BANKRUPTCY CITATIONS	------	

Notebook Catalog by Author

AUTHOR _____A-G_____   Holdings as of _____March 1985_____

Author	Author	Location
BLACK, HENRY C.	BLACK'S LAW DICTIONARY	c.1-Libn
		c.2-Indexes
		c.3-Smith
COLLIER, WILLIAM M.	COLLIER ON BANKRUPTCY	Bankr.
CALAMARI, JOHN D.	LAW OF CONTRACTS	Contracts

Notebook Catalog by Subject

SUBJECT _BANKRUPTCY_   Holdings as of _____March 1985_____

Subject	Author	Title	Location
Bankruptcy	-----	Chapter 11 Bus. Reorg.	KF 1544.29
	Collier, W.M.	Collier on Bankruptcy	KF 1524.C
	Murphy, P.A.	Creditor's Rights in...	KF 1524.M
Bankruptcy-- Forms	Collier, W.M.	Collier Bankr. Pract. Guide	KF 1524.C

FIGURE 10-15   Notebook-Style Catalog System

Source: *The Lawyer's Handbook*, 2d ed. (American Bar Association, copyright 1983). Reprinted with permission.

Computerized catalog systems can be created using almost any data-base management program. They are very easy to set up and are very flexible. There also are some commercially available library cataloging systems for many types of microcomputers. Other types of card catalog systems can be found in library supply catalogs. Figure 10-16 shows a list of some library equipment suppliers.

TRACKING THE COLLECTION—CIRCULATION

> *When an important book is missing from a law school [library], it is an occasion for concern. In a law office, the same loss can create a virtual state of siege. The cost in staff effort alone to find a single book that a lawyer [or legal assistant] has failed to sign out is enormous; in a large office it may require a search of over one hundred offices.*
>
> —**Richard Sloane,** "The Law Office Library," *The Lawyer's Handbook* (American Bar Association, 1983), B3-3.

A major task in any library is to know at any given time where each book or piece of material is. It is always a frustrating experience to reach for a book and find it is not available or is checked out to someone.

There are a variety of circulation and checkout systems. One of the simplest checkout systems is log-out sheet. Users simply sign a log of every book that is taken out of the library. Typically, the log contains the name of the book, the person checking it out, and the date. When material is returned, the entry is crossed off the log. One of the problems with this system is that to find a specific entry, you might have to look through the entire list.

A variation of a log-out sheet is to have a separate log-out sheet for each user. When a book is checked out, the user simply writes down the name, call number, and date on her own log sheet. These systems work in small law offices where volume is low.

Another circulation method is the familiar card system where the user completes a checkout card with the name of the book and author, etc., listed on the card. The advantage of this system is that it is very easy to see who has the book if it is not on the shelf by simply checking the card file.

**FIGURE 10-16
Library Equipment
and Supply Catalogs**

Gaylord Bros.
P.O. Box 4901
Syracuse, NY 13221-4901
1(800) 448-6160

Demco
P.O. Box 7488
Madison, WI 53707-7488
1(800) 356-1200

Brodart
1609 Memorial Ave.
Williamsport, PA 17705
1(800) 233-8959

Highsmith Co., Inc.
W5527 Highway 106
P.O. Box 800
Fort Atkinson, WI 53538-0800
1(800) 558-2110

A more expensive, but highly effective and quick, method is to use bar coding. Every book or piece of material is given a bar code. In addition, all users are given a card with a bar code on it. When a book is checked out, the user's and the book's bar codes are scanned into the computer. Thus, the computer knows at all times where the books or materials are. Unfortunately, bar code systems are fairly expensive.

The most difficult aspect of tracking books is not setting up a system but rather making the practitioners abide by. It is very simple for practitioners to walk out with a book instead of using the checkout procedures. Support from partners and administrators is essential.

Another circulation issue relates to whether all materials are available to be checked out of the library. Law offices can designate certain books that are heavily used to remain in the library. Although this procedure ensures that the book is available to all, it may not be convenient for the users. Some offices, on the other hand, allow all materials to be taken out of the library to encourage use. A balance must be struck between these two. A compromise might be to have several copies of heavily used books placed on "reserve" but purchase an additional "traveling" copy for individuals to check out.

MAINTAINING AND WEEDING OUT THE COLLECTION

An office library can be both a comfortable study center and a showplace for visitors, or it can be the site of a disorderly mass of unshelved books, and unsorted papers.

—**Richard Sloane,** "The Law Office Library," *The Lawyer's Handbook* (American Bar Association, 1983), B3-27.

Library maintenance is something that should be done on an ongoing basis. Such things as refiling material, keeping loose-leaf services up-to-date, and cataloging material are typical maintenance functions. Material that is outdated is not worth much and can actually be harmful. Another type of maintenance consideration is for periodicals, such as bar journals, magazines, and law journals, to be bound from time to time. Reducing separate periodicals to bound volumes makes the material easier to track and handle.

WEEDING OUT THE COLLECTION Weeding out a library collection is a needed task. Although many people, including attorneys, hate to throw anything away, there is no reason to pay rent on space to store books and materials that are no longer of use. Supplements and volumes that have been superseded should be thrown away, and books that are outdated or no longer of use should be discarded. In some cases, outdated texts may have misleading information that no longer applies. Some material that is being weeded out can be donated to public libraries and can earn the office some tax incentives.

PHYSICAL ASPECTS OF THE LIBRARY

A law library's space should be large enough for its readers or users, its staff, an expanding collection (including shelf space for books and documents), micrographic equipment, WESTLAW/LEXIS terminals or equivalent, and comfortable furniture.

Libraries should be comfortable, quiet places that are well lighted and arranged in a convenient layout so that information that is used time and again is easily accessible. Such material might include statutes, dictionaries, or reporters. For furniture such as tables and work surfaces, careful thought should be given to ensure that the surfaces are large enough so a user can spread out his material.

SHELVING AND STORAGE   Although CD-ROMs, micrographics, computer-assisted legal research (CALR), and other technologies are quickly emerging, books are still used in most law office libraries. Storage space can be a problem, especially in high-rent areas where space is a premium. In estimating shelf space, several factors should be considered, including: 1) the present number of books in the collection and the amount of shelf space they occupy and 2) the growth rate per year (an average of 5 percent to 10 percent is normal).[6] When estimating shelf space, there are about four to six books per linear foot of shelving. Thus, a typical three-foot-long shelf would hold an average of twelve to eighteen books. Also, most law books fit on shelves that are seven to eight inches deep. A few shelves ten to twelve inches deep will handle the few oversize books that come in.

Floor-load capacity also is a critical element. The minimum floor-load capacities for law libraries range from 175 to 250 pounds per square foot, depending on the type of shelving that is being used. Most buildings provide for floor-load capacities of 100 pounds per square foot. Thus, floor-load capacity should be carefully considered in designing a law library.

INSURANCE   Law office management should be careful to maintain proper insurance on the law library. Typical insurance usually includes smoke and water coverage in addition to the normal fire and theft insurance.

REDUCING LAW LIBRARY COSTS

One way to reduce law library costs is to carefully scrutinize each purchase, each renewal, and each update service. Publications should be canceled if they no longer reflect what the law office is doing. In some instances, a publication is purchased for a specific case. Once the case is over, there is little reason to continue updates and other costly material. It is estimated that approximately 85 percent of a law library's collection consists of reporters, statutes, loose-leaf services, and others that require supplements and that will continue to come in and cost the law office money unless canceled.

Law office staff should be required to justify why continuing supplements and publications should be purchased with responses other than "We have always subscribed to that." Instead, the question should be "What benefit does the publication currently give us?" Figure 10-17 contains other ways to reduce library costs.

BUDGETING   Careful tracking and budgeting is another way to reduce law library costs. A detailed budget in which every item is carefully considered and justified on its own merit will help the law office determine what items are the most important. A budgeting process that begins with last year's costs and then adds 5 percent for inflation or like amount does little to reduce costs. It is important to start from "scratch" each year and justify each anticipated expenditure.

- Charge back library costs, such as specific purchases and data-base costs (WESTLAW/LEXIS), to the client they benefit.
- Compare whether it is cheaper to buy certain treatises new each year rather than purchasing supplements.
- Consider canceling loose-leaf services that are available on WESTLAW/LEXIS, since you still have access to the information but it reduces overhead costs and allows the firm to charge the costs to the client the services benefit.
- Use an effective budgeting process such as a zero-based budget that forces the person purchasing books to justify the cost of the library every year and then to stick to the law library budget.
- Consider buying books used (such as reporters) instead of new.
- Carefully consider and scrutinize all purchases.

FIGURE 10-17
Ways to Reduce Library Costs

ACCOUNTING RECORDS Law offices also should develop an accounting system or use separate library software that tracks accounting information so they can determine exactly how much was spent on reporters and updating tax materials.

CHARGING LIBRARY COSTS BACK TO THE CLIENT Most law offices charge data-base costs, such as WESTLAW and LEXIS, back to the client. This technique also can be used for other library costs, such as charging the purchase price of a book to a client if the material is to be used for the client's case, cite-checking briefs and memorandums of law, or compiling bibliographies of books, articles, and documents on subjects directly related to particular client matters.

TECHNOLOGY AND THE LAW LIBRARY

COMPUTER-ASSISTED LEGAL RESEARCH (CALR) Computer-assisted legal research uses computers to search the words of cases, statutes, and documents themselves. Two familiar legal-information services include WESTLAW and LEXIS. Other legal-related services are VERALEX and Shepard's Citations. Legal professionals use their own computer or terminal and telecommunication equipment to access legal-information services. Services such as WESTLAW and LEXIS contain large data bases that have the full text of federal and state cases, statutes, and some legal periodicals. WESTLAW and LEXIS data bases, for example, allow the user to access nearly the same information that is available in a law library. The amount of information available depends on the specific service.

Because CALR systems use the full text of the document, there is no need for indices or digests. Instead, the user simply enters common words that describe the issue that might appear in the full text of the case or document and the system retrieves all cases and documents that meet the request. Since the information is stored on large mainframes, the data base can be searched and the documents quickly retrieved. The documents that are retrieved can be read on-line, can be sent off-line to your printer, or the full text can be downloaded to the user's computer. **On-line** *means that the user is connected to an information system and is running up charges.* **Off-line** *means that a user is no longer connected to an information service and that no charges are accruing except possibly a printing or downloading*

on-line
The user is connected to an information system and is running up charges.

off-line
The user is not connected to an information service and no charges are accruing except possibly a printing or downloading charge.

charge. Alternatively, a list of the appropriate cases or documents also can be printed or downloaded so that if the user likes, she can go to a library and examine the full text of the cases or documents.

CALR can be significantly quicker than using manual researching techniques. Further, when CALR is used correctly, it also can find or retrieve cases that might not otherwise have been found using manual methods because of poor indexing or other errors. CALR is also faster than manual methods, since it is possible to search many data bases (such as searching the case law of all fifty states on a specific subject). Using manual methods, the user would have to search through several sets of digests, supplements, and indices.

CALR, in addition to being quicker and sometimes being more accurate than manual researching, also can be more convenient. Nearly all legal-information services are available twenty-four hours a day, unlike many law libraries. Also, the research can be done from the legal professional's office. As mentioned before, when using a law library, it is possible that an important book might already be checked out or be unavailable. Sources are always available on-line with CALR. Another important factor to consider is that new cases are entered into legal-information services usually within a few days of being handed down or decided. Therefore, the information that is available on-line is almost always more up-to-date than information available in books.

Although CALR is both fast and convenient, it is not free. Most legal-information services charge a yearly subscription fee and a fee based on the amount of time connected to their system. Some services also charge a fee for every search that is done on their system. Some services have connect-time charges of more than two hundred dollars an hour. In addition, some services have a minimum monthly charge even if the service is not used. Because CALR is so expensive, new users can run up large bills quickly. Therefore, it is particularly important that new users have a thorough understanding of the CALR system they will be using. This is usually not a problem, since most CALR systems have off-line training tutorials. On the average though, most legal issues take approximately fifteen minutes to research. Most offices bill this expense back to their clients; some even do so at a higher rate than charged to help cover related expenses such as long-distance charges. The office must be careful, however, to not bill the client for general overhead costs. General overhead costs should already be figured in the office's attorney and legal assistant billing rate, so it would be inappropriate for the client to be billed for general overhead costs again.

CALR has many advantages over manual legal research, but there is room for both. Research experts recommend that one of the better ways to perform legal research is to combine the two methods by finding the cases on CALR and reading the text of the cases off-line in a library.

The 1992 IIT Chicago-Kent Large Firm Survey showed that more than 90 percent of all large law offices use some type of CALR system. The ABA's law office automation study of small law offices found that 48.2 percent of small law offices use CALR. Figure 10-18 contains some techniques for increasing productivity on CALR systems.

SUMMARY

Law offices of all types need a file system that allows them to store, track, and retrieve information about cases in a logical, efficient, an expeditious manner.

1. Use the Practice Data bases Offered in Many CALRs—WESTLAW and LEXIS both contain free training data bases. The practice data bases contain real cases, except that when you are connected to these data bases, no time is charged to your account. Use these data bases to try out new searching techniques; you have nothing to lose.

2. Do Not Read Cases On-Line—Get the Book—In most instances, do not read cases you have found on-line. If you have the book that the case appears in, simply get the cite, terminate the session, and read the text of the case from the book off-line.

3. Do Not Read Cases On-Line—Print Off-Line—As in number two, never read the cases you have found on-line. If you do not have access to the book, print the case off-line. When you are connected to many CALRs, you are incurring several charges including 1) an access service charge (i.e. Telenet, Tymenet, etc.) at $8 to $10 an hour; and 2) a data-base charge while you are in a CALR data-base (this charge can be anywhere from $150 an hour and up). If you read a case on-line, you are incurring both types of charges, the access service charge and the data-base charge. The cheapest way to get the full text of the case is to retrieve the case and print it "off-line."

4. Do Not Make Typos When Entering the Search—A typo in the search command can cost you several dollars as you wait for the CALR to run the search. Be sure and double-check your search command for typos before executing it.

5. Always Plan the Search—Always carefully plan out your search before going on-line and have several alternative searches ready.

6. Call the CALR's "Research Attorneys"—If you have a particularly difficult search to do, try calling one of the research attorneys provided by many CALR systems. In some cases, the call is toll-free. The research attorneys are experts at CALR and can help you prepare a successful search. In some cases, they will even run the search on-line for you to make sure their search query is correct.

7. Do Not Consider Unsuccessful Search Queries On-Line—If you have to run the searches you prepared on-line and still cannot get what you are looking for, exit the system and think of different alternatives. Remember, in many CALR systems, each time you issue a search command you are incurring another charge. Aimlessly entering search commands will only increase the costs.

FIGURE 10-18   Increasing Your Productivity on CALR Systems

When considering filing management techniques, each legal matter should be maintained separately and have its own case number. How a law office sets up its case numbering system is up to the office and its own needs. Alphabetical and numerical systems are common. In addition, the law office must decide whether files should be kept in a central location in the office or whether they should be kept throughout the office using a decentralized approach.

Color coding is a file management technique that is used to reduce the number of misfiled documents and lost files. Because most offices cannot keep all files indefinitely, an office should close inactive files and destroy the closed files from time to time to reduce file-storage requirements. There are many types of file storage equipment, including file drawers, shelf filing, mobile storage systems, automated filing equipment, micrographics, and imaging.

Nearly every law office has some type of law library. The law office library must be managed correctly to ensure that the law office gets its money's worth from it, especially when considering the high cost of maintaining a law library. Library management problems include development of a collection, proper cataloging and classifying a collection, tracking the collection, maintaining and weeding out the collection, and managing the physical needs of the library.

KEY TERMS

Alphabetic filing system
Bar coding
Centralized file system
Decentralized file system
File opening form
Shelf filing

Automated filing equipment
Micrographics
Imaging
Form file
On-line
Off-line

PROBLEM SOLVING QUESTIONS

1. Law libraries represent a large overhead cost to nearly every type of law office. List ways to reduce overhead costs of the library.

2. What types of filing systems have you dealt with? How did they work out? Was informa-tion ever lost? Why? In your experience, which filing systems were the easiest to learn and use?

KNOW YOUR ETHICS

1. Your supervising attorney hands you a case file that she would like you to do some work on. It appears from the file that the client saw the attorney on two different cases, the purchase of a piece of property and a medical malpractice matter. When you ask the attorney, she states that the client has recently raised the medical malpractice matter but that the client's primary focus is on the purchase of a piece of real estate. The attorney also states that she does not think the medical malpractice matter is significant and that is why a separate file is not being opened. The attorney tells you not to worry about it. To your knowledge, the attorney is not doing any research on the malpractice matter. How would you handle the situation?

2. The solo practitioner you worked for is moving across the country and thus wishes to close his law practice. The attorney is going to destroy all files related to the law practice because he does not want to have to rent storage space in a city he will no longer live in. The attorney is getting ready to dispose of the records by hauling them out to the Dumpster. What is your advice to the attorney?

3. Your office represents a client who is suing his former partner in a business deal venture that went sour. Your office has represented the client for two years and has put about three hundred hours in the case. In addition, your office has taken five depositions and paid for the transcripts. Your office also has hired an expert witness. The expert witness prepared a report that supports your client's case. The office has about thirty thousand dollars worth of fees and expenses in the case. One afternoon, the client comes into the office an gives the receptionist a letter stating that he is terminating the relationship with the law office and that he wants his files returned to him within one week. The attorney in the case states that there is no way he is going to hand over anything until the client pays the office's expenses. The attorney states that since the client has not paid for any work, the files are not legally his, and since the law office fronted the expenses, the law office at least owns the deposition transcripts and expert witness report. How would you handle the matter?

4. You have known for several months that your office's filing system is terrible. Documents are routinely lost, files are misplaced, and the filing is never filed in a timely manner. From an ethics and malpractice perspective, discuss the problems that may arise if a client's file or a piece of evidence regarding a client file is lost and cannot be found.

PRACTICE EXERCISES

1. The office you work for has recently added six attorneys and three legal assistants. The file system is no longer efficient. Finding files is slow and time-consuming. You have been asked to come up with a new filing system. The following are some of the details you should keep in mind when determining the new system:

- The three tax attorneys want to start their own department. The tax attorneys will shortly move their offices to the basement, and they want to keep their own files so they do not have to run up and down the stairs to get to them. None of the other attorneys use or need access to the tax files.
- Staff employees can be very reckless about the condition they leave files in.
- When a case is opened, all the documents are kept in a large expanding file folder.
- Documents tend to fall out of the files, and there is little organization to the case files.
- Many of the attorneys work on cases together and need access to the cases.
- People constantly are looking through the office trying to find a file.
- Last week the accounting department found out for the first time that the office has been handling a case for about four months. The client has never received a bill.
- The office wants a file system in which it can immediately tell when the case is filed, what type of case it is (the office mainly handles tax, probate, corporate, and general litigation matters) and which partner is responsible for the case (there are five part-

ners: Kathy Hines, Jonathan Hayes, Joseph Wagner, Cynthia Black, and Allen Hayes).

Please develop a strategy that will help eliminate these problems.

2. The partners in your office are displeased with the way the office's library is being maintained. They say that the library is hemorrhaging money with increased costs, which is crippling the office's profits. Your job is to draw up a plan to bring this situation under control. You have noticed the following:

- Several copies of books are purchased by different partners.
- The library is a mess most of the time. Books are kept in attorneys' and legal assistants' offices (they rarely check out the books and then fail to get them back to the library), there is not enough room for the materials the library does have, and books are stacked up on the floor. Many of the materials the library does have are outdated and no longer of use.
- You asked for several books, and, while you know they were ordered, you have not seen them yet.
- The library has no budget as such; purchases are made when the office thinks it needs them. In addition, when an attorney orders a book, the book is sometimes kept on the attorney's own bookshelf.
- All library costs, including WESTLAW and LEXIS are absorbed by the office.

NOTES

1. Deborah Heller and James M. Hunt, *Practicing Law and Managing People: How to Be Successful* (Butterworth, 1988), 60.

2. Gary A. Munneke, *Law Practice Management* (Saint Paul, Minnesota: West Publishing Co., 1991), 199.

3. *How to File and Find It*, Quill Business Library (Quill Corporation, 1989), 7.

4. Paul Hoffman, ed., *Law Office Economics and Management Manual*, vol. 3 (Clark, Boardman and Callaghan, Chicago 1992), sec. 41:04, p. 3.

5. Arentowicz and Bower, *Law Office Automation and Technology* (Matthew Bender and Company, 1992), sec. 10.01 [2].

6. Richard Sloane, "The Law Office Library," in *The Lawyer's Handbook*, "Revised Edition" (American Bar Association, 1983), B3-13.

Law Office Equipment, Space Management, Security, and Leases

CHAPTER OBJECTIVES

After you read this chapter, you will be able to:

- Discuss ways to research a major equipment purchase.

- Explain the concept of opportunity cost.

- Explain which equipment should be rented instead of purchased.

- Discuss why just-in-time inventory allows businesses to maximize cash flow.

- Distinguish between usable and rentable office space.

We've kept our investment strategy the same. We're committed to taking advantage of the benefits that technology offers to make us more responsive to our clients.[1]

Law practice management requires the development of some proficiency in choosing, acquiring, maintaining, and mastering the use of equipment. In other words, deciding what to buy and how to pay for it, knowing how long it will last, learning how to use it, teaching others to use it, and fixing or replacing it can be a full-time job.[2]

LAW OFFICE EQUIPMENT AND TECHNOLOGY

Law offices of all types have discovered the benefits of technology. Nearly all law offices have a variety of sophisticated equipment such as copy machines, computers, and facsimile (fax) machines. Using technology, staff members can increase productivity; that is, do more work with the same amount of effort. Thus, for legal assistants to be as productive as possible, they need to have a basic understanding of the technologies used in law offices.

In addition, in many instances technology allows a law office to increase the quality of the legal services that are provided. In large offices, it is not uncommon for millions of dollars to be spent on technology every year. Many managers think that by purchasing technology, they are investing in the future of the law office.

As law offices become increasingly technologically sophisticated, they must carefully choose the types of technologies that are purchased, since there are hundreds of options for nearly every piece of equipment. Offices also must manage the system implementation, staff training, how the equipment can be used most effectively, how it will be maintained, and how it will be paid for. Managing equipment and technology has become a major responsibility of managing law offices of all types. In some instances, legal assistants are the persons managing these resources. Different types of equipment are presented in this section, together with information on how equipment can be best purchased and managed.

Because computers are an integrated part of most law offices, they have been covered earlier in this text.

COPY MACHINES

Copy machines are a staple of every law office regardless of size or type. Law offices must routinely copy documents for internal files, clients, courts, opposing counsel, and others. It is not uncommon, even in a solo practitioner's office, to make tens of thousands of copies a year. Some larger offices have a centralized copy center or department that has its own staff. Other law offices have one or more copy machines located throughout the office that are self-serve. Some offices have both a centralized department, which handles large documents, and self-serve copy machines for smaller jobs.

As discussed in Chapter 5, photocopies that are necessary for a case are usually charged back to the client for reimbursement. Various systems are used to track these copies for reimbursement purposes, including maintaining copy logs and billing slips or entering the client's number into the copy machine for tracking purposes. Because all copy machines are different, new employees receive training on the machine shortly after being hired.

Copy machines come in many different shapes and sizes and with varying features. Figure 11-1 contains a selected list of some of the important features available. Price depends on the volume of the copier, the speed or pages per minute the copier can produce, and the extra features. There are hundreds of models of copy machines on the market, and competition is fierce. Prices range from a few hundred dollars for very low-volume copiers to five thousand to twenty thousand dollars for a medium-volume machine to more than one hundred thousand dollars for high-volume machines. Low-volume copy machines are rated to run about one thousand copies a month, medium-volume machines run four thousand to ten thousand copies a month, and high-volume machines are rated to run in excess of twenty thousand copies a month.

Two of the most important features of any copy machine are its reliability and the service provided by the company selling the machine.

We had a large and critical brief due to the Supreme Court that had to be copied immediately. Right in the middle of the job the copy machine broke. If the manufacturer had not provided us with quick and high-quality service, we would have had to take it to a printing service at a huge additional cost to our client. Quick and reliable service is a must for a law office copy machine.

—Law Office Management and Administration Report, Nov. 1992, p. 4

Volume also is an important consideration in selecting a copy machine, not just what the law office's volume is currently but what it might grow over the life of the copier. "To insure that a copy machine will accommodate an office's copy volume over the life of the machine, the rule of thumb is to add 67 percent to the office's present volume. Therefore, if a law office is presently producing 10,000 copies per month, the rule of thumb is to purchase a copier with the capacity to produce at least 16,700 copies per month."[3] Always plan purchases for future needs, especially large purchases like a copy machine.

Volume Capacity	— Refers to the number of copies typically made a month (e.g., low volume, sometimes called convenience copiers, 20,000 copies or fewer a month; medium volume, 20,000-50,000 copies; or high volume, 50,000 or more copies a month).
Speed/Pages Per minute	— Refers to the number of single copies the machine can make a minute. Low-volume copiers may start at 10 pages per minutes (ppm); medium-volume copiers typically start at 30 ppm; and many high-volume copiers exceed 120 ppm.
Automatic Document Feed (ADF)	— Refers to the machine's ability to automatically feed original pages into the machine without necessitating an individual to stand over the copy machine feeding documents into it.
Duplexing	— Automatically makes two-sided copies.
Stapling/Hole Punch	— Refers to the copy machine automatically stapling or punching holes (three-hole punch down the side or two-hole punch along the top) in the completed copies.
Sorter	— Most copy machines have an optional sorter (typically from 10-to 100-capacity sorter) that allows the machine to sort and collate copies automatically.
Reduction/Enlargement	— A standard feature on many copy machines that allows the machine to reduce or enlarge copies.
Multiple Paper Trays/Large Capacity	— Refers to the number of paper trays the copy machine has. Desirable in law offices that copy both legal size 8 1/2 × 14) and letter size (8 1/2 × 11). Large-capacity trays refers to the number of pages that can be held in each tray. Trays typically hold 500 sheets of paper; large-capacity trays can hold 1,500 or more in each tray.

FIGURE 11-1   Selected Copy Machine Features

automatic document feed (ADF)
Copier feature that feeds multipage documents into a copy machine either fully automatically or semiautomatically.

duplexing
The ability to automatically make two-sided copies.

An **automatic document feed (ADF)** *feeds multipage documents into a copy machine automatically.* Once the user places a multipage document like a brief or deposition in the ADF, he can leave the room and the machine will copy the document without additional help (see Figure 11-1).

Duplexing *is the ability to automatically make two-sided copies.* Duplexing is a nice feature for law offices because it saves additional paper costs. It saves in postage costs as well, since duplexed copies are lighter to mail than one-sided copies. In addition, some courts are considering using two-sided copies to reduce costs.

A reduction/enlargement feature can be helpful if the law office must make copies of oversized documents such as computer printouts. Some copies also have a built-in three hole punch and a stapler. These are needed features in many law offices.

Maintenance and supply costs also are important features to consider when purchasing copy machines. In most cases, a maintenance contract is desirable, since all copy machines eventually break. Some maintenance contracts include the costs of toner and other supplies. Careful consideration and/or cost projections should be made as to the costs of maintenance at different levels of volume and the cost per copy.

As an alternative to the high cost of purchasing and maintaining copy machines, some law offices have chosen to have their copiers supplied by facility management operations such as Xerox and others. Facility management operations provide the copy machine, maintenance, supplies, and personnel in an office. Costs range from five to seven cents per copy but relieve the office of the burden of choosing and maintaining its copiers.

When choosing copying machines, always ask for independent reviews from salespeople or subscribe to *Buyers Laboratory, Inc.,* (BLI) or to a newsletter such as *Law Office Management & Administration Report,* which routinely make copier recommendations. These independent recommendations and reviews will include tests on such things as reliability and ease of maintenance.

BILLING FOR CLIENT COPIES   Making sure that clients are properly billed for copies made for their case can be problematic given the larger number of cases and copies. Some offices have staff members complete expense slips detailing which client the copies were made for, how many copies were made, and why the copies were made. Some copy machines allow the user to enter a client identification number, which then tracks the number of copies to be billed to each client. Some copy machines use client copy cards to calculate the number of copies. The issue of tracking and billing clients for copies should be considered when purchasing a copier.

DICTATION EQUIPMENT

Although some lawyers and legal assistants use computers for drafting, many still use dictation. Dictation equipment is used in the legal environment to draft documents orally so that secretaries can transcribe the information. Dictation is faster than writing in longhand or shorthand, but it has a longer turnaround time than drafting on a computer. There are many types of dictation equipment with different-size tapes and tape machines. Small hand-sized tape recorders are popular for individuals who travel extensively. Dictation equipment usually has two components. The first is the recorder for the attorney or legal assistant, and the second is the transcribing machine that is used by the secretary. Dictation equipment costs from two hundred to twelve hundred dollars or more for both a recorder and a transcribing machine. Dictating is trickier than it sounds, and Figure 11-2 provides some tips on how to dictate effectively. As computers become more available and accessible, reliance on dictation in the law office will continue to decline.

TYPEWRITERS

Typewriters have had a place in a law office for the past hundred years. However, their use has greatly decreased with the widespread use of computers. Typewriters will continue to be used in law offices for forms, labels and envelopes (although there are some computerized methods of performing these tasks), and other miscellaneous purposes. Typewriters typically cost from one hundred to fifteen hundred dollars. There are many kinds of typewriters with a variety of features, including models that have spell-checking capability, memory capability, different fonts and type styles, automatic underlining, and bold facing.

- Organize your thoughts and ideas (using an outline may help).
- Enunciate and speak slowly and clearly.
- Listen to yourself from time to time to make sure the recorder is working properly and that you can be understood.
- Clearly dictate all punctuation including plurals and possessives.
- Use voice inflection just as you would in a normal conversation. Speaking in a monotone may put the transcriber to sleep.
- Spell out all proper names and other words that the transcriber might have trouble understanding.
- Spell out homonyms or word that sound alike (e.g. buy/by, invention/intervention; miner v. minor, parol v. parole, appellant v. appellate).
- Indicate to the transcriber how long the tape is.
- When changing topics on the tape, always announce the client/matter, case number, or other identifying information.
- Always dictate information in the proper order. It can be quite frustrating to the transcriber to perform a requested task and then later in the tape be told to disregard it, etc. If this happens, give the transcriber an accompanying note indicating to that he should simply disregard the request when it is given on the tape.
- Indicate symbols such as the section symbol, ampersand symbol (&), and formatting changes such as bold, underline, italics, etc.
- Avoid recording where background noise may be a problem such as with a radio and avoid other distracting noises such as clearing your throat, coughing, or eating.
- Start the tape by announcing the date and time of dictation (particularly in situations where multiple tapes are used).

FIGURE 11-2   Dictation Tips

POSTAGE MACHINES

Law offices use the U.S. Postal Service quite heavily. Given this large usage, most offices use a postage machine in lieu of using stamps. Although the machine itself can be either rented or purchased from office equipment supply stores, the law office must go to a local U.S. post office to have postage placed on the machine and the postage meter reset. In some cases the postage meter actually can have postage placed on the machine and be reset by phone. Once postage has been placed on the machine, users simply run an envelope or label through the machine and the postage seal and amount are stamped onto the envelope or label. There are many styles and types of postage machines based on the features and the volume of mail. Not only are postage machines more convenient to use than stamps, but one source indicates that metered mail skips nine steps in the automated postal system and can be delivered up to twenty-four hours sooner than mail with a postage stamp.[4] Postage costs, like long-distance and photocopying expenses, also are tracked and charged back to the client for reimbursement purposes by many law offices. Expense slips typically are used to charge this cost back to the client.

TELECOMMUNICATIONS

Telecommunications is a rapidly evolving area that has many aspects important to law offices. Among these are telephone systems, voice mail, facsimile equipment, modems, electronic mail, bulletin boards, computer-assisted legal research, and telex machines.

TELEPHONE EQUIPMENT   Telephones are important to any law office, since they are the means by which staff members communicate with clients, opposing counsel, courts, witnesses, and one another. Figure 11–3 includes a few features that are available on many phone systems. Smaller law offices use "key" systems. Large law offices use Private Branch Exchange (PBX) systems that allow the office to program the system as required and that generally are more flexible for needs of large offices.

> A PBX is like a private telephone company within your own office and offers significantly more flexibility and the use of many more lines. . . . Typically, a key system would be appropriate in law offices of up to 30–40 users. Beyond that a PBX may be more appropriate.
>
> —**Gary A. Munneke,** *Law Practice Management* (Saint Paul, Minnesota: West Publishing Company, 1991), 239, citing Gordon L. Jacobs, "Telephone and Communications Systems," 1987.

Telephone systems for law offices can cost from one thousand to one hundred thousand dollars or more depending on the number of phone stations needed and the number of outgoing lines needed. As with any equipment purchase, reliability is a key feature that must be researched carefully, which includes obtaining independent reviews of the equipment.

▪ Conferencing	Allows the user to connect two or more lines to form a telephone conference call.
▪ Intercom/Paging	Allows the telephone system to act as an intercom for internal communication within the office or to page individuals throughout the office.
▪ Hold	Allows the user to keep the caller connected without having to stay directly on the line.
▪ Speaker	Allows the user to talk and hear the caller without having to actually pick up the receiver.
▪ Speed Dialing	Allows the user to program often-called numbers into the phone system's memory and then call those numbers by either pushing a button or by entering a code.
▪ Busy Lamp Field	Allows users to see which stations or employees are currently on their phone.
▪ Direct Dialing	Allows a caller to call directly into a person's office without going through a receptionist.
▪ Client-Billing Options	Allows a user to enter a client code into the phone system when an outgoing call is made (such as a long-distance call) in order to bill that client for the reimbursement of the call.
▪ Call Forwarding	Allows users to automatically forward their calls to another station.

FIGURE 11-3   Selected Telephone Equipment Features

VOICE MAIL Voice mail is a computerized telecommunications system that stores and delivers voice messages. For example, if a caller tries to reach an individual who is not in, the caller is automatically forwarded to the person's voice "mailbox." The caller is able to leave a detailed message directly without going through a secretary or other individual where messages can be distorted or miscommunication can take place. The individual can then retrieve her messages by dialing her "mailbox." Voice mail also is available twenty-four hours a day, so clients can call and leave messages for people even when the office is not open. Voice mail systems can be expensive, ranging upward from five thousand dollars.

FACSIMILE (FAX) MACHINES Fax machines are used extensively by nearly every type and size of law office. Fax machines allow a user to electronically transmit a document's image, using telephone lines, to a receiving fax machine at another location, which prints the document that was sent. Fax machines are easy to operate and come in hundreds of styles with many features. Prices range from two hundred to two thousand dollars or more. Some fax machines work in conjunction with a computer system and are installed inside the computer system. This allows a user to fax a document, such as a word processing file, without even having to leave his desk.

One of the more important fax features is whether the fax machine will print incoming faxes on thermal paper or on plain paper or copy paper. Lower-cost fax machines print incoming messages on thermal paper. The thermal paper comes on a roll, and, depending on the machine, the machine may or may not cut the paper. In addition, thermal-paper faxes must be copied if the document is to be retained since thermal paper may erode and make the fax unreadable after time. Plain-paper faxes on the other hand, use regular copy paper, and do not have the drawbacks that thermal-paper faxes have. In general, thermal-paper fax machines cost approximately seven to eight cents per page, while plain-paper machines cost approximately three cents per page. Volume and transmission speed also should be considered when purchasing a machine.

Faxes have become so accepted in the legal community that many courts allow documents to be faxed if the documents are not more than ten to fifteen pages long.

In a pending asbestos case being heard in the Circuit Court for Baltimore, Maryland, a temporary secretary for one of the defense firms pushed the wrong precoded telephone number button on the fax machine's automatic dialer and mistakenly sent a top-secret report on the psychological profiles of prospective jurors to the opposing side. The plaintiff's counsel, in return, shared the report with the other plaintiffs' firms. As a result, Judge Marshall Levin felt compelled to dismiss all 51 jurors selected for the nation's largest consolidation of asbestos personal injury cases (9,032 plaintiffs and 10 defendants). In his oral opinion, Judge Levin said that, because the defense firm did not take reasonable precautions to prevent the mistake, the plaintiff's attorneys know the innermost thinking of the defense counsel.

—Michael P. Bentzen and Elizabeth A. Brandon-Brown, "Are You Sure Your Fax Transmissions Are Confidential?" *ABA Law Practice Management Publication Network,* vol. 1, no. 3, Winter 1993.

FAXES AND CONFIDENTIALITY   Faxes should be sent very carefully because an improper or misdirected fax transmission can lead to breach of client confidentiality, loss of attorney-client privilege, and legal malpractice. All fax cover pages for law offices should have some kind of confidentiality disclaimer on them such as the following:

> CONFIDENTIALITY NOTICE—This fax message contains legally confidential and privileged information intended for the sole use of the individual(s) or organizations named above. If you are not the intended recipient of this fax message, you are hereby notified that any dissemination, distribution, or copy of this message is strictly prohibited. If you have received this fax in error please notify us immediately by telephone and return this fax to us by mail.

Other precautions that can be taken to ensure fax information stays confidential include:

- Assuring that everyone using the fax machine knows how to use it correctly;
- Making sure that everyone operating the fax machine understands that a misdirected fax can destroy client confidentiality and the attorney-client privilege and can result in charges of malpractice;
- Requiring the sender to check to make sure the material has been received.

MODEMS AND INFORMATION SERVICES   A modem is a telecommunications device that allows remote computers to exchange information with one another using phone lines. Modems allow computers to access information services such as WESTLAW/LEXIS, and ABA/NET (ABA/NET is an on-line computer service that includes an "electronic bulletin board" and other services for attorneys). Modems are commonly used in law offices.

TELECOMMUNICATIONS AND CLIENT CONFIDENTIALITY   Client confidentiality should always be considered when dealing with phone systems. This is especially true considering the amount of time that legal assistants spend on the phone. Users should never broadcast client names over the law office's intercom/paging system. Users should be very careful about who is in the room when a client's case is being discussed on the phone. Conversations on mobile phones and cellular car phones should be limited if possible. Some radios/scanners have the ability to pick up these frequencies.

PAPER SHREDDERS

Paper shredders are a necessity in most law offices to ensure that client confidences are maintained. Paper shredders cost from one hundred to several thousand dollars. They are easy to use and safe (if they are used correctly). The size and volume of the shredder will dictate how many pieces of paper can be shredded at a time. Many shredders can "shred" staples, paper clips, diskettes, and cardboard as well.

PURCHASING EQUIPMENT AND SUPPLIES

It is not entirely uncommon for legal assistants to be involved in the purchase of equipment. Purchasing equipment is, of course, an important part of law office management, especially considering the mass use of technology. Making good purchasing decisions also is important considering the amount of resources and the dollar commitment that go into such purchases.

For example, if an office spends $10,000 on a computer system that never gets used or does not work properly, not only has the office lost the money that it invested, but also it has lost other opportunities as well. The office passed up an opportunity to purchase a computer that would have worked. This is called opportunity costs. The term **opportunity costs** *refers to the costs of forgoing or passing up other alternatives.* The law office's costs include the time and energy spent on the unsuccessful system but most importantly include the computer systems that were passed up that might have been successful and that could have raised the quality of the office's legal services.

Another important purchasing consideration is the useful life of the equipment being purchased. Suppose a law office is choosing between two equal pieces of equipment that both cost $10,000, but one has an estimated useful life of five years and the other has an estimated useful life of seven years. If the office chooses the equipment with the five year life, the office has large opportunity costs. Why? Because the cost per year to the office for the 5-year equipment is $2,000 ($10,000 divided by five equals $2,000), while the cost per year for the 7-year equipment is $1,428 ($10,000 divided by seven equals $1,428). Thus, it is very important that law offices use their money wisely and get as much out of their purchases as possible.

opportunity costs
The costs of forgoing or passing up other alternatives.

DETERMINE YOUR NEEDS

One of the first things that should be done when considering an equipment purchase is to clearly define what the needs are and to specify what problems the equipment will solve. Write down features or capabilities that the equipment should have. One way to do this is to talk to other members of the law office, from the lowest to the highest levels. In short, get input from others; they may think of things you might have forgotten. For example, if the office is purchasing a computer, determine what programs you want to use (i.e. the computer needs to be able to run this program and to do these things) and consider the needs of each user, since not all people will have the same needs.

SURVEY THE MARKET— DO YOUR HOMEWORK

One of the most important things a law office should do is to thoroughly research a purchase. Although this seems rather basic, many purchases are made on the word of a salesperson only. There are many ways to research a purchase, including some of the following:

CALL OTHER LAW OFFICES   An easy way to research purchases is to contact other law offices that are similarly situated and ask what kind of equipment they have, whether they like the equipment, what problems they have had, why they chose the equipment, and other such questions. It can be quite surprising how readily and how extensive such information may be given if you ask. When you call another law office, it is a mistake to simply talk to the office manager or administrator. Ask to talk to the person or persons who actually use the equipment. Remember, these are the people who probably know the most about the equipment, what it can do, and what it cannot do. Also, ask about maintenance and repair of the equipment, how often it has to be repaired, and how much it costs.

CONTACT OR JOIN ASSOCIATIONS OR OBTAIN PERIODICALS THAT REVIEW LAW OFFICE EQUIPMENT   Obtain product reviews from independent third parties that review office equipment or join Legal Management Associations that review office equipment.

TALK TO SALESPERSONS   Another way to get information is to contact dealers or salespersons. Salespersons are a tremendous source of information. Ask for brochures, specification sheets, and independent reviews that have been done on their product(s). Ask for demonstrations and information but do not commit to a purchase until after you have thoroughly researched your decision. Always ask for references. Try to make the vendor give you law office-related references, since law offices will tend to use the equipment in a similar fashion. Always call the references and ask detailed questions about concerns that you might have. Finally, try to test the equipment at your location. There is nothing like hands-on experience.

HIRE CONSULTANTS   Many offices, especially larger ones, hire consultants to help them make good purchasing decisions. Consultants can be expensive. However, if the consultant has had considerable experience in purchasing this type of equipment and large amounts of money are involved, the consultant's expertise might prove to be invaluable.

OBTAIN AS MANY BIDS AS POSSIBLE

Competition is an office's best ally. Most law offices do not take the time to negotiate with more than one vendor. When more than one vendor is capable of meeting an office's requirements, this strategy can be most effective. Even the slightest mention of comments and features of a competitive system will improve an office's negotiating position.

—Arentowica and Bower, *Law Office Automation and Technology* (Matthew Bender and Company, NY, 1992), sec. 1903[3].

One of the best things you can do to ensure that you get good equipment at a reasonable price is to generate as much competition as possible. Many offices issue requests for proposals (RFP). An RFP is a written request for bids that is sent to known vendors and that sets out the general specifications of the equipment, key contractual terms, and time frames. An RFP allows purchasers to obtain and compare like bids so that they know they are comparing "apples to apples."

MAKING THE PURCHASE DECISION

Careful thought and consideration should be made when making a purchase decision. Figure 11-4 shows a list of purchase factors that should be given consideration. Never rush into a decision. Whenever possible, try to project what

Does the equipment you are considering meet your needs?

- Ensure that the equipment truly meets your needs.
- Does the equipment have the ability to do the job now? What about your future needs? In two years? In five years?
- Is the equipment state-of-the-art?
- Will the equipment be obsolete in the near future?
- Is the equipment upgradable?

How long will the equipment last?

- What is the useful life of this piece of equipment?
- Is the product currently available?
- Is the equipment available now (not "soon" or "we are working on that")?

Financial considerations

- Is the equipment a good value?
- Can the firm afford the equipment? Is it within your means?
- Does new equipment or used equipment represent the best value?

Is the equipment/vendor reliable?

- Has sufficient evidence been produced to show that the equipment is reliable?
- Does the equipment have a maintenance contract? Is the maintenance contract affordable?
- Is the vendor who is selling the equipment reputable? How long in business?
- Were you given the opportunity to test the equipment?
- How much downtime is estimated with this machine?

Implementing considerations

- Will the equipment work in your law office (is there proper electricity, enough space, etc.)?
- Will the firm's staff need training on the equipment? If so, where will it come from? How much will it cost? How long will it take? How many staff members can attend (it is best to have at least three or more people to know how to operate each machine in case of staff turnover)?
- Is the equipment safe to operate?
- When will the equipment be delivered? How will it be installed? How will it be implemented or introduced into the office effectively?

FIGURE 11-4   Factors to Consider When Purchasing Equipment

your needs will be in three to four years. Obsolescence, especially when considering computers, can be a significant factor. Some computers are upgradable, which reduces the obsolescence factor (i.e. the microprocessor that runs the machine can be upgraded to newer, more powerful microprocessors).

When considering purchase decisions, make sure that the product is currently available. Generally, consider the product you see before you, not something a salesperson or an advertisement may offer you in the future.

One of the most compelling things to consider is, of course, the price of the product and whether or not it is a good value for the money. Remember that although price is important, so is common sense. If another product is a bit more expensive but is more reliable, is state-of-the-art, and is not subject to obsolescence as fast, it is usually wiser to spend the extra dollars to get exactly what you need.

Also whenever possible, have someone else look over your purchasing-decision rationale to consider factors you may have forgotten. Include others, especially those who will have to actually use the equipment, in the decision-making process. When others take responsibility in the project, they will accept it easier when it is being implemented. Proper training of staff members on the equipment is sometimes overlooked. The details of training should be discussed before the equipment is purchased. It also is important to try to have a minimum of three or four people trained on a piece of equipment so that the office is not without a person who knows how to properly run the equipment in the event of staff turnover.

People–not machines—do the work. If you install equipment without attending to the orientation and development of those who will use it, you are throwing your money away.

—Deborah Heller and James M. Hunt, *Practicing Law and Managing People: How to Be Successful* (Butterworth, 1988), 5.

DON'T FORGET TO PLAN

Major equipment decisions should be an integrated part of the planning and budgeting process. Because many equipment purchases require large amounts of cash or regular monthly payments in the form of lease or rental payments (which will affect monthly cash flow), it is important that these expenditures be budgeted and planned.

A law office's decision to change its technology requires significant planning.

—Margaret Cronin Fisk, "Capital Equipment Survey," *National Law Journal*, May 25, 1992, 15.

FINANCING DECISIONS

Once a law office has established what equipment to purchase, the office must then decide how to pay for it. The major alternatives for acquiring equipment include outright purchase, lease, and rental.

PURCHASE   When equipment is purchased, the buyer makes payment in full for the equipment (or obtains a separate loan) and subsequently takes title to the equipment. Outright purchase is the typical method for some types of law office equipment, such as dictation equipment or typewriters. The advantage to purchasing equipment is that the total cost is less than renting or leasing, since no finance or interest charges are incurred. The major disadvantage is that a purchase immediately reduces cash flow in the month that it is incurred. As noted earlier in this book, it is not uncommon for law offices to routinely suffer from cash-flow problems. Thus, the purchase of expensive equipment can exacerbate a cash-flow problem. Another disadvantage is that ongoing maintenance and/or support may suffer once equipment has been purchased, especially in the case of outdated equipment. Finally, in states that have high personal property taxes, purchase may be a disadvantage, since this form of acquisition would lead to increased property taxes.

RENTAL   In a rental agreement, the user typically pays a monthly rental fee, which usually includes maintenance and use of the equipment, but the vendor retains title to the equipment at all times. Rental agreements can be made for varying time periods but typically are six months to a year or more and usually include the ability to terminate the agreement with thirty to ninety days' notice. Advantages include the flexibility to cancel or terminate the contract when the equipment becomes dated in order to replace it with new equipment or, in cases where the office grossly underestimates its own needs, upgrade to a system that will meet its needs. Rental agreements also reduce the strain on cash flow, since payments are made over a period of time and without a large outlay of cash at any one time. Disadvantages of rental agreements include that rental payments typically are higher than purchase or lease, that rental prices may rise with little notice, and that after years of paying rent, the office never acquires title or interest in the equipment even though the payments may have paid for the equipment two or three times over.

LEASE   There are two main types of leasing arrangements. If equipment is purchased under an **operating lease,** the lessee (user) agrees to make payments for a specific period of time, typically one to five years or more. An operating lease is similar to a rental agreement except that the period is quite a bit longer. In a **lease-to-purchase** agreement, the lessee agrees to lease the equipment and make payments to the lessor for a specific period of time, but at the end of the lease term the lessee is given the option to purchase the equipment for its fair market value at the time or a prearranged figure such as 5 percent of the purchase price.

Equipment leases may be written with either the manufacturer or an independent leasing company. This distinction can be important, since if the leasing company is an independent, it may have little or no responsibility to complete agreements or promises of the vendor. The advantages of a lease include that leases provide for lower payments than do rental agreements and that certain tax advantages apply to some types of leases. The disadvantages of leases are that the period is usually longer than a rental agreement, there may be no ability to upgrade the equipment, and the lessee may or may not have any title to the equipment at the end of the lease period.

The type of financing used in any one situation will depend on the needs of the law office and the type of equipment being acquired. Generally, in situations where technology is changing rapidly, leasing or renting, if available, may be better than purchasing.

INVENTORY RECORDS AND INSURANCE

Once equipment is purchased and paid for, the equipment management process is not over. It is important to maintain inventory records of all equipment purchases, including information about the vendor, records of purchase/lease, serial number of the equipment, maintenance and service agreements, warranty information, installation instructions, and manuals. If regular maintenance is required, the law office should take care to calendar the appointments. It is in the office's best interest to maintain the equipment so as to get as many useful years out of it as possible. Inventory records also are important to establish and back up depreciation schedules for tax purposes and for establishing insurance losses in the case of theft, fire, etc.

Part of the maintenance effort is to ensure that all law office equipment is covered by adequate property loss insurance in case of theft, fire, or other catastrophe. Be sure that the property loss insurance allows for replacement costs if possible and adequately covers the property insured. The office does not want to be in the undesirable position of being underinsured. Also, be aware that electronic equipment such as computers are usually covered under separate insurance riders that require the office to list individually each piece of equipment with appropriate serial numbers.

OFFICE SUPPLIES

Law offices must maintain an adequate level of office supplies. Supplies includes everything from paper clips and pencils to legal pads, copy paper, staples, and envelopes (just to name a few). Management of office supplies is important, since offices rely quite heavily on them and in many cases cannot perform needed tasks without them. For example, if an office had a large document to be copied on a weekend and subsequently discovered it did not have enough paper to finish the job, this could cause significant problems. Law offices must regularly manage and keep track of office supplies so that shortages do not occur.

JUST-IN-TIME INVENTORY   There are many ways to manage office supplies, but they all usually require an individual to monitor the supply situation on a regular basis, such as every week or two, and make necessary orders as needed. Although law offices do not want to run out of supplies, they also do not want to tie up money or office storage space in supplies that sit month after month on the supply shelf. Just-in-time inventory is an inventory concept made popular by Japanese manufacturing companies. **Just-in-time inventory** *promotes the idea that offices should maintain minimum inventory levels. This allows the office to maximize its cash flow (i.e. it is not tied up in large inventories leading to higher financing charges, etc.), but just-in-time also promotes the idea that offices should build relationships with suppliers so that inventories can be ordered and received within a day or two of when they are needed.* Thus, just-in-time allows offices to have the supplies they need, when they are needed, and without shortages, while still maximizing their cash flow.

just-in-time inventory
An inventory concept that maximizes an office's cash flow by keeping low amounts of inventory on hand but having access to needed supplies by contracting with vendors that fill orders in one or two ways.

Just-in-time also points out the advantages of dealing with reputable suppliers who can be counted on and who give good service. It is important to find office suppliers who give reliable service without a large price markup. There are many office suppliers, both at the local level and at the national level, to choose from.

PILFERAGE   Nearly every law office manager or administrator will concede that many supplies are taken home by office employees and that copy machines, fax machines, and postage machines, are used for personal use by employees. This practice is commonly known as pilferage. Although pilferage probably will always exist, one way to limit it is to restrict access to whatever the item is, such as by locking supply rooms or having careful control over copy machines and other machines. Establishing strict policy guidelines can also help in this matter.

COST OF OFFICE SUPPLIES Law offices by their nature buy fairly large amounts of office supplies. It is important to shop around and get the best possible prices on items. Mail-order companies and large discount office supply stores typically offer the best prices. Beware of vendors giving large discounts. Discounts mean little, except that the vendor's everyday prices are quite high. Compare actual prices, then see who is least expensive, gives the best service, and stands behind their products.

LAW OFFICE LAYOUT, SPACE MANAGEMENT, SECURITY, AND LEASES

In this section a variety of office layout, space management, and law office leasing topics are discussed. These topics are sometimes referred to as facility management. **Facility management** *refers to law office management's responsibility to plan, design, and control a law office's own building or office space effectively.*

CONSIDERATIONS IN SELECTING NEW FACILITIES OR REMODELING OLD FACILITIES

Effectively controlling a law office's facilities is one area that law office management is responsible for, and legal assistants may be asked to play a role in choosing new office space, laying out their own office or a secretary's office, or moving a law office. In smaller law offices, legal assistants may play a larger role in this process. This section describes some of the considerations in selecting new facilities or remodeling existing facilities. From time to time, law offices must consider a move. Reasons include generally being unhappy with the office's current location, a need to expand beyond the capabilities of existing capacities, opening a new office, or merging with another law office.

REMODELING V. MOVING Consideration should be given to remodeling the office or expanding existing facilities v. moving the office entirely. The cost of moving and of losing some clients (if the office is moved, the new location may not be as convenient for everyone) should be taken into account when making such a decision.

BUILDING LOCATION Consideration should be given to the physical location of the law office, including whether the new building is on public transportation routes, is accessible from major highways, is convenient for existing clients to get to, is reasonably close or accessible to the courthouse(s) and law libraries, and whether the new location and surrounding area maintain and support the office's image. The type of law practice also should be considered. For example, corporate practices may need to be downtown, domestic-relation offices may want to be in suburbs, and some smaller-client-based firms may want to be in a mall. The type of client the firm is trying to attract may be a factor in building location.

PARKING Adequate parking for both employees and clients should be taken into consideration when choosing office space. Poor parking is a common complaint of law offices in downtown business districts.

---

facility management
A law office management's responsibility to manage, plan, design, and control an office's own building or office space effectively.

SPACE PLANNING

Office space is important for many reasons. Office space and office decor help define the image of the law office. It is important that the facility be functional, practical, and work for the particular law office's structure and needs.

One of the first aspects of space planning that must be considered is the organization of the law office. Law office management must decide what the needs of the office are. For example, management must decide whether practice groups will be grouped together or apart; whether computers, files, and other equipment will be centralized or decentralized; what types of offices are needed (e.g., number and size of conference rooms, kitchen area, and separate postage and copy areas); and whether the office will need to expand in the near future. An effective way of determining needs is to survey the staff members and ask them what they think they need and then use that information in the planning process. Some offices, especially medium- to larger-sized offices, hire consultants to help with these as well as other issues.

Estimating office space is not easy to do, but Figure 11-5 gives some rough estimates of the office space needed for law office personnel. You also can obtain a ballpark estimate of law office space needed by figuring that each lawyer needs 550 to 700 usable square feet in an office. Thus, a five-attorney office would need anywhere from 2,750 to 3,500 square feet.

[A] common mistake that law offices make. . .is to plan only for the existing legal personnel and clerical staff. Before making. . .plans, the office should make a thorough analysis of its present systems and equipment. Possible expansion should be taken into account. If the degree of expansion is uncertain, an office should always "overbuild" and lease part of the unused space.

—**Garth C. Grissom, Austin Anderson, and Mary I. Hiniker,** *The Lawyer's Handbook*, Rev. Ed. (American Bar Association, 1983), B1–4.

---

usable space
Space that is actually available for offices, equipment, furniture, or occupiable area. Usable space is what is important to law offices.

rentable space
Usable space plus common areas also known as a loss factor. Rentable space is what is important to landlords since this is what rental payments are based on.

loss factor
A tenant's pro-rata share of common spaces, including hallways, restrooms, etc., in a multitenant floor or building.

USABLE V. RENTABLE SPACE   **Usable space,** as the name implies, *refers to space that is actually available for offices, equipment, furniture, or occupiable area but does not include hallways, stairwells, and like areas. Usable space is what is important to law offices.*

Rental space, on the other hand, *is what rent is based on and includes usable space plus the tenant's pro-rata share of all common space on the floor such as hallways, stairwells, restrooms, etc., whether or not the space is occupiable. The tenant's pro-rata share of common space is called* a **loss factor** (also called a load factor). Rentable space is what is important to a landlord, since the tenant pays rent on the total rentable space. For example, if a tenant had 2,000 square feet of rentable space but only 1,750 square feet of usable space, the tenant would pay rent (usually so much per square foot) on the 2,000 square feet.

In buildings or floors where hallways, bathrooms, and elevators are shared by many tenants, each tenant is required to pay her loss factor. For example, if a tenant had 2,000 feet of usable space and the tenant's share of the loss factor was 5 percent, the tenant's rentable space (i.e. what she would pay rent on) would be 2,100 feet (2,000 times 1.05 equals 2,100). Load factors will, of course, vary from building to building.

COMPARING OFFICE SPACE Once a law office has a general estimate of the amount of space it needs, the next step is to evaluate different buildings. However, comparing alternative sites can be rather difficult. Figure 11–6 is a checklist/worksheet for comparing different alternatives, which includes rentable/usable square feet comparisons along with many other factors.

INDIVIDUAL OFFICES Figure 11-7 shows typical office layouts for partners, associates, and paralegals. Depending on the firm, paralegals may have private offices, share private offices with other legal assistants, or work in module partitions. Offices must, of course, have sufficient work space, be quiet, and provide for a usable working environment for the individual.

RECEPTION AREA Public spaces such as reception areas are important to the image of the office, since this area is the first one clients see when they come to the office. When designing the reception area, the office wants to project a comfortable but professional atmosphere, with comfortable chairs, a coatrack or closet, sufficient lighting for reading, and reading material a typical client would find interesting. Reception areas must not only provide space for guests but also accommodate a receptionist. A typical reception area for four guests is approximately two hundred square feet. If the receptionist has a computer, it should be placed so that the screen cannot be easily read by people coming into the office. Finally, for security reasons, a locked door to the firm's inner offices may be desired.

CONFERENCE ROOMS Most law offices also have one or more conference rooms of varying sizes depending on the office's type of practice, number of attorneys, and other factors. Smaller offices tend to have one conference room for every five to seven lawyers, while larger offices have one conference room for every seven to ten lawyers.[5]

LAW LIBRARY A law library also is a standard feature in most law offices. Some offices have a centralized library where all books are kept, while others have decentralized separate libraries based on subject matter. For example, the tax library might be next to the tax department. Libraries are used as quiet places to spread material and to perform research functions. Many offices also have WESTLAW and LEXIS, plus case law and state statutes on CD-ROM, in the library.

FILE ROOMS File rooms are heavily used in law offices. In some cases, law offices place file rooms in remote locations, since they do not need to be seen by the public. However, this is probably a mistake, since case files are used day in and day out and should be readily accessible to law office staff.

Files are the nerve center of every law office. If it is decided to have a single file room housing virtually all active files, the layout and design of this room must be considered. Once traffic patterns should be taken into account and the file room placed so as to be accessible to the greatest number of people.

—Garth C. Grissom, Austin G. Anderson, and Mary I. Hiniker, *The Lawyer's Handbook* (American Bar Association, 1983), B1–14.

Work Areas

Partners	180–240 sq. ft.
Associates	120–150 sq. ft.
Paralegals	80–100 sq. ft.
Secretaries with local files	80–100 sq. ft.
Administrators	Partner-or associate-size offices
Support department workers (individual work area only)	50–80 sq. ft.
Support department supervisors	80–100 sq. ft.
Librarian	100–120 sq. ft.
Each library staff member	75–90 sq. ft.

Heights

Desk	Approximately 28 1/2 in. above finished floor
Typing surface	Approximately 25–26 in. above finished floor
Computer keyboard	Approximately 27 in. above finished floor

Seating

Reception room seating/waiting area (to which must be added space for the receptionist and circulation)	Approximately 20 sq. ft. per visitor
Conference room seating at table	25–30 sq. ft. per person
Employee lunchroom seating (to which must be added space for kitchen facilities and storage)	15 sq. ft. per person

Library

Generally accepted live load for modern libraries with standard stack shelving	150 lb./sq. ft
Generally accepted live load for modern libraries with movable compact shelving	300 lb./sq. ft.
Library shelves considered full	When 3/4 utilized
Space used by 15–18 law books	3 ft. of linear shelving or 5–6 books/ft.
Bound periodical volumes	4–5/ft.
Annual growth for unbound periodical volumes	7–8 in./title
Each library shelf	12 in. high, 10–12 in. deep
Space required for each library shelving unit 12 in. deep and 36 in. wide which shares a 36 in.-wide aisle with another shelf	7 1/2 sq. ft.
Aisles—center or main	4–4 1/2 ft.
Aisles—between tables and wall	5 ft.
Aisles—between book stacks and between book stacks and wall shelving	2 1/2–3 ft. minimum—4–4 1/2 ft. for moderate to heavy use.
Aisles—in front of circulation desk, card catalog, and reference desk	5–6 ft.
Reading area	75 sq. ft./reader
Individual work areas should be provided for	Supporting 10 percent of the firm's lawyers
Minimum preferred	20–30 percent

File Cabinets (including Drawer Pullout Area)

Vertical standard letter (1.25 ft. × 5 ft.)	6.25 sq. ft.
Vertical standard legal (1.5 ft. × 5 ft.)	7.5 sq. ft.
Lateral 36 in. legal	9 sq. ft.

FIGURE 11-5   Summary of Space Requirements

Source: Marjorie Miller, *Designing Your Law Office* (American Bar Association, copyright 1988). Reprinted with permission.

	Present Space (If Applicable)	Alternative 1	Alternative 2	Alternative 3
I. Location—proximity to:				
A. Courts	_____	_____	_____	_____
B. Key clients	_____	_____	_____	_____
C. Transportation	_____	_____	_____	_____
D. Clubs, restaurants, etc.	_____	_____	_____	_____
E. Other (specify) ___	_____	_____	_____	_____
II. Rental rates				
A. Rates available	_____	_____	_____	_____
B. Periods during which rates will be effective	_____	_____	_____	_____
C. Escalation provisions	_____	_____	_____	_____
D. Base year for escalation	_____	_____	_____	_____
III. Rentable/usable square feet				
A. Rentable square feet available	_____	_____	_____	_____
B. Ratio of usable to rentable square feet	_____	_____	_____	_____
IV. Building core				
A. In square feet	_____	_____	_____	_____
B. As percentage of building	_____	_____	_____	_____
V. Satisfaction of firm's construction requirements (*Can the space be developed to meet the firm's requirements?*)				
VI. Security				
A. What type of security is provided?	_____	_____	_____	_____
VII. Concessions				
A. Work letter allowances toward construction	_____	_____	_____	_____
B. Other allowances or concessions	_____	_____	_____	_____
VIII. Timing				
A. When the firm needs the space	_____	_____	_____	_____
B. When the space is available	_____	_____	_____	_____
IX. Lease term				
A. Firm's long-term wishes regarding lease commitment	_____	_____	_____	_____
B. Lease terms available	_____	_____	_____	_____
X. Contiguous space, option space, right of first refusal on space				
A. Is contiguous space for future use?	_____	_____	_____	_____
B. When will such space be available?	_____	_____	_____	_____
C. Will the firm be granted options on that space?	_____	_____	_____	_____
D. Can the firm sublet space?	_____	_____	_____	_____
E. What rental rates and escalation provisions will apply to space rented in the future?	_____	_____	_____	_____
XI. Building characteristics				
A. Building core efficiency	_____	_____	_____	_____
B. Usable space efficiency	_____	_____	_____	_____
C. Heating, ventilation, air-conditioning, and sprinkler systems	_____	_____	_____	_____
D. Curtain wall	_____	_____	_____	_____
E. Floor loading	_____	_____	_____	_____
F. Lighting and ceiling	_____	_____	_____	_____
G. Infrastructure	_____	_____	_____	_____

FIGURE 11-6   Checklist for Analyzing Present and Alternative Spaces

H.	Connecting stair link	_____	_____	_____	_____
I.	Bathroom, plumbing, and wet columns	_____	_____	_____	_____
J.	Window treatments	_____	_____	_____	_____
K.	Elevators	_____	_____	_____	_____
L.	Emergency power supply	_____	_____	_____	_____
M.	Space planning	_____	_____	_____	_____
XII.	**Flexibility of firm**				
A.	To choose architect	_____	_____	_____	_____
B.	To choose contractors	_____	_____	_____	_____
XIII.	**Other**				
A.	Cleaning	_____	_____	_____	_____
B.	Parking	_____	_____	_____	_____
C.	Handicap accessible	_____	_____	_____	_____

FURNITURE   Furniture must not only project an office's image but also provide sufficient work surfaces, be comfortable and usable, and efficiently use the space the law office has. There are thousands of different kinds and types of furniture, including:

- Traditional—wood and plastic laminate;
- Contemporary—wood, metal, and laminate;
- High-tech—glass, wood, and metal;
- Ergonomic—laminate, wood, and metal.

Some offices use interior landscaping, also called system furniture or module design. **Interior landscaping** *uses movable partitions, or panels, and work surfaces, file cabinets, and drawers that attach to the partitions instead of interior walls.* The panels typically have electric cabling that runs through the bottom of each panel for electrical outlets. In this way, law offices can be completely flexible and use their space more wisely than ever before. The downsides of interior landscaping are increased noise and decreased privacy. The reason interior landscaping has gained in popularity is because of the increased cost of office space, and minimizing the amount of space a law office uses reduces rent and maintenance costs.

interior landscaping
Movable partitions, or panels, and work surfaces, file cabinets, and drawers that attach to the partitions.

Some studies have shown that the most negative feature of interior landscaping is not the increased noise problem but the lack of personal privacy, especially when short partitions are used that allow people to see over the top and where the entryways face out allowing others to see into the work space.

CORRELATION BETWEEN SPACE AND COST   Any office manager will tell you that there is a direct correlation between the amount of office space needed and cost. Office space has become increasingly more expensive, especially in metropolitan areas where costs went from seventeen dollars a square foot twenty years ago to anywhere from thirty to seventy dollars or more per square foot currently. The office lease represents the second largest nonlawyer expense, averaging 8.6 percent of gross income.[6] Lease payments represent a large overhead expense, which can put pressure on cash flow because it is a fixed cost, meaning that it is incurred every month without relation to whether or not the office is having a good month financially speaking. Thus, offices have struggled to become physically smaller and more compact and to use the space they have wisely.

PROFESSIONAL HELP   Many offices hire space planners, architects, designers, electricians, and consultants to help them lay out and design effective and functional law offices. This helps a law office avoid problems that other law offices have encountered.

FIGURE 11-7
Typical Partner, Associate and Paralegal Offices

Source: Marjorie Miller, *Designing Your Law Office* (American Bar Association, copyright 1988). Reprinted with permission.

Typical Partner's Office

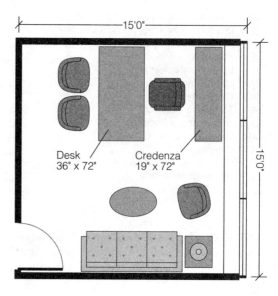

Typical Associate's Office

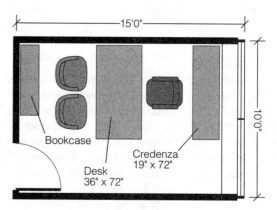

Typical Paralegal's Office

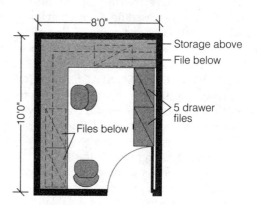

OTHER CONSIDERATIONS   When space planning, remember that there are considerations other than just taking measurements. Physical location of offices, lounges, and libraries and the effects on social relationships should all be taken into account. Consider the following:

A large law office was moving to new offices. It seemed natural and cost-effective to put all administrative services, including the office's administrator, on a specially designed administration floor of its own. The administrator had been a powerful force in the office—one who participated in major decisions and policy-making. Within a year of having been physically separated from the office owners, he began to notice that he was not being consulted as frequently as he had been. His credibility had begun to disintegrate. By the second year he was regarded by the partners as part of the accounting department. By the third year he was felt to be expendable and was asked to leave the office.

And another example:

A mid-size office. . .made a decision to eliminate a central lunch/lounge facility in its new offices. Each floor would have its own lunchroom and coffee area. The staff of the sixth, seventh, and eighth floors used to meet in the one large lunchroom. After the move they hardly saw one another. Gradually the camaraderie which used to exist among all personnel began to erode.[7]

Human factors and tendencies must be taken into account when space planning, or there may be unwanted side effects.

ENVIRONMENTAL CONSIDERATIONS

In addition to merely planning how space in a law office will be used, management must also consider environmental factors such as lighting, noise, climate control, color, image/appearance, elevators, electrical requirements, accessibility for persons with disabilities, and accessibility of the building to its clients, employees, and others. Figure 11-8 shows the results of a law office survey that was given to a variety of employees regarding environmental factors and shows that these factors do have an impact.

LIGHTING   Lighting is an environmental factor that is important when considering productivity. Studies have shown that lighting that projects downward, including bright fluorescent lights or large window lighting, creates glare and causes the eye to constantly adapt, resulting in eye fatigue. In addition, bright surfaces such as walls, floors, and equipment also can be a source of glare. High-quality light is free from glare and is dispersed throughout the room.

Many individuals prefer **task lighting,** *wherein lights are attached to work surfaces or furniture or are freestanding.* In many cases, task lighting also is adjustable

task lighting
Lights that are attached to work surfaces or furniture or that are freestanding.

Question	Response	
	Yes	No
1. Do you feel that a change in your working environment would have a positive effect on your productivity or efficiency?	92%	8%
2. Are you aware of the temperature in your office?	84%	16%
3. Are you aware of the lighting in your office?	52%	48%
4. Are you aware of the color in your office?	92%	8%
5. Do you feel these colors have any effect on you?	68%	32%
6. Would you like background music while you work?	68%	32%
7. Do you feel a change in your office environment would have a positive effect on your productivity or efficiency?	80%	20%

**FIGURE 11-8
Law Office Study Regarding the Importance of Environmental Factors**

Source: Marjorie Miller, *Designing Your Law Office* (American Bar Association, copyright 1988). Reprinted with permission.

so that light can be positioned when and where it is needed and projects light to the ceiling and other directions instead of straight down, which reduces glare. Also, soft lighting, especially in close quarters, is preferable to hard or bright lights.

A typical office will be outfitted with standard fluorescent lights. However, fluorescent lights can be fitted with diffusers that deflect light at a forty-five degree angle rather than having it come straight down. This is particularly helpful when employees use computer screens. Fluorescent lights, which typically have cool white fluorescent bulbs, can be replaced with warm white bulbs that put out a softer light. The effect of harsh lighting can also be reduced by additional sources of light such as natural light and task lighting.

NOISE   Noise also can visibly affect an employee's productivity. Studies have shown that unwanted noise produces tension, fatigue, higher error rates, decreased concentration, and low morale. In addition to productivity issues, confidentiality also should be a reason to control noise and to ensure that private conversations are kept private. Sound leakage is particularly a problem in offices with thin walls, walls that are not continuous, offices with hollow-core doors, and in offices that use interior landscaping. Ceiling panels, carpet, wall coverings, acoustical panels, and insulation can reduce and absorb unwanted noise.

Also, typewriters, printers, and other equipment that produce noise can be fitted with sound-absorbing hoods, and equipment such as copiers can be placed in soundproof rooms. However, most of the noise generated in a law office is by people. Soft background music also can be used to increase the pleasantness of office surroundings and to reduce unwanted and disrupting noise.

COLOR   Of the environmental conditions addressed in this section, color would seem to be one of the least important factors. This may or may not be the case. Many people are quite adamant about the colors that they find appealing and are the most comfortable with day in and day out. Some studies have found that surrounding colors can influence the effectiveness and productivity of workers. Figure 11-9 shows the effects of different colors on worker productivity. Color also can make an office more comfortable and make it more pleasing to the eye.

ELECTRICAL REQUIREMENTS   The electrical requirements are another environmental factor that should be researched before leasing or purchasing property. This is particularly true when an office has large computer equipment, copy machines, fax machines, printers, telephone systems, and other equipment. This type of equipment can strain building electrical systems, especially in older buildings. It is extremely important that a law office have a steady and reliable source of electricity that is sufficient to meet and exceed its needs.

CLIMATE CONTROL   Climate control, commonly referred to as heating, ventilation, and air-conditioning (HVAC), also is an environmental factor that should be considered carefully. The average office worker requires approximately two thousand cubic feet of fresh air per hour. An HVAC system should economically control an office's climate and provide clean and safe working conditions free of odors, dust, dirt, and smoke. Changes in air temperature also have been known to decrease worker productivity. Thus, the HVAC system must be stable and produce a constant temperature.

Color	Effects
Red	Overstimulates. Increases blood pressure. Creates feelings of physical warmth. Effective in areas where people spend short periods of time and stimulation is desired.
Black and brown	Create feelings of fatigue, often to the point of workers feeling ill. Decrease perception of light.
White	No strong reactions. Increases perception of light and space.
Blue	Very relaxing Reduces blood pressure and the effects of stress. Perceived, physically, as being cold. Sedative effect, occasionally to the point of depression. Overuse can cause sluggish behavior.
Yellow	No blood-pressure change. If tone is too bright or overused, can cause eyestrain. Is perceived as warm. Can stimulate a cheerful mood and often raises spirits.
Green	Considered the most normal color. No abnormal reactions. Can have a light sedative effect. May be perceived, physically, as cool or cold. In a test of rooms, each painted with a different color, a green room was selected as the favorite of the participants.

FIGURE 11-9
Effects of Color on Worker Well Being and Productivity

Source: Marjorie Miller, *Designing Your Law Office* (American Bar Association, copyright 1988). Reprinted with permission.

ACCESSIBILITY TO PERSONS WITH DISABILITIES   Whenever possible, law offices also should be accessible to persons with disabilities. Making law offices truly accessible to persons with disabilities is more complicated than might first be realized. Figure 11-10 contains a partial list of factors or changes that might be necessary in an office to make it accessible.

ELEVATORS   Elevators should be quick and responsive and large enough to handle the number of people who are using them, especially during peak times. Long elevator waits can be quite frustrating, especially if they happen on a regular basis.

MAINTENANCE AND CLEANING SERVICES   When considering a move, check on whose responsibility it is to take care of routine maintenance and other related issues such as whether the cleaning service is included with the lease or is contracted for separately with a third party. It is important to make sure that the cleaning service is bonded (bonded means that if the cleaning service steals from you, an insurance company will pay for the loss).

SPACE MANAGEMENT FOR THE LEGAL ASSISTANT

When setting up an office, resist the urge to throw everything in. Take the time to set up your office right; do it in the evening before work or early in the morning before work if you have to. Think about your particular work habits and how the office can be laid out to be functional and efficient for your particular needs.

OFFICE SPACES

- Provide wheelchair access and turnaround at entry. Clear turning space of 5 ft. (150 cm) needed for wheelchair maneuverability.
- Specify pedestal-base furniture. Avoid excessive leg and cross rail construction, sharp corners, and knob-type pulls.
- Place outlets, switches, equipment controls, thermostats, window closures, cabinet hardware, locks, handrails, and emergency equipment within reach of wheelchair user.
- Provide clear space of at least 2 ft. (60 cm) below countertops. Protect hazardous pipes and wiring from contact.

LIGHT SWITCHES

- Specify switches with easily operable positive action. Large rocker switches, palm- or arm-operated, are preferred.
- Locate switches 3 ft. to 3 ft. 3 in. (90 to 100 cm) above floor.
- Optimum outlet height is 1 ft. 8 in. to 2 ft. (50 to 60 cm) above floor.

DRINKING FOUNTAINS

- Upper edge of basin is 3 ft. (90 cm) above floor.
- Control and spouts should be hand-operated and placed up front. Time-delay lever below basin is also accessible.
- Recessed locations free passageways.
- Avoid spring-loaded shut-off mechanisms.

RAMPS

- Specify ramp gradient ratio. Width should not be less than 3 ft. 2 in. (95 cm).
- Maximum run to landing is 30 ft. (98 meters).
- Use nonslip surface.
- Provide rails on both sides at + 30 ft. (+90 cm) and intermediate rail at +2 ft. (+60 cm) from floor. Rails should not exceed 2 in. (5 cm) in diameter.

PUBLIC TOILETS

- Most local occupancy codes define proportionate requirements for public buildings, dormitories, etc.
- Place at least one specially designed toilet facility on each floor. Consider a separate disabled facility for both sexes rather than renovation.
- Include a toilet enclosure with enough room for wheelchair transfer *with* assistance of a second person.
- Minimum acceptable size of enclosure 5 ft. by 6 ft. (150 by 180 cm).
- Stall doors wing out and are a minimum width of 2 ft. 10 in. (85 cm). Use lever hardware, not recessed models.
- Toilets are centered with seat height at 19.5 in. (50 cm). Same measurement applies to urinal rims.
- Provide appropriate horizontal, vertical, and oblique grab rails of 1.5 in. (4 cm) diameter depending on disability.
- Dispensers, receptacles, mirrors, and accessory items should be within reach of wheelchair user and easily operable by handicapped persons.
- Locate towel racks, soap trays, and grab rails 2 ft. 10 in. to 3 ft. 3 in. (85 to 100 cm) above floor.
- Place tops of mirrors at 6 ft. 3 in. (190 cm) and bottom edges not greater than 2 ft. 8 in.(80 cm) above floor.

DOORS AND DOORWAYS

- All interior doorways must be accessible.

FIGURE 11-10   Disabled Accessibility

Source: Marjorie Miller, *Designing Your Law Office* (American Bar Association, copyright 1988). Reprinted with permission.

- Single doors should have minimum clear opening of 3 ft. (90 cm).
- Minimum accessible corridor/exit door opening should be 3 ft. 6 in. (108 cm).
- Vestibules should be at least 6 1/2 ft. (2 meters) long to prevent wheelchair entrapment.
- Door-opening areas must be free of any obstacles; 5 ft. (150 cm) in all directions.
- Door-opening pressure is not to exceed 9 pounds (4 kilos).
- Glazed doors should accommodate eye level of person in wheelchair.
- Door closers should be time-delay types only.
- Lever, push plate, and panic-bar hardware preferred. Hardware is normally mounted at 3 ft. (90 cm) above floor. Avoid knobs. Vertical pull-type handles are more suitable than horizontal pull-type handles. Center vertical handles at 3 ft. 6 in. (108 cm).
- Wheelchair space should be readily accessible to fire exits and emergency ramps.
- Sliding doors are more easily operated by handicapped persons. Avoid revolving doors or provide adjacent side-hung doors where they exist. Double-action swinging doors are hazardous.
- Illuminate and identify all exit/entrance doorways.
- Entry door thresholds and doormats should not project more than 0.5 in. (15 mm) above floor surfaces.
- Avoid entry carpets and grates with openings larger than 0.5 in. (15 mm).
- Use nonslip floors.
- Use audible communications signals and warning devices. Visual indicators should be provided for individually designed systems for specific needs/users.

ELEVATORS

- All elevators must be accessible.
- Elevators are the most efficient vertical transportation mode for disabled persons. Escalators, power ramps, and walks rarely accommodate persons with mobility impairment. Use of wheelchair lifts is not encouraged. Lifts may be incorporated where absolutely essential but never in new construction. Data on these devices relative to their safety and effectiveness are being evaluated by professional design groups.
- Buttons should be within reach of wheelchair operator at 2 ft. 6 in. to 4 ft. (75 to 120 cm) above floor.
- Emergency phone is essential. Place within wheelchair user's reach.
- Usable handrail height is 2 ft. 8 in. (80 cm).

Remember that you will be spending about 25 percent of your life in this office, day in and day out, so take the time to make it comfortable and practical. Every person and every office is different. Some employers will be willing to purchase things to make your office more efficient.

In the long run, it probably makes more sense to spend a little extra money to make the office practical and easy to work in. The long-term productivity gains save far more time and money in the end than not purchasing such items. Figure 11-11 will give you some ideas about setting up and managing your own office.

SECURITY AND SAFETY

Security is a topic that has previously not been taken very seriously by law offices. Unfortunately and tragically, violence to attorneys, legal assistants, legal secretaries, and court personnel has jumped at a dramatic and alarming rate in recent years. It is crucial that security be taken seriously. Disgruntled litigants

- **Work Space**—Legal assistants typically need as much usable work space as they can get to lay out documents they are working with, to organize files, and to do legal research (when drafting it is typical to have many books on your desk, including statutes and reporters). Maximize your usable work space whenever possible.
- **Mount Telephone on Wall**—Telephones typically sit on desks. However, nearly all telephones can be mounted on the wall. This gives you more usable work space on your desk and many times puts the phone closer to you anyway.
- **Replace Handset of Phone with Earpiece/Microphone**—Legal assistants can spend many hours on the phone. Most telephone headsets can be replaced with an earpiece/microphone unit with allows the user to talk on the phone hands free. They also are very comfortable to use and do not have the confidentiality problems that a speaker phone has.
- **Put Client Chairs Next to the Desk, Not Across the Desk**—Be sure to have an extra chair in the office if possible for clients and other people. Place the chair so that you do not have to talk across the desk to the client. This helps prevent you from being in a superior position to the client and creates a more amicable setting.
- **Keep Reference Books Next to You**—Keep reference books close by, such as *Black's Law Dictionary,* phone book, dictionary, form files, state statutes, and so forth so you do not have to get out of your chair to get them.
- **Background Music**—If you like music, many offices will allow you to play soft background music. This can set the mood or environment of your office as relaxed and also can reduce stress.
- **Comfortable Chair**—Do what you have to do to get a chair <u>that is comfortable to you,</u> even if it means bringing one from home or buying your own. Many times, people spend day in and day out in lumpy, worn out, uncomfortable, broken chairs and then wonder why they have backaches and do not want to come in for work. Easy chairs, secretarial chairs, get whatever chair is comfortable to you. Never let someone buy you a chair or get one for you without trying it out.
- **File Cabinet and Bookshelf**—If possible, get a file cabinet and a bookshelf and place them as close to your desk as possible. Legal assistants typically acquire important books, articles, and research material that should be saved. In addition, a file cabinet for the temporary storage of files while you are working with them will help keep you organized and keep your office from looking like a mess.
- **Glare Screen for Monitor**—If you use a computer, never put the monitor directly across from a window or directly under a fluorescent light, since either of these will create a large amount of glare. When possible, use a glare guard or some type of glare-reducing filter to place over the monitor. This can be purchased at most computer stores for a few dollars. Eyestrain can be a problem for legal assistants who work on a computer all the time.
- **Put Computer on Floor or on a Separate Desk**—If you are using a computer, never put the computer on the desk itself unless you absolutely have to since this will take up a great deal of space. Place the computer on the floor if possible and keep only the monitor and keyboard on the desk. If your computer cables are too short, cable extenders for all types of cables can be purchased at most computer stores. In addition, separate "keyboard drawers" can be purchased from most office suppliers for less than $20. Keyboard drawers allow you to mount the keyboard under the top of the desk and to pull the keyboard out when you need it and to push it back under the top of the desk when you do not (these only work if your desk does not have a "middle" drawer that goes over legs).

   If possible, separate and compact computer tables can be purchased for less than $100 at most office supply stores that have a place for the keyboard, monitor, computer, and printer.

FIGURE 11-11   Considerations When Setting Up a Legal Assistant's Office

assault all kinds of law offices all over the country from the rural solo practitioner to large firms in downtown skyscrapers. Figure 11-12 shows some extreme tragedies involving law offices.

There are many ways to provide security, including installing security systems, limiting access into private areas of the office using locked doors, installing locking doors with "buzzers" at reception areas, using security guards, installing security cameras, issuing identification and/or building passes, and limiting elevator service after certain hours. Law offices simply cannot afford to ignore the security issues that they are being faced with. Figure 11-13 contains some ideas of how law offices can tighten security. The type of security you use depends on the size of the firm, type of building, and many other factors.

SAFETY Safety also should be considered when looking for office space. Find out whether the building has a sprinkler system, fire alarms, emergency power/lighting, fire escapes, and other features that enhance safety.

- **Eight People Killed and Six Wounded When Gunman Attacks Law Firm**
  A man entered the 34th-floor law offices of a large downtown firm; under his suit jacket he had two guns, including a TEC-9 machine-gun-like pistol. In addition, he had a briefcase strapped to a dolly with hundreds of rounds of ammunition. Without speaking to anyone, he opened fire into a deposition room. He killed eight and wounded six before killing himself. The law firm represented the man's opponent in a lawsuit. The man had had his deposition taken earlier that morning in the office. Apparently the man thought he was going to lose the case. *San Francisco Daily Journal,* July 3, 1993; *ABA Journal,* September 1993, 20.
- **Attorney Gunned Down but Expected to Live—Pennsylvania**
  An attorney arrived at his office at 8:30 A.M. in a small town in Pennsylvania. He was gunned down as two horrified secretaries watched. The woman who allegedly shot him was the daughter of one of the attorney's clients. The attorney was representing the assailant's father in his attempts to have her civilly committed for mental illness. *National Law Journal,* Monday, July 26, 1993, 6.
- **Man About to Be Sentenced Assaults Federal Courthouse with Guns and Explosives—Kansas**
  A man who was about to be sentenced on federal drug charges arrived at the federal courthouse. He detonated a car bomb in the parking lot and proceeded to the fourth floor where the judges' chambers were. He killed one man and two others were injured in the clerk's office when an explosive that was strapped to his body went off. *Topeka Capital-Journal,* August 6, 1993.
- **Man Kills Four Clerks in New York—1992**
  A disgruntled child support payer shot and killed four clerks in the child support collection offices near the courthouse. *76 Judicature 315,* April-May 1993.
- **Two Appellate Court Judges, Two District Attorneys, and a Private Attorney Shot—Texas—1992**
  Two sitting appellate court judges and an assistant district attorney were shot and wounded, and another assistant district attorney and a private attorney were killed, during the rage of a litigant who recently lost a case. *76 Judicature 315,* April-May 1993.
- **Divorce Litigant Shoots Wife, Wife's Attorney, and His Attorney—Missouri—1992**
  A divorce litigant fatally shot his wife and wounded his wife's attorney, his own attorney, a bailiff, and a guard. *76 Judicature 315,* April-May 1993.

(continued)

FIGURE 11-12   Recent Legal Tragedies

- **Never Allow Free Access Throughout Your Office**—The golden rule of security is to **never** allow people free access throughout your office. Access to your office can be limited by restricting points of entry. If you are in a small building, lock the back door and don't allow the public to use it. Require the public to use the front door and have a receptionist there at all times monitoring the entrance.

    If your office is in a high rise, security stations can be posted at the entrance to the building and/or a receptionist at the entrance to your suite.

- **Limit the Public to a Waiting Room with a Locked Door to Inner Offices**—A good way to limit access to your office is to secure your waiting room. Simply put, the door from your waiting room to your inner offices should be locked and have a "buzzer" installed. By having a locked door to your inner offices, you restrict access and require the visitor to check in with the receptionist. This is similar to many doctor's offices, where a receptionist sits behind a sliding window and sounds a buzzer for you to come into the internal part of the office.

- **Issue Security Badges/Cards**—Another way to limit access in larger offices is to issue security cards or badges to personnel and to require visitors to check in and to issue them a "visitor" badge.

- **Monitor Entrances**—Entrances to the building or suites should be monitored when possible, by using security cameras, buzzers that go off when a person crosses the beam of light, posting security guards, or other such methods.

- **Remind Staff about Security Issues and Issue Policies**—Always remind staff about the importance of security issues and draft policies regarding security issues. Always be prepared.

- **Train Staff Members on Security Issues**—Whenever possible, staff members should be trained regarding safety awareness and security issues.

- **Large Buildings May Install Metal Detectors**—Metal detectors may be installed in large offices.

FIGURE 11-13   Strengthening Law Office Security

LAW OFFICE LEASE

Negotiating an office lease is a typical law office management duty. The state of the economy is a large factor when discussing bargaining position in a lease arrangement. When demand for office space is high, it is a seller's market, and the landlord can take a hard-line approach to the lease. However, when demand for space is down or if there is a glut of commercial property, it is a buyer's market, and buyers have a wide latitude in negotiating a lease. This section briefly covers the work letter and different types of leases.

work letter
The part of every lease that states what construction the landlord must perform before the tenant occupies the space.

THE WORK LETTER   *The* **work letter** *is the part of the lease that states what construction the landlord must perform before the tenant occupies the space.* An adequate work letter will set out the specifications of the office space the landlord will be required to supply to the tenant before the tenant takes possession. In effect, the work letter determines what the tenant is going to get for his money. Figure 11–14 shows a checklist of items to negotiate for when completing a work letter and/or lease. A typical work letter will cover the following areas.

HEATING, VENTILATION, AND AIR-CONDITIONING (HVAC)   The work letter should include information regarding acceptable temperature and humidity conditions to be maintained in each season, the quantity and quality of air to be delivered, how control of the temperature will be maintained and by

I. Matters involving the building
___ A. Lobby and lobby decoration
___ B. Elevators and elevator decoration
___ C. Exterior Windows
___ D. Standard building module
___ E. Parking availability
___ F. Washrooms
___ G. Size and location of freight elevator
___ H. Size and location of loading dock

II. Matters involving rent
___ A. Amount of *net* rent per square foot
___ B. Rentable space v. usable space
___ C. Date of rent commencement
___ D. Date of actual occupancy—access should be available no less than four to six months before rent commencement
___ E. Rent concessions
___ F. Procedure for resolving conflicts involving "market" rent
___ G. Availability of special parking rates

III. Matters involving development of the space
___ A. Standard walls
___ B. Walls with special sound attenuation
___ C. Height of walls above ceiling
___ D. Standard wall finish/covering
___ E. Special wall finish/covering
___ F. Glass walls
___ G. Standard doors and frames
___ H. Special doors and frames
___ I. Height of doors and frames
___ J. Painting
___ K. Standard hardware
___ L. Special hardware
___ M. Standard ceiling
___ N. Special ceiling
___ O. Height of ceiling
___ P. Standard flooring
___ Q. Special flooring
___ R. Standard base
___ S. Special base
___ T. Standard window covering
___ U. Special window covering
___ V. Overall—what is standard and what is extra

IV. Matters involving building systems
___ A. Duplex electrical outlets
___ B. Quadruplex electrical outlets
___ C. Strip electrical outlets
___ D. Power control for office automation systems
___ E. Telephone outlets
___ F. Standard lighting
___ G. Special lighting
___ H. Mechanical system

V. Matters involving standard and supplementary construction
___ A. Date by which construction documents are to be delivered to the landlord
___ B. Complete schedule leading to occupancy by tenant
___ C. Use of independent contractor(s)

___ D. Bids for work to be done
___ E. Fee of construction manager
___ F. Procedure for handling change orders

VI. Matters involving HVAC and electrical systems
___ A. Standard HVAC system
___ B. Special HVAC system for after-hours and computers
___ C. HVAC controls
___ D. Future expansion of HVAC system to meet growing needs
___ E. Smoke exhaust
___ F. Time periods during which building HVAC system is turned off
___ G. Time periods, if any, during which building electrical or lighting system is turned off
___ H. Procedure for tenant to request off-hours use of HVAC
___ I. Charge for off-hours use
___ J. Procedure for tenant to request off-hours use of electricity or lighting, if applicable
___ K. Charge for off-hours use

VII. Matters involving building services
___ A. Building services considered to be regular, i.e. covered by the lease and not separately billable to tenant
___ B. Schedule of all cleaning services
___ C. Building services considered to be special, i.e. not covered by the lease and, therefore, separately billable to tenant
___ D. Restrictions, if any, involving elevator service during tenant's move
___ E. Billing of electrical and utility costs—directly from the utility or passed through the landlord
___ F. Frequency with which landlord will repaint the leased premises

VIII. Matters involving pass-through of expenses
___ A. Base year for the purposes of calculating building services escalation
___ B. Items that make up the operation expense base
___ C. Pro forma financial statements showing operating expenses that will be incurred in future years
___ D. Operating expenses and taxes (expenses should be those which are incurred in a fully occupied building, and real estate taxes should be representative of comparable office buildings in the area)
___ E. Management fees (should be paid on the net, not gross, rent)

IX. Matters involving option space
___ A. Amount and schedule on which available
___ B. Demolition costs

X. Matters involving tenant's rights
___ A. What tenant is prohibited from doing
___ B. Right to sublease

XI. Definitions of terms used in the documents

FIGURE 11-14   Checklist for Negotiating a Lease and Work Letter

Source: Marjorie Miller, *Designing Your Law Office* (American Bar Association, copyright 1988). Reprinted with permission.

whom, and a description of the HVAC system. Poor HVAC systems can pose a problem in older buildings. HVAC also is important for law offices that have computer equipment that requires stable temperatures within a specified level. In addition, make sure the lease provides the days of the week and hours the HVAC system will run. This can be a problem if people may need to work late and no air is being circulated.

FLOORING/WALL COVERING Floor covering, floor-load capacities, and wall coverings also are covered in a work letter. Some computers require raised platforms for the computer room so that computer cables can be run under the floor and carpet. Other rooms, such as a law library or file room, require floor-load capacities of up to 125 pounds per square foot. **Floor-load capacity** *refers to the weight per square foot the floor can hold without collapsing.* Normal floor-load capacity is 75 to 100 pounds per square foot. If the floor-load capacity is not adequate, additional supports may be added. Carpet/floor tile allowances (if any) also are included. Wall covering such as paint and wallpaper also may be included.

floor-load capacity
The weight per square foot the floor can hold without collapsing.

CEILING Information regarding the type of ceiling tile may be included, especially if the tenants want acoustical ceiling tiles. Acoustical ceiling tiles are preferable, since they improve privacy and help to preserve confidential information. Ceiling heights also may be included here.

WINDOW COVERING The type of window covering (horizontal/vertical blinds or drapes) is covered in a work letter.

ELECTRICAL The amount of electrical power to be supplied also should be included. This is especially important if the law office has a great deal of computer equipment. Also, lighting requirements such as so many watts of fluorescent lighting per square foot, number of telephone and wall outlets, and like information are included in this section of the work letter.

DOORS/HARDWARE Doors and door hardware such as the type and size of doors (e.g., steel doors, hollow-core wood doors, solid wood doors, etc.), types of locks and door hinges, door closers, and door stops should be addressed in the work letter.

WALLS A work letter also refers to the types of walls ("partitions" in work letters). This may include ordinary Sheetrock walls but also may include special requirements, such as additional layers of Sheetrock for copy rooms, computer rooms, or kitchens/lounges with significant amounts of noise or other types of material for noise reduction.

LEASING When negotiating the lease and work letter, always know what concessions you want in advance and bargain for those items that are the most important. You should ask to see the plans and specifications of the building. Be prepared to negotiate not only on the items in the work letter but also on such matters as the term of the lease, the amount of rentable space and cost per square foot, parking spaces, whether signs are allowed and who pays for them, and how improvements are handled.

TYPES OF LEASES   There are a variety of types of leases. Among these are net leases and gross leases. In a **net lease,** *the tenant pays a base rent plus real estate taxes (either in whole or in part).* In some types of net leases, the tenant may also pay for insurance on the building and repair and maintenance charges. In a **gross lease,** *the tenant pays only for base rent, and the landlord covers all other building-related expenses (this may or may not include cleaning services, utilities, etc.).*

In both net and gross leases, the lease agreement typically will include annual increases. It is common for base rents to increase by a fixed amount, such as two percent to seven percent annually, or be tied to an increase in the Consumer Price Index or other such indices that track inflation. Some lease also will include increases regarding building repair and maintenance charges. Beware of complicated formulas for calculating increases that can be manipulated by the landlord. Some law offices hire leasing services to audit leases to determine whether the office was charged for services that exceeded the terms of the lease. One way to avoid some of these problems is to hire a leasing consultant or real estate broker to negotiate the terms of the lease for you. In many instances, the landlord pays the broker's commission without cost to the tenant.

net lease
A lease in which the tenant pays a base rent plus real estate taxes (either in whole or in part).

gross lease
A lease in which the tenant pays only for base rent, and the landlord covers all other building-related expenses.

MOVING CONSIDERATIONS

Moving a law office from one physical location to another may seem simple and easy, but that is rarely the case. The reason is that it takes a great deal of planning and organization to pull a move off successfully without:

- Offending clients who still expect their matters to be tended to;
- Losing or misplacing important information or files;
- Breaking or damaging important and expensive equipment;
- Paying an enormous amount for moving costs, employee downtime, and restoring office productivity.

The keys to a successful move are to plan thoroughly well in advance and to organize the moving process by leaving little to chance. Most law offices begin the planning process three to twenty-four months in advance of a move depending on their size.

Figure 11-15 contains a sample moving checklist of things to accomplish. When setting a moving date, be aware that weekend and holiday moves many times are done to reduce interference that might occur when trying to move during a normal workday. Selecting a mover is an important consideration and usually can be done by calling references. Always meet with the mover and communicate exactly what your moving plans are, including:

- An inventory of what the mover is going to move;
- Overall costs of the move including hourly rates;
- Whether the mover must provide boxes and cartons;
- Who will be responsible for coordinating the move with the new landlord;
- Detailed instructions to the mover including layout of each new office;
- Information regarding particularly heavy equipment, loose material, etc.

All boxes, equipment, and furniture should be tagged with a code number indicating where they go on a detailed map of the new location. The numbering system should take into account floor and room numbers. Copy machines and computer equipment can be very sensitive and should be moved by the vendor that services the equipment.

- Secure new office space
- Give notice to employees of the decision to move and get their input
- Assign office space, parking spaces, etc.
- Order new or upgrade telephone system
- Order new telephone number for new office if necessary
- Order new letterhead, envelopes, business cards, billing statements, checks, rubber stamp(s), mailing labels, etc.
- Order new sign for the office.
- Order furniture for the new office if necessary

- Establish who will coordinate and be responsible for the move
- Determine what dates and when the move will occur (e.g., weekends, holidays, evenings, etc.)
- Confirm moving dates with landlord
- Determine how long the move will take and place schedules accordingly
- Select a moving company

- Assemble a list of equipment and furniture to be moved
- Establish a list of equipment/furniture that will be sold, stored, or otherwise disposed of
- Establish packing requirements
- Prepare a basic move plan for the mover
- Confirm delivery dates of new furniture, vending machines, utilities
- Send out new address cards to clients, bar associations, other firms, judiciary, Martindale Hubbell, telephone directory, library subscription services, bank, vendors, post office, insurance carriers, utilities
- Order office keys
- Establish when staff will stop working on client matters and begin moving

- Secure needed packing materials, cartons, etc., if not provided by movers (always have a large supply of extras)
- Consider whether additional insurance will be needed if additional furniture or equipment is purchased
- Determining the order of the move (what gets moved first, moved last, set up first, etc.)
- Make necessary arrangements for moving of electronic equipment such as computers, copy machines, etc., and/or rental equipment. This equipment should usually not be moved by the moving company
- Test new phone equipment
- Distribute office keys to employees
- Clean out and throw away items not to be removed (housecleaning)
- Have employees remove personal property
- Request employees to close or put away as many files as possible
- Pack contents of offices, etc.
- Assign code numbers and tag equipment
- Cut over telephone system
- Move!
- Reduce access of employees to the new location until after everything is moved (will cut down on confusion)

FIGURE 11-15   Moving Details

Figure 11-16 gives a graphic account of a move for one office and shows how a move can be completed successfully.

---

20 years of Collecting "Stuff"

Moving a law firm is a daunting and traumatic event. Lewis and Roca moved 350 people from an office overstuffed from 20 years of doing business. Not only were we physically moving, we were simultaneously implementing a new computer system network, new software, and new telephone system and voice mail.

Teamwork is Needed at All Levels

You will need the cooperation and effort of every person in the law firm to conduct a successful move. We held periodic staff meetings, assigned activity coordinators, and generally tried to get all the employees on the team. This. . .allowed the administration to regularly communicate with the staff about tasks that needed to be completed on a timely basis. . . [and] helped us stay on schedule.

Planning

You simply can't overplan a move. . . . Think through as many of the details as you can and develop a schedule. We began planning a year in advance, but most of the real work was done in the five months prior to the move.

Clean Out "Stuff"—Be Ruthless!—11 Bottles of Whiteout in One Desk

Make decisions about what documents will be retained, what will be discarded, and what will be sent to storage. We gave each timekeeper a list of items he or she could keep and which types of material he or she could discard. Go through everything!! Be ruthless! Electronic documents can be cleaned out, too. 100,000 documents were cleared off the existing computer system. The savings in electronic and hard-copy storage space was dramatic.

Clean out those desks. Make the supplies hoarders return surplus supplies. One desk alone produced eleven bottles of Whiteout! You will be absolutely amazed at the amount of material that is squirreled away in lawyer's offices.

Have Letterhead Delivered to the New Location

Monitor levels of letterhead and other customized supplies so that there is not a large excess at move time. Plan to have the new letterhead delivered to the new location. . . .Don't pay to move it twice.

Personal Belongings Go Home

Insist that all personal belongings go home well in advance of the move. Moving personal belongings presents several problems, including insurance liability and unnecessary moving charges. Personal effects should not be returned until well after the move.

Communicate with Office Staff—Moving Is Traumatic—Solicit Staff Input at All Phases

Keep all firm personnel fully informed of the moving plans. Don't underestimate how traumatic a move can be. Our move updates were distributed on bright green paper. We also staged frequent staff meetings during which we provided status reports on our preparation progress. These meetings kept everyone informed and motivated. Solicit staff input at all phases of the planning process. Let them test equipment and furniture being considered.

Appoint an "Answer Person"

Several weeks prior to the move, appoint an experienced staff member to be the "Answer Person"— someone who can be trained to provide the answers on any question concerning the upcoming

(continued)

FIGURE 11-16   Blueprint for Relocating the Law Firm Office

move. Since many middle management will be unavailable during this point, having a stationary "Answer Person" to provide a triage of sorts to field the inevitable questions about parking, security cards, voice mail, supplies, etc., can really help to alleviate staff confusion and anxieties.

Communicate with Vendors

Meet with all your vendors and let them know your move timetable. It's a good idea to take equipment and service vendors on a tour of the new facility, in case. . . any changes in equipment are necessary. Some vendors insist on moving their own equipment. This is good to know and plan for in advance.

Provide Training on New Equipment to Staff

If you are changing a major system (adding voice mail, changing software, etc.), plan your training and documentation for several weeks prior to the move. This gives people a chance to become familiar with the new systems. . . . This is important even if the new equipment is not yet available to them.

Provide "Care Packages" to Staff

Provide detailed instructions about the move and information about the new location. We had a "care package" on everyone's chair that contained labeled floor plans, new telephone directories, a list of who to call for what, how to work the phones, and other helpful information to ease the anxiety of new surroundings and to minimize postmove work inefficiency.

Provide Documentation to the Movers

Provide adequate documentation for the movers. This includes portable maps of office/department layouts with preassigned room labels to help movers know where to go. Every room that is a destination for any box, equipment, furniture, or supplies should have a number assigned to it. There should be detailed library layouts specifying precisely where particular book sets should be shelved.

Take Care of the Telephone System Early

Telephone lines must be installed and operational before the phone company will assign phone numbers. If you want to maintain the same phone prefix for all your employees, you will have to be sure to reserve it well in advance of the move. The phone company won't guarantee the exact phone numbers you have reserved, but its your only chance to do so. Besides, you can't order the stationary, business cards, and other personalized supplies until those phone numbers are finalized. During the move, be sure to have the phone and computer vendors on hand to troubleshoot the inevitable malfunctioning cable, unprogrammed telephones, and the like. Don't let the vendor leave until the equipment works to your satisfaction. Hang on to them by their ankles if need be.

Install Technology in New Offices First

Arrange to install the computers, phones, copiers, and fax machines before the furniture and boxes are moved. This is critical for a number of reasons. The installers can work faster if they don't have to contend with the clutter of furniture or boxes. The movers can work faster if the "tekkies" are out of the way. Lastly, having the technology up and running allows a lawyer [and legal assistant] to begin work immediately upon moving. Of course, back up all computer and telephone systems before anything is moved.

The Move

Secure access to elevators in both the new and the old office locations. Don't let them assign you just the service elevator. Many a firm relocation has become a disaster due to inadequate elevator access. Allow only those persons directly involved in the physical move to be on the old or new premises. This means no partners, no associates, no children. Moreover, no one should be admitted to the new office location until the all-clear sign has been given. An office move is no time for spectators. Retain one fully functional office/secretarial station until after the move is completed. Include fax, word processor, a copy machine, and WESTLAW/LEXIS access. This will allow client business to continue during the most chaotic time.

(continued)

After the Move

Institute a six-month "No Complaints" period. This separates the anxiety-driven complaints from the rest and gives everyone a chance to get used to the new surroundings and troubleshoot the problems. Realize that the job is not over once moving day is finished. The key to any successful move is planning and working with all of your peers and your vendors so that everyone has the information they need to move in an efficient and effective way. Such an effort takes planning, teamwork, communication, and documentation.

Summary

Law offices of all types have discovered the increased productivity and increased quality of legal services that can be provided to clients by using technology that includes copy machines, dictation equipment, facsimile machines, and telecommunication equipment. Technology, however, must be carefully managed given its high cost. Every time a law office purchases equipment, an opportunity cost is involved. Opportunity cost refers to the cost of forgoing or passing up other alternatives. By carefully determining an office's current and future needs, researching the purchase, generating competition, and making purchase decisions wisely, a law office can go a long way toward making sure it is making intelligent purchases for equipment that will serve the office for many years to come.

Facility management refers to management's responsibility to manage, plan, design, and control a law office's own building or office space effectively. When choosing an office, careful consideration should be given to the building's location, effective space planning, space utilization, and environmental matters such as lighting, noise, color, climate, security, and safety. An office's usable space is actual occupiable area that the office can use for office, equipment, etc. A loss factor is the tenant's pro-rata share of common space in a multitenant floor or building. Rentable space is what a tenant pays rent on and includes usable space plus a loss factor. A work letter is a part of the lease that sets out the specifications of the office space the landlord will be required to provide. There are several types of leases, including net leases, where tenants pay a base rent plus other expenses such as real estate taxes, and gross leases, where the tenant pays only for base rent. When a law office must go through a move, it must be carefully planned well in advance with attention paid to all the necessary details

Key Terms

Automatic document feed (ADF)
Duplexing
Opportunity costs
Just-in-time inventory
Facility management
Usable space
Rentable space

Loss factor
Interior landscaping
Task lighting
Work letter
Floor-load capacity
Net lease
Gross lease

PROBLEM SOLVING QUESTIONS

1. Your law office recently purchased a piece of equipment. The equipment never worked properly and after three months the vendor picked it up. The vendor agreed to refund the office its money. Did the office lose anything? Comment on this situation. Would your answer change if the vendor did not refund the money and the office was forced to sue the vendor to recover the purchase price?

2. Your office needs to rent 5,000 square feet of usable office space. You have been given a great bid on an office with 5,000 square feet that suits your new and expanding image. The lease term can be a minimum of two years. However, within the next three years, the office is expecting to double its growth. The current space is a little cramped but could get you by for a year longer. Please discuss the office's situation. What do you recommend? Give reasons for your answer. What additional information would you like to have?

3. As the law office manager for a legal aid practice, you must consider how the office is going to finance a new copier it must have. The purchase price of a mid-size copier you are looking at is $7,500. The rental price on the machine is $250 per month. A lease-to-purchase agreement is $200 per month for four years; the office would have an option to buy the equipment under the agreement at 10 percent of the purchase price. The useful life of the copier is not more than five years. If the office purchased the machine, it would hurt its cash flow, but, on the other hand, the office doesn't want to pay a great deal extra if it uses the rent or lease option. Please list the factors that will influence your decision and present the approximate cost of the machine under each option. Discuss the pros and cons of each option.

4. You must purchase office supplies for your office. Nothing makes the partners more upset than to go into the supply room for supplies and be out of the item they are looking for. In fact, they like to see stacks of supplies. You are considering starting a just-in-time inventory system. Explain to the partners the benefits of this system. Also, explain how you will implement the system. They will specifically be curious to know how you will ensure that there are no supply shortages.

5. Recently, you notice that your office's secretarial pool is taking more and more sick days, that morale is dropping, that productivity is off, and that several secretaries are discussing filing workers' compensation claims. You have heard the secretaries complain about glare from their computer screens, the "institutional"-type atmosphere, and the uncomfortable, old secretarial chairs. You hear one of the administrators mentioning that the secretaries are just lazy and that their equipment is fine. However, to your recollection no one has checked the validity of their complaints. Please recommend to the administrator ways to handle the situation. The administrator will surely shoot down your ideas unless you are prepared to answer questions about how the cost of any new equipment could be justified to the partners.

6. As a legal assistant at a legal aid organization, you see all types and kinds of people. Although you are compassionate about their needs, you realize that some of the people coming into the office have extensive criminal records. Recently, you were working in your office when you heard one of the attorneys over the intercom call for "Help." A client was apparently threatening the attorney. In addition, several weeks ago one the new clients was making the receptionist feel "uncomfortable" by asking her for a date and not taking "no" for an answer. The legal aid organization does not have a great deal of money but is concerned about the safety of its staff. People are free to come and go as they like. The office is in a small building and has three doors leading in and out of the building. The front door opens into a small waiting room. The receptionist sits at a desk in the waiting room. The parking lot is very small and unlighted. Staff members must occasionally work late and typically leave the doors unlocked. Prepare a short memorandum to the director of the legal aid organization discussing your analysis of the security situation at the office. Prioritize a list of three things that could be done to increase the security at the building and include the cost of any such item. In addition to "gadgets," discuss policy issues and changes that could be made.

KNOW YOUR ETHICS

1.   Many of the attorneys in your office have cellular phones. Discuss from an ethical perspective the problem with cellular phones in that in some cases conversations can be intercepted using a simple radio scanner.

2.   Staff members in your office routinely use the office intercom systems all-call/paging feature that goes officewide to announce who is in the waiting room or who is on the phone needing to talk to a specific attorney. Is there any problem with this?

3.   Discuss the problems with fax machines from an ethical perspective.

4.   You are working on a particularly sensitive case for a good client. You are handling many sensitive documents, some of which need to be trashed. The office is small and thus does not shred all documents, just the ones that each employee thinks need to be shredded. The office shredder is several offices away. It is inconvenient for you to get up and shred a document every time you throw away a sensitive paper, so you have just been putting it in the regular trash can. Discuss the ethical considerations.

PRACTICE EXERCISES

1.   You have been charged with doing the research necessary to purchase a copier for your law office. You will research the purchase, get bids, and then present your recommendations to a committee. Your first step was to talk to law office staff members, and get their comments on what features they wanted in a machine and to generally research what size machine the office needed. Your research revealed the following:

- The law office appears to be making about 15,000 copies a month in high-volume months and about 10,000 in lower-volume months.
- The office handles cases in which employees must make as many as twenty separate copies of briefs and other large documents. Many of the briefs and documents eventually are mailed out.
- Everyone in the office agrees that having cost-saving features in the machine is important (both in time and in other costs) and that a machine should be purchased that is extremely reliable and large enough to handle the needs. Reliability is a feature that everyone agrees cannot be compromised on.

- The office wants to get a competitive maintenance contract that includes all supplies (other than paper) if possible.
- The office has a few instances in which legal-size paper is used, but the predominance of its paper need is letter size. This is especially true when copying large briefs.

What one additional piece of information is critical before you can really make this determination (think in terms of time)? Please prepare a brief specification sheet on the type of copier and/or features you might be looking for. The committee will be interested in your justification and support of the specifications you choose.

2.   As an office manager, you are considering the purchase of five typewriters. You have narrowed down to two greatly different machines. The first model costs $400 and has many features, including a maintenance agreement. The second machine costs $750, has substantially the same features plus some extra features the first machine does not have, and comes with a maintenance agreement. From reviews and other information, you estimate that the first machine will last about five years. Further, you estimate the second

machine will last ten years. Which machine would you purchase and why? Be specific.

3.   You have the task of researching the decision to purchase a phone system for your office. You will report to an office administrator, but the administrator expects you to do the legwork and to present her with good information that she can use to make the final decision and plan/budget for how to pay for the purchase. The administrator expects the system to cost not less than $10,000. Given the amount of money involved, you are a little nervous about the assignment. You, however, are determined to get every scrap of relevant information so that the administrator will have the information necessary to make a good decision. Please plan how you would complete the assignment, step-by-step.

4.   Your office has narrowed a search to two new office location alternatives, both of which are in multitenant office buildings. The first alternative has 2,000 square feet of usable space with a loss factor of 12 percent and a cost of $17 per square foot. The second alternative has 2,000 square feet of usable space with a loss factor of 7 percent and a cost of $22 per square foot. If everything else is equal, what do you recommend?

5.   The office you work for is considering a move. It would like you to do some preliminary work on its needs. The office has six attorneys, three legal assistants, four secretaries, one file clerk, and one copy clerk/runner. Please assume this is an "average" law office. The office will need offices, conference room(s), file room, reception room, kitchen, and library. Please estimate the total usable square footage it will need so it can begin looking for a new location. Also, please estimate the needed space for each office. Remember that space is expensive and should be used well.

6.   You have been appointed as the point person to arrange a solo practitioner's move to a new location. He put the decision off to decide to move or not until the last minute. It is now June 1. You must be out of your current building by June 30 and you can take possession of the new building on June 25. Time is of the essence, and you must quickly lay out a game plan to get the impossible done. The solo practitioner is changing his image and ordering three new desks and credenzas, which must be arranged with the office equipment company, and a new phone system. You must contact all necessary vendors and clients about the move. Please construct a detailed plan for your employer's move.

7.   Contact a law office in your area and discuss what it is doing to ensure the safety and security of its staff. Ask what its future plans are and what its philosophy on the topic is. Ask for examples of security or safety problems the office has had.

Notes

1. Margaret Cronin Fisk, "Capital Equipment Survey," *National Law Journal*, May 25, 1992, S5, quoting Charles E. Wharton, executive director of Los Angeles's O'Melveny & Myers.
2. Deborah Heller and James M. Hunt, *Practicing Law and Managing People: How to Be Successful* (Butterworth, 1988) 54.
3. Arentowicz and Bower, *Law Office Automation and Technology.* (Matthew Bender, 1992), sec. 9.05[5].
4. Paul Hoffman, ed., *Law Office Economics and Management Manual* (Clark Boardman, Callaghan, 1992), sec. 35.01, p. 3.
5. Marjorie A. Miller, *Designing Your Law Office* (ABA, 1988).
6. "How to Audit Your Lease Escalations", *Law Office Management Administration Report*, October 1992, 7.
7. Mary Ann Altman, "Hidden Factors in Space Planning," *Law Practice Management*, January/February 1990, 33.

A

SUCCESS STRATEGIES FOR THE NEW LEGAL ASSISTANT

The biggest reason we let legal assistants go is because they do not have the management skills necessary to perform adequately. They come out of school with a theoretical knowledge of law, but with few practical skills to manage themselves so as to succeed at our firm.[1]

In order to succeed, legal assistants must develop good management skills such as being accurate and thorough in everything they do, being routinely organized, prompt and prepared, being team players and communicating effectively. These things do not come naturally; most are learned the hard old-fashioned way, by trial and error, over years. Read this section with the idea that you can pick up some good ideas now that will save you many headaches once on the job. Some of the suggestions may sound simplistic. They really are not. The suggestions in this chapter come from many legal assistants and from many experiences. These suggestions really work; and while some are fundamental, all of them are still important.

ACCURACY, THOROUGHNESS, AND QUALITY

Accuracy and thoroughness are easy to say but hard to accomplish. However, high quality work is vital to the performance of a professional. A law office is a team, and everyone must be able to rely on the others; each client is paying for and deserves the absolute best work product the team can provide.

One element of quality work is careful documentation. It is important that when you talk to witnesses, clients, opposing counsel, or others that you keep written notes of your conversation and send a confirming letter that documents your conversation. Some cases can drag on for years; if proper notes are not kept in the file, vital information can be lost. Keeping proper documentation about the work you have done on a case is very important.

Mistakes happen. If something does slip by, do not try to cover it up. Admit and/or report the mistake, correct the mistake to the best of your ability as quickly as possible, take precautions to make sure it does not happen again, apologize, and go on. Because mistakes are natural and almost inevitable, being accurate and putting out quality work is a daily battle.

Ideas on how to improve the quality of your work:

- **Create Forms & Systems**–If you do a job more than once, create a system using forms and instructions for yourself. This will evoke your memories from the last time you performed the job and speed up the work.

- **Create Checklists**–Make a checklist for the jobs you regularly perform. Checklists will keep you from failing to perform specific details of a job that otherwise might be forgotten. In this way, the high quality of your work is maintained.

- **Be Careful and Complete**–Be prudent and careful in your work. Do not hurry your work to the degree that accuracy and thoroughness is compromised. Your work should always be neat and complete.

- **Keep Written Documentation and Notes**–Keeping proper documentation about work you have done on a case is very important.

- **Take Pride in Your Work**–Do not let work go out with your name on it that you are not proud to call your own.

- **Work Hard**–Accuracy and thoroughness is seldom reached by slothfulness. Work hard in what you do and your quality will always be better.

- **Ask for Peer Review**–If you have a particularly important project due and you have a question about the accuracy of your work have another legal assistant or other staff member look it over before it is turned in. While you do not want to become dependent on others or disrupt their productivity sometimes a second opinion can really help, especially if you are new to the organization.

- **Never Assume**–Do not assume anything. If you have the slightest doubt, check it out, research it, make sure that you pay attention to details, and double check the accuracy of your work.

THE ASSIGNMENT

> *A senior partner thinks he has told a legal assistant to take care of an important filing. In actuality, all he told the legal assistant to do was to draft the necessary documents to make the filing. The legal assistant drafts the documents and puts them in the senior partner's box for review. The filing deadline is missed. The senior partner blames the legal assistant for the job not being done properly.[2]*

When a task is being assigned, make sure you understand exactly what the assignment is and what the supervising attorney wants. Be absolutely certain that you understand the whole assignment; do not guess or extrapolate. One of the most common mistakes a new legal assistant makes is to not ask questions. It takes a certain amount of maturity to say "I do not understand", but it is absolutely critical. Your supervising attorney will not think any worse of you for it, and your chance of success on the task will be greatly enhanced. Also, it is a good idea to repeat the assignment back to the supervisor to make sure you understand all of the details of the assignment. If a task is extremely complicated, ask the supervisor to help you break it down into smaller parts. You might say: "This appears to be a fairly good sized job. Where do you recommend I start and how should I proceed; what steps should I take?"

It is also a good idea to write down your assignment. Have a pencil and a notebook or steno pad with you any time you talk to your supervisor about an assignment. A steno pad can serve as a journal allowing you to keep all of your assignments in one place. If you record assignments you will be able to refer back to them, if someone later has a question or problem about an assignment they gave you. Be sure to write down what the assignment is, who gave it to you, any comments the person made about the assignment, and when it is due. It is always a good idea to ask the exact date an assignment is due, not "sometime next week" or "whenever you get to it". Also be sure to write down when it was completed.

If an assignment gets a little fuzzy to you after you start it, ask the supervisor questions about it while you are still in the middle of it. Do not wait until the end of the assignment to realize you did something wrong; check in periodically and have the supervisor quickly review it. This is particularly important with large and complex tasks.

> *You start with real basic things like you bring a pad and pencil with you.*
> *You don't get grabbed in the hallway and get an oral assignment of some*
> *significance and not write it down.*[3]

Ideas on how to communicate effectively when receiving assignments:

- **Ask Questions When the Assignment Is Given**–Ask questions about the assignment until you fully understand what you are being asked to perform (Be aware that miscommunication problems occur more frequently regarding assignments you have never done before).

- **Repeat the Assignment Back**–Repeat the assignment back to the supervisor to make sure you understand all of the details of it.

- **Break Down Complex Assignments into Small Tasks**–On complex assignments ask the supervisor to help you break the assignment down into smaller tasks and help you organize the priority of the different tasks.

- **Have Pencil and Paper Ready**–Always have a pencil and paper (a steno pad works best) with you when you are being given as assignment. It allows you to remember when the assignment was given, by whom, any comments from the supervisor about it, and when it is due.

- **Always Ask for a Due Date**–Always ask for a specific due date. This prevents miscommunication regarding when an assignment should be completed.

- **Continue to Ask Questions and Check in Periodically**–As you work on the assignment continue to ask clarifying questions and periodically check in with your supervisor to keep her updated on your progress.

PREPARATION AND ORGANIZATION

Successful legal assistants are organized and prepared for everything they do. Being organized is not hard, it just takes planning and time. Always have an appointment calendar with you so that you can record important appointments and deadlines. In addition, use a "things to do" list each day and try to plan and prioritize things so that assignments and projects are never late. Prioritize your tasks so that you begin with the most important thing you have to do or with the task that has the most pressing deadline. When you are working on projects for two or more attorneys, ask someone to prioritize the tasks for you.

Ideas on preparation and organization:

- **Have an Appointment Calendar**–Carry an appointment calendar with you at all times. This way if you are caught in the hallway and given an assignment or meeting date you will know if you have a conflict.

- **Make a Things to do List**–Plan your day in advance, everyday. Make a "things to do" list and try to complete your list everyday, marking off items that are completed.

- **Prioritize Tasks**–When you are preparing your "things to do list", always prioritize the tasks so that you turn in assignments on time. Give priority to assignments that have the most pressing deadlines. If you have a question about what assignment needs to be done first, ask your managing attorney for direction.

- **Be on Time**–Always be on time when completing assignments, and attending meetings, and always take good notes when attending meetings so that you will remember important facts or information from the meeting.

MANAGE YOUR TIME

Are you using your time effectively, or wasting it? Time management and organization go hand in hand. Avoid procrastination by completing the things on your "to do list" day in and day out. Keep phone books, Rolodex, dictionaries and often-used reference manuals within arm's reach of your desk, so that time is not wasted looking for these materials. Be aware of people that come into your office and waste your time (be sure you are not guilty of doing this to others). Have the maturity to say: "That sounds very interesting and I would like to hear about it, but I have to get this assignment done right now—tell me about it at lunch". Avoid socializing in the office or hallways.

An effective way to manage your time, especially when you have large projects, is to make a Gantt chart. A **Gantt chart** *is a plan or timeline of projected begin dates and end dates for the various parts of a project.* Using a Gantt chart is an excellent way of planning a large project by breaking it into smaller tasks and allowing you to track the progress of the work. Large projects frequently require you to work on several tasks at one time, and the overlapping lines on a Gantt chart inform you of this fact.

Ideas on managing your time effectively:

- **Set Daily Objectives**–Always plan your day by setting daily objectives and prioritizing them accordingly. Try to stick to your plan and finish your objectives every day.

- **Do Not Waste Your Time on Irrelevant Tasks**–Do not waste your time on unnecessary tasks. When someone walks into your office to talk about an irrelevant subject and you have a job due, tell him politely to come back another time when you have free time.

▪ **Avoid Procrastination**–Do not put off what you can do today. Procrastination is unprofessional and leads to dissatisfied clients. Stick to your daily schedule and do not put things off unless you have a good reason.

▪ **Avoid Socializing in Hallways**–Socializing is not only a waste of your time, but also distracting to others around you. It also looks very bad to clients.

▪ **Make a Timeline or Gantt Chart**–When you have a large project, take the time to make a Gantt chart. A Gantt chart is a plan or timeline of projected begin dates and end dates for the various parts of a project. A Gantt chart will help you plan how you will complete the project and also allow you to track the progress of the work.

▪ **Have Reference Material Close By**–Lay out your desk and office so that important reference materials are located within arm's length to minimize time spent looking for things.

EFFECTIVE COMMUNICATION WITH ATTORNEYS

One of your most important tasks will be to establish mutual confidence between yourself and your supervisor. Because legal assistants and attorneys must work together very closely, good communication is an absolute necessity. Check in with the attorney on a daily basis if possible. If verbal communication is not possible, a short memo is very effective in keeping the attorney informed of what you are doing. Communication is especially important when decisions need to be made on a case, on how to do something, on how to handle a problem and the like.

> *If you want respect in this profession, you must command it. To command this respect, you must be an intelligent professional willing to take on responsibility without having to be asked. Find ways to make yourself even more valuable than you already appear to be. Don't sit and complain about the way things are. Take charge and change them.[4]*

One of the most important ways to improve communication is asking questions. Another important point for effective communicating is listening, really listening to others, what they are saying and what they are not saying. Remember, you cannot listen when you are talking.

One of the first things you should explore with the attorney is the limit of your authority in making decisions. This will take time for you to learn but it is very important. As the relationship grows you should begin to have mutual confidence in each other's work. You should be able to talk about important matters and make recommendations with confidence and effectiveness.

Ideas on communicating with attorneys:

▪ **Always Ask Questions**–If you do not understand something, ask questions.

▪ **Listen**–Do not forget to listen carefully when communicating with your supervising attorney. Listen and make notes so that you remember the details you will need to complete assignments.

- **Be Confident**–Do not be so intimidated by attorneys that you act timidly and fail to communicate. Carry yourself with confidence and authority. When you talk, always try to make eye contact.

- **Check In**–Check in with your supervising attorney on a daily basis so that she is informed of your progress on your assignments.

- **Do Not Make Important Decisions Unilaterally**–Include the supervising attorney in the decision-making process.

- **Establish Mutual Confidence**–Establishing mutual confidence with your supervising attorney is crucial. Your supervising attorney needs to have confidence in your work and you need have confidence in her work.

- **Establish Your Limit of Authority**–Ask your supervising attorney what your limit of authority is when making decisions. You need to know as clearly as possible when she should be involved in decisions and what types of decisions they are.

THE CLIENT COMES FIRST

When you are with a client, he should be given your undivided attention. Do not take phone calls, be interrupted, play with your nails, do anything else that would take your attention away from the client. Treat each client courteously and respectfully, and as if he is the only client you have.

While the needs of the client are very important, be careful not to overstep your bounds, by answering a question or giving legal advice that should be given by the attorney. Politely tell the client that you will have the attorney call him back with an answer to the question, or that you will talk to the attorney and call him back with the answer.

Finally, never talk about a client's case outside of work, ever. You owe the utmost confidentiality to your clients, and they expect it. Chapter Three deals in more depth with client-related issues.

Ideas on how to ensure that "the client comes first":

- **Give Clients Your Undivided Attention**–When you are with a client, be sure that you give the client your undivided attention, do not take phone calls, open mail or do anything else that would take your attention away from the client.

- **Give Clients Fast, Courteous, Respectful Treatment**–Treat the client courteously and respectfully at *all* times. Always return client phone calls as quickly as possible, but never later than the same day they called, and always try to answer their questions as quickly as humanly possible.

- **Treat Each Client As If He Were Your Only Client**–A client's case is very important to him and should be important to you. Let your clients know that their welfare genuinely concerns you.

- **Serve Clients But Do Not Overstep Your Bounds**–Do not let your zeal to serve clients cause you to overstep your bounds. Let the attorney answer complex client questions and give legal advice.

- **Client Confidence**–Always maintain the strictest standards regarding client confidentiality.

KEEP ACCURATE, CONTEMPORANEOUS TIMESHEETS

Attorneys and legal assistants keep time records for the amount of time spent on each case, so that management will know how much to bill each client. Many firms require legal assistants to bill a certain number of hours of billable time to clients a year or a month, so when you start with a firm always be sure to ask how many hours of billable time you are expected to have per month and annually. Also, ask when time sheets are due and when they are monitored for compliance (i.e. weekly, monthly, quarterly). It is a good idea to budget your time so that you know how many billable hours a month, week or even each day you will need to meet your goal, and then monitor yourself on your progress. Do not let yourself get behind, as you will not be able to make it up. If you are given a non-billable task, delegate the task as much as possible to secretaries and clerks. There are a few simple techniques to keeping accurate timesheets. Always record the necessary information on your timesheet *as the day progresses*. Do not try and go back at the end of the day or even week and try to remember what you did; write it down as you perform the work.

Timekeepers, especially new timekeepers, have a tendency to subjectively discount their hours because they feel guilty for billing their time to clients. Record the time you *actually* spent working on a client's case: if it took 6 hours to research a legal issue, record the whole 6 hours. If your supervisor does not believe the finished product is worth that much, he or she can adjust the time billed. Simply put, it is not your call to reduce your hours. Record your actual time and go on.

Ideas on keeping accurate time records:

- **Keep Track of Budgeted and Actual Billable Hours**–Your supervisor may tell you that you are responsible for billing a 100 hours a month (i.e. 25 hours a week). You want to be sure every week that the timesheets you turn in to management show as close to the amount budgeted as possible. You need to track this.

- **Keep a Timesheet near Your Phone**–Always keep a timesheet next to your phone, so when you pick up the phone you can record the time for it.

- **Fill out the Timesheet Throughout the Day**–Fill out your timesheet as you go throughout the day instead of trying to play the "memory game" to remember all the things you accomplished that day.

- **Record the Actual Time You Spent on a Case**–Always record the actual time it took you to perform the legal service. Let your supervisor make any decision to adjust or reduce time to be billed to the client.

- **Be Absolutely Honest and Ethical**–Never bill a client for administrative tasks or for time you did not actually spend working on his case.

WORK HARD & EFFICIENTLY

Everyone knows the difference between working hard and coasting. If you work hard, people will respect you and recognize you for it; if you do not, people will recognize this also and typically will resent you for it.

Do not be surprised if you must work overtime. The question as to whether legal assistants should be paid for overtime is a hot topic, some firms pay overtime compensation and some do not. In any event, if you have to work overtime, do it with a positive attitude. Be honest and sincere and work hard in everything you do. Also, try to work as efficiently as possible.

- **Pull Your Weight**–Work hard and pull your weight. Do what is asked of you and put out quality work.

- **Put in Overtime when Required**–Be ready to put in overtime when it is required. Try to be pleasant and professional about it.

- **Work Efficiently**–Work as a efficiently as possible. If you have access to a computer, it makes sense to use it instead of doing something by hand which may take longer.

POSITIVE ATTITUDE AND TEAM SPIRIT

> *The greatest key to success is something no one can give you—a good attitude! Enthusiasm has nothing to do with noise; it has more to do with motivation. It deals with our attitude. An attitude is something you can do something about, I can choose to be enthusiastic or I can choose not to be. Excitement is infectious; it's sort of like a case of the measles. You can't infect someone unless you have the real thing.[5]*

Essentially, a law office is a team that, to be successful, must rely on many different people to work together harmoniously. Approach your job with the goal of being a good team player and helping your team. Put the good of the firm above your own personal interest, and help the firm whenever you can, whether or not it is in your job description.

Good team players help other members of the team by passing along information and by cooperating on tasks. They are able to give and receive help when it is needed. Another aspect of being a team player is how to constructively criticize other players. First of all, be cordial and professional, never criticize another staff member in front of a client, an attorney or other staff members. Do not become emotional. Politely explain what the problem is and then suggest a reasonable solution for solving the problem. Treat the other person as an equal. When you are the one being criticized, do not take the criticism personally; look beyond the finding of fault and try to make the adjustments the firm is asking for. Listen carefully and ask questions so that you know exactly what the problem is.

Your own effectiveness as a legal assistant may well depend on how well you work with others at your own level on the team. There may be some people that you strongly dislike. You will need patience and interpersonal skills to learn to work with them and develop mutual trust and confidence.

Ideas on being a team player:

- **Put the Team First**–Always put the needs of the team before your own personal interests. In the long run, what is good for the team is good for you.

- **Delegate**–When possible delegate tasks to other team members. Use the team.

- **Help Other Team Members**–Always remember to take the time to help other team members. Otherwise, they will not be willing to help you when you need it.

- **Share Information**–Never horde information. Pass information along to other staff members, remembering to put the team first.

- **Constructively and Professionally Criticize Other Team Members**–Just because you are a team player does not mean you cannot constructively criticize others. Try to be respectful, professional, and non-emotional. Explain the criticism, then suggest ways to fix the problem. Treat others as equals.

- **Take Criticism Professionally**–Try to avoid getting defensive and listen to what is being said. As soon as possible, try to implement the suggestions of the other party.

- **Get Along With Those You Do Not Like**–It is probable that you will not like everyone you work with. But, for the good of the team, work at relationships and treat people with courtesy and respect anyway.

> *My secretary always backs me up, and she knows I'll back her up. One night she had a critical mailing to get out, and I stayed late with her so she could leave a little sooner. It's important to have a social relationship with her—you're concerned about her kids and she's concerned about how your weekend went.[7]*

- **Know the Employees of Your Firm**–Get to know the employees of your firm and treat all employees from the top to the bottom as you would like to be treated.

BE A SELF-STARTER

> *In order to advance as a paralegal, you must prove that you are capable of taking on greater responsibility by performing your present duties exceptionally well. Show your initiative by anticipating the next stage of any assignment and completing it before you are asked to do it.[8]*

Self-starters are valuable employees. Self-starters are people who do not need to be told what to do; they see a job that should be done or a need that could be fulfilled and they do the job or meet the need, without having to be told. They seek out and volunteer for new work, assume responsibility willingly, and anticipate future needs.

> *If you're in a meeting and everyone's talking about something, volunteer for it. Don't wait for them to point out, "That's something a paralegal could do."[9]*

Be flexible, open minded, and creative; be a problem solver. Do not hesitate to courteously suggest new ways of doing things as long as the idea is well thought out (not off-the-cuff) and would provide the firm with a real benefit over the present way. However, before you try to implement a new idea or approach be sure that you have researched, organized and planned the project well in advance and have assessed the chances or risk of failure and the consequences of such a failure. Get others involved in the project, ask for their help and input; this will help them accept the system later on.

Ideas on being a self-starter:

- **Anticipate**–Anticipate what jobs need to be done or what need is unfilled, and then do the job or fulfill the need without being asked to do it.

- **Seek Out and Volunteer for Assignments**–If a new assignment comes up (especially one with a lot of responsibility), volunteer for it.

- **Be Flexible and Open Minded**–Always be flexible, open minded and have a positive attitude. All businesses must change with the times; be adaptable.

- **Be Aware of the Risk**–Before taking on a new assignment, do some research and organization and planning. Assess your chances of success.

- **Get Others Involved**–Always include others in your development of new ideas. Get their thoughts and their feedback. Not only is the information helpful, but people are far more willing to implement an idea to which they have contributed.

> *Twenty years ago "pressure" and "stress" were primarily terms of physics, rather than terms of human behavior. Few will deny the pressure and stress that grips lawyers [and legal assistants] today.*[10]

STRESS MANAGEMENT

A law office is a very stressful place with lots of activities, deadlines, appointments, and problems. You must learn to manage your own stress or it will manage you. Do not be so consumed with your work to put it above your family or your own happiness. Learn to relax and participate in other activities that allow you to relax. A healthy lifestyle and exercise can also reduce your stress. You should also consider what causes your stress and how you can change your work environment to reduce your stress. Being a workaholic will only lead to burnout and frustration. Also, it is important that you take a vacation every year; everyone needs an extended rest at least once a year.

Ideas on managing stress:

- **Remember Your Family**–Do not let your work rule your life. To be a complete person, you must work hard but you also have responsibilities to your family. Try not to go too far in either direction, you need a balance.

- **Participate in Relaxing Activities**–Learn to relax and participate in activities you enjoy.

- **Exercise**–A healthy lifestyle and regular exercise is another good way to reduce stress.

- **Consider Your Environment**–Consider where your stress comes from and how you can change your work environment to reduce the cause of your stress.

- **Take a Vacation**–Take a vacation at least once a year. You need the rest and to get away from office from time to time.

CONCLUSION

There are many things that a successful legal assistant must have in addition to good technical skills. Being a team player, having a positive attitude, working hard, and keeping accurate records are just a few of the skills that legal assistants must have.

Everything in this appendix must be considered in light of the corporate culture of the particular law practice in which you are working. **Corporate culture** *refers to generally accepted behavior patterns within an organization.*[11] This will include the firm's values, personality, heroes, and mores. Most firms have a written procedures or staff manual that contains some of this information. However, many policies are never reduced to writing. Make it your business to understand your firm's position and how the firm views its clients, staff, and so on. Understanding how your particular firm looks at the world is very important.

NOTES

1. A legal administrator at a large Kansas City, Missouri firm.

2. William Statsky, *Introduction to Paralegalism,* West Publishing, 1992, p. 180, citing Sgarlat, *The Scape Goat Phenomenon,* 6 The Journal 10 (Sacramento Ass'n of Legal Assistants, June 1986).

3. Tokumitsu, "How to Avoid the Top 10 Mistakes Paralegals Make on the Job", *Legal Assistant Today,* Nov/Dec. 1991, p. 31.

4. William Statsky, *Introduction to Paralegalism,* West Publishing, 1992, p. 192, citing Roselle, *I Don't Get No Respect!,* 9 Nat'l Paralegal Reporter 2 (NFPA, November, 1984).

5. William Statsky, *Introduction to Paralegalism,* West Publishing, 1992, p. 192, citing Johnson, President's Message, *Newsletter* 1 (Arizona Paralegal Ass'n, July 1988).

6. Tokumitsu, "How to Avoid the Top 10 Mistakes Paralegals Make on the Job", *Legal Assistant Today,* Nov/Dec, 1991, p. 30.

7. Tokumitsu, "How To Avoid the Top 10 Mistakes Paralegals Make on the Job", *Legal Assistant Today,* Nov/Dec. 1991, p. 30.

8. William Statsky, *Introduction to Paralegalism,* West Publishing, 1992, p. 192, citing Coyne, *Strategies for Paralegal Career Development,* Nat'l Paralegal Reporter 20 (NFPA, Winter 1990).

9. Tokumitsu "How to Avoid the Top 10 Mistakes Paralegals Make on the Job", *Legal Assistant Today,* Nov/Dec, 1991, p. 29.

10. Thomas G. Bodie, *Practicing Competently,* Maryland Bar Journal, January/February, 1993, Volume XXVI, Number 1, p. 32.

11. Boone and Kurtz, *Management,* 3rd ed., Random House, 1987, p. 54.

NATIONAL LAW OFFICE MANAGEMENT, LEGAL ASSISTANT AND RELATED ASSOCIATIONS

Legal Administrators:
Association of Legal Administrators (ALA), 175 Hawthorn Parkway, Suite 325, Vernon Hills, IL 60061–1428 (708) 816–1212.

Legal Assistant Managers:
Legal Assistant Management Association (LAMA), 638 Prospect Avenue, Hartford, CT 06105–4298 (203) 232–4825.

General Legal Assistant Associations:
National Federation of Paralegal Associations, Inc., P.O. Box 33108, Kansas City, MO 64114–0108 (816) 941–4000.
National Association of Legal Assistants, Inc., 1601 South Main Street, Suite 300, Tulsa, OK 74119 (918) 587–6828.
American Association for Paralegal Education, P.O. Box 40244, Overland Park, KS 66204 (913) 381–4458.

Independent Legal Assistants:
The National Association for Independent Paralegals, 635 Fifth Street West, Sonoma, CA 95476 (800) 332–4557.

Legal Marketing Managers:
National Association of Law Firm Marketing Administrators, 60 Revere Drive, Suite 500, Northbrook, IL 60062 (708) 480–9641.

Filing and Records Management:
Association of Records Managers and Administrators, 4200 Somerset, Suite 215, Prairie Village, KS 66208, (913) 341–3808.

Law Libraries:
American Association of Law Libraries, 53 West Jackson Boulevard, Suite 940, Chicago, IL 60604 (312) 939–4764.

IBM-COMPATIBLE SOFTWARE PROGRAMS

This appendix identifies some of the IBM-compatible software programs that are available for law offices of all types. All the products are listed in alphabetical order.

The selection of any program used in this text should not be construed as an endorsement of the product by the author, editors, or publishers. In fact, the publisher herein expressly states neither good nor bad results regarding any of the programs listed.

These lists of programs are not to be construed as being expositive or complete. The publisher does not warrant that the product names, addresses, price information, and phone numbers have not changed since publication. If the list price is not given, it was not available.

A = Under $100
B = From $100 to $500
C = From $500 to $1,000
D = Over $1,000

LEGAL TIMEKEEPING AND BILLING

Alpine Legal Management	Alpine Datasystems, 7320 SW Hunziker Rd., Suite 310, Portland, OR 97223 (503) 624–0121, (800) 547–1837, List Price—D.
Compulaw	Compulaw, Ltd., 10277 West Olympics Blvd., Los Angeles, CA 90067 (800) 444–0020, List Price—D.
ISA Time, Billing	Prentice Hall Legal Practice Management, 300 Franklin Center, 29100 Northwestern Highway, Southfield, MI 48034–1095, List Price—C.
Juris	Juris, Inc., 5106 Maryland Way, Brentwood, TN 37207, (615) 377–3740, List Price—D.
PC Law	Alumni Computer Group, Ltd., 722–155 N. Michigan Drive, Chicago, IL 60601 (800) 387–9785, List Price—D.
Profit$ource	Software Technology, Inc., 1621 Cushman Drive, Lincoln, NE 68521 (402) 423–1440, List Price (single User)—C.

TABS	Software Technology, Inc., 1621 Cushman Drive, Lincoln, NE 68521 (402) 423–1440, List Price (Single User)—D.
TB–2000	Century Solutions & Software, Inc., P.O. Box 2565, Durango, CO 81302 (303) 247–7828, List Price—B.
Time Bridge	Bridge Software Systems, Inc., 800 Harbour Drive, Naples, FL 33940 (800) 446–1665, List Price—B.
Timeslips	Timeslips Corporation, 239 Western Ave., Essex, MA 01929 (508) 768–6100 or (800) 285–0999, List Price—B.
Verdict	Micro Craft, Inc., 688 Discovery Drive, Huntsville, AL 35806 (800) 225–3147, List Price—B.

DOCKET CONTROL SOFTWARE

Critical Date System	Software Technology, Inc., 1621 Cushman Drive, Lincoln, NE 68521 (402) 423–1440, List Price (Single User)—D.
Docket	Micro Craft, Inc., 688 Discovery Drive, Huntsville, AL 35806 (800) 225–3147, List Price—B.
Docket/Calendar Control System	Computer Law Systems, Inc., 11000 West 78th Street, Eden Prairie, MN 55344 (612) 941–3801, List Price—B.
Docket Calendar/ Critical Dates	Compulaw, Ltd., 10277 West Olympics Blvd., Los Angeles, CA 90067 (800) 444–0020, List Price—B.
Docket Control Systems	Precedent Systems, P.O. Box 5290, Woodland Park, CO 80866 (719) 687–6811, List Price—B.
Fast Tracker Plus/ Abacus Law	Abacus Data Systems, Inc., 6725 Mesa Ridge Rd., #204, San Diego, CA 92121 (619) 452–2073 or (800) 726–3339, List Price—B.
ISA Dates System	Prentice Hall Legal Practice Management, 300 Franklin Center, 29100 Northwestern Highway, Southfield, MI 48034–1095, List Price—B.
Law Office Manager	Avocat Systems, 1402 Riverview Tower, 900 S. Gay St., Knoxville, TN 37902 (800) 521–6588, List Price—B.
Legal Calendar	Tussman Programs, Inc., 24 Colorado Ave., Berkley, CA 94707 (800) 228–6589, List Price—C.
Pro	Clear Point Systems, Inc., 4 Point Clear Landing, Fairhope, AL 36532 (404) 237–9420, List Price—A.
Ticklex	Integra Computing, 910 Cobb Place Manor Dr., Marietta, GA 30066 (404) 426–5735, List Price—A.
Timeview	Timeslips Corporation, 239 Western Ave., Essex, MA 01929 (508) 768–6100 or (800) 285–0999, List Price—B.

CONFLICT CHECKING SOFTWARE

| ISA Files & Conflict System | Prentice Hall Legal Practice Management, 300 Franklin Center, 29100 Northwestern Highway, Southfield, MI 48034–1095, List Price—B. |

Conflict Resolution	Computer Law Systems, Inc., 11000 West 78th Street, Eden Prairie, MN 55344 (612) 941–3801, List Price—B.
Conflict of Interest	Precedent Systems, P.O. Box 5290, Woodland Park, CO 80866 (719) 687–6811, List Price—B.
Conflict of Interest Parties	Advanced Computers Systems Corporation, 1470 Marla Lane, Suite 200, Walnut Creek, CA 94596 (800) 543–3185, List Price—B.
Law Office Manager	Avocat Systems, 1402 Riverview Tower, 900 S. Gay St., Knoxville, TN 37902 (800) 521–6588, List Price—B.
Legal Master Conflict of Interest	Computer Software for Professionals, Inc., 1615 Broadway, Cathedral Building, 14th Fl., Oakland, CA 94612, (510) 444–5316, List Price—C.
Perfect Practice Conflict Checking	ADC Legal Systems, Inc., 1209 Edgewater Drive, Suite 100, Orlando, FL 32804–0086 (407) 843–8992, List Price—B.

LAW OFFICE ACCOUNTING SOFTWARE

General Ledger	Computer Law Systems, Inc., 11000 West 78th Street, Eden Prairie, MN 55344 (612) 941–3801, List Price—B.
General Ledger	Software Technology, Inc., 1621 Cushman Drive, Lincoln, NE 68521 (402) 423–1440, List Price (Single User)—D.
GLBridge	Bridge Software Systems, Inc., 800 Harbour Drive, Naples, FL 33940 (800) 446–1665, List Price—B.
ISA General Ledger & Trust System	Prentice Hall Legal Practice Management, 300 Franklin Center, 29100 Northwestern Highway, Southfield, MI 48034–1095, List Price—C.
PC Law Jr.	Alumni Computer Group, 300 Pearl St., Suite 200, Buffalo, NY 14202 (800) 387–9785, List Price—B.
Perfect Practice General Ledger	ADC Legal Systems, Inc., 1209 Edgewater Drive, Suite 100, Orlando, FL 32804–0086 (407) 843–8992, List Price—B.

TRUST ACCOUNTING SOFTWARE

Attorney Trust Account	Easy Soft, Inc., 475 Watchung Avenue, Watchung, NJ 07060 (908) 754–7638, List Price—B.
Pro Trust	SoftPro Corporation, P.O. Box 31485, Raleigh, NC 27622 (919) 848–0143, List Price—B.
Trust Accounting	Computer Law Systems, Inc., 11000 West 78th Street, Eden Prairie, MN 55344, (612) 941–3801, List Price—B.
Trust Accounting	Software Technology, Inc., 1621 Cushman Drive, Lincoln, NE 68521 (402) 423–1440, List Price (Single User)—B.
Plus Trust	Bridge Software Systems, Inc. 800 Harbour Drive, Naples, FL 33940 (800) 446–1665, List Price—B.
Perfect Practice Trust Management	ADC Legal Systems, Inc., 1209 Edgewater Drive, Suite 100, Orlando, FL 32804–0086 (407) 843–8992, List Price—B.

MACINTOSH SOFTWARE PROGRAMS

This appendix identifies some of the Macintosh software programs that are available for law offices of all types. All the products are listed in alphabetical order.

The selection of any program used in this text should not be construed as an endorsement of the product by the author, editors, or publishers. In fact, the publisher herein expressly states neither good nor bad results regarding any of the programs listed.

These lists of programs are not to be construed as being expositive or complete. The publisher does not warrant that the product names, addresses, price information, and phone numbers have not changed since publication. If the list price is not given, it was not available.

A = Under $100
B = From $100 to $500
C = From $500 to $1,000
D = Over $1,000

LEGAL TIMEKEEPING AND BILLING

Legal Billing	Satori Software, 2815 2nd Ave., Ste. 295, Seattle, WA 98121 (206) 443–0765.
MacEsquire	Synergy Marketing Communications, Inc., 11 Joseph Court, Ste., 213 Syosset, NY 11791–6702 (516) 935–9151.
MacLaw	Manhattan Software, 865 Manhattan Beach Blvd., Ste. 204, Manhattan Beach, CA 90266 (310) 545–6462.
Office Wiz	Oryx Associates, 1867 Union, Ste. B., San Francisco, CA 94123, (415) 563–9971.
Timeslips for The Mac	Timeslips Corporation, 239 Western Ave., Essex, MA 01929 (508) 768–6100, List Price—B
Time$aver Law Office Management System	Home Town Systems, P.O. Box 2306, Canada, V1G 4P2, (604) 782–3322

DOCKET CONTROL SOFTWARE

AgentDA	Team Building Technologies, 836 Bloomfield Ave., Outremont, Quebec, Canada H2V 3S6, (514) 278–3010, List Price B.
Automation Law	Lawteck Computer Systems, 333 25th St. E. #600, Saskatcheway, Saskatoon S7KOL4 (306) 934–1160.
Datebook	After Hours Software, Tri Center Plaza, 5990 Sepvulveda Blvd., Van Nuys, CA 94411 (818) 780–2220, List Price—B.
Daymaker	Pastel Development Corp., 113 Spring St., New York, NY 10012, (212) 941–7500, List Price—B.
Docket Time	Professional Software Designs, Inc., 3155 W. Belmont Ave., Phoenix, AZ 85051 (602) 841–4220.
Law Office Manager	Avocat Systems, 1402 Riverview Tower, 900 S. Gay St., Knoxville, TN 37902 (800) 521–6588, List Price—B.
Up To Date	Now Software, Inc., 520 S.W. Harrison, Suite 435, Portland, OR 97201 (503) 274–2800, List Price—B.

CONFLICT CHECKING SOFTWARE

Automation Law	Lawteck Computer Systems, 333 25th St. E. #600, Saskatcheway, Saskatoon S7KOL4 (306) 934–1160.
Law Office Manager	Avocat Systems, 1402 Riverview Tower, 900 S. Gay St., Knoxville, TN 37902 (800) 521–6588, List Price—B.

LAW OFFICE ACCOUNTING SOFTWARE

Accountant Inc.	Softsync, Inc., 800 SW 37th Ave., Ste. 765, Coral Gables, FL 33134 (305) 445–0903.
Automation Law	Lawtech Computer Systems, 333 25th St. E. #600, Saskatcheway, Saskatoon S7KOL4, (306) 934–1160.
MacMoney	Survivor Software, 11222 La Cienega Blvd., Ste. 450, Inglewood, CA 90304, List Price—B.
M.Y.O.B.	Teleware, Inc., 22 Hill Rd., Parsippany, NJ 07054 (201) 334–1154, List Price—B.
Quicken	Intuit, P.O. Box 3014, Menio Park, CA 94026 (800) 624–8742, List Price—B.

A MANUAL LAW OFFICE SYSTEM

TRAINING MANUAL OUTLINE:

- Welcome to Wallace & Sanders
- Introduction to This Training Manual
- Exercise 1: Completing a New File Form
- Exercise 2: Completing a Conflict-of-Interest Form
- Exercise 3: Completing Docket Entry Slips
- Exercise 4: Recording Trust Account Monies
- Exercise 5: Recording Time
- Exercise 6: Completing an Expense Slip
- Exercise 7: Preparing a Check Request and Trust Check
- Exercise 8: Preparing a Client Bill

WELCOME TO WALLACE & SANDERS

Welcome to Wallace & Sanders! We are an active and growing firm with four attorneys and two legal assistants. As you know, you have been hired as a legal assistant intern. We are very happy to have you on board; we can certainly use the help. Our internal systems are very important to the operation of this firm, and this training manual will help you learn some of our systems.

INTRODUCTION TO THIS TRAINING MANUAL

This training manual is provided to help you learn our systems, including how to open a new file, complete a conflict-of-interest form, complete a docket slip form, record monies in our trust account, complete a time record form, complete an expense-slip form, complete a check-request form, complete a trust check, and prepare a client bill. A sample client case, *Cindy and Joseph Forest v. Smithson*

Manufacturing, will be used throughout this manual to illustrate our systems. This manual shows you our forms and will help you with exercises on how to complete them. Only one form is included in this manual. Some exercises will require multiple copies of a form. Please make additional copies as needed.

EXERCISE 1: COMPLETING A NEW FILE FORM

Figure 1 contains our New File Form. This form must be completed on all new client cases that we are going to accept representation of. It is very important that this form be completed correctly. This form is used by our File Department to set up case files, is used by our partners to track new cases the firm is handling, and is used by our Accounting Department to help set up accounting files and proper billing procedures.

Please complete a New File Form for the case of *Cindy and Joseph Forest v. Smithson Manufacturing*. The facts of the case are presented below.

CINDY AND JOSEPH FOREST V. SMITHSON MANUFACTURING

Your supervising attorney, Shirley Wallace, asks you to complete a New File Form for Cindy and Joseph Forest, 2344 Washington Avenue (your city, state, and zip), home phone 233–2341. Wallace lets you know that she has represented the Forests before. A file number of 2342–2 has been assigned to this case. It appears that the Forests have a products-liability claim to be filed in court.

It seems that the Forests purchased a portable electric heater manufactured by Smithson Manufacturing approximately a year and a half ago. The heater seemed to work correctly and the Forests never had any problems with it. About three weeks ago, the Forests left the heater on in their house while they went out for dinner. The Forests house is quite old and is not insulated as well as it should be, and the central heater does not heat all of the house very well. Because it was particularly cold, the Forests left the heater on. Unfortunately for the Forests, when they returned from dinner there were two fire trucks fighting a fire at their house. Most of the interior and exterior was made of wood, so the house burned very quickly. Almost nothing was left from their house. Although the Forests had some insurance, they were underinsured and will not be able to replace everything they lost. Based on the investigation of the fire department, it was determined that the fire was started by a malfunction in the portable heater.

The Forests are making a five-thousand-dollar retainer to be held in the trust account for future attorney fees and expenses. The firm will bill the Forests at one hundred dollars an hour for attorney time and fifty dollars an hour for legal assistant time. The Forests would like to be billed monthly.

EXERCISE 2: COMPLETING A CONFLICT-OF-INTEREST FORM

Figure 2 contains our Conflict-of-Interest Form. This form must be completed on all new client cases that we are going to accept representation of. It is very impor-

Wallace & Sanders
NEW FILE FORM

Client Name: _____

Company: _____

Street: _____

City, State, Zip: _____

Telephone: Home _____ Work _____

Type of Client: (Check One) ___Individual ___Business ___Group of Individuals

___Litigation ___Nonlitigation

File Name: _____ File Number: _____

Opposing Party Name: _____

Type of Case: 1. Admin. Law   6. Real Estate   11. Workers' Comp.
(Circle One)   2. Bankruptcy   7. Personal Injury   12. Contract
                   3. Wills/Trusts/Estates 8. Criminal   13. Products Liability
                   4. Family Law   9. Labor Law   14. Discrimination/EEO
                   5. Collections   10. Tax   15. Other: _____

Description of Case: _____

_____

_____

Description of Case: _____ Managing Legal Assistant: _____

Referral Source: ___Existing/Past Client ___Another Attorney ___Advertising Name: _____

Fee Agreement: (Circle Applicable Ones) Hourly–Atty $ _____ , Legal Asst. $ _____ ;

Contingency _____%; Fixed Fee $ _____ Retainer $_____ .

Billing Frequency: ___Monthly ___Quarterly ___Semiannually ___Annually ___Other _____

Additional Remarks:

_____

_____

_____

FIGURE 1

Wallace & Sanders
CONFLICT-OF-INTEREST FORM

Case Name: _____

File Number: _____

Person Completing This Form: _____ Date Form Completed: _____

List Our Client(s), Opposing Parties, Opposing Counsel (if known), and Major Witnesses:

Name: _____

Street: _____

City, State, Zip: _____

Telephone: Home: _____   Work: _____

Name: _____

Street: _____

City, State, Zip: _____

Telephone: Home: _____   Work: _____

Name: _____

Street: _____

City, State, Zip: _____

Telephone: Home: _____   Work: _____

Name: _____

Street: _____

City, State, Zip: _____

Telephone: Home: _____   Work: _____

CONFLICT CHECK

Conflict Check Completed By: _____

Date of Conflict Check: _____

Check One:

_____No Conflicts were Found   _____Potential Conflicts with the Following Persons/Entities Were Found:

_____

FIGURE 2

tant that this form be completed correctly to ensure that the firm does not have any type of conflict that would prohibit it from representing the client. In addition, the firm's malpractice insurance carrier gives the firm a 7 percent discount on premiums if the firm routinely completes a conflict check on all new matters. This form is used by the File Department to check conflicts of interest against its computerized conflict-interest software program. Because our firm is relatively small, we also route the form to all staff members to make sure no one in the firm has a conflict problem.

Please note that Ms. Forest's maiden name is Jenkins and that Jerry Schneider also will probably be named in the products-liability suit to be filed in that Schneider is both the president of the company and designer of the portable heater. Please complete the Conflict-of-Interest Form for both clients, the defendant company, and Schneider (do not add addresses for this exercise). Please note that the File Department will complete the "Conflict Check" portion of the form.

EXERCISE 3: COMPLETING DOCKET ENTRY SLIPS

Figure 3 contains our Docket-Slip form. It is crucial that all important matters be recorded on a docket slip so that our file docket clerk can be sure to get the matter entered in the firm's docket.

- Your supervising attorney, Shirley Wallace, asks you to complete Docket Slips for the following items regarding the *Forest v. Smithson* case. When the new case was opened, Wallace asked you to enter the statute of limitations as next December 12. Although Wallace was sure the case would be filed immediately, she wanted to be sure that it was entered in the firm's docket to ensure that if problems arose and the case was not immediately filed, the deadline would not accidentally be missed. There is no "time" or "place" of events, but Wallace asked for thirty-, sixty-, and ninety-day reminders, and it is a top priority.
- Before any case is filed, it is extremely important that the case be adequately investigated. Before Wallace filed the case, she asked you to make sure that you had contacted any witnesses that might have seen the fire as it was starting that night and to be sure to get the fire department's investigation form and to get a signed statement from the fire department's investigator that concluded that the portable heater had started the fire. Wallace wanted this completed no later than February 28 of this year. Because the fire department investigator is hard to get in touch with, you think you had better give yourself fifteen-, ten-, and five-day reminders. This is a medium-priority matter.
- Before the case is filed, Wallace also wants to make sure she has an expert lined up who has reviewed the case file, the fire department's investigation report, and the fire department investigator's statement. She wants you to do some research and find a good products-liability expert witness with some specific expertise in portable heaters. She would like to file the case in early April, so the expert must be secured by March 20 or so. Because you think it will take some time to find an expert with this specialty, you decide to give yourself ten-, thirty-, and forty-five-day reminders. This is a medium-priority item.
- The case was filed on April 17. The defendants were served with the lawsuit on April 23. Wallace asks you to be sure to record when the

```
┌─────────────────────────────────────────────────────────────────────────┐
│  Wallace & Sanders              DOCKET SLIP                                │
│                                                                           │
│  Client/Case Matter: _____  File No.:_____   │
│                                                                           │
│  Event: _____   │
│                                                                           │
│  Date of Event: _____  Time of Event: _____     │
│                                                                           │
│  Place of Event: _____   │
│                                                                           │
│  To Be Handled By: _____  Reminder Dates:_____ _____ _____    │
│                                                                           │
│  Priority:  1 2 3 4 5  (Circle one, Top Priority is 1).  ┌──────────────┐ │
│                                                          │ Docket Clerk  │ │
│  Slip Completed By: _____ Date Slip Completed: _____ │  Use Only     │ │
│                                                          │ Date Entered in Docket: ___ │
│  Notes: _____        │ Entered By: _____ │
│                                                          └──────────────┘ │
└─────────────────────────────────────────────────────────────────────────┘
```

FIGURE 3

defendants' "Answer" is due. Under court rules, the defendant has thirty calendar days from the date of service to file an "Answer." No reminder is necessary.

- After the case was filed, Wallace and the defendants' attorney agreed to take the following depositions: Cindy Forest, June 2 at Wallace & Sanders, 10:00 A.M.; Joseph Forest, June 2 at Wallace & Sanders, 1:30 P.M.; and the defendant, Jerry Schneider, June 4 at 9:00 A.M. at Don Anderson's office (the defendant's attorney). Depositions are considered top-priority items. Wallace asks you to make fifteen-, ten-, and three-day reminders.

EXERCISE 4: RECORDING TRUST ACCOUNT MONIES

Figure 4 contains our Trust Account—Client Ledger form. Each individual who has money in the trust account must have a separate Trust Account—Client Ledger form. This ledger sheet documents the chronological activity for each client's account and maintains the client's balance in trust so that an accurate accounting of trust funds can be provided immediately upon request by the client or the managing attorney.

Wallace requests that you open a Trust Account—Client Ledger form on the *Forest v. Smithson* case and to record the five-thousand-dollar payment on the ledger sheet. The funds were received on January 15. Please keep in mind that a balance must be maintained on the client ledger sheet at all times.

EXERCISE 5: RECORDING TIME

Figure 5 contains the Time Record form we use for recording time. As with any business, we must make a profit to pay our employees, pay our expenses, pay

Wallace & Sanders
TRUST ACCOUNT – CLIENT LEDGER

Name of Client or Third Party_____
Legal Matte or Adverse Party_____
File or Case Number_____

Date	Description of Transaction	Check Number	Funds Paid	Funds Received	

FIGURE 4

ourselves, and to stay in business. Maintaining accurate and timely time records is an important part in this process. Timesheets are due to the Accounting Department every Friday by 4:00 P.M. Legal assistant interns are required to bill approximately fifteen hours a week. Full-time legal assistants must bill thirteen hundred hours a year. This averages to about twenty-five hours a week or five hours a day of billable time. Accurate billing is extremely important. We do not tolerate overbilling or unfair billing to our clients.

Wallace asks you to record the following time:

TIME RECORD

Professional Service Codes

A – Appearance, Hearing
B – Bar Associate/Community
   Activities, Client Development
C – Conference
D – Dictation

L – Letter
NC – Nonchargeable Time
O – Office Administration
P – Preparation

PB – Personal Business
R – Research
T – Travel
TC – Telephone Consultation

Time Conversion

6 Minutes = .1 Hour	36 Minutes = .6 Hour
12 Minutes = .2 Hour	42 Minutes = .7 Hour
15 Minutes = .25 Hour	45 Minutes = .75 Hour
18 Minutes = .3 Hour	48 Minutes = .8 Hour
24 Minutes = .4 Hour	54 Minutes – .9 Hour
30 Minutes – .5 Hour	60 Minutes – 1.0 Hour

DATE	CLIENT/CASE NAME	FILE NO.	ATTORNEY	PROFESSIONAL SERVICES CODE/DESCRIPTION	HOURS	TIME TENTHS

FIGURE 5

- Record one hour of your own time on January 16 for preliminary legal research in your state regarding the standard of proof in a products-liability case, the statute of limitations in such a case, and a general review of current products-liability cases in your state.
- Record four hours of your time on January 24 to locate three witnesses who live in the neighborhood who say they saw smoke rising out of the west side of the Forests' house where the portable heater was on the night of the fire, confirming the fire department's theory that the portable heater started the blaze.
- Record 2.5 hours of time that you spent on January 27 going to the fire department to copy the investigator's case file and report and to take the statement of the investigator.
- Record one hour of time you spent on January 29 for conducting legal research on WESTLAW. You entered "Smithson Manufacturing" in WESTLAW to see if there had been other reported cases against the manufacturer regarding this model of portable heater. You also researched portable heaters in WESTLAW to try to establish other cases where portable heaters had caused fires.
- Record five hours of time you spent on February 18 researching your files, calling other attorneys, and nailing down an expert witness.
- Record two hours of time on February 25 that you spent talking to an expert witness. You establish during the conversation that the expert, Robert Murray, has a degree in engineering from the Massachusetts Institute of Technology, and previously worked for a different manufacturer that manufactured portable heaters.
- Wallace passes you in the hall on April 14 and asks you to please record four hours of her time for reviewing the Forests' file, conducting legal research, meeting with the clients, and drafting the "Complaint."
- Wallace asks you to record 2.5 hours of time for June 2 to take the deposition of Cindy Forest, three hours of time on June 2 to take the deposition of Joseph Forest, and eight hours of time to take the deposition of the defendant Jerry Schneider on June 4. Please also record two hours of time on June 3 that Wallace spent with Robert Murray, the expert witness in the case, to help prepare her to take the deposition of Schneider.
- Finally, record four hours on June 26 that you spent summarizing the deposition of the Forests.

EXERCISE 6: COMPLETING AN EXPENSE SLIP

Figure 6 contains our Expense Slip form. It is important that all staff members routinely complete Expense Slips for costs associated with specific cases. This allows the firm to be reimbursed from clients for expenses such as copying charges, long-distance phone calls, and many other types of costs. If a staff member fails to complete an Expense Slip for items that could have been charged back to the client, our office "eats" the expense, which hurts our ability to make a profit.

Please record the following expenses:

- Twenty-five copies at twenty-five cents per copy on January 16 for copies of cases regarding standard of proof in a products-liability case in this state.
- Five dollars you spent from the Petty Cash Fund on January 27 to get a copy of the fire department's investigation report.

Wallace & Sanders
Expense Slip

Expense Type & Code:

1. Photocopies	4. Filing Fees	7. Facsimile	10. Travel
2. Postage	5. Witness Fees	8. Lodging	11. Overnight Delivery
3. Long Distance	6. WESTLAW/LEXIS	9. Meals	12. Other _____

Date:_____   Case Name:_____   File No._____

Expense Code:_____   Quantity_____   Amount _____   Billable/Non-Billable

Expense Code:_____   Quantity_____   Amount _____   Billable/Non-Billable

Expense Code:_____   Quantity_____   Amount _____   Billable/Non-Billable

Name of Person Making Expense Slip:_____

Description of Expense(s) incurred:

_____

_____

_____

_____

FIGURE 6

- Thirteen dollars postage costs to send information to the client on February 4.
- Ninety-three dollars of WESTLAW connect time on January 29 to find two other cases where Smithson Manufacturing was sued for products liability.
- Fourteen dollars you spent on long-distance phone charges finding an expert witness on February 18.
- Sixteen dollars for long-distance calls on February 25 you spent talking to your expert witness.

EXERCISE 7: PREPARING A CHECK REQUEST AND TRUST CHECK

Figure 7 contains our Check Request Form. Anytime you need a firm check or a trust check, you must complete this form so that we can establish a proper paper trail and so the Accounting Department knows who to write the check to, for what amount, and what the purpose of the check is.

Wallace & Sanders

CHECK REQUEST FORM

Client Name and File Number: _____

Date of Request: _____

Request Made by: _____

Bank Account: General Business Account   Trust Account   (Circle One)

Amount of Check $ _____

Check Should Be Made Payable To: _____

Address of Payee: _____

Detailed Description: _____

_____

_____

_____

_____

Accounting Use Only

Account No./Code: _____

Approved By: _____   Date: _____

FIGURE 7

Figure 8 contains a copy of a Client Trust Account check. Although this is typically done by the Accounting Department, it is a good idea for all staff members to know how to complete a check properly.

BANK 1

Wallace & Sanders
CLIENT TRUST ACCOUNT

_____ 19___

PAY _____ DOLLARS

┌   ┐
TO THE
ORDER
OF
└   ┘

$ _____

For: _____

Authorized Signature

FIGURE 8

- Please complete a Check Request Form and the accompanying check for the trust account for February 26 in the amount of one thousand dollars for an expert witness fee in *Forest v. Smithson*. Our expert witness, Robert Murray, 345524 Highway One, Malibu, CA 92523, requires a one-thousand-dollar fee up front before he will begin working on the case. The check number is 1,001 and should be recorded on the check in the upper right-hand corner.
- Please complete a Check Request Form and the accompanying check for the trust account for June 18 in the amount of six hundred dollars for deposition transcript fees in *Forest v. Smithson*. The check should be made payable to Smith & Seeley Court Reporting Services, P.O. Box 234234, (your city and state).
- Also, please record the two checks in the Forests' Trust Account—Client Ledger sheet showing appropriate balance left in trust.

EXERCISE 8: PREPARING A CLIENT BILL

Figure 9 contains our standard bill format. It is very important that members understand that when you record time, the client must eventually pay for the time. To emphasize this, please prepare a billing to the Forests for the legal services contained in Exercises 5, 6, and 7 using the format in Figure 9.

After you have prepared the client billing, please prepare a Check Request Form and a trust check (it should be numbered 1,003) from the trust account for the total amount of attorney fees and expenses. The check should be made payable to Wallace & Sanders Attorneys. Finally, please record the check in the Forests' Trust Account—Client Ledger and show the current balance in trust.

continuance Rescheduling an appointment or court date.

controlling The process of determining whether the law practice is achieving its objectives.

court awarded fees Attorneys fees given to the prevailing party in a lawsuit pursuant to certain federal and state statutes.

criminal fraud A false representation of a present or past fact made by a defendant.

cross-selling Refers to selling additional services to existing clients.

daisy wheel printer Printer that uses a daisy wheel or "print wheel."

data base A computer program that organizes, searches, and sorts data.

decentralized file system System in which files are kept in various locations throughout the law office.

desktop publishing Page layout and design using a computer.

docket A calendaring or scheduling system that tracks and organizes appointments, deadlines, and commitments.

dot-matrix printer Prints data by forming rows and columns of dots.

duplicating Duplicating is the ability to automatically make two-sided copies.

draw A payment to a partner that represents a share of a partner's anticipated net income. The draw is counted against the share of the partner's profits at the end of the year.

earned retainer An earned retainer is monies that the law office or attorney has earned and is entitled to deposit in the office's or attorney's own bank account.

employee assistant program A designated counseling service that an employer contracts with to provide counseling to its employees as a fringe benefits to employment.

employee attitude survey A survey that is given to an organization's employees and asks the employees to rate the effectiveness of the organization in many specific areas.

employment-at-will doctrine Doctrine that states than an employer and employee freely enter into an employment relationship and that either party has the right to sever the relationship anytime without reason.

equal employment opportunity Concept that means that employers make employment-related decisions without arbitrarily discriminating against an individual.

Equal Pay Act of 1963 Federal legislation that prohibits employers from paying workers of one sex less than the rate paid by employee of the opposite sex for work on jobs that require equal skill, effort, and responsibility and that are performed under the same working conditions.

escrow account A separate bank account (also called a trust account), apart from a law office's or attorney's operating checking account, where unearned client funds are deposited.

essential job functions Job duties or tasks that are necessary to the completion of the job and that will take up a significant part of the employee's time.

ethical rule A minimal standard of conduct.

expense A cost that the firm has incurred for the purpose of earning income.

expert witness A person who has technical expertise in a specific field and agrees to give testimony for a client at trial.

facility management Refers to law office management's responsibility to plan, design, and control a law office's own building or office space effectively.

Family and Medical Leave Act of 1993 Federal legislation that allows employees in certain circumstances to have up to twelve worksheets of unpaid leave from their jobs for family or health-related reasons.

feedback Information sent in response to a message.

financial management The oversight of a firm's financial assets and profitability to ensure overall financial health.

file opening form A standardized form that is filled out when a new case is opened.

flat fee   A fee for legal services that is billed as a flat or fixed amount.

floor load capacity   Refers to the weight per square foot the floor can hold without collapsing.

floppy disk drive   Device that stores data on a plastic magnetic disk called a floppy disk or diskette.

form file   A file that contains examples of documents used in a law office, including pleadings, contract, wills, and discovery documents.

freelance legal assistants   Self-employed legal assistants that market and sell their services to law offices on a per job basis.

Gantt chart   A plan or time line of projected begin dates and end dates of a project.

general counsel   The chief for a corporate legal department.

gross income   Monies that are received before expenses are deducted.

gross lease   The tenant pays only for base rent, and the landlord covers all other building-related expenses.

groupthink   The desire for group cohesiveness and consensus becomes stronger than the desire for the best possible decision.

hard disk   Device that stores data on a rigid magnetic material.

hardware   The actual physical components of a computer system.

hourly rate fee   A fee for legal services that is billed to the client by the hour at an agreed-upon rate.

human resource management   Recruiting, hiring, training, evaluating, maintaining, and directing the personnel that will provide quality legal services to the clients.

imaging   The capture, retrieval, and storage of document images.

impact printer   Prints data onto paper by physically impacting or striking the paper.

income   Something of value that a law office receives from a client in exchange for the law office providing professional legal services.

income budget   Estimate of how many partners, associates, legal assistants, and other will bill for their time, what the appropriate rates of hourly charge should be, and the number of billable hours each timekeeper will be responsible for billing.

ink-jet printer   Sprays ink onto a page to form letters.

input device   Enters information into a computer.

integrated software   Software that combines several application functions into one.

interior landscaping   Uses movable partitions, or panels, and work surfaces, file cabinets, and drawers that attach to the partitions instead of interior walls.

internal control   Procedures that an organization establishes to set up checks and balances so that no individual in the organization has exclusive control over any part of the accounting system.

just-in-time inventory   An inventory method that maintains minimum inventory levels to maximize cash flow.

laser printer   Uses a laser beam to form characters on a page.

lateral hire   Associate attorneys hired from other firms.

law clerk   A law student working for a law firm on a part-time basis while he or she is finishing a law degree. Law clerk duties revolve almost exclusively around legal research and writing.

law office information system   A combination of human involvement, computer hardware and software, and raw information that work together to solve problems in a law office.

law librarian   A librarian responsible for maintaining a law library. Maintenance includes purchasing new books and periodicals, classifying, storing, indexing, and updating the holdings, and coordinating computer-assisted legal research (i.e. WESTLAW, LEXIS, and other services).

leadership   The act of motivating or causing others to perform and achieve objectives.

lease-to-purchase   A lease where the lessee agrees to make payments for a specific period of time, but at the end of the lease term the lessee is given the option to purchase the equipment.

legal aid office   A not-for-profit law office that receives grants from the government and private donations to pay for representation of disadvantaged persons who otherwise could not afford legal services

legal assistants   A distinguishing group of persons who assist attorneys in the delivery of legal services. They have knowledge and expertise regarding the legal system and substantive and procedural law that qualifies them to do work of a legal nature under the supervision of an attorney.

legal assistant manager   One who supervises, recruits, trains, distributes, sets priorities, and directs the overall management of a group of legal assistants.

legal malpractice   Possible consequences when an attorney's or law office's conduct falls below the standard skill, prudence, and diligence that an ordinary lawyer would possess or that is commonly available in the legal community.

legal team   A group made up of attorneys, administrators, law clerks, librarians, legal assistants, secretaries, clerks, and other third parties. Each provides a distinct range of services to clients and each has a place on the legal team.

legal technicians   People who market their legal services directly to the public.

leveraging   The process of earning a profit from legal services that are provided by law office personnel (usually partners, associates, and legal assistants).

local area network   A multiuser system that links independent microcomputers together that are close in proximity for the purpose of sharing information, printers, and storage devices.

loss factor   The tenant's pro-rata share of common space.

mainframe computer   A large computer that is more powerful than a minicomputer and is capable of processing enormous volumes of data.

main memory   Holds or stores information that the computer is processing.

management   The use of people and other resources to accomplish objectives.

management by objectives   A performance program in which the individual employee and the employer agree on goals for the employee.

management reports   Reports used to help management analyze whether the office is operating in an efficient and effective manner.

managing partner   An attorney in a law firm chosen by the partnership or the shareholders to run the firm on a day-to-day basis, make administrative decisions, and set policies.

marketing   The process of educating consumers on the quality legal services that a law office can provide.

marketing plan   The goals that a marketing program is to accomplish and a detailed strategy of how the goals will be achieved.

memory chips   Tiny electronic circuits that store or hold information.

microcomputer   A small computer that is cheaper and less powerful than a minicomputer or a mainframe computer and is sometimes referred to as a personal computer of "PC."

micrographics   A means of storing files photographically using microfilm or microfliche on small pieces of film or plastic.

microprocessors   The processor chip used in microcomputers.

minicomputer   A medium-sized computer that is not as powerful as a mainframe computer but can still process large volumes of data.

mission statement   A general, enduring statement of what the purpose or intent of the law practice is.

Model Code of Professional Responsibility   American Bar Association (ABA) code of ethics published in 1983 which are self-imposed ethical standards for ABA members, but it can also serve as a prototype of legal ethic standards for state court systems.

Model Rules of Professional Conduct   American Bar Association (ABA) code of ethics published in 1969 which are self-imposed ethical standards for ABA members, but it can also serve as a prototype of legal ethical standards for state court systems.

modem   Peripheral that allows computers in different locations to communicate with one another using telephone lines.

monochrome monitor   Monitor that displays information in one color, usually green, amber or white.

mouse Device used to move the cursor on a monitor and otherwise enter information into a computer.

multitask operating system System that allows the execution of several application programs at the same time.

negligent hiring Hiring an employee without sufficiently and reasonably checking the employee's background.

net income Monies that are left after expenses are deducted from gross income.

net lease The tenant pays a base rent plus real estate taxes.

noise Any situation that interferes with or distorts the message being communicated from the sender to the receiver.

nonbillable time Time that cannot be directly billed to a paying client.

nonequity partner A partner who does not share in the profits or losses of the firm but may be entitled to certain benefits not given to associates.

nonimpact printer Prints data onto paper without physically striking the paper.

of counsel An attorney affiliated with the firm in some way such as a retired or semiretired partner.

office manager Manager who handles day-to-day operations of the law office, such as accounting, supervision of the clerical support staff, and assisting the managing partner.

office sharing An arrangement in which two or more sole practitioners share office space and sometimes share support staff but do not share profits.

"off-the-shelf" software Preprogrammed software not written by the user.

off-line The user is not connected to an information service and no charges are accruing except possibly a printing or downloading charge.

on-line The user is connected to an information system and is running up charges.

operating system software Instructs the computer how to operate its circuitry and how to communicate with input, output, and storage devices.

operating lease A lease where the lessee agrees to make payments for a specific period of time.

opportunity costs Refers to the costs of forgoing or passing up other alternatives.

optical character recognition scanner Device that scans or reads printed material into a computer's memory.

organizing The process of arranging people and physical resources to carry out plans and accomplish objectives.

output device A piece of equipment that outputs processed information from a computer.

outside counsel Refers to when a corporate or governmental law practice hires a private law office to help them with legal matters.

overhead General administrative costs of doing business, including costs such as rent, utilities, phone, and salary costs for administrators.

partner An owner in a private law practice that has the partnership form of business structure that shares in the practice's profits and losses.

peripheral devices Pieces of equipment that are connected to a computer to perform specific functions.

personnel handbook A manual that lists the formal personnel policies of an organization.

planning The process of setting objectives, assessing the future, and developing courses of action to achieve that objectives.

policy A specific statement that sets out what is or is not acceptable.

powerful managing partner A management structure in which a single partner is responsible for managing the firm.

practice management Management decisions about how a law office will practice law and handle its cases.

prepaid legal service A plan that a person can purchase that entitles the person to receive legal services either free or at a greatly reduced rate.

presentation graphics software Software that allows a computer to produce professional-quality charts and diagrams.

printer Peripheral that produces data on paper.

pro bono Legal services that are provided free to charge to a client who is not able to pay for the services.

procedure A series of steps that must be followed to accomplish a task.

processor chip Performs the actual arithmetic computations of the computer.

programmer A person who writes computer programs.

pure retainer A fee that obligates the office to be available to represent the client throughout the time period agreed upon.

rainmaking The ability to bring in new clients to a law office.

random access memory (RAM) Temporary memory that is used to store application programs and data that are entered into a computer.

read only memory (ROM) Permanent, unchanging memory that is used internally by the computer to operate itself.

reasonable accommodation Accommodating a person with a disability, which may include making existing facilities readily accessible, restructuring the job, or modifying work schedules.

realization Amount a firm actually receives in income as opposed to the amount it bills.

recurring entry A calendar entry that recurs typically either daily, weekly, monthly, or annually.

rephrasing A technique used to improve communication by repeating back to a person what your understanding of the conversation was.

rental space Is what rent is based on and includes usable space plus the tenant's prorata share of all common space on the floor such as hallways, stairwells, and bathrooms.

retainer for general representation Retainer typically used when a client such as a corporation or school board requires continuing legal services throughout the year.

rule by all partners/shareholders A management structure in which all partners/shareholders are included in decisions that affect the firm.

rule by management committee/board Management structure that uses a committee structure

to make management decisions for the firm.

rule by three Billing formula that says for a fee earner to be profitable, he/she should bill at three times his/her pay.

secretaries Employees who provide assistance and support to the law office staff by taking dictation, performing typing and filing functions, and aiding in scheduling of appointments.

service bureau An outside or third-party office that sells computer time—usually mainframe computer time—to others.

settlement A mutual agreement to resolve a dispute on specified terms.

sexual harassment Unwelcome sexual advances, requests for sexual favors, and other verbal or physical conduct of a sexual nature that creates an intimidating, hostile, or offensive working environment.

shareholder An owner in a private law practice that is a corporation that shares in the practice's profits and losses.

shelf filing Method in which files are stored on a shelf, much like books in a library would be stored.

single-task operating system Permits the computer to operate only one application program at a time.

single-user system A computer that can accommodate only one person at a time and is not linked to other systems or computers.

spreadsheet software Computer software that calculates and manipulates numbers, using labels, values, and formulas.

staff attorney An attorney hired by a firm with the knowledge and understanding that he or she will never be considered for partnership.

staffing plan Estimate of how many employees will be hired or funded by the firm, what positions or capacities they will serve in, what positions will need to be added, what old positions will be deleted, and how much compensation each employee will receive.

statute of limitations A statute or law that sets a limit on the length of time a party has to file a suit. If a case is filed after the statute of limitations, the claim is barred and is dismissed as a matter of law.

storage capacity The maximum amount of data that can be stored on a device.

storage device Stores data that can be retrieved later.

Strategic planning The process of determining the major goals of a firm and then adopting the courses of action necessary to achieve those goals.

substantive task A task that relates to the process of actually performing legal work for clients.

system A consistent or organized way of doing something.

task lighting Where lights are attached to work surfaces or furniture or are free standing.

terminal A keyboard and monitor that are used to communicate with computers.

time to billing percentage System of adjusting downward the actual amount that will be billed to clients during the budget process, taking into account the fact that timekeepers are not always able to bill at their optimum levels.

timekeeper productivity report Report showing how much billable and nonbillable time is being spent by each timekeeper.

timekeeping The process of tracking how attorneys and legal assistants use their time.

timekeeping and billing service bureau A company that for a fee processes attorney and legal assistant timesheets (usually a monthly basis), generates billings, and records client payments for a law practice.

timesheet/timesheet A record of information about the legal services professionals provide to each client.

total quality management A management philosophy based upon knowing the needs of each client and allowing those needs to drive the legal organization at all levels of activity, from the receptionist to the senior partner.

trust account A separate bank account (also called an escrow account), apart from a law office's or attorney's operating checking account, where unearned client funds are deposited.

unearned retainer Monies that are paid up front by the client as an advance against the attorney's future fees and expenses. Until the monies are actually earned by the attorney or law office, they actually belong to the client.

usable space Space that is actually available for offices, equipment, furniture, or occupiable area but does not include hallways, stairwells, and like areas.

value billing A type of fee agreement that is based not just on the time required to perform the legal work but also on the complexity of the matter and the expertise of the attorneys required to perform it.

wide area network A multiuser system that can link independent microcomputers together that are located thousands of miles apart.

word processing program Program used to edit, manipulate, and revise text to create documents.

work days System of calculating deadlines that refers to only days when the court is open.

work letter The part of the lease that states what construction the landlord must perform before the tenant occupies the space.

wrongful termination A lawsuit in which a former employee alleges than an employer unlawfully terminated the employee.

zero-based budgeting A type of budget that forces everyone in the organization to justify and explain his or her budget figures in depth without using prior year's figures as justification.

INDEX

ABA (American Bar Association), 6, 45
ABA Committee on Ethics and Professional
    Responsibility, 63
ABA *Law Practice Staff Manual*, 88
ABA *Model Code of Professional Responsibility*, 45
ABA *Model Rules of Professional Conduct*, 45
ABA *Model Guidelines for the Utilization of Legal
    Assistant Services*, 52
ABA/NET, 373
ABA *Office Automation in Smaller Law
    Offices*, 178
Access time, 354
Accounting software, 364
Activity hourly rate, 150
Adequate preparation, 265
Administrative management, 30, 31
Administrators, 6
Administrative task, 34
Advertising, 104, 301
Age Discrimination in Employment Act, 332
Aged accounts receivable, 183
Alphabetic filing, 384
Ambulance chasing, 104
Americans with Disabilities Act (ADA), 300, 333
Application software, 347
Asphalt Engineers, Inc. v. Galusha, 47
Associate attorney, 4
Association of Legal Administrators, 6
Attitude survey, 124, 317
Attorney-client privilege, 55
Attorneys, 3, 4
Attorney hourly rate, 148
Automated document feed, 420
Automated filing equipment, 396

Bar coding, 387
Billable hours, 171

Billable time, 168
Billing, 147, 174
Billing practices, 178
Bills not paid, 187
Blended hourly rate fee, 148
Blind ads, 302
Bona fide occupational qualification, 333
Budgeting, 240
Bug, 375

CD-ROM, 355
Calendar, 269
Calendar days, 262
Card system
Case retainer, 156
Case type productivity report, 185
Cash advance, 155
Cash flow, 244
Central processing unit, 348
Centralized filing, 388
Check request, 251
Chinese Wall, 60
Civil Rights Act, 332
Clerks, 18
Client funds, 231
Client hourly rate, 148
Client interviews, 134
Client property, 398
Client relationships, 121
Client surveys, 124
Coaching technique, 312
Commingling of client funds, 235
Communication, 126, 266
Communication barrier, 126
Communication device, 358
Competence, 265
Compuserve, 373

Computer, 347
Computer assisted legal research, 411
Computerized docket control, 269
Computer programs, 347
Confidentiality, 55
Confidentiality policy, 58
Conflict checking, 59
Conflict of interest, 57, 398
Conflict of interest of policy, 60
Contingency fee, 150, 159
Continuance, 259
Contract attorney, 5
Controlling, 33
Copy machines, 419
Court awarded fees, 157
Court rules, 261
Criminal fraud, 162
Cross-selling, 100

Dabney v. Investment Corp. of America, 55
Daisy wheel printer, 359
Database management, 365
Decentralized filing, 388
Defense firms, 25
Deming, Edwards W., 90
Desktop publishing, 365
Dictation equipment, 421
Diligence, 266
Disengagement letters, 74
Docket, 259
Docket control, 259
Docket control entries, 262
Document receipt date, 264
Dot-matrix printer, 357
Double billing, 163
Draw, 4, 247
Duplexing, 420

Earned retainer, 155
Equipment, 418
Embezzlement, 248
Employee attitude survey, 317
Employee assistance program, 326
Employment applications, 302
Employment-at-will-doctrine, 327
Equal employment opportunity, 316
Equal Pay Act, 332
Equity partner, 4
Escrow account, 155
Essential job functions, 298
Ethics, 43, 89, 158, 232, 252, 265, 398
Ethical rule, 45
Exempt employees, 330
Expenses, 164, 237

Expert witness, 18
Evaluations, 313

Facility management, 432
Fair Labor Standard Act, 330
Family and Medical Leave Act, 330
Fee agreements, 147
Feedback, 128
Fee disputes, 72
File cabinet, 395
File date, 264
File management, 383
File management equipment, 395
File opening form, 388
File retention, 394
Financial management, 31
Flat fee, 153
Floor load capacity, 448
Floppy disk, 354
Form files, 399
Freelance legal assistants, 7

Gantt chart, 112
General counsel, 19
Government law practices, 20
Gross income, 236
Gross lease, 449
Group communication, 133
Groupthink, 134

Hard disk, 355
Hardware, 347
Hiring, 298
Hourly rate fee, 148
Human resource management, 33, 298

Imaging, 398
Impact printer, 357
In re Complex Asbestos Litigation, 62
Income, 236
Income budget, 242
Incompetence, 72
Ink-jet printer, 359
Input device, 347, 356
Integrated software, 369
Internal control, 247
Interior landscaping, 337
Interviewing, 134,
ITT Chicago-Kent Survey of Large Law Offices, 178

Job descriptions, 298
Job interviewing, 304
Job interview check list, 305
Just-in-time inventory, 431

Lack diligence, 267
Large law firm, 24
Laser printer, 358
Lateral hire, 4
Law clerk, 17
Law librarian, 18
Law office information system, 348, 375
Leadership, 33, 129, 132
Lease, 446
Lease to purchase, 430
Legal assistant code of ethics, 49, 50
Legal aid office, 21
Legal assistant manager, 6
Legal assistants, 6
Legal assistant salaries, 12
Legal assistant hourly rate, 148
Legal expenses, 164
Legal malpractice, 67, 268
Legal team, 4
Legal technicians, 52
LEXIS, 18, 372, 411
Leveraging, 177
Library management, 400
Lighting, 439
Limited liability company, 27
Listening, 128, 129
Litigation support, 368
Local area network, 353
Loss factor, 433

Mail date, 264
Mainframe computer, 350
Main memory, 349
Malpractice, 67, 268
Malpractice claim data, 70
Management, 31
Management by objectives, 317
Management reports, 183
Managing partner, 4
Manual docket control, 269
Marketing, 33, 93
Marketing plan, 101
Medium law firm, 24
Megafirm, 22
Microcomputer, 352, 360
Micrographics, 396
Microprocessor, 349
Microsoft Windows, 370
Minicomputer, 351
Mission statement, 106
Missouri v. Jenkins, 16, 175
Mobile storage system, 396
Model Code of Professional Responsibility, 45
Model Rules of Professional Conduct, 45

Modem, 349
Monitor, 357
Moving considerations, 449
Mouse, 357
Multitask operating system, 362

National Association of Legal Assistants, 16, 48, 49
National Federation of Paralegal
    Associations, 16, 48, 50
Negligent hiring, 308
Net income, 236
Net lease, 449
New employee checklist, 311
Noise, 126
Nonbillable time, 169
Nonequity partner, 5
Nonexempt employees, 330
Nonimpact printer, 359
Nonrefundable retainer, 155
Numerical filing, 387

Of counsel, 6
Office managers, 17
Office sharing, 23
Office supplies, 431
Open-ended questions, 305
Operating lease, 430
Operating system software, 347
Opportunity costs, 426
Optical character recognition, 356
Organization, 33
Output device, 347, 357
Outside counsel, 186
Overhead, 169

Partner, 4
Partnership, 26
Payroll, 239
Performance evaluations, 310
Peripheral devices, 354
Personnel policies, 326
Personnel handbook, 326
Personnel law, 327
Plaintiff firms, 25
Planning, 33, 105, 106
Planning process, 110
Policy, 87
Positive discipline, 326
Powerful managing partner, 27
Practice management, 30, 246
Prepaid legal services, 157
Pregnancy Discrimination Act, 332
Presentation graphics, 369
Printer, 357

Pro bono, 169
Procedure, 87
Processor chip, 349
Professional corporation, 26
Profit, 238
Profit distribution, 247
Programmer, 349
Progressive discipline, 322
Pure retainer, 157

Rainmaking, 101
Random access memory, 350
Read only memory (ROM), 349
Realization, 243
Reasonable accommodation, 333
Reasonable fee, 160
Receiving documents, 261
Recruiting,
Recurring entry, 272
Reference check, 308
Rental space, 433
Rephrasing, 130
Resume, 302
Resume evaluation, 303
Retainer fees, 153
Retainer for general representative, 155
Rivera v. Chicago Pneumatic, 61
Rule by management committee/board, 27
Rule by all partners/shareholders, 27
Rule of Three, 177

Secretaries, 18
Security, 443
Seniority system, 247
Service bureaus, 185, 350
Settlement, 232
Sexual harassment, 333
Sexual harassment policy, 329
Shareholder, 4
Shelf filing, 396
Single-task operating system, 362
Single-user system, 353
Small law firm, 24

Sole practitioner, 22
Sole proprietorship, 26
Solicitation, 104
Spreadsheets, 252, 364
Staff attorney, 5
Staffing plan, 243
Staff manuals, 81, 82, 86
Staff manual - prototype, 88
Statute of limitations, 259
Storage device, 347, 354
Strategic planning, 108, 109
Substantive task, 34

Tape backup, 355
Telecommunications, 372
Terminal, 351
Termination, 320
Termination checklist, 323
Tickler card system, 269
Timekeeper Productivity Report, 185
Timekeeping, 146, 166
Timesheet, 166
Time to billing percentage, 242
Total quality management (TQM), 89
Troubled employees, 324
Trust account, 155, 231
Typewriters, 421

Unauthorized Practice of Law, 48, 51
Unearned retainer, 155
Usable space, 433

Value billing, 158
Virus, 375

WESTLAW, 18, 372, 411
Wide area network, 353
Windows, 370
Word processing, 366
Workdays, 262
Work letter, 446
Zero-based budgeting system, 244